Resilience in Deaf Children

Debra H. Zand · Katherine J. Pierce
Editors

Resilience in Deaf Children

Adaptation Through Emerging Adulthood

 Springer

Editors
Debra H. Zand
Missouri Institute of Mental Health
5400 Arsenal
St. Louis, MO 63139
USA
debbie.zand@mimh.edu

Katherine J. Pierce
Department of Psychiatry
Washington University School of Medicine
660 South Euclid Ave.
St. Louis, MO 63110
USA
piercek@psychiatry.wustl.edu

ISBN 978-1-4419-7795-3   e-ISBN 978-1-4419-7796-0
DOI 10.1007/978-1-4419-7796-0
Springer New York Dordrecht Heidelberg London

Library of Congress Control Number: 2011922988

Printed on acid-free paper

Springer is part of Springer Science+Business Media (www.springer.com)

For Hannah & Abrahm – our child guides to understanding the resilience pathway

Foreword

Throughout much of history, deaf people have been misunderstood and misrepresented by societies that magnify their inabilities and try to change these to abilities that will allow for their seamless merging into the hearing population. For deaf people, this is a frustrating odyssey that often results in an inadequate sense of belonging within the auditory environment swirling around them. Communicating and relating to others in ways that do not match the surrounding society's expectations of typical communication usually results in negative responses and distancing from others. It is no wonder that hearing parents are weighted down with concern and worry when they discover that their infants/toddlers are deaf.

Refreshingly, the past few decades have witnessed an astounding explosion of publications that explore the ways in which deaf people have forged ahead with their lives. These publications have accelerated the shift away from the perception of deaf people as a subgroup at risk for maladaptive lives if they don't "overcome their disability" to focus on their ability to survive and manage their lives competently, all things being equal. This relatively recent focus on strengths, healthy functioning, and positive psychology has been a long time coming.

The authors contributing to this book, *Resilience in Deaf Children: Adaptation Through Emerging Adulthood*, have continued this trend away from the historically negative framework by focusing on the concept of resilience as a positive attribute that each one of us has the capacity to possess. Resilience is a concept with multiple definitions, as has been made abundantly clear throughout the chapters. Most typically, resilience has been defined in terms of the ability to withstand adversity. Other approaches to this construct rely on a dynamic paradigm that incorporates developmental and transactional processes between oneself and the various environmental influences that mold and reshape the ability to confront the various vagaries that life offers.

Reading through the chapters, I could not help but reflect on my own life story and how my own resilience evolved. As it should for many deaf people, the critical points made by the contributing authors resonated with me. I was not identified as deaf until the age of 2. I was blessed by parents who provided warmth, affection, and access to communication and language after overcoming a week's worth of mourning for the loss of their idealized hearing child. Utilizing the steadfast support of a therapist experienced in working with young deaf children, my parents spent untold hours ensuring a language-rich environment for me, even though both had to work full time. They made it comfortable and "normal" for me to be deaf. They affirmed my desire to be with deaf friends as well as hearing peers. When my academic and social abilities as a deaf girl who spoke differently were questioned, the principal of my elementary school fought against entrenched opinions that I as a deaf student could not succeed in challenging post-elementary educational environments. These dynamic ecological influences, and more, conspired to form within me a resilient, solid, and coherent sense of self capable of facing indifference, doubt, opposition, and outright discrimination as well as the joys of life.

My experiences and the perceptions of the various authors in this book highlight the importance of considering not only individual characteristics but also the ecological systems that surround the individual. Edna Simon Levine's (1981) seminal book, *The Ecology of Early Deafness*, was one of the early significant texts to bring attention to the critical importance of the interactive role of self and environment in enhancing the development of deaf persons. She noted how an unaccommodating, noninclusive environment could result in individual deficiencies, even when the deaf child had significant potential. The importance of reforming the environment to enhance communication access and appropriate development was a constant theme for her.

How accommodating environments could be created has been highlighted by a parade of books that followed Dr. Levine's. For example, *Deaf in America: Voices from a Culture* (Padden & Humphries, 1988) taught the public how culturally Deaf people created an approach to life that was functional and full of human connections, enhanced by visual ways of communicating. This approach is grounded in an environment that accommodated their communication and social needs in ways that were normal for them. Creating a new center of normality that can stand alongside the normality of people who hear was a critical contribution to the notion that deaf people are capable of full lives and dealing with risks in their own ways just like everyone else. This new center reinforced the expectation that deaf children could be well-adjusted and resilient given appropriate access to the world around them.

With that expectation in mind, books such as *The Deaf Child in the Family and at School* (Spencer, Erting, & Marschark, 2000) began to look at the nature of interactions between the deaf child and the family/community/school systems as well as the philosophies that guide these systems. The book you are holding in your hands has taken this scrutiny of accommodating environments and theoretical frameworks one step further. Its authors have proposed various system constellations that contribute positively to the deaf child's evolving resilience. A number of them focus on Urie Bronfenbrenner's (e.g., 2005) theoretical paradigm that encompasses the critical bidirectional influences of distant systems such as culture and government and more immediate systems such as schools or the medical establishment, for example, as these directly and indirectly influence the deaf child via family and neighborhood systems, and vice versa. How these systems are shaped can have powerful influences on resilience and sense of self as the child transitions to adolescence and young adulthood. This is a dynamic process that requires some goodness of fit between individual characteristics and the various systems in order to enhance the potential for resilience. Although the complexities of this process are daunting, the power to mold the child demands that it be carefully attended to. In this book, the authors successfully break down the complexities into components that readers can try to apply in their own situations.

Again and again in this book, the contributing authors refer to the family system as a centerpoint that serves (as it did for me) to pave the way to the incredible possibilities of being a resilient deaf person. Based on research documentation, strongly emphasized throughout the book, the nature of attachment, relationships, and family communication – whether via a signed or spoken language – are key components for the development of resilient deaf children. Given professional support to encourage them to work on strong family relationships and communication, parents are more likely to be intuitive in meeting their child's needs. Using this as a foundation, the authors provide practical suggestions that will enhance the ways multiple systems (family, community, neighborhood, school, workplace, and so on) can facilitate social support and resilience, thereby enhancing the deaf child's capacities for relatedness, competence, and self-determination.

This book is a welcome addition to the burgeoning literature that focuses on the strengths and capabilities of deaf people for managing their lives. It provides a refreshing look into how these positive attributes can be developed throughout the early phases of the life course. It provides us with theoretical paradigms that help us conceptualize how resilience can be fostered in any deaf child, whatever the internal attributes and external circumstances may be. And it provides hope that society can and will recognize that deaf people can and do make significant contributions to the fascinating diversity of human lives.

Gallaudet University   Irene W. Leigh, Ph.D.
Washington, DC, USA

References

Bronfenbrenner, U. (Ed.). (2005). *Making human beings HUMAN: Bioecological perspectives on human development*. Thousand Oaks, CA: Sage Publications, Inc.

Levine, E. S. (1981). *The ecology of early deafness; Guides to fashioning environments and psychological assessments*. New York: Columbia University Press.

Padden, C., & Humphries, T. (1988). *Deaf in America: Voices from a culture*. Cambridge, MA: Harvard University Press.

Spencer, P. E., Erting, C. J., & Marschark, M. (2000). *The deaf child in the family and at school*. Mahwah, NJ: Lawrence Erlbaum.

Acknowledgements

This book was meant to stimulate thought and discussion regarding the manner in which resilience among the deaf may be similar, and yet again distinctly different, than that of the hearing population. This conceptualization created the canvas on which many of the works in the book were painted. We would like to take the time here to thank all of the authors for their timely and generous contributions to the content of this book and making the "picture" as complete as possible at this juncture in time.

We would also like to thank Dr. Danny Wedding for acting as a mentor and as a sounding board for our ideas about which direction the book should take as it was developing over time.

Finally, we would be remiss if we did not thank the people at Springer, for without them this book would have never made it to production and into your hands to read.

Contents

About the Editors

Dr. Zand is a clinical psychologist and Research Associate Professor at the University of Missouri–Columbia, Medical School, Department of Psychiatry. For the past 14 years, her work has focused on child and adolescent mental health and resilience. During this time, she has been responsible for writing, designing, and directing multiple federally funded longitudinal grants. Her most recent project focuses on fostering bonding between medically fragile, developmentally disabled young children and their caregivers. Dr. Zand has taught both graduate and undergraduate courses in research methods and mental health policy, mentored graduate students and junior faculty, published in peer-reviewed journals, and presented findings in local, state, and national forums. Recently, she was accepted into the American Psychological Association's Leadership Institute for Women in Psychology.

Dr. Kathy Pierce, a clinical psychologist at Washington University's School of Medicine – Department of Psychiatry, specializes in novel interventions for persons with treatment-resistant depression. Over the past 6 years, Dr. Pierce has worked on both industry and federally funded clinical trials, serving as a supervisor, psychometrician, treater, statistician, co-author, and/or grant writer. Prior to working at Washington University, Dr. Pierce was the Evaluation Director for a nonprofit agency providing care for AIDs patients, and co-led Missouri's "Deaf Mental Health PAH," a statewide deaf mental health advocacy group.

About the Contributors

Elizabeth B. Adams, M.A., received her M.A. in psychology from Gallaudet University and is currently pursuing a Ph.D. in clinical psychology from Gallaudet University. She is a co-editor of the *Gallaudet Chronicle of Psychology*, a student-run journal that truly reflects the working, living, and learning that takes place at Gallaudet and within the Deaf community.

Shirin D. Antia, Ph.D., is a full professor at the University of Arizona in the Department of Disability and Psychoeducational Studies. She was born and educated in India and has considerable international and intercultural experiences in special education. Her research interests are in the area of peer interaction, social integration, and best practices in inclusion of Deaf and Hard of Hearing children. She has authored numerous research articles and chapters on these topics. Most recently, she was the principal investigator of a research grant to examine the social and academic status and progress of deaf and hard of hearing students in public schools over a 5-year period.

Patrick J. Brice, Ph.D., received his Ph.D. in clinical and developmental psychology in 1983 and has been at Gallaudet University since that year. He first completed a postdoctoral fellowship in psychology at Gallaudet in 1983, taught in the Department of Counseling from 1984 until 1995, and since 1995 has been a professor in the Department of Psychology. He has been the Clinical Psychology Ph.D. Program Director since 2001. In addition to his teaching at Gallaudet, Dr. Brice has studied various aspects of development in deaf children, including social cognition, self-regulation and executive functions, social–emotional development, and parent–child attachment. He is a reviewer for The *Journal of Deaf Studies and Deaf Education* and the *Journal of the American Orthopsychiatric Association* and also serves as a grant reviewer for various funding agencies. Dr. Brice has also been a consulting psychologist to the Lab School of Washington, St. Elizabeth's Hospital, The National Health Care Foundation for the Deaf, and the Family Service Foundation in Maryland. He maintains an independent practice of psychology in Maryland and District of Columbia He specializes in parent–child attachment, adult attachment, social and cognitive development of deaf children, psychological assessment, and individual psychotherapy.

Cindi Cassady, Ph.D., a clinical psychologist in private practice in San Diego, CA, has worked with deaf and hard of hearing individuals and their families for the past 20 years. She is co-clinical director of mental health services at Deaf Community Services, as well as clinical supervisor at the Bridgman Group Home, which serves emotionally and behaviorally disturbed youth, ages 12–18. Dr. Cassady also specializes in working with perpetrators and victims of domestic violence and is certified by the Department of Adult Probation to facilitate a 52-week domestic violence group for deaf male perpetrators.

Rachel Gali Cinamon, Ph.D., is an associate Professor in the Department of Counseling and Special Education, School of Education, Tel Aviv University and is also Head of the special program for career counseling for young adults, Tel Aviv University.

Susan Daniels, OBE is the chief executive of the National Deaf Children's Society, UK.

Johannes Fellinger, M.D., is a neuropsychiatrist, pediatric neurologist and Head of the Neurological Institute for Language and Senses – Health Center for the Deaf of the Hospital of St. John of God in Linz, Austria.

Lorraine Green, Ph.D., is a lecturer in social work at the University of Manchester. Her main research interests include gender and child welfare, abuse, and children in vulnerable settings or circumstances.

Peter C. Hauser, Ph.D., is an Associate Professor of Research and Teacher Education at the National Technical Institute for the Deaf at Rochester Institute of Technology, Rochester, New York where he is the Director of the Deaf Studies Laboratory (DSL). His laboratory follows three strands of inquiry that focus on the (a) separate effects of sign language fluency and different levels of hearing on cognition, including attention, executive functions, memory, and reading processes; (b) psychosocial development of deaf students and the impact of audism on education; and (c) development of sign language assessment instruments. He is also the Director of the Neurocognitive Foundations of Vision for Language and Communication Research Initiative at the National Science Foundation Science of Learning Center on Visual Language and Visual Learning at Gallaudet University, Washington, DC.

Daniel Holzinger, Ph.D., is a clinical linguist and Head of the Centre for Language and Communication of the Neurological Institute for Language and Senses – Hospital of St. John of God in Linz, Austria.

Susan Kashubeck-West, Ph.D., is a licensed psychologist and Associate Professor at the University of Missouri–St. Louis. Dr. Kashubeck-West's primary research interests fall into two main areas: body image and eating disorders, and multicultural issues (broadly defined). She is interested in issues related to sexual orientation, race/ethnicity, and gender, primarily as they relate to psychological well-being.

Erin A. Kennedy, Ph.D., is a Developmental Psychologist and Assistant Professor in the Department of Psychology at Lock Haven University in Lock Haven, PA. She has conducted research on bullying in adolescence, socio-emotional adjustment of children with siblings who have been diagnosed with serious illnesses, self-esteem and academic motivation in college students with learning disabilities, and issues related to gender-typed behavior in childhood.

Lynne Sanford Koester, Ph.D., is a Developmental Psychologist who specializes in infant development and parent–infant interactions, particularly with children who are deaf. She worked previously at the Max-Planck Institute for Psychiatry in Munich, Germany, and at Gallaudet University in Washington, DC. Her current position is at The University of Montana–Missoula, where she is a Professor in the Department of Psychology.

Janet E. Kuebli, Ph.D., is a Developmental Psychologist and Associate Professor at Saint Louis University where she also directs the Undergraduate Studies Program in psychology. Her research interests include emotion development, including the role of family discourse in emotion socialization; children's health/safety socialization; and the psychology of parenting.

Jason Listman, M.S., is currently a faculty member in the Department of American Sign Language and Interpreting Education at the National Technical Institution of the Deaf. Prior to becoming an ASL instructor, he worked at the Deaf Studies Lab (DSL) from 2004 to 2009, working closely with Dr. Peter Hauser in areas such as linguistics, cognition, and psychosocial factors relating to the deaf experience. Mr. Listman hopes to begin his doctoral program in Education in 2012, with his primary research interest being resilience in deaf adolescents.

John Luckner, Ed.D., is a professor and the coordinator of the Deaf Education teacher preparation program in the School of Special Education and the Director of Research for the Bresnahan/Halstead Center at the University of Northern Colorado. Dr. Luckner was a classroom teacher of students who are deaf or hard of hearing for 9 years. His primary research interests include literacy, social–emotional development, teacher preparation, and the provision of appropriate services for students who are deaf or hard of hearing and their families.

Pamela Luft, Ph.D., is an Associate Professor of Special Education at Kent State University in Ohio and the Director of the Deaf Education program. She received her M.Ed. in Deaf Education from McDaniel College, her M.S. in Technology for Persons with Disabilities from the Johns Hopkins University, and her Ph.D. from University of Illinois at Urbana–Champaign in Special Education. She worked in public, special day and residential schools as a teacher, behavior specialist, career coordinator, and program administrator before getting her doctorate. Her research and grant projects have focused on transition services and rehabilitation services for the deaf. She has published on issues related to transition, technology employment of persons with disabilities, special education policy, and instructional practices.

Jennifer Lukomski, Ph.D., is an Associate Professor at Rochester Institute of Technology School Psychology Program. She teaches for RIT as well as consults with Greater Rochester school districts regarding school programming for deaf and hard of hearing youth. She also has a clinical practice. Her research focus includes social–emotional issues related to deaf and hard of hearing learners.

Linda Risser Lytle, Ph.D., is an associate professor and director of the Summers Only School Counseling Program in the Department of Counseling at Gallaudet University. She also maintains a private practice, working with deaf and hard of hearing individuals and their families. Dr. Lytle is interested in issues surrounding the development of deaf female identity. She is currently intrigued by the richness and complexity of using narrative inquiry as a research tool and how the use of stories influences both teller and listener.

Nicole McCray, Ph.D., is a recent graduate of the Developmental Psychology graduate program at The University of Montana–Missoula. Her research focuses on parent–infant interactions and interventions with at-risk populations.

Jill Meyer, M.S., is a licensed clinical professional counselor conducting research at the Missouri Institute of Mental Health in St. Louis, MO. She is also a doctoral candidate at the University of Missouri–St. Louis. Her background is in rehabilitation counseling and counseling education. Ms. Meyer's primary research areas are disability issues (including deaf studies) as they relate to rehabilitation and well-being.

Rinat Michael is a doctoral student in the Department of Counseling and Special Education, School of Education, Tel Aviv University.

Tova Most, Ph.D., is an associate Professor, and Head of the Department of Counseling and Special Education, School of Education, Tel Aviv University.

Gina A. Oliva, Ph.D., was a professor in the Department of Physical Education and Recreation at Gallaudet University until her retirement in 2009. She continues to be active professionally through publications, presentations, and consultations.

Gina's first book, *Alone in the Mainstream: A Deaf Woman Remembers Public School* (Gallaudet University Press) was published in 2004. Her current research and writing interests include deaf–hearing friendships and alliances, the development of social capital in summer and weekend programs, and the social needs of youth with cochlear implants.

Joan M. Ostrove, Ph.D., is an associate professor of psychology at Macalester College in St Paul, Minnesota. Her research concerns the connections between individual psychology and social structure. She is currently working on projects related to the ways in which social class background shapes people's experiences in higher education and about how people build alliances across differences related to social identity. Her work on alliances is focused on relations between Deaf and hearing people, and between people of color and white people. She is currently on leave from Macalester and is a student in the Interpreter Preparation Program at Ohlone College in Fremont, CA.

Susanne Reed, Ph.D., is a researcher at the University of Arizona. She taught deaf and hard of hearing students in public and center-based programs, preschool through high school for 18 years. Her research interests are in the area of best practices for inclusion of Deaf and Hard of Hearing students. Dr. Reed is the author or co-author of several peer-reviewed articles and a book entitled, *"Itinerant Teachers of Students Who are Deaf and Hard of Hearing: Their Beliefs and Practices for Developing Literacy."*

Katherine D. Rogers, M.Res., is a NIHR (National Institutes of Health Research) doctoral fellow working within the Social Research with Deaf People group at the University of Manchester. Her main research interests include the mental well-being of deaf children and mental health assessment in Sign Language.

Linda R. Shaw, Ph.D., is a Professor and Department Head, in the Department of Disability and Psychoeducational Studies at the University of Arizona. Prior to her current position, Dr. Shaw was Director of the Rehabilitation Counseling Program at the University of Florida. A licensed mental health counselor, Dr. Shaw's research focuses on disability, human rights, rehabilitation ethics, and professional issues in rehabilitation counseling. Dr. Shaw has published and presented widely on issues related to disability-related job discrimination and the correlates of professional ethical behavior.

Martha A. Sheridan, Ph.D., is a professor of social work at Gallaudet University where she teaches courses in human behavior and the social environment, social work practice, and field instruction. She has worked as a clinical social worker in school, community mental health, and private practice settings, and as an administrator, educator, consultant, and advocate. Her publications include *Inner lives of deaf children: Interviews and analysis* (2001) and *Deaf adolescents: Inner lives and lifeworld development* (2008).

Nicole Renick Thomson, Ph.D., is a Developmental Psychologist and Research Assistant Professor of Psychiatry at the University of Missouri St. Louis's Missouri Institute of Mental Health in St. Louis, MO. Her research interests include the etiology and prevention of youth alcohol use, socio-emotional development in early childhood, parenting, moral development and gender identity. Her recent publications have appeared in *Sex Roles, Pediatrics, and Journal of Adolescence.*

Christine Yoshinaga-Itano, Ph.D., is a Professor in the Department of Speech, Language and Hearing Sciences at the University of Colorado, Boulder. Professor Yoshinaga-Itano has certification as both an educator of the deaf and an audiologist and has conducted research on the development of young children with hearing loss and their families since the 1970s. She has focused on the interrelationship between language and communication skills, cognition and social–emotional development.

Alys Young, Ph.D., is a Professor of Social Work Education and Research at the University of Manchester and director of SORD (Social Research with Deaf People). She has published extensively on families with deaf children and service development and evaluation.

Part I
Introduction

Chapter 1
Critical Issues in the Application of Resilience Frameworks to the Experiences of Deaf Children and Young People

Alys Young, Katherine D. Rogers, Lorraine Green, and Susan Daniels

Abstract In this chapter, the authors take a critical look at the application of resilience-based frameworks to the experience of deaf children/young people. They begin by discussing three key issues: the implications of defining deafness as risk or adversity, in the face of which one is required to be resilient; the significance of the socially constructed nature of outcome-oriented definitions of resilience in the context of deaf children; and the extent to which the individualization of resilience may obscure significant aspects of deaf children's experience in society. They go on to look in detail at how factors and processes associated with resilience may be difficult or differently achieved in the case of deaf children arguing that research is not yet adequate to investigate from d/Deaf people's perspective how they might define what it is to be resilient. The chapter reviews the small amount of specific research that does exist in relation to resilience and deaf children, but questions whether a concern with resilience is not just ultimately a rebranding of the evidence and insights of the much broader corpus of research concerning deaf children's optimum development.

Resilience is an enticing concept. It focuses attention on what it is that enables people to bounce back despite numerous setbacks; it forces us to understand how and why children might succeed despite adversity; and it offers the hope that early disadvantages, harm or pain do not determine a negative trajectory for children's futures. Thus to understand resilience – why one may have it and one may not – is potentially to understand what might make a positive difference, what might enable success, and how to engender greater coping resources in all. Certainly, the study of resilience has flourished in many fields and resilience-building interventions are increasingly common. However, the application of resilience-based frameworks to the lives of deaf children and young people is new. Very little research that directly addresses resilience has been carried out in this context, although as will become

A. Young (✉)
Social Research with Deaf People Programme, School of Nursing, Midwifery and Social Work
University of Manchester, Manchester, UK
e-mail: alys.young@manchester.ac.uk

D.H. Zand and K.J. Pierce (eds.), *Resilience in Deaf Children: Adaptation Through Emerging Adulthood*, DOI 10.1007/978-1-4419-7796-0_1,
© Springer Science+Business Media, LLC 2011

apparent from this book, there is much that could be said to be related to resilience, or which implicitly addresses resilience.

In 2007, the authors were commissioned by the National Deaf Children's Society (NDCS) in the UK to write a comprehensive literature review on deaf children and resilience (Young, Green, & Rogers, 2008). NDCS, the largest organization in the UK representing deaf children and their families, was considering a program of work aimed at maximizing deaf children's resilience. Understanding the available literature was an important first step. However, as we began the work, it became apparent that the application of resilience-based frameworks to the lives of deaf children and young people was not without its problems. At a theoretical level, we began both to interrogate the validity of the concept in this particular context and to investigate how the experiences of deaf children and young people might bring something new to mainstream understandings of resilience. In this chapter, we will outline some of the theoretical challenges this confluence of resilience and deafness raises for us as a contribution to critical debate and critical practice. As a postscript to this chapter, the original commissioner of the literature review will offer her reflections on the issues we have raised.

The Problems of Deafness as "Risk" in the Face of Which One Is Resilient

In general terms, resilience is used to refer to the factors, processes, and mechanisms that in the face of significant risk, trauma, adversity, stress, or disadvantage, nonetheless, appear to work to enable an individual, family, or community to survive, thrive, and be successful (however those outcomes may be defined). Differing constituencies of interest will approach resilience with differing emphases. Resilience may be seen as the counterweight to psychopathology (Rutter, 2000), as a generally required adaptability to significant challenges (Singer & Powers, 1993), as inherent traits or acquired skills (Bartelt, 1994; Rigsby, 1994), as specific to particular processes in particular contexts (Cohler, 1987; Jacelon, 1997; Ungar, 2004), or as synonymous with desirable outcomes (Jackson & Martin, 1998; Olsson, Bond, Burns, Vella-Brodrick, & Sawyer, 2003). However, regardless of such differences, one thing remains constant, namely, the definition of something as risk/adversity/stress/trauma/disadvantage, in the light of which we recognize resilience. Rutter (2000) makes a telling point in suggesting that one of the methodological problems with much research on resilience is that it does not clearly enough define or justify that source risk. Has the adverse experience or disadvantage really been proven to be such, so that consequent identified features and processes of resilience are valid? In this respect, we must ask ourselves how and why deafness may be regarded as risk in the face of which a child and/or their family may be resilient and what the implications might be of that definition for how we define and promote resilience.

We do know that deafness in childhood (particularly early childhood and severe to profound deafness) is linked developmentally with a greater likelihood of a host of

less than optimal outcomes, be they in the domains of literacy (Conrad, 1979), mental
health (Hindley, 1997; Hindley, Hill, McGigan, & Kitson, 1994; Hindley & Kitson, 2000;
Sinkkonen, 1998), social and cognitive functioning (Greenberg & Kusche, 1989;
Marschark, 1993), educational achievement (Powers & Gregory, 1998), vulnerability
to abuse (Obinna, 2005; Sullivan, Brookhouser, & Scanlon, 2000), or future employment and socioeconomic opportunity (Dye & Kyle, 2000). However, this is not the
same as saying deafness itself is a risk factor for such outcomes. Rather deafness in
a range of familial, social, and institutional contexts may interact with variables and
processes that make its potential negative effects more likely.

   A classic example in this respect is that of child protection. Deafness does not
necessarily render deaf children more vulnerable to abuse, but care and educational
circumstances where there are fewer opportunities to be able to communicate effectively with adults to discuss protection and/or disclose abuse might make deaf children more likely targets for abusers (Kennedy, 1989; Sullivan, Vernon, & Scanlon,
1987). These types of interactions between trait and environmental contexts are
what Rutter (2000) describes as "proximal risk mechanisms" (p. 653). The key
distinction here is that deafness may be a risk indicator, but is not of itself a risk
mechanism. Nonetheless, some studies persist in failing to make that distinction.
For example, Kramer, Kapteyn, and Houtgast (2006) in a study of occupational
performance conclude that "…hearing impairment should be considered as a risk
factor for fatigue and mental distress which may lead to sick leave" (p. 510). Yet
their own study addresses how it is interaction with features of the workplace that
may create disadvantageous experiences for deaf workers, not the fact that they
have a hearing loss per se.

   The second issue in thinking about deafness as risk in the face of which one
wishes to develop resilience questions the nature of the relationship between deafness and disadvantage from a sociopolitical perspective. If one accepts the notion
of Deafness as a defining feature of cultural-linguistic identity (Lane, Hoffmeister, &
Behan, 1996; Padden & Humphries, 1988), rather than an audiological impairment,
then the nature of the risk associated with it concerns the failure to enable deaf
children to have developmental opportunities to realize that identity. Paradoxically,
from this perspective, resilience could be defined in terms of outcome as the
achievement of a signing Deaf identity and membership in the Deaf community,
despite the range of hearing-oriented discourses and institutionalized preferences
(oral education, cochlear implantation, medical model understanding of deafness as
impairment) that might work against such achievement through one's childhood
(Ladd, 2003). In other words, resilience could be defined as resistance to conformity or to imposed normative expectations, a little-explored approach in the mainstream literature (Grover, 2002; McAdam-Crisp, 2006 are rare exceptions).

   This particular paradox became literally transparent when two of the authors
first discussed the original literature review project in British Sign Language (BSL).
One used a sign for resilience akin to that of "protection" with the direction of the
movement of the sign toward the body. For her, a primary meaning of resilience was
the opposite of risk – what was it that acted to protect the individual against adverse
consequences of stressful, traumatic, or disadvantageous life experiences? It drew
attention to the individualized and to some extent internalized nature of psychosocial

features such as repertoires of coping skills and positive cognitions. The other took up the discussion and used a sign akin to that of "resistance," with an outwards movement of a closed fist away from the body and upwards. For her, resilience was that which enabled one to fight back and continue to dismiss those features of a world that might seek to diminish all of which one was capable. It drew attention to the influence of societal attitudes and structures which could discriminate and disadvantage.

Indeed in BSL, there is no consistently recognized sign for "resilience" (yet) and in the course of the project we remained alert to those used by others and what they might betray about how resilience was understood in relation to deafness and its conceptualization (or not) as risk, disadvantage, and vulnerability. In ASL too, there is yet to be a conventional sign but one often used emphasizes the notion of bounce-backability.

The third issue in considering the relationship between deafness as risk/disadvantage/trauma and resilience concerns how comfortable or not we might feel about defining deafness as an undesirable trait to be overcome or survived (Woolfe & Young, 2006). Within such a framework, resilience becomes evidenced by having done so. Yet as the disability movement has successfully critiqued, the discourse of overcoming one's disability as evidenced through achievement renders any kind of achievement exceptional, thus reinforcing the normative low expectations that society might otherwise have. It diminishes what may be of value in simply being who one is capable of being (rather than having to be a heroic figure who overcomes despite the odds).

Our point here is that resilience, if used to indicate a remarkable or exceptional trajectory for deaf children, runs the risk, paradoxically, of reinforcing low expectations for the majority and making success unexpected rather than normal. Also, as has been pointed out in another context, to align resilience with the definition of success is potentially to open the door to withdrawal of support for individuals no longer deemed to need it if regarded as resilient (Rigsby, 1994).

The Problem of Resilience as Outcome in the Context of Deaf Children

Commonly in the mainstream literature, predefined *outcome* definitions of resilience dominate analyses of process (how someone becomes resilient) without questioning the definition of the resilient outcome in the first place. A study of resilient care leavers (i.e., foster care children) (Jackson & Martin, 1998) is a case in point, but this is a methodological problem that spans a great many studies (e.g., Hampson, Rahman, Brown, Taylor, & Donaldson, 1998). In the Jackson and Martin study (1998), resilience is defined by the display of exceptional academic success against the odds. Consequently, research subjects are classified into a successful or unsuccessful group against this criterion, and then differences between the two groups are investigated. What differentiates the groups against the agreed outcome provides the definition of what constitutes resilience.

The problem is the a priori definition of what counts as a resilient outcome constrains the nature of the analysis. Rather two-dimensional connections are sought between variables that might differ between the two groups and the outcome. Also, as Rutter (2000) argues, a variable is hardly a mechanism (it does not explain the pathway to an outcome) and while the presence of enabling factors may be taken as connected with resilient outcomes, this is absolutely not the same as saying their absence accounts for why a resilient outcome is not achieved.

Furthermore, we may want to question the definition of resilience used in the first place. It has been well argued (McAdam-Crisp, 2006; Serafica, 1997; Ungar, 2004) that one of the problems of much resilience literature is that it fails to acknowledge the socially and culturally constructed nature of the outcome definitions of resilience that are used (e.g., academic success as normative social good). Grover (2002, 2005), for example, argues children's attempts at survival and being resilient with dignity under difficult conditions are often interpreted as evidence of psychopathology or conduct disorder, particularly if they involve the breaking of legal rules. Yet their behavior may be clear evidence of resilience, if we were to positively value its manifestations.

For example, children protesting against institutionalized care conditions by running away or completely rejecting the value of education, rules, or social conformity could be seen as resilient, but according to different outcomes and criteria from those normally evoked (Cirillo, 2000; Green, 1998; Morgan, 1998). A similar point could be made in relation to deaf children in oral schools where signing was banned and children punished for its use, yet they still learned to sign from their deaf peers and still valued it as essential to their personhood.

In relation to deaf children, therefore, a pertinent question becomes what counts as a resilient outcome and what are the assumptions and values that underpin its definition and by whom? To ask such a question is not necessarily to deny resilience as an entity, but is to draw attention to the fact that outcomes perceived as evidence of resilience are themselves socially and culturally constructed. Unfortunately, the few research studies specifically related to resilience in deaf children/young people have taken a less critical approach to the problem of a priori definitions of resilience based on outcome markers.

Applying a strict definition of resilience in deafness research (i.e., one that specifically utilizes resilience theory and models), we were only able to locate two publications (Charlson, Bird, & Strong, 1999; Rogers, Muir, & Evenson, 2003) that empirically applied resilience as a framework for their investigations. One was, however, founded on a data set previously collected, Charlson, Strong, and Gold (1992) and we further identified one publication that argues for resilience as evidential from deaf adults' narratives of childhood (Steinberg, 2000), which we discuss later.[1]

Charlson et al. (1999) use a rather simple outcomes-derived approach to investigating resilience in deaf young people. That is to say, they identify (through others' nomination) deaf young people regarded as "outstandingly successful" (taken from

[1] It should be noted that resilience in the context of deafness has acquired some currency in the field of sign linguistics where it is a term used to denote those features of language that appear in deaf children's communication systems whether or not they have been exposed to a conventional language model (Goldin-Meadow, 2003, Chap. 16). These linguistic sources are not regarded as relevant for this purpose.

Charlson et al., 1992) then investigate a subsample of three of them (through case study) to identify those factors associated with success, which are then presumed to be synonymous with resilience.

To be fair, the authors do not themselves define a successful outcome for deaf children, they allow those who nominate relevant deaf young people to set that definition. It is, however, noticeable that in so doing, the nominators predominantly reinforce the notion of resilience being associated with exceptional achievement (e.g., in education and sports), rather than resilience being associated with the successful acquisition of those skills and abilities that enable one successfully to respond to stressful or adverse life events *as a matter of course*. This alternative, nonexceptional approach to what is resilience has been neatly summed up elsewhere as "ordinary magic" (Masten, 2001).

Rogers et al. (2003), while also taking a predefined outcomes approach to the investigation of resilience, go one step further and begin to consider what might be an appropriately defined "successful" outcome *specifically* for young Deaf people. In their case study of three Deaf young people they:

> "...define resilience as the exemplary ability to bridge the Deaf and hearing worlds both socially (i.e., through leadership roles in the Deaf community) and in terms of work success (i.e., working a combined total of 40 hours weekly in one or more hearing settings), despite the risk and challenges that may be associated with audiologic and linguistic differences" (p. 223).

Although, in this study, the social and political construction of what counts as a resilient outcome is acknowledged in its definition being so precise and context specific, there is little justification for why that particular definition is seized upon. Within the highly contested field of deafness, where multiple paradigms (medical, social, and cultural) compete to define what it is to be d/Deaf, one cannot imagine that Rogers et al.'s (2003) definition of a resilient outcome is one that would be shared by proponents of all communication methodologies, nor indeed by all culturally Deaf insiders.

Our point here is fundamentally that in the deafness field there is still much basic research work to be done on exploring *what is resilience (including a resilient outcome) as understood and constructed by deaf children and adults themselves*, even before we seek to understand those factors and processes that may promote, sustain, or indeed reduce it. That said, this small corpus of work does offer some insight into processes, traits, and mechanisms seen from d/Deaf perspectives that the authors associate with the resilient outcomes they have predefined. We return to these issues later.

The Problem of the Individualization of Resilience in the Context of Deaf Children

A further potential problem in applying resilience-based frameworks to understanding the situation of deaf children concerns what we are terming the individualization of resilience. A great deal of mainstream literature concerning resilience, particularly from psychological/psychopathological perspectives (e.g., McCreanor & Watson, 2004), is concerned with accounting for why individuals may vary in their capacity to cope with/adapt to/overcome adverse circumstances and identifying how individuals can acquire (or be equipped with) the knowledge, skills, and practical techniques (Gilligan, 1998) that enable them to be more resilient. There are legions of work that identify such resilience-building or resilience-enabling factors that lie within the mastery of the individual (e.g., Oliver, Collin, Burns, & Nicholas, 2006; Tuttle, Campbell-Heider, & David, 2006) to be recognized, acquired, or deliberately taught. Our argument is not that these individual-based traits and characteristics are irrelevant in the case of deaf children and their families; indeed we will go on to examine why some of them may be particularly important and/or particularly difficult to influence in relation to deaf children. Rather, our point at this stage is that the *individualization of resilience* distorts significantly the life context of deaf children in which they may be seeking to be resilient.

Deaf children, in common with children with disabilities and other marginalized groups, are subject to the considerable influence of institutional and structural discrimination as well as the social processes of stigma, and additionally, the consequences of communication disadvantage. For example, we know that in the UK context, deaf adults are less likely to enter higher education (Powers & Gregory, 1998); to be significantly under and unemployed in comparison with their hearing peers (Dye & Kyle, 2000); and to face barriers to employment that are a consequence of communication ability/preference as well as hearing loss (RNID, 2006). More generally, in what has famously been termed phonocentrism (Corker, 1998), the hearing world is not one that is easy to navigate for those who do not rely on hearing and in which they may be cast as outsiders (Higgins, 1979). This attention to the socio-structural context is important in reminding us that the roots of risk and resilience do not wholly, nor perhaps should even be primarily understood, to lie within the individual.

This insight challenges a trajectory of resilience building that exclusively seeks to educate and equip a child/young person with tools to better navigate the potentially adverse consequences of their deafness without also fundamentally tackling the contribution of social systems to that risk and disadvantage. Indeed, the wider debate exists about whether in focusing on resilience we are in fact inappropriately transferring both blame and responsibility onto individuals to function well, rather than dealing with some of the overriding factors associated with their risk of not thriving, which create the processes and contexts of adversity in the first place. If we follow this argument to its logical conclusion, we should quite rightly question approaches to understanding and building resilience that assume to know what it is in terms of the individual and how to build it in them:

> "In the past, there has sometimes been a wish to search for the hallmarks of resilience, as if once one knew what it "looked like," it should be a relatively straightforward matter to design intervention to bring it about. That no longer appears a sensible aim" (Rutter, 2000, p. 675).

If we are to move toward a more sophisticated understanding of resilience in the context of deaf children, then this must to some extent include an understanding of both risk and resources lying within the domain of social relations and social policy (distal mechanisms). From this perspective, resilience is not just a personally acquired or individual characteristic; it is also an issue of social challenge and social change. How can we enable children's familial and social environments (including the educational environment) to be ones that foster resilience by actively challenging processes of disadvantage and discrimination that result from how society is organized and behaves?

In this respect, an interesting example is provided by the parent-driven organization Hands and Voices (http://www.handsandvoices.org). One of their cofounders Janet DesGeorges (2003) in writing, as a hearing parent, about the processes of coming to terms with her daughter's deafness, reminds us that the end point is "advocacy" not "acceptance." She argues that parents have a responsibility to equip themselves[2] with the skills to advocate for their deaf children in all domains (social, educational, and community) to ensure that barriers are brought down and children have access to those resources and opportunities that they need to develop and flourish through childhood. The emphasis is not on equipping the child to cope with the difficulties they are bound to face, but in challenging the origins of those difficulties where they need not exist.

To understand resilience as personally acquired and personally identifiable characteristics that delineate a resilient individual from one who is not, runs the risk of directing our attention to building resilience in the individual at the expense of enabling resilience by challenging the distal mechanisms that work against its engendering. In making this point, we are not necessarily arguing against programs supporting children in building skills and experiences that foster greater resilience (as we discuss later). We are cautioning against seeing such individualization as the sum of what fostering resilience might be about.

A Closer Look at Factors Associated with Resilience: Protection and Navigation Within the Deaf Experience

Much of the mainstream resilience literature concerns itself with identifying those factors (be they internal and/or environmental) that enable resilient processes and outcomes to occur. Attention has been paid to identifying these even if exactly how they operate is not necessarily well understood, nor how they might be promoted necessarily straightforward.

From one perspective, factors associated with resilience are factors associated with protection (protective mechanisms). Namely what it is that obviates against risk, or reduces the likely adverse consequences of the risk to which the individual may be vulnerable (Dyer & McGuiness, 1996; Hill, 1998; Rutter, 1995). Resilient individuals (or in some cases groups) are thus those found to have such characteristics,

---

[2] Hands and Voices provide parent to parent training in this respect.

or those with such characteristics are associated with being resilient. We state this point both ways to indicate that "association" is just that; without causal explanation of mechanisms it is unclear what is affected and how. Studies vary considerably in the extent to which they investigate the direction, strength, and complexity of the mechanisms of association they might identify. Nonetheless, there are recurring categories of "protective and promotive" factors (Ostazewski & Zimmerman, 2006) associated with resilience in the mainstream literature.

In this respect, attention has been paid to (1) internal psychological characteristics and personality traits: intelligence, positive cognitive processing of negative experiences, good self-esteem, strong self-efficacy, effective coping strategies, internal locus of control, sense of purpose/goal orientation, optimism, creativity, perseverance, self-understanding, authenticity, and desire to learn (e.g., Bland, Sowa, & Callahan, 1994; Gillham & Reivich, 2004; Valentine & Feinauer, 1993; Waaktaar, Christie, Borge, & Torgersen, 2004); (2) interpersonal repertoires of psychosocial competencies: prosocial behavior, good communication including problem solving communication, good naturedness in such a way as to gain other's positive attention, and social competence (Bland et al., 1994; Dyer & McGuiness, 1996; Joseph, 1994; Olsson et al., 2003); and (3) sociocultural characteristics: positive values, such as faith, spirituality, and religious belief, and ideological commitment (Hill, 1998; Valentine & Feinauer, 1993; Walsh, 1998).

From a different perspective, significant factors associated with resilience are those that provide assets and build resources for the successful navigation of day-to-day experience in such a way that experience impacts positively, or one can overcome its potentially negative effects. Sometimes referred to in the literature as "environmental assets" (Rogers et al., 2003), this perspective would include (1) factors associated with experiential learning such as the expansion of opportunities for new experiences, in terms of both quality and quantity, strengths-based experiences that confirm competence and promote positive self-esteem, opportunities for the completion of important life transitions, experiences of taking responsibility, opportunities for the development of problem-solving attitudes and behaviors, and experiences of participation in a wide variety of social contexts (Floyd, 1996; Gilligan, 2000; Hill, 1998; Johnson, 2003) and (2) familial, educational, and social conditions as a resource for the development of the competencies to negotiate the challenges of everyday life: emotional and practical family support resources and systems, role models and mentors, positive peer groups and peer support, good teachers, and a trusted adult either in or outside the direct family (Beltman & MacCallums, 2006; Gilligan, 1998; Grover, 2005; Waaktaar et al., 2004). As Walsh (2002, 2003) has suggested, from this perspective, resilience is not an achieved outcome, or incident specific response, but a life-long way of being.

Clearly, these two perspectives of traits that protect and assets that enable are not mutually exclusive. Prosocial behavior may be both an individual characteristic found to be protective against risk and a tool for navigating relationships that serves successfully to expand social horizons. As Rutter (1993, 1999), writing about protective mechanisms, suggests, resilience is perhaps best understood as the *cumulative successful handling* of manageable difficulties, which may inoculate against some future stresses. Nonetheless, the distinction between protective factors (including notions of protective processes) and what we are terming factors associated with the successful navigation of experience is helpful in thinking about the context of deaf children/young people. It is about reframing. If we are quite rightly questioning the validity of rather simplistic notions of deafness as risk, and resilience as evidence of the individual's success despite the adversity of being deaf, then it is pertinent to reframe resilience in terms of *the successful navigation of the experience of being deaf in a world that creates risks that might impede self-fulfillment, safety, and well being*. From this perspective, we can begin to think about what it is about deaf children's experiences that make the resilience-related factors we have identified and their associated processes and pathways difficult to achieve, or only differently achieved.

However, in reaching this point in our argument, we have also hit a paradox. Although there is very little specific work on resilience and deaf children (see below for further discussion), there are volumes of research that one might associate with the question we are posing, namely what might make these resilience-related factors difficult or differently achieved in the case of deaf children? So is this focus on resilience and deaf children simply a rebranding of preexisting knowledge without any additional insights?

For example, the seminal work of Greenberg and colleagues is focused on the promotion of the cognitive, social, and emotional development of deaf children/ young people (e.g., Calderon & Greenberg, 1993; Greenberg & Kusche, 1993; Greenberg, Kusche, Cook, & Quamma, 1995; Greenberg, Lengua, & Calderon, 1997). It contains many features coherent with a focus on resilience: an emphasis on positive psychology (skills building, not deficit remediation); an attention to the need for psychological, behavioral, social, and communicative resources that better suit and challenge less than optimum environmental conditions; and a methodology expressly designed for their acquisition and sustainability. The following would not be out of place in much resilience-framed work:

> "A…challenge for deaf youth is meeting the demand presented by daily hassles in a way that allows them to have positive interactions with others and to negotiate the hearing world. To meet these challenges and to show healthy social adjustment and relation with both deaf and hearing peers and adults, effective integration of affective, cognitive and behavioral skills is essential. This is likely to require active problem solving, effective utilization of support systems, and cognitive strategies that enhance one's beliefs about control and efficacy" (Greenberg et al., 1997, p. 318).

Indeed, one could argue that much of this particular volume is devoted to the application of deaf child/adult-related scholarship to the theoretical frameworks of resilience (from whatever perspective) regardless of whether that work would originally have been engendered from a resilience perspective/theoretical basis. Such application of knowledge and association of ideas is nonetheless helpful. It forces critical attention onto the fact that there is no easy translation of the conclusions of the resilience-based corpus of knowledge into the context of deaf children and young people. Careful consideration is needed of how their experiences of being deaf (and how society's responses to deafness and d/Deaf people) impact on those issues that resilience scholarship has identified as vital. Such seemingly fundamental issues as learning to take responsibility, being mentored, developing social competence, exploring new experiences, and so forth can all be problematic when mediated by, for example, the challenges of communicative competence and access to information.

That said, are there perhaps highly specific features of deaf children and young people's experience of the world, that might lead us to identify different factors and processes associated with resilience that are unique to that experience, rather than their experience being applied to what is already known about resilience? This is a rather frontier question because, as already discussed, there is little published literature that has sought specifically to use resilience-based frameworks to understand deaf children and young people's experience. Nonetheless, what exists does begin to offer some new insights.

Is There Evidence of Specifically Different Deaf Experience-Related Resilience Factors and Processes?

Charlson et al. (1999) and Rogers et al. (2003) mostly claim to have identified that the factors associated with resilience in deaf young people are highly consistent with those identified in children and young people in the nondeaf-related literature and in a wide variety of risky, disadvantaged, and adverse conditions. Of course, these conclusions may be an artifact of simply applying well-established resilience frameworks as the basis for the analysis of the data (one decides in advance what one is looking for and seeks to establish fit or variation). Nonetheless, from the data shared in these papers, one can recognize the universal significance of such characteristics as perseverance, self-belief, the importance of a mentoring adult, and positive peer relationships, which are common to a whole raft of studies in other spheres. Perhaps, this gives us an indication that there is more that unites the experience of deaf children with that of those who are not deaf than distinguishes their experience?

Yet if one looks closely into the same papers, one finds testimony of aspects of familial and social relations that are consequential on deafness such as extreme communication deprivation between some children and their parents and the stress of communication mismatch in a range of hearing contexts. This raises the question of whether there are "special" conditions surrounding the deaf child experience that *transform the significance and operation* of some of the identified resilience features that are seemingly consistent with the nondeaf literature. Very little has been considered in this respect.

Rogers et al. (2003) begin to take us along this road in identifying "comfort with solitude" being vital to the resilience repertoire for deaf young people and not a feature one would ordinarily find common to other populations. However, Wagnild and Young (1990) identified "existential aloneness" as a protective factor among those regarded as resilient. Is this different from the experience of deaf young people? Rogers et al. (2003) also suggest that "impression management" might be a resilience-reducing factor of particular relevance for young deaf people because: "Strong needs to conceal flaws while creating favorable social impressions may present an overwhelming challenge to Deaf persons who are already taxed by the burden of communicating with hearing people" (p. 231).

Certainly, Steinberg (2000) argues strongly that "Deafness serves as an exceptional model for the study of adaptation and resilience, particularly in relation to the emergence of a sense of self" (p. 105). Taking as her starting point the commonly disrupted and degraded nature of communication between deaf children and their hearing parents/developmental environments, she argues that one of the most enduring effects of deafness is the inability to create, explore, understand, or express narratives about oneself and others in childhood. If shared communication between child and caregiver is poor and inconsistent, and the world is one where information is difficult to share/obtain, and knowledge/experience through language hard to acquire, then she argues deaf children are potentially faced with few internal resources to make sense of the world around them. They are typically faced with the inappropriate burden of responsibility for trying to make communication with others work, a lack of access to the emotional lives of others, reduced experiences of empathic communication, and consistent social experiences of isolation.

For Steinberg (2000), the adaptations to these common experiences revealed in the narratives of d/Deaf adults looking back (whether drawn from research or clinical populations) are both evidence of, and definitions of, resilience in the context of deaf childhoods. In this respect, Steinberg's emphasis on narrative experience is consistent with an approach to resilience that is based on understanding the resources and strategies for the navigation of experience, rather than one that has sought post hoc to identify factors and mechanisms that can be associated with any given outcome one has classified as evidence of resilience.

Interestingly, for Steinberg (2000), resilience may quite legitimately encompass strategies that, looked at through a normative developmental psychology lens, might be regarded as significantly maladaptive or even disturbed. However, she emphasizes throughout her work that if such strategies were all that was available to that particular child, then the fact that they utilized them was evidence of that child's resilience – they did not go under in the most adverse conditions of communication deprivation.

In this respect, Steinberg recounts the story of an 8-year-old child who was sent home from school because her father had died, but there was nobody who could explain this to her, and there was almost no communication in the family. All she knew was that her father had disappeared:

> "Confused and bereft of landmarks or ways of responding, she placed her father's rowboat on the lake, sat on the boat near the dock and described everything to the moon. She recalled that the moon comforted her and answered her questions… This quiet dialog with the moon *exemplifies the resilient child* who invents a 'God of listening' to quell the 'yearning for witnessed significance' (Fleischman, 1989)" (Steinberg, 2000, p. 98, emphasis mine).

Clearly the question we have posed – whether there are features of the deaf child's experience that transform the significance and operation of factors and processes universally identified as consistent with resilience – is yet to be comprehensively addressed. In the little literature we have reviewed in this section, some issues are emerging that might begin to shed light on it – principally connected with the impact of communicative resources/skills and less than optimum communicative environments. It is not, however, a question that has been investigated in depth and, as previously discussed, may actually be obscured through the application of methodologies that are based on what is already known from the mainstream.

That said, it is equally important to establish the extent to which features of resilience (whether regarded as protection and/or navigation) may be of universal significance for this population also. However, in the course of establishing the veracity of such a position, it would still be important to consider carefully whether, although the features are universal, they are perhaps differently achieved in the case of deaf children/young people.

Resilience Enabling[3]: Deaf Children and Future Research

Our review, thus far, has identified some of the potential difficulties in applying resilience frameworks to the situation of deaf children and young people; has identified the factors and processes that consistently recur when considering both protective/promotive and navigatory understandings of what we may mean by enabling resilience; and has considered in relation to them that there is much work in deafness-related research of implicit relevance; however, research concerning deaf children/young people, which is specifically resilience-led, is rather restricted. So, does this bring us to the point where it is possible to identify those strategies, interventions, behaviors, or conditions that might promote resilient families of deaf children, and ultimately resilient young deaf people?

Certainly this "what works" kind of question is of contemporary interest as evidenced in Newman's (2004) review "What Works in Building Resilience" in which he reviews over 300 studies in varying contexts to define "resilience building" features and strategies that have direct implications for professional practice. (It is perhaps of note within such a comprehensive review only two identified studies even tangentially involved disabled children and none involved deaf children.) However, as Newman (2004) remarks: "The difficulties of translating the theory of resilience into concrete strategies should not be underestimated, especially where children are facing severe adversities or unpredictable life paths" (p. 68). In other words, there is a step between identifying what is of relevance and actually seeking to operationalize that in practice and subsequently evaluate the effects of such. Just because we know, for example, that encouraging risk taking within a supportive structure might be helpful in building resilience we do not necessarily know how to translate this

---

[3] We prefer the term resilience enabling to resilience building to avoid any overly narrow assumptions of equipping the individual without acknowledging the significance of socio-structural factors in the facilitation of resilience (such as challenging discriminatory attitudes).

knowledge into a practice that might encourage such an effect. Furthermore, where research has been undertaken on the application of theory-into-practice for resilience (e.g., Buchanan, 2004; Raybuck & Hicks, 1994; Wasmund & Copas, 1994), the extent to which those findings are context-bound is of vital importance. As we have reviewed, there is a host of added considerations in deaf children's experience that would need to be accounted for in resilience-enabling interventions. Increasing evidence is emerging of differences in deaf children's learning styles, in comparison with hearing children, for example. How would these be taken into account in designing resilience enabling interventions?

We would argue this is exactly the kind of research that is yet to be undertaken in relation to deaf children/young people where currently we have the rather paradoxical situation of (1) research that by proxy is highly relevant to the enabling of resilience but which fundamentally is not framed as resilience (e.g., Greenberg & Kusche, 1993); (2) many studies in other domains that individually are about features or processes that resilience enabling work identifies as important, for example, work on the influence of deaf role models on family support and deaf child development (e.g., Sutherland, Griggs, & Young, 2003), but the impact of which is not considered in terms of resilience; (3) resilience-specific work that is beginning to open up, at a theoretical level, the identification of resilience-related characteristics and strategies in deaf young people, but which says nothing about the application of these to practice (e.g., Rogers et al., 2003); and (4) little, if any, interrogation of professional practice associated with deaf children and young people from the perspective of resilience theory/theories.

On the one hand, these types of conclusions would seem to point in the direction of the need for the development of resilience-based professional practice in relation to deaf children and young people. On the other hand, it has been argued in some nondeaf-related contexts that while resilience may be a helpful theoretical perspective, it can be so over-generalized to be of little use in practice (Gorell Barnes, 1999).

Conclusions

Having thus reviewed the concept and application of resilience and resilience frameworks in the mainstream literature and considered its intersections with the deaf children's experiences and extant deaf-specific resilience literature, what are our conclusions? The following summarizes the main issues to emerge:

1. In considering the dynamics of how resilience may operate and be promoted, it is more helpful to consider the proximal risk mechanisms associated with deafness rather than thinking about deafness itself as a risk factor.
2. Outcome-oriented definitions of resilience focusing on achievement against the odds or despite being deaf, emphasize success as exceptional rather than normative and paradoxically may reinforce low expectations. Resilience understood from an outcomes perspective also runs the risk of being reductionist in its construction

of what might count as thriving for deaf children and of promoting particular preferred ways of being for deaf children.

3. Resilience associated with outcomes of success (however defined) is not an apolitical approach. Indeed, from some perspectives resilient deaf children may be those who successfully resist a perceived normative pressure to develop/communicate in a particular way that is regarded as synonymous with resilience.

4. A focus on the individual becoming equipped to be resilient fails adequately to account for the socio-structural mechanisms that may create and reinforce risk and adversity for deaf children and young people, including discrimination. Placing responsibility with the individual to be resilient can easily deemphasize the responsibility of society to create the conditions for resilience in how it behaves toward and supports its deaf citizens. Both would need to be pursued in tandem for optimum effect.

5. Reframing resilience in terms of the capacity to positively navigate the experience of being deaf in a world that may create risk and adversity in its response to deafness and d/Deaf people, is a helpful way to assist deaf children/young people to move forward. It brings together the importance of personal repertoires of skills and resources, with an understanding of resilience that acknowledges the social construction of risk and outcome, while emphasizing the increased vulnerability of deaf children to many factors that may work against them becoming resilient.

6. Many factors known to be protective and promotive in enabling resilience are ones that may be difficult to or differently achieved for deaf children, e.g., repertoires of coping styles, positive self-esteem. There is, therefore, no easy application of mainstream knowledge without careful consideration of how the context of deaf children's experience may challenge or modify preexisting approaches to resilience building. This is potentially a significant future area of both research and professional practice.

7. Some known resilience building strategies may be highly applicable in the case of deaf children (mentoring, opportunities for responsibility, expansion of experience including risk taking, etc.), but how they might be achieved may be different. For example, the mismatch of communication preference, ability, skill, capacity between deaf children and those around them may mean that there are experiences that are: denied to them (through assumed needs to be protective), unavailable in the same way (learning through peer social groups), or not considered relevant (the range of experiences from which deaf children may benefit will be reduced by the assumptions of others). We have no clear empirical evidence of such mechanisms in respect to resilience and deaf children. These conclusions are extrapolations that would require empirical verification.

The empirical evidence base for resilience and deaf children is very small, although many inferences can be made (as above). This may be because there is a host of work happening to support the abilities of deaf children and young people to navigate their world effectively and avoid unnecessary risk and adversity that simply have not been branded as resilience (e.g., Greenberg & Kusche, 1993). This raises the question of whether, therefore, it is of any help to apply a resilience framework to this context. In other fields, one of the strongest arguments for its application has been that it begins to orient practitioners and families toward positive psychology. That is to say, the recognition of and building of strengths in situations of adversity, rather than an emphasis on the pathological and dysfunctional requiring remediation. In supporting deaf children/young people, it may indeed be very helpful to use resilience as a means of reframing professional assessment and intervention, but research of the effects of such would also have to be undertaken.

There is a small amount of evidence that is beginning to suggest (1) that while the same issues associated with resilience are applicable to the deaf context, we understand very little about how variables associated with that context may modify the dynamics of resilience (whether understood in terms of factors, processes, mechanisms, or pathways); (2) there may be context-specific realizations of resilience that grow out of the experience of being deaf that are highly original to that experience, and that, in turn, may inform the more mainstream understanding of resilience (e.g., a factor such as comfort with solitude and how it operates effectively). However, we are in our infancy in exploring such questions.

Resilience, although with many caveats, might be a helpful way forward in focusing people's minds (professionals, parents, those who work with deaf young people) on being more deliberate in their attention to strategies and resources that build capacity in the individual *and* which challenge the structures and approaches that do not optimally enable or reveal the resilience of deaf young people. Individual and sociostructural efforts must go hand in hand to avoid the divisive potential of resilience as an approach that separates the successful from the failing and that reinforces normative standards of what it is to be successful that work against the diversity of d/Deaf people.

Acknowledgements Parts of this chapter first appeared in Young et al. (2008). The original work was funded by the National Deaf Children's Society, UK to whom we extend particular thanks for their vision in recognizing the timeliness of the topic.

Afterword by Susan Daniels, OBE, Chief Executive of the National Deaf Children's Society (NDCS), UK

NDCS is the UK's largest organization representing deaf children and their families in the UK (http://www.ndcs.org.uk). Its vision is: "A world without barriers for every deaf child." Empowerment is central to our mission, so that families can achieve the best outcomes for their deaf children and deaf children and young people are able to reach their true potential. In 2007, we began to consider the relevance of "resilience" to our goals, prompted by the work of Tony Newman (2004) who had reviewed evidence about what works in building resilience among a whole variety of children growing up in different circumstances. Yet within that review, there was scarcely a mention of any work that had been done in relation to deaf children and their families. As an organization, NDCS is committed to the development of new approaches in our own family support services and those of statutory providers as well as the provision of good evidence to support parents' decision making. We therefore began to wonder if the mainstream work on resilience and resilience building had anything to offer deaf children and their families.

For us, there were three objectives:

- Explore whether the concept of resilience used within mainstream child and family support is relevant to deafness.
- Promote the concept of resilience among professionals working with deaf children and their families.
- Explore the type of interventions that can help to build resiliency in families of deaf children and deaf children themselves.

To these ends, we commissioned the literature review that forms the basis of the preceding chapter; we organized a national conference that brought together experts in the resilience field and experts working with deaf children and their families; and we embarked on a project to make a DVD about resilience with deaf children and their families.

The literature review raised for us some difficult questions. Anecdotally we knew that many deaf adults could identify with the concept of resilience as being one of successfully navigating through the challenges of being deaf in a hearing world. Indeed, looking back, some deaf people can identify what it was that gave them the strength, determination, creativity, skills, and confidence to make life work for them. However, the literature review challenged us to think further. It drew our attention to the potential problem of labeling some children as resilient and others as not. It asked us to consider the relationship between resilience and success and whether there was a danger of equating the two, therefore, potentially reinforcing success as exceptional for deaf children, when it should be the norm. We had many hours of discussion about whether the concept of "resilience" really added anything to our work with deaf children and families. In the end, did it not all come back to quality communication and interaction as the bedrock of the relationships and experiences that support deaf children's development? This is the underpinning premises on which NDCS' family support work is based.

Yet on the other hand, resilience is easily graspable as a working idea that can inform the actions of professionals, the goals of deaf young people, and help families make sense of the investment they put into their children's optimum development. Many concepts that are underlined in work relating to resilience, all seemed relevant to work with deaf children and their families: the importance of enabling deaf children to access a wide range of experiences and opportunities; taking part in family decision making at the earliest possible opportunity; expressing feelings and emotions; developing independent thought and the ability to problem solve; as well as being able to draw on a range of strategies to manage less than optimum situations. However, to pursue this track, we knew that we should consider more precisely what we meant by resilience when talking specifically about deaf children and young people. If we are going to work to build it, we need to be able to share what we think it is.

These thoughts led us to the DVD project. We commissioned DeafWorks, a deaf-led consultancy specializing in education and training, to make an experimental DVD which could be used by parents and professionals, showing a range of children demonstrating some of the strategies mainstream literature suggest contribute to the development of resilience. The DVD was unscripted and took a "fly on the wall" approach to filming in the children's homes. One of the major challenges was to avoid any suggestion that the children in the DVD were "resilient" and that those we decided not to include in the final product were not. This was not a judgement it was appropriate for us to make. It was clear in the filming that the children used were able to draw on a range of strategies in their interaction with their environment. Unsurprisingly, it also demonstrated the importance of effective communication in the home and the involvement of the child in decision making from the earliest possible stage. The purpose of this pilot DVD was to provoke discussion by families and professionals about these strategies and how parents in particular could help their children to develop a range of ways of managing and responding to challenges they encounter.

Clearly, there is still a long way to go in understanding resilience among deaf children/young people and in working toward resilience building strategies in families, communities, and wider society. In this author's view, there is a need to gather deaf children's own views about which factors contribute to their sense of well-being and happiness, consider these factors in the light of the existing evidence about resilience and analyze the extent to which they overlap. In this way, it might be possible to move away from simply applying existing knowledge about resilience and expand the concept to incorporate the experience of being deaf.

It is hoped that this book, with its expanse of scholarship, will make an important contribution to that goal. I am delighted that work NDCS commissioned on behalf of deaf children and their families can take its place within this volume and look forward to further discussion and research on a topic which has the potential to offer a different way of capturing the challenges of providing effective support to deaf children and young people.

References

Bartelt, D. W. (1994). On resilience: Questions of validity. In M. C. Wang & E. W. Gordon (Eds.), *Educational resilience in inner city America: Challenges and prospects* (pp. 97–108). Hillsdale, NJ: Lawrence Erlbaum Associates.

Beltman, S., & MacCallums, J. (2006). Mentoring and the development of resilience: An Australian perspective. *International Journal of Mental Health Promotion, 8*(1), 21–32.

Bland, L. C., Sowa, C. J., & Callahan, C. M. (1994). An overview of resilience in gifted children. *Roeper Review, 17*(2), 77–80.

Buchanan, A. (2004). Learning to LUMP it? How to improve the mental health of children in public care Is it just a matter of buildings resilience? *International Journal of Child and Family Welfare, 7*(4), 197–206.

Calderon, R., & Greenberg, M. (1993). Consideration in the adaptation of families with school-aged deaf children. In M. Marschark & M. D. Clark (Eds.), *Psychological perspectives on deafness* (pp. 27–47). Hillsdale, NJ: Lawrence Erlbaum.

Charlson, E., Bird, R. L., & Strong, M. (1999). Resilience and success among deaf high school students: Three case studies. *American Annals of the Deaf, 144*(3), 226–235.

Charlson, E., Strong, M., & Gold, R. (1992). How successful deaf teenagers experience and cope with isolation. *American Annals of the Deaf, 137*(3), 261–270.

Cirillo, I. (2000). *The relationship of constructive aggression to resilience in adults who were abused as children.* Unpublished doctoral dissertation, Smith College for Social Work, Northanpton, MA, cited in Ungar, M. (2004). A constructionist discourse on resilience: Multiple contexts, multiple realities amongst at-risk children and young children and youth. *Youth and Society, 35*(3), 341–365.

Cohler, B. J. (1987). Adversity, resilience and the study of lives. In E. J. Anthony & B. J. Cohler (Eds.), *The invulnerable child* (pp. 363–424). New York: Guilford Press.

Conrad, R. (1979). *The Deaf schoolchild: Language and cognitive functioning.* London: Harper & Row.

Corker, M. (1998). *Deaf and disabled or deafness disabled – Towards a human rights perspective.* Buckingham, England: Open University Press.

DesGeorges, J. (2003). Family perceptions of early hearing, detection and intervention systems: Listening to and learning form families. *Mental Retardation in Developmental Disability Research Review, 9*(2), 89–93.

Dye, M. W. G., & Kyle, J. G. (2000). *Deaf people in the community: Demographics of the Deaf community in the UK.* Bristol: Deaf Studies Trust.

Dyer, G. D., & McGuiness, T. M. (1996). Resilience: Analysis of the concept. *Archives of Psychiatric Nursing, 10*(5), 276–282.

Floyd, C. (1996). Achieving despite the odds: A study of resilience among a group of African American high school seniors. *Journal of Negro Education, 65*(2), 181–189.

Gillham, J. E., & Reivich, K. J. (2004). Cultivating optimism in childhood and adolescence. *Annals of Political and Social Science, 591*(1), 146–163.

Gilligan, R. (1998). Enhancing the resilience of children and young people in public care by mentoring their talent and interests. *Child and Family Social Work, 4*(3), 187–196.

Gilligan, R. (2000). Adversity, resilience and young people: The protective value of positive school and spare time experiences. *Children and Society, 14*(11), 37–47.

Goldin-Meadow, S. (2003). How do the resilient properties of language help children learn language? In S. Goldin-Meadow (Ed.), *The resilience of language: What gesture creation in deaf children can tell us about how all children learn language* (pp. 185–198). New York: Psychology Press Inc.

Gorell Barnes, G. (1999). Operationalizing the uncertain: Some clinical reflections. *Journal of Family Therapy, 21*(2), 145–153.

Green, L. (1998). *Caged by force, entrapped by discourse: A study of the construction and control of children and their sexualities in residential children's homes.* Unpublished doctoral dissertation, University of Huddersfield, Huddersfield.

Greenberg, M., & Kusche, C. (1989). Cognitive, personal and social development of deaf children and adolescents. In M. C. Wang, M. C. Reynolds, & H. J. Walberg (Eds.), *Handbook of special education: Research and practice* (pp. 484–526). Oxford: Pergamon Press.

Greenberg, M., & Kusche, C. (1993). *Promoting social and emotional development in deaf children: The PATHS project.* Seattle: University of Washington Press.

Greenberg, M. T., Kusche, C. A., Cook, E. T., & Quamma, J. P. (1995). Promoting emotional competence in school-aged deaf children: The effects of the PATHS curriculum. *Development and Psychopathology, 7*, 117–136.

Greenberg, M. T., Lengua, L. J., & Calderon, R. (1997). The nexus of culture and sensory loss: Coping with deafness. In S. A. Wolchik & I. N. Sandler (Eds.), *Handbook of children's coping: Linking theory and intervention* (pp. 301–331). New York: Plenum Press.

Grover, S. C. (2002). Conduct disordered behaviour as an adaptive response to stress. *Ethical Human Sciences and Services: An International Journal of Critical Inquiry, 4*(3), 1–6.

Grover, S. (2005). Advocacy by children as a causal factor in promoting resilience. *Childhood, 12*(4), 527–538.

Hampson, J. E., Rahman, M. A., Brown, B., Jr., Taylor, M. E., & Donaldson, C. J., Jr. (1998). Project self – Beyond resilience. *Urban Education, 33*(1), 6–33.

Higgins, P. C. (1979). Outsiders in a hearing world: The deaf community. *Journal of Contemporary Ethnography, 8*(1), 3–22.

Hill, R. B. (1998). Enhancing the resilience of African American families. *Journal of Human Behavior in the Social Environment, 1*(2–3), 49–61.

Hindley, P. A. (1997). Psychiatric aspects of hearing impairment. *Journal of Child Psychology and Psychiatry, 38*(1), 101–117.

Hindley, P. A., Hill, P. D., McGigan, S., & Kitson, N. (1994). Psychiatric disorder in deaf and hearing-impaired children and young people: A prevalence study. *Journal of Child Psychology and Psychiatry, 35*(5), 917–934.

Hindley, P. A., & Kitson, N. (2000). *Mental health and deafness: A multidisciplinary handbook.* London: Whurr.

Jacelon, C. S. (1997). The trait and process of resilience. *Journal of Advanced Nursing, 25*(11), 123–129.

Jackson, S., & Martin, P. Y. (1998). Surviving the care system: Education and resilience. *Journal of Adolescence, 21*(5), 569–583.

Johnson, N. G. (2003). On treating adolescent girls: Focus on strengths and resiliency in psychotherapy. *Journal of Clinical Psychology, 59*(11), 1193–1203.

Joseph, J. M. (1994). *The resilient child: Preparing today's youth for tomorrow's world.* New York: Plenum Press.

Kennedy, M. (1989). The abuse of deaf children. *Child Abuse Review, 3*(1), 3–7.

Kramer, S., Kapteyn, T. S., & Houtgast, T. (2006). Occupational performance: Comparing normally-hearing and hearing-impaired employees using the Amsterdam checklist for hearing and work. *International Journal of Audiology, 45*, 503–512.

Ladd, P. (2003). *Understanding Deaf culture: In search of Deafhood.* Clevedon: Multilingual Matters.

Lane, H., Hoffmeister, R., & Behan, B. (1996). *A journey into the Deaf-World.* San Diego, CA: Dawn Sign Press.

Marschark, M. (1993). *Psychological development of deaf children.* New York: Oxford University Press.

Masten, A. S. (2001). Ordinary magic: Resilience processes in development. *American Psychologist, 56*(3), 227–238.

McAdam-Crisp, J. (2006). Factors that can enhance and limit resilience for children of war. *Childhood, 13*(4), 459–477.

McCreanor, T., & Watson, P. (2004). Resiliency, connectivity and environments: Their roles in theorizing approaches to promoting the well-being of young people. *International Journal of Mental Health Promotion, 6*(1), 39–42.

Morgan, R. H. (1998). *The relationship between resilience factors and behavioral outcomes of children in residential treatment centers.* Unpublished doctoral dissertation, School of Social Services, Fordham University, USA, cited in Ungar, M. (2004). A constructionist discourse on resilience: Multiple contexts, multiple realities amongst at-risk children and young children and youth. *Youth and Society, 35*(3), 341–365.

Newman, T. (2004). *What works in building resilience.* Ilford, Essex: Barnardo's.

Obinna, J. (2005). Researching sexual violence in the deaf community. *Sexual Assault Report, 8*(3), 33–38.

Oliver, K. G., Collin, P., Burns, J., & Nicholas, J. (2006). Building resilience in young people through meaningful participation. *Australian e-Journal for the Advancement of Mental Health, 5*(1). Retrieved May 12, 2009, from http://www.ausient.com/vol5iss1/oliver.pdf

Olsson, C. A., Bond, L., Burns, J. M., Vella-Brodrick, D. A., & Sawyer, S. M. (2003). Adolescence resilience: A concept analysis. *Journal of Adolescence, 26*(1), 1–11.

Ostazewski, K., & Zimmerman, M. A. (2006). The effects of cumulative risks and promotive factors on urban adolescent alcohol and other drug use: A longitudinal study of resiliency. *American Journal of Community Psychology, 38*(3–4), 237–249.

Padden, C., & Humphries, T. (1988). *Deaf in America. Voices from a culture.* Cambridge, MA: Harvard University Press.

Powers, S., & Gregory, S. (1998). *The educational achievements of Deaf children.* London: Department for Education and Employment.

Raybuck, E. S., & Hicks, G. F. (1994). KIDS CARE: Building resilience in children's environments. *Journal of Alcohol and Drug Education, 39*(3), 34–45.

Rigsby, L. C. (1994). The Americanization of resilience: Deconstructing research practice. In M. C. Wang & E. W. Gordon (Eds.), *Educational resilience in inner city America: Challenges and prospects.* Hillsdale, NJ: Lawrence Erlbaum Associates.

RNID. (2006). *Opportunity blocked: The employment experiences of deaf and hard of hearing people.* London: RNID. Retrieved May 12, 2009, from http://www.rnid.org.uk/VirtualContent/84923/2476_Opportunity_Blocked1.pdf

Rogers, S., Muir, K., & Evenson, C. R. (2003). Signs of resilience: Assets that support deaf adults' success in bridging the deaf and hearing worlds. *American Annals of the Deaf, 148*(3), 222–232.

Rutter, M. (1993). Resilience: Some conceptual considerations. *Journal of Adolescent Health, 14*(8), 626–631.

Rutter, M. (1995). Psychosocial adversity: Risk, resilience and recovery. *Southern African Journal of Child and Adolescent Psychiatry, 7*(2), 75–88.

Rutter, M. (1999). Resilience concepts and findings: Implications for family therapy. *Journal of Family Therapy, 21*(2), 119–144.

Rutter, M. (2000). Resilience reconsidered: Conceptual consideration, empirical findings, and policy implications. In J. P. Shonkoff (Ed.), *Handbook of early intervention* (pp. 651–682). Cambridge: Cambridge University Press.

Serafica, F. C. (1997). Psychopathology and resilience in Asian American children and adolescents. *Applied Developmental Science, 1*(3), 145–155.

Singer, G. H. S., & Powers, L. E. (1993). Contributing to resilience in families. In G. H. S. Singer & L. E. Powers (Eds.), *Families, disability and empowerment: Active coping skills and strategies for family intervention* (pp. 1–25). Baltimore, MD: Paul H. Brookes Publishing Co.

Sinkkonen, J. (1998). Mental health problems and communication of children with hearing loss in Finnish special schools. In A. Weisel (Ed.), *Issues unresolved: New perspectives on language and deaf education.* Washington, DC: Gallaudet University Press.

Steinberg, A. (2000). Autobiographical narrative on growing up deaf. In P. E. Spencer, C. J. Erting, & M. Marschark (Eds.), *The deaf child in the family and at school: Essays in honor of Kathryn P. Meadow–Orlans* (pp. 93–108). New Jersey: Lawrence Erlbaum Associates Publishers.

Sullivan, P. M., Brookhouser, P., & Scanlon, J. (2000). Maltreatment of deaf and hard of hearing children. In P. Hindley & N. Kitson (Eds.), *Mental health and deafness* (pp. 149–184). London: Whurr.

Sullivan, P. M., Vernon, M., & Scanlon, J. (1987). Sexual abuse of deaf youth. *American Annals of the Deaf, 132*(4), 256–262.

Sutherland, H., Griggs, M., & Young, A. M. (2003). Deaf adults and family intervention projects. In C. Gallaway & A. M. Young (Eds.), *Deafness and education in the UK: Research perspectives.* London: Whurr.

Tuttle, J. N., Campbell-Heider, N., & David, T. M. (2006). Positive adolescent life skills training for high-risk teens: Results of a group intervention study. *Journal of Pediatric Health Care, 20*(3), 184–191.

Ungar, M. (2004). A constructionist discourse on resilience: Multiple contexts, multiple realities amongst at-risk children and young children and youth. *Youth and Society, 35*(3), 341–365.

Valentine, L., & Feinauer, L. L. (1993). Resilience factors associated with female survivors of childhood sexual abuse. *American Journal of Family Therapy, 21*(3), 216–224.

Waaktaar, T., Christie, H. J., Borge, A. I. H., & Torgersen, S. (2004). How can young people's resilience be enhanced? Experience from a clinical intervention project. *Clinical Child Psychology and Psychiatry, 9*(2), 167–183.

Wagnild, G., & Young, H. M. (1990). Resilience among older women. *Image: Journal of Nursing Scholarship, 22*(4), 252–255.

Walsh, F. (1998). *Strengthening family resilience*. London: The Guilford Press.

Walsh, F. (2002). Bouncing forward: Resilience in the aftermath of September 11. *Family Process, 41*(1), 34–36.

Walsh, F. (2003). Family resilience: A framework for clinical practice. *Family Process, 42*(1), 1–17.

Wasmund, W., & Copas, R. (1994). Problem youths or problem solvers? Building resilience through peer helping. *Journal of Emotional and Behavioral Problems, 3*(2), 50–52.

Woolfe, T., & Young, A. M. (2006). Deafness, deaf people and genetics. *Bio-Sciences Review,* 21–23.

Young, A. M., Green, L., & Rogers, K. D. (2008). Resilience and deaf children: A literature review. *Deafness and Educational International, 10*(1), 40–55.

Part II
Infancy and Toddlerhood

Chapter 2
Attachment Formation Between Deaf Infants and Their Primary Caregivers: Is Being Deaf a Risk Factor for Insecure Attachment?

Nicole Renick Thomson, Erin A. Kennedy, and Janet E. Kuebli

Abstract The overarching goal of this chapter is to examine attachment formation between deaf infants and their primary caregivers. Our approach is to consider, through integration of attachment theory with the empirical literature on the development of both hearing and deaf infants, *whether* and *how* deafness could negatively impact the development of a secure attachment. Beginning with an overview of mainstream attachment theory and its significance for development, characteristics of the developing infant are explored, with a discussion of how congenital deafness plays a role in the infant's attempts to seek proximity and need fulfillment from caregivers. Next, the discussion focuses on parenting/caregiving behavior and how this may be influenced by the infant's deafness, followed by examination of some contextual factors that may be important for the developing attachment relationship, such as social support, and how these factors may operate among in deaf infant–hearing caregiver dyads. The chapter concludes with a discussion of the implications of considering attachment processes among the deaf within a risk-resilience framework. Directions for future research are offered throughout the chapter.

Arguably one of the most important relationships that human beings enter into begins immediately at birth with the primary caregiver, most often the biological mother. Though Freud initially theorized about the importance of early experience and early relationships, John Bowlby elaborated on the critical importance of the infant–caregiver relationship through his ethological-evolutionary theory of attachment, paving the way for decades of research. Van IJzendoorn and Sgi-Schwartz (2008) summarized the core hypotheses of attachment theory as follows: (1) attachment is universal; all infants become attached to one or more specific individuals (excepting infants with severe neurophysiological impairment); (2) attachment security is normative; (3) attachment security is dependent on sensitive caregiving; (4) attachment security is predictive of differences in competencies, such as emotion regulation.

N.R. Thomson (✉)
University of Missouri – St. Louis's Missouri Institute of Mental Health, St. Louis, MO, USA
e-mail: nicole.thomson@mimh.edu

D.H. Zand and K.J. Pierce (eds.), *Resilience in Deaf Children: Adaptation Through Emerging Adulthood*, DOI 10.1007/978-1-4419-7796-0_2,
© Springer Science+Business Media, LLC 2011

The second proposition, the "normativity hypothesis," is largely the focus of the present chapter. Given that some studies have classified up to 35–40% of US infants as insecurely attached (van IJzendoorn & Kroonenberg, 1988), the true "normative" nature of attachment security is not fully understood; it is unclear, for example, whether infants with a disability such as deafness are at risk for being overrepresented in the insecurely attached group. The overarching goal of the present chapter, therefore, is to examine attachment formation between deaf infants and their primary caregivers. Our approach is to consider, through integration of attachment theory with the empirical literature on the development of both hearing and deaf infants, *whether* and *how* deafness could negatively impact the development of a secure attachment.

To accomplish the goal of the chapter, characteristics of the deaf infant with potential implications for the attachment relationship are considered within the broader context of a dynamic, social-ecological system. Bronfenbrenner's (1979) ecological systems theory, which examines children's development as a function of interrelated contextual factors, and Belsky and Vondra's (1989) determinants of parenting model guided our chapter's contents. In particular, Belsky and Vondra's premise is that the quality of infant–caregiver attachment, along with other developmental outcomes, is "*multiply determined* [emphasis added] by factors emanating from within the parent, the child, and the social context in which parent and child are embedded" (Belsky, Rosenberger, & Crnic, 1995, p. 116). Further, Belsky's model assumes that developmental outcomes are proximally determined by the child's characteristics and parenting behavior. Distal factors that exert direct and indirect influences on parenting behavior and, in turn, child development, include a parent's own developmental history and personality, work, marital relations, and social network. It is our contention that these theoretical frameworks are important for considering development in general, and provide a structure for examining how nonnormative circumstances (including, but not limited to, deafness) may impact developmental outcomes.

Consequently, this chapter examines these proximal and distal factors as they specifically relate to the formation of attachment between deaf infants and their caregivers. The chapter begins with an overview of mainstream attachment theory and its significance for development, as well as issues pertaining to measurement and classification of attachment security. Next, characteristics of the infant are explored, with a discussion of how congenital deafness plays a role in the infant's attempts to seek proximity and need fulfillment from caregivers, followed by a section on parenting/caregiving behavior and how this may be influenced by the infant's deafness. The fourth section of the chapter examines contextual factors, such as social support, and how these factors may operate among infant–caregiver dyads. The chapter concludes with a discussion of the implications of considering attachment processes among the deaf within a risk-resilience framework.

It is important to note that the complicated nature of this topic necessitated limiting the scope of this discussion. For example, although approximately 50% of infants with congenital deafness/hearing loss will also exhibit one or more additional risk factors, such as malformations of the head and neck, hyperbilirubinemia, or Usher's syndrome in which visual loss may also occur (North Dakota Chapter of American

Academy of Pediatrics, 2008), the chapter's discussion is limited to infants who do not have co-occurring disorders or multiple risk factors. Moreover, since the process of forming a secure attachment may be different for an infant who loses hearing later in infancy or early childhood, the present discussion assumes that the infant was born with profound hearing loss. Further, while it is plausible that parental deafness may have a unique impact on parenting behavior and the development of an attachment, the majority of parents of deaf infants are hearing (90%; Vaccari & Marschark, 1997); therefore, our discussion primarily examines hearing parent–deaf infant dyads. Finally, the purpose of this chapter is not to make recommendations about how parents should handle a diagnosis of hearing loss in their infant to "maximize" attachment outcomes. Our discussion proceeds with the premise that parents have a range of options available to them for communicating with their deaf child, ranging from spoken language to visual language and/or a combination of strategies. Our approach was to integrate the currently available empirical findings from studies conducted with deaf infants and their caregivers, regardless of which communication mode was used by the dyads, to discern general implications for the formation of a secure attachment. We also limited the majority of the discussion to the period of infancy spanning approximately 0–2 years old, the age range encompassing the time prior to and immediately after a diagnosis of hearing loss is typically made. This age range also corresponds to the first three phases of attachment formation (i.e., preattachment through clear-cut attachment) originally conceptualized by John Bowlby (1969/1982).

Overview of Attachment Theory and Its Developmental Significance

John Bowlby's Attachment Theory

The fundamental principal that originates from Bowlby's (1969/1982, 1973) ethological-evolutionary attachment theory is that an infant's attachment to a primary caregiver, who is usually but not necessarily the mother, is an innate mechanism that ensures that the helpless human infant is protected from danger and will survive at least until reproductive age. Attachment is a biologically-based drive to seek proximity to the person who is perceived to be most likely to keep the infant safe. Bowlby claimed that the infant's attachment behaviors are organized into an "attachment behavioral system," which functions to regulate proximity to the caregiver. The attachment behavioral system is comprised of a variety of signals – clinging, smiling, crying, reaching, babbling, grasping – and is most likely to be activated in situations that evoke fear in the infant, such as when the availability of the caregiver is threatened or danger is perceived, as well as in situations that evoke the infant's desire to explore the environment (Kobak, Cassidy, Lyons-Ruth, & Ziv, 2006). Bowlby noted that a well-attached infant is likely to show some degree of distress upon separation. Conversely, little or no sign of anxiety may signal a problem with the attachment relationship. He also pointed out that virtually all infants will become attached, even those who are reared in deplorable caregiving situations; however, not all infants become *securely* attached – a notion that was further elucidated by the work of Ainsworth and Wittig (1969).

The essence of Bowlby's account of the development of an attachment between the infant and primary caregiver can be summarized as proceeding through four phases (Bowlby, 1969/1982): (1) Birth to 2 months: indiscriminate responsiveness to humans in which infants emit signals (e.g., crying, clinging, etc.) and begin associating relief of distress and/or need fulfillment with particular caregivers; (2) 2 to 6–8 months: discriminating sociability in which the infant shows preference for the caregiver(s) who has responded consistently to provide comfort and need fulfillment; (3) 6–8 months to 2–3 years: autonomy and responsibility in interactions with attachment figures in which young children are more capable (physically and cognitively) of actively and purposefully seeking proximity to their caregivers, and more likely to show stranger and separation anxiety; and (4) 2–3 years and up: the final phase of attachment, marked by children's developing capacity to infer attachment figure's goals, feelings, and motives, laying the groundwork for a more complex, goal-corrected partnership.

An infant's attachment *behavior* (behavior that promotes proximity to a caregiver) is distinguishable from an attachment *bond* (an affectional tie; Cassidy, 2008). Mary Ainsworth, the first to study the development of infant–mother attachment empirically, described the attachment bond as a particular type of affectional bond with clear defining characteristics. An affectional bond between infant and caregiver(s) exists if it is persistent, involves specific person(s), is emotionally significant, compels the infant to seek proximity to that person(s), and engenders distress upon separation from that person(s). According to Ainsworth (1989), one additional criterion for the existence of an attachment bond is that the infant relies on the caregiver for security and comfort.

Mary Ainsworth: Measurement and Classification of Attachment Patterns

Ainsworth developed a standardized laboratory procedure known as the Strange Situation (Ainsworth & Wittig, 1969), which helped to further validate and refine the different "attachment types" that she postulated. The Strange Situation involves the mother and her infant in a laboratory playroom where they are joined by a female stranger. While the stranger engages the infant in play, the mother leaves the room briefly (first separation) and then returns (first reunion). Next, both the stranger and the mother leave the room (second separation), then both return (second reunion). Ainsworth came to realize the critical importance of the patterns of behavior exhibited by the infants during the two reunion phases. Infants who appeared angry, ambivalent, or avoidant during the reunions tended to be the same infants who had less than optimal relationships with their mothers when observed at home.

Ainsworth's work resulted in the identification of individual differences in infant behavioral patterns that she believed were the result of the quality of caregiving they had received. Thus, Ainsworth identified several attachment types that can be viewed as varying in terms of quality of the attachment relationship (as opposed to quantity). In general, attachment relationships can be described as either *secure* or *insecure* (Ainsworth, Blehar, Waters, & Wall, 1978; Bowlby, 1973). Key behavioral characteristics of *securely* attached infants include the following: using their mothers as a "secure base" from which to explore their environment, displaying distress upon separation from their mothers, and proximity-seeking, distress-reduction upon reunion with their mothers. Insecure attachment relationships may correspond to one of three patterns: avoidant, resistant, or disorganized/disoriented. *Avoidant* infants rarely cry during periods of separation from their attachment figure and clearly show avoidant behavior upon reunion. *Resistant* babies show signs of anxiety manifested as seeking closeness to the caregiver and failing to explore. When reunited with the mother after a separation phase, these infants tend to resist their mothers and may display anger toward her, even to the point of hitting her. The *disorganized/disoriented* classification is considered to be the least common as well as the most insecure attachment pattern. These infants show contradictory behaviors with their attachment figure, seeking closeness yet with flat or depressed affect or dazed facial expressions. They may also show apprehension toward the caregiver. In general, this classification indicates that the infant lacks the ability to effectively elicit supportive interactions from the caregiver in stressful situations.

As it turns out, the quality of an infant's attachment to a primary caregiver has important implications that extend well beyond a survival instinct. What begins as a biological proclivity toward safety-seeking results in mental representations of the self, the caregiver, and dyadic interactions with the caregiver that are generalized as either positive/supportive or negative/unsupportive. As Sroufe (2000) characterized it, dyadic emotional regulation in early childhood becomes the prototype for later individual emotional regulation. These mental representations, or internal working models, serve to organize the child's behavior in new contexts as he/she becomes less reliant on the attachment figure for guidance and support and when confronted with situations that would typically evoke attachment behavior (e.g., fear-provoking situations). Ultimately, it is the internal working model that provides the foundation for the quality of the child's other social relationships (Craig, 2000).

Developmental Significance of Individual Differences in Attachment Quality

The early attachment relationship was hypothesized (Ainsworth, Bell, & Stayton, 1974; Bowlby, 1969/1982, 1973; Sroufe, 1988; Weinfield, Sroufe, Egeland, & Carlson, 2008) to exert its primary influence on socioemotional aspects of development. Well-designed longitudinal studies have found that early attachment relationships are indeed related to specific socioemotional constructs, including dependency, self-reliance, self-efficacy, anger, empathy, and social competence. Children with secure attachments, as compared to those whose attachments are characterized as insecure, are better at establishing peer group belongingness, are less socially anxious, are more persistent in their play, have higher self-esteem, show greater empathic concern for others, are more self-reliant, are more self-confident, and have greater capacity for emotional regulation (Bohlin, Hagekul, & Rydell, 2000; Sroufe, Egeland, Carlson, & Collins, 2005). Meaningful differences among the insecure attachment subtypes have also emerged. For example, children with avoidant attachment histories tend to show more conduct problems, while those with resistant histories display more anxiety-related disturbances. Disorganized attachment appears to be predictive of more severe psychiatric symptoms including conduct disorder and dissociative tendencies (Sroufe, 2005).

Despite the compelling nature of these findings, however, it is also important to point out that not all studies find links between attachment and developmental outcomes, and when significant associations are found they tend to be modest. There are a multitude of possible reasons for the inconsistencies found in the literature, including different ways of conceptualizing and measuring the outcome variables, assessments that do not occur early enough in the child's life and/or assessments that are repeated too infrequently, as well as multidetermination of outcomes (Thompson, 2008; Weinfield et al., 2008). Overall, investigation of attachment and its developmental sequelae are challenging, requiring studies that span long periods of time and that adequately capture the complex and dynamic nature of development.

As others have noted, it is useful to think about the significance of the attachment relationship in terms of developmental pathways, a general metaphor for describing individual differences in typical and atypical outcomes across developmental periods (Cicchetti, 1993; Rutter & Sroufe, 2000). This framework views individual differences in terms of distinctive developmental trajectories that require support to be maintained, yet remain open to modification (Weinfield et al., 2008). On the one hand, there are reasons to expect continuity in individual trajectories, which is consistent with what Bowlby (1973) termed the "homeorhetic" nature of development, the tendency for individuals to return to their developmental trajectories after changes or variations have occurred. Major sources of continuity in developmental trajectories are the internal working models of the self, the caregiver, and the caregiving relationship. These mental representations are likely to be self-perpetuating because they are the lens through which people interpret their social interactions and relationship experiences (Thompson, 2008). Conversely, there are also reasons to expect discontinuity in individual trajectories. For example, disruptions in the child's relationship with his/her attachment figure that occur across the life span may lead to discontinuity, that is, the benefits of a secure attachment formed in infancy may wane over time, and the child's current life circumstances grow increasingly important in the prediction of psychosocial functioning (Thompson, 2008). Attachment theory, therefore, is not a critical period theory as internal working models are continually elaborated and changed (Sroufe, 1988).

Quality of Attachment as a Risk or Protective Factor

When considering whether quality of attachment is a risk or a protective factor, it is important to remember the predictive limitations of the attachment construct in general. As mentioned previously, some studies have not found a link between attachment and developmental outcomes, and even significant associations tend to be modest. Moreover, although the presence of even one secure attachment may facilitate a positive developmental trajectory (Cassidy, 2008), or at least provide some protection for the child in the presence of stress or other risk factors, it is still not a guarantee of eventual adaptive functioning. Likewise, insecure attachment does not guarantee negative socioemotional outcomes. Insecure attachments of the avoidant and resistant subtypes may be more appropriately considered "moderate risk factors" for psychological disturbance in later life (Sroufe, 2005). Many studies show that attachment insecurity does not by itself have a direct impact on the development of psychopathology, but in combination with other risk factors substantially increases the risk for poor outcomes (Greenberg, 2005). The disorganized attachment subtype appears to be the only one that is clearly related to psychopathology (Van IJzendoorn, Schuengel, & Bakermans-Kranenburg, 1999). Therefore, although attachment is clearly an important developmental construct, it is also important to acknowledge limitations in its scope of influence on child outcomes. Indeed, the influence of attachment on development is extremely complex, and fully accurate conclusions cannot be drawn when it is considered in isolation from other circumstances in the child's life.

Characteristics of the Deaf Infant and Implications for Attachment

Given that the developing attachment relationship is, at least in part, predicated upon characteristics and behavior of the infant (e.g., the infant signals the caregiver when seeking safety and/or need fulfillment), it is important to consider the characteristics that may be specific to deaf infants, thereby having the potential to influence the formation of secure attachment relationships with caregivers. Independent of studies of attachment, researchers' interest in hearing mothers' interactions with their deaf children can be traced back at least to the late 1970s. Marschark (1993) cited Marvin's (1977; Greenberg & Marvin, 1979) research with preschoolers as the first to suggest that a child's deafness could compromise communicative exchanges with caregivers and influence the development of attachment. Marschark (1993) noted that synchronous and reciprocal parent–child interactions were very likely supported by infants' own early abilities to maintain attention to their caregivers' voices and faces. He reasoned that deaf infants' early failure or limitations to orient to their mothers' voices might undermine sensitive caregiving prior to when a child's deafness is often first diagnosed and when attachment is still developing. Marschark (1993) speculated that this could explain the tendency reported in earlier studies for hearing mothers with deaf children to be more tense, controlling, and intrusive in their interactions with their deaf children as compared to matched hearing and deaf dyads.

This section begins with a brief overview of the current status of newborn hearing loss diagnosis and subsequent intervention, followed by an examination of infant behaviors that may serve to facilitate or compromise the formation of a secure attachment. Next, research on the prenatal development of the sense of hearing and the implications of these findings for newborns' preference for their mothers' voices are summarized. The various strategies that could be utilized by a deaf infant in an effort to achieve and maintain proximity to a caregiver, such as vocal, tactile, and visual methods, are also discussed. Third, research related to the relationship between language development in hearing and deaf infants and attachment formation is summarized along with issues related to language-based interventions for children born with hearing loss. Finally, the continuing role of language development, and the supplementary roles of tactile and, especially, visual communication, in the formation of attachment security in toddlerhood are examined.

Diagnosis and Intervention for Newborn Hearing Loss

As recently as 10 years ago, infant hearing loss often went undiagnosed until at least 30 months of age. With the advent of state and federal guidelines and mandates for Early Hearing Detection and Intervention (EHDI), the average age of diagnosis has dropped to 3 months (White, 2006). In 2006, nearly 93% of newborns were screened for hearing loss, up from just 3% in 1993 (NCHAM, 2006), and the number of children per year who receive early intervention has increased by an average of 17% (White, 2006), suggesting that EHDI is effective when adequately supported by pediatricians, audiologists, hospital chief executive officers, and parents (Finitzo, Albright, & O'Neal, 1998).

The EHDI process can be quite successful. As Yoshinaga-Itano (2003) pointed out, EHDI is the only newborn screening that does not require a blood test and that has a primarily education-based, rather than medical, follow-up. Yoshinaga-Itano (2003) reported that newborn hearing screening in Colorado hospitals resulted in earlier intervention; most cases of hearing loss were identified within 3 months and intervention began, on average, within 2 months of identification. Given that the aim of intervention is to help deaf children develop communication skills that predict social and academic outcomes, the Joint Committee on Infant Hearing (2000) recommended that intervention efforts start by 6 months of age. Intervention programs typically include the provision of assistive listening devices (hearing aids or cochlear implants) as well as teaching the type of language chosen by the parents, with options ranging from those closest to spoken language (auditory-verbal and auditory-oral) to those closest to visual language (American Sign Language; Gravel & O'Gara, 2003; White, 2006).

However, intervention typically does not begin until infants are at least 6 months old, and the process of perfecting the functioning of hearing aids and cochlear implants is both complicated and time-consuming (McKinley & Warren, 2000). If hearing loss is not definitively diagnosed until the infant is 3 months old (or later in some instances), and intervention does not occur until at least 6 months of age, it is important to consider what might occur during the first several months of life that would either help or hinder the formation of secure attachments between deaf infants and their primary caregivers.

Phase 1: Preattachment/Indiscriminate Signaling

Sound

It is well known that the inner ear is partially developed and begins to function at about the 28th week of gestation (Saffran, Werker, & Werner, 2006). Fetuses demonstrate both movement and increased heart rate in response to sound at 26–28 weeks gestational age (Kisilevsky & Low, 1998). Sound conduction to the fetus is limited by the mother's body, the amniotic fluid surrounding the fetus, and the underdeveloped auditory system. Nevertheless, Vouloumonos and Werker (2007) found that newborn babies demonstrated a behavioral bias for speech, the foundation of which forms prenatally. Specifically, when presented with a special pacifier that, when sucked at different rates, produced speech or nonspeech sounds, newborns sucked the pacifier more to listen to the speech sounds, suggesting that they likely have a prenatally acquired preference for the sounds of human speech.

Additionally, research has demonstrated that newborns actually prefer the sound of their own mothers' speech, a preference that may serve to prepare the infant to begin developing an attachment relationship with the mother at birth. Evidence for this comes from DeCaspar and Fifer's (1980) landmark study, in which infants sucked harder (on special nipples i.e., worked harder) to hear their mothers' voices after, at most, 12 h of contact with them. The hypothesis that infants prefer their mothers' voices from birth was further supported by Spence and DeCaspar's (1987) finding that 38- to 60-h-old newborns were able to discriminate between filtered versions of their mothers' voices (e.g., a simulation of the input that would be received in the womb) and unfiltered versions of their mothers' voices (e.g., a simulation of mothers' voices as heard after birth) but did not show a preference for either, suggesting a level of familiarity with their mother's voice both before and after birth.

Given the findings that prenatal exposure to the mother's voice can influence postnatal preference for the mother's voice, it is important to consider the role that this preference plays in the formation of an attachment relationship. Indeed, DeCaspar and Fifer (1980) suggested that "mother–infant bonding [is] best served by (and may even require) the ability of a newborn to discriminate its mother's voice from that of other females" (p. 1174). As hearing infants develop the ability to understand and produce language, they use this ability to aid in the formation of a synchronous and reciprocal relationship with their environments (Marschark, 1993), one in which the bidirectional communication between mother and child, for example, is clear and unobstructed. Though the specific implications of these findings are not known for infants who are born with congenital hearing loss, infants who are unable to hear their mothers' voices in utero do not initially enter into the formation of an attachment relationship having a preference for their mother's voice. The deaf infant is nonetheless born with behavioral abilities related to vocalizations, touch, and vision that may serve as proximity-seeking signals and that may compensate for the failure to hear their mother in utero.

Early prelingual vocalization is a common way for the newborn infant to signal to obtain proximity to the caregiver: "If infants do not vocalize in order to perfect their ability to speak…and they do not use words in order to convey information to others, what *are* their motives?" (Locke, 2001, p. 298, italics in original). In fact, Locke agreed with Bowlby's (1969/1982) original premise that infants use vocalizations, such as crying, cooing, or grunting, to maintain proximity to the parent as they form an attachment. He further described infant vocalization as analogous to the testing of a microphone; vocalization serves as an attempt to evaluate the existence of an open channel of communication, a necessity for survival. Overall, deaf and hearing infants have not been found to differ greatly in terms of quantity of vocalization, and generally, there are more similarities than differences in the quality of vocalizations produced by deaf and hearing infants (Oller, 2006). While deaf infants cry longer or louder than hearing infants, perhaps in an effort to receive feedback from caregivers (Masataka, 2006), deaf infants appear to be similar overall to hearing infants in their use of prelingual vocalizations (Oller, 2006) to achieve proximity to a caregiver.

Auditory/verbal communication from the parent to the infant is disrupted, however, among deaf newborns and their caregivers. Thus, it is important to consider how alternative modes of need-signaling and communication may impact the developing attachment relationship. As Koester (1994) reported, "the mediating effect of other forms of contingent responsiveness may help to overcome these obstacles…as evidenced by the deaf infants' generally secure attachment ratings" (p. 58). Two important alternative sensory modalities through which the deaf infant can "request" caregiver attention and "receive" it when it is offered are touch and vision.

Touch

In the early phases of attachment formation, tactile-based need-signaling (e.g., clinging, reaching, and grasping) is another method that infants can use effectively to maintain proximity to the caregiver. Indeed, newborns are highly sensitive to touch at birth and the role of touch in the formation of a parent–child relationship is well established in empirical literature. In his classic research with rhesus monkeys, Harlow (1959) determined that touch, or contact comfort, is more important for the establishment of a mother–infant relationship than are feeding and nourishment. A method of skin-to-skin and chest-to-chest contact immediately after birth called "kangaroo care" has been demonstrated to be beneficial for both preterm and full-term infant development (Feldman & Eidelman, 2003; Walters, Boggs, Ludington-Hoe, Price, & Morrison, 2007). In their examination of the role of touch in the mother–infant social relationships, Stack and Muir (1992) used a common still-face procedure in which mothers interacted normally with hearing infants, then adopted a neutral and nonreactive facial expression, and then again interacted normally. When this procedure was modified to include tactile stimulation during the still-face portion of the procedure, infants smiled more in the still-face interaction when they were being touched than when they were not, suggesting that tactile stimulation is a powerful component of social interaction. For deaf infants in particular, touch may be especially important in the first few months of life when they are not mobile, and close physical contact with parents is a necessary component for the development of a secure attachment (Koester, 1994) and as a method of communication (Lederberg & Mobley, 1990). Additionally, while hearing babies may respond negatively to too much tactile stimulation (Pipp-Siegel et al., 1998), deaf babies likely have a higher threshold for tactile stimulation and benefit from high levels of active touching (touching with moving contact, such as tapping or stroking).

Signaling with Sight

In addition to touch, communication through visual means is likely to be especially important in the first months of life. Koester (1994) outlined the importance of the visual system for effective mother–child interaction. Infants can use their visual abilities to exert a great deal of control over their environment; for example, infants who no longer desire to engage with caregivers can easily close their eyes or avert their gazes. Deaf infants in particular use visual information (e.g., attention to parents' lip movements and facial affective cues) to obtain information when communicating with parents (Harris & Chasin, 2005). However, for deaf infants, breaking visual contact can elicit discomfort due to the lack of auditory contact with the caregiver, an explanation for the finding that deaf infants break eye contact in face-to-face interaction less often than do hearing infants (Koester, 1994). Deaf infants also spend more time continually looking at their mothers (as opposed to looking back and forth between the mother and the environment). Eye contact and gaze aversion consequently have been used to indicate the extent of synchrony/reciprocity between mother and infant (Koester, 1995).

In Stack and Muir's (1992) study of tactile stimulation during still-face infant–mother interaction, it was notable that infants responded to their mother's touch by smiling. This adaptive proximity-seeking behavior serves to ensure that a visually attentive primary caregiver remains in close physical contact with the infant. Beginning at about one month of age, infants display exogenous smiles, smiles that appear reflexively in response to external stimulation, including tactile and visual stimulation (Wolff, 1963). Though this type of smile is reflexive, it serves as an important component of visual interaction between the caregiver and the infant that is likely to ensure that the caregiver remains present in the interaction, thus facilitating the formation of a secure attachment. Starting at about 6 weeks of age, infants smile in response to social stimuli, such as seeing the preferred caregiver's face, a response that is solidified by about 12 weeks. Smiling serves as a means by which an infant can signal positive affect to the caregiver, which, again, may facilitate the formation of a secure attachment (Feldman & Rimé, 1991). It is unlikely that hearing and deaf infants differ in terms of their smiling behavior and timing; indeed, Koester (1995) found no significant difference in frequency of smiling as a function of hearing status. Hence, deaf infants can use smiling to achieve and maintain proximity to the caregiver.

Thus far, this section has described the ways in which the sensory capabilities of a hearing infant are similar to and different from those of a deaf infant with implications for the indiscriminate signaling phase of the developing attachment relationship. Together, the existing literature on both hearing and deaf infants suggests that most of the attachment behaviors in the infant's repertoire for signaling the caregiver do not appear to differ drastically as a function of hearing status. When tactile and visual stimulation and support from parents is present at appropriate levels (which will be addressed in the following section), the current body of evidence suggests that deaf infants enter the world prepared to enter into an attachment relationship with their primary caregiver.

Phase 2: Attachment-in-the-Making/Discriminate Signaling

From approximately 6–8 weeks through the eighth month of life, infants begin to demonstrate a preference for the caregiver(s) who has responded most consistently to their bids for proximity and need fulfillment. During this phase, the typically developing infant is smiling and laughing more, and begins to show clear signs of language development, such as the start of babbling. During this phase, infants also begin to form expectations about how caregivers will respond to their needs. For deaf infants, it is during this phase that diagnosis is likely to occur along with the start of professional intervention, which includes support for language development and may include the provision of assistive listening devices.

Because language comprehension develops before language production, it is useful to contrast deaf and hearing infants' abilities to receive language input from parents. For hearing infants, reciprocal spoken communicative interactions are a major component of infant–parent interactions, and specifically, the way in which mothers communicate with their hearing infants is an important mechanism for ensuring optimal interaction. Infant-directed speech, the exaggerated, slowed, high-pitched language style that adults worldwide use with infants, serves to engage the infant's attention in an attempt to maintain social interaction (Fernald, 1992; Masataka, 2006) well before language development and comprehension become the major focus. Furthermore, infants demonstrate a preference for infant-directed speech from birth (Cooper & Aslin, 1990). Miall and Dissanayake (2003) expand on the spoken-only quality of infant-directed speech with their concept of babytalk, which appears at about 6 weeks and lasts until about 24 weeks. Babytalk refers to the dyadic engagement between a caregiver and an infant that consists of visual and body language behaviors in addition to prelingual vocal behaviors. They suggest that the babytalk "conversation" – especially the infant's ability to *react* to caregivers and *elicit* reactions from caregivers – provides the foundation for a coordinated social-emotional relationship involving mutuality and the infant's expectation that caregivers will be responsive to their expressions of need for proximity and protection (e.g., crying) as outlined by Bowlby (1969/1982).

Vocal turn-taking, a more advanced and reciprocal form of verbal communication than infant-directed speech and babytalk, may also be important for the development of a secure attachment (Masataka, 2006). Masataka's research suggests that conversational turn-taking begins in hearing infants as early as 3 months after birth, which closely parallels the phase of attachment formation when the infant begins to respond preferentially toward familiar caregivers. In vocal turn-taking, infants actively "turn off their own voice" to hear the voice of the preferred caregiver (Masataka, 2006, p. 43). Interestingly, Masataka suggested that interactions that involve turn-taking are likely to be phylogenetically inherited, which would suggest that given the proper environmental support, deaf infants would be just as likely to exhibit this behavior with caregivers as would hearing infants. Oller (2006) pointedly explains that research has not yet demonstrated major differences in the amount or quantity of language produced by deaf and hearing infants, except for the finding that deaf infants use more glottal sequences (syllable sequences that are not well enunciated and are broken up by glottal stops, as in the separation between the two syllables in "uh-oh"). There does, however, appear to be a difference in the time of onset of babbling, a major milestone in language development that serves as a precursor to meaningful speech. In hearing infants, babbling refers to sounds that approximate repeated consonant–vowel combinations, but may also include squeals, growls, or "raspberries" (Oller, 2006). Oller further explains that "canonical" babbling refers to vocalizations that combine clearly formed consonants and vowels (e.g., bababa). Given the appropriate amount and type of stimulation, hearing infants are likely to begin to babble around 6–8 months of age.

When considering delays in the onset of babbling in deaf infants, Oller (2006) addresses the importance of degree of hearing loss by explaining that even profoundly deaf infants have some amount of auditory input, though small. When auditory input is combined with information from other sensory modalities (e.g., lip-reading), mildly and severely deaf infants show only minor delays in the onset of babbling. However, profoundly deaf infants who do not receive sign language input enter the babbling stage much later than do hearing children; for these children, canonical babbling may not occur until well after the child's first birthday. Additionally, Oller (2006) addresses the shortage of research evaluating the different vocal patterns in deaf and hearing infants in actual social interactions. It appears, though, that if deaf infants' language production abilities in infancy are similar enough to those of hearing infants, attachment formation should not be irreversibly disrupted. Again, however, deaf infants need adequate support from their environment, particularly the primary caregiver, to ensure that interaction proceeds smoothly.

One component of intervention programs involves training parents, especially hearing parents, to communicate effectively with their infants. Because most parents choose to communicate with their children using auditory/oral-based language (White, 2006), it is important to examine whether parents of infants with assistive listening devices communicate in a similar manner as do parents of hearing infants. Bergeson, Miller, and McCune (2006) found that mothers of infants with cochlear implants also used typical infant-directed speech patterns (e.g., increases in pitch, changes in pitch, fewer words per utterance, more pauses between utterances, and a slower rate of speech) and that the use of these patterns was more highly related to the length of hearing experience (e.g., time since implantation) than to the age of the child. In other words, infant-directed speech is not necessarily relevant only for young hearing infants but also for older infants who were born deaf but who have begun to receive auditory input as a result of assistive listening devices. As addressed previously in this section, a major function of mothers' infant-directed speech is the engagement of the child's attention, which is a key component of the reciprocity necessary for the development of a secure attachment relationship.

Phase 3: Clear-Cut Attachment

During this phase of attachment formation, infants are even more active in seeking contact with their caregivers, and they take greater responsibility for initiating interactions through burgeoning language and motor skills (e.g., crawling and walking). It is also during this time that infants may display separation and/or stranger anxiety upon their caregivers' departure. Infants who have developed a secure attachment thus far use their caregivers as a "secure base" from which they can explore and master their environment, yet seek protection and comfort when these needs arise (Siegler, DeLoache, & Eisenberg, 2003). Within the age-range of this attachment phase (i.e., 6–8 months to 1½ to 2 years), infants born with congenital deafness have likely made some strides in establishing a shared language with their caregiver, whether it is based on manual communication, oral communication, or a combination of both. Language, as one basis for greater reciprocity in interactions with a caregiver, indeed becomes an increasingly important component of hearing parent–deaf child interactions.

Language development and attachment require similar levels of reciprocity between parents and children so that it is useful to examine the relationship between the two concepts. In a meta-analysis of seven studies, van IJzendoorn, Dijkstra, and Bus (1995) found a significant relationship between attachment security and language competence (both measured at ages ranging from 11 to 42 months). However, three studies in the meta-analysis assessed attachment security and language concurrently, and the remaining four assessed attachment security prior to language competence. As a result, it is difficult to draw conclusions from this meta-analysis about the predictive influence of language development on attachment security. Importantly, attachment security and language development seem to be most directly related only in high-risk samples (Cohen, 2001; van IJzendoorn et al., 1995). Additionally, few studies have examined the causal influence of language on attachment security, a relationship of particular importance when considering the language competence of a deaf infant. Vaccari and Marschark (1997) suggest that spoken language may not be necessary or sufficient for attachment; however, they are clear that some level of competent communication between mother and child is required for the development of a secure attachment. The importance of language is also underscored by Wedell-Monnig and Lumley's (1980) finding that deaf toddlers were less active than, but similar in responsiveness to, hearing children in mother–child interactions and when children were playing independently. Their data revealed a trend toward lower levels of interaction over a time period of 2 months between mothers and their deaf children, which may suggest that mothers get frustrated as their children enter toddlerhood (approximately 24 months) and engage less in the expected language interaction. Thus, difficulties in communication between the deaf child and parent may be minimized by language development resulting from early intervention.

Importantly, effective communication is not limited to oral communication; without the benefit of typically developing language capabilities, the deaf infant may be able to compensate using the tactile and visual modalities to facilitate and/or maintain a secure attachment. Physical contact, eye contact, and facial expressions are essential for effective communication. Parents may also wish to learn sign language to facilitate communication with their deaf children. Unfortunately, many hearing parents use sign language inconsistently, and they tend to only use signs when speaking directly to the child; many parents do not use manual communication at all (Stuckless & Birch, 1997). Interventions designed to help parents understand the importance of visual strategies in addition to language (e.g., parents must ensure that they have children's attention before attempting to sign) can be effective in ensuring that parents are sensitive to their deaf children's communication needs.

Indeed, high levels of family involvement in intervention efforts are crucial for language development (Moeller, 2000). Yoshinaga-Itano (2003), for example, reported that the probability of language falling in the normal range is higher for newborns born in hospitals that have screening programs and that offer early intervention programs. When children born in such hospitals were evaluated between 12 and 60 months, they demonstrated higher language quotients (language age compared to chronological age), vocabulary development (number of words), speech ability (clarity and intelligibility of speech sounds), and syntax ability (sentence length). Furthermore, for children whose hearing loss identification and intervention occurred within the first 12 months, all aspects of language were more similar to those of their age-matched hearing peers than to those of their deaf peers who had not received intervention (Yoshinaga-Itano, 2001).

Yoshinaga-Itano, Sedey, Coulter, and Mehl (1998) examined language ability in children ranging in age from 1 to 3 years who were enrolled in an intervention program within 2 months of their initial diagnosis. About half of the sample had been diagnosed before 6 months of age, while the rest were diagnosed after 6 months of age. Also, about half of the sample used spoken language only, while the rest used a combination of spoken and sign language. For children with cognitive levels in the typical range, those who were diagnosed before 6 months demonstrated more advanced expressive (simple and complex gestural and verbal behaviors) and receptive language abilities. Furthermore, regardless of which mode of communication was used, children who had been diagnosed prior to 6 months were at an advantage in terms of language ability.

Assistive listening devices, such as cochlear implants, may be an effective approach to fostering deaf infants' language development, more so than hearing amplification (e.g., hearing aids). For example, Geers (2006) cites research stating that children whose hearing loss is treated using only hearing amplification (e.g., hearing aids) combined with oral communication techniques have been found to develop language production abilities at about half the rate of their hearing counterparts. On the other hand, children who receive cochlear implants are more likely to develop language at the same rate as hearing children (see also Horn, Houston, & Miyamoto, 2007). The age at which children receive cochlear implants appears to be an important factor, however. McKinley and Warren (2000) concluded, in their review of research on the effectiveness of cochlear implantation in children who were prelingually deaf, that children who received cochlear implants prior to 3 years of age performed better on measures of language ability than did children who received the implants after age 3; over a 3-year period, the language and vocabulary development of children with cochlear implants was similar to that of hearing children. Furthermore, Nicholas and Geers (2007) (see also Svirsky, Robbins, Kirk, Pisoni, & Miyamoto, 2000) assessed the outcomes of cochlear implantation in severely to profoundly deaf children (ages 3½ and 4½) who received implants at an average age of about 23 months. Their results suggested that children who receive cochlear implants and spoken language education before 2 years of age are likely to catch up to their hearing peers in spoken language skills by the age of 5. In general, it appears that the earlier the age at which children receive cochlear implants, the better the expected language outcomes.

Any level of language development that occurs for the deaf infant should continue to facilitate the formation and maintenance of a secure parent–child attachment relationship. Additionally, both hearing and deaf toddlers alike will continue to benefit from the use of tactile and visual communication in interactions with caregivers. For example, face-to-face visual communication in infancy is an important foundation of "joint attention," or shared visual attention, an infant's ability to attend to a partner as well as to a shared experience. Around 6 months of age, time spent in face-to-face interactions decreases as children become more interested in other objects in the environment (Adamson & Chance, 1998). With joint attention, infants and caregivers can share their experiences. Based on the understanding that deaf infants necessarily must obtain the majority of information about their environments via the visual system, Spencer (2000) examined whether hearing ability is necessary for the development of shared visual attention abilities. Data indicated that hearing ability alone does not influence visual attention, but that deaf children need attention-directing signals from their mothers (e.g., tapping to signal communication) as well as rich visual environments. However, hearing mothers may be less likely than deaf mothers to engage in such behaviors or to provide such environments, especially in the period of time immediately following diagnosis, before the mother has adjusted to the situation. Prezbindowski, Adamson, and Lederberg (1998) examined the role of language in the development of joint attention and found that both deaf and hearing infants increased the amount of time they spent in joint attention tasks from 18 to 22 months of age. As this increase occurs before major improvements in language ability, the authors suggested that language is not necessary for the development of joint attention, a finding particularly relevant for deaf infants. However, in light of Lederberg and Mobley's (1990) finding that deaf children were more likely to end communication as a result of not seeing or hearing the mother's last communication, it is likely that synchronous visual attention is important for effective communication and attachment security. Finally, while Koester and MacTurk (1991), (as cited in Koester, 1994) found no significant differences in attachment security between deaf and hearing infants, they did find that deaf infants displayed more proximity-seeking behaviors (e.g., looking, gesturing, and touching) upon reunion with mothers, providing further evidence that other modalities of communication are extremely important to the developing attachment relationship between deaf infants and their caregivers.

Theoretical and empirical evidence suggests that deaf infants are likely to be just as prepared at birth as their hearing counterparts to form secure attachments with their caregivers. The attachment behavioral system of deaf infants for signaling their needs to caregivers is much the same as that of hearing infants, including clinging, smiling, crying, reaching, babbling, and grasping. Some evidence suggests that they may bid for their caregiver's attention more frequently than do hearing infants (e.g., by crying more), but whether this signifies a potential problem with attachment formation (e.g., that the deaf infant's bids are less effective at garnering a response) is unclear. Deaf infants also respond very well to other modalities of communication, particularly the visual and tactile modalities. Perhaps most importantly, deaf infants and children who receive intervention in the form of a combination of cochlear implantation and verbal communication before the age of 2 are less likely to demonstrate the language delays that could possibly influence attachment development. All in all, it appears as though the conditions for the formation of a secure attachment among deaf infants are more similar to than different from those of hearing infants, insofar as the deaf infant can utilize a variety of strategies for eliciting caregiver's responses. The following section is devoted more specifically to the role of the caregiver's behavior in the development of a secure attachment relationship.

Caregiver Characteristics and the Caregiving Process

Just as it is important to consider how an infant's hearing impairment may influence signaling to the caregiver when seeking safety and/or need fulfillment, it is equally important to consider characteristics of the caregiver and how caregivers' behavior has the potential to influence the formation of a secure attachment. Indeed, attachment is a *relational* quality, rather than an individual difference dimension. Both child and caregiver contribute to the quality of the relationship and are jointly responsible for the attachment bond between them. Despite some attention to child factors (e.g., temperament), more research overall has investigated the impact of maternal caregiving on attachment style. This is because of Ainsworth's original emphasis on identifying maternal behaviors that facilitated secure attachment as opposed to insecure attachment styles (Ainsworth et al., 1971, 1974, 1978).

Maternal Sensitivity

Ainsworth particularly drew attention to the consequences of sensitive maternal behavior toward the infant. In two *American Psychologist* articles, Ainsworth (1979; Bowlby & Ainsworth, 1991) repeatedly emphasized the importance to secure attachment of interactions between infants and mothers in which mothers *promptly*, *contingently*, and *appropriately* responded to their infants' signals in ways that permit infants to "build up expectations of the mother and, eventually, a working model of her as more or less accessible and responsive" (p. 934). By the early 1990s, sufficient attachment research had been conducted to permit a preliminary "descriptive" meta-analysis (van IJzendoorn, Goldberg, Kroonenberg, & Frenkel, 1992) comparing maternal and child contributions to attachment across studies with both typically developing and clinical samples. The authors concluded that maternal problems (i.e., mental illness, maltreatment, teenage motherhood) posed the primary risk for development of insecure attachment. Child problems, by contrast, appeared to influence the specific style of insecure attachment that developed.

Over the past decade, attachment researchers have grappled with how best to operationally define maternal sensitivity (De Wolff & van IJzendoorn, 1997; Donovan, Leavitt, Taylor, & Broder, 2007; Keller, Lohaus, Volker, Cappenberg, & Chasiotis, 1999; Meins, Fernyhough, Fradley, & Tuckey, 2001; Thompson, 2008; van den Boom, 1997). As Meins et al. (2001) aptly argued, confusion about this construct has arisen, in part, out of a lack of consensus among researchers regarding which specific behaviors constitute maternal sensitivity. Some researchers have proposed expanding the maternal sensitivity construct to include other maternal behaviors in addition to those identified by Ainsworth. For example, Nievar and Becker (2008) have recently presented compelling theoretical and empirical evidence that sensitivity is a stronger predictor of attachment security than previous studies have demonstrated (see De Wolff & van IJzendoorn, 1997) when it is defined by maternal behaviors that are "correctly timed (i.e., synchronous) and mutually rewarding (p. 104)." They argued that defining sensitivity as a *unidirectional* phenomenon (e.g., the ability of the mother to perceive the infant's signals accurately and respond promptly and appropriately) produces only weak correlations with attachment security and does not entirely represent what is fundamentally a dyadic construct.

Other Important Aspects of Maternal Sensitivity and Caregiving

Other aspects of mothers' parenting behavior that have been examined by developmental psychologists within the context of the attachment relationship include sensory sensitivity, emotional availability, interactional synchrony, and, more recently, mind-mindedness and parental reflective function. Research conducted with hearing infants has demonstrated that these factors are associated with attachment outcomes and that they supplement Ainsworth's concept of maternal sensitivity.

Sensory Sensitivity

Developmental researchers have begun to delve more deeply into the components of maternal sensitivity, as seen in the work by Martha Donovan and her colleagues on maternal *sensory* sensitivity. They have identified two important conceptual predictors of whether or not a mother will respond appropriately to the signals of her infant: her ability to detect signal differences at the sensory level and her decision to enact a behavioral response. In other words, variations in maternal sensitivity may be explained by differences in mothers' sensitivity to signals from her infant at the sensory level (e.g., the mother's ability to detect the infant's positive and negative facial expressions), as well as differences in decision-making processes. This is a relatively new line of inquiry, and additional studies investigating the potential link between sensory sensitivity and the developing attachment relationship are needed. Evidence from Donovan et al. (2007) that mothers' sensory sensitivity to infant affective signaling at 6 months of age predicted mothers' behavior and affect during interactions with her child at 2 years of age indicates this is a promising area of work. Importantly, Donovan et al. has demonstrated that it is possible to measure mothers' sensory sensitivity as a component of responsiveness, which could have significant implications for future research with hearing mothers of deaf infants. If mothers differ in their ability to detect signals from their infants at the sensory level, and if deaf infants' signaling behaviors are atypical as a function of their impairment, then maternal sensitivity and, ultimately, the attachment relationship could be adversely affected.

Emotional Availability

Maternal emotional availability has been recognized as being important for the infant's development of affect tolerance and regulation of distress (Sroufe, 1995), and emotional expression (e.g., Cassidy, 1994). Emotional availability emphasizes the emotional features of the parent–child interaction, with parents' ability to detect their infant's emotional signals and how they emit their own emotions playing critical roles (Biringen, 2000). In Pauli-Pott and Mertesacker's (2009) recent study with hearing infants, 89 infant–mother dyads were videotaped at 4, 8, and 12 months of age during 10-min interactions (such as diaper changes and playing with age-appropriate toys together) that were subsequently scored for maternal positive and negative affect expression and openness of affect expression. Infant positive and negative expressions were also coded from the videotaped interactions. At 18 months of age, mother–infant dyads returned to the laboratory for the Strange Situation procedure. Several interesting findings emerged from this study, including the fact that the relationship between mother's emotional expression and infant's attachment security changed with age. At 4 months of age, highly positive maternal affect together with negative or neutral infant affect significantly predicted attachment insecurity. However, at 12 months, low emotional authenticity (i.e., ambiguous emotional communication/ attempts to mask negative emotion) predicted insecure infant attachment. These findings concur with earlier studies of maternal affect (e.g., Izard, Haynes, Chisholm, & Baak, 1991) in samples of hearing infants, demonstrating that mothers of insecure infants were less "genuine" in displays of affect, with more attempts to conceal negative emotions than displayed by mothers of secure infants. It is optimal, therefore, for the mother's affect to be appropriate and genuine, producing congruence between her verbal and nonverbal communication. Interestingly, Pipp-Siegal, Blair, Deas, Pressman, and Yoshinaga-Itano (1998) found that mothers' emotional openness with their 2-year-old child did not differ as a function of the child's hearing status, but significantly more mothers of children who were deaf or hard of hearing displayed hostility toward them than did mothers of hearing children. Likewise, Meadow-Orlans and Steinberg's (1993) ratings of mothers' affective displays during unstructured play with 18-month-old infants were more negative overall for mothers of deaf infants versus mothers of hearing infants. Maternal negative affect alone is not likely to impede attachment security, assuming these emotions are "authentic" and not severe enough to translate into less appropriate and sensitive caregiving (such as caregiving associated with clinical levels of depression).

Mind-Mindedness and Reflective Function

Meins et al. (2001) argued that it is necessary to also examine caregiving that occurs specifically in response to the infant's mental states. Meins and her colleagues use the term "mind-mindedness" to describe the extent to which a mother views her child as a living being with mental states, rather than with only physical and emotional needs. If a caregiver is unable to differentiate her own affect/emotional state from her infant's, perhaps because she does not view her infant as a separate being with mental states and intentions, the result may be "distortion, misattribution, and otherwise misattuned responsiveness to infant distress" (Grienenberger, Kelly, & Slade, 2005, p. 302). Therefore, a mother's ability to "mentalize" is crucial to affect regulation, since mentalizing symbolizes her understanding that affective states are changeable (e.g., fear can be allayed). Meins et al. (2001) study of mind-mindedness and attachment indicated that mothers' comments about their infants' knowledge, thoughts, and desires that were relevant to the given situation predicted attachment security.

Similar to the concept of mind-mindedness is reflective function (Slade, 2005) defined as "the capacity to link mental states to behavior in meaningful and accurate ways" (p. 275). Slade argued that caregivers and children alike must develop reflective function, as it is a necessary foundation for the development of self-understanding and an understanding of others, both of which are components of attachment. When caregivers appropriately acknowledge and respond to their children's affective states, children develop an understanding of their own emotions and how their emotions develop as a result of interactions with caregivers. Slade further proposed that the child's development of reflective function is partially contingent on talking; that is, the mothers' ability to recognize and respond to her child's changing mental states "first in gesture and action, and later in words and play" is critical for children's development of self-understanding (Slade, 2005, p. 271). An important question, however, is to what extent *parental* reflective function is related to attachment security. A mother's capacity for reflective function is closely tied to her responsiveness to the infant's signals, particularly when either the mother or the infant is experiencing strong negative emotion. Preliminary evidence supports an inverse relationship between parental reflective function and "atypical" maternal behavior (e.g., intrusiveness, withdrawal, failure to offer comfort to crying infant, etc.) which, in turn, predicts infant attachment security (Grienenberger et al., 2005).

To date, no studies on mind-mindedness or parental reflective function have included samples of deaf infants. By implication, prior to having a formal diagnosis of hearing impairment, mothers of deaf infants may be intuitively aware of having difficulties "connecting" with their baby as a result of their infant's deafness. Mothers may feel frustrated by this, and their negative affect may manifest as aggressiveness or intrusiveness or they may become fearful and withdrawn (Marschark, 1993). Postdiagnosis, mothers of deaf infants may have difficulty coping with the fact of the child's impairment. While she is adjusting to this situation and its accompanying negative emotions, a mother who can step back from her own affective experience and view her infant's subjective intentions and other mental states (i.e., a mother with a greater capacity for reflective function) is more likely to engage in sensitive caregiving and respond appropriately to the bids of the infant. In this way, reflective function capacity within the caregiver may be viewed as a protective factor for the development of a secure attachment and, therefore, a promising new line of research particularly for dyads that may be at risk for attachment insecurity.

Interactional Synchrony

The focus of the interactional synchrony construct is on the timing and rhythm of mother–infant interactions, with the mother's role being to mirror her infant's behavior and adjust the rhythm and tempo of her own behavior to that of her infant (Beckwith, Rozga, & Sigman, 2002). In spite of this emphasis on the mother's behavior, it is nonetheless viewed as a reciprocal process that relies as much upon infants' initiations and bids for attention as upon mothers' responses. Perhaps more relevant to the population of hearing mothers and deaf infants is the notion of interactive *dyssynchrony* proposed by Biringen, Emde, and Pipp-Siegal (1997). The thesis of Biringen et al. is that even under the best of circumstances, mother–infant interactions are not without some conflict and discord. Interactive dyssynchrony is described as "subtle interruptions in the flow of interaction" (p. 6), such as when the infant turns away from the mother or vice versa. "Repair" occurs when one or the other member of the dyad resumes the interaction. Movement from synchrony to dyssynchrony to repair/reinitiation of synchrony is considered optimal; alternatively, dyssynchrony without successful resolution is maladaptive. An important avenue for future research will be to examine whether dyssynchronous interactions are more likely to occur among hearing mother–deaf infant dyads compared to other dyads. In addition, an understanding of infant and/or maternal behaviors that result in successful repair and reinitiation when dyssynchrony occurs has the potential to greatly inform the development of effective interventions.

Studies of Hearing Mother–Deaf Infant Interactions

Overall, research examining interactions between deaf infants and their caregivers, particularly with a focus on attachment outcomes for the infant, is very sparse. Lederberg and Mobley (1990) were the first to directly test links between maternal behaviors and attachment with children who were deaf. They compared toddlers aged 18–25 months whose hearing impairments were diagnosed at 10 months of age with a matched group of hearing children. The majority of the hearing impaired toddlers were profoundly deaf, and all came from families who were participating in a parent education program for families raising a deaf child. In addition to observing mother–child free play, Lederberg and Mobley assessed attachment using Ainsworth's Strange Situation standard procedure. Counter to van IJzendoorn et al.'s (1992) later conclusion, they reported that the distribution of secure and insecure attachment classifications within each group was similar for both hearing and impaired children. Qualitative ratings of dyads during play further indicated that mothers with deaf children did not differ in terms of sensitivity or teaching and that the children in the two groups did not differ in terms of their "initiative, compliance, affect, attention span, pride in mastery, or creativity" (Lederberg & Mobley, 1990, p. 1602). However, the two groups did differ in some aspects of mother–child interactions. Whereas mothers of deaf children initiated more interactions than did those with hearing children, deaf children terminated play more often, and their interactions with their mothers were of a shorter duration than those of the hearing group. Lederberg and Mobley speculated that insecure attachment among deaf children was not automatic when early diagnosis and intervention occurred.

More studies have examined the quality and/or characteristics of hearing mother–deaf infant interactions without regard to the impact of these interactions on attachment security. Meadow-Orlans and her colleagues were among the first to study mother–child interactions in families with deaf infants. In a longitudinal study, MacTurk, Meadow-Orlans, Koester, and Spencer (1993) compared hearing mothers who had either deaf or hearing infants when the children were 9, 12, 15, and 18 months. Videotapes of brief play interactions between mothers and infants showed that at both 9 and 18 months, mothers with deaf infants displayed fewer contingent nonverbal behaviors than did mothers of hearing infants. A global interaction measure, derived from separate ratings of mothers' sensitivity, involvement, flexibility, affect, and consistency, was also significantly lower for mothers with deaf infants. Notably, however, maternal nonverbal responsiveness at 9 months predicted the 18-month global interaction ratings more strongly for dyads in which the child was deaf.

Mothers' attention to their infants' object-directed eye gazes were of interest in another study of mother–child interaction (Spencer, Bodner-Johnson, & Gutfreund, 1992). When caregivers are responsive to children's looks, joint attention, which is thought to support various desirable developmental outcomes, becomes possible. Object-directed gazing is, therefore, an infant signal to which mothers may attend. Spencer et al. (1992) compared three groups: hearing mothers of deaf children, deaf mothers of deaf children, and hearing mothers of hearing children. Frequency of infant object-directed gazes did not differ among these groups. However, the researchers found that responsiveness to their infants' object-directed gazes was significantly less for hearing mothers of deaf children than for mothers in the other two groups, which did not differ. The causal mechanism for the lower rate of responsiveness among hearing mothers of deaf infants is not clear from this study, nor is it clear whether or not mothers' lower level of responsiveness would jeopardize their infant's attachment security. Future studies of joint attention among hearing mothers and deaf infants would benefit from incorporating measures of sensory sensitivity (Donovan et al., 2007) and/or parental reflective function (Slade, 2005), as well as of attachment security. It would be highly informative, for example, to examine whether maternal responsiveness is mediated by hearing mothers' ability to detect their deaf infant's object-directed eye gazes or by the extent to which they mentalize what their deaf baby is thinking about during object gazing.

Some research offers indications of dyssynchronous interactions that occur in hearing mother–deaf infant relationships. For example, Koester, Karkowski, and Traci (1998) examined the "repair process" after 9-month-old hearing and deaf infants broke eye contact with their deaf or hearing mothers during face-to-face interactions. Participants were four groups (all possible hearing/deaf combinations) of ten mother–infant dyads. Videotaped interactions between the dyads were coded for instances in which the infant looked away from the mother, and then for the immediately following maternal strategy: observing/waiting, vocal response, tactile/vibratory response, or visual response. "Success" scores were also derived, based on the number of times the mothers' strategy resulted in the infant regaining eye gaze. Results indicated no significant differences in infant gaze aversion by group;

however, for each episode, it was the deaf infants with hearing mothers that looked away *least* often, supporting the notion that visual attention plays an important role for deaf infants and their caregivers. Deaf mothers were more likely to use visual strategies to regain infants' attention than were hearing mothers, regardless of the hearing status of their infant. Hearing mothers (of both deaf and hearing infants) were more likely to use vocalization than were deaf mothers. No group differences emerged in use of tactile/vibratory strategies. In terms of success, the most successful strategy used by hearing mothers of deaf infants to regain their infants' visual attention, when compared to the other three groups of dyads, was vocal. It appears that it is not the vocalizations per se to which success can be attributed, but to the nonverbal movements that often accompany vocalizing such as head movement and changes in facial expression. These nonverbal behaviors are apparently responsible for capturing the deaf infant's attention, even when the mother is only peripherally visible.

Nonetheless, hearing mothers of deaf infants make some adjustments in their interactional styles, namely, by incorporating visually accessible forms of communication such as finger play and tactile contact along with vocalizations (Koester, 1995; Koester, Brooks, & Traci, 2000). Further, Koester (1995) offered an interesting glimpse into hearing mother–deaf infant patterns of synchrony/dyssychrony in her use of the still-face paradigm following normal interaction. Mothers were instructed to face their 9-month-old infant without responding to him/her in any way for 2 min. During the still-face episode (i.e., dyssynchrony), deaf infants *reduced* their signaling efforts (though they did show a marked increase in arm, leg, and torso movements), while hearing infants *increased* their signaling efforts. Koester reasoned that the decreased signaling behavior of deaf infants when their mothers became nonresponsive could be a reflection of an uncoordinated interaction history through which the deaf infant has learned to cope by turning inward. Moreover, Pipp-Siegel et al. (1998) found that both parents and deaf infants used touch more often during free-play sessions; additionally, the use of touch increased commensurate with the severity of the child's hearing loss (ranging from mild to profound). Child-initiated and/or mother-initiated touch was mostly used to get the other individual's attention. Furthermore, mothers and children who interacted in a hostile manner with one another touched each other less, which may suggest that touch is an important method of communication only when mother–child relationships are secure. Koester et al. (2000) also highlighted the importance of touch as a method of communication, particularly when it was used in an effort to achieve or maintain the infant's visual attention. They suggested that it is the quality of touch (e.g., active vs. passive touch), rather than the quantity of touch, that is important, especially when the hearing status of the parent and child is mismatched. Specifically, while hearing babies may respond negatively to too much tactile stimulation (Pipp-Siegel et al., 1998), deaf babies likely have a higher threshold for tactile stimulation and benefit from high levels of active touching (touching with moving contact, such as tapping or stroking).

Koester (1992) has also proposed that research on interactions between mothers and deaf infants would benefit from being viewed through the intuitive parenting model (originally proposed by Papousek & Papousek, 1987), especially to inform interventions for dyads involving a deaf partner. The focus of the intuitive parenting construct is on *nonconscious* parental behaviors, those "natural" behaviors that parents enact with their infants but are generally not able to report on verbally. These natural behaviors include: babytalk, touching infants to examine their muscle tone as an indicator of wakefulness, visual distance regulation to ensure that the parent is within the infant's optimal range, adjustment of stimulation to the infant's tolerance level as well as timing, repetitions, and rhythms of stimulation in all modalities (e.g., vocalizations are often paired with tactile, kinesthetic, and visual stimulation). In her application of this model to interactions involving deaf infants, Koester raises important questions about whether hearing parents can intuitively compensate for their infants' more limited repertoire of communication strategies and/or whether certain intuitive behaviors are resistant to change. Empirically driven answers to these compelling questions are quite limited. The available data in the literature thus far indicate that hearing mothers do intuitively compensate by increasing their visual communication strategies with their deaf infants; however, as already noted, some researchers have suggested that hearing parents may risk overcompensating by being overly directive and intrusive with deaf children (e.g., Marschark, 1993; Spencer et al., 1992).

Together, research that has included hearing mothers with deaf infants has yielded a mixture of findings, with some studies suggesting there is no difference in interactional style/quality among these dyads, and other studies concluding that hearing mothers and deaf infants do in fact have different interactional styles when compared to other dyad types (i.e., hearing mothers with hearing infants, deaf mothers with deaf infants, etc.). Documented differences in interactional styles (e.g., increasing use of tactile strategies with vocalizations) does not necessarily imply, however, that the quality of the interaction suffers. Researchers who have examined quality of interactions have tended to show that hearing mothers of children who are deaf or hard of hearing are less sensitive, more intrusive, and more hostile (Marschark, 1993). Unfortunately, the ability to integrate the existing literature and extract general implications for deaf infants is impeded by a variety of factors, such as very low sample sizes and lack of consistency in operational definitions of constructs. Most important, virtually nothing is known about whether and how hearing mother–deaf infant interactions, even if different or somewhat lower in quality compared to interactions with hearing infants, ultimately have any adverse impact on attachment security.

The Development of Attachment Within Context: Discussion of Distal Factors

A full account of attachment security pertaining to the deaf infant cannot be achieved without consideration of contextual factors. From an ecological perspective, the development of an infant–caregiver attachment is embedded within a family system which, in turn, is embedded within the broader community (Belsky, 1995, 2006; Bronfenbrenner, 1979). While this is true for hearing and deaf populations alike, it is possible that the broader ecology influences the deaf infant–caregiver dyad in unique ways. For the purposes of this chapter, distal factors that are considered are those that could exert influence on parent–child interaction patterns, and therefore, the developing attachment relationship.

According to Belsky's (1984) process model of parenting, factors including parents' work, the marital relationship, and their social network can each exert both direct and/or indirect influences (via parents' personalities) on the quality of parenting behavior, thereby having the potential to impact the attachment relationship. Moreover, each of these distal factors is inextricably interrelated (i.e., job satisfaction may impact marital quality (or vice versa; marital quality is related to individuals' broader social networks, etc.). However, it is important to keep in mind that the parenting system operates in such a way that any single source of vulnerability (e.g., low marital quality) is less likely to adversely affect the parent–child attachment relationship; the greatest risk for adverse outcomes is present when there are *multiple* vulnerabilities in the system (Belsky, 2006). Given the multitude of factors that could impact parent–child interactions and the complex interrelationships among these factors, the goal of this section is to provide a relatively brief overview of the issues that may be particularly important for attachment formation among hearing caregivers and deaf infants and have received some empirical attention. Specifically, these issues include stress experienced by primary caregivers, mothers' reaction to their infant's diagnosis and societal expectations for her response, social support, and societal/institutional conditions.

Although not directly addressed by Belsky's model, parenting stress is nonetheless an important part of parenting to consider in terms of its causes and subsequent impact on parenting behavior and the attachment relationship, particularly for families caring for an infant with a disability. In particular, studies of stress levels in parents of children who are deaf compared to parents of hearing children reveal a pattern of mixed findings. Some studies indicate no difference in parental stress level between these groups (e.g., Asberg, Vogel, & Bowers, 2008; Meadow-Orlans, 1994), whereas others report greater stress among parents of deaf children (e.g., Quittner, Glueckauf, & Jackson, 1990). Interestingly, one study actually reported slightly *lower* stress levels among parents of deaf children (Pipp-Siegel, Sedey, & Yosinaga-Itano, 2002). Pipp-Siegel et al. (2002) administered the Parental Stress Index/Short Form (PSI/SF) to 184 hearing mothers of children (ranging in age from 6 months to 5 years) with hearing loss. The PSI/SF consists of three subscales: Parental Distress (i.e., amount of stress the parent feels due to personal factors such as lack of social support or depression), Parent–Child Dysfunctional Interaction (i.e., whether or not the child is seen as a positive or a negative element in the parent's life), and Difficult Child (i.e., behavioral characteristics of the child reflecting whether the child is difficult to manage due to temperament and/or learned patterns of defiance). The investigators also measured mothers' "daily hassles," level of social support, and the child's expressive language ability via mother report. Comparison of their data to a large, normative sample of 800 parents of hearing children indicated that stress levels among mothers of children who were deaf/hard of hearing were not clinically higher than those among mothers of hearing children. For the Parental Distress subscale in particular, the mothers of children who were deaf/hard of hearing reported *less* stress than did mothers of hearing children. A variety of factors may potentially explain this finding, including the fact that the sample of mothers with a deaf child had been receiving intervention services (i.e., social support). Pipp-Siegel et al. also reported that the following characteristics could put mothers at higher risk for experiencing clinical levels of stress: (a) perception of greater intensity of daily hassles, (b) having a child with a disability in addition to deafness, (c) having a child with a language delay, (d) having a child with less severe hearing loss (perhaps because mothers' discount their child's mild hearing loss and do not modify their expectations or behavior), (e) lower family income, and (f) low levels of perceived support from others. The attachment relationship was not assessed, but conceivably any of the risk factors identified in this study (or a combination of them) could comprise attachment formation if maternal sensitivity and/or the quality of mother–child interaction suffered.

The scarcity of studies investigating infant deafness and its relationship to parenting stress, coupled with the fact that the samples/methods used for these studies differ in other important ways (i.e., age of the children and age of their hearing loss diagnosis, socioeconomic status, measurement differences, etc.) makes it difficult to make definitive conclusions about the relationship between parenting a deaf infant and stress level. Although stress is not an inevitable outcome of parenting a child with a disability, there is enough evidence within the parenting literature to indicate nonetheless that parents, particularly mothers who tend to be the primary caregivers, can feel overwhelmed by the additional demands of providing care for a special-needs child (e.g., Hassall, Rose, & McDonald, 2005; McLinden, 1990). The implications of increased stress for parents are not entirely straightforward; in terms of the attachment relationship, it will likely depend upon the extent to which the quality of the mother's interactions with her infant suffers as a result. Studies with hearing infants have suggested, for example, that stress can result in more negative interactional patterns and insecure infant attachment (e.g., Crnic & Greenberg, 1990; Jarvis & Cressey, 1991).

A factor that is unique to the family ecology of parents with infants diagnosed with hearing impairment is their initial reaction to, and subsequent adjustment to, the diagnosis itself. Researchers have documented that parents initially experience negative emotional reactions to their child's diagnosis of profound hearing loss (Calderon & Greenberg, 2000). Marvin and Pianta (1996) suggested a theoretical framework for making predictions about how parental reactions to their child's diagnosis of a chronic disability may influence attachment security. Drawing from Bowlby's work on loss and mourning and subsequent studies by Lyons-Ruth, Block, and Parsons (1993), and Main and Hesse (1990), this framework suggests that parents go through a period of mourning and grieving, even trauma, when their child's diagnosis is initially received and subsequently must change their internal working models of self and child from those representing a healthy child to those representing a child with a chronic medical condition. Parents who are unable to successfully reorient to the present reality and modify their internal working models accordingly, would be considered "unresolved," resulting in caregiving difficulties and increased risk of insecure attachment. Marvin and Pianto examined this theoretical framework empirically with mothers of infants (median age = 22 months) who received a diagnosis of cerebral palsy. With data collected from the Strange Situation and the Reaction to Diagnosis Interview (RDI), the researchers found that 82% of mothers classified as "resolved" vs. 19% of mothers classified as "unresolved" on the RDI had securely attached children. This study was the first to demonstrate that mothers' resolution of their grief reactions to their child's diagnosis may be important for the formation of a secure attachment and has clear implications for offering early intervention services to these families. Sheeran, Marvin, and Pianta's (1997) subsequent study further showed that mothers' resolution of their child's diagnosed chronic medical condition related to lower parenting stress and greater marital satisfaction from their partners' points of view. Further, while mothers' resolution status had no bearing on their need for social support, "resolved" mothers found their support systems to be more helpful than did "unresolved" mothers. Very few studies, however, have focused exclusively on deaf infants and their caregivers.

Social support, one of the determinants of parenting behavior in Belsky's model, may be viewed as a protective factor for the family system and for individual parents. Not only can social support provide a buffer from the stress that may arise from caring for a deaf child but in the form of a solid support network it can provide broader protection against stress incurred from other sources within the system as well, such as from work and/or the marital relationship. Specific to the developing infant–parent attachment relationship, social support is likely to exert indirect effects on attachment either through parents' internal working models or via parenting behavior (see Belsky et al., 1995; Berlin & Cassidy, 1999, for reviews). Social support can mitigate the negative consequences that the birth of an infant with a disability such as deafness may bring to the family system; by the same token, lack of social support can have a direct impact on maternal sensitivity which, in turn, can have a negative influence on the attachment relationship (Crockenberg, 1981; MacTurk et al., 1993). Indeed, Meadow-Orlans (1994) found a significant inverse/negative relationship between parenting stress and social support for mothers of deaf infants. This relationship was marginally significant for fathers of deaf infants, and not statistically significant for parents of hearing infants. Studies suggesting that hearing mothers of deaf infants and children are less sensitive and more intrusive than mothers of hearing infants also report that these differences are not evident when level of social support for the mother is considered (e.g., Meadow-Orlans & Steinberg, 1993). From an intervention standpoint, it is important that Meadow-Orlans and Steinberg (1993) indicated that receipt of support near the time of the child's diagnosis and total level of support (rather than number of support sources) are vital in terms of positively impacting maternal behavior. Their findings also leave open the possibility that social support has some direct benefits to the child as well. They studied mother–child interactions when infants were 18-months of age and noted no statistical difference between deaf and hearing infants on most of the behaviors that were measured, specifically, their level of compliance, affect, and involvement. One potential explanation for this that has not been tested empirically is that mothers' support systems may provide direct benefits to the infant via additional adults with whom to have positive interactions (e.g., father, extended family, teachers/professionals, etc.).

Some researchers are beginning to turn their attention toward even broader aspects of the social-ecological system, guided by the belief that fully understanding caregiving and developing effective interventions can only be accomplished with a consideration of how social and institutional conditions affect families (e.g., Ray, 2003). The period of time immediately following diagnosis is often very challenging, as parents are dealing with their own strong emotions while trying to learn about their infant's diagnosis and make decisions about early intervention. Parents will likely feel pressure to quickly adapt to the situation and learn how to navigate the advice they are receiving from the various professionals they are encountering, while even the professionals themselves may not completely agree on the best approach or intervention for the family (Calderon & Greenberg, 2000). In her secondary analysis of interview data from 30 parents of children with chronic health conditions, Ray reported on some of the negative circumstances that parents felt had impacted their stress level and ability to parent effectively. These circumstances included parents encountering negative attitudes among health professionals (e.g., lack of support or respect for the role of the parent), difficulties with government or agency guidelines for eligibility for services, lack of information on caring for their child or available resources, lack of funding for social services, lack of coordination among professionals and their agencies, and significant bureaucratic red tape. Further, Ray's study sheds light on circumstances that make parenting a special-needs child challenging, but that are not often acknowledged, such as the stigma associated with disability, varying opinions on "who" is responsible for the care of special-needs children (i.e., the society or the family), and the feminization of caregiving, which often translates into the mother taking on the majority of the caregiving duties (and most often being the partner who leaves a paid job to do so).

Clearly, much of the work on parenting and the family ecology have focused on mothers as the primary caregiver, rather than on fathers. Gregory (1991) provides a compelling argument that the way in which "mothering" is conceptualized within Western culture may also negatively impact their emotional well-being and stress level, with subsequent implications for a mother's relationship with her child. For example, Gregory (1991) argued that Western society's message to mothers of disabled children is, at least implicitly, "to make their child be, or seem to be, as 'normal' as possible" (p. 127). Through interviews conducted with mothers of deaf children during the 1970s, Gregory noted that after their children were diagnosed as deaf, mothers reported having to adjust to feelings of being different from other mothers and having to handle their fears about the reactions of others when the diagnosis is revealed to them. Hence, mothers expressed feelings of isolation and lack of social support as they came to terms with the fact that their children were "different." Gregory further contended that the influence of attachment theory was to heighten the responsibility that mothers felt for their children's healthy socioemotional development, adding to the pressure on mothers to be "good" and to the likelihood that any perceived failure of the child's development is their fault. Advice from professionals is often based on laboratory studies of child development and therefore runs the risks of being too far removed from real-world contexts, at odds with mothers' own intuitions, or of not fully accounting for the ways that deaf children make sense of their world. As a result, mothers may become overly self-conscious in their interactions with their children, and therefore, the interactions with their infants may be less natural and thereby potentially less sensitive and synchronous.

In consideration of the influence of distal factors on the attachment relationship, it is important to restate Belsky's proposition that the parent–child relationship and the family system in general are well buffered. As yet, there is no justification for expecting that the broader ecology would differentially impact the caregiver–deaf infant relationship. Some empirical evidence suggests that mothers of children with a disability, though not necessarily deafness specifically, do experience additional stress that may be directly attributable to dealing with the fact of their child's diagnosis and/or providing care for a child with special needs. The extent to which this stress translates into insecure infant attachment will depend on a multitude of other factors including, but certainly not limited to, the caregiver's social support network and coping skills, marital quality, job stress, and the quality and timing of professional intervention.

Conclusion

The overall purpose of this chapter is to consider whether infant deafness is a risk factor for insecure attachment. Consideration of the issue of resilience implies that deafness is an adversity to be overcome, though perhaps it is more useful and accurate to conceptualize deafness as an adversity only under certain circumstances (see Rutter, 2000). Ultimately, the resilience of deaf infants in the context of attachment formation cannot be addressed with a "one-size-fits-all" answer because of the complex nature of attachment and its multiple predictors. In line with Young, Green, and Roger's (2008) notions of resilience and the deaf, congenital deafness within the context of attachment formation may be a "risk indicator," but only when it interacts with other contexts and processes (e.g., neglectful, insensitive parenting) that "render its disadvantaging effects more likely" (Young et al., 2008, p. 4). The weight of the empirical evidence thus far does not provide an overwhelmingly compelling case for believing that infant deafness alone would result in an insecure attachment. The other environmental/contextual factors and processes that need to be considered in addition to deafness include, but are certainly not limited to other characteristics of the child (e.g., whether the child has another medical or psychiatric diagnosis), the caregiver (e.g., maternal sensory sensitivity), the quality of their interactions (e.g., synchronicity), and the broader social ecology within which the child and the family is situated (e.g., community/social support network;

availability of timely and accurate diagnosis and subsequent intervention). Finally, it is important to bear in mind that even if a deaf infant (or any infant) developed an insecure attachment (though again it is doubtful that it could be directly attributed to deafness alone), his/her developmental trajectory is not necessarily enduring; other protective factors within the familial and social-ecology of that individual could help to buffer the individual with an insecure attachment from seriously negative outcomes.

Given the limited amount of research currently available, there is a tremendous opportunity for investigators to examine attachment formation in deaf infants. The available research on the development of attachment in deaf infants is limited not only in terms of quantity but also in terms of quality and scope. Existing studies tend to have small samples and are outdated; older studies, for example, do not reflect current trends in diagnosis and intervention and whether these trends have any bearing on attachment security (e.g., most research available appears to have been conducted before the onset of EHDI). Moreover, it is difficult to integrate existing study findings to extrapolate a cohesive picture of deaf infant attachment due to differences in measurement and sample characteristics. Rather than a focus on attachment per se, studies have addressed mother and/or deaf infant characteristics and behaviors, as well as interactional quality of the dyad. Only a few have incorporated measures of attachment security to examine whether interactional differences translate into less secure attachment. There is also a great need for studies that incorporate longitudinal designs as attachment security can change, either positively or negatively, depending on other circumstances within the family that may change and therefore impact caregiving quality (e.g., parental employment status, divorce, etc.). A general critique of the attachment literature, including studies with hearing infants, is that too few studies have examined fathers, extended family members or nonrelative caregivers as attachment figures. Both Bowlby and Ainsworth recognized that attachment to caregivers in addition to the mother is possible, yet this aspect of attachment theory has received little research attention (Howes & Spieker, 2008). The deaf literature in particular would benefit from consideration of infants' additional attachment relationships as yet another potential protective factor or buffer against poor developmental outcomes. Finally, while there are several intervention programs with specific focus on the attachment relationship, particularly for at-risk families [e.g., Steps Toward Effective, Enjoyable Parenting (STEEP), the Seattle program (Greenberg & Speltz, 1988; Speltz, 1990), The Ann Arbor Approach (1993), Circle of Security (COS, Marvin, Cooper, Hoffman, & Powell, 2002), etc.], none of these were developed with the specific needs of families with deaf infants in mind. A comprehensive program that addresses auditory assistance in addition to the family ecology (e.g., parenting stress and social support), sensitive caregiving, and attention to the developing attachment relationship [c.f. Counseling and Home Training Program for Deaf Children (CHTP), implemented in British Columbia (Greenberg, 1983)] is likely to be the most effective for families with deaf infants.

Additional dialogue about the normativity of attachment as it pertains to the relationship between hearing parents and their deaf infants would be useful as well.

For example, Keller (2008) has argued that whether or not attachment security is indeed adaptive cannot be determined without considering contextual information; that is, are the behaviors associated with secure attachment healthy strategies given the environment within which the child and family are situated? Keller argues that security of attachment is actually a moral ideal insofar as it provides a pathway to developmental outcomes that are valued within Euro-American middle-class culture, such as self-confidence, curiosity, and psychological independence. Maternal sensitivity, she argues, becomes a judgment of how good or bad mothers are. In fact, there may be environmental contexts in which an intrusive and controlling mother is the ideal of good parenting, as in non-Western cultures (Keller, 2007). Perhaps behavioral strategies utilized by the deaf infant/hearing mother are adaptive within the context of deafness, even if they would be formally classified as insecurely attached. Future research that focuses on whether the deaf infant's behavior and the mother's responses are in fact adaptive strategies in that they ultimately lead to desirable outcomes might be more enlightening than focusing exclusively on attachment styles per se. In line with Keller's argument, Marschark (1993) suggests that the Strange Situation may not be a valid measurement procedure for deaf infants as the deaf and hearing communities may not have identical behavioral standards for mother–infant attachment. For example, a deaf infant's indifference to his/her mother's departure could be due to the infant either not being aware of her departure or not understanding her departure in the same way as a hearing infant. Indeed, a deaf infant–hearing mother relationship that appears to be "out of sync" in comparison to hearing infants/hearing mothers may in fact be a different pattern of synchrony and reciprocity not well captured by current attachment measurement techniques.

Since Bowlby initially set forth the theoretical tenets of attachment theory, decades of research has contributed greatly to current understanding of the importance of the infant–caregiver relationship. Unfortunately, implementation of well-designed studies of attachment formation among deaf infants and their caregivers has lagged considerably behind studies designed with hearing infants. More questions than answers remain about the exact nature of the deaf infant–hearing parent relationship; the time is here for new investigations of attachment formation among the deaf.

Acknowledgement The authors would like to thank Mark Greenberg, PhD for his feedback on an earlier version of this chapter.

References

Adamson, L. B., & Chance, S. (1998). Coordinating attention to people, objects, and symbols. In A. M. Wetherby, S. F. Warren, & J. Reichle (Eds.), *Transitions in prelinguistic communication: Preintentional to intentional and presymbolic to symbolic* (pp. 15–37). Baltimore: Brookes.
Ainsworth, M. D. S. (1979). Attachment as related to mother–infant interaction. *Advances in the Study of Behavior, 9*, 2–52.

Ainsworth, M. D. S. (1989). Attachments beyond infancy. *American Psychologist, 44*, 709–716.

Ainsworth, M. D. S., Bell, S. M., & Stayton, D. (1971). Individual differences in strange situation behavior of one-year-olds. In H. R. Schaffer (Ed.), *The origins of human social relations* (pp. 17–57). London: Academic Press.

Ainsworth, M. D. S., Bell, S. M., & Stayton, D. (1974). Infant–mother attachment and social development. In M. P. Richards (Ed.), *The introduction of the child into a social world* (pp. 99–135). London: Cambridge University Press.

Ainsworth, M. D. S., Blehar, M. C., Waters, E., & Wall, S. (1978). *Patterns of attachment: A psychological study of the strange situation.* Hillsdale, NJ: Lawrence Erlbaum Associates.

Ainsworth, M. D. S., & Wittig, B. A. (1969). Attachment and exploratory behavior of one year-olds in a strange situation. In B. M. Foss (Ed.), *Determinants of infant behavior* (Vol. 4, pp. 111–136). London: Methuen.

Asberg, K. K., Vogel, J. J., & Bowers, C. A. (2008). Exploring correlates and predictors of stress in parents of children who are deaf: Implications of perceived social support and mode of communication. *Journal of Child and Family Studies, 17*(4), 486–499.

Beckwith, L., Rozga, A., & Sigman, M. (2002). Maternal sensitivity and attachment in atypical groups. *Advances in Child Development and Behavior, 30*, 231–274.

Belsky, J. (1984). The determinants of parenting: A process model. *Child Development, 55*, 83–96.

Belsky, J. (1995). Expanding the ecology of human development. In P. Moen, G. H. Elder, K. Luscher, & U. Bronfenbrenner (Eds.), *Examining lives in context: Perspectives on the ecology of human development* (1st ed., pp. 545–561). Washington, DC: American Psychological Association.

Belsky, J. (2006). Determinants and consequences of infant–parent attachment. In L. Balter & C. S. Tamis-LeMonda (Eds.), *Child psychology: A handbook of contemporary issues* (2nd ed.). New York: Psychology Press.

Belsky, J., Rosenberger, K., & Crnic, K. (1995). Maternal personality, marital quality, social support and infant temperament: Their significance for infant–mother attachment in human families. In C. Pryce, R. Martin, & D. Skuse (Eds.), *Motherhood in human and nonhuman primates: Prosocial determinants* (pp. 115–124). Basel: Karger.

Belsky, J., & Vondra, J. (1989). Lessons from child abuse: The determinants of parenting. In D. Cicchetti & V. Carlson (Eds.), *Child maltreatment: Theory and research on the causes and consequences of child abuse and neglect* (pp. 153–202). New York: Cambridge University Press.

Bergeson, T. R., Miller, R. J., & McCune, K. (2006). Mothers' speech to hearing-impaired infants and children with cochlear implants. *Infancy, 10*(3), 221–240.

Berlin, L. J., & Cassidy, J. (1999). Relations among relationships: Contributions from attachment theory and research. In J. Cassidy & P. R. Shaver (Eds.), *Handbook of attachment: Theory, research, and clinical applications* (pp. 688–712). New York: Guilford Press.

Biringen, Z. (2000). Emotional availability: Conceptualization and research findings. *American Journal of Orthopsychiatry, 70*(1), 104–114.

Biringen, Z., Emde, R. N., & Pipp-Siegal, S. (1997). Dyssynchrony, conflict, and resolution: Positive contributions to infant development. *American Journal of Orthopsychiatry, 6*(1), 4–19.

Bohlin, G., Hagekull, B., & Rydell, A. M. (2000). Attachment and social functioning: A longitudinal study from infancy to middle childhood. *Social Development, 9*(1), 24–39.

Bowlby, J. (1969/1982). *Attachment and loss: Vol. 1. Attachment.* New York: Basic Books.

Bowlby, J. (1973). *Attachment and loss: Vol. 2. Separation.* New York: Basic Books.

Bowlby, J., & Ainsworth, M. D. S. (1991). An ethological approach to personality development. *American Psychologist, 46*(4), 333–341.

Bronfenbrenner, U. (1979). *The ecology of human development: Experiments by nature and design.* Cambridge, MA: Harvard University Press.

Calderon, R., & Greenberg, M. T. (2000). Challenges to parents and professionals in promoting socioemotional development in deaf children. In K. P. Meadow-Orlans, P. E. Spencer,

C. Erting, & M. Marschark (Eds.), *The deaf child in the family and at school: Essays in honor of Kathryn P. Meadow-Orlans*. Mahwah, NJ: Lawrence Erlbaum Associates.

Cassidy, J. (1994). Emotion regulation: Influences of attachment relationships. In N. Fox (Ed.), *The development of emotion regulation. Monographs of the society for research in child development, 59*(2–3, Serial No. 240) (pp. 228–249).

Cassidy, J. (2008). The nature of the child's ties. In J. Cassidy & P. R. Shaver (Eds.), *Handbook of attachment: Theory, research, and clinical applications*. New York: Guilford Press.

Cicchetti, D. (1993). Developmental psychopathology: Reactions, reflections, projections. *Developmental Review, 13*(4), 471–502.

Cohen, N. J. (2001). *Language impairment and psychopathology in infants, children, and adolescents: Vol. 45. Developmental clinical psychology and psychiatry*. Thousand Oaks, CA: Sage Publications.

Cooper, R. P., & Aslin, R. N. (1990). Preference for infant-directed speech in the first month after birth. *Child Development, 61*, 1584–1595.

Cooper, G., Hoffman, K., Powell, B., & Marvin, R. (2005). The circle of security intervention: Differential diagnosis and differential treatment. In L. J. Berlin, Y. Ziv, L. Amaya-Jackson, & M. T. Greenberg (Eds.), *Enhancing early attachments: Theory, research, intervention, and policy* (pp. 127–151). New York: Guildford Press.

Craig, W. (2000). *Childhood social development: The essential readings*. Malden, MA: Blackwell Publishing.

Crnic, K. A., & Greenberg, M. T. (1990). Minor parenting stress with young children. *Child Development, 61*, 1628–1637.

Crockenberg, S. B. (1981). Infant irritability, mother responsiveness, and social support influences on the security of mother–infant attachment. *Child Development, 52*, 857–865.

DeCaspar, A. J., & Fifer, W. P. (1980). Of human bonding: Newborns prefer their mothers' voices. *Science, 208*(4448), 1174–1176.

De Wolff, M. S., & van IJzendoorn, M. H. (1997). Sensitivity and attachment: A meta-analysis on parental antecedents of infant attachment. *Child Development, 68*, 571–591.

Donovan, W., Leavitt, L., Taylor, N., & Broder, J. (2007). Maternal sensory sensitivity, mother–infant 9-month interaction, infant attachment status: Predictors of mother–toddler interaction at 24 months. *Infant Behavior & Development, 30*, 336–352.

Feldman, R., & Eidelman, A. I. (2003). Skin-to-skin contact (Kangaroo Care) accelerates autonomic and neurobehavioural maturation in preterm infants. *Developmental Medicine & Child Neurology, 45*(4), 274–281.

Feldman, R. S., & Rimé, B. (1991). *Fundamentals of nonverbal behavior*. Cambridge: Cambridge University Press.

Fernald, A. (1992). Human maternal vocalizations to infants as biologically relevant signals: An evolutionary perspective. In J. H. Barkow, L. Cosmides, & J. Tooby (Eds.), *The adapted mind: Evolutionary psychology and the generation of culture* (pp. 391–428). New York: Oxford University Press.

Finitzo, T., Albright, K., & O'Neal, J. (1998). The newborn with hearing loss: Detection in the nursery. *Pediatrics, 102*(6), 1452–1460.

Geers, A. E. (2006). Spoken language in children with cochlear implants. In P. E. Spencer & M. Marschark (Eds.), *Advances in the spoken language development of deaf and hard-of-hearing children* (pp. 244–270). Oxford: Oxford University Press.

Gravel, J. S., & O'Gara, J. (2003). Communication options for children with hearing loss. *Mental Retardation and Developmental Disabilities Research Reviews, 9*, 243–251.

Greenberg, M. T. (1983). Family stress and child competence: The effects of early intervention for families with deaf infants. *American Annals of the Deaf, 128*, 407–417.

Greenberg, M. T. (2005). Enhancing early attachments: Synthesis and recommendations for research, practice, and policy. In L. Berlin, Z. Yair, & L. Amaya-Jackson (Eds.), *Enhancing early attachments: Theory, research, intervention and policy* (pp. 327–343). New York: Guilford Press.

Greenberg, M. T., & Marvin, R. S. (1979). Attachment patterns in profoundly deaf preschool children. *Merrill-Palmer Quarterly, 25*(4), 265–279.

Greenberg, M., & Speltz, M. L. (1988). Contributions of attachment theory to the understanding of conduct problems during the preschool years. In J. Belsky & T. Nezworski (Eds.), *Clinical implications of attachment* (pp. 177–218). Hillsdale, NJ: Lawrence Erlbaum Associates.

Gregory, S. (1991). Challenging motherhood: Mothers and their deaf children. In A. Phoenix, A. Woollett, & E. Lloyd (Eds.), *Motherhood: Meanings, practices and ideologies* (pp. 123–142). London: Sage.

Grienenberger, J., Kelly, K., & Slade, A. (2005). Maternal reflective functioning, mother–infant affective communication, and infant attachment: Exploring the link between mental states and observed caregiving behavior in the intergenerational transmission of attachment. *Attachment & Human Development, 7*(3), 299–311.

Harlow, H. F. (1959). Love in infant monkeys. *Scientific American, 200*(6), 68–74.

Harris, M., & Chasin, J. (2005). Visual attention in deaf and hearing infants: The role of auditory cues. *Journal of Child Psychology and Psychiatry, 46*(10), 1116–1123.

Hassall, R., Rose, J., & McDonald, J. (2005). Parenting stress in mothers of children with an intellectual disability: The effects of parental cognitions in relation to the child characteristics and family support. *Journal of Intellectual Disability Research, 49*, 405–418.

Horn, D. L., Houston, D. M., & Miyamoto, R. T. (2007). Speech discrimination skills in deaf infants before and after cochlear implantation. *Audiological Medicine, 5*(4), 232–241.

Howes, C., & Spieker, S. (2008). Attachment relationships in the context of multiple caregivers. In J. Cassidy & P. R. Shaver (Eds.), *Handbook of attachment: Theory, research, and clinical applications*. New York: Guilford Press.

Izard, C. E., Haynes, O. M., Chisholm, G., & Baak, K. (1991). Emotional determinants of infant–mother attachment. *Child Development, 62*(5), 906–917.

Jarvis, P. A., & Cressey, G. L. (1991). Parenting stress, coping, and attachment in families with an 18-month old. *Infant Behavior and Development, 14*, 383–395.

Joint Committee on Infant Hearing. (2000). Year 2000 position statement: Principles and guidelines for early hearing detection and intervention programs. *American Journal of Audiology, 9*, 9–29.

Keller, H. (2007). *Cultures of infancy*. Mahwah, NJ: Lawrence Erlbaum Associates.

Keller, H. (2008). Attachment – past and present. But what about the future? *Integrative Psychological Behavior Science, 42*, 406–415.

Keller, H., Lohaus, A., Völker, S., Cappenberg, M., & Chasiotis, A. (1999). Temporal contingency as an independent component of parenting behavior. *Child Development, 70*, 474–485.

Kisilevsky, B. S., & Low, J. A. (1998). Human fetal behavior: 100 years of study. *Developmental Review, 18*, 1–29.

Kobak, R., Cassidy, J., Lyons-Ruth, K., & Ziv, Y. (2006). Attachment, stress, and psychopathology: A developmental pathways model. In D. Cicchetti & D. Cohen (Eds.), *Developmental psychopathology Vol. 1: Theory and method*, Wiley (pp. 333–369).

Koester, L. S. (1992). Intuitive parenting as a model for understanding parent–infant interactions when one partner is deaf. *American Annals of the Deaf, 137*(4), 362–369.

Koester, L. S. (1994). Early interactions and the socioemotional development of deaf infants. *Early Development and Parenting, 3*(1), 51–60.

Koester, L. S. (1995). Face-to-face interactions between hearing mothers and their deaf or hearing infants. *Infant Behavior and Development, 18*, 145–153.

Koester, L. S., Brooks, L., & Traci, M. A. (2000). Tactile contact by deaf and hearing mothers during face-to-face interactions with their infants. *Journal of Deaf Studies and Deaf Education, 5*(2), 127–139.

Koester, L. S., Karkowski, A. M., & Traci, M. A. (1998). How do deaf and hearing mothers regain eye contact when their infants look away? *American Annals of the Deaf, 143*(1), 5–13.

Lederberg, A. R., & Mobley, C. E. (1990). The effect of hearing impairment on the quality of attachment and mother–toddler interaction. *Child Development, 61*, 1596–1604.

Locke, J. L. (2001). First communion: The emergence of vocal relationships. *Social Development, 10*(3), 294–308.

Lyons-Ruth, K., Block, D., & Parsons, E. (1993, March). *The disturbed caregiving system: Conceptualizing the impact of childhood trauma on maternal caregiving behavior during infancy*.

Paper presented at the biennial meeting of the Society for Research in Child Development, New Orleans, LA, USA.

MacTurk, R. H., Meadow-Orlans, K. P., Koester, L. S., & Spencer, P. E. (1993). Social support, motivation, language, and interaction: A longitudinal study of mothers and deaf infants. *American Annals of the Deaf, 138*(1), 19–25.

Main, M., & Hesse, E. (1990). Is fear the link between infant disorganized attachments status and maternal unresolved loss? In M. Greenberg, D. Cicchetti, & E. M. Cummins (Eds.), *Attachment in the preschool years* (pp. 161–182). Chicago: University of Chicago Press.

Marschark, M. (1993). Origins and interactions in social, cognitive, and language development in deaf children. In M. Marschark & M. D. Clark (Eds.), *Psychological perspectives on deafness* (pp. 7–26). Hillsdale, NJ: Lawrence Erlbaum Associates.

Marvin, R. S. (1977). An ethological-cognitive model of the attenuation of mother–child attachment. In T. M. Alloway & L. Krames (Eds.), *Advances in the study of communication* (pp. 25–60). New York: Plenum Press.

Marvin, R., Cooper, G., Hoffman, K., & Powell, B. (2002). The circle of security project: Attachment-based intervention with caregiver-preschool child dyads. *Attachment & Human Development, 4*(1), 107–124.

Marvin, R. S., & Pianta, R. C. (1996). Mothers' reactions to their child's diagnosis: Relations with security of attachment. *Journal of Clinical Child Psychology, 25*(4), 436–445.

Masataka, N. (2006). Development of communicative behavior as a precursor of spoken language in hearing infants, with implications for deaf and hard-of-hearing infants. In P. E. Spencer & M. Marschark (Eds.), *Advances in the spoken language development of deaf and hard-of-hearing children* (pp. 42–63). Oxford: Oxford University Press.

McKinley, A. M., & Warren, S. F. (2000). The effectiveness of cochlear implants for children with prelingual deafness. *Journal of Early Intervention, 23*(4), 252–263.

McLinden, S. E. (1990). Mothers' and fathers' reports of the effects of a young child with special needs on the family. *Journal of Early Intervention, 14*, 249–259.

Meadow-Orlans, K. P. (1994). Stress, support, and deafness: Perceptions of infants' mothers and fathers. *Journal of Early Intervention, 18*(1), 91–102.

Meadow-Orlans, K. P., & Steinberg, A. G. (1993). Effects of infant hearing loss and maternal support on mother–infant interactions at 18 months. *Journal of Applied Developmental Psychology, 14*, 407–426.

Meins, E., Fernyhough, C., Fradley, E., & Tuckey, M. (2001). Rethinking maternal sensitivity: Mothers' comments on infants' mental processes predict security of attachment at 12 months. *Journal of Child Psychology and Psychiatry, 42*(5), 637–648.

Miall, D. S., & Dissanayake, E. (2003). The poetics of babytalk. *Human Nature, 14*(4), 337–364.

Moeller, M. P. (2000). Early intervention and language development in children who are deaf and hard of hearing. *Pediatrics, 106*(3), e43. doi:10.152/peds.106.3e43.

National Center for Hearing Assessment and Management (NCHAM). (2006) *State summary statistics: Universal newborn hearing screening*. Retrieved November 24, 2008, from http://www.infanthearing.org/status/unhsstate.html.

Nicholas, J. G., & Geers, A. E. (2007). Will they catch up? The role of age at cochlear implantation in the spoken language development of children with severe to profound hearing loss. *Journal of Speech, Language, and Hearing Research, 50*, 1048–1062.

Nievar, M. A., & Becker, B. J. (2008). Sensitivity as a privileged predictor of attachment: A second perspective on DeWolff and vanIJzendoorn's meta-analysis. *Social Development, 17*(1), 102–114.

North Dakota Chapter of American Academy of Pediatrics (NDAAP). (2008) *Facts on newborn hearing loss*. Retrieved December 30, 2008, from http://www.ndaap.org/hearing.htm.

Oller, D. K. (2006). Vocal language development in deaf infants: New challenges. In P. E. Spencer & M. Marschark (Eds.), *Advances in the spoken language development of deaf and hard-of-hearing children* (pp. 22–41). Oxford: Oxford University Press.

Papousek, H., & Papousek, M. (1987). Intuitive parenting: A dialectic counterpart to the infant's precocity in integrative capacities. In J. D. Osofsky (Ed.), *Handbook of infant development* (2nd ed., pp. 669–720). New York: John Wiley & Sons.

Pauli-Pott, U., & Mertesacker, B. (2009). Affect expression in mother–infant interaction and subsequent attachment development. *Infant Behavior and Development, 32,* 208–215.

Pipp-Siegel, S., Blair, N. L., Deas, A. M., Pressman, L. J., & Yoshinaga-Itano, C. (1998). Touch and emotional availability in hearing and deaf or hard of hearing toddlers and their hearing mothers. *The Volta Review, 100*(5), 279–298.

Pipp-Siegel, S., Sedey, A. L., & Yoshinaga-Itano, C. (2002). Predictors of parental stress in mothers of young children with hearing loss. *Journal of Deaf Studies and Deaf Education, 7*(1), 1–17.

Prezbindowski, A. K., Adamson, L. B., & Lederberg, A. R. (1998). Joint attention in deaf and hearing 22 month-old children and their hearing parents. *Journal of Applied Developmental Psychology, 19*(3), 377–387.

Quittner, A. L., Glueckauf, R. L., & Jackson, D. N. (1990). Chronic parenting stress: Moderating versus mediating effects of social support. *Journal of Personality and Social Psychology, 59*(6), 1266–1278.

Ray, L. D. (2003). The social and political conditions that shape special-needs parenting. *Journal of Family Nursing, 9*(3), 281–304.

Rutter, M. (2000). Resilience reconsidered: conceptual consideration, empirical findings, and policy implications. In J. P. Shonkoff (Ed.), *Handbook of early intervention* (pp. 651–682). Cambridge: Cambridge University Press.

Rutter, M., & Sroufe, L. A. (2000). Developmental psychopathology: Concepts and challenges. *Development and Psychopathology, 12*(3), 265–296.

Saffran, J. R., Werker, J. F., & Werner, L. A. (2006). The infant's auditory world: Hearing, speech, and the beginnings of language. In D. Kuhn & R. Siegler (Eds.), *Handbook of child psychology: Vol 2. cognition, perception, and language* (6th ed., pp. 58–108). Hoboken, NJ: Wiley.

Sheeran, T., Marvin, R. S., & Pianta, R. C. (1997). Mothers' resolution of their child's diagnosis and self-reported measures of parenting stress, marital relations, and social support. *Journal of Pediatric Psychology, 22*(2), 197–212.

Siegler, R., DeLoache, J., & Eisenberg, N. (2003). *How children develop* (1st ed.). New York: Worth Publishers.

Slade, A. (2005). Parental reflective functioning: An introduction. *Attachment & Human Development, 7*(3), 269–281.

Speltz, M. L. (1990). The treatment of preschool conduct problems: An integration of behavioral and attachment constructs. In M. Greenberg, D. Cicchetti, & M. Cummings (Eds.), *Attachment in the preschool years: Theory, research and treatment* (pp. 399–426). Chicago: University of Chicago Press.

Spence, M. J., & DeCaspar, A. J. (1987). Prenatal experience with low-frequency maternal-voice sounds influence neonatal perception of maternal voice samples. *Infant Behavior and Development, 10,* 133–142.

Spencer, P. E. (2000). Looking with listening: Is audition a prerequisite for normal development of visual attention during infancy? *Journal of Deaf Studies and Deaf Education, 5*(4), 291–302.

Spencer, P., Bodner-Johnson, B., & Gutfreund, M. (1992). Interacting with infants with a hearing loss: What can we learn from mothers who are deaf? *Journal of Early Intervention, 16,* 64–78.

Sroufe, L. A. (1988). The role of infant-caregiver attachment in development. In J. Belsky & T. Nezworski (Eds.), *Clinical implications of attachment* (pp. 18–38). Hillsdale, NJ: Lawrence Erlbaum Associates.

Sroufe, L. A. (1995). *Emotional development: The organization of emotional life in the early years.* New York: Cambridge University Press.

Sroufe, L. A. (2000). Early relationships and the development of children. *Infant Mental Health Journal, 21*(1–2), 67–74.

Sroufe, L. A. (2005). Attachment and development: A prospective, longitudinal study from birth to adulthood. *Attachment & Human Development, 7*(4), 349–367.

Sroufe, L. A., Egeland, B., Carlson, E., & Collins, W. A. (2005). *The development of the person: The Minnesota study of risk and adaptation from birth to adulthood.* New York: Guilford.

Stack, D. M., & Muir, D. W. (1992). Adult tactile stimulation during face-to-face interactions modulates five-month-olds' affect and attention. *Child Development, 63*, 1509–1525.

Stuckless, E. R., & Birch, J. W. (1997). The influence of early manual communication on the linguistic development of deaf children. *American Annals of the Deaf, 142*(3), 71–79.

Svirsky, M. A., Robbins, A. M., Kirk, K. I., Pisoni, D. B., & Miyamoto, R. T. (2000). Language development in profoundly dead children with cochlear implants. *Psychological Science, 11*(2), 153–158.

Thompson, R. (2008). Early attachment and later development: Familiar questions, new answers. In J. Cassidy & P. R. Shaver (Eds.), *Handbook of attachment: Theory, research, and clinical applications*. New York: Guilford Press.

Vaccari, C., & Marschark, M. (1997). Communication between parents and deaf children: Implications for social-emotional development. *Journal of Child Psychology and Psychiatry and Allied Disciplines, 38*(7), 793–801.

van den Boom, D. C. (1997). Sensitivity and attachment: Next steps for developmentalists. *Child Development, 64*, 592–594.

van IJzendoorn, M. H., Dijkstra, J., & Bus, A. G. (1995). Attachment, intelligence, and language: A meta-analysis. *Social Development, 4*(2), 115–128.

van IJzendoorn, M. H., Goldberg, S., Kroonenberg, P. M., & Frenkel, O. (1992). The relative effects of maternal and child problems on the quality of attachment: A meta-analysis of attachment in clinical samples. *Child Development, 63*, 840–858.

van IJzendoorn, M. H., & Kroonenberg, P. M. (1988). Cross-cultural patterns of attachment: A meta-analysis of the strange situation. *Child Development, 59*(1), 147–156.

van IJzendoorn, M., Schuengel, C., & Bakermans-Kranenburg, M. (1999). Disorganized attachment in early childhood: Meta-analysis of precursors, concomitants, and sequelae. *Development and Psychopathology, 11*, 225–250.

van IJzendoorn, M. H., & Sgi-Schwartz, A. (2008). Cross-cultural patterns of attachment: Universal and contextual dimensions. In J. Cassidy & P. R. Shaver (Eds.), *Handbook of attachment: Theory, research, and clinical applications*. New York: Guilford Press.

Vouloumonos, A., & Werker, J. F. (2007). Listening to language at birth: Evidence for a bias for speech in neonates. *Developmental Science, 10*(2), 159–171.

Walters, M. W., Boggs, K. M., Ludington-Hoe, S., Price, K. M., & Morrison, B. (2007). Kangaroo care at birth for full time infants: A pilot study. *MCN: The American Journal of Maternal/Child Nursing, 32*(6), 375–381.

Wedell-Monnig, J., & Lumley, J. M. (1980). Child deafness and mother–child interaction. *Child Development, 51*, 766–774.

Weinfield, N. S., Sroufe, L. A., Egeland, B., & Carlson, E. A. (2008). Individual differences in infant-caregiver attachment: Conceptual and empirical aspects of security. In J. Cassidy & P. R. Shaver (Eds.), *Handbook of attachment: Theory, research, and clinical applications* (2nd ed.). New York: Guilford Press.

White, K. R. (2006). Early intervention for children with hearing loss: Finishing the EHDI revolution. *The Volta Review, 106*(3), 237–258.

Wolff, P. H. (1963). Observations on the early development of smiling. In B. Foss (Ed.), *Determinants of infant behavior* (Vol. 2, pp. 113–138). London: Methuen.

Yoshinaga-Itano, C. (2001). Early identification, communication modality, and the development of speech and spoken language skills: Patterns and considerations. In P. E. Spencer & M. Marschark (Eds.), *Advances in the spoken language development of deaf and hard-of-hearing children* (pp. 298–327). Oxford: Oxford University Press.

Yoshinaga-Itano, C. (2003). Early intervention after neonatal hearing screening: Impact on outcomes. *Mental Retardation and Developmental Disabilities Research Reviews, 9*, 252–266.

Yoshinaga-Itano, C., Sedey, A. L., Coulter, D. K., & Mehl, A. L. (1998). Language of early- and later-identified children with hearing loss. *Pediatrics, 102*, 1161–1171.

Young, A., Green, L., & Roger, K. (2008). Resilience and deaf children: A literature review. *Deafness and Education International, 10*(1), 40–55.

Chapter 3
Deaf Parents as Sources of Positive Development and Resilience for Deaf Infants

Lynne Sanford Koester and Nicole McCray

Abstract In this chapter, we explore the idea that deaf parents may play a particularly important role in the lives of deaf infants and provide evidence to support this particularly in relation to social–emotional development. Consistent with the overall theme of this volume, we assert that deaf parents might well be considered "protective factors" in the lives of young deaf children and that hearing parents, as well as early intervention professionals, can benefit from the knowledge gained through observing and understanding the many intuitively appropriate behaviors incorporated by deaf parents into their daily interactions with deaf children.

The chapter begins with a brief discussion of risk and resiliency, specifically in relation to several important aspects of infant development: temperament, emotional regulation, and attachment to significant caregivers. Sameroff's (Hum Dev, 18:65–79, 1975) Transactional Model is then introduced to emphasize the reciprocal nature of early parent–child interactions and to draw attention to the contributions made by each participating member – in this case, parent and infant – of the interacting dyad. For purposes of illustrating these concepts and to focus on the role of deaf parents, two vignettes are included, which describe hypothetical interactions between a deaf infant and either a deaf or hearing parent.

The theory of Intuitive Parenting (Papoušek & Papoušek, *Psychobiology of the human newborn*, pp. 367–390, 1982; Papoušek & Papoušek, *Handbook of infant development*, 2nd ed., pp. 669–720, 1987) is included as a means of explaining the many nonconscious behaviors often used by both deaf and hearing parents to facilitate communication with a prelingual infant. Prior to a discussion of implications and conclusions, the chapter also addresses the importance of social support for parents of deaf infants and the child's later development of empathy and literacy skills.

L.S. Koester (✉)
Department of Psychology, The University of Montana, Missoula, MT, USA
e-mail: lynne.koester@umontana.edu

D.H. Zand and K.J. Pierce (eds.), *Resilience in Deaf Children: Adaptation Through Emerging Adulthood*, DOI 10.1007/978-1-4419-7796-0_3,
© Springer Science+Business Media, LLC 2011

*Imagine for the moment a hearing American couple adopting an 18-month-old hearing toddler from Korea. Bridging the language gap with children younger than 18 months seems like it would be relatively easy: The child will have some words and a few simple sentences in Korean, but not too many. The new family and the community then flood the child with language, both intentionally and unintentionally, and eventually she becomes fluent in English rather than Korean. At the same time, of course, she learns more than just a particular language. Through the spoken language that she hears, the child also learns who people are, about social rules and customs, about objects and events in the world, and about the uses of communication... **Now consider the situation of a child who cannot hear.***

Marschark (2007, p. 12)

Young children learn more than can be imagined simply by observing others in their social world; much of this involves the incidental, informal learning that takes place without any intentional instruction from others. Messages about appropriate social interactions, display rules, expression of emotions, and participating in dialogs or conversations are often conveyed by both verbal and nonverbal means of communicating. Unless these messages are accessible in the visual-gestural modality, they are likely not to be discerned by the deaf child, who, therefore, is at the risk of missing these early lessons in socialization, interactions, and communication. In this chapter, we focus on those deaf children whose parents are also deaf, in an effort to highlight some of the important but subtle interactive dynamics thought to enhance the positive development of these children.

In recent years, the field of developmental psychology has joined the larger trend of focusing on strengths rather than deficits, protective rather than risk factors, and sources of support that can help families cope with the stressors that may accompany child-rearing. These emphases are particularly important in relation to the disabilities literature, as the historical tendency has typically been to concentrate on presumed weakness or disadvantages. In the case of hearing loss, for example, there is historical evidence that deaf parents in the USA were previously deemed inadequate, particularly as parents of a hearing child (Padden & Humphries, 1988). Interestingly, the same attitude has not usually existed in regard to hearing parents of deaf children, despite the fact that essentially the same disparity of communication styles exists in these dyads. The purpose of this chapter is to highlight the strengths and resources that deaf parents bring to the family system in which one or more children are also deaf. Although some later developmental outcomes (e.g., in middle childhood and adolescence) will be mentioned, the primary age ranges to be addressed will be infancy, toddlerhood, and the early preschool years.

According to Thompson et al. (2001), approximately 5,000 American families experience the birth of a deaf infant each year. Several research teams have addressed the potential protective factors that may be present for those children who adapt most successfully to deafness, regardless of the hearing status of their parents (e.g., Erting, Prezioso, & Hynes, 1990/1994; Sass-Lehrer & Bodner-Johnson, 2003; Yoshinaga-Itano, Sedey, Coulter, & Mehl, 1998). Other studies have emphasized the heterogeneity of individual, family, and contextual differences and the range of supports available for deaf children and their families (e.g., Meadow-Orlans, Mertens, & Sass-Lehrer, 2002; Spencer, 2003). Much of the information and applications generated by these studies are more relevant for families with hearing parents, which constitute approximately 90% of those with deaf children (Marschark, 1993). Since fewer rigorous studies have been carried out with deaf parents of deaf children, much of the information presented here will be somewhat speculative, but is based on the well-substantiated theory of Intuitive Parenting developed by Papoušek and Papoušek (1982, 1987) and Papoušek and Bornstein (1992). This theory draws attention to many naturally occurring caregiving behaviors that appear to be especially well suited to the developmental needs of a young infant; in the case of a child with hearing loss, deaf parents may be particularly adept at reading an infant's signals, understanding body language, and responding accordingly. This theory has, therefore, been applied in research with this population and provides a useful explanatory tool for explaining the dynamics of interactions with deaf infants.

Risk/Resilience

Researchers have traditionally used the term resilience to describe three types of phenomena (Werner, 2000). First, resilience has been used to explain positive developmental outcomes in children from high-risk backgrounds, such as poverty or abuse, who have overcome great odds. Next, resilience has been used to explain sustained competence under stressful circumstances, such as parental divorce. Finally, resilience has been used to describe individuals who are able to successfully recover from serious childhood trauma such as war or famine (Werner, 2000). Thus, in each of these cases, resilience is predicated on some form of risk. The presence of a disability in either the parent or a child has often been thought to represent a risk factor, as documented by Meadow-Orlans (1995).

When attempting to explain outcomes in the face of stress, researchers have focused on identifying protective factors that may moderate the stress a child is experiencing and therefore enhance positive developmental outcomes. Protective factors are generally conceptualized as factors within the child, family, or community that serve as buffer against negative experiences (Werner, 2000). There are many conceptualizations of risk and resilience. In this chapter, we view resilience as a developmental and transactional process, rather than a quality of individual children. More specifically, resilience can be viewed as an ongoing process of gathering resources that allow the individual to adaptively deal with stressful events, and one that provides a foundation for dealing with future challenges as well as recovering from stress (Yates, Egeland, & Sroufe, 2003). We will assert that deaf parents, by virtue of having learned to function (in most cases) in both the deaf and hearing world, can serve as important sources of resilience for deaf children, thus protecting them from many of the potentially adverse effects of growing up with a hearing impairment. This argument will be developed by providing evidence from the literature regarding early social–emotional development, parent–child attachment, effective communication patterns, and later identity formation.

However, it is also important to acknowledge that risk factors do exist in these families, as in all families. For example, there may well be negative effects associated with being members of a stigmatized or marginalized group, with having limited access to ideal educational environments for those with hearing loss, or with having to face numerous difficult choices about medical procedures and schooling. Background variables such as poverty, unemployment, parental mental health concerns, domestic violence, and so forth may all be just as prevalent in these families, such that having parents who are deaf in and of itself may not function as a strong protective factor for the deaf child when multiple risk factors are present.

Nevertheless, for deaf children, the hearing status of their parents may play a role in determining future developmental trajectories in a variety of domains. All human infants are born with a predisposition to communicate with others, either by spoken or visual-gestural language, and to participate as partners in social interactions. According to Marschark (2007, p. 5), "effective parent–child communication early on is the best single predictor of success in all areas of deaf children's development." Much of the research on risk factors for deaf children focuses on those with hearing mothers. Difficulties in early communication, reactions to identification of a deaf child (usually perceived as stressful by hearing parents), and the question of whether the child will later seek to be part of a deaf community have been identified in previous studies as factors that may contribute to diminished developmental outcomes in these children.

For deaf infants whose parents are also deaf, such risk factors may not exist. Therefore, when attempting to explain outcomes for this group of deaf children, researchers must examine factors beyond the hearing status of the parent that may influence developmental outcomes. Would the child benefit from hearing aids or cochlear implants, and if so, are the parents open to these choices? Does the child have other disabilities or learning differences that might exert a more powerful influence over their academic achievement and social development? Does the family live in close enough proximity to a residential school for the deaf, so that the child's attendance there is feasible if the parents prefer this option? Since the family is a dynamic system, it must be recognized that all of these choices, decisions, opportunities, and potential constraints will be the result of complex factors including the prior experiences of the parents and the current characteristics of the child. Biological predispositions, often thought of as temperament, are among the first innate characteristics that an infant brings to early interactions with the social environment.

Temperament

When assessing risk and protective factors within an individual child, temperament frequently emerges as a quality that may have either a positive or negative effect on interactions between parent and infant. Temperament is a biologically based quality of infants that emerges early and remains relatively stable (although not unchangeable) as the individual develops (Thompson, 1999). All current conceptualizations of temperament share a common belief that infants have constitutionally based tendencies to react to environmental stimuli and affective experiences in particular ways. Such predispositions interact with the caregiving environment to form relatively predictable patterns of behavior over time (Barton & Robins, 2000).

An infant's temperament manifests itself behaviorally in the form of agreeability (activity level, sociability, and emotionality), reactivity/arousal, and self-regulation or the ways in which arousal is managed. Thomas and Chess developed three classifications of infant temperament: *Easy, Difficult, and Slow to Warm Up* to describe the behaviors observed in daily interactions (Thompson, 1999). Such behaviors may have a tremendous effect on the developing relationship between parent and child. For example, an infant's temperament can have an effect on parental feelings of competency as parents interpret the feedback they receive from their infant. In particular, a child who is difficult to soothe because of a more reactive temperament might contribute to parental feelings of frustration and incompetence.

Temperament itself does not seem to have a direct effect on children's adjustment. Instead, the match between temperament and environmental demands or "goodness of fit" seems to play a much larger role in determining later outcomes. "Goodness of fit" is, in part, determined by how parents interpret infants' behaviors (Thompson, 1999), and this interpretation of behavior may be especially important in the case of deaf infants. For hearing parents, in particular, many of the deaf child's communicative efforts may need to be inferred from body language, facial expressions, gestures, or nonlinguistic vocalizations. If the child becomes easily frustrated as a result of not being able to communicate his or her needs effectively, the escalation of emotions and negative behaviors can lead the parents to think of the child as being "difficult" or even unmanageable. The risk of this counter-productive spiral occurring is likely to be minimized in a family in which the parents can communicate with the deaf child in the visual-gestural mode from the beginning, thus providing the child with the means of expressing – and therefore regulating – emotions more readily.

It is possible that other behaviors used by deaf children to communicate or interact with their environments may also be interpreted as a manifestation of a reactive or difficult temperament. For example, the heightened activity levels of deaf infants, observed by some researchers, may be perceived by hearing parents as indicating a difficult temperament (Koester & Meadow-Orlans, 1999). Thus, both temperament and disability can have an effect on the readability of an infant's signals. If these parents perceive their deaf child as "difficult" based on observed daily interactions, such an interpretation might make an already stressful situation even more taxing. In an examination of hearing mothers' perceptions of their 9-month-old infants' temperament, Koester and Meadow-Orlans (2004a, b) found that hearing mothers of deaf infants tended to perceive infant behavior characteristics such as repetitive motor activity and frequent looking away from the partner as "difficult." In contrast, deaf mothers did not perceive heightened activity levels in deaf babies as reflecting a difficult temperament as readily as hearing mothers. Instead, they seemed to view this type of activity as a positive effort on the part of the infant to interact, to communicate, and to influence the environment.

Temperament can provide a buffer against stressors by eliciting positive responses, or it can exacerbate a child's vulnerability to stressors by eliciting negative responses from adults, regardless of whether a child has a disability or not. "The difficult child [with a disability] is at greatest risk for evoking aversion in others...New situations, people, and routines evoke withdrawal and protest and adaptation takes a long time... When stresses occur stormy interactions are all too likely" (Chess & Thomas, 1996, p. 175).

Emotional Regulation

In addition to affecting the response they receive from caregivers, infants' temperament or reactivity may also interact with caregiver behaviors to influence the infant's emerging regulatory strategies. The development of characteristic patterns of behavior in early childhood is rooted in children's ability to regulate their emotional state and formulate a behavioral response to their experience (Barton & Robins, 2000). Emotional regulation is one of the most important tasks for an infant's social–emotional development, in part because the strategies infants develop to regulate emotion during the first year are thought to underlie secure attachments (Crockenberg & Leerkes, 2000). Caregivers play an important role in facilitating emotional regulation by providing strategies for self-regulation that are eventually internalized by the developing child. These strategies that arise in the context of early interactions generalize over time to include the regulation of affective states, arousal, attention, and the organization of complex behaviors needed for social interaction (Barton & Robins, 2000). Early integration of experience includes the regulation of arousal, activity, affect, and attention; the signals associated with the regulation of these play a central role in nonverbal communication (Papoušek, 2008). It is assumed that effective modulation of emotions may be learned sooner by deaf infants with deaf parents, as a result of a more immediate communicative connection that allows these infants access to important messages and feedback about their reactivity and behavioral manifestations of emotions. In the case of deaf infants with hearing parents, this process may take somewhat longer and may be highly dependent on the proficiency with which the parents are able to communicate with the infant.

Emotional regulation describes individuals' attempts to monitor, evaluate, and modify their emotional reactions. It involves internal and external processes, such as the maintenance and modification of physiological arousal or internal feeling states (Crockenberg & Leerkes, 2000). Emotional regulation emerges in the context of parent–infant interaction, such as when parents help children to reduce negative emotions by soothing or distraction. Caregivers also reinforce positive emotions, structure the environments in which children experience emotions, and influence how infants interpret situations through social referencing. By 7–9 months, infants are able to detect differences in affective states in social partners and use these states to regulate their own emotions and behaviors (Crockenberg & Leerkes, 2000).

Parents help infants to regulate their emotions by paying attention to infants' emotion-related behaviors (muscle tone, facial expression, quality of vocalizations, and so forth) that serve as indicators of internal states. Infants can modify these overt expressions to achieve a goal, such as being held or played with (Crockenberg & Leerkes, 2000). The process of regulation can be seen as both physiological and emotional responses when babies encounter new situations. Ideally, infants receive support from caregivers in regulating this arousal, rather than becoming overwhelmed. These emotion-related behaviors can be linked with emotional reactivity or the intensity, onset, and duration of infant emotional arousal. This infant reactivity determines, in part, the intensity of signals to which parents themselves react. In turn, this reciprocal process contributes to the intensity of signals the infant produces to get his/her needs met. For example, some parents may respond to infants' signals only when they reach a particular intensity, while others respond before they reach that same level. Infants then learn which signals they can use most effectively to get their needs met (Crockenberg & Leerkes, 2000). If an infant learns that it is only by using extreme methods (e.g., temper tantrums) that his or her needs are responded to, then this pattern of interaction is likely to become increasingly prevalent and may lead to a cycle of coercive, out-of-control behaviors. Of course, this scenario can easily unfold in any family, but it is more probable in situations involving poor communication for whatever reason; for purposes of this chapter, we would assert that it may be more predictable in families of deaf children and hearing parents, unless easily accessible communication is established early on.

Infants vary widely in their capacity for effective emotional regulation. One explanation for this variability is that infants differ in their physiological reactivity, an internal characteristic that, in combination with external factors, contributes to differences in emotional regulation. Another explanation is that parents vary in attunement and responsiveness to infant emotional cues. When caregivers and infants are engaged in a contingent cycle of signals and responses, i.e., "attunement," the conditions needed to promote emotional regulation exist (Stern, 1985). For a positive contingent cycle to exist, parents need to be aware of and respond appropriately to their infant's affective states and cues and vice versa. When such awareness and responsiveness co-occur, regulation is present or in the process of being established. However, when there is a mismatch between infant signals and maternal responses, behavioral and physical disorganization in the infant is likely to result (Crockenberg & Leerkes, 2000). Failures in the development of self-regulatory capacities are believed to underlie a variety of behavior problems such as attention deficits, oppositional behavior, and frequent tantrums (Barton & Robins, 2000). Once again, it seems likely that deaf parents may be able to achieve this attunement somewhat more effortlessly than hearing parents, due to their own history of reading "body language," communicating in a visual-gestural modality, and responding to subtle cues regarding the mental and physical states of a social, interactive partner. Regardless of whether these deaf parents have had previous experience with young children, their own upbringing may have provided a good foundation for understanding the social–emotional needs of a deaf child.

Attachment

Attachment theory evolved from the work of John Bowlby and Mary Ainsworth to explain the seemingly contradictory infant behaviors of proximity seeking and exploration (Bretherton, 1992). The goal of the attachment system is security, and the behaviors associated with it are most likely to be activated when the child is frightened, fatigued, or ill and less obvious when the child feels protected, helped, or soothed. For example, if children become frightened during exploratory activities, they will then seek proximity to and reassurance from trusted caregivers, thus allowing for continued exploration under safe conditions. Through repeated experiences of proximity seeking and exploration within the "secure base" of caregivers, infants also develop internal working models of their social world and of the self. Internal working models are formed early in life and operate outside of conscious awareness, but are revised frequently in early childhood when development is rapid (Bretherton, 1985).

Parental responsiveness has emerged as a major determinant of relationship quality, and one of the most important factors contributing to attachment security in infants (Juffer, Bakermans-Kranenburg, & van Ijzendoorn, 2007; Lounds, Borkowski, Whitman, Maxwell, & Weed, 2005). This characteristic involves the parent's ability to provide contingent, consistent, and appropriate responses to the infant's cues (Ainsworth, Blehar, Waters, & Wall, 1978). Responsive parents are aware of their infant's signals, respond promptly, display flexibility in behavior and thought, exert appropriate levels of control, and are able to negotiate between the sometimes conflicting goals of their infants (Lounds et al., 2005). Similarly, responsiveness reflects the degree to which parents' actions are sensitive and child focused and is evident in both daily care and social interactions between parents and children. Attachment theory, therefore, suggests that early responsiveness provides the foundation that allows children to feel secure, to develop basic trust in their caregivers, and to explore their environments with initiative and confidence.

This early parental responsiveness requires an understanding of and sensitivity to children's individual developmental abilities, such that parents do not over- or underestimate their children's skills (Hans & Wakschlag, 2000). Parental characteristics such as personality type and feelings of effectiveness in interactions with infants, as well as situational factors such as perceived social support and life stress, may all influence parental responsiveness. In addition, attributes within the infant such as temperament, readability, and predictability are associated with levels of parental responsiveness (Bornstein & Lamb, 1992).

In the areas of attachment, quality of maternal affective behavior, and parental control, the impact of childhood deafness on the parent–child social relationship is not necessarily negative (Lederberg & Prezbindowski, 2000). It appears that most parents are quite resilient and, given adequate support, can adjust to the diagnosis of an infant's hearing loss without long-term negative effects on the parent/child attachment relationship. Nevertheless, it is also possible that this process will take somewhat longer to develop when the parents are hearing and the child is deaf;

in situations involving both parents and child who are deaf, the ease with which early communication is established is likely to contribute to more rapid establishment of responsive parenting and mutually satisfying parent–infant relationships. For these parents, the presence of a deaf child is not considered atypical and is in fact often desired, and they have a lifetime of personal experience to call upon to inform their parenting (Koester, Brooks, & Traci, 2000). On the other hand, parents with anxious or conflicted attitudes toward deafness have been shown by some (e.g., Hadadian, 1995) to have deaf children whose attachment styles are less secure.

The Transactional Model of Early Interactions

The Transactional Model proposed by Sameroff (1975) enables us to better understand the development of young children by examining ways in which parents and infants reciprocally respond to one another and influence each others' behaviors. For example, Sameroff emphasizes the contributions of both partners – each with his or her unique attributes and styles – so as to better understand the reciprocal nature of these relationships. In the case of a deaf infant, this perspective seems especially important as it allows us to explore the differential roles of deaf and hearing parents in the development of their infants.

A major assumption of this model is that every interaction represents a dynamic transaction in which each partner is altered through the experience of interacting with the other. In terms of parent–infant relationships, this assumption means that while the caregiving environment influences the infant, the infant also influences his or her caregiving environment (Sameroff, 1975). That is, rather than simply looking at parental behaviors and child responses separately, it is important to examine the cues and feedback that the child is providing and how the parent interprets such feedback, which in turn will affect subsequent parental behaviors. The Transactional Model reflects an understanding of the critical role of individual differences, which are particularly important to consider in the case of deaf infants and their deaf or hearing parents.

Deaf Parents as Protective Factors

Hintermair's (2006) "resource-oriented" approach is consistent with our assertion that deaf parents may actually be an asset for a deaf child, having themselves experienced the dilemmas as well as the achievements and satisfactions that may be relevant for their child's social–emotional and cognitive development. It is clear from the literature (Hintermair, 2004, 2006; Meadow-Orlans, 1995; Quittner, 1991) that high levels of parental stress are often associated with social–emotional problems in children, but it is also important to search for *strengths* rather than deficits when examining family interactions. In Hintermair's work, the focus is on *resource orientation*, such as asking what parents bring to the situation in terms of their own capabilities and experiences, what the child brings to the situation as well, and finally, how others can reinforce what is available, healthy and strong within this family system. In other words, early interventionists, educators, and policy makers alike need to concentrate on strengthening existing resources rather than belaboring perceived deficits. To fully understand the coping process within a given family, one must consider the following contributing factors as described by Hintermair (2006):

1. Family variables (e.g., SES, cohesion, roles, available resources, proximity to extended family, number and ages of children)
2. Parent variables (e.g., quality of relationships, time available, schedules, and communicative competency with a deaf child)
3. Child variables (e.g., degree of hearing loss, additional health issues, age, temperament, language and cognitive development, and social–emotional maturity)
4. External variables (e.g., social support, geographical location, educational opportunities, contact with professionals, and contact with others in the deaf community).

The diagnosis of a child's hearing loss may actually bring a sense of relief for deaf parents, as they often feel more equipped to interact easily with a child who shares their own communicative needs (Orlansky & Heward, 1981). To illustrate this concept, deaf parents have been shown to incorporate more visual and tactile strategies rather than emphasizing vocal behaviors, thus intuitively fostering the deaf infant's visual attention skills (Koester, Brooks, & Karkowski, 1998; Koester et al., 2000; Mohay, 2000; Swisher, 1992; Waxman & Spencer, 1997).

In contrast, Meadow-Orlans (1995) describes the reaction of many hearing parents, asserting that "diagnosis of a disability in an infant or young child is almost always a shock experienced by parents as a tragedy. From that point onward, parental reactions vary enormously, but grief, depression, and guilt are common…which can interfere with effective parenting" (p. 61). What are the implications then, when the birth of a deaf child is actually *welcomed* by deaf parents, rather than being viewed as unfamiliar, stressful, or even "tragic?" To illustrate some of these concepts, we now present two imagined vignettes representing a deaf child with either hearing or deaf parents.

Case Example of Deaf Child with Deaf Parents

In the first case example, both parents are deaf: Brittany, the mother, is a law student, and Timothy, the father, works for a construction firm. Both attended residential schools for the deaf and have a large network of friends in the deaf community near their home in urban St. Louis. Their first child, Benjamin, was diagnosed soon after birth as also having a profound hearing loss; his parents did not think twice about using sign language with him and assume that he will eventually attend a residential school as well. They are committed to having their son develop a strong sense of identity with the deaf culture and are adamant about the importance of his becoming proficient at American Sign Language. Brittany and Timothy also recognize the value of having Benjamin being able to function in the hearing world and hope that his English language skills and literacy will prove to make this possible.

During a typical, playful interaction between 1-year-old Benjamin and his father, one can observe the following: Timothy frequently repositions himself so as to maintain easy eye contact with his son and uses exaggerated facial expressions (wide open mouth and eyes, eyebrow shifts, etc.) to emphasize his own emotional reactions and to elicit his son's attention. When Benjamin is looking away, Timothy makes sure to tap lightly on his baby's shoulder or arm before signing to him and gives Benjamin plenty of time to visually or physically explore the physical world before trying to communicate about those objects of interest. As a result, when Timothy does communicate, such as by labeling or describing objects or people, his deaf infant is likely to be attentive to his signing and also able to connect the messages with those things that have attracted his interest.

Brittany puts in many long hours as a law student, and as a result is sometimes less patient than she would like with her young son. Occasionally, she witnesses Benjamin's strong emotional outbursts, and although she realizes that these may be typical for a toddler she is nevertheless concerned lest they become a pattern. In an effort to help him soothe himself when distressed and to modulate his emotional reactions more effectively, Brittany uses calming tactile contact, close face-to-face interactions, and signs to him about how he may be feeling when these outbursts occur. She also tries to model ways of calming herself when she becomes upset or overly tired, so that he will indirectly observe and detect a variety of mechanisms for controlling his emotions in the future.

Case Example of Deaf Child with Hearing Parents

In the second case example, both parents are hearing: Jessica, the mother, is a stay-at-home mom to 3-year-old Emma, who is hearing. David, the father, is a dermatologist. David and Jessica live in Philadelphia and are comfortably middle class. They had always planned on having two children and were very excited when they found out their second child would be a boy.

When a newborn hearing screening revealed that their son, Josh, was deaf, Jessica and David were stunned. They had no experience with deafness and had never even known anyone who was deaf. Jessica immediately began researching deafness and contacting specialists, while David immersed himself in his work. After consulting with numerous specialists, Jessica began learning sign language; she wanted to be prepared to help Josh to communicate as soon as possible. David, on the other hand, began researching cochlear implants and firmly believed that Josh would need to learn to communicate in spoken English, if he was to have any chance of leading a normal life.

Over the first year of Josh's life, the stress level in his home was quite high. David took several months to adjust to the fact that the son he had always wanted was a little different than he had expected. He and Jessica argued frequently about his withdrawal from family life. They also disagreed about the appropriate way to communicate with their son. Jessica is a sensitive mother, but initially struggled to find ways to soothe Josh. Most days, she found it overwhelming to care for both Emma and Josh, while also learning sign language and meeting with Josh's doctors. Jessica eventually found three other mothers whose children were also deaf and began meeting with them on a weekly basis for play dates.

During a typical play interaction between Josh and his mother, one can observe the following: Jessica frequently offers Josh toys and demonstrates their proper use. She talks throughout the interaction, often using the same melodic "motherese" she had used so effectively with Emma, and occasionally introduces a sign to label an object. She works hard to get Josh's attention visually, but seems to overlook the opportunities to incorporate tactile stimulation into their interactions. Occasionally, she misses the mark completely and tries to engage him in play that is somewhat inappropriate given his abilities. For example, she tries to play telephone with Josh and does not quickly pick up on the fact that this activity is completely lost on him.

When David is home, he enjoys the typical rough-and-tumble play that he had always imagined with his son, and Josh reciprocates by giggling and showing that he enjoys these special moments as well. However, when David tries to read to Josh, a frustrating struggle usually ensues even with books that are primarily pictures. While Josh is focused on the pictures, touching them and pointing and sometimes babbling, his father tries to narrate the story or describe the images without first eliciting his son's visual attention. Occasionally, Josh looks up at his father's face inquisitively, but David typically follows only with further vocalizations and quickly loses his son's attention once more. Only when David's face or gestures are highly animated during the storytelling does Josh seem to be able to maintain his attention, quickly alternating his gaze between the picture book and his father's face.

David has little contact with the other families who have deaf children and expresses little interest in meeting with them or seeking support for his frustrations as a parent. He clearly loves both of his children deeply and makes every effort to provide for his family well, but he nevertheless feels overwhelmed by the contradictory information they often receive about signed communication versus oralism. His long work hours provide a convenient excuse for expecting Jessica to take the primary responsibility for the two children, especially in relation to learning sign language and communicating with their deaf son. Josh is securely attached to his parents and interacts easily with the other deaf children in his play group. We might anticipate, however, that in the next few years there will be evidence of delays not only in his language and literacy development, but also in his ability to express and regulate his own emotions, his ability to understand other people's states of mind and the quality of his social interactions.

The purpose of including these two hypothetical examples is to provide illustrations of some of the subtle dynamics that may differentiate the characteristic interactions between deaf and hearing parents with their deaf infant or toddler. Parents who are able to pick up on their child's cues and respond quickly and appropriately, often without conscious thought, may have a better chance of helping their child learn how to regulate his or her emotional reactions – an important skill to emerge in the early years. Similarly, parents who are able to follow the child's lead, respond to the child's visual attention, and pace their interactions accordingly are more likely to maintain the child's attention when giving instructions, communicating, labeling objects and events, or reading to the child. These are all important features of the deaf child's experiences during the first few years, and they help to lay the foundation for later social competence, focused attention, literacy, and even academic skills. In many cases, these behaviors may appear more automatically or intuitively when the parent is deaf, as will be described further in the next section.

The Concept of Intuitive Parenting

The human newborn, whether hearing or deaf, comes into the world with integrative and communicative capacities that predispose the infant to respond to human social stimuli such as touch, voices, faces, and smells (DeCasper & Fifer, 1980; Fagan, 1979; Schaffer, 1979). Such early behaviors help the otherwise helpless newborn to become established quickly as a reciprocating member of its social environment. However, in order for these competencies to fully develop, responsive (and often nonconscious) parental behaviors are needed to assist the infant in becoming an effective communicative and interactive partner over time (Koester, Papoušek, & Papoušek, 1987; Papoušek & Papoušek, 1982, 1987). As Bornstein (1995) states, the concept of intuitive parenting can be understood as follows:

> The parent (and the caregiver in general) is biologically predisposed as the more experienced partner to lead the infant toward a fundamental sociocultural integration and, for this purpose, toward the acquisition of a proper cultural communication. The dialogic character of this lead is evident in respect to intrinsic motivations in infants, on the one hand, and to their developmental constraints in behavioral regulation, on the other. The dosage and complexity of didactic interventions are adjusted, according to feedback cues in infant behaviors. Efforts for eliciting and maintaining infant communication are obvious… Intuitive caregiving aims not only at hygienic, autonomic, and emotional needs of infants, but also at the needs to be together with someone, to share experience, to acquire adequate means of communication, and to create novel symbols… (p. 132).

Communication: Intuitive Strategies Used by Deaf Parents

Parents typically adjust their own communication and efforts to elicit the infant's attention (Papoušek & Papoušek, 1982), such as by modifying the complexity, timing, and speed of their infant-directed communication (Koester 1992, 1995; Koester, Papoušek, & Smith-Gray, 2000; Papoušek & Papoušek, 1987). This is true not only in the case of spoken language, but in visual-gestural communication as well. Deaf parents have been found to modify their sign language input to infants (both deaf and hearing) to include more exaggerated visual, tactile, and facial components than usual (Erting et al., 1990/1994; Erting, Thumann-Prezioso, & Benedict, 2000; Koester, Lahti-Harper, & McCray, 2009); it is hypothesized that this occurs because of their own intuitive understanding of the sensory needs of a child learning language in the visual-gestural mode.

Other examples of intuitive parenting behaviors by deaf parents have been reported by Swisher (2000), who describes the strategies of tapping on the child's body to elicit attention, or waving within the child's visual field before communicating with signs or gestures. Earlier studies of infant-directed signing (e.g., Harris, Clibbens, Chasin, & Tibbits, 1989; Kyle & Ackerman, 1990; Launer, 1982; Maestes y Moores, 1980) have yielded similar conclusions: deaf parents modify their signed communications to infants, making them especially salient by using large movements, holding signs longer than usual, incorporating an unusual amount of repetition, producing signs slowly, physically orienting their infants so as to facilitate visual attention, tapping the infant's body before signing, and often signing directly on the infant's face or body.

Other researchers have taken this a step farther by examining strategies for gaining mutual attention (Prendergast & McCollum, 1996) – a particularly important concern in relation to early interactions with deaf children. Pizer and Meier (2006) focused on attention-getting strategies used by deaf mothers with deaf infants and found modifications such as an expanded signing space, increased repetitions, and modified placement of signs. All of these are thought to reflect a deaf mother's sensitivity to the deaf child's need to learn to alternate his or her gaze between the (signed) communication and its referent. Visual attention is an important component of successful interactions with a deaf child and is a skill that needs to be facilitated early in their development. It is suggested that for an infant born into a signing family this need is accommodated easily by deaf parents; in the case of hearing parents, however, the task is likely to be less intuitive and somewhat more difficult.

Thus, in families where both parents and child are deaf, parents are easily able to incorporate intuitive behaviors that are well adapted to meet the cognitive, socioemotional and linguistic needs of the child with a hearing loss. As Mohay (2000) has pointed out, it is important to recognize that language delays, poor educational achievement, and difficult interactions with family members and peers are not typically observed in deaf children with deaf parents. Mohay and colleagues have identified specific behaviors used by deaf parents that may facilitate communication with their deaf children, such as gaining visual attention before communicating (often using touch and longer pauses for this purpose), reinforcing this attention, and making language an especially salient part of parent–child interactions. These intuitive, effective modifications of communicative behaviors by deaf parents are particularly important in making a visual-gestural language accessible, and have, therefore, been used as the basis for interventions with hearing parents of a deaf child (Mohay, 2000; Spencer, 2003).

Social Support and Membership in a Deaf Community

From a "resource-oriented" perspective, the availability of personal and social resources plays an important role in determining how both parents and children adapt and cope with the realities of childhood deafness. Again, in the case of deaf parents, these resources and knowledge about decisions, support services, and educational options will have already been mastered to a large degree as a result of their own developmental experiences. If these parents have grown up surrounded by hearing family members, they may have learned to manage and to succeed in the face of difficult communication, inadequate educational or social networks, and even stigma or prejudice within their communities. Thus, the coping skills they themselves have developed can be passed on to their own children, making this pathway an easier one for the next generation to traverse if their offspring also experience a hearing loss. It should be reiterated, however, that hearing parents are certainly entirely capable of providing the nurturance, support, love, and even language input to facilitate the healthy development of either a deaf or a hearing child. Our point is simply that deaf parents have often been overlooked as potential models and sources of strength and resilience for deaf children and that there is much still to be learned from this population. Parents who feel competent and relaxed about raising a deaf child are likely to experience less stress and to have more resources already available to make the child-rearing process less daunting.

Hintermair (2004) has also found that social support helps to reduce parental stress and that a "sense of coherence" in the lives of parents with deaf children is particularly important. The presence of additional handicapping conditions for the child may intensify the mother's stress, but the chosen mode of communication with a deaf child apparently has less impact on stress levels within the family.

Later Sense of Self in the Deaf Child

In their study of deaf college students, Jambor and Elliott (2005) explored various factors related to deafness that may affect self-esteem, such as communication patterns at home, degree of hearing loss, and coping styles. Results indicated that those with higher identification with the deaf community tended also to have higher self-esteem, defined as one's personal assessment of worthiness as an individual. According to the authors, self-esteem has a powerful influence on multiple areas of development, including motivation, emotions, and overt behaviors; in addition, it is proposed that a healthy self-esteem can serve as a buffer for possible discrimination that is sometimes faced by individuals with disabilities. Among these groups, support from family members plays an important role in determining the social–emotional outcomes related to feelings of self worth. Interestingly, although it might be expected that deaf children would suffer from low self-esteem as a result of being members of a marginalized, or perhaps devalued group, this expectation has not always been supported by empirical evidence (Jambor & Elliott, 2005).

Of course, this process begins much earlier in a child's development and is influenced in many ways as the child's individual characteristics are responded to and shaped by the social environment and everyday interactions. It is likely that deaf children with deaf parents have many opportunities to observe, model, and develop their own effective coping strategies for dealing with a world that is not always ready to accommodate their needs. Jambor and Elliott's findings (2005) reveal that a strong identification with other deaf individuals is related to positive self-esteem and that those students with strong bicultural skills (that is, those who are able to cope well in both worlds, hearing and deaf) tend to have the healthiest assessment of their own self-worth.

> If parents have been overly protective, as is sometimes the case with children who have disabilities, the child is not given sufficient opportunity to develop strategies for coping, for solving problems independently; that is, when parents are all too ready to step in and "rescue" the child from difficult or awkward situations (often surrounding issues related to deafness and communication), then the child is less likely to be able to develop these skills and rely on them when the parent is not available (Meadow-Orlans & Steinberg, 1993). Thus, social–emotional competence encompasses the quality of the child's interactions and functioning within a broad spectrum of domains, with the foundations laid during early parent–infant interactions setting the stage for later relationships with other children, caregivers, extended family members, teachers, schoolmates, and others in the larger community. (Koester, Middleton, Traci, & Klöhn, 2008, p. 135).

Nikolaraizi and Hadjikakou (2006) studied the role of educational experiences in the development of deaf identity, with a focus on the school context in Greece. They assert that a deaf child who is raised and educated in an environment with other deaf people is likely to be immersed in deaf culture, rather than isolated from it. As a result, many of these children develop a "bicultural" identity, one in which they are comfortable interacting with both deaf and hearing individuals. Exposure to and competent use of sign language was found to be a powerful factor in defining the social identity of these deaf children. As the authors point out, however, there are also cases in which deaf youngsters feel caught between these two worlds, or for whom educational experiences are primarily negative; these children are likely to experience rejection, social stigma, loneliness, being bullied, and other damaging developmental events.

Development of Theory of Mind in Deaf Children

Schick, de Villiers, de Villiers, and Hoffmeister (2007) recently examined the role of language in Theory of Mind (ToM) development with a large sample of deaf children. Although these children typically develop the same array of social, emotional, and cognitive skills as their hearing peers, the ability to understand others' behaviors and mental states may be delayed due to the lack of access to speech or to skilled signing. Studies examining ToM understanding in deaf children of hearing parents have found that these children often have skills that are quite significantly delayed compared with their hearing peers; in some cases, these deaf children do not reliably demonstrate an understanding of "false-belief" tasks (a common method for assessing ToM) until early adolescence. In contrast, deaf children of deaf parents develop language according to normal trajectories and tend to perform significantly better on ToM tasks than do their deaf peers with hearing parents.

This appears to be a case in which deaf parents, who provide their children with natural access and exposure to sign language, facilitate the deaf child's acquisition of ToM skills. The mechanism here seems to be the richness and accessibility of the child's language environment. In other words, through much direct and indirect language learning, a deaf child with fluently signing parents is more likely to develop ToM skills at the expected rate and timetable. Thus, deafness itself may not hinder this process, but lack of early language acquisition certainly appears to play an important role. Hearing parents who are learning sign language clearly enhance this process for a deaf child, although they may not yet have the fluency to engage in elaborate mental state talk with a young child. This latter point may hold the key to understanding deficiencies in ToM skills by some deaf children – just as a paucity of experiences with conversation about other peoples' states of mind may lead to similar results in hearing children.

Educational Achievement: Attaining Literacy by the Deaf Child

Goldin-Meadow and Mayberry (2001) have identified two separate but related skills that are fundamental to the process of reading: knowledge and use of a language, and the ability to map between that language and its printed representation. Since this is usually based on sound, a firm working knowledge of spoken language usually helps once the child has solved the puzzle of how the two are connected. In both of these cases, a child with profound hearing loss is likely to be at a disadvantage. Nevertheless, although many of these children do not perform well on reading tasks, some do in fact master this skill quite well. As Goldin-Meadow and Mayberry ask, how do they do this and what can we learn from them about the process?

Perhaps the answer can be found by again considering those deaf children whose parents are also deaf, such that the children are easily learning sign language from birth. However, Goldin-Meadow and Mayberry (2001) describe another problem that arises with this approach: "Unfortunately for the potential deaf reader, ASL is not English... The bottom line for many deaf children born to deaf parents is that, although they are native (and fluent) users of a language (sign language), that language is not the language they are learning to read" (p. 223). Nevertheless, it is noteworthy that the best deaf readers are often those born to deaf parents, but for quite different reasons than might first be expected: (1) their hearing loss is likely to be identified early (although this has in the meantime become more common in other families as well), leading to appropriate educational opportunities and good social–emotional support within the family and (2) they have the advantage of becoming fluent in at least one language at an early age.

Again, according to Goldin-Meadow and Mayberry (2001), the deaf child's signing ability is probably the best predictor of eventual reading and overall literacy skills. Children the world over acquire spoken and signed languages with relatively little conscious effort, simply by being immersed in their language communities. In contrast, reading is a skill that must be taught, and it is still not evident exactly how and with what pedagogical strategies parents and educators can best help deaf students become effective readers.

Conclusions and Implications

In this chapter, we have provided evidence along with some speculation that the presence of deaf parents in the lives of deaf children can be a source of positive influence; we assert that this may even serve as a protective factor against the potential difficulties often faced by individuals with hearing loss, particularly during the early years. Infancy is an unusually important time in a child's life during which emotional regulation, an understanding of the rules and expectations of the social world, and the beginnings of language should all emerge. Of course, these developments all co-occur with the child's initial sense of self, of other trusted individuals, and of the limits and challenges of the physical world. The infant's exploration of not only the physical but also the social environment is inevitably intertwined with emerging communication skills, but if these are delayed or compromised then all realms of development can be affected.

Deaf parents, who have typically experienced the need to communicate via non-vocal modalities and to be highly attentive to visual cues during social interactions, may be especially adept at perceiving, interpreting, and responding to a deaf infant's behavioral signals. Although historically it has been the case that parents with physical, sensory, or cognitive disabilities have been deemed inadequate as parents, we would assert that the opposite may be true of deaf parents with deaf infants. That is, through their intuitive understanding of the world of a deaf child, deaf parents may in fact be better equipped to provide the necessary communicative and interactive skills that will enhance that child's opportunities for becoming an effective communicator.

Several caveats are in order, however: (1) This conclusion should not be interpreted to imply that hearing parents are less than competent to rear a deaf child; rather, the implication is that deaf adults can be excellent models for the subtle interactive behaviors that will make the early experiences with a deaf child all the more rewarding and effective; (2) It is also not our intent to imply that exposure to hearing individuals or to spoken language is unimportant, but we would contend that most children in today's Western societies are surrounded by sounds (i.e., spoken communication via radio, television, and the public environment in general) regardless of the hearing status of their parents; and (3) Simply having deaf parents does not, by any means, ensure the healthy or optimal development of a deaf child, just as having hearing parents does not inevitably lead to a child who is insecurely attached or a poor communicator; it may, however, act as a buffer for the child in light of a potential risk factor such as early deafness.

It is important to shift the focus in the literature to strengths rather than deficits, when considering either deaf or hearing parents. Early interventionists and family support specialists can play a crucial role in facilitating successful outcomes for deaf infants and toddlers by becoming aware of the interactive behaviors used by many deaf parents, which are so well attuned to the needs of a deaf child. In most cases, hearing parents make impressive efforts to interact effectively with their deaf child, regardless of the chosen mode of communication. Therefore, rather than needing a major overhaul, it may only be necessary to provide ideas for fine-tuning and making minor adjustments to these interactive behaviors in order for hearing parents to adequately meet the needs of the very young deaf child.

References

Ainsworth, M. D. S., Blehar, M. C., Waters, E., & Wall, S. (1978). *Patterns of attachment: A psychological study of the strange situation*. Hillsdale, NJ: Lawrence Erlbaum Associates.

Barton, M. L., & Robins, D. (2000). Regulatory disorders. In C. H. Zeanah Jr. (Ed.), *Handbook of infant mental health* (2nd ed., pp. 311–325). New York: The Guilford Press.

Bornstein, M. H. (1995). *Handbook of parenting*. Mahwah, NJ: Lawrence Erlbaum Associates.

Bornstein, M. H., & Lamb, M. E. (1992). Social development in infancy. In M. Bornstein & M. Lamb (Eds.), *Development in infancy: An introduction* (pp. 409–447). New York: McGraw-Hill.

Bretherton, I. (1985). Attachment theory: Retrospect and prospect. *Monographs for the Society for Research in Child Development, 50*, 3–35.

Bretherton, I. (1992). The origins of attachment theory: John Bowlby and Mary Ainsworth. *Developmental Psychology, 28*, 759–775.

Chess, S., & Thomas, A. (1996). *Temperament: Theory and practice*. Philadelphia, PA: Brunner/ Mazel.

Crockenberg, S., & Leerkes, E. (2000). Infant social and emotional development in family context. In C. H. Zeanah Jr. (Ed.), *Handbook of infant mental health* (2nd ed., pp. 60–90). New York: The Guilford Press.

DeCasper, A. J., & Fifer, W. P. (1980). Of human bonding: Newborns prefer their mothers' voices. *Science, 208*, 1174–1176.

Erting, C. J., Prezioso, C., & Hynes, M. (1990/1994). The interactional context of deaf mother-infant communication. In V. Volterra & C. J. Erting (Eds.), *From gesture to language in hearing and deaf children* (pp. 97–106). Heidelberg/Washington, DC: Springer (1990)/Gallaudet University Press (1994).

Erting, C. J., Thumann-Prezioso, C., & Benedict, B. S. (2000). Bilingualism in a deaf family: Fingerspelling in early childhood. In P. Spencer, C. J. Erting, & M. Marschark (Eds.), *The deaf child in the family and at school: Essays in honor of Kathryn P. Meadow-Orlans* (pp. 41–54). Mahwah, NJ: Lawrence Erlbaum Associates.

Fagan, J. F. (1979). The origins of facial pattern recognition. In M. H. Bornstein & W. Kessen (Eds.), *Psychological development from infancy* (pp. 83–113). Hillsdale, NJ: Lawrence Erlbaum and Associates.

Goldin-Meadow, S., & Mayberry, R. I. (2001). How do profoundly deaf children learn to read? *Learning Disabilities: Research & Practice, 16*(4), 222–229.

Hadadian, A. (1995). Attitudes toward deafness and security of attachment relationships among young deaf children and their parents. *Early Education and Development, 6*, 181–191.

Hans, S. L., & Wakschlag, L. S. (2000). Early parenthood in context: Implications for development and intervention. In C. H. Zeanah Jr. (Ed.), *Handbook of infant mental health* (2nd ed.). New York: The Guilford Press.

Harris, M., Clibbens, J., Chasin, J., & Tibbits, R. (1989). The social context of early sign language development. *First Language, 9*, 81–97.

Hintermair, M. (2004). Sense of coherence: A relevant resource in the coping process of mothers of deaf and hard-of-hearing children? *Journal of Deaf Studies and Deaf Education, 9*(1), 15–26.

Hintermair, M. (2006). Parental resources, parental stress, and socioemotional development of deaf and hard of hearing children. *Journal of Deaf Studies and Deaf Education, 11*(4), 493–513.

Jambor, E., & Elliott, M. (2005). Self-esteem and coping strategies among deaf students. *Journal of Deaf Studies and Deaf Education, 10*(1), 63–81.

Juffer, F., Bakermans-Kranenburg, M. J., & van Ijzendoorn, M. H. (2007). Methods of the video-feedback programs to promote positive parenting. In F. Juffer, M. J. Bakermans-Kranenbury, & M. H. van Ijzendoorn (Eds.), *Promoting positive parenting: An attachment based intervention* (pp. 11–22). New York: Lawrence Erlbaum Associates.

Koester, L. S. (1992). Intuitive parenting as a model for understanding parent-infant interactions when one partner is deaf. *American Annals of the Deaf, 137*(4), 362–369.

Koester, L. S. (1995). Characteristics of face-to-face interactions between hearing mothers and their deaf or hearing 9-month-olds. *Infant Behavior and Development, 18*(2), 145–153.

Koester, L. S., Brooks, L. R., & Karkowski, A. M. (1998). A comparison of the vocal patterns of deaf and hearing mother-infant dyads during face-to-face interactions. *Journal of Deaf Studies and Deaf Education, 3*(4), 290–301.

Koester, L. S., Brooks, L. R., & Traci, M. A. (2000). Tactile contact by deaf and hearing mothers during face-to-face interactions with their infants. *Journal of Deaf Studies and Deaf Education, 5*(2), 127–139.

Koester, L. S., Lahti-Harper, E., & McCray, N. (2009, April). *Infant-directed signing and intuitive behaviors of Deaf mothers during interactions with their infants.* Poster presented at the Biennial Meetings of the Society for Research in Child Development, Denver, Co.

Koester, L. S., & Meadow-Orlans, K. P. (1999). Responses to interactive stress: Infants who are deaf or hearing. *American Annals of the Deaf, 144,* 395–403.

Koester, L. S., & Meadow-Orlans, K. P. (2004a). Attachment behaviors at 18 months. In K. P. Meadow-Orlans, P. E. Spencer, & L. S. Koester (Eds.), *The world of deaf infants: A longitudinal study* (pp. 134–146). New York: Oxford University Press.

Koester, L. S., & Meadow-Orlans, K. P. (2004b). Interactions of mothers and 9-month-old infants: Temperament and stress. In K. P. Meadow-Orlans, P. E. Spencer, & L. S. Koester (Eds.), *The world of deaf infants: A longitudinal study* (pp. 57–65). New York: Oxford University Press.

Koester, L. S., Middleton, M., Traci, M. A., & Klöhn, B. (2008). Von der Kindheit zum jungen Erwachsenenalter: Entwicklungspsychologische Verläufe gehörloser Kinder ("From early childhood to adolescence: Developmental pathways of deaf children"). *Heilpädagogische Forschung, XXXIV*(3), 132–146.

Koester, L. S., Papoušek, H., & Papoušek, M. (1987). Psychobiological models of infant development: Influences on the concept of intuitive parenting. *Psychobiology and Early Development, 46,* 275–287.

Koester, L. S., Papousek, H., & Smith-Gray, S. (2000). Intuitive parenting, communication, and interaction with deaf infants. In P. Spencer, C. Erting, & M. Marschark (Eds.), *The deaf child in the family and at school: Essays in honor of Kathryn P. Meadow-Orlans* (pp. 55–71). Mahwah, NJ: Lawrence Erlbaum Associates.

Kyle, J. G., & Ackerman, J. (1990). Signing for infants: Deaf mothers using BSL in the early stages of development. In W. H. Edmondson & F. Karlsson (Eds.), *SLR '87: Papers from the Fourth International Symposium on Sign Language Research, Lappeenranta, Finland, July 15–19, 1987* (pp. 200–211). Hamburg: Signum.

Launer, P. (1982). *Early signs of motherhood: Motherese in American Sign Language.* Paper presented at the American Speech-Language Hearing Association, Toronto, Canada.

Lederberg, A. R., & Prezbindowski, A. K. (2000). Impact of child deafness on mother-toddler interaction: Strengths and weaknesses. In P. E. Spencer, C. J. Erting, & M. Marschark (Eds.), *The deaf child in the family and at school. Essays in honor of Kathryn P. Meadow-Orlans* (pp. 73–92). Mahwah, NJ: Lawrence Erlbaum Associates.

Lounds, J. J., Borkowski, J. G., Whitman, T. L., Maxwell, S. E., & Weed, K. (2005). Adolescent parenting and attachment during infancy and early childhood. *Parenting: Science and Practice,* *5,* 91–118.

Maestes y Moores, J. (1980). Early linguistic environment: Interactions of deaf parents with their infants. *Sign Language Studies, 26,* 1–13.

Marschark, M. (1993). *Psychological development of deaf children.* New York: Oxford University Press.

Marschark, M. (2007). *Raising and educating a deaf child* (2nd ed.). New York: Oxford University Press.

Meadow-Orlans, K. P. (1995). Sources of stress for mothers and fathers of deaf and hard of hearing infants. *American Annals of the Deaf, 140,* 352–357.

Meadow-Orlans, K. P., Mertens, D. M., & Sass-Lehrer, M. A. (2002). *Parents and their deaf children: The early years.* Washington, DC: Gallaudet University.

Meadow-Orlans, K. P., & Steinberg, A. (1993). Effects of infant hearing loss and maternal support on mother-infant interactions at 18 months. *Journal of Applied Developmental Psychology, 14,* 407–426.

Mohay, H. (2000). Language in sight: Mothers' strategies for making language visually accessible to deaf children. In P. E. Spencer, C. J. Erting, & M. Marschark (Eds.), *The deaf child in the family and at school: Essays in honor of Kathryn P. Meadow-Orlans* (pp. 151–166). Mahwah, NJ: Lawrence Erlbaum Associates.

Nikolaraizi, M., & Hadjikakou, K. (2006). The role of educational experiences in the development of deaf identity. *Journal of Deaf Studies and Deaf Education, 11*(4), 477–492.

Orlansky, M. D., & Heward, W. L. (1981). *Voices: Interviews with handicapped people.* Columbus, OH: Charles E. Merrill.

Padden, C., & Humphries, T. (1988). *Deaf in America: Voices from a culture.* Cambridge, MA: Harvard University Press.

Papoušek, H., & Bornstein, M. H. (1992). Didactic interactions: Intuitive parental support of vocal and verbal development in human infants. In H. Papoušek, U. Jurgens, & M. Papoušek (Eds.), *Nonverbal vocal communication: Comparative and developmental approaches* (pp. 209–229). New York: Cambridge University Press.

Papoušek, H., & Papoušek, M. (1982). Integration into the social world: Survey of research. In P. Stratton (Ed.), *Psychobiology of the human newborn* (pp. 367–390). New York: John Wiley & Sons.

Papoušek, H., & Papoušek, M. (1987). Intuitive parenting: A dialectic counterpart to the infant's integrative competence. In J. D. Osofsky (Ed.), *Handbook of infant development* (2nd ed., pp. 669–720). New York: John Wiley & Sons.

Papoušek, M. (2008). Disorders of behavior and emotional regulation: Clinical evidence for a new diagnostic concept. In M. Papoušek, M. Schieche, & H. Wurmser (Eds.), *Disorders of behavioral and emotional regulation in the first years of life* (pp. 53–84). Washington, DC: Zero to Three.

Pizer, G., & Meier, R. P. (2008). Child-directed signing in ASL and children's development of joint attention. In R. M. de Quadros (Ed.), *Proceedings of the 9th international conference on theoretical issues in sign language research, 2006, Florianopolis, Brazil.* Petrópolis/RJ. Brazil: Editora Arara Azul.

Prendergast, S. G., & McCollum, J. A. (1996). Let's talk: The effect of maternal hearing status on interactions with toddlers who are deaf. *American Annals of the Deaf, 141,* 11–18.

Quittner, A. L. (1991). Coping with a hearing-impaired child: A model of adjustment to chronic stress. In J. H. Johnson & S. B. Johnson (Eds.), *Advances in child health psychology* (pp. 206–223). Gainesville, FL: University of Florida.

Sameroff, A. S. (1975). Transactional models in early social relations. *Human Development, 18,* 65–79.

Sass-Lehrer, M., & Bodner-Johnson, B. (2003). Early intervention: Current approaches to family-centered programming. In M. Marschark & P. E. Spencer (Eds.), *Deaf studies, language, and education* (pp. 65–81). New York: Oxford University Press.

Schaffer, H. R. (1979). Acquiring the concept of the dialogue. In M. H. Bornstein & W. Kessen (Eds.), *Psychological development from infancy: Image to intention* (pp. 279–305). Hillsdale, NJ: Lawrence Erlbaum Associates.

Schick, B., de Villiers, J., de Villiers, P., & Hoffmeister, R. (2007). Language and theory of mind: A study of deaf children. *Child Development, 78*, 376–396.

Spencer, P. E. (2003). Parent-child interaction: Implications for intervention and development. In B. Bodner-Johnson & M. Sass-Lehrer (Eds.), *The young deaf or hard of hearing child: A family-centered approach to early education* (pp. 333–371). Baltimore, MD: Paul H. Brookes.

Stern, D. N. (1985). *The interpersonal world of the infant: A view from psychoanalysis and developmental psychology*. New York: Basic Books.

Swisher, M. V. (1992). The role of parents in developing visual turn-taking in their young deaf children. *American Annals of the Deaf, 137*, 92–100.

Swisher, M. V. (2000). Learning to converse: How deaf mothers support the development of attention and conversational skills in their young deaf children. In P. E. Spencer, C. J. Erting, & M. Marschark (Eds.), *The deaf child in the family and at school: Essays in honor of Kathryn P. Meadow-Orlans* (pp. 21–39). Mahwah, NJ: Lawrence Erlbaum Associates.

Thompson, D. C., McPhillips, H., Davis, R. L., Lieu, T. A., Homer, C. J., & Helfand, M. (2001). Universal Newborn Hearing Screening: Summary of evidence. *Journal of the American Medical Association, 286*, 2000–2010.

Thompson, R. A. (1999). The individual child: Temperament, emotion, self, and personality. In M. H. Bornstein & M. E. Lamb (Eds.), *Developmental psychology: An advanced text book* (4th ed.). Mahwah, NJ: Lawrence Erlbaum Associates.

Waxman, R. P., & Spencer, P. E. (1997). What mothers do to support infant visual attention: Sensitivities to age and hearing status. *Journal of Deaf Studies and Deaf Education, 2*, 104–114.

Werner, E. (2000). Protective factors and individual resilience. In J. P. Shonkoff & S. J. Meisels (Eds.), *Handbook of early childhood intervention*. Cambridge: Cambridge University Press.

Yates, T. M., Egeland, B., & Sroufe, L. A. (2003). Rethinking resilience: A developmental process perspective. In S. S. Luthar (Ed.), *Resilience and vulnerability: Adaptation in the context of childhood adversities* (pp. 243–266). New York: Cambridge University Press.

Yoshinaga-Itano, C., Sedey, A. L., Coulter, D. K., & Mehl, A. L. (1998). Language of early- and later- identified children with hearing loss. *Pediatrics, 102*, 1161–1171.

Chapter 4
Risk and Resiliency of Infants/Toddlers Who Are Deaf: Assessment and Intervention Issues

Christine Yoshinaga-Itano

Abstract With the advent of universal newborn hearing screening, earlier identification of hearing loss, and earlier entrance into early intervention services, the focus has been on the advances in amplification technology, surgically implanted technology, genetic research, and neuroscience and physiological studies. However, despite all of these scientific discoveries, the outcomes of children with hearing loss are dependent upon optimal and successful communication interactions, initially between parents and children and ultimately between the children and the surrounding world. This chapter tries to highlight those aspects gleaned from research on children with hearing loss in Colorado. The research highlights critical components of intervention for families that have children with hearing loss. Communication development begins in infancy through the social–emotional foundation established through the reciprocal relationship between parent and child. The diagnosis of hearing loss within the first few weeks of a child's life could potentially disrupt this social–emotional development. It is critical that appropriate assessment is part of the intervention program to insure that an optimal social–emotional foundation is established from the beginning of the child's and family's journey. This chapter provides an overview of what is known about the social–emotional relationship of a child with deafness and his/her parent(s), intervention strategies, and the ramifications of the characteristics of the parent–child relationship upon risk and resiliency of infants and toddlers with hearing loss.

Chapter Overview

With the advent of universal newborn hearing screening (UNHS), earlier identification of hearing loss, and earlier entrance into early intervention services, the focus has been on the advances in amplification technology, surgically implanted technology,

C. Yoshinaga-Itano (✉)
Department of Speech, Language and Hearing Sciences,
University of Colorado, Boulder, CO, USA
e-mail: christie.yoshi@colorado.edu

D.H. Zand and K.J. Pierce (eds.), *Resilience in Deaf Children: Adaptation Through Emerging Adulthood*, DOI 10.1007/978-1-4419-7796-0_4,
© Springer Science+Business Media, LLC 2011

genetic research, and neuroscience and physiological studies. All these areas have had exciting discoveries, many of them within the last decade. However, despite all of these scientific discoveries, the outcomes of children with hearing loss are dependent upon optimal and successful communication interactions, initially between parents and children and ultimately between the children and the surrounding world. The focus has been on sensitive periods of development because our Colorado study (Yoshinaga-Itano, Sedey, Coulter, & Mehl, 1998) reported significant differences in language outcomes for children identified with hearing loss prior to the age of 6 months and enrolled into appropriate early intervention services. Many researchers and professionals immediately focused upon their belief that the sensitive period of development in the first year of life was auditory/speech based, though our study included children from a vast array of communication methods and modes of communication. The Colorado children were enrolled in a statewide early intervention program with a highly developed transition of care from diagnosis/confirmation of hearing loss to enrollment into early intervention, and early intervention was provided by individuals who are highly skilled and knowledgeable about deafness and hearing loss. Our research laboratory in Colorado continued to publish research on successful outcomes including a series of articles investigating many social–emotional factors such as grieving (Yoshinaga-Itano, 2002; Yoshinaga-Itano & Abdala de Uzcategui, 2001), parental stress (Pipp-Siegel, Sedey, & Yoshinaga-Itano, 2001b), emotional availability (Pressman, Pipp-Siegel, Yoshinaga-Itano, Kubicek, & Emde, 2000), mastery motivation (Pipp-Siegel, Sedey, VanLeeuwen, & Yoshinaga-Itano, 2003), personal–social development (Yoshinaga-Itano, 2002), and the significant relationship between these variables and language development within our population. Unfortunately, since that first article in 1998, no other programs in the USA have published outcome data that replicates the development of the Colorado children with hearing loss from infancy through school age. A study in England also found children who were early identified had better receptive language development at 8 years than those who were later identified (Kennedy et al., 2006). All of the presentations on research in the USA to date have found that maternal level of education and maternal bonding are two of the most significant predictors of successful outcomes across the USA, and these variables seem to overtake the potential benefit of earlier identification and intervention. Perhaps the most significant finding from the series of Colorado studies is that maternal level of education does not predict language outcomes in the first 3 years of life when Colorado provides parent–infant intervention services to all families whose children have early-identified hearing loss. The families in the Colorado Home Intervention Program, a statewide program providing service to over 90% of the children with bilateral hearing loss between the ages of birth and 3 years, can demonstrate that there is a high level of parent satisfaction in the services offered, that the levels of parental stress are similar to the parents of hearing children, that their emotional availability, a measure of maternal bonding, is similar to parents of hearing children, and that their children have age-appropriate personal social and emotional skills within the first 3 years of life. Intervention efficacy is difficult to prove because there are so many different strategies used by early intervention providers in the Colorado Home Intervention Program (e.g., the program individualizes the intervention for each family and child). The historic emphasis on social–emotional factors and the significant in-service training of early intervention providers in counseling skills must play a significant role in the successful outcomes of this population. It is hoped that programs will focus not only on the auditory skill development, spoken language strategy, or the sign language method and instructional technique, but also on the care and support that families need after the diagnosis of any disability, particularly in the infant period.

This article tries to highlight those aspects gleaned from research on the children with hearing loss in Colorado. The research highlights critical components of intervention for families that have children with hearing loss. Communication development begins in infancy through the social–emotional foundation established through the reciprocal relationship between parent and child. The diagnosis of a hearing loss within the first few weeks of a child's life could potentially disrupt this social–emotional development. It is critical that appropriate assessment is part of the intervention program to insure that an optimal social–emotional foundation is established from the beginning of the child's and family's journey. This article provides an overview of what is known about the social–emotional relationship of the child with deafness and his/her parent(s), intervention strategies, and the ramifications of the characteristics of the parent–child relationship upon risk and resiliency of infants and toddlers with hearing loss.

The Importance of Newborn Hearing Screening

Pathways for risk and resilience of infants and toddlers with hearing loss begin at birth and, because of UNHS, it is now possible to investigate this issue beginning as early as the newborn period. Infants and toddlers who are deaf and their families are "at-risk" for developmental delays in language, speech, and social–emotional development and for negative impact on the quality of life of the family. This risk for developmental delay is magnified because the infants are typically born into a hearing, not a deaf, world and their hearing parents have little knowledge about deafness. The hearing parent typically does not have the knowledge or skills to be able to appropriately respond to the child's needs and wants at a critical time period. The child may not have auditory access to spoken language, and the child may not communicate these needs and wants through auditory vocal communication, but through visual or tactile modalities. Because the parent may not recognize and interpret this communication, the child's communication may not be responded in a manner that acknowledges and satisfies the child's emotional needs. Parents who hear and have infants who hear learn to soothe their infants through their voice, even when out of view, from another room. Such communication may not be possible as it may be inaccessible to a child who is deaf. This response may initially be unavailable to an infant with hearing loss because it is not audible without the aid of technology. Even after an infant with hearing loss receives appropriate amplification technology, s/he still does not access all sounds available to hearing infants at the volume received by a hearing infant. Theoretically, then, vision and touch play a more significant role in the emotional development of infants and children with hearing loss than for their hearing peers.

Moses (1983) theorized that infants and children with hearing loss are "at-risk" emotionally, because they may not fulfill the expectations or dreams of the parent who is hearing and may begin life with parents who are grieving, in denial, depressed, or angry. Studies on grief with children with hearing loss and children with other disabilities have found that this attention to grief may leave fewer emotional resources available to the child (Sheeran, Marvin, & Pianta, 1997; Yoshinaga-Itano & Abdala de Uzcategui, 2001).

The earlier the diagnosis of hearing loss, the greater the opportunity that more immediate early intervention services are provided. In addition, the parent can learn appropriate strategies to read and respond to the child's requests for emotional comfort. These skills should reduce the likelihood that congenital hearing loss will impact the emotional development of the child. Although there have been historical studies that have identified the high rate of social and emotional delays and disorders in children with hearing loss (Furstenberg & Doyle, 1994; Hintermaier, 2006; Mitchell & Quittner, 1996; van Eldik, 2005), the social and emotional development of the child with hearing loss in Colorado has been found to be age appropriate when the child is early identified and provided with appropriate intervention (Yoshinaga-Itano, 2002; Yoshinaga-Itano & Abdala de Uzcategui, 2001).

Both internal and external factors interact to determine how emotionally resilient the child with hearing loss will be to his/her language learning environment and his/her life experiences. Parent and child variables play a role to either support or erode this resilience. The directionality of the causality loops appears to be reciprocal, indicating that resilience could be enhanced through the parent's influence, the child's influence, or the interaction between the parents and the child. Internal factors within the child may also impact this resilience, but studies are not yet available to identify these factors. In 2007, often within hours after birth, 94% of all newborns in the USA were screened for hearing loss (http://www.cdc.gov/ncbddd/ehdi/documents/DataSource2007.pdf). UNHS/early hearing detection and intervention (EHDI) programs began in three states (Rhode Island, Hawaii, and Colorado) in 1992. If the infant does not pass the screening test, the infant is referred for additional testing. From this moment, the parents' reaction to the referral or "fail" of the screening test could begin to alter the normal sequence of events and the emotional response of the parent to the birth and the newborn child. If the families receive immediate and appropriate counseling, the family may be able to respond in a manner that is emotionally and positively responsive to the infant (Pressman, 2000; Pressman, Pipp-Siegel, Yoshinaga-Itano, & Deas, 1999).

Detection/Case Identification

Since 1992, in the USA, when the first UNHS programs were initiated, many changes have occurred in the population of children who are deaf and their families.

Prior to 1992, infants and children with hearing loss were identified through a variety of mechanisms: screening in the newborn intensive care units, concern of the parents, physicians, or other family members, or preschool hearing screening programs. The average age of identification for children with severe and profound hearing loss ranged from 18 months to 3 years, while children with mild and moderate hearing losses were commonly not identified until they were 5, 6, or 7 years. Today, 94% of the approximately four million children born each year in the USA are screened for hearing in the newborn period, within the first month of life, predominantly prior to hospital discharge. Though there are still some delays in the identification of hearing loss, because of the lack of documentation or follow-up, at least half of all infants with congenital hearing loss are being identified at least by 12 months. All 50 states have instituted a UNHS/EHDI program and are in various stages of development.

Characteristics of the Colorado Home Intervention Program

Colorado is a unique example of UNHS/EHDI program development because it began with a highly developed statewide parent–infant program that was offered to all families of newly identified infants and children. Because of UNHS programs, the age of identification of hearing loss is much less variable by the degree of hearing loss or type of hearing loss. The initiation and intensity of intervention still has some variability but, for example, in the state of Colorado, about two-thirds of the infants are confirmed with hearing loss within the first few months of life and almost all of them by 6 months of life with an immediate initiation of intervention services after diagnosis of the hearing loss.

The diagnosis of hearing loss can contribute to significant grieving within a vulnerable period for the parents (Kurtzer-White & Luterman, 2003; Moses, 1983). There are several factors that seem to ameliorate the negative consequences of such an early diagnosis of hearing loss. Recall that the Colorado population of children with hearing loss is the only one in the USA to have demonstrated significantly better developmental outcomes through 7 years (Baca, 2009). They are a unique population because the parental stress and maternal bonding as measured through emotional availability and social–emotional development of the children are identical to hearing dyads.

For instance, the children and families in the Colorado studies (Baca, 2009; Pipp-Siegel, Blair, Deas, Pressman, & Yoshinaga-Itano, 2001a; Pipp-Siegel et al., 2003; Pressman, 2000; Pressman et al., 1999; Yoshinaga-Itano and Abdala de Uzcategui, 2001; Yoshinaga-Itano et al., 1998) share many things in common: (1) average age of identification is 6–8 weeks of age, (2) immediate contact by early intervention services, within 48 h after the diagnosis of hearing loss, with a highly specialized early intervention provider, (3) services provided by early interventionists who are skilled in grief counseling and family systems theories, (4) regular monitoring of developmental progress, including social–emotional development, (5) home intervention services once per week with early intervention providers who have knowledge and skills about deafness and hearing loss, (6) connections with individuals who are deaf, and (7) parent-to-parent support. To my knowledge, no other state program has all of these characteristics.

Intervention process. To assure a seamless transition from confirmation/diagnosis of hearing loss to early intervention services in Colorado, care/service coordination is provided within 48 h of the confirmation of hearing loss. Families have immediate contact information with a Co-HEAR coordinator, one of nine specialists who is trained to do first contact with each family of an infant diagnosed with hearing loss. The Co-HEAR coordinators were selected because they are the most highly qualified and experienced early intervention specialists with parents who have infants and children with hearing loss. The qualifications of these care coordinators are based upon a philosophical belief that the first contact for parents with newly identified children with hearing loss should be an individual with the highest level of knowledge and skills, with the capability of providing families with appropriate knowledge to answer questions that parents have and provide them with the support they need to make decisions about amplification, early intervention programs, and methods of communication.

Co-HEAR contact and counseling. The Co-HEAR specialist has specific training in grief counseling and has extensive experience in parent–infant intervention with families and children who are deaf, as well as extensive training and knowledge about the development of deaf children. Families typically have an average of about 10 h of intervention with the Co-HEAR coordinator prior to choosing an intervention specialist. The amount of early intervention services provided is dependent on the needs of each individual family. Unfortunately, parents report that many state programs do not provide care coordination in a timely manner to families, and they may be provided by professionals who are not knowledgeable about deafness and hearing loss and cannot answer questions that parents ask. The lack of immediate and appropriate care coordination for families and the manner and content of the information provided to families has been reported to significantly impact parental stress levels and grieving (Young & Tattersall, 2007).

The Effect of Hearing Loss Diagnosis on the Social/Emotional Relationship Between Parent and Child

Following the diagnosis of hearing loss, the primary priorities of the family are dealing with the emotional impact of the diagnosis, gathering information, and making decisions about what will be best for their infant and family. The time of diagnosis is a very sensitive period for the family. The initial emotional response to the diagnosis could be intense and could require immediate and appropriate support. Because there is a significant relationship among parental stress, parental grief, parental attachment, and language development, it is important to begin the family's journey with the highest level of professional expertise.

It is critically important that parent–infant providers learn counseling strategies appropriate to the task of supporting families from the diagnosis of the hearing loss through the intervention process. Learning nonjudgmental strategies, appropriate techniques for working with culturally diverse families, and assisting families with their acquisition of information in a nonbiased manner are important skills. Counseling skills alone are not sufficient because the parent also expects a high level of knowledge about deafness and hearing loss that the provider possesses in this initial infant period.

The interaction between social–emotional aspects and language begins the journey for parents and interventionists at the point of identification of the hearing loss. Those who have first contact with families will begin their interactions assisting families with the social–emotional impact of the information. Although there are significant questions about the diagnosis of hearing loss, causes of hearing loss, and amplification, initially, the grief expressed by parents/families is significant and parents may find that these emotions interfere with how they would normally have bonded with their newborn, as well as their comprehension of information and expectations. This highlights the need for early intervention providers to understand how to provide appropriate support to parents/families helping to bring them back to the joy that they would have experienced had they not been told in this sensitive period that their child had a hearing loss.

The affective climate of a parent–child relationship has been hypothesized to be a necessary context for the unfolding of child development in many domains including exploration and competence in the physical, social, and linguistic world (Emde, 1988, 1996; Emde, Biringen, Clyman, & Oppenheim, 1991; Emde & Easterbrooks, 1985). The diagnosis of hearing loss, especially within the first few weeks of life, can have a significant impact upon the emotional balance of the family. The unanticipated information about the diagnosis of hearing loss can result in a response of grieving that can be of varying intensity and duration. How the family deals with their grief and its resolution will ultimately impact the emotional relationship of parent and child and can either facilitate or be detrimental to the language development of the child (Pipp-Siegel, 2000).

A profile of the social–emotional component has been accomplished in Colorado made through examining the following variables. In future, other variables with high relationship to the development of children with hearing loss may also be identified. The relevant variables are as follows:

1. Characteristics of the parents:

   (a) Parental grief
   (b) Parental stress
   (c) Parental needs
   (d) Parental hassles
   (e) Parental involvement

2. Characteristics of the child:

   (a) Personal–social development
   (b) Mastery motivation
   (c) Development of self

3. Qualities of reciprocal relationships:

   (a) Emotional availability of parent to child and child to parent
   (b) Touch interactions.

A high priority of intervention is to provide support to the family so that the family can rediscover the "magic" of the birth and the awe of shepherding a new life through the trials and tribulations of everyday experiences. The early years of a child's life should be filled with joy and wonder. The professional's ability to support parents at this critical juncture in their child's life has significant ramifications for the successful development of communication skills.

Characteristics of the Parent

Parental grief. Pianta and Marvin (1993) developed the RDI, Reaction to Diagnosis Intervention, that probes for episodic recall of events and experiences at the time of diagnosis. Parents are asked to relate the emotions associated with that experience, the change in these emotions since the time of diagnosis, and their search for reasons for this experience. These families report changes in their emotions since the diagnosis of the hearing loss. They indicate that they are able to move on in life and have suspended the search for a reason. Families that have resolved their grief (Pianta & Marvin, 1993) are able to provide accurate representations of their child's abilities and provide balanced statements regarding the benefits to self. The resolution of grief can be evidenced through feelings, actions, or thoughts.

Those families with unresolved grief indicate one or several of the following characteristics: (1) being emotionally overwhelmed, (2) being angrily preoccupied, (3) neutralizing their emotions, (4) having feelings of depression or passivity, (5) expressing cognitive distortions, which may include unrealistic beliefs, denial, or pursuit of wished-for-realities such as a different diagnosis, and (6) displaying disorganization or confusion. Families with unresolved grief actively search for reasons for their child's deafness as the primary focus of their emotional energy. In these cases, attention to the reality of the child's needs is displaced by the need to find a reason for their child's disability. This need is often so strong that it distracts the parent from attending to painful emotions. This search often continues even after parents are repeatedly told by professionals that there is a high probability that no reason will be found and that knowing the cause would likely not change the diagnosis or prognosis. Consistent with the study of Yoshinaga-Itano et al. (1998), the Colorado longitudinal database of over 1,000 infants and toddlers continued to show that the cause of hearing loss during the first 3 years of life was "unknown" in 50–60% of the children with hearing loss. New advances in genetics may change this statistic. In some instances, however, knowledge of the cause of the hearing loss can lead to intense guilt.

A variety of reactions to the diagnosis of deafness may be observed among families. Some families, who are unable to resolve their grief, may be stuck in the past or cut-off from the experience of the diagnosis, indicating no emotion at the time.

Their story about the diagnosis may be confused and disorganized making it difficult to understand. Emotionally overwhelmed families have strong expressions of sadness and/or pain. There is an enlistment of sympathy and a feeling that the crisis continues in the present. Families that are angrily preoccupied are those that express active and thematic anger and enlist endorsement of this anger from the professional. Families that have neutralized their emotions report no perception of negative emotion associated with the diagnosis. Some families have clear distortion of the expectations regarding their child's condition and future. They may express unbalanced perceptions regarding the benefits versus negative aspects of the experience either idealizing the experience or painting a picture of no hope. Families may express confusion or incoherence through indications of contradiction in the content of their presentation of the story about their experiences. Some families lose their train of thought and need to be reoriented by the professional. They may ramble or oscillate between polarized perceptions, i.e., all good or all bad, all painful or all beneficial.

The interaction of professionals particularly at the beginning of the family's journey can either provide significant support to ameliorate the grief or exacerbate the grieving. Unfortunately, many families report that exacerbation of grief is more often a reflection of their own personal experience. In a study of 16 families, conducted by Pipp-Siegel (2000), there was a strong trend toward a significant finding based on the child's age at identification. Of these 16 families, ten had resolved their grieving, while six had not. The average age of identification for the resolved group was 8.1 months and for the unresolved group was 16 months. The interview was conducted at a mean of 37.72 months since the identification of hearing loss for the resolved group and 39 months since the identification of hearing loss for the unresolved group. No differences by caregiver education, gender, or degree of hearing loss were evident. The families that had resolved their grief had children with expressive language skills that were 6 months better than the families with unresolved grief. Although there is a need for significantly more research data, there is a strong indication that the resolution of grief may be highly related to the language development of the child with the hearing loss. Theoretically, higher language development will be associated with communication interactions that are closest to typical development. The ability to communicate in the typical range of development should reduce the family's grief related to their feelings of disorder and delay. A family that must devote significant resources to grief has reduced resources for developing a positive emotional relationship between parent and child and for supporting the child's development of language.

Families should have immediate contact with an individual who is knowledgeable about hearing loss (preferably within 48 h of the diagnosis of hearing loss). The first contact person should be able to answer questions posed by the family, including a re-explanation of the screening and diagnostic evaluation results, the rationale for urgency, information about amplification device options, methods of communication, potential for speech, language, literacy, and social–emotional development. The first contact person should also be able to provide grief counseling with knowledgeable information as well as to begin immediate intervention services informing parents/family about how to assist their infant's access to sounds in the environment, especially their voices, when the family has chosen a goal of spoken language. If the family has chosen a goal of sign language acquisition either in addition to spoken language or as an alternative to spoken language, the intervention provider needs to be able to provide the family with information that will facilitate their learning of a visual communication system. It is critically important that the initial contact with the family provides information based on evidence in the literature and not completely on personal opinion and belief of the professionals from their experiences.

Parental stress. Parental stress has been found to be highly related to a child's language development and additional disabilities (Hintermaier, 2006; Kushalnagar et al. 2007; Pipp-Siegel et al. 2001a). In addition to parental grieving, parental stress has been identified as a significant factor for families with children, who have hearing loss, who were identified with hearing loss prior to the establishment of UNHS programs (Lederburg & Golbach, 2001; Quittner, 1991). Some studies after institution of UNHS programs have reported increased family stress at the time of the diagnosis and continuing to 18–24 months (Vohr et al., 2008). Diagnosing hearing loss during the newborn period could potentially amplify parental stress and was a primary caution from individuals who were not initially supportive of establishing UNHS programs. Stress of the mother/father could be magnified by parental grieving. Parental stress can become exacerbated by change in lifestyle that can accompany a diagnosis of hearing loss. The ability of each parent to accept and understand hearing loss could impact the marital relationship. In addition, the ability of each parent to bond with and communicate with their newborn infant will depend upon the family's ability to learn strategies that will help to form a normal communication relationship with their child. The child's language ability is highly related to the level of parental stress for families with children who are deaf (Pipp-Siegel et al., 2001a).

The most commonly used measure of parental stress is the Parental Stress Inventory (PSI) (Abidin, 1995). Abidin (1995) differentiated three different types of parenting stress and developed an assessment procedure, the PSI. Stress can be caused by (1) parental distress: parental characteristics known to affect parenting ability, such as depression or lack of social support; (2) difficult child: child characteristics, such as a difficult temperament which might include learned patterns of defiance, noncompliance, or demanding behavior; and (3) parent–child dysfunctional interaction: difficulties in interacting with the child, such as the parent feeling rejected, abused by, or disappointed in the child, a result of the parent–child bond being either threatened or not adequately established. The parental stress score is derived from subscales of items related to depression, role restriction, isolation, and stress related to the individual's spouse. The parent–child dysfunctional interaction score is derived from subscales consisting of items related to an individual's feelings of acceptability, parenting ability, and attachment of the parent to the child. The difficult child score is derived from subscale items that are related to the child's temperament, the child's adaptability, how demanding the parent perceives the child to be, the general mood of the child, and the child's distractability/hyperactivity. The PSI is a clinical tool and families should be referred for psychological counseling services, if they respond at a clinical level.

In addition to the PSI, several inventories have been used by researchers to determine the level of parental stress and what causes increased stress. The Parenting Events Scale (Crnic & Greenberg, 1990) consisted of 20 statements about daily routines (i.e., being nagged, whined at, complained to, or difficulty getting privacy). Parents were asked to rate the frequency of the occurrence on a four-point scale and the degree to which the behavior is a "big hassle" or "no hassle." The responses on this scale were highly related to the PSI and can be used to guide intervention. This assessment scale can provide information about how the family is coping with daily stresses.

The Family Support Scale (Dunst, Jenkins, & Trivette, 1984) consists of 18 sources of family support (parents, friends, spouse, etc.). Families rated the availability of the source of support and whether the support is helpful. Their responses on this instrument were also significantly related to parental stress levels and assist in the development of appropriate intervention strategies. This instrument is an assessment tool that provides information for the early intervention provider about the families' needs for support.

In a study of 184 hearing mothers of children with hearing loss, ages of birth through 72 months (Pipp-Siegel et al., 2001b), parental stress was measured by the short form of the Parental Stress Index (Abidin, 1986). The 184 mothers in this study did not demonstrate significantly higher stress levels than the control group of the instrument. Lederberg and Golbach (2001) reported a longitudinal study of perceptions of stress and social support by 46 hearing mothers of deaf and hearing children between the ages of 22 months and 4 years. They found that at the 22-month age level, mothers of deaf toddlers expressed more stress as measured by the Revised Questionnaire on Resources and Stress [QRS-R developed by Holroyd (1974) and revised by Friedrich, Greenberg, and Crnic (1983)]. This instrument has 52 items providing information on four factors: Parent and Family Problems, Pessimism, Child Characteristics, and Physical Incapacitation. It has been used as a measurement of stress for families with children who have disabilities. At 3- and 4-year age levels, the amount of stress experienced by mothers of deaf children was comparable to the control group of hearing children and to the norms established for the PSI for the general population. Mother-related stress had the most direct and significant effect on how mothers perceived and evaluated their life. These results are consistent with those reported by Pipp-Siegel et al. (2001b) in their study of 184 children who were deaf between the ages of 6 and 67 months measured by the Parental Stress Index/Short Form (Abidin, 1995).

Both results differ significantly with those reported by Quittner, Glueckauf, and Jackson (1990) who reported high degrees of stress among a large sample (96) of mothers of deaf children and 118 hearing controls in the province of Ontario during a time when early identification and intervention were infrequent. The children were between the ages of 2 and 5 with an average age of 4 years. Quittner et al. (1990) reported that mothers of deaf children were significantly more stressed than mothers of hearing controls. Quittner reported that in five of six subscales of stress the average was at or above the clinical cut-off.

Thus, with parent–infant intervention techniques that include a strong counseling component, the parental stress levels can be similar to the general public for both early and later-identified children. If stress levels are high, focus of intervention should be to assist the family in reducing these stress levels. Relief of stress could result from respite care, reduction of financial concerns, or feelings of support from intervention. This intervention may involve referral to individuals with specialty in these areas. Language levels of the child have been found to be highly related to parental stress (Pipp-Siegel et al., 2001a). A reciprocal relationship probably exists in which lowered parental stress can result in a faster rate of child language development and increased child language development can result in reduced parental stress.

Stress of parents of children who are deaf did not differ significantly from stress of parents of children who are hearing on either Difficult Child or Parent–Child dysfunctional analysis. Hearing mothers of children who are deaf reported greater stress due to parent characteristics than hearing mothers of children who hear. Thirteen percent of the families were at or above the clinical cut-off level, indicating the need for mental health services. Parental distress on the PSI increased as the intensity and frequency of hassles on the Parenting Events Scale increased, as the parent perceived less amount of social support (Family Needs Survey) and had less income. Parents of younger children tended to report higher parental distress. Mothers of children with multiple disabilities and mothers with greater intensity of hassles in the home, mothers of children whose expressive language quotients decreased (indicating that the gap between language and chronological age is greater), and mothers of children who had mild *hearing loss* were more stressed in the parent–child dysfunctional interaction. It is extremely interesting that mothers of children with mild hearing loss, who typically have higher language levels and greater auditory skills, report greater stress in their interactions. Mothers of children with mild hearing loss seem to judge their children's inappropriate behavior, hyperactivity, failure to comply, etc., as due to the fact that they are being "naughty," refusing to obey, rather than due to inability to understand or hear correctly. The milder the hearing disability, the more likely mothers do not take their hearing disability into account when behavior is not as anticipated. Theoretically, if mothers of very young children find their children with mild hearing loss to be difficult children and feel that they have greater stress in their interactions, one would anticipate that there might be a higher internalization by the child that they are "bad" children or "unacceptable children." Mothers reported marginally more parent–child dysfunctional interaction stress the younger children (Pipp-Siegel et al., 2001a), with parents of younger children being more stressed than parents of older children.

Parenting Events Scale. When a high percentage of daily routines is rated as a "big hassle," the parent also rated themselves as more highly stressed on the PSI than those who found daily routines to be less of a hassle. When parents reported that they lacked sources of social support from family, friends, spouse, or agencies, they also experienced higher degrees of parental stress. Parental distress also increased the greater the discrepancy between age and language development or the lower the expressive language quotient. Discrepancies between language development and chronological age can occur because of secondary disabilities, later-identification of hearing loss, or intervention procedures that have not been successful. Mothers had significantly more stress in their interactions when their children had major medical conditions in addition to hearing loss, and as the intensity of hassles in the home increased so did a mother's perception that her child was difficult (Pipp-Siegel et al., 2001b). However, it is interesting to note that although 40% of the sample had additional disabilities, the number of mothers whose stress levels were at the clinical level was significantly lower than those at 16%.

The degree of parental stress reported by these mothers was similar to the findings of Meadow-Orlans (1994) and colleagues (1995). Parents of children with hearing loss experience stress at similar levels to parents of children with cerebral palsy (Pipp-Siegel et al., 2001b), unless their children have additional disabilities with low expressive language quotients. Development of counseling strategies that will assist providers in decreasing parental stress should be a focus for training of early intervention providers.

Intervention providers need to be trained to determine when the family's needs can be adequately addressed by professionals in the area of deafness and hearing loss or through a clinical specialist in grief. Instruction regarding making referrals to appropriate resources should be part of in-service education.

Stress caused by internal parent stress. Intervention should focus on helping families obtain appropriate support. Behavior management strategies may be appropriate for families that perceive a high frequency and intensity of daily hassles. Alternate approaches to dealing with daily stresses may be discussed with the family.

Stress caused by the perception that the child is difficult. Sometimes perception that the child is difficult is related to behavior difficulties, communication issues, or significant multiple disabilities. The focus of intervention may be directed toward behavior management, improving language skills, and providing support to reduce stress in daily living caused by multiple disabilities. Families may need a deeper understanding about how a child could hear conversational speech but still not always understand. Even when a child has a mild hearing loss, the hearing loss could significantly and negatively effect the child's understanding.

Stress caused by the perception that the parent–child interaction is dysfunctional. Parent–child interaction is most affected by language delays. Improvement of language should have a significant impact upon parent–child interaction. Inability to communicate desires and needs can significantly impact the behavior of the child, leading to temper outbursts, tantrums, and aggression toward parents and other family members, because the child is unable to express how s/he is feeling through words.

Parental involvement. The degree to which a family is able to engage in the intervention services provided has been believed to be highly related to the individual child's success and developmental outcomes. Moeller (2000) reported that later-identified children were more likely to have language levels that were similar to early identified children if their families were rated as having high parental involvement.

Because the relationship between social and emotional development in the infant/toddler period has only recently begun to appear in the research on deaf and hard-of-hearing children, it is anticipated that recommendations for assessment and intervention will begin to emerge.

Assessment procedures developed by Moeller (2000) can be done through the Family Participation Rating Scale (see Table 4.1).

It is important to note that the assessment of Family Involvement is not a "blind" procedure, as the intervention provider is aware of the child's language development and other demographic variables of the family and child. Therefore, it is possible that the intervention provider's knowledge of the child's ability to communicate

Table 4.1 Family participation rating scale

Family Participation Rating Scale

Rating 5 (ideal participation):
Family appears to make a good adjustment to the child's deafness. The family is able to put the child's disability in perspective within the family. Family members actively engage in sessions. They attend sessions and meetings regularly and pursue information on their own. They serve as effective advocates for their child with professionals/school districts, etc. Family members become highly effective conversational partners with the child and serve as strong and constant language models. Family members become fluent/effective users of the child's mode of communication. They are capable in applying techniques of language expansion. Extended family members are involved and supportive.

Rating of 4 (good participation):
Family members make a better than average adjustment to the child's deafness. Family members regularly attend parent meetings and sessions. Parents take an active role (perhaps not the lead) in Individual Family Service Plans and Individual Education Plans. Family members serve as good language models for the child and make an effort to carry over techniques at home. Some family members have fairly good facility in the child's communication mode and/or in techniques for language stimulation. Efforts are made to involve extended family members.

Rating of 3 (average participation):
Family is making efforts to understand and cope with the child's diagnosis. Family members participate in most sessions/meetings. Busy schedules or family stresses may limit opportunities for carryover of what is learned. Family may find management of the child challenging. Family attends IFSP and IEP meetings but may rely primarily on professional guidance. Family attempts to advocate but may be misdirected in some of their efforts. Selected family members (e.g. mother) may carry more than their share of responsibility for the child's communicative needs. Family members develop at least basic facility in child's communication mode. Family members are willing to use language expansion techniques but need ongoing support and direction.

Rating of 2 (below average):
Family struggles in acceptance of the child's diagnosis. The family maybe in inconsistent in attendance. They may be inconsistent in maintaining the hearing aids and keeping them on the child outside of school. They may have some significant life stressors that interfere with consistent carryover at home. Management of the child presents daily challenges to the family. Communicative interactions with the child are basic. Family lacks fluency in the child's mode of communication.

Rating of 1 (limited participation):
Family faces significant life stresses that may take precedence over the child's needs (e.g., domestic abuse and homelessness). Family has limited understanding of deafness and its consequences for the child. Participation may be sporadic or less than effective. Parent/child communication is limited to very basic needs.

Published with permission from Moeller (2000)

could significantly impact how they rate/judge the family's involvement in intervention. It seems likely that an intervention provider would attribute a child's higher language development to better parental involvement, although it is possible that other variables such as the child's innate cognitive potential and the degree of hearing loss could play important roles in how quickly the child learns language.

Interestingly, the family involvement scores appeared to have a much lower impact on language levels for the children who were enrolled into early intervention services within the first 11 months, when compared with those enrolled through the next 5 years, indicating that earlier access to intervention, to language and audition, results in higher language levels even when family involvement is lower. The average language levels for children with earlier intervention were within the low-average range for typically hearing children at 5 years. If the child is later identified, the child was found to be less resilient to language delay when the family involvement was low. When a child makes slow or invisible advancement in development, this slow development could create increasing discouragement and poorer involvement in intervention. The interventionist should be careful not to judge the "cause" of poorer parental involvement as the lack of investment of the family, because it could be due to the family's feelings of helplessness, disappointment, or discouragement.

Characteristics of the Child

Personal–social development. The Minnesota Child Development Inventory includes a subtest that measures personal–social development (Ireton & Thwing, 1972). These items include social skills, emotional, and behavioral development. Many, but not all of these items, are language dependent. Over 70% of the variance in personal–social skill development is accounted for by the symbolic play development, expressive language development, and degree of hearing loss of the child.

Early identified children had better personal–social quotients in the first 3 years of life than later-identified children. The age of identification effect was found by gender, degree of hearing loss category, mode of communication, and at each testing age. There is a strong relationship between language development and symbolic play development of children with hearing loss and their personal–social development. Symbolic play and expressive language, however, do not account for all of the variance in personal–social development. Degree of hearing loss also contributes information. Interestingly, parents report that children with mild hearing loss have poorer personal–social skill development than children with moderate-to-profound hearing loss when they are later identified. Thus, the relationship of early identification/intervention to personal–social skill development is the strongest for children with mild hearing loss. These children are most at-risk with later identification to have the greatest delays in personal–social development than children with greater degrees of hearing loss (Yoshinaga-Itano & Abdala de Uzcategui, 2001).

Some have argued that children with mild hearing loss do not demonstrate significant enough developmental delay to warrant newborn hearing screening.

The personal–social skill difference appears to counter this argument. An implication for intervention for later-identified children is that a much greater emphasis needs to be placed upon remediation of delays in this developmental area.

Mastery motivation. The question about how temperament can impact language development has been addressed in the literature of children with normal hearing and typical development (Dichter-Blancher, 1999). The role of temperament in normal language development did not reveal significant relationships. However, it was hypothesized that for children with atypical development, those with disabilities, temperament, specifically mastery motivation could play an important role in language development. This is a reasonable possibility.

One temperament characteristic that matches teacher, parent, and early intervention provider observations with many children with hearing loss is a child's "mastery motivation." A core component of mastery motivation is a "disposition to persistently attempt to attain a goal in the face of moderate uncertainty about whether the goal can be achieved" (McCall, 1995, p. 227). Mastery motivation involves several types of persistence, including persistence when playing with objects, persistence in the social and symbolic domain, and persistence in mastering gross-motor skills (Barrett & Morgan, 1995). Children who demonstrated high object-oriented persistence tend to examine and work with toys and other objects for extended periods of time in an attempt to use them successfully (e.g., putting a puzzle together properly). Those with high levels of social-symbolic persistence make repeated attempts at interacting with others and engaging in pretend play, such as how persistent a child will be in getting an idea across, in understanding language of an adult or peer, and in using language to successfully solve social problems, such as entering into group play. High levels of gross-motor persistence are seen in children who will repeat motor tasks until they can do them well (e.g., throwing and climbing).

In general, high-risk children demonstrate less persistence than low-risk children. For example, less persistence has been reported for children with physical disabilities (Jennings, Connors, & Stegman, 1988; Jennings, Connors, Stegman, Sankaranarayan, & Mendelson, 1985), spina bifida (Landry, Copeland, Lee, & Robinson, 1990), and cystic fibrosis and congenital heart disease (Goldberg, Washington, Morris, Fischer-Fay, & Simmon, 1990) and for premature infants (Harmon & Culp, 1981; Harmon, Morgan & Glicken, 1984). Persistence, however, seems to be related to cognition (Jennings, Harmon, Morgan, Gaiter, & Yarrow, 1979; Yarrow, Morgan, Jennings, Harmon, & Gaiter, 1982) with differences between children with and without medical diagnoses disappearing after controlling for cognitive ability (Goldberg et al., 1990). For example, no significant differences in persistence were found between children with Down syndrome and typically developing children when cognitive ability was controlled (MacTurk, Hunter, McCarthy, Vietze, & McQuiston, 1985)

Studies assessing mastery motivation levels of children with hearing loss have produced mixed results. MacTurk (1993) examined infants at 9 and 12 months and reported no significant difference in levels of *persistence* or social smiles (an indication of "task pleasure") between children with and without hearing loss. The social interactions for a child of 9–12 months do not yet require a significant amount of language communication. In contrast, decreased motivation was reported in older, 8- to 12-year-old, boys with hearing loss when compared with a group of hearing children of the same age (Stinson, 1974). Taken together, these studies suggest that decreases in mastery motivation in children with hearing loss may emerge later in development.

In addition to persistence, another core feature of mastery motivation is the pleasure children obtain when mastering a task. *Mastery pleasure* refers to the expressive aspect of mastery motivation, entailing affective reactions observed during or upon completion of a child's attempt to master a challenging task (Morgan, MacTurk, & Hrncir, 1995). Low correlations between task persistence and mastery pleasure have been reported (Barrett, Morgan, & Maslin-Cole, 1993; Yarrow et al., 1982). Unlike persistence, children with medical conditions demonstrate less mastery pleasure compared with children without medical conditions even when cognitive ability is controlled (e.g., MacTurk et al., 1985).

Mastery motivation has also been shown to be linked to language development. Dichter-Blancher (1999), for example, studied typically developing hearing toddlers and reported that object and social mastery motivation were positively related to children's receptive, expressive, and grammatical language development.

Because the acquisition of language presents special challenges in this population, the role of mastery motivation may be particularly strong. Those children who are intrinsically more persistent may be at an advantage in terms of gaining increased access to language. In an attempt to master language (either via sign or in oral form), for example, tenacious children will persist in asking others to repeat themselves until they understand the communication and will be persistent in ascertaining that their communication to others is understood. Thus, persistence in the face of moderate uncertainty of success may play a significant role in children with hearing loss.

The relation between mastery motivation and expressive language was studied in 200 young children with hearing loss between 7 and 67 months. Hearing mothers assessed their children's expressive language (Minnesota Child Development Inventory, Ireton & Thwing, 1974) and several aspects of mastery motivation including mastery pleasure and three components of mastery persistence (*gross motor*, object oriented, and social/symbolic) by using the Dimensions of Mastery Motivation Questionnaire (Morgan et al., 1992). Simple correlations revealed significant relations between expressive language and all mastery motivation scales. When demographic and hearing loss variables were entered into a regression equation, only increased *social/symbolic persistence* significantly predicted and increased language development, while *object-oriented persistence* marginally predicted increases in expressive language quotients. Expressive language quotients also increased as child age, age of identification, and degree of hearing loss decreased and as maternal ratings of her child's general competence increased. There was a significant relationship between the development of symbolic play, symbolic interaction with objects and people in the environment, and mastery motivation (Pipp-Siegel et al., 2003).

Development of self. Studies of the development of self-concept in early childhood have focused on self-recognition (Lewis & Brooks-Gunn, 1979), self-evaluation (Stipek, 1983), or self-regulation (Kopp, 1982). Stipek, Gralinski, and Kopp (1990) developed a parent-report questionnaire about self-concept development.

Self-description/evaluation and self-regulation are two factors examined through this Self-Concept Questionnaire.

Pressman et al. (1999) and Pressman (2000) in a study on the early self-development of children with hearing loss found that both self-recognition and self-description/evaluation developed between 14 and 40 months. Deaf and hard-of-hearing children always passed the self-recognition items prior to the self-description/evaluation items, similar to the development of children with normal hearing. Self-recognition scores increased significantly from 14 to 40 months when children were deaf. Expressive language completely accounted for the development of self-recognition as the child grew older. Self-description/evaluation also increased significantly with age and decreased significantly as the age at which hearing loss was identified increased, even when child and family characteristics were controlled. Expressive language partially, but not completely, mediated the relation between self-description/evaluation and both age and age of identification. Thus, age of identification, even beyond the effects of improvement of language, had a significant relationship with the development of self (Pressman et al., 1999).

The development of self, believed to be precursors of self-esteem and self-concept, has both language and social–emotional and/or nonverbal components. Language development, as found with other aspects of social–emotional development, is highly related to the development of self. When hearing loss is later identified, children have a reduced ability to identify self and describe self. These abilities are the foundation for the development of self-concept and self-esteem. While language accounts for a significant amount of the relationship with the development of self, indicating that children can identify and describe self as their language development is stronger. Age of identification impacts not only the language development but also the grief, stress, and parental bonding, which may also have a significant impact on self-identification and -description.

The Reciprocal Relationship Between Parent and Child

Emotional reciprocity. Several measures of parental bonding have been used in the literature to compare parent/child interactions of D/HH children of hearing parents with hearing children of hearing parents and deaf children of deaf parents. Our research laboratory uses the Emotional Availability Scales (EAS) (Pipp-Siegel & Biringen, 2000) because the scale captures the emotional characteristics of the interaction. The instrument has been useful for the study of typical development and can be translated into both intervention goals and strategies.

The assessment of emotional availability is accomplished through the analysis of videotaped interactions of mother/father and child and is a measure of parental bonding. The EAS (Biringen & Robinson, 1991; Biringen, Robinson, & Emde, 1988) can be used to rate parent–child interaction. The EAS rates mothers/fathers on two separate subscales and children on two separate subscales. Parents are given global ratings on sensitivity and structuring/intrusiveness. Sensitivity is defined as the parent's ability to (1) read child cues and respond appropriately, (2) resolve parent–child conflict, misunderstanding, or affective mismatch, and (3) tolerate a wide range of affect, while keeping interactions predominately positive in tone. The qualities are assessed on a scale from 1 (highly insensitive) to 9 (highly sensitive). Maternal/paternal structuring/intrusiveness is defined as the degree to which a parent provides optimal support to encourage learning, exploration, and play while at the same time avoiding overwhelming a child's autonomy with a structure that is rigid, fosters infantile behaviors, or is disruptive. Structuring/intrusiveness is a seven-point scale rating a parent on a range from 1 (non) to 5 (optimal) to 7 (overly high). The EASs include two child subscales: responsiveness and involvement. Child responsiveness is defined as the ability of the child to react to his/her parents and the corresponding affect. Children's responses range from 1 (unresponsive) negative, emotionless, showing boredom or withdrawn to 7 (optimally responsive) showing appreciation and pleasure in a parent's company. Child involvement is defined as the degree to which the child attempts to engage parents in play, showing an age-appropriate balance between autonomy (independence) and connectedness on a scale from 1 (uninvolving) to 7 (highly involving).

In a study comparing D/HH and hearing children's language gains at Time 1 and Time 2 and the corresponding emotional availability of the children and their mothers, the following results were obtained (Pressman et al., 1999; Pressman et al., 2000):

- Colorado D/HH children did not have significantly different interaction with their mothers than mothers and children who had normal hearing. Their interactions were not more negative.
- Positive child emotional availability (responsiveness and involvement) predicted language gain from Time 1 to Time 2 in both D/HH and hearing children.
- Positive maternal emotional availability had a significant positive effect on language gain in the D/HH group than the hearing control group meaning that for children with hearing loss, the more positive maternal emotional availability, the greater the language growth from Time 1 to Time 2.
- Both maternal and child effects made independent predictions of language gain of the D/HH children. Thus, both the mother's emotional availability and the child's emotional availability contributed to language gain.
- There is minimal research conducted on the relationship of father and child with a significant hearing loss. Hopefully, in future, this relationship will be further explored.

These results are consistent with a reciprocal model of child and parent effects on language (Clarke-Stewart, 1988; Davis, Stroud, & Green, 1988; Dunham & Dunham, 1992; Richards, 1994; Whitehurst et al., 1988).

Higher maternal emotional availability's positive impact on the language development of D/HH children may reflect the extra flexibility and sensitivity necessary to make compensatory adjustments to the communicative needs of a D/HH child (Koester, 1994; Lederberg & Mobley, 1990).

The implications of these studies are that the improvement of the maternal emotional availability to the child should result in increased rate of language development, and increases in the child's language development should result in improved emotional availability of parent to child and child to parent.

Parents can learn to identify their own positive interactions and videotaped observations are often very beneficial. Positive interactions are extremely difficult when parents are experiencing significant stress in their lives and depression. When grief is not resolved, the parents' ability to be emotionally available to their children is compromised. Parents can be helped to identify the types of activities that are the most enjoyable for themselves and their children.

The Use of Touch and Emotional Availability

The use of touch can be analyzed through the coding of videotaped interactions of mother and child. One examines the types of touch used by the parent in communication, the frequency of the touches, and the impact of the touches (supportive and intrusive).

The use of touch in mother–child interactions of 2 years old children was found to negatively affect the emotional availability of hearing dyads but not the D/HH dyads. This finding supports the hypothesis that touch is intrusive to hearing toddlers because of their developing sense of autonomy, while touch remains an important modality of communication of D/HH toddlers and their hearing mothers (Pipp-Siegel et al., 2001a).

Mothers of D/HH toddlers touched their children and initiated touches more often than hearing dyads. They touched more positively than hearing dyads and used touch in more and different ways than mothers of hearing toddlers. At the 2-year-old period, increase in touch from mother to child increases frustration and hostility in relationships of parents and their children who have normal hearing, while touch at this age is used communicatively and appears to provide comfort in relationships of mothers and their children with hearing loss (Pipp-Siegel et al., 2001a).

If touch is used inappropriately as a means of getting attention from the child, interactions can become negative. Strategies to help parents use a variety of different attention-getting devices can be used to replace techniques, such as excessive tapping on the child's shoulder or turning the child's head to get attention thereby diverting the child's attention from the activity. Natural techniques of drawing the child's attention to either the sounds of speech or the face of the speaker or the sign of the communicator can be used.

Summary of Assessment Strategies that Could Be Used to Investigate the Emotional Well-Being of the Parents and Child

Parental Stress Index (Abidin, 1995) can be used to assess clinical levels of parental stress for families with infants through school-aged children. Data from this instrument can provide valuable information about referral for specialized counseling services. *Revised Questionnaire on Resources and Stress* (Friedrich et al., 1983) can be used specifically for parents who have children with disabilities from birth.

Child Behavior Checklist. The revised Child Behavior Checklist 1.5–5 years contains 99 items as Not True, Somewhat or Sometimes True, or Very or Often True. Achenbach and Rescorla (2000) identified seven factors: emotionally reactive (9 items), anxious/depressed (8 items), somatic complaints (11 items), withdrawal (8 items), sleep problems (7 items), and an externalizing problems score formed by attention problems (5 items) and aggressive problems (19 items). A total problem score is derived from 67 items of the 7 syndromes, 32 items that represent other problems, and 1 item added by the parent/caregiver. This instrument is used in the diagnosis of emotional–behavioral disorders.

Parenting Events Index (Crnic & Greenberg, 1990), the hassles index, can provide the intervention provider with valuable information about issues in daily life that are creating stress. The provider can then work collaboratively with the family to determine alternative modifications in daily routines or approaches can ameliorate the intensity of the hassles.

Parent needs survey (Dunst et al., 1984) was designed for use with families that have children with significant disabilities between the ages of birth and 5 years. The information can be helpful in intervention by helping professionals recognize and support parental need for resources. The provider can identify resources that the parent may need, such as respite care or building a social support system.

Parent Involvement Index (Moeller, 2000) was found to be highly related to language development and was particularly significant in children with later-identified hearing loss. The scale itself does not provide information about what strategies could be used to improve parental involvement, but can help to identify a priority for developing counseling strategies appropriate for an individual family.

The Personal–Social subscale of the Minnesota Child Development Inventory (Ireton & Thwing, 1974) can be used for a general index of personal and social development for children between the ages of birth and 7 years. Personal–social development is highly related to language development of the child with significant hearing loss. This instrument is a quick index, through a parental questionnaire, of how similar the social and emotional skills of the child are to the child with normal hearing and typical development.

Conclusion

This article summarizes the research from our Colorado research on children with early identified hearing loss since the institution of UNHS and presents a model for consideration of the social–emotional aspects of infants/children and their families and their interrelationships with language development. The role of social–emotional variables has been sorely neglected in the discussion of important foci for early intervention services for parents and their children with hearing loss. Emphasis for children who are early identified with hearing loss has focused predominantly on amplification technology and whether the method of communication is through auditory, visual, or combined modalities. Regardless of the chosen technology or method of communication, a family's investment and involvement in using technology consistently and their ability to learn and apply communication strategies, the development of language may depend upon the emotional resources that they have to focus on the intervention. The emotional well-being of the parents, the child, other children in the family, as well as the ease and pleasure of interaction from both the parent and the child perspectives may either facilitate or slow down the child's language, communication, and social–emotional development.

References

Achenbach, T. M., & Rescorla, L. A. (2000). *Manual for the ABESPA preschool form and profiles*. Burlington, VT: University of Vermont, Research Center for Children, Youth and Families.

Abidin, R. R. (1986). *Short form of the Parental Stress Index*. Odessa, FL: Psychological Assessment Resources.

Abidin, R. R. (1995). *Parenting Stress Index* (3rd ed.). Odessa, FL: Psychological Assessment Resources.

Baca, R. (2009). *A longitudinal language growth model for young children with hearing impairment*. Unpublished doctoral dissertation, University of Colorado, Boulder, Co.

Barrett, K. C., & Morgan, G. A. (1995). Continuities and discontinuities in mastery motivation in infancy and toddlerhood: A conceptualization and review. In R. H. MacTurk & G. A. Morgan (Eds.), *Mastery motivation: Origins, conceptualizations, and applications* (pp. 57–93). Norwood, NJ: Ablex.

Barrett, K. C., Morgan, G. A., & Maslin-Cole, C. (1993). Three studies on the development of mastery motivation in infancy and toddlerhood. In D. Messer (Ed.), *Mastery motivation in early childhood: Development, measurement and social processes* (pp. 83–108). London: Routledge.

Biringen, Z., & Robinson, J. (1991). Emotional availability in mother-child interactions: A reconceptualization for research. *American Journal of Orthopsychiatry, 61*, 258–271.

Biringen, Z., Robinson, J. L. & Emde, R. N. (1988). *Manual for scoring the emotional availability scales*. Unpublished manuscript, University of Colorado Health Sciences Center.

Clarke-Stewart, K. A. (1988). Parents' effects on children's development: A decade of progress? *Journal of Applied Developmental Psychology, 9*, 41–84.

Crnic, K. A., & Greenberg, M. T. (1990). Minor parenting stress with young children. *Child Development, 61*, 1628–1637.

Davis, H., Stroud, A., & Green, L. (1988). The maternal language environment of children with language delay. *British Journal of Disordered Communication, 23*(3), 253–266.

Dichter-Blancher, T. B. (1999). *The role of language and parenting behaviors in the development of mastery motivation in toddlers*. *ETD Collection for Fordham University*. New York: Fordham University. Paper AAI9926891. Retrieved from http://fordham.bepress.com/dissertations/AAI9926891.

Dunham, P., & Dunham, F. (1992). Lexical development during middle infancy: A mutually driven infant-caregiver process. *Developmental Psychology, 28*, 414–420.

Dunst, C. J., Jenkins, V., & Trivette, C. M. (1984). The Family Support Scale: Reliability and validity. *Journal of Individual, Family, and Community Wellness, 1*, 45–52.

Emde, R. N. (1988). Development terminable and interminable: I. Innate and motivational factors from infancy. *International Journal of Psychoanalysis, 69*, 23–42.

Emde, R. N. (1996). Thinking about intervention and improving socio-emotional development. *Zero to Three, 17*, 11–16.

Emde, R. N., Biringen, Z., Clyman, R. B., & Oppenheim, D. (1991). The moral self of infancy: Affective core and procedural knowledge. *Developmental Review, 11*, 251–270.

Emde, R. N., & Easterbrooks, M. A. (1985). Assessing emotional availability in early development. In W. K. Frankenburg, R. N. Emde, & J. W. Sullivan (Eds.), *Early identification of children at risk: An international perspective* (pp. 70–101). New York: Plenum.

Friedrich, W. N., Greenberg, M. T., & Crnic, K. (1983). A short-form of the questionnaire on resources and stress. *American Journal of Mental Deficiency, 88*(1), 41–48.

Furstenberg, K., & Doyle, G. (1994). The relationship between personal-behavioral functioning and personal characteristics on performance outcomes of hearing impaired students. *American Annals of the Deaf, 139*, 410–414.

Golbach, T., & Lederburg, A. (1999). *Social support and parenting stress in hearing mothers of deaf preschoolers: A longitudinal study*. Proceedings of the Society of Research in Child Development, Albuquerque, NM.

Goldberg, S., Washington, J., Morris, P., Fischer-Fay, A., & Simmons, R. J. (1990). Early diagnosed chronic illness and mother-child relationships in the first few years. *Canadian Journal of Psychiatry, 35*, 726–733.

Harmon, R. J., & Culp, A. M. (1981). The effects of premature birth on family functioning and infant development. In I. Berlin (Ed.), *Children and our future* (pp. 1–9). Albuquerque, NM: University of New Mexico Press.

Harmon, R. J., Morgan, G. A., & Glicken, A. D. (1984). Continuities and discontinuities in affective and cognitive-motivational development. *Journal of Child Abuse and Neglect, 8*, 157–167.

Hintermaier, M. (2006). Parental resources, parental stress and social emotional development of deaf and hard of hearing children. *Journal of Deaf Studies and Deaf Education, 11*(4), 493–513.

Holroyd, J. (1974). The questionnaire on resources and stress: An instrument to measure family response to a handicapped member. *Journal of Community Psychology, 2*, 92–94.

Holroyd, J. (1976). *Manual for the questionnaire on resources and stress*. Los Angeles: UCLA Neuropsychiatric Institute.

Ireton, H., & Thwing, E. (1972). *The Minnesota Child Development Inventory*. Minneapolis, MN: University of Minnesota.

Ireton, H., & Thwing, E. (1974). *The Minnesota Child Development Inventory* (2nd ed.). Minneapolis, MN: Pearson Education, Inc.

Jennings, K. D., Connors, R. E., & Stegman, C. E. (1988). Does a physical handicap alter the development of mastery motivation during the preschool years? *Journal of the American Academy of Child and Adolescent Psychiatry, 27*, 213–317.

Jennings, K. D., Connors, R. E., Stegman, C. E., Sankaranarayan, P., & Mendelson, S. (1985). Mastery motivation in young preschoolers: Effect of a physical handicap and implications for educational programming. *Journal of the Division for Early Childhood, 9*, 162–169.

Jennings, K., Harmon, R., Morgan, G., Gaiter, J., & Yarrow, L. (1979). Exploratory play as an index of mastery motivation: Relationships to persistence, cognitive functioning, and environmental measures. *Developmental Psychology, 15*, 386–394.

Kennedy, C. R., McCann, D. C., Campbell, M. J., Law, C. M., Mullee, M., Petrou, S., et al. (2006). Language ability after early detection of permanent childhood hearing impairment. *New England Journal of Medicine, 354*(20), 2131–2141.

Koester, L. S. (1994). Face-to-face interactions and the socioemotional development of deaf infants. *Early Development and Parenting, 3*, 51–60.

Kopp, C. B. (1982). Antecedents of self-regulation: A developmental perspective. *Developmental Psychology, 26*, 199–214.

Kurtzer-White, E., & Luterman, D. (2003). Families and children with hearing loss: Grief and coping. *Mental Retardation Developmental Disabilities Research Review, 9*(4), 232–235.

Kushalnagar, P., Krull, K., Hannay, J., Mehta, P., Caudle, S., & Oghalai, J. (2007). Intelligence, depression and behavioral adaptability in deaf children being considered for cochlear implantation. *Journal of Deaf Studies and Deaf Education, 12*(3), 335–349.

Landry, S. H., Copeland, D., Lee, A., & Robinson, S. (1990). Goal-directed behaviors in children with spina bifida. *Journal of Developmental and Behavioral Pediatrics, 11*, 306–311.

Lederberg, A. R., & Mobley, C. E. (1990). The effect of hearing impairment on the quality of attachment and mother-toddler interaction. *Child Development, 61*, 1596–1604.

Lederberg, A., & Golbach, T. (2001). Social support and parenting stress in hearing mothers of deaf preschoolers: A longitudinal study. *Journal of Deaf Studies and Deaf Education, 7*, 330–335.

Lewis, M., & Brooks-Gunn, J. (1979). *Social cognition and the acquisition of self.* New York: Plenum Press.

MacTurk, R. H. (1993). Social and motivational development in deaf and hearing infants. In D. J. Messer (Ed.), *Mastery motivation: Children's investigation, persistence and development* (pp. 149–167). London: Rutledge.

MacTurk, R. H., Hunter, F., McCarthy, M., Vietze, P., & McQuiston, S. (1985). Social mastery motivation in Down syndrome and non-delayed infants. *Topics in Early Childhood Special Education, 4*, 93–109.

McCall, R. B. (1995). On definitions and measures of mastery motivation. In R. H. MacTurk & G. A. Morgan (Eds.), *Mastery motivation: Origins, conceptualizations, and applications* (pp. 273–292). Norwood, NJ: Ablex Publishing Co.

Meadow-Orlans, K. (1994). Stress, support, and deafness: Perceptions of infants' mothers and fathers. *Journal of Early Intervention, 18*, 91–102.

Meadow-Orlans, K. P., Smith-Gray, S., & Dyssegaard, B. (1995). Infants who are deaf or hard of hearing, with and without physical/cognitive disabilities. *American Annals of the Deaf, 140*, 279–286.

Mitchell, V. T., & Quittner, A. L. (1996). Multimethod study of attention and behavior problems in hearing impaired children. *Journal of Clinical Child Psychology, 25*, 83–96.

Moeller, M. P. (2000). Early intervention and language development in children who are deaf and hard of hearing. *Pediatrics, 106*, E43.

Morgan, G. A., Harmon, R. J., Maslin-Cole, C. A., Busch-Rossnagel, N. A., Jennings, K. A., Hauser-Cram, P., & Brockman, L. (1992). *Assessing perceptions of mastery motivation: The dimensions of mastery questionnaire, its development, psychometrics and use.* Unpublished manuscript, Colorado State University, Fort Collins, CO.

Morgan, G. A., MacTurk, R. H., & Hrncir, E. J. (1995). Mastery motivation: Overview, definitions and conceptual issues. In R. H. MacTurk & G. A. Morgan (Eds.), *Mastery motivation: Origins, conceptualizations, and applications* (pp. 1–18). Norwood, NJ: Ablex Publishing Co.

Moses, K. (1983). The impact of initial diagnosis: Mobilizing family resources. In J. A. Mulick & S. M. Pueschel (Eds.), *Parent-professional partnerships in developmental disability services* (pp. 11–34). Cambridge, MA: Academic Guild Publishers.

Pianta, R. C., & Marvin, R. S. (1993). *Manual for classification of the reaction to diagnosis interview.* Unpublished manuscript, University of Virginia.

Pipp-Siegel, S. (2000). *Resolution of grief of parents with young children with hearing loss.* Boulder, CO: University of Colorado. Unpublished manuscript.

Pipp-Siegel, S., & Biringen, Z. (2000). Assessing quality of relationships between parents and children: The Emotional Availability Scales. In Yoshinaga-Itano, C. & Sedey, A. (Eds.) *The early years-language, speech and social-emotional development: Deaf and hard-of-hearing children of hearing parents. The Volta Review, 100*(5), 237–250.

Pipp-Siegel, S., Blair, N., Deas, A., Pressman, L., & Yoshinaga-Itano, C. (2001). Touch and emotional availability in hearing and deaf or hard of hearing toddlers and their hearing mothers. *The Volta Review, 100*(5), 279–298.

Pipp-Siegel, S., Sedey, A., & Yoshinaga-Itano, C. (2001). Predictors of parental stress in mothers of young children with hearing loss. *Journal of Deaf Studies and Deaf Education, 7*(1), 1–17.

Pipp-Siegel, S., Sedey, A. L., VanLeeuwen, A., & Yoshinaga-Itano, C. (2003). Mastery motivation predicts expressive language in children with hearing loss. *Journal of Deaf Studies and Deaf Education, 8*(2), 133–145.

Pressman, L. (2000). *Early self-development in children with hearing loss.* Unpublished doctoral dissertation, University of Colorado, Boulder, CO.

Pressman, L. J., Pipp-Siegel, S., Yoshinaga-Itano, C., Kubicek, L., & Emde, R. M. (2000). A comparison of the links between emotional availability and language gains in young children with and without hearing loss. *The Volta Review, 100*(5), 251–277.

Pressman, L., Pipp-Siegel, S., Yoshinaga-Itano, C., & Deas, A. (1999). The relation of sensitivity to child expressive language gain in deaf and hard-of-hearing children whose caregivers are hearing. *Journal of Deaf Studies and Deaf Education, 4*, 294–304.

Pressman, L., Pipp-Siegel, S., Yoshinaga-Itano, C., Kubicek, L., & Emde, R. N. (1999). A comparison of links between emotional availability and language gain in young children with and without hearing loss. *The Volta Review, 100*, 251–277.

Quittner, A. L., Glueckauf, R. L., & Jackson, D. N. (1990). Chronic parenting stress: moderating versus mediating effects of social support. *Journal of Personality & Social Psychology, 59*(6), 1266–1278.

Quittner, A. L. (1991). Coping with a hearing-impaired child: A model of adjustment to chronic stress. In J. H. Johnson & S. B. Johnson (Eds.), *Advances in child health psychology* (pp. 205–223). Gainsville: University of Florida Press.

Richards, B. J. (1994). Child-directed speech and influences on language acquisition: Methodology and interpretation. In C. Gallaway & B. J. Richards (Eds.), *Input and interaction in language acquisition* (pp. 74–106). New York: Cambridge University Press.

Sheeran, T., Marvin, R. S., & Pianta, R. C. (1997). Mothers' resolution of their child's diagnosis and self-reported measures of parenting stress, marital relations, and social support. *Journal of Pediatric Psychology, 22*(2), 197–212.

Stinson, M. S. (1974). Relations between maternal reinforcement and help and the achievement motive in normal-hearing and hearing-impaired sons. *Developmental Psychology, 10*, 348–353.

Stipek, D. (1983). A developmental analysis of pride and shame. *Human Development, 26*, 42–54.

Stipek, D. J., Gralinski, H., & Kopp, C. B. (1990). Self-concept development in the toddler years. *Developmental Psychology, 26*, 972–977.

Van Eldik, T. (2005). Mental health problems of deaf youth with hearing problems as shown on the youth self report. *American Annals of the Deaf, 115*, 11–16.

Vohr, B. R., Jodoin-Krauzyk, J., Tucker, R., Johnson, M. J., Topol, D., & Ahlgren, M. (2008). Results of newborn screening for hearing loss: Effects on the family in the first 2 years of life. *Archives of Pediatrics and Adolescent Medicine, 162*(3), 205–211.

Whitehurst, G. J., Fishel, J. E., Lonigan, C. J., Valdez-Menchaca, M. C., DeBaryshe, B. D., & Caulfield, M. B. (1988). Verbal interaction in families of normal and expressive language-delayed children. *Developmental Psychology, 24*, 690–699.

Yarrow, L., Morgan, G., Jennings, K., Harmon, R., & Gaiter, J. (1982). Infants' persistence at tasks: Relationships to cognitive functioning and early experience. *Infant Behavior and Development, 5*, 131–141.

Yoshinaga-Itano, C. (2002). The social-emotional ramifications of universal newborn hearing screening, early identification and intervention of children who are deaf or hard of hearing. In R. C. Seewald & J. S. Gravel (Eds.), *A sound foundation through early amplification 2001. Proceedings of the Second International Pediatric Audiology Amplification UK* (pp. 221–232). Chicago, IL: St. Edmundsbury Press Conference.

Yoshinaga-Itano, C., & Abdala de Uzcategui, C. (2001). Early identification and social-emotional factors of children with hearing loss and children screened for hearing loss. In E. Kurtzer-White & D. Luterman (Eds.), *Early childhood deafness* (pp. 13–28). Baltimore, MD: York Press Inc.

Yoshinaga-Itano, C., Sedey, A. L., Coulter, D. K., & Mehl, A. L. (1998). The language of early- and later-identified children with hearing loss. *Pediatrics, 102*(5), 1161–1171.

Young, A., & Tattersall, H. (2007). Universal newborn hearing screening and early identification of deafness: Parents' responses to knowing early and their expectations responses of child communicative development. *Journal of Deaf Studies and Deaf Education, 12*(2), 209–220.

Part III
Childhood

Chapter 5
Developing a Concept of Self and Other: Risk and Protective Factors

Patrick J. Brice and Elizabeth B. Adams

Abstract There is very little research that has been done with deaf children, specifically with the concept of resilience in mind. There are, however, data on a number of developmental factors that can be examined for the roles they play as protective factors and in providing deaf children with the skills necessary to adapt to and cope with a complex and demanding world. In particular, we argue that developing a strong sense of self and an accurate and objective understanding of other people, rooted in a caring and secure parent–child attachment, provides a foundation for deaf children to thrive. We also review the challenges for deaf children in developing the skills to understand others and feel positively about one self, including delayed language acquisition, concluding that the relationship context is most crucial.

H.L. Mencken reportedly once pointed out that for every complex and difficult problem there is a simple and elegant solution that is completely wrong. Most problems that are truly interesting and important are complex, with many different factors interacting in both predictable and random ways to influence the dynamics. This is as true for human behavior and human development as it is for quantum physics. Studying how people adapt to and cope with their ever-changing world requires consideration of many different characteristics. The reductionism of science, breaking development into "areas" that are studied independently, ultimately falls short of actually explaining anything. This is perhaps most true in studies of resilience in children, which started with the observation that some children with numerous risk factors developed into quite well adjusted people. This was a surprise to a number of researchers, leading to the broader study of resilience in the face of what should be overwhelming obstacles.

Understanding resilience in deaf children is even more complicated, starting with the very question, "Where does resilience lie?" Does resilience lie in the children themselves, such that it is an inherent characteristic of the child? Or, does resilience lie in the environment surrounding the child? Moreover, might resilience

P.J. Brice (✉)
Department of Psychology, Gallaudet University, Washington, DC, USA

D.H. Zand and K.J. Pierce (eds.), *Resilience in Deaf Children: Adaptation Through Emerging Adulthood*, DOI 10.1007/978-1-4419-7796-0_5,
© Springer Science+Business Media, LLC 2011

lie in the transactions that occur between the child and his/her environment? As Bronfenbrenner (1979, 2005) pointed out, we all exist in a series of nested environments, influencing and being influenced by those close to us and by factors that are quite distal such as cultural attitudes and practices. But out of those interactions and transactions with our families, our communities, and cultures, an organized pattern of behaving develops, triggered by environmental cues and responses and fostered by interpersonal connections between child and caregivers.

Sroufe, Egeland, Carlson, and Collins (2005) present data on one of the most ambitious of longitudinal research projects, the Minnesota Study of Risk and Adaptation. They followed 180 children born into high-risk situations, including poverty and young motherhood, from birth to adulthood. One of their primary interests was in studying and learning how organized patterns of development come about and determining whether those patterns were consistent over the lifespan, at least throughout childhood and adolescence. They wanted to study that person who has, "...emerged out of the relationships matrix" (Sroufe et al., 2005, p. 121). A striking finding in their rich dataset was that the attachment style that developed between the child and the parent – secure, anxious-avoidant, or anxious-resistant – was a strong predictor of child adjustment, peer relationships, and even academic test performance throughout life. The internalized conceptualization of human relationships and interpersonal interactions that young children (i.e., before the age of 3) develop continue to influence how they behave and how well they adjust. These characteristics are not set in stone, and can be changed, both positively and negatively, by continued interactions and experiences, but nonetheless they are powerful.

Resilience is the process of changing both one's self and the environment so that development proceeds in such a way as to optimize resources and achievements. Because of the demonstrated power of the internalized conceptualizations of self and other for optimal development, the current chapter reviews the extant research available investigating attachment styles and Theory of Mind (the understanding of other), and self-concept/self-esteem (the understanding of one's self). Additionally, we will look at research on deaf children's ability to self-regulate, a characteristic or skill that is central to being able to develop a sense of self and other.

The research on development in deaf children has very few comprehensive longitudinal studies from which to draw. Nothing like the Sroufe et al. (2005) project exists. Schlesinger and Meadow (1972) continued to study children from their classic study in the Bay Area of California for some years, and Meadow-Orlans, Spencer, and Koester (2004) report on an ambitious 15-year study of deaf infants, looking at differences between deaf children with hearing vs. deaf parents. While there are few of these ambitious projects, there is a slowly growing body of research on several lines of development in deaf children. There is a history of research looking at impulsivity or behavior problems in deaf children, and more recent research which has reconceptualized impulsivity in terms of executive functioning. Additionally, there is research on attachment styles in deaf children as well as their parents, including data on the relationships between deaf parents and their deaf and hearing children (from an attachment perspective). We are learning more about self-concept in deaf children and the various factors that affect how deaf children come to think of themselves and where they see themselves most positively. And, we are also learning about how deaf children come to understand what other people might be thinking, feeling, or intending. Taken together, these data begin to suggest something about what makes a child, or a child–environment unit, resilient and what may be some of the risk factors. Central to our argument will be the idea that developing a strong sense of self that is built from a history of secure attachment paves the way for a child to exhibit resilience. Furthermore, parents and families that are willing communicators – open to trying to understand not just the overt language, but the underlying affective tone – encourage more positive development in children regardless of the decision made about how to communicate. We hope to show that while there is complexity, certain not-surprising patterns can be discerned.

Attachment and Development of Deaf children

All aspects of human development occur in a context of relationships with others, and thus discussing the beginnings of that relationship context is a fine place to start our discussion. Attachment theory is noted to be one of the most empirically founded frameworks in the fields of social and emotional development (Cassidy & Shaver, 2008) and is one of the most widely used theoretical approaches to understanding and exploring complex behavioral patterns. With far reaching clinical implications from infancy into old age, attachment is one of the most influential and important variables in development (Cassidy & Shaver, 1999). Research has demonstrated that attachment is related to social adjustment, quality of interpersonal relationships, and self-esteem (Weinfield, Sroufe, Egeland, & Carlson, 1999).

Research utilizing the framework of attachment theory to understand development has been an integral component of developmental psychology. Although the number of studies utilizing attachment theory to examine patterns in deaf children is limited, the available research provides an interesting understanding of how we conceptualize risk and resilience in the development of deaf children.

Young, Green, and Rogers (2008) pointed out that when considering risk and resilience, there are two possible ways to frame these constructs. One perspective emphasizes characteristics within the deaf child, protecting him/her from an environment that is not necessarily suited to foster their development. This perspective also considers the characteristics within the child that promote resilience, despite the potential disadvantages that being deaf may present. A contrasting perspective emphasizes the environment, focusing on the factors outside the child, such as the parent or the school, that foster resilience in the face of risk. From this perspective, being deaf is not considered the risk, but rather the onus of risk lies in the environment. Similarly, it is also the environment that will promote resilience within the child. A consideration of attachment and deaf children includes both of these perspectives, taking into consideration characteristics of the child, as well as the child's environment and primary relationships.

Some of the available research examining attachment patterns between deaf children and their parents reveals that in general, the overall patterns of these dyads are not different than those of hearing children and their parents. Meadow, Greenberg, and Erting (1984) completed a study focused on attachment patterns of deaf children from deaf families. The attachment classifications of the sample of deaf children were compared to the distribution of attachment patterns found in hearing samples. Results indicated that the distribution of attachment styles found in the population of deaf children and deaf parent dyads was similar to the distributions found in hearing samples. However, this study has been criticized for its use of the Strange Situation Procedure with children outside the validated age range.

Research examining the relationship between hearing parents and deaf children in the context of attachment patterns is extremely limited and yields inconclusive results. Lederberg and Mobley (1990) compared hearing child–mother dyads with deaf child and hearing mother dyads. The researchers examined security of attachment and ratings of maternal and child behavior during free play. The Strange Situation Procedure was used to assess attachment classification.

Results of the study revealed no significant interaction between hearing status and attachment. Children with hearing loss were not more likely to be classified as insecure or disorganized and overall were not rated to be more difficult to classify than hearing children. Hearing loss was also not shown to impact the quality of the relationship between the mother and the child (Lederberg & Mobley, 1990). This study also has been criticized for use of the strange situation with children outside the validated age range. Despite the limitations of these studies, it is interesting to note that hearing loss, as an isolated variable, does not seem to contribute to an increased incidence of insecure attachment patterns. These results support the idea that although we may hypothesize that children with hearing loss would be more likely to form insecure attachments, this is not the case. In the face of hearing loss, these children are resilient, at least with respect to forming secure attachments.

While general patterns of attachment security have not been shown to relate to hearing loss, research in the area of attachment with deaf children has emphasized the role of communication in the formation of attachment patterns. Greenberg and Marvin (1979) utilized a "goal-directed" coding approach to the Strange Situation Procedure in one study with deaf children. The results suggested that communication proficiency influences the attachment classification for deaf child and hearing mother dyads. They found that deaf preschoolers and hearing mothers with poor communication were likely to be insecurely attached, whereas deaf preschoolers and hearing mothers with effective communication were more likely to be securely attached (Greenberg & Marvin, 1979).

Although Lederberg and Mobley (1990) generally found no difference between hearing and deaf children in their distribution of attachment patterns, they did notice that toddlers with hearing loss spent less time interacting with their hearing mothers and more time in solitary play compared to hearing toddlers. Mothers of deaf children were more likely to initiate interaction, and deaf children were more likely to terminate an interaction, reportedly because the children did not hear the communication (Lederberg and Mobley, 1990).

Both the Greenberg and Marvin (1979) and the Lederberg and Mobley (1990) studies point to factors of risk and resilience that lie both within the child and within the environment. The Greenberg and Marvin (1979) study highlights the importance of language use and effective communication in fostering a secure parent–child attachment pattern. It is important to note that the particular mode of communication was not considered to be the defining variable but rather the effectiveness of the communication. Thus, communication effectiveness should be considered when reviewing factors of risk and resilience. Parents of children with hearing loss report choosing a mode of communication and that navigating family communication is one of the most difficult decisions they confront (Meadow-Orlans, Mertens, & Sass-Lehrer, 2003). The choice of communication method may need to be evaluated and re-examined at several points in the child's development, as communication needs change. Regardless of the communication mode chosen, effective communication is key in the development of quality family relationships and emotional development of the child. In terms of resilience, effective communication may be an important variable to healthy development. Effective communication is developed based on both characteristics of the child and the environment. The language skills of the child as well as the communication match with the environment are both critical for effective growth and attachment.

In terms of attachment during childhood, a consideration of language and communication is particularly relevant. As a child becomes older, and thus develops a capacity for linguistic communication, the importance of language in the relationship increases. As highlighted in the Lederberg and Mobley (1990) study, language mediation will impact the nature of play and other interactions as the child becomes older. Interactions and responses to situations are eventually expressed through symbolic language. A closer examination of research on attachment and deaf children may reveal that in infancy, fewer differences exist between deaf and hearing children. However, as children begin the fourth stage outlined in Bowlby's (1969/1982) trajectory of attachment development, this may change. In the fourth stage, the key attachment task is negotiating a parent's departure and return, which can require a more developed mastery of language.

While the limited research on attachment patterns of deaf children has emphasized the importance of effective communication in the development of healthy attachment patterns, a number of other variables have also been identified. While these variables have not been isolated and extensively examined in the limited research examining attachment patterns in deaf children, it is likely that they contribute to the development of healthy attachment patterns in this population. In particular, two studies have looked at the effects of parental attitudes toward deafness and parental coping with diagnosis as they relate to attachment security.

Hadadian's (1995) study investigated deaf children of hearing parents' security of attachment as it relates to parental attitudes about deafness. The study included 30 deaf children. In addition to attachment measures, parents also completed an Attitude Toward Deafness Scale. Results revealed a negative correlation between parents' scores on the Attitude Toward Deafness Scale and child attachment security. The correlation revealed that more negative attitudes toward deafness were negatively correlated with security. This finding suggests that parental attitudes about deafness can impact the quality of the attachment relationship.

Another study by Spangler (1988) investigated the role of parental characteristics in the development of attachment security in deaf infants. Specifically, the study investigated the influence of parental grief and coping abilities on the development of attachment security. Twenty hearing mother and deaf child dyads were included in the study. The dyads completed the Strange Situation Procedure, and the parents were asked to complete a modified version of the Texas Revised Inventory of Grief (Faschingbauer, 1981), the Beck Depression Inventory (BDI; Beck, 1978), and a grief inventory developed by the researcher. Analyses revealed that mother–child pairs with nonsecure attachment classifications had Texas Inventory of Grief classifications that were less resolved and also had significantly lower scores on the coping inventory developed by the researcher.

The Hadadian (1995) and Spangler (1988) studies both highlight how characteristics of parents influence the development of attachment security in deaf children. Research supports the importance of parental behaviors in the formation of healthy attachment patterns. Mothers of secure children demonstrate more genuine delight in their child (Britner, Marvin, & Pianta, 2005) and interactions are more reciprocal, synchronous, and mutually rewarding (Isabella & Belsky, 1991). In general, parents of securely attached children provide more protection for their children and also help to support positive exploration (Britner et al., 2005).

These findings demonstrate the important connection between parental behavior and child attachment status, reinforcing the concept of attachment as representative of the relationship between the parent–child dyad. While much of the research on attachment theory has focused on the attachment status of the child, it is critical to remember that the attachment classification of the child is dependent on the relationship with the primary attachment figure and the attachment figure's responsiveness to the child.

Research has shown that trauma in adulthood can also cause changes in the attachment representations of the caregiver (Main & Hesse, 1990; Marvin & Pianta, 1996). When caregivers experience a traumatic event, they may change the way they interact with their child. The caregiver may become overwhelmed with the task of dealing with his/her own trauma and become emotionally unresponsive or otherwise become unable to meet the needs of the child. As a result, the child's perceptions about the caregiver may change, thus impacting the attachment relationship (Lyons-Ruth & Spielman, 2004; Main & Hesse, 1990; Marvin & Pianta, 1996). Research has also shown that parental internal working models may be negatively affected by variables such as changes in the child's responses to the parent, quality of parent–child interactions, and difficulties associated with parenting (Amber, Belsky, Slade, & Crnic, 1999). Keeping these findings in mind, parental attitudes toward deafness and parental coping related to the grief associated with receiving a diagnosis of deafness are likely to influence the attachment relationship.

In terms of risk and resilience, these findings support the idea that a potential risk for the child lies in the attitude and response of the parent. In terms of raising resilient deaf children, fostering a supportive and accepting environment for the deaf child will also foster healthy attachment patterns. Additionally, helping parents to manage and resolve the grief and difficulties associated with receiving a diagnosis of deafness will also help to foster securely attached deaf children, and thus children who are more resilient.

The importance of parental responsiveness, and parental states of mind in general, was highlighted in a meta-analysis exploring the relative effects of maternal and child problems on the quality of attachment in hearing children (Van IJzendoorn, Goldberg, Kroonenberg, & Frenkel, 1992). This meta-analysis explored 34 clinical studies investigating attachment classifications. The study investigated whether maternal problems, such as mental illness, led to more insecure attachment classifications in children compared to "child problems," or specific areas of concern in the child such as mental illness or physical disability. The two groups were compared with a baseline of attachment classification derived from 21 studies including nonclinical samples. The analysis revealed that groups with a primary identification of maternal problems showed more deviating attachment classifications when compared to the nonclinical sample. The groups with a primary identification of "child problems" showed distributions similar to that found in the normal sample (Van IJzendoorn et al., 1992). This research highlights the importance of parental support and adjustment in the formation of healthy attachment patterns above "problems" identified in the child.

Previous research has also explored attachment status in deaf adults. Considering the limited number of studies examining attachment patterns in deaf children, we can further understand attachment patterns in deaf children by understanding the attachment patterns of deaf adults. One of the most fascinating components of attachment theory is the finding that attachment patterns remain relatively stable throughout the lifespan. Thus, children identified as securely attached in childhood are likely to grow into adults who demonstrate secure/autonomous attachment patterns.

One study administered the Adult Attachment Interview (AAI; George, Kaplan, & Main, 1984, 1985, 1996) to 50 deaf adults who were fluent in American Sign Language (ASL; Chovaz McKinnon, Moran, & Pederson, 2004). It was hypothesized that many of these adults may have insecure attachment styles because at the time of the study many of them reported communication difficulties with their parents who did not know ASL. Additionally, it was common for many children to be separated from their parents for extended periods of time as they attended residential schools for the deaf from a young age. However, results revealed that the majority of the deaf adults were classified as secure/autonomous in rates equal to hearing adults (Chovaz McKinnon et al., 2004; Leigh, Brice, & Meadow-Orlans, 2004).

Many questions remain surrounding the nature of parent–child attachment patterns in the deaf population. Attachment is a critical theoretical perspective and developmental framework for understanding healthy development. The research on attachment security in deaf children and in deaf adults is largely positive. Despite the potential risks posed to deaf children for forming secure attachments, the majority of deaf children and deaf adults form secure attachments. A review of the attachment literature focusing on the deaf population reveals that in spite of the proposed "risk" of being deaf, as it relates to attachment security, deaf individuals are resilient.

Theory of Mind and Development of Deaf Children

As children grow, the attachment behavioral system becomes an internalized mental representation of attachment figures and other important figures in their lives. These representations contain the beliefs about and scripts for how to behave with other people. The first attachment relationships guide children as they develop their "theories" of what other people are like. The ability to understand the mental states of others is an important skill that is used daily as children decide how to behave when interacting with others and is critical successful relationships with others. This ability to understand other people has been termed "theory of mind" (Flavell, 1999; Premack & Woodruff, 1978). A number of studies have examined the development of theory of mind in deaf children, providing an interesting picture on how deaf children develop this skill, along with particular considerations for encouraging its development in this population. Similarly, a number of studies have also examined deaf children's understanding of facial expressions and other emotional cues in general as a way of studying how deaf children understand others.

When considering risk and resilience in deaf children, a review of literature in the area of understanding others' emotions is helpful. Accurately understanding others is a skill that is needed when playing or working with others as well as when attempting to solicit support or help from caregivers. Research focusing on these constructs in deaf children has demonstrated that development of this skill may be challenging, particularly for deaf children with limited language development. Understanding the emotions of others is a broad topic that can be conceptualized and measured in various ways. Understanding emotions in others, at a basic level, requires a child to observe a person's behavior and infer what their internal emotional state is, then apply a label to that experience. Previous research has demonstrated that by the age of 3, children have some basic understandings of mental thought. They are able to identify mental states as a characteristic of humans and themselves and use facial expressions to label emotions. A number of studies have examined these preliminary skills of understanding others' emotions through the examination of deaf children's ability to recognize emotion.

Emotion recognition is considered a primary skill needed for social adaptation, that, if undeveloped, impedes social interaction and the ability to understand emotions in more complex ways. The available research on emotion recognition in deaf children provides mixed results. Early studies demonstrated that deaf children are more likely than their hearing counterparts to make errors in recognition of emotional facial expressions (Bachara, Raphael, & Phelan, 1980). The number of errors in this study was related to age of onset of hearing loss. Results demonstrated that children who were deaf before they acquired language performed more poorly than those who lost their hearing after language acquisition (Bachara et al., 1980).

Similar results were found in another study that compared deaf children and adolescents with blind and hearing and sighted controls (Dyck, Farrugia, Shochet, & Holmes-Brown, 2004). Results indicated that while deaf adolescents performed better on emotion recognition tasks than deaf children, their performance was lower than both blind and hearing and sighted adolescents. The authors also noted that deaf children performed with deficits equal to children with autism (Dyck et al., 2004).

Other studies, however, have shown no difference in deaf and hearing children's ability to recognize emotion. One study found no differences between deaf and hearing children when the task required that the children match the emotion rather than identify it alone (Russell et al., 1998). Another study reported similar findings. In their sample, 6- and 10-year old deaf children were as accurate as hearing children in predicting and evaluating the emotional responses of others (Rieffe, Meerum Terwogt, Martens, & Smit, 2000). The research participants, however, were involved in emotion awareness training.

However, emotion recognition is only a part of the complex cognitive task of understanding another person. Between the ages of 4 and 5, typically developing children acquire a more complex understanding of mental states. At this age, children have the capacity to understand that different people can have differing perspectives, beliefs, and perceptions. Children also begin to understand that their beliefs, and mental states, as well as those of others can change, and that it is possible to have more than one perspective on things (Wellman, 1990). This also allows the child to understand that some of the mental representations that people have, or they have themselves, may be false or inaccurate (Flavell, Miller, & Miller, 1993; Wellman, 1990) and can influence behavior. These abilities are considered to be the cornerstone of theory of mind.

In research investigating theory of mind, the ability is measured in a number of ways. One of the most popular methods is the false belief task (Wimmer & Perner, 1983). In these tasks, children are typically told a story about a person who holds a false belief and are then asked to predict their behavior. A correct answer would be one demonstrating that the child understands that the individual in the story would act according to that false belief (Wellman, 1988). Perspective-taking tasks (Flavell, Everett, Croft, & Flavell, 1981) are also a popular measure of theory of mind as are appearance-reality distinction tasks (Flavell, Flavell, & Green, 1983).

Peterson and Siegal published the earliest research examining 8–13-year-old deaf children's theory of mind in 1995. They reported that the majority of the children were unable to successfully complete the task, which is typically achieved by most 4-year-old hearing children. The study was then replicated in 1997 with a larger sample and produced similar results (Peterson & Siegal, 1997). This study has been criticized, however, because the children were only required to complete one task, and the study itself did not provide information on why the children had difficulty in completing the task.

Available research is not unanimous in the finding that deaf children possess a less developed sense of theory of mind compared to their peers, as demonstrated in the previously mentioned studies by Russell et al. (1998) and Rieffe et al. (2000). However, research replicating these findings has not been widely published. Additionally, these studies did not provide specific information on what made these children successful on the chosen measurement of theory of mind. Subsequent research on theory of mind in deaf children has more closely examined and compared deaf children with different backgrounds in an attempt to increase our understanding of how theory of mind is developed and fostered in deaf children with differing language and developmental backgrounds.

Several studies have noted differences in development of theory of mind between deaf children who are native signers or deaf children of deaf parents, and deaf children of hearing parents. One study compared the performance of 59 deaf children and 22 autistic children to 21 hearing children on a theory of mind task (Peterson & Siegal, 1999). The researchers found varying performance on theory of mind measures depending on the linguistic background of the child. Results revealed that native signers and oral deaf children from deaf families performed similarly to hearing children on the theory of mind task. Deaf children from hearing families, however, performed significantly worse (Peterson & Siegal, 1999).

As a result of research findings demonstrating differences between native signers and deaf children of hearing parents, subsequent research closely examined the role of language competency in theory of mind. It was proposed that the noted differences between native signers and deaf children of hearing parents likely resulted from their differing backgrounds in language exposure. Researchers have argued that development of theory of mind is connected to language, and certain mastery of language syntax must be present to develop this skill (de Villiers & de Villiers, 2000). It has also been proposed that in addition to language comprehension, exposure to discussion about theory of mind or the emotional states of others is critical for its development in children (Siegal, Varley, & Want, 2001).

Several studies have attempted to control for the linguistic demands of many theory of mind tests in an effort to see if modifying the test itself would produce more equivalent results between deaf of deaf and deaf of hearing children. Woolfe, Want, and Siegal (2002) conducted two studies investigating the role of language ability on theory of mind. They compared native deaf signers with deaf children raised by hearing parents who were classified as "late signers." In order to reduce the language demand of traditional theory of mind tests, the participant's ability to understand other people's thoughts, desires, and beliefs were tested using a series of "thought pictures."

Results revealed that even when controlling for factors of language, such as syntax and mental age in spatial ability, as well as controlling for executive functioning, deaf late signers still showed deficits in concepts of theory of mind when compared with deaf native signers and hearing children (Woolfe et al., 2002). In fact, despite the fact that the chronological age of the native signers was younger than the late signers, the former group of children still outperformed the latter. The researchers argue that this is evidence that theory of mind is primarily developed through social interaction and exposure to conversations regarding mental states. Other researchers have also demonstrated that deaf children raised in a spoken language environment show a developmental delay in theory of mind when compared to native signers (Peterson & Siegal, 1995; Russell et al., 1998; Schick, de Villiers, de Villiers, & Hoffmeister, 2007).

More specific investigations of language modalities of deaf children have been carried out as well. Meristo et al. (2007) compared children from various language modalities and linguistic educational environments. Using children from three countries, Italy, Estonia, and Sweden, he showed that children in the bilingual program performed best and the native signers in the bilingual program outperformed the bilingually instructed late signers as well as native signers attending oral-only programs (Meristo et al., 2007). The researchers hypothesized that access to sign language in a bilingual environment produces more opportunity to participate and observe conversations about abstract emotions and thus supports development of theory of mind, especially for native signers (Meristo et al., 2007).

In a study by Frey (1998), deaf children as a whole were compared with hearing children in a study that controlled for the linguistic demands of traditional theory of mind tests. Frey administered two theory-of-mind tasks to deaf children between 3 and 10 years of age. The tasks minimized linguistic demands in both administration and response. Results indicated that, particularly in older deaf children, general linguistic ability, assessed separately, was more influential to performance on the task than chronological age (Frey, 1998).

With the emphasis on language acquisition and mastery as it relates to theory of mind, it is not surprising that research has begun to emerge investigating theory of mind in deaf children with cochlear implants. Peterson (2004) examined theory of mind in 26 oral deaf children, half with hearing aids and half with cochlear implants. Within each of these groups, half of the children attended oral-only schools and the other half attended signing and oral schools. No significant differences were found between any of the groups. As a whole, the deaf children performed at a level equivalent to their peers with autism, and the hearing control group scored higher than all other groups (Peterson, 2004). Another study investigating theory of mind in deaf children with cochlear implants found that, controlling for age, theory of mind was positively correlated with language ability (Macaulay & Ford, 2006). This study, however, did not include a comparison group of deaf children without cochlear implants.

The current research on theory of mind in deaf children with cochlear implants is extremely limited. As the number of children with cochlear implants continues to grow, inclusion of this population in studies of this nature is needed. At least one of the research studies in this area initially hypothesized that because cochlear implant children have access to sound, their development of theory of mind could differ from, and perhaps exceed, that of children without cochlear implants (Macaulay & Ford, 2006). The available research thus far has not demonstrated that children with cochlear implants have superior or differing understandings of theory of mind. This is likely due to the fact that currently there is no conclusive evidence that children with cochlear implants have superior language skills compared to deaf children without cochlear implants (Spencer & Marschark, 2003).

Parental hearing status will influence both choice of communication mode and quality of communication. Courtin and Melot (1998) suggest that deaf children of deaf parents have an advantage over other deaf children in a number of ways. These children receive early exposure to language and experience the benefit of a more natural communication match compared to deaf children of hearing parents. In addition, the researchers argued that the linguistic components of sign language might also promote development of theory of mind. Specifically, they suggest the use of spatial mapping in signed languages helps promote perspective taking. Additionally, beyond language skill (although perhaps because of it), deaf children of deaf parents participate in more complex interactions, are exposed to more conversations about mental states, and engage in more pretend play. The researchers also propose that deaf children of deaf parents may exhibit lower levels of impulsiveness, have increased self-concept, and develop critical cognitive skills earlier, and more completely, than deaf children with hearing parents (Courtin & Melot, 1998).

Deaf children of hearing parents have a vastly different experience. These children are exposed to language later and, as noted in previous research, often have less developed language skills as a result. In addition, the communication between the parent and child is less rich, less abstract, and less abundant (Courtin & Melot, 1998). Additionally, hearing parents of deaf children have been shown to be more controlling of their child's play, and language is restrained. As a result, the interaction between the parent–child dyad may negatively impact the child's cognitive flexibility and thus theory of mind (Courtin & Melot, 1998).

While the effects of each of these variables was not measured individually and conclusively determined to be directly related to development of theory of mind, Courtin & Melot (1998) point out an important consideration when interpreting existing research on theory of mind in deaf children. They suggest that we look not only at language skill but also how and why language skill influences development of theory of mind and how it interacts with other variables. Relationship variables between the mother and child (attachment security), characteristics of the mother (anxiety levels, resolution of grief, and attitudes about deafness), and characteristics of the parents (self-esteem, emotional regulation, and executive functioning) should also be explored.

In terms of risk and skills that help protect children, the available information provides us with some insights as they relate to theory of mind. First, the characteristic of deafness, in the audiological sense, is not itself an isolated risk for deaf children in the development of theory of mind. This has been demonstrated in several studies indicating that deaf native signers, despite their hearing loss, have performed at levels equivalent to hearing peers. We also know that a number of factors (language skill and others) influence the development of theory of mind. These factors can be conceptualized as risks (e.g., limited language, lack of exposure to conversation about other people's emotions) and as skills that protect children and thereby foster resilience (e.g., improving the quality of play between deaf children and hearing parents). We also know that although research has demonstrated deficits in some deaf children's theory of mind, it can be improved through training and education and frequently improves with age. Theory of mind has important implications for development and functioning throughout the lifespan, and it can be said that children with developed theory of mind have an additional skill set that is critical for positive social interaction. This, in turn, increases the likelihood that these children will be resilient when encountering developmental challenges. As our understanding of theory of mind in deaf children increases, so will our knowledge of how to encourage and promote it, fostering more resilient deaf children.

Self-Concept and Sense of Self

In addition to developing schema that represent other important people, children also develop schema that represent themselves. Self-concept refers to this psychological representation of oneself, the internal representation of one's strengths, weaknesses, likes, dislikes, habits, and personality. Self-esteem, as Harter (1982, 1999) notes, refers to the evaluations we make of ourselves in different areas and the importance that we attach to that area (for example, how important is it to be good at sports, and how good at sports am I?). Both self-concept and self-esteem are forged in social interactions where children (and adults) use the appraisals they see in others around them to make judgments about their own worth. Parents and, later, peers, become the mirrors which the child uses to come to an understanding of the self. Positive feedback on one's efforts and accomplishments, acceptance by important people, and a differentiation of characteristics leads to a coherent and positive sense of one's self.

Numerous theorists and researchers have discussed the importance of self-esteem for psychological adjustment (Erikson, 1968; Rogers, 1951, 1980; Sullivan, 1947). Having a coherent and strong sense of self can free up energy to focus on learning skills, allow individuals to take risks (such as trying new activities or joining new groups), and allow one to look objectively at one's own behavior, changing that behavior as needed (Mikulincer & Shaver, 2008).

Current investigators tend to view self-concept as multidimensional, involving different aspects of oneself (Harter, 1982; Piers & Harris, 1984; Shavelson, Hubner, & Stanton, 1976). Children, as well as adolescents and adults, view their various characteristics differently and begin to assess themselves as being complex and varying. This development requires the ability to coordinate differing views of the same person, which is typically not established in children until later preschool ages or elementary school. Harter (1982) demonstrated that, by age 8, the majority of children could clearly distinguish between different types of specific self-esteem. They can separately evaluate academic competence, athletic abilities, and social self-worth. Yetman and Brice (2002) found that deaf children also distinguish between different areas of self-esteem, and like hearing children, exhibit lower self-esteem when their evaluation of their competence in a particular area contrasts with their perception of how important it is to be competent in that area.

Models of self-esteem generally attribute great importance to peer relations in the formation and maintenance of self-esteem. The ability to form successful relationships with peers is seen as integral in the development of positive feelings about the self (Altshuler, 1974). Further, good peer relations in childhood are good predictors of adjustment in adolescence and adulthood (Parker & Asher, 1987; Patterson, Capaladi, & Bank, 1990; Serbin, Schwatzman, Moskowitz, & Ledingham, 1990). Past investigators discovered significant correlations between self-esteem and popularity (Coie, Dodge, & Cappotelli, 1982; Withycombe, 1973). Cantrell and Prinz (1985) found the relationship between these two variables to be curvilinear. Peers accepted children with moderately high levels of self-esteem more than children with low self-esteem. However, as self-esteem increased beyond a reasonable level, peer acceptance decreased.

Yetman and Brice (2002) investigated the self-concept/self-esteem of deaf children in inclusion or mainstream educational programs in the USA looking particularly at whether the number of deaf children in the program made a difference for self-esteem. She found that the number of hours per week spent in classes with primarily hearing children is a very important variable. Those deaf students who spent the greatest amount of time in classes with hearing peers reported lower levels of global self-esteem as well as academic, social, and behavior self-esteem in comparison to those deaf students who spent the least amount of time in regular classrooms. Furthermore, their hearing peers typically ignored the vast majority of deaf children attending those public school programs when all students were asked about their peers. As opposed to being chosen as popular or unpopular, deaf students were uniformly overlooked completely.

van Gurp (2001) also looked at self-concept in deaf students in Canada. She compared three school settings, segregated (schools for the deaf), congregated (a deaf program in a public school), or resource. General school self-esteem was better in resource than in congregated or segregated schools, a finding that was not predicted. However, it was found that segregated settings appeared to offer some other advantages. Children in those settings appeared to have stronger self-concepts in the area of physical appearance, peer relationships, and general self-worth. Teachers noted that when deaf students changed to the congregated or resource settings, that they began to dress differently, attempting to blend in with the fashions of the new school.

This last finding could be related to the fact that in Yetman and Brice's (2002) data, deaf children who used hearing children as their referent groups for comparison had significantly lower levels of self-esteem than those deaf children who compared themselves with other deaf peers. The present results suggest that the more hours a student spends in a special education classroom, the more likely that student is to use fellow deaf peers as a referent group. If deaf students do not feel part of the hearing class, then the lack of friendships or connections may not bother them. However, for the deaf child who receives all or the majority of his/her education in a regular classroom and gets pulled for support only for a brief period each day, such removal may serve to create feelings of disconnection and isolation from hearing classmates. Since such a student spends the majority of his/her time with hearing peers, the hearing group becomes the reference group and self-esteem appears to be negatively affected.

These data fit with results that Gregory reported on approximately 80 families with deaf children that have been followed longitudinally for 25 years (Gregory, 1998). Gregory documented that the vast majority of deaf young people gravitate toward other deaf people as their friends and mates. While hearing students and youth are finding their friends in school, deaf youth are finding them in deaf clubs and at formal and informal deaf events. This can be influenced by the communication pattern that a deaf person uses as they grow up. Oral deaf youth may spend less time with other deaf mates and instead report more hearing friends.

A study conducted by Esposito (2005) investigated the social functioning and self-esteem of deaf children who had received cochlear implants and were being educated in hearing school environments. She found that, according to both the children themselves and their parents, social functioning with hearing children was "adequate." She stated, "…it can be inferred that the majority of these children feel relatively at ease in the presence of other hearing children, generally get along well with hearing peers, and have more than one close hearing friend from school" (Esposito, 2005, p. 80). Furthermore, these children appeared to have levels of self-esteem that ranged from medium to high on all subscales of the Self-Perception Profile for Children and reported high levels of overall or global self-worth. Esposito concluded that the results highlighted the importance of good communication "matches" between parents and children.

Beyond type of school setting, self-concept in deaf children has been assessed to determine its standing relative to hearing children. The question is whether deaf children, by nature of not hearing are more likely to have lowered levels of self-esteem or self-concept. Here, the data is less clear, with measurement issues clouding the data. Bat-Chava (1993), for example, showed that in self-report measures, written vs. signed method of measure administration made a significant difference in the results. Prout (1999) also argued that standard self-report measures may not be appropriate because the deaf adolescents she interviewed in her research on self-understanding showed that deafness and hearing loss was a major part of their self-understanding. This is not a characteristic that is typically included in most self-report measures of self-concept or self-esteem.

Obrzut, Maddock, and Lee (1999 reviewed 18 studies available at the time that investigated self-concept in deaf children. Their conclusions were first that deaf children from deaf families do better with respect to self-esteem. Secondly, they concluded that deaf children from residential schools had self-esteem levels that were most closely aligned with hearing children.

Prout's (1999) study, while based on a small sample size, is highly relevant to a discussion of resilience and challenges in deaf children and youth. When deaf children are younger, deafness tends to be defined in terms of external characteristics such as use of hearing aids. However, by the time they are adolescents, deafness as an issue of identity is integral. Given that data seems to generally support the notion that deaf children may feel more isolated and neglected in their school settings, that self-esteem may decrease with age for oral deaf students (Silvestre, Ramspott, & Pareto, 2007), and peers gain in importance, it is logical to conclude that deaf children have more challenges to developing a coherent sense of self than nondeaf children.

Self-Regulation and Executive Functioning

A last topic to be discussed turns from a discussion of internal cognitive understandings to a behavior management skill. The ability to self-regulate, monitor, and modulate one's own behavior is critical for overall adjustment and positive sense of self.

Developing the ability to relate to others in a positive manner, forming a positive and coherent sense of self, and an understanding of other people all require that the child attend to the experiences they are having and, to some extent, reflect on them. Self-regulation is that ability to stop and think before acting, allowing cognitive processes to enter the situation and determine various alternatives, along with an evaluation of the efficacy of those alternatives. Self-regulation comes under the umbrella term of executive functioning, which has become a topic of intense theoretical and research interest in the past 15 years.

Historically, research with deaf children has reported data that is less than optimistic in terms of self-regulation development. Meadow and Schlesinger (1971) in their groundbreaking research on deaf children found that, according to teachers and counselors, behavior problems in the deaf students at schools for the deaf in California were five times the rate of those in the Los Angeles school system. Altshuler, Deming, Vollenweider, Rainer, & Taylor (1976) administered what they termed measures of impulsivity to deaf adolescents and found that the deaf youngsters in their sample were more impulsive, less mature, and less flexible than the hearing participants. It should be noted that some of these measures may have had questionable use as instruments for measuring impulsivity.

Freeman, Malkin, and Hastings (1975) looked at psychosocial development in hearing families with deaf children, collecting data from mothers and teachers. They reported that the mothers, in particular, described their children as being more difficult, having problems in compliance with adult requests, and being more restless. Chess and Fernandez (1980) also reported that children who were deaf secondary to maternal rubella showed higher levels of impulsive behavior, even if there were no other documented cognitive deficits. Reivich and Rothrock (1972) studied 327 children from a state school for the deaf and found that there was a higher frequency of behaviors rated in the hyperactive "dyscontrol" factor, related to conduct, in both deaf girls and boys.

These studies almost uniformly concluded that deaf children had more struggles with self-regulation than their hearing peers. One limitation of many of these studies, however, was the reliance on reports of adults regarding the child's behavior. This is especially critical since none of the measures used had norms that included a well-developed deaf sample, and hearing adults may not always be sensitive to the sorts of behaviors that deaf children exhibit which are part and parcel of the Deaf world and living as a Deaf person in the world. Mitchell and Quittner (1996) assessed attention and related behaviors in deaf children using several performance measures of attention including a Continuous Performance Test (the Gordon CPT) as well as child behavior rating scales for parents and teachers. More of the deaf children performed in the "Borderline to Abnormal" range on the three subtests (Delay, Vigilance, and Distractibility) of the CPT than their hearing counterparts. Mitchell and Quittner (1996) concluded that difficulties on these tasks were related to impulsivity and sustained attention or memory.

Sporn (1997) studied ADHD in deaf children, specifically investigating the performance of deaf children on the Test of Variables of Attention (TOVA), one of the widely used continuous performance tests as well as studying how these children were rated by their teachers using the Conner's Teacher Rating Scale. She found that children in her sample demonstrated more difficulty on the TOVA than their hearing peers, with both more errors of inattention and errors of impulsivity. Furthermore, the children who performed the worst were also rated by their teachers as having more attention related problems than deaf children who were more skilled on the TOVA. These data are important as the TOVA does not use any language-based stimuli and does not involve short-term memory demands, which may confound results for deaf children.

One explanation for the findings that deaf children struggle more with self-regulation and controlling or inhibiting impulses involves the delays with language that many deaf children exhibit. Language, specifically pragmatic language, has been implicated in the development of executive functioning skills, as well as self-concept and identity. The internal dialogue in which children engage about them-selves allows for the development of self-regulation. Studies with hearing children have found a connection between language difficulties and Attention Deficit Hyperactivity Disorder (ADHD) (Bain, 2001; Gizzo, 2002; Kim, 2000). Children diagnosed with ADHD have been shown to score lower on measures of pragmatic language. Kim's (2000) study is illustrative. Young hearing children (6–8 years old) with ADHD had similar semantic knowledge as their non-ADHD peers, but made many more communication errors, including interrupting, not answering or responding to their partner's questions or comments, and providing less feedback. Torres and Arocho (2001) in their study of language in planning and problem solving found that ADHD children had more verbal and off-task interruptions. They sug-gested that these behaviors interfered with the use of language as a tool for monitoring, evaluating, and regulating one's own behavior.

There is research with deaf children that bears directly on Barkley's (1997) hybrid model and his notion of the role of language in executive functions and self-regulation. First, Harris (1978) studied deaf children of deaf parents in comparison with deaf children who had hearing parents; it was assumed that the children of deaf parents had better developed language than those deaf children with hearing parents. In his study, the results suggested strongly that deaf children of deaf parents had greater control over their own behaviors and that they had a better developed ability to reflect on the task in which they were engaged.

Kalback (2004) set out to study specifically the link between language develop-ment and executive functioning in deaf children. In her earlier work (Rhine [Kalback], 2002), she found that deaf children were rated as having more trouble in three specific aspects of executive functioning: inhibition of impulses, flexibly shifting tasks, and working memory. These scores were based on parent ratings from the Behavior Rating Inventory of Executive Functioning (BRIEF). The inhibit and working memory scales, in particular, are effective predictors of ADHD in hearing children. In her second study, Kalback administered a range of language measures as well as a number of measures of executive functioning, including the BRIEF once again and hands-on measures of planning and organization and prob-lem solving. She found that both pragmatic aspects of language and simple vocabu-lary knowledge in sign language were significantly related with a summary measure of executive functioning as well as with specific measures of inhibitory control. Kalback (2004) concluded that her data were consistent with Barkley's (1997) ideas about internal speech being used to help with self-regulation and organization of behavior.

Furthermore, Kalback's (2004) data revealed that language and executive functioning, taken together, significantly predicted ratings of social skills, with executive functioning explaining more than language measures. Children with better developed executive functioning skills also were rated as having better developed social skills; in turn, executive functioning was predicted by better language development.

The data available to date suggest a complex and most likely bidirectional relationship between various aspects of development. Self-concept is related to a significant degree with feedback from the social world. Better adjustment in the social world and better skills to deal with the social world are predicted by executive functioning and self-regulation, which is aided by language development. Better self-regulation also allows for better language development by facilitating joint attention and longer and more complex conversations about more complicated and subtle aspects of the world. This in turn also provides the child with the tools necessary to reflect more deeply about their experiences and integrate them into a sense of self and a sense of other, particularly being able to predict the affective responses of others.

Conclusion

At this point, we return to the scientist who quipped that for every complex problem there is a simple solution that is completely wrong. The dynamics at play between various factors in a deaf child's development are complex, multiply determined, and subject to influences that cannot be predicted. Risk, protective factors, and resilience can be seen as independent, though related, constructs. Children experience different levels of risk. Some children with limited internal resources and born into impoverished families struggling with mental health issues may be at very high risk; those with great internal resources born into families that are well supported and capable may experience less risk. Similarly, some children may show themselves to be highly resilient, apparently coping with any number of challenges; others seem to struggle even when there is great support. When exploring risk and resilience, it is critical to explore potential factors that lie within the child and in the environmental context. What demands are placed on a child by the environment and what skills are needed to manage those demands?

The data regarding development in deaf children is woefully incomplete and does not provide any unequivocal answers regarding risk or resilience in deaf children. Yet, it appears that deaf people as adults demonstrate resilience. In a study with deaf mothers, Leigh et al. (2004) analyzed transcripts from the AAI, a semi-structured interview that asks about relationships with both parents as well as a series of questions about the changes in those relationships. The transcripts were then evaluated for narrative coherence, not the content that is recalled. What was striking was that in the 32 deaf women who participated, even those with hearing parents, were overwhelmingly forgiving of their parents. There was acknowledgement of problems in communication or differences of opinion regarding school choices, but these women explained that their parents generally did the best they could. Experiences that could have led to frustration, anger, and depression had been transformed into something more positive. In other words, what may have been considered factors of risk were not perceived as detrimental in reflections of adult deaf women.

In our review of relevant research, we explored the development of skills fostering understanding self (self-concept and self-regulation) and understanding others (theory of mind and attachment). It is our belief that acquired skills in these domains have major implications for the overall development of the child. Within each of these constructs, we examined factors of risk and factors of resilience. The message we can take from the research presented here is that the relationship context is crucial.

A common theme throughout the research reviewed in this chapter is an emphasis on language mastery, parent–child reciprocity and interaction, and communication. While there is still much we need to know, research has identified specific patterns in these domains that encourage healthy development and promote (or can alone be considered factors of) resilience. Within each section reviewed, there was an emphasis on communication. Communication and formal language must grow from a relationship. The relationships that are founded upon sensitivity and attunement provide the opportunity to develop a joint language. In turn, language as an effective tool provides the means whereby children can develop more elaborated schemas of other people. Language seems to be the path toward mastering one's own impulses, which makes space for children to reflect on others, developing their theories of what other people may think and feel, and how that differs from their own experience. This then leads to children developing a coherent and organized sense of self and a sense of general satisfaction with that sense of self. All of these emerge from the relationship context.

A major implication of this hypothesis is that helping deaf children to be resilient means helping that parent–child or caregiver–child unit. We know that children are easily sensitive to emotions in others, especially their parents or other very important people. It is not enough for parents to just say that they enjoy their children. They must truly enjoy them. It is not enough to say that they have learned a great deal from having a deaf child. They must truly be open to learning.

We are encouraged by all of the positive findings that the literature reports. Many deaf children have secure attachments to parents (hearing and deaf alike), develop understandings of others, and come to feel positively about themselves. The clinics of our cities are not filled to capacity with deaf adults who cannot cope with their worlds. It is our responsibility now to provide families with the support they need to enhance the protective environmental factors that all children need to develop to their full potential.

References

Altshuler, K. Z. (1974). The social and psychological development of the deaf child: Problems, their treatment and prevention. *American Annals of the Deaf, 119*, 365–376.

Altshuler, K. Z., Deming, W. E., Vollenweider, J., Rainer, J. D., & Taylor, R. (1976). Impulsivity and profound early deafness: A cross-cultural inquiry. *American Annals of the Deaf, 121*, 331–345.

Amber, J. L., Belsky, J., Slade, A., & Crnic, K. (1999). Stability and change in mothers' representations of their relationship with their toddlers. *Developmental Psychology, 35*, 1038–1047.

Bachara, G. H., Raphael, J., & Phelan, W. J. (1980). Empathy development in deaf preadolescents. *American Annals of the Deaf, 125*(1), 38–41.

Bain, J. L. (2001). Language development in children with attention deficit disorder. *Dissertation Abstracts International, Section B: The Sciences and Engineering, 61*, 10-B.

Barkley, R. A. (1997). *ADHD and the nature of self-control*. New York: Guilford.

Bat-Chava, Y. (1993). Antecedents of self-esteem in deaf people: A meta-analytic review. *Rehabilitation Psychology, 38*(4), 221–234.

Beck, A. T. (1978). *The depression inventory*. Philadelphia: Center for Cognitive Therapy.

Bowlby, J. (1969/1982). *Attachment* (Attachment and loss, Vol. 1). New York: Basic.

Britner, P. A., Marvin, R. S., & Pianta, R. C. (2005). Development and preliminary validation of the caregiving behavior system: Association with child attachment classification in the preschool strange situation. *Attachment and Human Development, 7*(1), 83–102.

Bronfenbrenner, U. (1979). *The ecology of human development*. Cambridge: Harvard University Press.

Bronfenbrenner, U. (2005). Interacting systems in human development. In U. Bronfenbrenner (Ed.), *Making human beings human: Bioecological perspectives on human development* (pp. 3–15). Thousand Oaks, CA: Sage.

Cantrell, V. I., & Prinz, R. J. (1985). Multiple perspectives of rejected, neglected, and accepted children: Relation between sociometric status and behavioral characteristics. *Journal of Consulting and Ethical Psychology, 53*(6), 884–889.

Cassidy, J., & Shaver, P. R. (Eds.). (1999). *Handbook of attachment: Theory, research, and clinical application*. New York: Guilford.

Cassidy, J., & Shaver, P. R. (Eds.). (2008). *Handbook of attachment: Theory, research, and clinical application* (2nd ed.). New York: Guildford.

Chess, S., & Fernandez, P. (1980). Impulsivity in rubella deaf children: A longitudinal study. *American Annals of the Deaf, 125*, 505–509.

Chovaz McKinnon, C., Moran, G., & Pederson, D. (2004). Attachment representations of deaf adults. *Journal of Deaf Studies and Deaf Education, 9*(4), 366–386.

Coie, J. D., Dodge, K. A., & Cappotelli, H. A. (1982). Dimensions and types of social status: A cross-age perspective. *Developmental Psychology, 18*, 557–569.

Courtin, C., & Melot, A. (1998). Development of theories of mind in deaf children. In M. Marschark & M. D. Clark (Eds.), *Psychological perspectives on deafness* (Vol. 2, pp. 79–102). Mahwah: Lawrence Erlbaum.

de Villiers, J. G., & de Villiers, P. A. (2000). Linguistic determinism and the understanding of false beliefs. In P. Mitchell & K. Riggs (Eds.), *Children's reasoning and the mind*. Hove, UK: Psychology Press.

Dyck, M. J., Farrugia, C., Shochet, I. M., & Holmes-Brown, M. (2004). Emotion recognition/understanding ability in hearing or vision-impaired children: Do sounds, sights, or words make the difference? *Journal of Child Psychology and Psychiatry, 45*(4), 789–800.

Erikson, E. H. (1968). *Identity, youth and crisis*. New York: W.W. Norton.

Esposito, L. J. (2005). *Oral communication ability, social functioning, and self-esteem among mainstreamed deaf children with cochlear implants: A longitudinal study*. Unpublished doctoral dissertation, Gallaudet University, Washington, DC.

Faschingbauer, T. R. (1981). *Texas revised inventory of grief manual*. Houston: Honeycomb.

Flavell, J. H. (1999). Cognitive development: Children's knowledge about the mind. *Annual Review of Psychology, 50*, 21–45.

Flavell, J. H., Everett, B. A., Croft, K., & Flavell, E. R. (1981). Young children's knowledge about visual perception: Further evidence for the level 1–level 2 distinction. *Developmental Psychology, 17*, 99–103.

Flavell, J. H., Flavell, E. R., & Green, E. L. (1983). Development of the appearance-reality distinction. *Cognitive Psychology, 15*, 95–120.

Flavell, J. H., Miller, P. H., & Miller, S. (1993). *Cognitive development* (3rd ed.). Englewood Cliffs: Prentice-Hall.

Freeman, R. D., Malkin, S. F., & Hastings, J. O. (1975). Psychosocial problems of deaf children and their families: A comparative study. *American Annals of the Deaf, 120*, 391–405.

Frey, R. J. (1998). General linguistic competency in the deaf: A prerequisite for developing a theory of mind? [Dissertation] *Dissertation Abstracts International Section A: Humanities and Social Sciences, 59*, 1903.

George, C., Kaplan, N., & Main, M. (1984). *The Berkeley adult attachment interview*. Unpublished manuscript, University of California at Berkeley.

George, C., Kaplan, N., & Main, M. (1985). *The Berkeley adult attachment interview*. (2nd ed.). Unpublished manuscript, University of California at Berkeley.

George, C., Kaplan, N., & Main, M. (1996). *The Berkeley adult attachment interview*. (3rd ed.). Unpublished manuscript, University of California at Berkeley.

Gizzo, D. P. (2002). Conversation skills and peer rejection among ADHD and comparison boys. *Dissertation Abstracts International: Section B: The Sciences & Engineering, 62*(8-B).

Greenberg, M. T., & Marvin, R. S. (1979). Attachment patterns in profoundly deaf school children. *Merrill-Palmer Quarterly, 25*, 265–279.

Gregory, S. (1998). Deaf young people: Aspects of family and social life. In M. Marschark & D. Clark (Eds.), *Psychological perspectives on deafness* (Vol. 2). Mahwah, NJ: Lawrence Erlbaum.

Hadadian, A. (1995). Attitudes toward deafness and security of attachment relationships among young deaf children and their parents. *Early Education and Development, 6*(2), 181–191.

Harris, R. I. (1978). The relationship of impulse control to parent hearing status, manual communication, and academic achievement in deaf children. *American Annals of the Deaf, 123*, 52–67.

Harter, S. (1982). The perceived competence scale for children. *Child Development, 53*(1), 87–97.

Harter, S. (1999). *The construction of the self: A developmental perspective*. New York: Guildford.

Isabella, R. A., & Belsky, J. (1991). Interactional synchrony and the origins of infant–mother attachment: A replication study. *Child Development, 62*, 373–384.

Kalback, S. R. (2004). *The assessment of developmental language differences, executive functioning, and social skills in deaf children*. Unpublished manuscript, Gallaudet University.

Kim, O. H. (2000). Language characteristics of children with ADHD. *Communication Disorders Quarterly, 21*(3), 154–165.

Lederberg, A. R., & Mobley, C. E. (1990). The effect of hearing impairment on the quality of attachment and mother–toddler interaction. *Child Development, 61*, 1596–1604.

Leigh, I. W., Brice, P. J., & Meadow-Orlans, K. (2004). Attachment in deaf mothers and their children. *Journal of Deaf Studies and Deaf Education, 9*(2), 176–188.

Lyons-Ruth, K., & Spielman, E. (2004). Disorganized infant attachment strategies and helpless-fearful profiles of parenting: Integrating attachment research with clinical intervention. *Infant Mental Health Journal, 25*, 318–335.

Macaulay, C. E., & Ford, R. M. (2006). Language and theory-of-mind development in prelingually deafened children with cochlear implants: A preliminary investigation. *Cochlear Implants International, 7*(1), 1–14.

Main, M., & Hesse, E. (1990). Parents' unresolved traumatic experiences are related to infant disorganized attachment status: Is frightened and/or frightening parental behavior the linking mechanism? In M. T. Greenberg, D. Cicchetti, & E. M. Cummings (Eds.), *Attachment in preschool years: Theory, research, and intervention* (pp. 161–184). Chicago: University of Chicago Press.

Marvin, R. S., & Pianta, R. C. (1996). Mothers' reactions to their child's diagnosis: Relations with security of attachment. *Journal of Clinical Child Psychology, 25*, 436–445.

Meadow, K. P., Greenberg, M. T., & Erting, C. (1984). Attachment behavior of deaf children with deaf parents. In S. Chess & A. Thomas (Eds.), *Annual progress in child psychiatry & child development* (pp. 176–187). New York: Brunner-Mazel.

Meadow, K. P., & Schlesinger, H. (1971). The prevalence of behavioral problems in a population of deaf school children. *American Annals of the Deaf, 116*, 346–348.

Meadow-Orlans, K. P., Mertens, D. M., & Sass-Lehrer, M. (2003). *Parents and their deaf children: The early years*. Washington, DC: Gallaudet University Press.

Meadow-Orlans, K. P., Spencer, P. E., & Koester, L. S. (2004). *The world of deaf infants*. New York: Oxford University Press.

Meristo, M., Falkman, K. W., Hjelmquist, E., Tedoldi, M., Surian, L., & Siegal, M. (2007). Language access and theory of mind reasoning: Evidence from deaf children in bilingual and oralist environments. *Developmental Psychology, 43*(5), 1156–1169.

Mikulincer, M., & Shaver, P. R. (2008). Adult attachment and affect regulation. In J. Cassidy & P. R. Shaver (Eds.), *Handbook of attachment, second edition: Theory, research, and clinical applications*. New York, NY: Guilford.

Mitchell, T. V., & Quittner, A. L. (1996). Multimethod study of attention and behavior problems in hearing-impaired children. *Journal of Clinical Child Psychology, 25*(1), 83–96.

Obrzut, J. E., Maddock, G. J., & Lee, C. P. (1999). Determinants of self-concept in deaf and hard of hearing children. *Journal of Developmental and Physical Disabilities, 11*, 237–251.

Parker, J. G. H., & Asher, S. R. (1987). Peer relations and later personal adjustment: Are low accepted children at risk? *Psychological Bulletin, 102*(3), 357–389.

Patterson, G. R., Capaladi, D., & Bank, L. (1990). An early starter model for predicting delinquency. In D. Pepler & K. Rubin (Eds.), *The development and treatment of childhood aggression* (pp. 139–168). Hillsdale, NJ: Lawrence Erlbaum.

Peterson, C. C. (2004). Theory of mind development in oral deaf children with cochlear implants or conventional hearing aids. *Journal of Child Psychology and Psychiatry, 45*, 1096–1106.

Peterson, C. C., & Siegal, M. (1995). Deafness, conversation and theory of mind. *Journal of Child Psychology, Psychiatry and Allied Disciplines, 36*, 458–474.

Peterson, C. C., & Siegal, M. (1997). Domain specificity and everyday biological, physical, and psychological thinking in normal, autistic, and deaf children. In H. M. Wellman & K. Inagaki (Eds.), *The emergence of core domains of thought: Children's reasoning about physical, psychological, and biological phenomena* (pp. 55–70). San Francisco: Jossey-Bass.

Peterson, C. C., & Siegal, M. (1999). Representing inner worlds: Theory of mind in autistic, deaf, and normal hearing children. *Psychological Science, 10*, 126–129.

Piers, E. V., & Harris, D. B. (1984). *Piers-Harris children's self-concept scale, revised manual*. Los Angeles: Western Psychological Services.

Premack, D., & Woodruff, G. (1978). Does the chimpanzee have a theory of mind? *Behavioral and Brain Sciences, 1*(4), 515–526.

Prout, T. A. (1999). *The development of self-understanding in deaf children*. Unpublished doctoral dissertation, University of Pittsburgh.

Reivich, R. S., & Rothrock, I. A. (1972). Behavior problems of deaf children and adolescents: A factor-analytic study. *Journal of Speech and Hearing Research, 15*, 93–104.

Rhine, S. E. (2002). *Assessment of executive functioning in deaf and hard of hearing children*. Unpublished masters pre-dissertation, Gallaudet University, Washington, District of Columbia.

Rieffe, C., Meerum Terwogt, M., Martens, E., & Smit, C. (2000). The 'theory of mind' of deaf children: The priority of desires [Dutch]. *Pedagogische Studien, 77*(1), 21–32.

Rogers, C. R. (1951). *Client centered therapy: Its current practice, implications and theory*. Boston: Houghton Mifflin Company.

Rogers, C. R. (1980). *A way of being*. Boston: Houghton Mifflin Company.

Russell, P. A., Hosie, J. A., Gray, C. D., Scott, C., Hunter, N., Banks, J. S., et al. (1998). The development of theory of mind in deaf children. *Journal of Child Psychology and Psychiatry, 39*, 903–910.

Schick, B., de Villiers, P., de Villiers, J., & Hoffmeister, R. (2007). Language and theory of mind: A study of deaf children. *Child Development, 78*, 376–396.

Schlesinger, H. S., & Meadow, K. P. (1972). *Sound and sign: Childhood deafness and mental health*. Berkeley, CA: University of California Press.

Serbin, L. A., Schwatzman, A. E., Moskowitz, D. S., & Ledingham, J. E. (1990). Aggressive, withdrawn & aggressive/withdrawn children in adolescence: Into the next generation. In D. Pepler & K. Rubin (Eds.), *The development and treatment of childhood aggression* (pp. 139–168). Hillsdale, NJ: Lawrence Erlbaum.

Shavelson, R. J., Hubner, J. J., & Stanton, J. C. (1976). Self-concept: Validation of construct interpretations. *Review of Educational Research, 46*, 407–441.

Siegal, M., Varley, R., & Want, S. C. (2001). Mind over grammar: Reasoning in aphasia and development. *Trends in Cognitive Sciences, 5*(7), 296–301.

Silvestre, N., Ramspott, A., & Pareto, I. D. (2007). Conversational skills in a semi-structured interview and self-concept in deaf students. *Journal of Deaf Studies and Deaf Education, 12*, 38–54.

Spangler, T. H. (1988). Exploration of the relationship between deaf children's attachment classification in the strange situation and effects of parents' success in grieving and coping. *Dissertation Abstracts International, 49*(1-B), 244.

Spencer, P. E., & Marschark, M. (2003). Cochlear implants: Issues and implications. In M. Marschark & P. E. Spencer (Eds.), *Oxford handbook of deaf studies, language and education* (pp. 434–450). Oxford: Oxford University Press.

Sporn, M. B. (1997). *The assessment of the test of variables of attention with deaf children*. Unpublished pre-dissertation project, Gallaudet University, Washington, DC.

Sroufe, L. A., Egeland, B., Carlson, E. A., & Collins, W. A. (2005). *The development of the person: The Minnesota study of risk and adaptation from birth to adulthood*. New York, NY: Guilford.

Sullivan, H. S. (1947). *Conceptions of modern psychiatry*. Oxford, England: William Alanson White Memorial Lectures.

Torres, M. A. M., & Arocho, W. C. R. (2001). The use of language by boys and girls with characteristics of attention deficit disorder and hyperactivity while planning a task. *Revista Interamericana de Psicologia, 35*(1), 143–162 [From PsychInfo Database, 2002, Article No. 2001-05067-007].

van Gurp, S. (2001). Self-concept of deaf secondary school students in different educational settings. *Journal of Deaf Studies and Deaf Education, 6*(1), 54–69.

Van IJzendoorn, M. H., Goldberg, S., Kroonenberg, P. M., & Frenkel, O. J. (1992). The relative effects of maternal and child problems on the quality of attachment: A meta-analysis of attachment in clinical samples. *Child Development, 63*(4), 840–858.

Weinfield, N. S., Sroufe, L. A., Egeland, B., & Carlson, E. A. (1999). The nature of individual differences in infant–caregiver attachment. In J. Cassidy & P. R. Shaver (Eds.), *Handbook of attachment: Theory, research, and clinical applications* (pp. 68–88). New York: Guilford.

Wellman, H. M. (1988). First steps in the child's theorizing about the mind. In J. Astington, P. Harris, & D. Olson (Eds.), *Developing theories of mind* (pp. 64–92). New York: Cambridge University Press.

Wellman, H. M. (1990). *The child's theory of mind*. Cambridge: MIT.

Wimmer, H., & Perner, J. (1983). Beliefs about beliefs: Representation and constraining function of wrong beliefs in young children's understanding of deception. *Cognition, 13*, 103–128.

Withycombe, J. (1973). Relationships of self-concept, social status and self-perceived social status and racial differences of Paiute Indian and white elementary school children. *Journal of Social Psychology, 91*, 337–338.

Woolfe, T., Want, S. C., & Siegal, M. (2002). Signposts to development: Theory of mind in deaf children. *Child Development, 73*, 768–778.

Yetman, M., & Brice, P. J. (2002). *Peer relations and self-esteem among deaf children in a mainstream school environment*. Unpublished manuscript, Gallaudet University.

Young, A., Green, L., & Rogers, K. (2008). Resilience in deaf children: A literature review. *Deafness and Education International, 10*(1), 40–55.

Chapter 6
Risk and Resilience for Social Competence: Deaf Students in General Education Classrooms

Shirin D. Antia, Susanne Reed, and Linda Shaw

Abstract Increasing numbers of deaf students receive most of their education in general education classrooms. These students may not have easy access to peers and adults with whom they can communicate; consequently professionals have expressed fears that these students will be socially isolated and lack opportunities to develop the social competence necessary for success. We briefly review the available literature on social competence of deaf students in general education classrooms, paying particular attention to student-related, school-related, and family-related factors that influence risk and resiliency. Student-related risk factors include the presence of a hearing loss (however mild) and lack of social maturity due to age; resilience factors include an outgoing personality, good communication skills, and the ability to self-advocate. School-related risk factors include school transitions (e.g., from elementary to middle school); resilience factors include opportunities to work collaboratively and become familiar with hearing peers; access to extra-curricular activities; and stable, continuing services from teachers of the deaf. Family-related risk factors include lack of resources; resilience factors include parental communication with school personnel and social coaching by parents. Case studies of three deaf students are provided to illustrate the effects of risk and resilience factors. Although there continue to be gaps in our knowledge of the social competence of deaf students in general education classrooms, the current literature indicates that these students are not necessarily lonely or isolated. However, additional research on how to minimize risk and increase resilience is needed.

Deaf children have long been considered a population at risk for difficulties in developing social competence because of the negative effects of hearing loss on language and communication development. This is particularly true for deaf children of hearing parents. In a classic article, Meadow (1980) suggested that the communication and language difficulties experienced by many deaf children result

S.D. Antia (✉)
Department of Disability and Psychoeducational Studies,
University of Arizona – Tucson, Tucson, AZ, USA

D.H. Zand and K.J. Pierce (eds.), *Resilience in Deaf Children: Adaptation Through Emerging Adulthood*, DOI 10.1007/978-1-4419-7796-0_6,
© Springer Science+Business Media, LLC 2011

in experiential deficiencies that, in turn, negatively influence their social maturity (Meadow, 1980). Specific areas of social delay may include the development of emotional understanding, and predicting the motivation and feelings of others (Greenberg & Kusche, 1993). More recently, researchers studying the development of Theory of Mind suggest that language focuses children's attention on mental explanations of behavior and provides them with a vocabulary for abstract concepts such as thoughts and feelings (Schick, deVilliers, deVilliers, & Hoffmeister, 2007). Such a vocabulary, in turn, plays an important role in understanding the feelings, motivation and actions of others that is essential to the development of social relations. The lack of full accessibility to language and communication therefore can negatively influence deaf children's social development.

Deaf children's difficulties in acquiring social competence can also be attributed to their inability to pick up incidental cues about social behavior from the people around them and from "linguistic overprotection" (Calderon & Greenberg, 2003; Greenberg & Kusche, 1993). Most children learn social behavior by incidental and passive exposure to events such as adult discussions, or siblings' and parents' talk about the resolution of social difficulties. Such incidental learning may be unavailable to many deaf children who cannot access communication not specifically directed toward them. Linguistic overprotection occurs when the adults (parents or teachers) do not provide extended or complete verbal explanations to the deaf child regarding the child's own actions, the actions of the adults themselves, or the actions of other individuals. Thus, deaf children may not always understand the reasons for specific actions; neither may they understand that specific behaviors might have social consequences or affect social relationships. The paucity of explanation may occur because the adult believes that the deaf child's communication abilities would prevent comprehension of the explanation or because the adult feels insecure communicating with the child. Such insecurity may be most acute for parents whose children use sign language.

In the past, most deaf students attended residential or day schools. The signing environment at these schools allowed deaf students access to communication and opportunities to interact with multiple deaf peers. Since the 1970s, however, deaf students have increasingly been attending their local public schools. In the USA, data collected by the Gallaudet Research Institute (GRI) indicated that, in 2006–2007, 75% of deaf children nationwide attended local public schools and 44% of deaf students attended general education classrooms for 16 or more hours per week (Gallaudet Research Institute, 2006). These children may not have easy access to peers and adults with whom they can communicate. Professionals have expressed fears that these children will consequently be socially isolated and not have opportunities to develop the social competence necessary for success (Stinson & Kluwin, 2003).

Although hearing loss may place deaf students in public schools at risk for poorer social outcomes, there are many factors that can mitigate against those risks. A body of research has emerged examining factors that influence individual reactions to adverse life events. Those factors that enhance one's ability to successfully cope with difficult or traumatic life circumstances are collectively referred to as "resilience." Resilience has been defined in many different ways but is perhaps best described as "the individual's capacity for adapting successfully and functioning competently despite experiencing chronic stress or adversity, or following prolonged or severe trauma" (Cicchetti & Rogosch, 1997). Resilience literature has identified numerous factors that appear to exert a "protective" effect that allows individuals in adverse conditions to achieve a variety of positive outcomes. These factors range from a wide range of personality factors such as self-efficacy, self-esteem, a sense of humor, prosocial values, and an optimistic attitude (Brooks, 1999; Cicchetti & Rogosch, 1997; Peng, 1994; Rutter, 1990; Werner, 1993) to relationships with parents, counselors, teachers, and others (Cicchetti & Rogosch, 1997; Gilligan, 2000; Masten, 1994; Wolin & Wolin, 1993). Community participation and access to various needed resources are also seen as important contributors to resiliency (Gilligan, 2000; Sandler, 2001).

In this chapter, we will review the literature on social competence for deaf students in general education classrooms, examine factors that contribute to risk and resilience and present three case studies of deaf students in public schools that illustrate the contribution of various risk and resiliency factors to social outcomes.

Social Competence

Social competence is a complex concept that includes the ability to appropriately communicate with others; the knowledge of the rules governing interactions within a variety of social contexts; the ability to take multiple perspectives in different situations; an understanding of the feelings and motivations of others; and the ability to use these skills and abilities to maintain healthy social relationships (Antia & Kreimeyer, 1992; Calderon & Greenberg, 2003). Social competence can therefore be measured in a variety of ways. Researchers have examined deaf children's social interaction with peers (Antia, 1982; Arnold & Tremblay, 1979; Lederberg, 1991; Lederberg, Ryan, & Robbins, 1986; Minnett, Clark, & Wilson, 1994; Rodriguez & Lana, 1996); social acceptance by peers (Bowen, 2008; McCain & Antia, 2005; Nunes & Pretzlik, 2001; Wauters & Knoors, 2008), their ability to make and keep friends (Musselman, Mootilal, & MacKay, 1996; Stinson & Kluwin, 1996; Stinson & Whitmire, 1991, 1992), and their social skills as rated by teachers, parents, and themselves (Antia et al., 2008).

Peer Social Interaction

Early observation studies of social interaction of deaf children with hearing peers found that preschool and elementary-age deaf children in integrated settings (i.e., with hearing children present) interacted less frequently with peers, spent less time in interaction with peers, and interacted with fewer peers than hearing children (Antia, 1982; Antia & Kreimeyer, 2003; McCauley, Bruininks, & Kennedy, 1976;

Vandell & George, 1981). Deaf children were also found to engage significantly less in associative/cooperative play than hearing children (Antia & Dittillo, 1998). Early studies of high school students using self reports of social interaction and participation also indicate that deaf students reported more frequent in-school interaction with deaf than hearing peers (Stinson, Whitmire, & Kluwin, 1996). Antia and Kreimeyer (2003) provide a comprehensive review of deaf children's social interaction with peers. In this chapter, we will focus on the factors that appear to facilitate peer interaction.

Peer interaction is influenced by familiarity, gender, and mode of communication. Lederberg et al. (1986) observed preschool deaf children in dyadic play with peers. They reported that deaf children had more successful initiations and engaged in more physical communication and pretend play with familiar than with unfamiliar hearing partners. Studies of high school students also indicate that those deaf students who spend more time with hearing students in general education classrooms also report higher social participation with hearing students. Stinson and Whitmire (1991) obtained student self-ratings from 84 deaf adolescents in secondary and postsecondary programs in England using the Social Activity Scale (Stinson & Whitmire, 1992). Results indicated that the deaf students rated themselves as interacting more frequently with hearing than with deaf peers during in-classroom and out-of-school social activities, and equally frequently with deaf and hearing peers for in-school social activities (e.g., eating lunch with friends). As the number of general education classes increased, a corresponding increase in the amount of time interacting with hearing peers was reported. Students who spent the least amount of time in general education classrooms reported significantly less interaction with hearing peers in class and in school than those who spent the most amount of time in general education classes.

The positive effect of peer familiarity can also be seen in studies of the interaction of deaf students in coenrolled classrooms. In coenrollment models deaf and hearing students are educated in the same classroom by a team of two teachers, a general education teacher and a teacher of deaf students, who collaborate to provide instruction to all the students. A typical coenrollment classroom may consist of an approximately 2:1 ratio of hearing and deaf students. In many coenrollment classrooms, the teachers and students frequently use both spoken English and sign language thus allowing communication access for all students and deaf children can become familiar with their hearing peers as they participate together in all classroom activities (Kluwin, 1999; Kluwin & Gonsher, 1994; Kreimeyer, Crooke, Drye, Egbert, & Klein, 2000). Kreimeyer et al. (2000) examined the social interaction of five deaf students in a coenrolled third/fourth grade classroom. The authors obtained observational data throughout the school year on the frequency of peer interaction between five deaf students and their deaf and hearing classmates in the classroom and in the lunchroom. The results indicated that, after the first week of school, each of the deaf students increased positive interactions with their hearing peers in the classroom. Four of these five children also increased their interaction with hearing peers in the lunchroom. Unfortunately, because no comparative data were obtained of the frequency of peer interaction of hearing students in either setting, it was not possible to know whether the deaf students engaged in peer interaction as frequently as the hearing students. It is conceivable that although the rate of interactions between hearing and deaf students increased, the deaf students may have continued to have low rates of peer interaction when compared with that of hearing students. Because the presence of supportive relationships seem to increase resilience, opportunities that enhance the quality and quantity of social interactions among peers might be particularly important to the development of resilience among deaf students.

In addition to familiarity, gender may influence the amount of interaction between deaf students and their hearing peers (Musselman et al., 1996). In a study of Canadian high school youth, Musselman et al. (1996) administered the Social Activity Scale to 72 deaf and 88 hearing high school students. This study included three groups of deaf students: those who attended no general education classes, those who attended 1–4 general education classes, and those who attended five or more general education classes. The researchers found that both in-class and out-of-school social participation with hearing peers increased for deaf girls with increased time in general education classrooms. However, this was not true for deaf boys who demonstrated comparable levels of in-class and out-of-school social participation regardless of the amount of time in general education classes.

As one might expect, a shared mode of communication facilitates the quantity and quality of peer interaction. Researchers examining the interaction of deaf adolescents report that those who use oral communication are more likely to have interaction with hearing peers than those who use sign communication (Bat-Chava & Deignan, 2001; Stinson & Kluwin, 1996; Stinson & Whitmire, 1992). Bat-Chava and Deignan examined the oral language and social relationships of elementary-aged deaf children with cochlear implants who spent most of their day in general education classrooms. Parents of children whose oral communication improved post implant also reported that their children were more willing and able to interact with hearing peers. Conversely, children whose oral communication did not improve were reported to have difficulties in social relationships with hearing peers. Two early studies (Stinson & Kluwin, 1996; Stinson & Whitmire, 1992) of adolescents also examined the relationship between mode of communication and peer interaction. Stinson and Kluwin (1996) collected self-reported data on the social activity, speech and signing skills of deaf adolescents in 15 public high schools while Stinson and Whitmire (1992) reported on deaf adolescents participating in a summer camp. In both studies, those who rated themselves as having a preference for oral communication reported more interaction with hearing peers. Adolescents who rated themselves high in signing skills or with a preference for sign communication reported interacting mostly with other deaf adolescents.

Social Acceptance and Friendships

Socially accepted students are known and liked by their classmates, thus not rejected by peers. However, students can be neglected or minimally accepted by peers without being socially rejected. Social acceptance by peers is one outcome (although not an inevitable outcome) of positive interaction with peers. Social acceptance is typically measured through the use of peer nomination and peer rating scales. Peer nomination scales require students to specifically name their friends, while peer rating scales provide students with a list of peers to be rated, usually on a scale such as "don't like," "like a little," "like a lot" (Bierman, 2004). However, social acceptance is not synonymous with friendships. A child could be socially neglected, but have one close friend. Friendship patterns can be examined either by student self report, parent reports of friendships, or by examining sociometric networks in the classroom for reciprocal friendship choices. Studies of social acceptance of deaf students in public schools have yielded varying results. Factors that appear to influence social acceptance and provide resilience include the amount of time that deaf students spend with hearing peers, and the age of the children (Antia & Kreimeyer, 1996; Bowen, 2008; Cappelli, Daniels, Durieux-Smith, McGrath, & Neuss, 1995; Nunes & Pretzlik, 2001).

Antia and Kreimeyer (1996) examined the social acceptance of 45 preschool through first grade deaf children who were in public schools but spent only part of the school day with their hearing peers. These children were participants in a study to determine whether a social skills intervention or an intervention that promoted only familiarity with hearing peers would result in increased interaction and acceptance between deaf and hearing children. All children completed a peer rating scale prior to and after the intervention. The researchers found that deaf children were significantly less accepted than their hearing peers before and after the intervention. However, despite the lower levels of acceptance, the hearing children did not reject deaf children as playmates. Instead, one could characterize the deaf children as being minimally accepted.

Cappelli et al. (1995) studied 23 first- through sixth-grade oral deaf students and 23 hearing classmates matched for gender. All students completed peer rating and peer nomination measures. Results indicated that the deaf students received significantly lower likeability and social preference ratings than their hearing classmates. These researchers reported that a higher percentage of the younger students (first to third grade) were rejected by hearing classmates than the older students (fourth to sixth grade) suggesting that age might be associated with resilience due to increasing social maturity and better developed social skills, leading to increased social acceptance.

In a more recent study of students in England, Nunes and Pretzlik (2001) examined the social status of nine oral fourth and fifth grade deaf students and their hearing classmates in two public schools in England. Results indicated that the deaf students were no more likely than their hearing peers to be disliked. No significant differences in the proportion of students identified as *popular* or *rejected* were found between deaf and hearing students. However, the proportion of deaf students identified as *neglected* was significantly higher than that of hearing classmates. Moreover these researchers reported that the deaf students were significantly less likely than their hearing classmates to have a friend in their classroom.

In a study conducted in the Netherlands, Wauters and Knoors (2008) gave a sociometric assessment to 18 elementary deaf students who attended general education classrooms, and 344 hearing classmates. These researchers found no differences between the social status (popular, rejected, neglected, controversial, or average) of deaf and hearing students, or how much students were liked or known within the classroom. Moreover, data collected over a 2-year period showed that these outcomes remained stable over time. They also found no differences between deaf and hearing students in the number of mutual friendships.

Adolescent friendships have been typically studied using a rating scale that examines deaf students' emotional security with both hearing and deaf peers. Stinson and Whitmire (1991) examined the emotional security of 84 deaf adolescents in England who spent varying amounts of time in general education classrooms. All students, including those who spent most of the day with hearing peers in general education classrooms reported feeling more emotionally secure with deaf than hearing peers. However, as with social interaction, those deaf students who spent more time in general education classrooms also reported significantly greater emotional security with hearing peers. Stinson et al. (1996) also studied friendships of 220 deaf adolescents in the USA who attended public schools but spent varying amounts of time in general education classrooms with hearing peers. Again, students reported that they felt more emotionally secure with deaf than hearing peers. However, their ratings of emotional security with hearing peers increased as they spent more time in the general education classroom. Thus, access to deaf peers may aid in increasing resilience among deaf adolescents.

As mentioned earlier, coenrolled classrooms may provide a facilitative social environment for deaf students. In these classrooms students have access to both hearing and deaf peers, while in general education classrooms deaf students may have access to only hearing peers. It is possible that the coenrolled classrooms provide the deaf children the security of having deaf peers similar to themselves as well as access to familiar hearing peers. In contrast to students who spend only some of their time in the general education classroom and thus may be perceived as visitors in the classroom social structure, students in the coenrolled classroom are likely to be perceived as members of the classroom. Studies of social acceptance in these classrooms have indicated positive social outcomes for the deaf students (Bowen, 2008; Kluwin, 1999; Kluwin & Gonsher, 1994).

Kluwin and Gonsher (1994) examined social acceptance among 17 hearing and 7 deaf kindergartners in a coenrolled classroom using a peer nomination procedure to provide a measure of popularity and a description of the social networks in the classroom. They reported that there were no significant differences in the popularity of the hearing and deaf children. Moreover, the deaf children were in the middle to upper range of the classroom social system throughout the year. Finally, they also found that the number of reciprocal friendship nominations between deaf and hearing children increased during the school year.

Kluwin (1999) examined the self-perceived popularity, and social isolation of deaf and hearing elementary and middle school students (grades 4–8) in coenrolled classrooms. Students completed a series of questionnaires that included a self-concept scale and a loneliness scale. No differences were found between the hearing and deaf students on their perception of their own popularity among peers, or on their feelings of loneliness, leading Kluwin to conclude that coenrollment was a facilitator of social outcomes for deaf students.

Bowen (2008) also explored the friendship patterns of deaf and hearing students in a fourth/fifth grade coenrolled program. Students completed a friendship sociogram where they responded to eight positive and eight negative questions with peer nominations. Each student was ranked based on the nominations. The author reported no statistically significant differences in the rankings of deaf and hearing students. Deaf students received more positive and negative nominations from their peers in the co-enrolled class than from peers in a traditional class (i.e., from familiar rather than unfamiliar peers). Unfamiliar peers only gave one positive nomination to a deaf student. Thus, being a member of the classroom can lead to friendships as well as antipathies. However, coenrollment classrooms seem to facilitate peer relationships.

As with social interaction, the ability to communicate easily with peers can affect the social status and friendship patterns of deaf students in general education classrooms. Deaf students who have good oral ability may be more likely to gravitate toward hearing peers than those who do not have such ability. A survey study of friendship patterns of 100 profoundly deaf oral students in Australia (Roberts & Rickards, 1994) reported that 83% of the students who attended general education programs reported having mostly hearing friends. However, the hearing status of their friends appeared to be related to how well their speech could be understood. Similarly, in a summary of research findings on the social relationships of deaf adolescents Stinson and Whitmire (1992) concluded that students who preferred oral communication had a high need for closer relationships with hearing peers.

Social Skills

Social skills are often measured through teacher, student, and parent rating scales (Andersson, Rydell, & Larsen, 2000; Antia et al., 2008; Mejstad, Heiling, & Svedin, 2008/2009). Andersson et al. (2000) compared the social competence of 48 elementary-age deaf students in Sweden, most of who were enrolled in general education classrooms, with data collected previously on a normative sample of hearing children. Teachers and parents completed the Social Competence Inventory (Rydell, Hagekull, & Bohlin, 1997) and the Children's Behavior Questionnaire (Achenbach, 1991). These rating scales measured prosocial orientation, social initiative, externalizing, internalizing, and concentration problems. The authors reported no differences between the groups on any of the scales except parent-reported social initiative, on which the deaf children had significantly lower scores than the hearing norms.

Antia et al. (2008) completed a 5-year longitudinal study of 197 deaf students in general education classrooms. The students' hearing levels ranged from mild to profound; they were in grades 2–8, and 85% spent three or more hours per day in the general education classroom at the beginning of the study. The researchers obtained teacher ratings of social skills and problem behaviors of deaf students annually for 5 years using the Social Skills Rating System (SSRS) (Gresham & Elliott, 1990). The Social Skills scale of the SSRS requires teachers to rate students' cooperation, assertion, responsibility, empathy, and self-control. The Problem Behaviors scale requires teachers to rate behaviors such as inappropriate aggression, anxiety, sadness, loneliness, and hyperactivity. Antia and her colleagues found that, over the 5-year period, between 79 and 86% of students were rated as displaying average or above-average social skills, a percentage comparable to that of the typical hearing normative group. In addition, 86–94% of students were rated as displaying average or below-average problem behaviors, which was better than expected of the normative group. Teacher ratings of social skills remained constant as students moved into middle and high school, while ratings for problem behaviors significantly declined as students became older.

Mejstad et al. (2008/2009), in a large-scale study of mental health and self image of Swedish students, examined prosocial behaviors through questionnaires completed by teachers, parents, and students themselves. The participants in this study were 111 Swedish students between the ages of 11 and 18, who attended a public school, a special school for hard-of-hearing students, or a special school for deaf students. Mejstad et al. reported that the deaf students had similar scores to the hearing norms obtained in other Nordic countries. Moreover, students attending the public school program had significantly higher scores on prosocial behavior than those at schools for the deaf, suggesting that being in general education classrooms did not put deaf students at risk socially.

McCain and Antia (2005) also used the SSRS to compare the social behavior of 10 deaf and 18 hearing students in a multigrade (third to fourth to fifth grades) coenrolled classroom. They found that the deaf students who had no additional cognitive or attentional learning problems scored within the normal range and had scores similar to their hearing classmates. In contrast, teachers rated the deaf students with additional problems in the below average range for social skills and these students also scored significantly lower than their hearing classmates. Thus, it appears that hearing loss alone did not depress social skills of these students.

Risk and Resilience Factors Influencing Social Outcomes

Several researchers have examined resilience in deaf children/adolescents. While the characterization of deafness as "adversity" or "risk" has, perhaps justifiably, been criticized as an unsubstantiated assumption (Young, Green, & Rogers, 2008), there seems little doubt that there are a number of factors that may serve to result in improved outcomes for deaf children. Although the literature in deafness is limited, there are a number of factors that are important in helping deaf children and adults to achieve a variety of kinds of successful outcomes. Rogers, Muir, and Everson (2003) have provided an excellent review of the literature in deafness and resilience. Unfortunately, there exist only a few studies and most of these are theory-based or use a case study approach. However, these authors identified 13 factors that they grouped into three general categories of "assets." These are (1) Interpersonal Assets, which include a good sense of humor, caring, responsible and committed to worthy goals, a strong sense of social bonds, emotionally self-perceptive, awareness of strengths, and comfort with solitude; (2) Environmental Factors, which include quality time with caring mentors in school, positive learning partnerships with peers in college, supportive family environment, and rich opportunities for participation in the community; and (3) Behavioral Assets, including self-advocacy, self-reliant, goal-directed behaviors and persistent problem solving, and authentic presentation of self.

We have categorized risk and resilience factors into similar categories but not identical, to the categories used by Rogers et al. (2003). Instead of interpersonal, environmental, and behavioral factors we have categorized factors as being student-related; school-related, or family-related. Student-level factors include both interpersonal assets and behavioral assets, while environmental factors include both school and family factors. Individual students will experience a combination of favorable and unfavorable factors, some of which are subject to change while others are not.

Student-Related Factors

Student factors influencing outcomes include communication, gender, and age. Good communication skills positively influence social outcomes and clearly are factors that can promote resilience. Preliminary data presented by Antia and her colleagues (Antia, 2009; Luckner, Antia, & Kreimeyer, 2009) indicates that students' communication participation in the classroom as measured by a questionnaire (Antia, Sabers, & Stinson, 2007), and students' expressive and receptive communication ability as rated by their teacher of deaf are significantly related to social skills scores. Students who rated themselves as understanding teachers and peers, and having higher positive affect in the general education classroom, received higher social skills scores and lower problem behavior scores than students who rated themselves lower in these areas. Students who were rated by their teachers as having good receptive and expressive communication (regardless of communication mode) also received higher social skills scores than those who had poorer communication skills. Although the correlations were significant, the magnitude of the correlations was modest to low (between 0.15 and 0.38). The communication ratings tapped children's general communicative competence, which could be broadly thought of as including not only language skills (vocabulary syntax, etc.) but also pragmatic communication skills such as communication assertiveness, repair, and the ability to match communication mode and register to one's audience. Good communication skills (separate from *mode* of communication) equip students to participate effectively in an interpersonal, dynamic social context and thus can be thought of as promoting resilience.

Although oral communication is neither sufficient nor necessary for social competence, good oral communication (receptive and expressive) allows for ease of social interaction between deaf students and hearing peers and thus appears important to the resilience of deaf students in general education classrooms (Stinson & Kluwin, 1996). Moreover, oral communication may also make it easier for deaf students to pick up social cues and learn social skills by overhearing communication among hearing parents and adults regarding acceptable social behavior. However, lack of oral communication skills does not preclude friendships with hearing peers. Studies in coenrollment classrooms indicate that hearing students can become reasonably fluent in sign communication (Bowen, 2008; Kluwin & Gonsher, 1994), thus breaking down communication barriers with deaf peers. Additionally, interpreters can help facilitate peer interaction by interpreting for the deaf and hearing students in social communication situations, and, more importantly, teaching sign language, formally or informally, to the hearing students (Antia & Kreimeyer, 2001).

Another student factor that influences social outcomes is gender. Musselman et al. (1996) reported that deaf boys and girls showed different patterns of participation with hearing peers with increased time in general education. For girls, increased time resulted in increased participation with hearing peers, while boys reported similar levels of participation with hearing peers regardless of the amount of time in general education classrooms. Martin and Bat-Chava (2003) using parental interviews to examine friendships, found that, while there were no differences between elementary-age boys' and girls' success in relationships with hearing peers, they used different social strategies to establish these relationships. An effective strategy for girls was the ability to assert their needs, an important resiliency-related skill, while for boys the single most effective strategy was to excel in sports (a resiliency factor that, while student-related, could be enhanced by access to school extracurricular activities).

Age also affects social outcomes perhaps, in part, because friendships of younger children may depend on proximity, while those of adolescents are more dependent on shared interests and perceived similarity. Elementary-age deaf students appear to have more positive relationships with hearing peers than deaf adolescents (Nunes & Pretzlik, 2001; Stinson et al., 1996; Wauters & Knoors, 2008). However, teachers' ratings of students' social behaviors remained positive over a 5-year period, indicating that students do not seem to have additional social problems as they got older (Antia et al., 2008).

Degree of hearing loss is often mentioned as a factor influencing social and academic outcomes. However, few studies have actually examined the influence of varying degrees of hearing loss on social behavior or outcomes. Typically, researchers have included only students with severe or profound hearing loss (Musselman et al., 1996; Stinson & Kluwin, 1996) or have not specifically examined the effect of different degrees of hearing loss on social behavior (Antia, 1982; Wauters & Knoors, 2008). When degree of hearing loss is examined, it has been found to have modest but significant correlations (of between 0.12 and 0.14) with teacher-rated social skills, although, when one examines functional hearing (students' use of audition with appropriate amplification) rather than degree of hearing loss the correlations are much higher (between 0.22 and 0.27) (Antia, 2009; Antia et al., 2008). These data indicate that deaf students in general education classrooms, who have greater degree of hearing loss, or whose use of audition is less efficient, are likely to have lower social skills ratings. Similarly, Most (2004) reported a significant correlation of 0.34 between degree of hearing loss and teacher-rated social behavior. However, one must also take into consideration that the mere presence of a hearing loss is a risk factor. Students with mild hearing loss have been reported to have higher rates of dysfunction in social/emotional behavior (Bess, Dodd-Murphy, & Parker, 1998; Most, 2006) than hearing students.

Charlson, Bird, and Strong (1999) reported on the case histories of three deaf students who had achieved success despite stressful circumstances. Although the researchers did not specifically focus on social success, they identified the following student characteristics as important to resilience: a good nature, responsible commitment to worthy goals, optimism, a meaningful life philosophy, keen social perceptions of others, self-awareness of assets, self-reliant determined attitudes, assertive self-advocacy, and active problem-solving skills.

School-Related Factors

School factors influencing social outcomes include the amount of time deaf students spend with their hearing peers, and the resulting familiarity with these peers. Schools can also positively influence social outcomes by providing appropriate mentoring, opportunities for community participation, access to school extracurricular activities, and instruction in self-advocacy and other skills that promote student resilience.

Deaf students who spend most of their time in the classroom with hearing peers tend to make friends and feel comfortable with them. Coenrollment programs where a group of deaf students spend all their time in the same classroom as their hearing peers have shown consistently positive results; in these classrooms no differences have been found between deaf and hearing students in terms of social acceptance, friendship, or social competence (Bowen, 2008; Kluwin & Gonsher, 1994; Kluwin, Gonsher, Silver, & Samuels, 1996; McCain & Antia, 2005). One reason for the social success of deaf students in coenrollment classrooms may be because all students, deaf and hearing, are equal members of the classroom; in other words, the deaf students are not merely visitors to the classroom. As classroom members, each student's learning, communication, and social needs get consideration. As a result all students can enter fully into the social life of the classroom (Antia, Stinson, & Gaustad, 2002).

Another school factor that can positively influence students' social outcomes is access to school extra-curricular activities. Schools provide opportunities for social interaction and resulting friendships through planned extra-curricular activities such as sports and clubs; these in turn facilitate development of community. These extra-curricular activities may also positively influence socialization because they give the deaf students an opportunity to engage with others in mutually interesting activities in which they might shine. However, engagement in extra-curricular activities can be limited by the unwillingness or inability of schools to provide sign language interpreters for nonacademic events. Often deaf students in the school do not attend their neighborhood schools; in these cases transportation is often a problem (Stewart & Stinson, 1992). Finally, although there is little literature specifically on deaf students, schools can promote resilience by teaching students such skills as self-advocacy and social skills (Battle, Dickens-Wright, & Murphy, 1998; Bierman, 2004; English, 1997; Fiedler & Danneker, 2007).

Family-Related Factors

While some data are available on the influence of family factors on academic outcomes of deaf students (Antia, Jones, Reed, & Kreimeyer, 2009; Bodner-Johnson, 1986) the effect of family factors on students' social outcomes, have not been extensively studied. Antia et al. (2008) found that parental participation in their child's education is significantly but modestly correlated with student and teacher ratings of students' social behavior. These authors obtained information on parental participation by having teachers indicate the kinds of school activities in which parents were involved. These activities included attending IEP meetings, taking sign language classes, communicating with school personnel, volunteering at the school, attending parent–teacher conferences, attending school events and taking parent classes or workshops. From these data, the authors created a parental participation score by summing all the school activities in which parents or guardians were involved. Exploratory analyses showed correlation coefficients of 0.18 between parental participation and teacher-rated social skills scores, and 0.20 between parental participation and students' self-rated social skills. Thus, parental participation exerted a protective influence that clearly contributed to students' social outcomes. However, the authors only examined parental participation in the school context. Parental involvement with their children obviously goes far beyond school involvement and is likely to include the quality and quantity of parent–child communication, parents' encouragement of their children's participation in extra-curricular activities, or their ability to encourage children's friendships. These qualities were not taken into consideration.

The quality and quantity of interaction between parents and children is likely to influence social outcomes. Parents can serve as social "coaches" for their children by discussing strategies for handling peer problems or by demonstrating competent social interaction with a variety of people (Bierman, 2004). Parental resources (both money and time) are likely also to have an effect on child social outcomes. Parents who can afford to have their children involved in social activities, and who can transport their children to these activities, can provide their children multiple opportunities for socializing with peers. However, parents' work schedules may also prevent them from transporting children to social activities outside of school. While these parental involvement issues affect all children, they are crucial for socialization of deaf children in public schools, especially if their school socialization experiences are limited.

Case Studies

In order to illustrate the social lives of deaf students in public schools and to explore risk and resilience factors contributing to social outcomes, three case studies are presented in the following section. These case studies are part of a longitudinal study completed by Antia et al. (2008) on the academic and social status and progress of deaf students in general education classrooms. The authors completed case studies on a subset of 25 student participants. For each of the 25 students participating in the case studies, the researchers interviewed the following individuals who were involved with the students: the teacher of deaf who provided service to the student; interpreters (when applicable); one or two general education teachers who were judged by the teacher of deaf to know the student well; school administrators; parents; and the case study students themselves. Interview protocols were developed and used that addressed issues particular to each person's role. For example, administrators were asked about school-wide social initiatives, teachers were asked to describe the students' social relationships at school, while parents described social relationships outside of school. Three sets of interviews were conducted over the 5-year period so that the researchers were able to obtain information about students' social change over time. In addition to the interviews, researchers obtained academic achievement data from state achievement tests, functional data from the Gallaudet Functional Rating Scales (Karchmer & Allen, 1999), teacher-rated and student-rated social skills data, and teacher-rated problem behavior data from the Social Skills Rating Scale (Gresham & Elliott, 1990). For this chapter, three cases were selected to illustrate student, school, and family factors that influenced social outcomes. All names and other identifying information are changed to protect privacy and confidentiality.

Frank

Frank was in his first year of high school, in ninth grade, at the time of the initial interviews. He had a unilateral profound hearing loss. The researchers were not able to obtain information on the age of identification of his hearing loss, nor when he first received services. Although he had been in the same school district and had received services from the same teacher of deaf since fifth grade, his teacher of deaf and his mother noted that services had been interrupted several times while he was in elementary and middle school, because his family moved frequently. He was rated as functioning normally in the areas of attention, as well as expressive and receptive communication, but as being mildly limited in the area of thinking and reasoning. In ninth grade, he spent most of his school day in a special education classroom with hearing students who had cognitive disabilities. However, by 11th and 12th grade he was spending increasing amounts of time in a resource room for students with learning disabilities. In 12th grade he was required to take the state achievement test, and received scores far below expectations (the lowest ratings possible) in all three content areas of reading, math, and language. In ninth grade, his general education teachers rated his social skills at the low average level and his problem behaviors as above average. However, in the following years his social skills and problem behaviors were rated as average by his teachers. He rated himself average in social skills throughout the time that he participated in the study.

In ninth grade, Frank seemed to be a withdrawn and shy person. He did not participate in any extra-curricular activities and disliked sports. It was difficult for him to stay after school because no transportation was provided for these activities and he lived quite a distance away from the school. He had few friends and when asked about his favorite person at school, he named his teacher of deaf. His teachers and his mother characterized him as shy and a loner. During this time his classroom peers were in special education and Frank reported that he did not like spending time with them. Outside of school he socialized mainly with his sisters. He disliked wearing his hearing aids, (his teacher mentioned that he had stopped wearing them in eighth grade), and also did not use his FM system. His teachers mentioned that he did not want to wear these because he hated to wear anything that might make him different from other students.

Thus, in his first year of high school Frank presented a profile of a deaf student who was lonely and isolated, not unlike the picture painted in the literature. However, during follow-up interviews in two subsequent years (his junior and senior years in high school) he presented quite a different profile. In his junior year he started driving and was able to take a job at a restaurant. His teacher and his mother reported that having a job gave him confidence and made him feel better about himself. He was described as having come out of his shell and having made friends (both boys and girls). By his senior year, he seemed to be a happy sociable person. He worked at the school copy center, where he was liked and encouraged, and for which he received a school award. He was well-known in his school, felt confident about himself and was reported as participating in class discussions, and good at collaborative classroom activities. The job at the school copy center gave him the opportunity to go to different classrooms and meet different students. As a consequence he reported having several hearing friends at school. During his senior interview, Frank stated that he had decided just to be himself and start talking to people, and to stop being shy. He seemed, at this time, to become aware of his assets and to capitalize on them by being more assertive. He was involved in school extra-curricular activities and took a leading role in some of these activities. His main activity outside of school was work – he worked at two different restaurants sometimes till late at night. His mother reported that he was well liked at work and was seen as a responsible worker. Work seemed to be an important resilience factor for Frank as it provided him with the opportunity to engage in goal-directed behaviors. These goal-directed behaviors seemed to carry over to school in his work at the copy center and school extra-curricular activities.

When examining risk and resilience factors for Frank, it became clear that the presence of even a minimal hearing loss created a perceived difference from peers, and therefore negatively influenced his social relationships. His teacher of deaf mentioned that Frank "struggled …. to admit he had a problem with his hearing." He refused to wear his hearing aid or use the FM system because he believed this focused attention on his hearing loss. Although his expressive and receptive communication skills were rated as normal in comparison to his peers, and his preferred mode of communication was oral, he clearly had difficulties with literacy; difficulties that prompted his teacher of deaf to attempt to teach him to sign. Again, however, Frank was highly resistant to any activity that focused attention to his hearing loss. His teacher reported the following:

> …he would not participate, not lift his hands, not look… at one point he welled up with tears and actually started crying … he was so embarrassed that I was doing sign language and there was other people present.

It would appear that his shyness was due to his fear of being different.

Participation in extra-curricular sports activities appears to be a facilitator for social outcomes in boys (Martin & Bat-Chava, 2003). As Frank was not interested in sports he did not seem to have opportunities to interact with hearing peers in this area. His social life in ninth grade seemed to revolve around adults not peers, as he mentioned that the teacher of deaf was his favorite person at school. Such a preference for adults over peer interaction has been noticed before in deaf children (Antia, 1982). However, with increasing age he had access to transportation that allowed him to participate in a wider range of activities. Once he could drive, Frank was able to work; work appeared to provide him a sense of self-worth and a way to interact with a wide range of people. Jobs seemed to develop self-confidence, an important factor in resiliency.

When we examined school factors, we found that Frank was the only student with a hearing loss at his school. We speculate that this might have contributed to his sense of isolation. His peers were limited to the students in his self-contained special education classroom. His mother was aware of his isolation and mentioned that students picked on him and the other special education students because of their perceived differences. She thought that the school should have some disability awareness training for the entire student body.

During freshman year, Frank had limited opportunities to interact with peers outside the special education classroom in which he spent most of his day. The school did not provide transportation for after-school activities, and Frank did not join general education classes. In Frank's junior and senior years he moved out of the special education classroom to the resource room. Such a move provided him an opportunity to interact with classmates who were not cognitively limited. His work in the school copy room also provided him with opportunities to socialize with a wider range of peers than he had access to in ninth grade. Thus, access to a wide range of peers in a context where he was successful (the copy room) led to increased self-confidence, and more social interaction and relationships, which appeared to facilitate social success.

Finally, Frank appeared to have many family facilitators. He was reported to be very close to his mother and to his siblings. His mother supported his working outside of school. She was also aware of the support services provided to him by his teacher of deaf and communicated regularly with her. She welcomed other children to their home (but mentioned that there were no youth in the neighborhood who were Frank's age, or who went to his school). Frank initially presented a profile of an isolated student, with few friends. However, access to a wider group of peers in school, the ability to be successful at work, and a supportive home environment resulted in a positive social outcome.

Santiago

Santiago was in middle school, in grade 7, at the time of the initial interviews. He had a mild bilateral hearing loss and had received his elementary and middle school education in the same rural school district. He had always been fully included in the general education classroom and his hearing loss was identified at 1 year of age, he received amplification at age 5, and school services started at age 7, in elementary school. Santiago was followed from grade 7 through grade 11. He was rated by his teacher of deaf as functioning normally in expressive and receptive communication, attention, and thinking/reasoning. He was bilingual in Spanish and English; his home language and his parents' preferred language was Spanish. He was a high achieving student scoring above the 50th percentile in math, and close to the 50th percentile in reading and language on state achievement tests. During the 5 years that he participated in the research study, he received average social skills and problem behavior ratings from his teachers. He self-rated his social skills as average during grades 7 and 8 but above average in grades 9–11.

Santiago was described by his teachers and his parents as a very social person. Friendships were important to him and he had many friends through school, church, and through his extra-curricular activities. He was very concerned that he appear similar to other students and through the entire 5 years refused to wear either hearing aids or glasses. In seventh grade his teachers described him as a typical seventh grade boy who was unruly and uncooperative at times. By eighth grade he gravitated toward a group of boys who were trouble-makers; consequently he had been in trouble in school several times resulting in detention and a behavior program. By the time he was in high school, his teacher of deaf mentioned that his social skills were "too good" and that he sometimes hung out with his friends instead of going to class. However, he continued to be popular, friendly, and participatory in class. His parents reported that the phone was always ringing for him, that he went to many parties. In 11th grade he had a weekend job working for a friend of his father's who was a carpenter. He had his own transportation (a motor bike) and was saving up to buy a car. He had responsibilities in the home to look after his young sibling after school.

Apart from the hearing loss itself, Santiago seemed to have few risk factors and many protective factors that facilitated positive social outcomes. At the individual level, he had good oral communication skills resulting in ease of communication with his hearing peers. He was involved in, and enjoyed, sports; sports provide an arena for deaf boys to interact on an equal footing with hearing peers. One aspect that might have put him at risk was his embarrassment and subsequent refusal to use amplification or to wear glasses even though he admitted that he needed both. His teachers and parents mentioned that this refusal affected his academic work, but that he was not open to any change. It appeared to be extremely important to him that he not appear different from his peers.

At the school level, many protective factors seemed to be in place. He had received services continuously since age 7. In high school, many of the general education teachers mentioned that they used cooperative learning strategies in the classroom, and encouraged students to work with one another. The high school itself appeared to be a friendly community. One teacher mentioned that it was small enough that the students knew one another quite well and she did not see as many "cliques" as she had in other schools. The school population was largely Hispanic, and the students, including Santiago, conversed in Spanish outside of the class-room. Although some of the teachers appeared to see the predominant use of Spanish as a problem for the students academically, it appeared to be "social glue" for the students themselves and provided Santiago with opportunities for participation in the school community. Thus, his Spanish communication skill was clearly a resilience factor for him. Although the school was in a rural area, he lived close enough to be able to see his friends after school.

Santiago was one of only two deaf students in the school. Although he was not a particular friend of the other deaf student, the presence of another student meant that he was not totally isolated; the teacher of deaf mentioned that the two students had talked with one another about using amplification in the classroom. The presence of more than one deaf student also seemed to have raised teachers' awareness of deaf students in the school.

Santiago's family was very involved with him. There were no language barriers between him and his parents as they could converse in oral Spanish. His parents encouraged him to become involved in a number of after-school activities; he played several different sports and his father encouraged him to join the school band and learn to play an instrument. All Santiago's teachers stated that his parents were supportive of him, that they had expectations that he would do well in school, and be respectful of his teachers. His parents gave the interviewers many instances of how they expected him to behave socially. His father encouraged him to express himself and speak his mind:

> If he feels anger let it be known, ... if he has something to say he should say it so that people can pay attention to him and listen to him.

They also let him know when they disapproved of his friends. They responded to teachers when they complained about Santiago's behavior in class and set contingencies for Santiago's good behavior. At the same time, they allowed him to spend time with his friends and attend parties. Santiago presented a profile of a student who was well integrated socially and who had few social risk factors and many social facilitators.

Sheila

Sheila was in elementary school, in third grade, at the time of the initial interviews and in seventh grade at the time of the final interviews. She had a profound bilateral hearing loss that was identified before she was 1 year old. The researchers were not able to get information about the age at which she first received services, but she had spent some time at a school for the deaf. She was rated by her teachers of deaf as functioning normally in receptive and expressive communication, attention, and thinking/reasoning. She spent almost the entire school day in the general education classroom and received services from a teacher of deaf and a sign language interpreter. Her preferred language was American Sign Language (ASL). She was able to take the state standardized achievement tests in math and language/writing at grade level, and scored at the 50th percentile for math, and the 35th percentile for language/writing. Her reading scores, however, were below average. Her general education teachers rated her as above average in social skills and below average in problem behaviors during her years in elementary school (third to fifth grades). After she moved to middle school (sixth grade), teachers rated her as average in social skills and problem behaviors; thus, her social skills ratings decreased and her problem behavior ratings increased, though they remained within normal levels. Sheila's self-ratings mirrored those of her teachers; she rated herself above average in social skills in elementary school but average in middle school.

In early elementary school Sheila was a popular child. Teachers commented that she was extremely well liked by both peers and teachers, that everyone wanted to be around her, and that she was always invited to all the birthday parties. The teacher of deaf reported that Sheila had no problems with friendships because "she just has warmth like sunshine." She had both deaf and hearing friends. She had a close deaf friend with whom she spent time outside school hours. Her family reported that they would drive some distance to ensure that she could play with her friend. They also tried to find other deaf playmates for her.

She visited with her school friends both after school and on weekends. Her hearing friends were reported as having learned to sign by interacting with her. The teacher of deaf mentioned that her hearing girlfriends did a good job signing and interpreting for Sheila, though the communication might be "a little heavy on fingerspelling." There was also a sign language club in place. During this time Sheila was active in after-school activities. She attended an after-school program where she completed homework and participated in recreational activities. Her friends interpreted for her in this after-school program, as there was no interpreter. By fourth grade, she was also involved in a private gymnastics program and went to the campus of the school for the deaf to play volleyball. At the gymnastics program she had no interpreter but managed by watching all the other students do the movements before she took her turn.

By fifth grade, however, Sheila stated that she wanted to attend the school for the deaf because she was lonely. She was the only deaf child in her grade and told the interviewer that the other children ignored her and that she had trouble communicating with them:

> I had friends but I couldn't communicate with them totally. I could communicate with them but it was not good communication, it was like spelling out words.

She reported that she wanted to be part of the group and involved in many activities. The move to sixth grade (middle school) in the subsequent year left her with few friends and a feeling of depression. During her interview, she stated that people should have more than one friend.

> There should be a variety of people [available for friendship] with no limitations on who you know and who you socialize with.

However, by seventh grade she was happier. Her parents attributed part of her happiness to having a boyfriend who helped her have "a more typical middle school experience" according to her general education teacher. She once more had hearing friends in the general education classroom and chose to work with them during classroom small group activities. In middle school, Sheila reported that she had deaf friends who lived near her. She also was friends with another deaf girl who was in some of her seventh grade classes. She and her deaf friend started a sign language club attended by 12–13 hearing students. These hearing students also became friends with whom she could communicate.

Sheila presented an interesting picture of risk and resilience factors at the individual, school, and family level. At the individual level, clearly her profound hearing loss and her preference for ASL was a risk factor because it hindered communication with her hearing peers. However, she was reported to be a well-adjusted person, and her outgoing and friendly personality was facilitative in developing friendships with hearing peers. She was motivated to be in public school and stated that while she could communicate better with her friends at the school for the deaf, she was glad she was in public school for the academics. Thus, she had a commitment to her goals, a resilience factor that helped her during difficult times at school. As she got older, she seemed to have more difficulties socially, and was more aware of the need for fluent communication with friends. However, again, a resilience factor was her ability to engage in active problem solving and her self-reliant attitude that was seen when she took on the task of helping her hearing peers learn sign language through a school sign language club. Having close deaf friends appeared to be a protective factor, as was having a close relationship with her boyfriend.

School facilitative factors included the sign language club, the presence of interpreters, and the presence of at least one other deaf peer in her class at middle school. Another important facilitator was that opportunities for socialization were written into her IEP, which called for promoting socialization, meeting deaf people, and learning about deaf culture. In fourth grade, her teacher of deaf helped her obtain a TTY. Her mother reported that with this machine, "her world got expanded...she feels she can communicate with the entire world and that has helped a lot." The sign language club appeared to be important in encouraging sign language learning among hearing students. However, it was most successful in facilitating peer relationships when Sheila and her friend took major responsibility for managing the club in middle school. The presence of deaf peers was important to Sheila's social life. The school participated in an annual middle school get together for all the deaf students in the region. The teacher of deaf created opportunities for Sheila and another deaf student on her caseload by giving them a chance to "chat" and communicate on the computer.

As one would expect, Sheila's interpreters were key to her communication with hearing teachers and peers in school. Sheila mentioned that she enjoyed being herself and communicating when she had interpreters

Without interpreters it is really hard, not fluent, and not smooth. [It is] not natural. I enjoy being myself and communicating and being able to let myself shine and show myself...

During school, her interpreters were flexible and sensitive to her need to communicate with her peers. When the class was engaged in small group work, the interpreter would interpret when there were no hearing peers who could sign, but when peers could sign, she did not interpret very much and "let them work things out for themselves." The interpreter reported that she let Sheila "be in charge of when she wants an interpreter there and when she doesn't."

The absence of interpreters appeared to be the largest single risk factor for Sheila. The interpreters were present for those after-school activities that were related to Sheila's Individual Education Plan (IEP). Unfortunately, in fifth grade, Sheila could not participate in some after-school activities, because interpreters were not always available. Neither were interpreters available during the students' lunch break.

Sheila's close family relationships were clearly a protective factor. Her parents were able to communicate with her fluently in ASL. Her home languages were Spanish and ASL; because her father was a Child of Deaf Adults, sign language was always part of her life. Her parents went to considerable lengths to facilitate socialization, driving her to meet her deaf friends and including her boyfriend on family trips. They had always been involved in her education, moving the family several times in order to provide her the best services possible.

Risk and Resilience Factors Across Cases

These case studies illustrate risk and resilience factors that contribute to the social outcomes of students who are deaf and in general education classrooms. Individual student factors include communication competence, gender, age, the interpersonal assets of responsibility, and commitment to goals, and behavioral assets of problem solving, self-reliance and goal-directed behaviors. School factors include teacher support and mentoring, peer learning partnerships, and access to out-of-classroom activities. Family factors include family bonds, communication between parents and the deaf student, and support for socialization.

The ability to communicate with peers is clearly a factor that promotes positive social outcomes. Communication competence goes beyond mode, and, as mentioned earlier includes such pragmatic skills as comfort and ability in communicating in different situations with a variety of individuals. Thus, Frank, although he has a minimal hearing loss and uses oral communication, had difficulty communicating with peers, while Santiago did not. Santiago's use of Spanish with his friends facilitated friendships in his school environment. Sheila was a competent communicator but needed an interpreter to communicate comfortably with peers who did not sign. However, social resilience involves more than the ability to communicate. Both Santiago and Sheila were socially aware and socially perceptive of others, traits which allowed them to positively engage with their peers. Such social perception has been found to be a resilience factor in deaf children (Charlson et al., 1999).

Both boys, Frank and Santiago, were happiest when they were involved in extra-curricular activities. Santiago was involved in sports, while Frank, in his last years of high school, had a job, which seemed to provide the same advantage as involvement in sports. While Sheila participated in extra-curricular activities, these apparently did not play as important a role for her. She seemed happiest when she had a group of friends to "chat with."

Age seemed to influence social relationships. All three students were reported to have social problems around their middle school years. Frank had difficulties in middle and early high school, Santiago started showing some problem behavior in late middle school, while Sheila, who had many friends in third and fourth grade, started feeling the lack of close relationships during fifth and sixth grade. However, over time the social issues appeared to resolve themselves. Frank expanded his peer circle once he could work; Sheila had a boyfriend by seventh grade. No specific reasons were provided for Santiago's improved social behavior in tenth grade; however, his parents communicated to him clearly about his responsibilities and their disapproval of some of his friends.

A student-related risk issue was "appearing different" from peers. This was the case for both boys, who did not want any attention called to their hearing loss. Santiago reported that he was embarrassed by having to wear hearing aids and glasses though he admitted he needed both. He even went so far as to refuse services so he wouldn't appear to be different, while Frank cried when a teacher used sign language to communicate with him in front of other people.

Interpersonal assets and personality are important in promoting resilience in deaf students (Charlson et al., 1999; Rogers et al., 2003). Sheila and Santiago were described as being friendly and outgoing individuals who could make friends easily. The opposite was true for Frank who, in ninth grade, was reported to be very shy. However, later he made a decision to "be himself" and start talking to people, thus showing that he was emotionally self-perceptive. Sheila's motivation for academic excellence and her own goals for her future kept her in public school even though she was aware that she might have more friends if she attended the school for the deaf. Again, her commitment to her established goals seemed to help her through difficult times.

School resiliency factors included familiarity with peers, opportunities to work collaboratively in learning partnerships with peers within the classroom, access to extra-curricular activities, and services from teachers and interpreters. Although the literature suggests that peer familiarity is a resiliency factor, these case studies show that familiarity can also be a risk factor. Santiago had been with the same peers, and in relatively small schools, since elementary school. His high school was small, apparently with few cliques, where most students knew one other. For him, familiarity with peers promoted resilience. Frank, also in a small rural school district, had been with the same peers from fifth grade. In his case, however, he had not been well accepted by these peers. He apparently needed a wider circle of peers with whom he could share interests. Within the classroom itself, working within collaborative small groups appeared to facilitate peer familiarity and interaction. Several general education teachers reported this strategy and all three students participated readily in collaborative activities with peers.

Access to extra-curricular activities was an important factor affecting social outcomes. School extra-curricular activities gave these students access to peers with similar interests. Lack of transportation and lack of interpreting were barriers to access and negatively impacted social outcomes. Once these issues were resolved, social outcomes improved. An important extra-curricular offering that affected Sheila was the sign language clubs in her public school program that were organized either by the teacher of deaf, the interpreter, or Sheila herself. These clubs provided her a means of access to hearing peers who could communicate with her. By seventh grade, Sheila started and organized the club with her friends, without the need for an adult presence thus, showing her ability to solve a problem (lack of sufficient signing peers) and her ability to engage in goal-directed behaviors.

School transitions seemed to be a risky time for each of these students. Unfortunately, we did not obtain information about how teachers or other adults eased the transition between elementary and middle school and again between middle school and high school. The easiest transition (from middle to high school) was Santiago's, apparently because he had already been accepted by the small school community in the elementary grades. Frank, who was not so well accepted, was isolated his first year in high school. Despite being accepted in elementary school, Sheila had a rough transition to middle school, possibly because she alone among the three attended a large urban school district.

Consistent and stable services to the deaf student presumably assist the student to develop the communication skills necessary to succeed socially and academically. Frank seems to exemplify issues common for students with unilateral hearing loss. He was identified late, received services late, and services were unstable until he was in fifth grade. The reports of the degree of his hearing loss varied, and his mother expressed frustration at the lack of services available to him during his early years. His unilateral hearing loss did not seem to generate the urgency for services that Sheila's profound bilateral hearing loss did. Santiago and Sheila both received stable services from a teacher of deaf from the time they entered school (and perhaps earlier). A resilience factor for deaf students is time with caring mentors (Rogers et al., 2003). Teachers of deaf appeared to serve as mentors at school for all three students. Frank clearly liked his teacher and spent time with her and Sheila's teacher opened up her world by assisting her to obtain a TTY.

Sign language interpreters are clearly necessary for students who use ASL as their primary language. Typically, interpreters in school translate the teacher's speech but may not always translate the speech of classmates. Sheila expressed unhappiness with one of her interpreters who would interpret academic but not social speech. She once petitioned her teacher for a different interpreter for a class presentation, and asked friends (instead of the interpreter) to interpret for her so she could make a point to her general education teacher. At other times, she expressed appreciation of an interpreter who allowed her to access her "natural language and natural world." The lack of interpreting services for extra-curricular activities was a risk for Sheila because it prevented her from joining activities where she might have met peers with common interests. Finally, the presence of even one additional deaf student seemed to be a protective factor because it made teachers aware of the needs of deaf students.

All three families were important to the eventual positive social outcomes for these students. Family factors included communication with their child, parental participation in the school and communication with school personnel, and parental resources to support their child's socialization. Communication and close bonds with their parents was a resiliency factor for all three students. Frank was very close to his mother and sisters. Santiago's father was a great social coach who gave him clear guidelines about how he should behave and encouraged Santiago to express himself. Sheila's parents signed; thus, they were able to communicate with her, though they admitted that they did not sign all their conversation.

All three families reported that they communicated frequently with school personnel. Frank's mother reported that she could always contact his teachers. Although Santiago's family typically only communicated with the school when he had a problem, his teachers knew they could contact the family if needed. Sheila's family was in constant contact with the teachers or administrators by phone, in person, and by email.

The three families had very different resources available to support their deaf child. Frank's family could not provide transportation for extra-curricular activities; consequently, he was not able to participate in these activities until he was able to drive himself. Santiago's family had sufficient resources to buy him his own motorbike allowing him to go to parties and spend time at his friends' homes. Sheila's parents spoke about their constant search for deaf peers with whom she could interact. In order to facilitate her social life the family spent considerable resources transporting Sheila, her boyfriend, and other friends (who lived some distance away). Finally, students' social responsibilities in the home seemed to facilitate outcomes. Frank was responsible for accompanying his younger sisters to their activities, while Santiago was responsible for the care of his young sibling after school when his parents were not at home.

Conclusions

There continue to be gaps in our knowledge about the social competence of deaf students in public schools, and, specifically, those who spend most of their time with hearing peers in a general education setting. In general, it appears that these students are not necessarily lonely or isolated, but, of course, their social outcomes vary depending on the combination of risk and resilience factors present in their lives. Although student-related, school-related, and family-related factors all contribute in various ways to social outcomes, we do not yet have a substantial body of research that examines the severity of the various risk factors, nor how risk factors interact to produce outcomes. We know very little about factors that make a positive contribution to the resilience of students and how to promote resilience in deaf students, despite factors that might put them at risk. Such research would be invaluable to professionals who work with deaf students and their families.

At the student level, communication proficiency appears to be a key resiliency factor. Communication should be thought of broadly as including not only facility with language but also the ability to communicate appropriately with a wide variety of individuals. Communication proficiency is not necessarily related to mode of communication or speech intelligibility. Mode of communication is also a factor that influences outcomes. Although oral language proficiency can be a resilience factor, such proficiency by itself does not remove the risk of poor social outcomes, as illustrated by the case studies. A preference for sign language can be a risk factor if schools do not make appropriate provisions for interpreters both for classroom and extra-curricular activities. Elementary and secondary deaf students have different social needs, but the data do not show that students are more socially isolated or have poorer social outcomes as they move from younger to older grades. A gap in the research is that few data are available on the effects of personality, locus of control, or other student traits on social outcomes. The case studies suggest that these traits, as well as other traits identified in the resilience literature may be important mediators of social outcomes in deaf students.

At the school level, the presence of additional deaf peers seems to be a protective factor. The most consistently positive social outcomes are reported for those deaf students who are in coenrolled classrooms where they have access to both deaf and hearing peers, and all students are members of, rather than visitors to, the classroom. In these situations sign language appears not to be a barrier to peer communication. However, for students who sign, school personnel need to be aware of the necessity of providing interpreters for noninstructional as well as extra-curricular activities. We also need research on whether the presence of interpreters for these activities promotes social outcomes for students in public schools. Transitions from school to school create stresses for all students, but may create particular social stresses for deaf students and their families, because support services and personnel may need to be re-created at each school transition. Thus, effective transitions will need to be studied and addressed. Research at the classroom level is also needed, to determine how classroom instruction can promote peer collaboration and enhance social relationships. We also need research on whether instruction in self-advocacy and problem solving can improve behaviors that promote resilience.

Families play an important role in a variety of ways: by providing access to friends, by acting as social coaches for deaf children, and by promoting independence and resilience. Ideally, we need information on how professionals and families can work together to promote social outcomes for deaf students. Professionals who work with young children often have the time, skills, and inclination to work with families; however, close coordination between school and home often decreases as students get older. The field needs to develop service models where teachers of deaf students are expected to work not only with the student and teachers at school but are also given time to communicate and work with families. The field also needs to develop strategies to reach out to, and involve families who are disinclined to be involved or unable to communicate with school personnel.

An area that has not been explored is how participation of deaf students in the community outside of school might create resilience and be a protective factor for social outcomes. When students who are deaf are invisible to the community in which they live, they may also be at risk for poor social outcomes. All deaf students will not have families that help them to access their community, and schools may have to take on this role. The presence, accessibility, and affordability of community interpreters, for example, might allow deaf students to volunteer in their local community and obtain and maintain after-school employment. When deaf students are visible to the larger hearing community, they may have better opportunities for developing community bonds.

References

Achenbach, T. M. (1991). *Manual for the child behavior checklist.* Burlington, Vermont: University of Vermont Press.

Andersson, E. O., Rydell, A., & Larsen, H. C. (2000). Social competence and behavioral problems in children with hearing impairment. *Audiology, 39,* 88–92.

Antia, S. D. (1982). Social interaction of partially mainstreamed hearing-impaired children. *American Annals of the Deaf, 127,* 18–25.

Antia, S. D. (2009). *Social skills of hard-of-hearing and deaf students in general education classrooms: Longitudinal data.* Paper presented at the Society for Research on Child Development Preconference: Research on children with mild to severe hearing loss.

Antia, S. D., & Dittillo, D. A. (1998). A comparison of the peer social behavior of children who are deaf/hard of hearing and hearing. *Journal of Children's Communication Development, 19,* 1–10.

Antia, S. D., Jones, P. B., Reed, S., & Kreimeyer, K. H. (2009). Academic status and progress of deaf and hard-of-hearing students in general education classrooms. *Journal of Deaf Studies and Deaf Education, 14,* 293–311.

Antia, S. D., Jones, P., Reed, S., Kreimeyer, K. H., Luckner, J., & Johnson, C. (2008). Longitudinal study of Deaf and Hard of Hearing students attending general education classrooms in public schools. Final report submitted to Office of Special Education Programs for grant H324C010142, University of Arizona.

Antia, S. D., & Kreimeyer, K. H. (1992). Social competence intervention for young children with hearing impairments. In S. L. Odom, S. R. McConnell, & M. A. McEvoy (Eds.), *Social competence of young children with disabilities* (pp. 135–164). Baltimore: Paul H. Brookes.

Antia, S. D., & Kreimeyer, K. H. (1996). Social interaction and acceptance of D/HH children and their peers. *The Volta Review, 98*, 157–180.

Antia, S. D., & Kreimeyer, K. H. (2001). The role of interpreters in inclusive classrooms. *American Annals of the Deaf, 146*, 355–365.

Antia, S. D., & Kreimeyer, K. H. (2003). Peer interactions of deaf and hard-of- hearing children. In M. Marschark & P. Spencer (Eds.), *Handbook of deaf studies and deaf education* (pp. 164–176). Oxford, UK: Oxford University Press.

Antia, S. D., Sabers, D., & Stinson, M. S. (2007). Validity and reliability of the classroom participation questionnaire with deaf and hard of hearing students in public schools. *Journal of Deaf Studies and Deaf Education, 12*, 158–171.

Antia, S. D., Stinson, M. S., & Gaustad, M. G. (2002). Developing membership in the education of deaf and hard of hearing students in inclusive settings. *Journal of Deaf Studies and Deaf Education, 7*, 214–229.

Arnold, D., & Tremblay, A. (1979). Interaction of deaf and hearing preschool children. *Journal of Communication Disorders, 12*, 245–251.

Bat-Chava, Y., & Deignan, E. (2001). Peer relationships of children with cochlear implants. *Journal of Deaf Studies and Deaf Education, 6*, 186–199.

Battle, J., Dickens-Wright, L. L., & Murphy, S. C. (1998). How to empower adolescents: Guidelines for effective self-advocacy. *Teaching Exceptional Children, 30*(3), 28–33.

Bess, F. H., Dodd-Murphy, J., & Parker, R. A. (1998). Children with minimal sensorineural hearing loss: Prevalence, educational performance, and functional status. *Ear and Hearing, 19*, 339–354.

Bierman, K. L. (2004). *Peer rejection: Developmental processes and intervention strategies.* New York: The Guilford.

Bodner-Johnson, B. (1986). The family environment and achievement of deaf students: A discriminant analysis. *Exceptional Children, 52*, 443–449.

Bowen, S. (2008). Coenrollment for students who are deaf or hard of hearing: Friendship patterns and social interactions. *American Annals of the Deaf, 153*, 285–293.

Brooks, R. B. (1999). Fostering resilience in exceptional children: The search for islands of competence. In V. L. Schwean & D. H. Saklofske (Eds.), *Handbook of psychosocial characteristics of exceptional children* (pp. 563–586). New York: Kluwer Academic/Plenum.

Calderon, R., & Greenberg, M. T. (2003). Social and emotional development of deaf children: Family, school and program effects. In M. Marschark & P. Spencer (Eds.), *Oxford handbook of deaf studies, language, and education* (pp. 177–189). New York: Oxford University Press.

Cappelli, M., Daniels, T., Durieux-Smith, A., McGrath, P. J., & Neuss, D. (1995). Social development of children with hearing impairments who are integrated into general education classrooms. *The Volta Review, 97*, 197–208.

Charlson, E. S., Bird, R. L., & Strong, M. (1999). Resilience and success among deaf high school students: Three case studies. *American Annals of the Deaf, 144*, 226–235.

Cicchetti, D., & Rogosch, F. A. (1997). The role of self organization in the promotion of resilience in maltreated children. *Development and Psychopathology, 9*, 799–817.

English, K. (1997). *Self-advocacy for students who are deaf or hard of hearing.* Austin, TX: Pro-ed.

Fiedler, C. R., & Danneker, J. E. (2007). Self-advocacy instruction: Bridging the research-to-practice gap. *Focus on Exceptional Children, 39*(8), 1–20.

Gallaudet Research Institute. (2006). *Regional and national summary report of data from the 2006-2007 Annual Survey of Deaf and Hard of Hearing Children and Youth.* Washington, DC: GRI Gallaudet University.

Gilligan, R. (2000). Adversity, resilience and young people: The protective value of positive school and part-time experiences. *Children and Society, 14*, 37–47.

Greenberg, M. T., & Kusche, C. A. (1993). *Promoting social and emotional development in deaf children: the PATHS project.* Seattle: University of Washington Press.

Gresham, F. M., & Elliott, S. N. (1990). *Social skills rating system.* Circle Pines: American Guidance Service.

Karchmer, M., & Allen, T. (1999). The functional assessment of deaf and hard of hearing students. *American Annals of the Deaf, 144*, 68–77.

Kluwin, T. N. (1999). Coteaching deaf and hearing students: Research on social integration. *American Annals of the Deaf, 144*(4), 339–344.

Kluwin, T. N., & Gonsher, W. (1994). A single school study of social integration of children with and without hearing losses in a team taught kindergarten. *ACEHI/ACEDA, 20*, 71–86.

Kluwin, T. N., Gonsher, W., Silver, K., & Samuels, J. (1996). Co-teaching: Education together. *Teaching Exceptional Children, 29*, 11–15.

Kreimeyer, K. H., Crooke, P., Drye, C., Egbert, V., & Klein, B. (2000). Academic and social benefits of a coenrollment model of inclusive education for deaf and hard-of-hearing children. *Journal of Deaf Studies and Deaf Education, 5*, 174–185.

Lederberg, A. R. (1991). Social interaction among deaf preschoolers: The effects of language ability and age. *American Annals of the Deaf, 136*, 53–59.

Lederberg, A. R., Ryan, H. B., & Robbins, B. L. (1986). Peer interaction in young deaf children: The effect of partner hearing status and familiarity. *Developmental Psychology, 22*, 691–700.

Luckner, J., Antia, S. D., & Kreimeyer, K. H. (2009). *Teacher and student perceptions of social skills and problem behaviors of students who are DHH in general education classrooms.* Paper presented at the Association of College Educators-Deaf Hard of Hearing.

Martin, D., & Bat-Chava, Y. (2003). Negotiating deaf-hearing friendships: Coping strategies of deaf boys and girls in mainstream schools. *Child Care, Health and Development, 29*, 511–521.

Masten, A. S. (1994). Resilience in individual development. Successful adaptation despite risk and adversity. In M. C. Wang & E. W. Gordon (Eds.), *Educational resilience in inner city America: Challenges and prospects* (pp. 3–26). Hillsdale, NJ: Erlbaum.

McCain, K., & Antia, S. D. (2005). Academic and social status of hearing, deaf, and hard-of-hearing students participating in a co-enrolled classroom. *Communication Disorders Quarterly, 27*, 20–32.

McCauley, R. W., Bruininks, R. H., & Kennedy, P. (1976). Behavioral interactions of hearing impaired children in regular classrooms. *Journal of Special Education, 10*, 277–284.

Meadow, K. (1980). Early manual communication in relation to the deaf child's intellectual, social, and communicative functioning. *American Annals of the Deaf, 113*, 29–41.

Mejstad, L., Heiling, K., & Svedin, C. G. (2008/2009). Mental health ad self-image among deaf and hard of hearing children. *American Annals of the Deaf, 153*, 504–515.

Minnett, A., Clark, K., & Wilson, G. (1994). Play behavior and communication between deaf and hard of hearing children and their hearing peers in an integrated preschool. *American Annals of the Deaf, 139*, 420–429.

Most, T. (2004). The effects of degree and type of hearing loss on children's performance in class. *Deafness and Education International, 6*, 154–166.

Most, T. (2006). Assessment of school functioning among Israeli Arab children with hearing loss in the primary grades. *American Annals of the Deaf, 151*, 327–335.

Musselman, C., Mootilal, A., & MacKay, S. (1996). The social adjustment of deaf adolescents in segregated, partially integrated and mainstreamed settings. *Journal of Deaf Studies and Deaf Education, 1*, 52–63.

Nunes, T., & Pretzlik, U. (2001). Deaf children's social relationships in mainstream schools. *Deafness and Education International, 3*, 123–136.

Peng, S. S. (1994). Understanding resilient students: The use of national longitudinal databases. In M. C. Wang & E. W. Gordon (Eds.), *Educational resilience in inner city America: Challenges and prospects* (pp. 73–84). Hillsdale, NJ: Erlbaum.

Roberts, S. B., & Rickards, F. W. (1994). A survey of graduates of an Australian integrated auditory/oral preschool. Part II Academic achievement, utilization of support services, and friendship patterns. *The Volta Review, 96*, 207–236.

Rodriguez, M. S., & Lana, E. T. (1996). Dyadic interactions between deaf children and their communication partners. *American Annals of the Deaf, 141*, 245–251.

Rogers, S., Muir, K., & Everson, C. R. (2003). Signs of resilience: Assets that support deaf adults' success in bridging the deaf and hearing worlds. *American Annals of the Deaf, 148*, 222–232.

Rutter, M. B. (1990). Psychosocial resilience and protective mechanisms. In J. Rolf, A. S. Masten, D. Cicchetti, K. H. Neuchterein, & S. Weintraub (Eds.), *Risk and protective factors in the development of psychopathology* (pp. 181–214). New York: Cambridge University Press.

Rydell, A., Hagekull, B., & Bohlin, G. (1997). Measurement of two social competence aspects in middle childhood. *Developmental Psychology, 33*, 824–833.

Sandler, I. (2001). Quality and ecology of adversity as common mechanisms of risk and resilience. *American Journal of Community Psychology, 5*, 19–57.

Schick, B., deVilliers, P., deVilliers, J., & Hoffmeister, R. (2007). Language and theory of mind: A study of deaf children. *Child Development, 78*, 376–396.

Stewart, D. A., & Stinson, M. S. (1992). The role of sport and extracurricular activities in shaping socialization patterns. In T. Kluwin, D. F. Moores, & M. Gonter Gaustad (Eds.), *Toward effective public school programs for deaf students* (pp. 129–148). New York: Teachers College Press.

Stinson, M. S., & Kluwin, T. N. (1996). Social orientations toward deaf and hearing peers among deaf adolescents in local public high schools. In P. C. Higgins & J. E. Nash (Eds.), *Understanding deafness socially* (pp. 113–134). Springfield: Charles C. Thomas.

Stinson, M. S., & Kluwin, T. (2003). Educational consequences of alternative school placements. In M. Marschark (Ed.), *Oxford handbook of deaf studies, language and education* (pp. 52–64). New York: Oxford University Press.

Stinson, M. S., & Whitmire, K. (1991). Self-perceptions of social relationships among hearing-impaired adolescents in England. *Journal of the British Association Teachers of the Deaf, 15*, 104–114.

Stinson, M. S., & Whitmire, K. (1992). Students' views of their social relationships. In T. N. Kluwin, D. F. Moores, & M. G. Gaustad (Eds.), *Towards effective public school programs for deaf students: Context, process, and outcomes* (pp. 149–174). New York: Teachers College Press.

Stinson, M. S., Whitmire, K., & Kluwin, T. N. (1996). Self perceptions of social relationship in hearing-impaired adolescents. *Journal of Educational Psychology, 88*, 132–143.

Vandell, D. L., & George, L. (1981). Social interaction in hearing and deaf preschoolers: Successes and failures in initiations. *Child Development, 52*, 627–635.

Wauters, L., & Knoors, H. (2008). Social integration of deaf children in inclusive settings. *Journal of Deaf Studies and Deaf Education, 13*, 21–36.

Werner, E. (1993). Risk, resilience, and recovery: Perspectives from the Kauai longitudinal study. *Development and Psychopathology, 5*, 503–515.

Wolin, S., & Wolin, S. (1993). *The resilient self: How survivors of troubled families rise above adversity*. New York: Villard.

Young, A., Green, L., & Rogers, K. (2008). Resilience and deaf children: A literature review. *Deafness and Education International, 10*, 40–54.

Chapter 7
Enhancing Resilience to Mental Health Disorders in Deaf School Children

Johannes Fellinger and Daniel Holzinger

Abstract This chapter examines the results of a large cross-sectional research program examining mental health, language development, and cognitive abilities of a representative sample of deaf (hearing loss at least 40 dB) school children in Upper Austria ($n=99$). Prevalence of mental health disorders was found to be about twice as high in deaf children as in the general pediatric population, with prevalence increasing to four times as likely in children who have problems making themselves understood in the family. Practical experiences are described, and findings are linked to practical recommendations, to improve resilience to mental health disorders in deaf children.

It is perhaps quite unusual to start a chapter in a scientific book as first author in a very personal way. But as this book is about resilience in deaf people, my father's life came up more and more in my mind. His deafness made me enter the world of people who cannot hear or have difficulties hearing, and he being deaf in such a positive way also had a strong influence on my relationship to deaf people. So I start this chapter, which I would like to dedicate to him (he passed away 7 years ago), with a description of his life and discuss features of his life with a perspective on recent concepts of resilience and especially resilience in deaf people. After this I describe the development of my involvement in the field of deafness. This is also the background for the second section of our chapter – the empirical work we did regarding deaf school children in Upper Austria. The last section of this chapter (i.e., recommendations) is based on the practical experiences described in part one and on the findings of the study shown in part two. To facilitate comprehension of the salient points of each section, we provide summary boxes at the end of each section.

J. Fellinger (✉)
Neurological Institute for Language and Senses-Health Center for the Deaf,
Hospital of St. John of God, Linz, Austria
e-mail: johannes.fellinger@bblinz.at

D.H. Zand and K.J. Pierce (eds.), *Resilience in Deaf Children: Adaptation Through Emerging Adulthood*, DOI 10.1007/978-1-4419-7796-0_7, © Springer Science+Business Media, LLC 2011

My Father's Life: An Example of Resilience

My father Matthew Fellinger was born in 1924. When he was 5 years old, his father died. His life circumstances became quite severe. Nevertheless, his reports of his early years were always quite positive. He had to work hard during school time, but he had friends, was good at sports, and liked to play music. At age 15 he contracted meningitis. After recovering he was completely deaf and lost his sense of balance. At that time he withdrew completely from his social environment and was very depressed. Plans for his future to become a forester were destroyed. He spent most of the time on his own, could not understand other people and was increasingly less able to speak. When he was on his own he preferred to draw or paint. His occupational outlook was quite poor and humiliating for him; he had to become a wood shoemaker and later on an assistant to a dentist. He could not go further due to his deafness. Later on he started to work as a painter of ceramics. The artists who he painted for discovered his talents and suggested that he should study in Vienna at the academy of fine arts. Although his mother was deeply concerned, he went to Vienna, which at that time was completely destroyed after the war. He started to study and made his living by working hard at night. He was also physically ill (stomach ulcer) and described himself as "full of bitterness" due to many disappointments in human relationships. However, he was ambitious to show others that he would also be able to achieve something in life. His anger about his deafness turned into a more thankful attitude when he started to read the Gospel and realized that he was a beloved person. He stated that when he became a Christian, he found a new direction for his life. He continued with his studies and started to work as an independent artist. In 1956 he married my mother, a hearing lady, against the will of her family. Step-by-step his work was recognized by the public. He was able to make a living out of his fine arts and became quite famous in Upper Austria. My mother contributed a lot to his success by constantly being by his side as an interpreter of lip reading and finger spelling when he had to negotiate with architects etc.

We, as his sons (three boys), did not experience anything of the bitterness he reported experiencing during his adolescence and early adult years. We enjoyed a very warm and thankful father. He was thankful to everyone and nearly for everything. He did not see his deafness as a disability anymore, but as an advantage. It helped him to remain focused on his work. In his late years when he realized how his deafness had become a starting point for meaningful services for deaf people in Austria, his thankfulness of having become deaf even increased.

In the light of recent literature on resilience, my father was a living example for what Antonovsky (1979) described as a "sense of coherence." He defined a "sense of coherence" as follows:

> ...a global orientation that expresses the extent to which one has a pervasive, enduring though dynamic feeling of confidence that one's internal and external environments are predictable and that there is a high probability that things will work out as well as can reasonably be expected.
>
> Antonovsky; cited by Sullivan, 1993

In other words it is a mixture of optimism and control. It has three components – comprehensibility, manageability, and meaningfulness. Comprehensibility is the extent to which events are perceived as making logical sense that they are ordered, consistent, and structured. Manageability is the extent to which a person feels that he/she can cope. Meaningfulness is how much one feels that life makes sense and that challenges are worthy of commitment. This concept of "sense of coherence" Antonovsky (1979) explained why some people are more resilient against severe distress than others. It arose from the salutogenic approach, that is, the search for the origins of health rather than the causes of disease. His concept is now widespread and applied across cultures.

In my father's case a concept of resilience related to positive patterns of adaptation in the context of adversity can easily be applied. The main adversity, the sudden hearing loss at age 15, can easily be identified, and the list of adaptive systems that shows a striking consistency in world literature on resilience (Masten & Obradović, 2006) can be applied to his life.

Deafness as a Threat

But is it correct to apply the term "threat" to deafness in general? What does deafness actually mean for a person who was born deaf to deaf parents and grew up in a deaf community? Young, Green, & Rogers, 2008 have addressed these questions in a very unique way in their review article "Resilience and deaf children" (Young et al., 2008). We have to keep these questions in mind when we study literature, which is mainly reporting that deafness in childhood is linked with a greater likelihood of mental health problems in children (Hindley, 1997; van Gent, Goedhart, Hindley, & Treffers, 2007) and adults including physical symptoms and lower quality of life (Fellinger et al., 2005; Fellinger, Holzinger, Gerich, & Goldberg, 2007).

Background

Before we describe the findings of a recent research project on mental health and quality of life in deaf school children in Upper Austria, we would like to give some background information on Austria and our personal professional involvement in the field of deafness.

Austria, a part of the European Union, is a highly developed industrial country. Eight million people are living in Austria; about 350,000 of them are diagnosed with a hearing loss, and about 8,000 people are members of the signing community (http://www.oeglb.at/). The first school for deaf children was founded by the end of the eighteenth century. By the end of the nineteenth century, as in most countries at that time, the oral approach became the official way of deaf education. Nevertheless, sign language was used by the children visiting boarding schools. In the last

20 years many children with different degrees of hearing loss are in regular school settings, but there are still enough children that attend special schools for deaf children.

Recently almost all children with profound hearing loss have received cochlear implants (CI). Since 2005 sign language is an official language in Austria (http:// www.oeglb.at/). Bilingual approaches are still rare in the education of deaf children in spite of strong support by the deaf community.

During his internship in neurology and psychiatry in Linz, Austria, the first author observed deaf patients who were experiencing unsatisfying and unacceptable relationships with their doctors. This situation finally brought him to the setting up of a walk-in clinic for deaf people. In this clinic children and adults are treated by a signing multidisciplinary team in the fields of physical, mental, and social health. Since the very beginning a fourth dimension has also been part of the whole concept of the health centre – the development of communication abilities. This department is led by the second author. Several deaf people also wished to improve their skills in signed, spoken, or written language. It was obvious that these skills were underdeveloped compared to their cognitive abilities. This special clinic has been in existence for over 20 years now. Daily clinical work has provided lots of opportunities to observe the mental health of the deaf and hard of hearing over their life span.

This health centre for the deaf was also the basis for two other important services. The problems of deaf people with additional handicaps very soon became obvious. At the places they were accommodated, some were with their parents, others were in institutions for people with mental retardation or old-aged people – there were no provisions to ensure adequate communication. It was interesting that even if they came only once a week to have training in communication, improvement could be observed. Some also participated in our therapeutic ceramic workshop. These observations encouraged us to fight for a facility where deaf people with additional handicaps could live together and work together in an environment where visual communication is guaranteed. In 1999, it was finally done: "Lebenswelt Schenkenfelden," a "living environment" was set up in the centre of a village. Since then 30 deaf people with additional handicaps work and live together according to the concept of a therapeutic community. Responsibility for each other and the intensive involvement in reconciliation after or during conflicts are the key elements, which are derived from the Gospel of Christ, and lead to a harmonious and open atmosphere.

In order to get a deaf staff, a 3-year training was established for deaf people to become professionals working in the field of people with deafness and additional handicaps. Since 1997 32 deaf professionals have received this qualification with an officially recognized diploma as pedagogues and assistants for visual communication. Since the very beginning an increasing number of children have been admitted to be assessed in a comprehensive way. Since 2003 early intervention for deaf children in Upper Austria became part of our department's responsibility. Since that time there is also a team of therapists directly involved at the special school of the deaf.

In 2004 a study focusing on positive outcomes of deaf children covering the field of psychosocial well-being and academic skills was started – the CHEERS study. This study was not primarily designed on concepts of resilience in general but had a strong emphasis on mental health and quality of life, which can be considered characteristics of life most people desire. Therefore, factors which are correlated to a higher prevalence of mental health problems or mental health disorders can be considered as potential risk factors of which some might be influenced by appropriate measures. As there is a lack of longitudinal studies on resilience of deaf school children, we feel free to share our cross-sectional study data on mental health in this book.

CHEERS Study

Sample Description

Upper Austria is one of nine Austrian provinces and has 1,380,000 inhabitants (http://www.aeiou.at/aeiou.encyclop.o/o111888.htm). Only in Upper Austria all pupils are screened for their hearing in the first year of school attendance. All children with hearing loss are registered at the centre for special education for children with sensory impairments. The centre provides support for these children in mainstream settings all over the country, as well as education at the special school for children with hearing or visual impairments, in Linz, the capital town of Upper Austria. Consequently, the educational authorities of Upper Austria have access to an epidemiologically complete sample of deaf children.

From a population of 145,000 pupils attending the first to ninth grades during the school years 2003–2004 and 2004–2005, all 186 children with bilateral hearing loss of at least 40 dB were invited by the educational authorities of Upper Austria to participate in the study. The size of this group of children with severe and profound hearing loss was very close to the expected population prevalence of one in 750 children (Davis & Wood, 1992; Davis et al., 1997; Thompson et al., 2001).

The principal caregivers of 116 children gave written informed consent, leading to a response rate of 62.4%. The study was approved by the Ethics Committee of the Hospital of St. John of God in Linz (Austria) and was conducted in accordance with the ethical standards stipulated in the 1964 Declaration of Helsinki.

The sample was representative for the population of children with hearing loss in Upper Austria in terms of demographic characteristics (Fellinger, Holzinger, Sattel, & Laucht, 2008; Fellinger, Holzinger, Beitel, Laucht, & Goldberg, 2009). Loss of subjects due to refusal to participate in the study was not selective with regard to gender or age, and those who did not take part did not differ from participants in terms of not having German as their native language. However, children with profound hearing loss were significantly overrepresented among the participants as compared to the nonparticipants, while those with moderate hearing loss were underrepresented. As the degree of hearing loss was a critical factor for the subsequent analyses, this oversampling of children with very little hearing provided the advantage that groups divided by severity of hearing loss had an adequate size to permit reliable comparisons.

The current investigation included 99 children (53 boys, 46 girls) with performance $IQ \geq 70$ (see measures). The characteristics of this sample are presented in Table 7.1. The severity of hearing loss as categorized from recent audiological records varied from moderate (40–69 dB HL: $n = 44$) to severe (70–94 dB HL: $n = 24$) and profound (>94 dB HL: $n = 31$) according to the pure-tone thresholds at 500, 1,000 and 2,000 Hz (Parving, 1995). Within the group of the profoundly deaf ($n = 31$, see Table 7.1), there were 18 children with CI, (average age at implantation 4.5 years). Profoundly deaf children with and without CI did not differ with regard to gender, age, SES (socioeducational status – measured as parental educational level on a five-point scale varying from "without school leaving certificate" to "university degree"), and nonverbal IQ. The mean age at assessment was 11.1 years (range 6.5–16.0). Performance IQ was in the normal range (i.e., within 1 standard deviation of the norm). Spoken language was the preferred means of communication (as reported by the parents) for almost all children with moderate hearing loss and for less than half of the profoundly deaf. In most of the remaining cases ($n = 25$ children), sign language or sign-supported speech was used as an alternative. There were significant differences with regard to severity of hearing loss in the preferred means of communication, the age at identification of hearing loss and the first fitting of hearing aids. Children with a higher degree of hearing loss tended to use sign communication more often, and hearing loss was detected earlier. The majority of participants (58, corresponding to 58.6%) attended a regular school in their local community as single pupils with hearing loss or together with other children with disabilities. Eighteen (18.2%) visited the special school for the deaf in Linz (the capital of the province) following a group mainstream concept. This means that hearing children are also attending the special school for children with sensory impairments. So a group of about 15 hearing children is taught together with a group of about five children with hearing loss by two teachers. The remaining 23 children (23.2%), who mainly had profound hearing loss, attended special classes with about only four to seven deaf children. Results are shown for those who completed the assessments (see tables).

Summary

This large cross-sectional research program in Upper Austria examined mental health, language development, and cognitive abilities of a representative sample of 99 pupils with hearing loss of at least 40 dB. They attended classes from grade one to grade nine at different types of school settings.

Table 7.1 Characteristics of the study sample

Hearing loss	Moderate (40–69 dB) $n=44$	Severe (70–94 dB) $n=24$	Profound (95+ dB) $n=31$	Total $n=99$	Significance level[a]
Gender: n (%) females	24 (54.5)	12 (50.0)	17 (54.8)	53 (53.5)	n.s.
Age in years: M (SD)	11.0 (2.44)	11.7 (3.00)	10.7 (2.95)	11.1 (2.74)	n.s.
SES: M (SD)	3.6 (0.87)	3.9 (0.75)	3.3 (0.89)	3.3 (0.87)	n.s.
Nonverbal IQ: M (SD)	98.64 (16.81)	95.67 (15.61)	98.65 (13.76)	97.92 (15.52)	n.s.
Native language not German[b]: n (%)	8 (18.2)	4 (16.7)	4 (12.9)	16 (16.2)	n.s.
Spoken language preferred: n (%)	42 (95.5)	17 (70.8)	15 (48.4)	74 (74.7)	$p<0.001$
Age at diagnosis of hearing impairment in months: M (SD)	40.64 (28.73)	32.83 (23.06)	14.46 (12.36)	31.05 (25.89)	$p<0.001$
Age at first fitting of hearing aids in months: M (SD)	48.61 (31.38)	37.87 (24.65)	22.23 (20.89)	37.91 (28.97)	$p<0.001$

[a] Results of ANOVAs and χ^2 tests, respectively, comparing groups defined by hearing loss
[b] Like Turkish, Serbo-Croatian and languages from other Eastern European and former Soviet countries

Measures

Mental Health Problems

To assess behavioral problems in children and adolescents, German versions of the Strengths and Difficulties Questionnaire (SDQ) (Woerner et al., 2002) were used. The SDQ is a short assessment instrument that addresses positive and negative behavioral attributes of children and adolescents and generates scores for clinically relevant aspects. The SDQ can be completed by parents or teachers or as a self-report by children aged 11 years or older. First presented by Goodman (1997) the SDQ is now applied worldwide, and a considerable body of reliability and validity data has been published (Becker, Woerner, Hasselhorn, Banaschewski, & Rothenberger, 2004; Klasen, Woerner, Rothenberger, & Goodman, 2003).

The results of the four problem subscales of the SDQ (emotional symptoms, conduct problems, hyperactivity/inattention, and peer problems), the combined total difficulties score, and the positive scale assessing prosocial behavior were computed. Normative reference data have been provided for the German parent version (Woerner, Becker, & Rothenberger, 2004). Of children and adolescents in the community, approximately 10% scored within the borderline range and a further 10% within the abnormal range of the total difficulties score (slightly lower percentages of caseness were chosen for the five subscales).

There are positive experiences using the SDQ in the field of deafness. For instance, Hintermair (2007) assessed parents' perceptions of German deaf children's emotional problems (Hintermair, 2007). A translation in Swedish sign language has also been used in a survey on abuse in deaf adolescents (Malmberg, Rydell, & Smedje, 2003). A standardized sign language version for the SDQ does not exist for Austrian sign language. If the level of literacy was not sufficient, the SDQ was used as a structured interview in the preferred mode of communication, whether in sign language or simplified German. All parents completed the parent SDQ, and teachers completed the teacher SDQ.

Mental Health Disorders

The Kinder-DIPS (Diagnostisches Interview für psychische Störungen) (Unnewehr, Schneider, & Margraf, 1998) is a German structured diagnostic interview derived from the Diagnostic Interview Schedule for Children (DISC-R) (Shaffer et al., 1993). The parent version was used to diagnose Axis I disorders according to ICD-10 and the (DSM-IV TR) for lifetime and point-prevalence in children from age 6 to 19 years. The Kinder-DIPS is a reliable and valid structured interview.(Unnewehr et al., 1998) The Kinder-DIPS assesses all anxiety disorders of childhood or adolescence, panic disorders (with and without agoraphobia), agoraphobia without history of panic disorder, simple phobia, major depression, dysthymia, attention-deficit hyperactivity disorder, oppositional defiant disorder, conduct disorder, enuresis, and encopresis. The parents' version was used in the present study. Our use of current diagnosis allows us to examine the relationship between each diagnosis and children's scores on the Strengths and Difficulties Questionnaire (SDQ), (Becker et al., 2004; Klasen et al., 2003; Woerner et al., 2002, 2004) but is confined to an arbitrary point in the child's life. We, therefore, also considered lifetime diagnosis, since this provides information about relapsing disorders such as depression.

Quality of Life

The Inventory of Life Quality in Children and Adolescents (ILC) was handed out to children and their parents to assess basic aspects of quality of life in deaf children (Mattejat & Remschmidt, 2006). The ILC comprises seven areas (school, family, social contacts with peers, interests and recreational activities, physical health, mental health, and global), which are rated in terms of their quality of life on a five-point scale from "very good" to "very bad" using "smiley" icons as anchors. In addition, an LQ total score is computed, with high scores reflecting better quality of life. Parents and adolescents were given the questionnaire version, while children were interviewed to complete the children's report form. Satisfactory test–retest reliability was reported with coefficients of about $r_{tt} = 0.60$ for most scales (Mattejat & Remschmidt, 2006). Norms are available for different samples including community and clinical samples.

Hearing Loss

The severity of hearing loss was categorized from recent audiological records (within the preceding year) as moderate (40–69 dB hearing loss), severe (70–94 dB hearing loss), or profound (>95 dB hearing loss) according to the pure-tone thresholds at 500, 1,000 and 2,000 Hz (Parving, 1995).

Cognitive Abilities

All children were assessed for their nonverbal intelligence using the Hamburg Wechsler Intelligence Scales, third revision (HAWIK) (Tewes, Rossman, & Schallberger, 1999). The assessments were carried out in the preferred mode of communication of the child. Norms for the general population were used.

Language Measures

Spoken and sign language level. Deaf children may be using more than one method of communication, i.e., spoken and/or signed language. The Profile of Multiple Language Proficiencies (PMLP) (Goldstein & Bebko, 2003) was created by Goldstein and Bebko to assess language skills in both modalities by use of a single scale that represents eight different stages of language development. These stages of language development can be rated independently for spoken and signed language. They describe developmental steps of languages from a prelinguistic level, basic one or two word/sign utterances, full simple sentences up to consistent and fluent use of grammatical rules without any errors. Children with no use of signed language at all were rated at the lowest level of signed language proficiency. To determine the language level according to the PMLP, videotaped structured conversations in signed and/or spoken language were rated by experienced linguists and a deaf psychologist. The PMLP is used as our measure of language used in peer communication.

Spoken language grammar: Spoken language grammar was assessed by a task of sentence imitation included in the Heidelberger Sprachentwicklungstest (HSET) (Grimm & Schöler, 1991). German sentences with increasing complexity were presented orally once or twice in an optimal face-to-face situation, which permits the use of lip reading. The sentences as repeated by the children were evaluated for grammatical correctness. This procedure, therefore, represents a mixed measure of expressive grammar, language perception, and speech articulation. German norms for children up to an age of 9:11 years are available. Therefore, the age norms of 9:11-year-old children were used as a point of reference for the study sample older than 9:11 years.

Expressive vocabulary. Vocabulary knowledge was assessed via a word list of the German version of the Wechsler Intelligence Scales (Hawik III) (Tewes et al., 1999). The children were presented a word in spoken and written form and asked to explain its meaning. To convey this explanation the children used their preferred mode of communication, i.e., spoken and/or signed language.

Intelligibility Spoken language intelligibility was assessed by videotaping children as they pronounced 20 different digits from 0 to 99 and counting the percentage of number words understood by a naïve listener watching the tape afterward.

Reading Comprehension To assess reading comprehension a standardized German reading test (Grissemann & Baumberg, 2000) was used. The child is required to read short texts with increasing complexity and to answer multiple choice questions.

Parents' and Teachers' Interviews

For the parent and teacher interview, extended structured interviews were performed with parents and teachers, including medical history, family background, the child's situation at school, and the child's preferred mode of communication at school and home. Parents and teachers were asked to evaluate the children's ability to make themselves understood with the question: "How do you estimate the child's ability to make him/herself understood in the family?"

Teachers provided information on the child's peer acceptance by answering questions such as: "How frequently has he/she had negative experiences like being teased: often/sometimes/rarely/never?" The assessments and interviews were

administered in the children's regional schools by a multiprofessional team with
extensive experience in working with deaf children. The team consisted of two
linguists, one psychologist, and one neuropsychiatrist, who also conducted the
Kinder-DIPS interviews.

Summary

To assess mental health aspects a set of standardized questionnaires like the
SDQ and the ILC, as well as a structured psychiatric parent interview (Kinder
DIPS), was used together with extended interviews with parents and teachers
including medical history, family background, the child's situation at school,
the child's communicative abilities, and family communication.

In a field study these instruments, with well established norms for the
general population, were found to be applicable for a population of children
with different degrees of hearing loss; for the self-report versions the level
and mode of language was adapted to the individual subjects needs.

Results

Parent and Teacher Reports on Deaf Children's Mental Health (SDQ)

Table 7.2 shows the average scores and the percentages of children who scored
within the borderline or abnormal range on the different SDQ scales obtained for
parent ratings. Data are presented for the entire sample as well as separately for
groups defined by degree of deafness as compared with a normative German hearing
sample aged 6–16 years (Woerner et al., 2004). Deaf children scored significantly
higher than hearing controls on all subscales, with the exception of hyperactivity/
inattention. Accordingly, rates of deaf children with scores in the borderline or
clinical range exceeded those of normative samples with regard to emotional problems, conduct problems, and peer problems. Results for the total difficulties indicate that more than one third of the deaf children were rated as borderline or
abnormal by parents, which is approximately twice as much as among controls.
Comparison between deaf groups revealed no significant overall differences, either
in SDQ scores or in percentage of cases. In addition, there were no significant differences between profoundly deaf children with and without CI. Upon closer
inspection scores and rates for conduct problems and hyperactivity/inattention were
found to be significantly higher among children with severe hearing loss than in
those with moderate and profound deafness, respectively.

Table 7.3 presents the teacher-rated mean SDQ scale scores and percentages of
borderline/abnormal cases for the deaf sample (total group and separately according
to degree of hearing loss) as compared to a normative British hearing sample aged

Table 7.2 Variation in parent SDQ ratings by degree of deafness in the child: means, SD, and % disturbed (borderline and abnormal cases)

SDQ scale	Moderate (40–69 dB) n=41	Severe (70–94 dB) n=22	Profound (95+ dB) n=29	Total n=92	German hearing sample n=930	p (between deaf groups)[a]	p (between deaf and hearing)[a]
Emotional symptoms	3.12 (2.66)	3.41 (2.24)	2.90 (2.27)	3.12 (2.43)	1.53 (1.75)	0.760	<0.001
	34.1%	45.4%	34.5%	37.0%	14.0%	0.639	0.001
Conduct problems	2.22 (1.85)	3.0 (1.95)	2.03 (1.86)	2.35 (1.90)	1.82 (1.62)	0.167	0.009
	43.9%	59.1%	37.9%	45.7%	15.3%	0.309	0.001
Hyperactivity/ inattention	3.56 (2.42)	4.09 (2.47)	2.97 (2.41)	3.5 (2.44)	3.19 (2.28)	0.260	0.226
	19.5%	31.8%	10.3%	19.6%	14.7%	0.160	0.188
Peer problems	1.93 (1.85)	2.41 (2.56)	2.69 (2.21)	2.28 (2.15)	1.59 (1.68)	0.330	0.003
	39%	27.3%	51.7%	40.2%	13.3%	0.207	0.001
Prosocial behavior	8.27 (1.90)	8.36 (1.89)	7.48 (2.26)	8.04 (2.03)	7.55 (1.92)	0.198	0.022
	9.8%	9.1%	10.3%	9.8%	15.6%	0.989	0.124
Total difficulties	10.83 (6.47)	12.91 (6.01)	10.59 (6.47)	11.25 (6.37)	8.13 (5.33)	0.374	<0.001
	36.6%	45.5%	27.6%	35.9%	18.4%	0.416	<0.001

[a] Statistical tests in the following order: ANOVA and t-test, respectively; χ^2 test

Table 7.3 Variation in teacher SDQ ratings by degree of deafness in the child: means, SD, and % disturbed (borderline and abnormal cases)

SDQ scale	Moderate (40–69 dB) n=42	Severe (70–94 dB) n=19	Profound (95+ dB) n=28	Total n=89	British hearing sample n=8,208	p (between deaf groups)[a]	p (between deaf and hearing)[a]
Emotional symptoms	1.73 (2.29)	1.63 (2.34)	1.77 (2.14)	1.72 (2.23)	1.4 (1.9)	0.908	0.204
	11.9%	15.8%	14.3%	13.5%	14.4%	0.909	0.805
Conduct problems	1.12 (1.45)	1.94 (1.77)	1.50 (1.74)	1.39 (1.61)	0.9 (1.6)	0.218	0.008
	16.7%	31.6%	21.4%	21.3%	14.1%	0.420	0.049
Hyperactivity/ inattention	1.85 (1.68)	2.75 (2.20)	2.27 (2.66)	2.15 (2.10)	2.9 (2.8)	0.076	0.002
	2.4%	15.8%	10.7%	7.9%	17.5%	0.157	0.017
Peer problems	2.05 (2.29)	1.56 (1.50)	2.45 (2.22)	2.06 (2.13)	1.4 (1.8)	0.584	0.007
	21.4%	5.3%	28.6%	20.2%	12.1%	0.144	0.019
Prosocial behavior	6.63 (2.89)	6.63 (2.03)	7.82 (1.89)	6.96 (2.51)	7.2 (2.4)	0.171	0.403
	35.7%	42.1%	14.3%	30.3%	26.4%	0.073	0.399
Total difficulties	6.85 (6.09)	7.88 (5.40)	8.00 (7.00)	7.38 (6.18)	6.6 (6.0)	0.606	0.265
	16.7%	26.3%	21.4%	20.2%	18.7%	0.672	0.712

[a] Statistical tests in the following order: ANOVA and t-test, respectively, χ^2 test

5–15 years (Meltzer, Gatward, Goodman, & Ford, 2000). This comparison group was chosen as a substitute for a still lacking representative German sample. Deaf children rated by their teachers received significantly higher scores than hearing controls on the subscales assessing conduct problems and peer problems, as well as lower scores on the hyperactivity/inattention subscale. Similar results were obtained for the percentages of cases, with the rate of deaf children above threshold on total difficulties being only slightly higher than among controls. As was the case for the parents' reports, differences between groups according to degree of deafness turned out to be rather small. Once again, somewhat higher scores and rates for "externalizing" problems were observed in children with severe hearing loss compared to those with moderate and profound deafness. No significant differences were observed among profoundly deaf children with and without CI, although teachers generally reported fewer problems in children with CI than in those without CI on all SDQ scales (reaching a trend for conduct problems).

A further analysis examined the differences and agreements between the parents' and teachers' ratings of the children. Results indicated that parents were more likely than teachers to rate their deaf children as having difficulties ($F_{(1,179)} = 28.78$, $p < 0.001$), with significantly higher scores on all SDQ subscales (all $p < 0.004$) except for peer problems ($p = 0.149$). In addition, agreement between parent and teacher reports was determined and compared with cross-informant correlations from a normative British hearing sample (Meltzer et al., 2000). Table 7.4 shows the correlations between parent and teacher SDQ scores separately for subscales and total difficulties in the deaf sample and in hearing controls. As can be seen, correlations in the deaf sample were generally moderate, with the exception of prosocial behavior and conduct problems, which yielded slightly lower coefficients. There were no significant differences between correlations from deaf and hearing samples. Cross-informant agreement on deaf children's mental health was as high (or low) as among hearing controls. Regarding emotional symptoms, agreement on deaf children even tended to be superior to that on hearing controls.

Table 7.4 Cross-informant correlations for SDQ scores between parents and teachers (comparison with British normative sample)

SDQ scale	Deaf sample $n=87$	British normative sample $n=7,313$	p (between deaf sample and British normative sample)
Emotional symptoms	0.41	0.27	0.148
Conduct problems	0.28	0.37	0.359
Hyperactivity/inattention	0.41	0.48	0.426
Peer problems	0.53	0.37	0.066
Prosocial behavior	0.10	0.25	0.158
Total difficulties	0.48	0.46	0.815

Current and Lifetime Diagnoses

It was possible to obtain clinical diagnoses for 95 children, as the parents of four children did not keep their appointments. Both current and lifetime diagnoses were found to be unrelated to severity of deafness (Table 7.5), although the lifetime rates for "any diagnosis" fell just short of significance at the 5% level. Type of school attended was not related to current or lifetime diagnoses of any mental disorder.

Within the profoundly deaf group CI (average age at implantation 4 years 5 months) had no impact on any lifetime or current diagnosis, nor were there differences in terms of gender, German as first language, or ability to make oneself understood within the family. However, the extent of hearing loss had been diagnosed about 1 month earlier (Mann–Whitney $U=42.5$, $p<0.029$), and they were also more likely to use spoken speech. Five children of the profoundly deaf group without an implant used only sign language, and three preferred spoken language. The equivalent numbers for those with an implant are 0 and 10 ($\chi^2=8.67$, $p<0.013$).

Table 7.5 shows that 32.6% had a current diagnosis, and 45.3% had a diagnosis in their lifetime from the Kinder-DIPS examination. It can be seen that 7.4% of the children are currently depressed, and over a quarter had been depressed at some time. These closest comparable figures for lifetime diagnosis of German-speaking children with normal hearing are 18% for any diagnosis and 3.4% for depression. However, no diagnosis is related to the degree of deafness (Ihle, Esser, Schmidt, & Blanz, 2000; Ihle & Esser, 2002).

Parent and Child Reports on Quality of Life (ILC)

Parent-rated ILC scores for the deaf sample and a normative German sample aged 6–15 years (Mattejat & Remschmidt, 2006) are presented in Table 7.6. Higher scores on subscales reflect a poorer quality of life, while a higher LQ total score reflects a better quality. Parents of deaf children did not differ from parents of hearing controls with regard to the total score. However, significant differences in subscale scores were found, indicating that parents of deaf children were more satisfied with their children's quality of life regarding the areas of family, interests and recreational activities, and physical health compared to parents of hearing controls. In contrast, they tended to score lower than controls on satisfaction with their children's peer contacts. There were no significant differences in ILC scores between groups according to degree of hearing loss or between profoundly deaf children with and without CI, with one exception: parents of children with CI were significantly more satisfied with their children's quality of life in terms of family than parents of children without CI ($p=0.038$).

The self-rated ILC scores reveal a more complex picture (see Table 7.7).

Compared to hearing controls, deaf children reported that they were less satisfied with their quality of life in general (marginally significant), as well as with

Table 7.5 Current and lifetime clinical diagnoses by degree of deafness (excl. IQ<70)

	Degree of hearing impairment			Results	
Current clinical diagnosis by KINDER DIPS	Moderate n=44	Severe n=23	Profound n=28	Sig. of statistical test[a]	Total n=95
Depression F30	n=4 9.1%	n=3 13.0%	n=0 0	p=0.17	7 7.4%
Anxiety disorders F93/F40	n=4 9.1%	n=5 21.7%	n=6 21.4%	p=0.25	15 11.6%
Internalizing disorder F30/F93/F40	n=8 18.2%	n=6 26.1%	n=6 21.4%%	p=0.75	20 20.2%
Hyperactivity F90	n=4 9.1%	n=4 17.4%	n=3 10.7%	p=0.59	11 11.6%
Oppositional defiant disorders F91/F92	n=6 13.6%	n=1 4.3%	n=1 3.6%	p=0.24	8 8.4%
Externalizing disorder F90/F91/F92	n=8 18.2%	n=5 21.7%	n=4 14.3%	p=0.79	17 17.9%
Any diagnoses	n=14 31.8%	n=10 43.5%	n=7 25.0%	p=0.37	n=31 32.6%
No diagnosis	n=30 68.2%	n=13 56.5%	n=21 75.0%	p=0.37	n=64 67.4%
Lifetime Clinical diagnosis by KINDER DIPS	Moderate n=44	Severe n=23	Profound n=28	Sig. of statistical test[b]	Total n=95
Depression F30	n=13 29.5%	n=6 26.1%	n=6 21.4%	p=0.758	25 26.3%
Anxiety/phobia F93/F40	n=5 11.4%	n=5 21.7%	n=6 21.4%	p=0.41	16 16.8%

Internalizing disorder F30/F93/F40	$n=15$ 34.1%	$n=8$ 34.8%	$n=8$ 28.6%	$p=0.86$	31 31.3%
Hyperactivity F90	$n=4$ 9.1%	$n=6$ 26.1%	$n=3$ 10.7%	$p=0.145$	13 13.7%
Oppositional defiant disorders F91/F92	$n=7$ 15.9%	$n=1$ 4.3%	$n=1$ 3.6%	$p=0.14$	9 9.5%
Externalizing disorder F90/F91/F92	$n=9$ 20.5%	$n=7$ 30.4%	$n=4$ 14.3%	$p=0.37$	20 20.2%
Any diagnoses	$n=21$ 47.6%	$n=14$ 60.9%	$n=8$ 28.6%	$p=0.06$	43 45.3%
No diagnosis	$n=23$ 53.4%	$n=9$ 39.1%	$n=20$ 71.4%	$p=0.06$	52 54.7%

Percentages refer to the percentage within each group of hearing loss. Children may have multiple disorders

[a] χ^2-test, two tailed

[b] χ^2-test, two tailed between different degrees of hearing loss

Table 7.6 Variation in parent ILC ratings by degree of deafness in the child: means and SD (in parenthesis)

ILC scales	Moderate (40–69 dB) n=37	Severe (70–94 dB) n=20	Profound (95+ dB) n=24	Total n=81	German hearing sample n=315	p (between deaf groups)[a]	p (between deaf and hearing)[a]
School	2.03 (0.99)	2.35 (0.89)	2.08 (0.97)	2.12 (0.95)	2.01 (0.73)	0.466	0.288
Family	1.35 (0.72)	1.50 (0.69)	1.25 (0.53)	1.36 (0.66)	1.64 (0.68)	0.459	<0.001
Peer contacts	1.73 (0.80)	2.10 (1.02)	2.21 (0.98)	1.96 (0.93)	1.77 (0.62)	0.107	0.065
Interests and recreational activities	1.70 (1.00)	1.55 (0.69)	1.79 (0.83)	1.69 (0.88)	1.92 (0.83)	0.662	0.021
Physical health	1.46 (0.65)	1.35 (0.75)	1.35 (0.59)	1.41 (0.65)	1.73 (0.71)	0.800	<0.001
Mental health	2.19 (0.85)	2.40 (1.00)	2.21 (0.72)	2.25 (0.85)	2.14 (0.74)	0.650	0.258
Global rating	1.81 (0.85)	1.85 (0.88)	1.92 (0.72)	1.85 (0.81)	1.77 (0.60)	0.885	0.365
LQ total score	22.73 (3.20)	21.90 (3.82)	22.17 (3.66)	22.36 (3.47)	22.01 (4.95)	0.661	0.370

[a] Statistical tests in the following order: ANOVA and t-test, respectively, χ^2 test

Table 7.7 Variation in children's ILC ratings by degree of deafness in the child: means and SD (in parenthesis)

ILC scales	Moderate (40–69 dB) $n=40$	Severe (70–94 dB) $n=22$	Profound (95+dB) $n=29$	Total $n=91$	German hearing sample $n=315$	p (between deaf groups)[a]	p (between deaf and hearing)[a]
School	1.75 (0.91)	1.91 (1.02)	1.76 (0.87)	1.79 (0.88)	2.03 (0.74)	0.772	0.011
Family	1.44 (0.97)	1.64 (1.00)	1.38 (0.62)	1.47 (0.88)	1.67 (0.74)	0.565	0.030
Peer contacts	1.55 (0.71)	1.41 (0.67)	1.45 (0.99)	1.48 (0.79)	1.59 (0.70)	0.771	0.204
Interests and recreational activities	2.42 (1.39)	2.68 (1.43)	2.55 (1.66)	2.53 (1.48)	1.94 (0.94)	0.801	<0.001
Physical health	2.00 (1.09)	2.23 (1.07)	2.07 (1.25)	2.08 (1.13)	1.65 (0.76)	0.753	0.001
Mental health	2.03 (0.87)	2.14 (0.83)	2.14 (0.97)	2.09 (0.89)	2.04 (0.79)	0.836	0.597
Global rating	1.59 (0.72)	1.48 (0.75)	1.66 (0.90)	1.58 (0.78)	1.67 (0.62)	0.729	0.303
LQ total score	21.90 (3.33)	21.32 (3.86)	21.86 (3.34)	21.75 (3.43)	22.42 (5.29)	0.800	0.065

[a]Statistical tests in the following order: ANOVA and t-test, respectively, χ^2 test

their interests and recreational activities and their physical health in particular. On the other hand, they scored significantly higher than controls on satisfaction with the areas of school and family. All differences between deaf groups were far from being statistically significant, with the exception of one area. Profoundly deaf children with and without CI did not differ with regard to their self-rated ILC scores. Compared to those without CI, children with CI were significantly less satisfied with their quality of life regarding school ($p=0.008$).

Further evidence on the differences between parents and deaf children in their perceptions of quality of life can be derived from analyses of the differences and agreements in terms of the ILC scales between these groups. Results revealed that in three areas (school, peer contacts, and total quality) parents were significantly less satisfied than their children (all $p<0.02$), while in two areas (interests and recreational activities, physical health) children reported less satisfaction than their parents (all $p<0.001$). Agreement between parents' and children's ratings of life quality was generally low and statistically insignificant, with the exception of two areas (family: $R=0.320$, $p=0.004$ and school: $R=0.207$, $p=0.066$).

These discrepancies between parents' and children's view of their quality of life are corroborated by findings on the relationship between quality of life and children's mental health. While parent-rated SDQ scores were strongly associated with parent-rated ILC scores (SDQ total difficulties and LQ total score: $R=-0.583$, $p<0.001$), they were found to be unrelated to self-rated ILC scores ($R=-0.164$, $p=0.126$).

Family Communication

Thirty-three percent of the parents reported that their child had difficulties making him/herself understood in the family. Twenty-five percent of the children preferred the use of sign language, but only 50% of their parents reported that they were using sign language on a regular basis in family communication. Only 25% of the parents in families with children whose preferred communication was sign language rated their competence in sign language as good.

Mental Health and Language in the Teenager Subgroup

Sample

The study sample ($n=43$) did not show any significant difference regarding sex, age, and mother tongue other than German from the nonparticipants. Children with severe/profound hearing loss were more likely to participate ($p=0.008$). The average age of the sample was 13:5 years (SD 1:6) (age range from 10:7 to 16), 60.5% were female. Average performance IQ was 99.26 (SD 15.1). 21.4% of the children had a multilingual family background. Spoken language was the preferred means of communication for 34 children (79%). The others primarily used sign language. Thirty-three children (77%) were mainstreamed together with classmates with normal hearing. Ten children, who had significantly higher degrees of hearing loss ($p = 0.009$) attended small classes exclusively for the deaf in the school for the deaf. The majority of them (seven out of ten children) used sign language as their preferred means of communication. They were more often from a family with a mother tongue other than German ($p = 0.023$). No differences regarding sex, age, socioeconomic status (SES), as measured by educational level of the mother, and nonverbal IQ were found between these ten children and the 33 mainstreamed children.

Language

Children with bilateral permanent hearing loss showed significantly impaired language skills as compared to the reported norms for each test, which are based on hearing children (Table 7.1). All the language skills reported except intelligibility of speech are highly correlated with the degree of hearing loss. For our sample with a mean age of 13:5 years, the equivalent age level for vocabulary knowledge is only 10:2 years. Grammatical skills as assessed by the HSET showed a mean standard score of 30.1 as compared to a norm of 8–9:11-year-old German children with normal hearing. Reading comprehension scores were below average but within the range of 1 standard deviation (standard score 45.1).

All spoken language measures showed significantly worse results for the children in the school for the deaf (Table 7.8). However, these children demonstrated more elaborated sign language skills as compared to those in the mainstream. On the other hand, in a mode-independent comparison of language level by use of the

Table 7.8 Language results by school settings: means and SD

Language test results	Mainstream ($n = 33$)	Segregated ($n = 10$)	Total ($n = 43$)	p^a
HAWIK III: passive vocabulary age of reference (SD)	11.14 (3.35)	7.21 (1.30)	10.23 (3.43)	<0.001
HSET, grammar standard score (SD)	33.33 (14.59)	19.50 (7.91)	30.12 (14.51)	0.001
Intelligibility: percentage of correct numbers (SD)	94.84 (7.13)	55.56 (36.78)	86.0 (24.34)	0.013
Reading comprehension standard score (SD)	48.73 (11.34)	34.71 (1.81)	45.14 (11.58)	<0.001
PMLP spoken language level: raw score (SD)	5.88 (1.36)	3.60 (1.65)	5.35 (1.72)	<0.001
PMLP sign language level: raw score (SD)	1.76 (1.69)	4.30 (1.16)	2.35 (1.91)	<0.001

[a]Mainstream vs. segregated

PMLP, the sign language level of the children in special classes for the deaf was found to be significantly lower ($p=0.001$) than the spoken language level of the mainstreamed students.

Mental Health

As compared to the norms, parents perceived more emotional, conduct, and peer relationship problems and thus reported higher total problem scores on the SDQ. The deaf adolescents themselves only showed a significantly higher rate of peer relationship problems (Tables 7.9 and 7.10).

Summary

Prevalence of mental health disorders is about twice as high as in the general population. SDQ, DIPS:

1. No significant differences in mental health were observed between groups according to the degree of hearing loss. But on a descriptive basis parents and to a lower extent teachers reported more problems in children with severe deafness than in those with moderate or profound deafness (especially so-called externalizing problems). The lifetime rates for "any diagnosis" fell just short of significance at the 5% level.
2. Parents reported more problems than teachers, who mainly reported more conduct and peer problems but less problems with hyperactivity and inattention.
3. Over a quarter of all children had been depressed at some time (26.3%), but there was no difference regarding the degree of hearing loss.
4. Children with CI (15 out of 31 within the profoundly deaf group), (mean implantations age: 48, 2 months SD 32, 6 months) did not show significant differences in problem behavior of lifetime diagnoses.
5. Type of school attended was not related to lifetime diagnoses of any mental disorder (57 normal schools, 38 special schools).
6. Findings on "Quality of Life" showed that parents tend to have a more positive view of their children's "Quality of Life" compared to the children's self-reports showing problems of isolation and physical complaints.
7. SDQ self-reports by adolescents showed increased scores in peer relationship problems, whereas parents reported higher rates of mental distress in general.

Table 7.9 SDQ: Parents' ratings by school settings: means, SD and % above the threshold of the scale for "borderline range"

SDQ scale	Mainstream n=31	Segregated n=9	Total n=40	German norm sample n=930	Significance of mean difference			
					p^a	p^b	p^c	p^d
Emotional symptoms	3.00 (2.68) 32.3%	4.11 (2.15) 44.4%	3.25 (2.59) 35.0%	1.53 (1.75) 14.0%	<0.001	0.005	0.007	0.262
Conduct problems	2.35 (2.11) 25.9%	2.78 (1.20) 22.2%	2.45 (1.93) 25.0%	1.82 (1.62) 15.3%	0.046	0.168	0.044	0.450
Hyperactivity and inattention	3.16 (2.61) 22.6%	3.56 (1.67) 11.1%	3.25 (2.42) 20.0%	3.19 (2.28) 14.7%	0.876	0.952	0.529	0.672
Peer problems	2.97 (2.33) 29.0%	2.67 (1.80) 33.3%	2.90 (2.21) 30.0%	1.59 (1.68) 13.3%	0.001	0.003	0.111	0.723
Prosocial behavior	8.13 (1.78) 6.4%	7.56 (2.69) 11.1%	8.00 (2.00) 7.5%	7.55 (1.92) 15.6%	0.163	0.081	0.995	0.456
Total difficulties	11.48 (6.93) 40.0%	13.11 (4.46) 50.0%	11.85 (6.44) 42.2%	8.13 (5.33) 18.4%	0.001	0.011	0.010	0.512

[a]Total study sample vs. British norm
[b]Mainstream vs. British norm
[c]Segregated vs. British norm
[d]Mainstream vs. Segregated

Table 7.10 SDQ self-ratings by school settings: means, SD, and % above the threshold of the scale for "borderline range"

SDQ scale	Mainstream (n=33)	Segregated (n=10)	Total (n=43)	British norm sample (n=4,228)	Significance of mean differences			
					p^a	p^b	p^c	p^d
Emotional symptoms	2.73 (2.24) 9.1%	3.80 (2.78) 30.0%	2.98 (2.39) 14.0%	2.8 (2.1) 11.2%	0.630	0.853	0.285	0.217
Conduct problems	2.15 (1.62) 9.1%	3.10 (1.97) 30.0%	2.37 (1.73) 14.0%	2.2 (1.7) 10.6%	0.518	0.865	0.182	0.131
Hyperactivity and inattention	3.33 (1.07) 6.0%	3.90 (1.59) 10.0%	3.47 (1.97) 7.0%	3.8 (2.2) 11.5%	0.271	0.205	0.847	0.432
Peer problems	2.55 (1.82) 36.4%	3.60 (1.96) 50.0%	2.79 (1.88) 39.5%	1.5 (1.4) 3.6%	<0.001	0.002	0.008	0.122
Prosocial behavior	8.03 (1.47) 15.2%	7.10 (2.69) 40.0%	7.81 (1.83) 20.9%	8.0 (1.7) 20.9%	0.508	0.906	0.317	0.161
Total difficulties	10.76 (5.19) 18.02%	14.40 (6.19) 40.0%	11.60 (5.59) 23.3%	10.3 (5.2) 16.5%	0.133	0.616	0.066	0.070

[a] Total study sample vs. British norm
[b] Mainstream vs. British norm
[c] Segregated vs. British norm
[d] Mainstream vs. segregated

Correlates

Quality of Life and Mental Health Problems

These discrepancies between parents' and children's view of their quality of life are corroborated by findings on the relationship between quality of life and children's mental health. While parent-rated SDQ scores were strongly associated with parent-rated ILC scores (SDQ total difficulties and LQ total score: $R = -0.583$, $p < 0.001$), they were found to be unrelated to self-rated ILC scores ($R = -0.164$, $p = 0.126$).

Mental Health Problems and Mental Health Disorders

The association between current clinical diagnosis and scores on the SDQ is shown in Table 7.11. The SDQ total score is related to all the diagnoses listed, but depression, anxiety, and phobias are also linked to the SDQ emotional problems score. Depressed children have poor peer relationships, while anxious children are also hyperactive. Internalizing disorders as well as externalizing disorders are related to all SDQ scales except peer relationship problems.

Further analyses explored the association between mental distress in deaf children and characteristics of their family and peer relationships. A lifetime diagnosis of mental distress is related to the parent's rating of the child's ability to make himself or herself understood in the family: 7.7% ($n = 4$) of those without a diagnosis sometimes had problems, but all the others ($n = 48$) reported no problems. In contrast, 18.6% ($n = 8$) of those with a diagnosis sometimes had problems, and a further 7% ($n = 3$) could "almost never" make themselves understood (no problems vs. sometimes/almost always problems, odds ratio 4.12 [1.2–14.1], $p = 0.020$). This difference remains after controlling for IQ and degree of deafness.

Parents and teachers were asked whether the child had ever been teased, isolated, or maltreated. As can be seen in Table 7.12, ratings by both teachers and parents indicated that children with a lifetime diagnosis of an internalizing disorder had odds ratios of 3.2–6.4 of having been teased, maltreated, or isolated when compared to those without such a diagnosis. For lifetime externalizing disorders only parents reported that their child had been teased significantly more often than those without a lifetime diagnosis. There were no differences concerning other characteristics of interpersonal relationships and regarding teachers' ratings.

Ratings by parents of children not being able to make themselves understood correlated with being teased +0.34 ($p < 0.001$), with being isolated +0.26 ($p = 0.013$), and with being maltreated +0.22 ($p = 0.03$). Ratings by teachers of children being able to make themselves understood correlated with being accepted by others +0.22 ($p = 0.03$). Logistic regression shows that failure to make oneself understood in the family is the best predictor of being teased (Table 7.13). Although a lifetime clinical diagnosis is most important for the explanation of being teased in terms of explained

Table 7.11 Current clinical diagnosis against SDQ scores for 90 children with complete records; showing the biserial correlation between the diagnosis and the scale together with its significance, and the percentage of children with that diagnosis who have a score above the threshold of the scale for "borderline range"

Clinical diagnosis	Emotional n=90	Conduct n=90	Hyperactivity n=90	Peer n=90	Total score n=90
Depression / F30	0.316 (0.002)** 100.0%	0.142 (0.181) 80.0%	0.043 (0.684) 40.0%	0.254 (0.016)* 80.0%	0.303 (0.004)** 20.0%
Anxiety/phobias / F93/F40	0.237 (0.024)* 69.2%	0.197 0.063 61.5%	0.286 (0.006)** 38.5%	−0.018 0.867 38.5%	0.251 0.017* 53.8%
Any internalizing disorder	0.362** 0.000** 76.5%	0.214 0.043* 64.7%	0.240 0.023* 35.3%	0.148 0.164 52.9%	0.363 0.000** 64.7%
Hyperactivity / F90	0.168 0.114 40.0%	0.161 0.129 50.0%	0.352 0.001** 60.0%	0.099 0.353 60.0%	0.275 0.009** 70.0%
Opp. Def. Disorder / F91/F92	0.159 0.136 62.5%	0.285 0.000** 87.5%	0.225 0.033* 25.0%	0.058 0.586 50.0%	0.265 0.012* 75.0%
Any externalizing disorder	0.239 0.023* 50.0%	0.290 0.006** 68.7%	0.417 0.000** 43.7%	0.051 0.635 50.0%	0.362 0.000** 68.3%
Any Kinder DIPS Dx	0.398 0.000** 63.0%	0.337 0.001* 66.7%	0.451 0.000** 37.0%	0.078 0.463 48.1%	0.473 0.000** 66.7%

*p<0.05, **p<0.01

Table 7.12 Percentage of children with a lifetime disorder who are sometimes or frequently teased/maltreated/isolated, or never, seldom, or only sometimes accepted by other children

	Teased	Maltreated	Isolated	Less accepted by peers
Internalizing disorders				
Parents	*46.7%*	*33.3%*	*31.0%*	28.6%
	4.5 [1.7–11.7]	*4.5 [1.5–13.1]*	*5.3 [1.7–16.2]*	1.3 [0.4–3.1]
	(0.002)**	*(0.006)***	*(0.003)***	(0.557)
Teachers	*38.0%*	*24.1%*	*31.0%*	34.5%
	3.2 [1.1–8.1]	*4.3 [1.3–12.4]*	*6.4 [1.4–24.8]*	2.5 [0.8–6.2]
	(0.023)*	*(0.013)**	*(0.012)**	(0.075)
Externalizing disorders				
Parents	*50.0%*	25.0%	21.0%	26.3%
	3.7 [1.3–10.4]	1.6 [0.5–5.2]	1.8 [0.5–5.7]	1.1 [0.3–3.3]
	(0.014)*	(0.440)	(0.355)	(0.584)
Teachers	26.3%	15.8%	10.5%	31.6%
	1.6 [0.4–3.9]	0.77 [0.1–2.6]	2.1 [0.4–7.3]	1.8 [0.6–5.2]
	(0.498)	(0.704)	(0.272)	(0.311)

Children with a lifetime disorder compared with those without one with an odds ratio
*$p<0.05$, **$p<0.01$

Table 7.13 Logistic regression showing nonverbal intelligence, any lifetime diagnosis, communicational abilities, and degree of hearing impairment as predictors of "being teased"

	Odds ratio	p Value
Nonverbal intelligence (HAWIK)	1.03 [0.99–1.06]	0.070
Any diagnoses (lifetime)	3.44 [1.33–8.89]	0.011
Ability to make oneself understood	9.61 [1.86–49.7]	0.007
Degree of hearing impairment	0.99 [0.97–1.01]	0.228

Summary

Mental health disorders are about four times more likely to be found in children who have problems making themselves understood in the family. Children with a lifetime diagnosis of an internalizing disorder are more likely to have been teased, maltreated, or isolated. Ratings by parents of children not being able to make themselves understood correlated significantly with being teased, isolated, or maltreated. Ratings by teachers of children being able to make themselves understood correlated significantly with being accepted by others.

variance, the ability to make oneself understood remains significantly associated with being teased, but not with the degree of hearing loss. After controlling for nonverbal intelligence the ability to communicate and the presence of a lifetime clinical diagnosis account for additional 20.2% of variance in this model.

Table 7.14 Pearson correlations between language and communication skills and children's self-SDQ by school setting

	Total difficulties (SDQ)			Peer problems (SDQ)		
	Mainstream	Segregated	Total	Mainstream	Segregated	Total
HAWIK III: passive vocabulary age of reference	−0.130 (0.470) n=33	−0.097 (0.789) n=10	−2.36 (0.128) n=43	−0.019 (0.916) n=33	0.067 (0.853) n=10	−0.126 (0.423) n=43
HSET, grammar standard score	−0.259 (0.146) n=33	−0.477 (0.163) n=10	−0.360* (0.018) n=43	−0.255 (0.152) n=33	−0.108 (0.767) n=10	−0.300 (0.051) n=43
Intelligibility percentage of numbers correct	−0.298 (0.104) n=31	0.250 (0.517) n=9	−0.214 (0.185) n=40	−0.233 (0.208) n=31	0.225 (0.560) n=9	−0.152 (0.350) n=40
Reading comprehension standard score	−0.028 (0.887) n=29	0.545 (0.103) n=10	−0.146 (0.374) n=39	0.231 (0.227) n=29	0.451 (0.191) n=10	0.029 (0.860) n=39
PMLP spoken language level raw score	−0.388* (0.026) n=33	0.388 (0.267) n=10	−0.288 (0.061) n=43	−0.350* (0.046) n=33	0.635* (0.048) n=10	−0.205 (0.187) n=43
PMLP signed language level raw score	0.390* (0.025) n=33	−0.282 (0.430) n=10	0.363* (0.017) n=43	0.155 (0.388) n=33	−0.627 (0.052) n=10	0.153 (0.328) n=43

Values in italic are significant at the $p < 0.05$ level. Values are represented as R (p)
SDQ strengths and difficulties questionnaire

Language and Mental Health in the Subgroup of Deaf Teenagers

No significant relationship was found between the degree of hearing loss and linguistic results on one hand and SDQ parents scales and the SDQ self-report scales on the other hand. Whereas the linguistic results did not correlate with the SDQ parents' scales, the relationship between the linguistic data and the mental health problems shown on the SDQ self-report was complex and varied by type of school (Table 7.14). For the whole sample only the findings on grammatical competence in German (HSET) showed a significant negative correlation with total difficulties on the SDQ, whereas a higher level of sign language competence was associated with higher total difficult scores. Dividing the sample by school settings showed a negative relationship between higher levels of spoken language competence (PMLP) and the SDQ scores for total difficulties and peer problems in mainstreamed children, but a reverse correlation with peer problems in segregated children. Children in classes for the deaf who had a higher command of sign language demonstrated almost significantly less peer relationship problems ($p = 0.052$). However, mainstreamed children with higher sign language competence showed more total difficulties on the SDQ. Reading comprehension, which is strongly correlated with general knowledge and academic skills, was not significantly correlated with mental health problems. Furthermore, it was not specific linguistic parameters such as intelligibility, spoken language comprehension, or vocabulary knowledge that proved to be associated with mental health problems (Fig. 7.1).

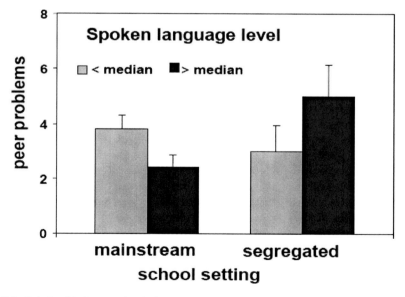

Fig. 7.1 Relationship between level of spoken language and peer relationship problems by school setting

It could be that it is the specific characteristics of children in deaf school settings such as higher degree of hearing loss or higher percentage of children with migrant background that explain the higher rate of peer relationship problems. To determine the specificity of the influence of language level in different environments on the peer problems' dimension of the SDQ, a linear regression analysis was performed. In the first step the following control variables were entered: age, sex, hearing loss, performance IQ, and SES. In step 2 the school setting, whether mainstream or school for the deaf, was added to the model. In step 3 the language level, either in sign language or in spoken language, was entered. Linguistic variables that are applicable only for spoken language were not included. In the final step the interaction between school setting (segregated or mainstreamed) and functional language proficiency in spoken language and sign language was entered. After controlling for the above mentioned parameters, the regression analysis confirmed that proficiency of language in the mode used in the type of school influences peer relationship problems ($\delta R^2 = 0.213$; $F = 2.17$, $p = 0.047$).

Summary

Problems in peer relationships do not correlate with the degree of hearing loss or discrete linguistic skills, but with the level of language used in conversation with peers at school whether signed or spoken language.

Some Characteristics of Children Without Any Lifetime Diagnosis of a Mental Health Disorder

Children who did not show any lifetime diagnosis of a mental health disorder (and the figures are nearly the same for those who did not show any lifetime depressive disorder) differed significantly from those who had one or more lifetime mental health disorder in the following characteristics, which to some extent can be regarded as factors of resilience, as they confirm what is known from literature about health in early infancy. These characteristics include a pregnancy without problems, no problems during or postbirth, and no abnormalities of motor and cognitive development.

Characteristics of mentally healthy children in general, like getting along very well with classmates and peers, were found also in our sample of children with deafness (getting along very well two times more frequent, $p = 0.045$), and having many friends (2.7 times more frequent, $p = 0.029$). Teachers reported that the self-esteem of those without a lifetime diagnosis was 3.6 times more likely to be well developed compared to those with a lifetime diagnosis ($p = 0.022$).

A factor specifically related to consequences of deafness is the ability to make oneself understood in the family and among peers. Those without a lifetime diagnosis were 4.2 times more likely to have no problems with making themselves understood in their family. Adolescents with good peer relationships had higher levels of competence of the language mode of their peers, whether spoken or signed. Finally, with regard to the early years, it is interesting to report that 2.4 times more parents of children without a lifetime diagnosis reported to have been supported in a sufficient way after diagnosis ($p = 0.053$).

How Can These Data Be Linked to a Concept of Resilience?

As already mentioned, the data of the CHEERS study are cross-sectional data so far and therefore only of limited scientific value when questions of resilience are to be discussed. Nevertheless, we want to share thoughts about our findings in relation to Antonovsky's model of sense of coherence with its subcomponents – comprehensibility, manageability, and meaningfulness. These components are not so much focusing on genetic and environmental preconditions, but rather on acquired attitudes and capabilities to cope with a diversity of challenges. Each of these three dimensions can be linked to certain aspects of communication like *comprehending* how things are linked to each other, being able to *manage* by expressing what you think and you want, and to *gain meaning* from what you are doing by being able to deal with things beyond the here and now.

The main finding of the CHEERS study in our eyes is the relationship between mental health problems and problems in communication within the family and with peers. The impact of these specific deafness-related findings is addressed in the following paragraphs according to the three dimensions of the Sense of Coherence.

Comprehensibility

As it is well known from longitudinal studies with language impaired children and adolescents (e.g., Tomblin, 2008), a lack of communicative abilities brings about a lack of general knowledge and understanding. Deaf children often have less knowledge about the way events in the world are logically connected. This lack of information makes the world less predictable. As clinical experience shows, anxiety, behavior problems, or helplessness are frequent reactions of deaf children to events that cannot be explained. An understanding of the way things are linked together cannot be acquired by mere direct perception of events but needs linguistic explanations by others.

Manageability

Lack of communication within the family or peer group involves that deaf children are not sufficiently able to make themselves understood and thus express their needs and manage the situations in life. This lack of communicative control of their environment often leads to the reaction of overprotection by parents and others and further decreases the chance to experience the feeling of "*I can!*" Although causality cannot be determined, it is interesting that having problems in family communication is correlated to negative experiences with peers at school as a victim and with higher rates of mental health disorders. Adolescents with higher level of the language mode of their peers (whether spoken or signed) reported better peer relationships.

Meaningfulness

To experience that life is meaningful is always connected to some extent to the development of a healthy self-esteem and the possibility to develop perspectives of a future dimension. To deal with future concepts is associated not only with a certain developmental stage of cognition but also with a level of command of language, which in our study sample was not age-appropriate.

We think that our findings, which we have discussed now in the light of possible impact of communicative deprivation on the development of a strong sense of coherence, cannot fully explain the high rates of mental health problems associated to deafness regardless of its degree. We consider this finding also to show the impact of deafness per se on the General Resistance Resources (GRR) in Antonovsky's model (Antonovsky, 1979).

In the last section of our chapter, we want to share recommendations for improving resilience to mental health disorders in deaf school children, which we derive from a continuously ongoing interaction between research and our clinical experience. It is not a complete list of recommendations and does not specifically address the very first years of childhood when secure attachment has to develop, which generally is regarded as a key element of resilience.

Recommendations for Improving Resilience to Mental Health Disorders in Deaf Children

Concerning Parents

- Priority has to be given to the provision of opportunities for the child to express him/herself in a way that makes him/her feel understood by his family, as well as making sure the child understands what is told to him/her.
- Parents need to spend some time together with the deaf child giving him/her space to listen.
- Deaf children should be encouraged to take an active responsibility in family communication.
- Children's clear signals to express lack of comprehension should be highly evaluated by their parents.

- Children need to learn to reflect more about communication processes. Parents should make them think about the quality of family communication.
- INCLUSION on any level for all family members should be a family rule.
- The checking of what is understood by the communication partner by making him summarize the main contents is a useful exercise.
- Working together on a diary is helpful (using pictures, drawings, text, etc.) to address emotional aspects and differentiate them.
- If body language is giving reasons for concern, negative experiences should be directly asked for (they are frequently associated with feelings of shame and therefore not uttered spontaneously).
- Sometimes environmental factors have to be assessed carefully even if the child does not directly report about having been teased, isolated, or maltreated.
- If satisfying peer contacts do not develop by themselves, it is more than justifiable that parents strive for possible groups their deaf child can become a member of. For most deaf and hard of hearing children it is very important to meet other children who are deaf. To provide such opportunities for supporting the development of their identity in some cases means to overcome long travel distances.
- When school placement decisions have to be made, the language level of the child concerned has to be carefully evaluated in comparison to the language level of the language mode preferred by peers, whether spoken or signed language. If signed language is the preferred means of communication, a signing peer environment is recommended.
- Parents whose children prefer sign language should develop sufficient sign language skills to be able to carry out full conversations with their deaf child.

Concerning Teachers

- As deafness is frequently associated with mental health problems, which sometimes remain unrecognized for a long time, teachers of deaf pupils should become familiar with frequently occurring mental health disorders to provide access to professional help.
- Common symptoms of mental distress in the context of deafness deserve special attention. Deeper understanding can be gained by an extended but guided exposure to self-experience as described below.

Experiment of Self-experience for Teachers of Deaf Children

The participants are asked to close their ears with earwax. By this a moderate hearing loss is simulated. Participants are told that their ears have to stay closed for at least 2 h and that they should write down whatever they notice during two lessons, which are structured in the following way. During the first

(continued)

(continued)

unit (lasting exactly as long as a typical unit at school) quite interesting stuff is presented first orally only. After that first lecture a break of 15 min is planned during which they are asked to interact with each other as they would usually do.

The next unit starts again with only speaking to them in a not very pronounced way. Statements about how important it would be to know the exact contents of the lectures given to pass the exam cause additional stress to the audience. Later on the intensity of eye contact and the use of additional visual material varies. Then a more interactive part follows. The participants are asked to report to the group what they have been experiencing so far. Any observation is collected and written down and grouped according to the dimension symptoms, reflections about the type of presentation and social interactions.

It is interesting to report that in almost all of these sessions the author has been given a nearly complete list of physical and mental symptoms of distress. Complaints included headache, abdominal discomfort, getting feelings of anger, and the loss of the ability to concentrate. After this rather stressful experience for the whole group (and it is important to mention that the author also keeps his ears closed while he is teaching), the ear wax is removed.

Then it is comparatively easy to discuss the different ways to teach in a less distressing way by analyzing their own experiences:

- Teachers have *the* important role in the prevention of bullying and other adverse behaviors, but they are usually not prepared to run effective programs. Therefore, specific training and support in implementation are required.
- The same is true for prevention of sexual abuse.
- Programs like the PATHS curriculum (Greenberg & Kusché, 1998) have been successfully used to give deaf pupils better access to their emotional experiences.
- Teachers in special schools for the deaf have to become prepared to serve a complex group of pupils with additional cognitive, mental, and social handicaps.
- Working together in a multidisciplinary team including experts in mental health has proved to be effective in accompanying single children with very special needs.
- Finally, a high standard of sign language competence has to be kept up in specialized schools, which usually requires a constant involvement of native signers.
- Deaf role models in early intervention programs, kindergartens, and schools and opportunities of peer counseling for deaf adolescents are of high importance in the development of an identity and self-consciousness.

Concluding Remarks

Considering the main results of our CHEERS study in the light of the question how to increase resilience to mental health disorders in deaf school children, we came down to the important factors of family communication and peer communication.

We could show that not language skills per se have an impact on mental health but also communication and the ability to make oneself understood in his or her social environment. This being understood by others seems to have priority over being able to understand what others are saying. Efforts to deeply understand a deaf child have to exceed the dimensions of the here and now. According to the concept of "sense of coherence" this understanding has to include questions with a long perspective like meaning in life and also the religious dimension.

But healthy family communication is not only characterized by aspects of understanding and being understood but also by opportunities for the development of a strong self efficiency. When a child perceives that his/her communicative attempts has impact on his/her social environment, the component of manageability is enhanced.

Later on satisfying work can contribute a lot to the development of a sense of coherence by giving the individual opportunities to answer the question "what am I good for." In practice parents and teachers are asked to understand the deaf child's gifts and talents to accompany him or her in a meaningful educational and occupational direction. Although the importance of strengths is frequently mentioned in pedagogic contexts, intensive and systematic research to identify these strong points even in children with great difficulties is frequently lacking or not documented in school reports.

To give deaf children opportunities to become responsible givers instead of receivers of help, efforts have to start early. Time in school could be of greatest value in transforming learned helplessness (which sometimes is a product of deep parental concern) to skilled helpfulness. So the success children have supports them to realize how valuable they are. Thus, the resilience to distressing conditions and experiences of a life in a world that is mostly not adapted to the needs of deaf people can be strengthened. Positive deaf role models will also have the highest impact in improving the living conditions in society for those who are deaf.

References

Antonovsky, A. (1979). *Health, stress, and coping.* San Francisco: Jossey-Bass.

Becker, A., Woerner, W., Hasselhorn, M., Banaschewski, T., & Rothenberger, A. (2004). Validation of the parent and teacher SDQ in a clinical sample. *European Child and Adolescent Psychiatry, 13*(Suppl 2), II11–II16.

Davis, A., Bamford, J., Wilson, I., Ramkalawan, T., Forshaw, M., & Wright, S. (1997). A critical review of the role of neonatal hearing screening in the detection of congenital hearing impairment. *Health Technology Assessment, 1*, i-176.

Davis, A., & Wood, S. (1992). The epidemiology of childhood hearing impairment: Factor relevant to planning of services. *British Journal of Audiology, 26*, 77–90.

Fellinger, J., Holzinger, D., Beitel, C., Laucht, M., & Goldberg, D. P. (2009). The impact of language skills on mental health in teenagers with hearing impairments. *Acta Psychiatrica Scandinavica, 120*, 153–159.

Fellinger, J., Holzinger, D., Dobner, U., Gerich, J., Lehner, R., Lenz, G., et al. (2005). Mental distress and quality of life in a deaf population. *Social Psychiatry and Psychiatric Epidemiology, 2005*(40), 737–742.

Fellinger, J., Holzinger, D., Gerich, U., & Goldberg, D. (2007). Mental distress and quality of life in the hard of hearing. *Acta Psychiatrica Scandinavica, 115*, 243–245.

Fellinger, J., Holzinger, D., Sattel, H., & Laucht, M., (2008). Correlates of mental distress among children with hearing impairments. *Europeau Child and Adolescent Phychiatry, 51*, 635–641.

Goldstein, G., & Bebko, J. M. (2003). The profile of multiple language proficiencies: A measure for evaluating language samples of deaf children. *Journal of Deaf Studies and Deaf Education, 8*, 452–463.

Goodman, R. (1997). The strengths and difficulties questionnaire: A research note. *Journal of Child Psychology and Psychiatry, 38*, 581–586.

Greenberg, M. T., & Kusché, C. A. (1998). *Blueprints for violence prevention: The PATHS project* (Vol. 10). Boulder, CO: Institute of Behavioral Science, Regents of the University of Colorado.

Grimm, H., & Schöler, H. (1991). *Heidelberger Sprachentwicklungs test*. Verl. für Psychologie: Hogrefe.

Grissemann, H., & Baumberg, W. (2000). *Leseverstandnistest ZVLT*. Bern: Hans Huber.

Hindley, P. (1997). Psychiatric aspects of hearing impairments. *Journal of Child Psychology and Psychiatry, 38*(1), 101–117.

Hintermair, M. (2007). Prevalence of socioemotional problems in deaf and hard of hearing children in Germany. *American Annals of the Deaf, 152*, 320–330.

Ihle, W., & Esser, G. (2002). Epidemiologie psychischer Störungen im Kindes- und Jugendalter: Prävalenz, Verlauf, Komorbidität und Geschlechtsunterschiede. [Epidemiology of mental disorders in childhood and adolescence: prevalence, course, co-morbidity and gender differences]. *Psychologische Rundschau, 53*, 159–169.

Ihle, W., Esser, G., Schmidt, M., & Blanz, B. (2000). Prävalenz, Komorbidität und Geschlechtsunterschiede psychischer Störungen vom. *Zeitschrift fur Klinische Psychologie und Psychotherapie, 29*, 263–275.

Klasen, H., Woerner, W., Rothenberger, A., & Goodman, R. (2003). German version of the strength and difficulties questionnaire (SDQ-German) – overview and evaluation of initial validation and normative results. *Praxis der Kinderpsychologie und Kinderpsychiatrie, 52*, 491–502.

Malmberg, M., Rydell, A. M., & Smedje, H. (2003). Validity of the Swedish version of the strengths and difficulties questionnaire (SDQ-Swe). *Nordic Journal of Psychiatry, 57*, 357–363.

Masten, A. S., & Obradović, J. (2006). Competence and resilience in development. *Annals of the New York Academy of Sciences, 1094*, 13–27.

Mattejat, F., & Remschmidt, H. (2006). *ILK inventar zur erfassung der lebensqualität bei kindern und jugendlichen. Ratingbogen für kinder, jugendliche und eltern*. Bern: Huber.

Meltzer, H., Gatward, R., Goodman, R., & Ford, F. (2000). *Mental health of children and adolescents in Great Britain*. London: The Stationery Office.

Parving, A. (1995). Factors causing hearing impairment: Some perspectives from Europe. *Journal of the American Academy of Audiology, 6*, 387–395.

Shaffer, D., Schwab-Stone, M., Fisher, P., Cohen, P., Placentini, J., Davies, M., et al. (1993). The diagnostic interview schedule for children – revised version (DISC-R): I. Preparation, field testing, interrater reliability, and acceptability. *Journal of American Academy of Child & Adolescent Psychiatry, 32*(3), 643–650.

Sullivan, G. C. (1993). Towards clarification of convergent concepts: Sense of coherence, will to meaning, locus of control, learned helplessness and hardiness. *Journal of Advanced Nursing, 18*, 1772–1778.

Tewes, U., Rossman, P., & Schallberger, U. (1999). *Wechsler intelligence test for children, HAWIK-III*. Bern, Switzerland: Huber.

Thompson, D. C., McPhillips, H., Davis, R. L., Lieu, T. L., Homer, C. J., & Helfand, M. (2001). Universal newborn hearing screening: Summary of evidence. *JAMA, 286*, 2000–2010.

Tomblin, J. B. (2008). Validating diagnostic standards for specific language impairment using adolescent outcomes. In C. F. Norbury, J. B. Tomblin, & D. V. M. Bishop (Eds.), *Understanding developmental language disorders* (pp. 93–116). New York: Psychology Press.

Unnewehr, S., Schneider, S., & Margraf, J. (1998). *Kinder-DIPS: Diagnostisches interview bei psychischen störungen im kindes und Jugendalter* (Germanth ed.). New York: Springer.

van Gent, T., Goedhart, A. W., Hindley, P. A., & Treffers, P. D. A. (2007). Prevalence and correlates of psychopathology in a sample of deaf adolescents. *Journal of Child Psychology and Psychiatry, 48*(9), 950–958.

Woerner, W., Becker, A., Friedrich, C., Klasen, H., Goodman, R., & Rothenberger, A. (2002). Normal values and evaluation of the German parents' version of strengths and difficulties questionnaire (SDQ): Results of a representative field study. *Zeitschrift für Kinder und Jugendpsychiatrie und Psychotherapie, 30*, 105–112.

Woerner, W., Becker, A., & Rothenberger, A. (2004). Normative data and scale properties of the German parent SDQ. *European Child and Adolescent Psychiatry, 13*(Suppl 2), II3–II10.

Young, A. M., Green, L., & Rogers, K. D. (2008). Resilience and deaf children: A literature review. *Deafness and Educational International, 10*(1), 40–55.

Chapter 8
Promoting Resilience: Suggestions for Families, Professionals, and Students

John Luckner

Abstract The majority of children who are deaf mature and become healthy adults who have fulfilling relationships and meaningful careers and they contribute to society. Unfortunately, the professional literature in the field of deaf education tends to be oriented toward deficiencies and problems. This chapter stresses a strength-based perspective and begins by presenting the results of three small-scale studies that examined the perceptions of successful students, adults, and families. Central themes from those studies are presented and then interwoven with a summary of practical suggestions for promoting resilience.

Resilience is a conceptual term used to describe the positive psychological outcomes that occur for some individuals even though they have been exposed to environmental risk experiences, stress, and adversity (Masten & Obradovic, 2006; Rutter, 2006). In contrast, the terms at-risk and vulnerable are often used to describe individuals who experience a maladaptive downward spiral in their response to adversity (Luthar, Cicchetti, & Becker, 2000).

Writers and researchers have characterized individuals who are deaf as being at-risk and vulnerable for the past 100 years. This pathological perspective of hearing loss has led to a focus on deficiency, dysfunction, and deviance, with limited attention to strengths, optimal adjustment, or resilience (Luckner & Stewart, 2003; National Association of the Deaf, 2000).

Unfortunately, the concentration on pathology and difference has masked the fact that many individuals with a hearing loss have overcome obstacles, achieved happiness, and attained life success. These individuals have exercised their strengths rather than concentrating on their challenges. In an effort to offset the prevalent viewpoint of focusing on the maladaptive development of individuals who are deaf, my colleagues and I undertook a series of three small-scale studies to look at successful individuals and families. This chapter begins with a brief

J. Luckner(✉)
School of Special Education, Bresnahan/Halstead Center,
University of Northern Colorado, Greeley, CO, USA
e-mail: john.luckner@unco.edu

D.H. Zand and K.J. Pierce (eds.), *Resilience in Deaf Children: Adaptation Through Emerging Adulthood*, DOI 10.1007/978-1-4419-7796-0_8, summary of each study and concludes with specific suggestions for families, professionals, and students based on the results of those studies as well as recommendations from other writers and researchers who have addressed the topics of resiliency, protective factors, and success.

Successful Students in General Education Settings

The majority of students who are deaf currently are being educated in general education settings alongside their hearing peers. This practice has increased annually since the enactment of Public Law 94-142, the Education of All Handicapped Children Act of 1975. Additionally, this course of action is likely to continue to occur in the future because of (a) newborn hearing screening programs, early intervention, and the related positive effects on the development of language skills (Yoshinaga-Itano, Sedey, Coulter, & Mehl, 1998); (b) the decrease in severe to profound deafness (Holden-Pitt & Diaz, 1998); (c) the closing of several state schools for the deaf; (d) the increase in the number of children who are deaf receiving cochlear implants (National Institute on Deafness and other Communication Disorders, 2007); and (e) federal legislation (e.g., Individuals with Disabilities Education Improvement Act of 2004) which contains several provisions directed at providing students with disabilities greater access to the general education curriculum.

Luckner and Muir (2001) undertook a study to identify successful students who are deaf who received the majority of their educational services in general education settings in an effort to identify the factors that contributed to their success. A letter was sent to every teacher of students who are deaf in the state of Colorado explaining the purpose of the study. In the letter, teachers were asked to nominate students who are deaf (better ear average 75 dB or higher), who were in upper elementary school through high school, and who met the following criteria of success (a) age-appropriate academic skills in most subjects, (b) relationships with friends, and (c) positive self-perceptions. This three-component definition of success used for this study was determined after reading several other studies that were undertaken with successful business executives (Covey, 1989; Garfield, 1986), successful adults with learning disabilities (Gerber, Ginsberg, & Reiff, 1992), and successful individuals with physical disabilities (Powers, Singer, & Todis, 1996). Each study used a different definition of success, yet they included elements that focused on the three components of achievement, social skills, and self-perceptions.

Twenty-seven students were nominated to participate in the study. We received 20 signed permission slips from parents. Thirteen females and seven males, ranging in ages from 12 to 19, participated in the study. Ten students used speech and sign, nine used speech, and one used sign to communicate.

Each student was observed in the general education setting. In addition, we interviewed (a) the 20 students; (b) 13 deaf education teachers, 9 educational interpreters, and 2 paraprofessional notetakers who worked with the students; (c) 19 general education teachers who worked with the students; and (d) 19 parents of the students. Each interview was audio or videotaped and then transcribed at a later time. The transcribed interviews and the observation data were coded. Themes were identified by their reoccurrence across observations as well as from the interviews with each group of respondents (i.e., students, parents, deaf education professionals, and general education teachers) and were placed into categories based on similar content and meaning. Once all data were evaluated, conclusions were derived and documented. The ten factors that emerged as positively influencing a student's success were:

1. Family involvement.
2. Students were self-determined.
3. Each student was involved in some type of extracurricular activity.
4. Each student had friends and good social skills.
5. Students knew how to self-advocate for their needs.
6. Collaboration and consultation occurred regularly across service providers.
7. Deaf education professionals consistently supplemented the lessons being taught in the general education classroom through a three-step process of pre-teach, teach, and postteach.
8. Each student was identified early and his or her family participated in some form of early intervention.
9. Students were strong readers.
10. Families and professionals maintained high expectations for student performance.

Successful Deaf Adults

Luckner and Stewart (2003) conducted a study to gather information from successful deaf adults about their perceptions of the factors that contributed to their success. For the purposes of the study, the subjective construct of success was defined across five variables (a) education – completed a postsecondary training program, (b) income – earned more than $30,000 a year, (c) employment – was currently employed, (d) social – had friends and was respected by his or her peers, and (e) self-confidence – exhibited positive self-perceptions.

The target population was identified through a nomination process. The Association of the Deaf in Colorado mailed letters to each of its 400 members. The letter contained information that (a) described the purpose of the study, (b) explained the criteria for being selected as a successful adult who is deaf, and (c) had instructions for nominating adults who are deaf to participate in the study.

Twenty-two individuals were nominated. Many of those individuals were nominated multiple times. Each individual was contacted and asked to participate in the study. Everyone was willing to participate, but several could not find time in their busy schedules to participate in the videotaped interview. Fourteen individuals were interviewed. Ten were female, four were male. They ranged in age from 27 to 74. Twelve had hearing parents and two had parents who were deaf. They were involved in a wide range of professional endeavors (e.g., social worker, chemist, university instructor, engineer, teacher, technician, librarian, printer, and counselor). Individuals participated in a videotaped, semi-structured interview that focused on their perceptions of the ingredients that helped promote their success as well as recommendations for students, parents, and service providers. After the interview, the videotapes were transcribed and coded by the authors. Following are the most frequently reported responses regarding their own success, advice for students, parents, and professionals.

Factors contributing to their success:

1. They worked hard.
2. They received ongoing support from their family.
3. Their family accepted the hearing loss.
4. Their family emphasized education, specifically learning to read and write.
5. They were motivated.
6. They enjoyed overcoming challenges.

Advice for students:

1. Set goals.
2. Develop friendships.
3. Become skilled at reading and writing.
4. Learn to advocate for yourself.

Advice for parents:

1. Communicate with their child.
2. Provide ongoing support and be involved in their child's life.
3. Expose children to many different activities and experiences.

Advice for professionals:

1. Be caring and have high expectations for students.
2. Improve their sign communication skills.
3. Be involved with the Deaf community.

Healthy Families

The findings of the two studies described above strengthened our understanding of the central role that families play in fostering individuals' success. As a result, Luckner and Velaski (2004) studied healthy/successful families of children who are deaf based on similar research that had been undertaken with hearing families (e.g., Gottman, 1994; Haddock, Zimmerman, Ziemba, & Current, 2001; Wallerstein & Blaleslee, 1995). The intention of the study was to identify healthy families of children who are deaf and to identify the factors that contributed to their health as well as to solicit from them suggestions for other families who have a child who is deaf and for professionals in the field of deaf education.

For the purposes of the study, a family was defined as "two or more people who regard themselves as a family and who perform some of the functions that families typically perform. These people may or may not be related by blood or marriage and may or may not usually live together" (Turnbull & Turnbull, 2001, p. 12). Simultaneously, the term "healthy" was used instead of successful based on the research cited above. The term healthy was not limited to the narrow medical definition, but rather encompassed a much broader meaning that focused on positive family identity, satisfying and fulfilling interactions, and successful functioning so that both individual and family's needs were met (Lin, 1994). Specifically, the working definition of a healthy family was:

1. Communication among all members is clear and direct.
2. Roles and responsibilities are clearly delineated, and the family allows for flexibility in role allocation.
3. The family members accept limits for the resolution of conflict.
4. Intimacy is prevalent and is a function of frequent, equal-powered transactions.
5. There is a healthy balance between change and maintenance of stability (Luterman, 1987, p. 8).

All teachers of students who are deaf within Colorado were sent a letter asking them to nominate a healthy family who had a child who is deaf. The letter included information describing (a) the purpose of the study, (b) the definition of a family, (c) the definition of a healthy family, and (d) a request for them to nominate any family that has a child who is deaf (better ear average 75 dB or higher, ages 4–18) and who met these criteria.

Nineteen families participated in the semi-structured interviews. Participation within the interviews varied. In some cases, one member of the family, usually the mother, responded to the questions. In other cases, the family discussed the questions prior to the interview and one family member communicated their responses. In several instances, the entire family responded.

In a manner similar to the studies described above, the interviews were transcribed and analyzed. Information was systematically transformed into naturally occurring meaning units through the process of coding.

When asked to reflect on the factors that contribute to being a healthy family who has a child who is deaf the following five reasons were identified:

1. Commitment to family.
2. Learning to sign with their child.
3. Support from extended family, friends, and members of the community.
4. Support from the professionals working at the educational program their child attends.
5. High expectations for the child with a hearing loss.

The most frequent responses when asked to offer advice for other families with children who are deaf were:

1. Gather information to identify resources and learn what rights your child has.
2. Have high expectations for your child.
3. Learn sign language.
4. Be involved in your child's education.
5. Love and encourage your child daily.

Recurrent advice for professionals consisted of:

1. Be supportive, understanding, and encouraging.
2. Remember parents know their child and family needs best.
3. Be a resource for families.
4. Get to know the child.

Limitations and Implications

The studies described above were small in scale, conducted by one group of researchers, with participants from one state. Consequently, generalization needs to occur with caution. However, given the fact that the field of education of students who are deaf suffers from a paucity of research (i.e., quantitative, qualitative, mixed-method, single subject, and case study) (Easterbrooks, 2005; Luckner, 2006; Schirmer & McGough, 2005), it is appropriate to view the results of these studies as preliminary investigations that need to be replicated by different investigators in different places. Simultaneously, for the purposes of this chapter, the cumulative results of the studies described above are used as a springboard to link other research and literature in the development of practical suggestions that can be field-tested in future studies.

General Suggestions

To begin the discussion of actions that can be undertaken to promote resilience, it is valuable to initially consider the universal needs of human beings and how these needs influence behavior. Several authors (e.g., Blocher, Heppner, & Johnston, 2001; Ormrod, 2008; Ryan & Deci, 2000) suggest that in addition to our basic physiological needs (e.g., oxygen, water, food, warmth, exercise, and rest) and safety needs (i.e., to feel protected and secure), humans have three growth needs:

1. Relatedness – We are social creatures; people of all ages have a fundamental need to feel socially connected and to secure the love and respect of others.
2. Competence – We need to believe that we can deal effectively with our environment. Our self-worth is enhanced by achieving success on a regular basis or by avoiding failure. Consequently, people often avoid tasks they expect to do poorly and/or make excuses to justify their poor performance.

3. Self-determination – We want to have a sense of autonomy regarding the things we do and the directions our lives take.

Unfortunately, a hearing loss during early childhood has the potential to negatively impact each of these three critical developmental aspects (please see Young, Green, & Rogers, 2008 for a more in-depth discussion about resilience risk indicators and individuals who are deaf). Identifying actions that can be taken to address each of these essential needs as well as integrating suggestions from the general literature on resilience is the focus of the remainder of this chapter.

Suggestions for Families

It is well understood that families are the critical element in the development of healthy, competent, and caring children (Clarke-Stewart & Dunn, 2006). The quality of family life affects the success of children and adolescents in school, the community, and significantly influences how well they will function as adults (Masten & Shaffer, 2006; Seligman & Darling, 1997; Singer & Irvin, 1989).

Families who have a child with a hearing loss experience many of the same successes and challenges as other families. Yet, having a child with a hearing loss tends to change family dynamics and the home environment (Meadow-Orlans, Mertens, & Sas-Lehrer, 2003; Spencer, 2001). While family and parenting issues are fundamentally the same, the hearing loss tends to impose greater complexity on the process, requiring more thought and greater care (Luterman, 1987). Three specific issues noted by Luckner and Velaski (2004) that are often different for families who have a child with a hearing loss are:

1. Most (95%) children with a hearing loss are born to hearing parents (Mitchell & Karchmer, 2004). Almost all of these adults use spoken language as their primary means of communicating with others. In addition, because hearing loss is a low-incidence disability, most parents have never come in contact with a person who is deaf. Moreover, they have a limited understanding of what it is like to have a hearing loss. Sound is so much a part of their lives that they cannot imagine a world where speech is always unintelligible, distorted, too soft, or not heard at all. Through spoken language most of these parents unconsciously learned to interact with others, developed language, acquired academic and world knowledge, and developed the prerequisite skills that helped them become literate.

2. When hearing parents learn their child has a hearing loss, they usually experience a range of reactions and face a variety of challenges (Luterman, 1987). Some of those challenges include understanding the impact of a hearing loss, finding appropriate services and support, and developing communication strategies. Whether families choose to use an oral approach, a sign system, or American Sign Language (ASL) to communicate with their child, they will need to learn new skills as well as make significant changes in how they interact with their child. Hence, during the critical years of learning language, the primary caregivers

of children who are deaf are often dealing with the emotional and pragmatic implications of the identified hearing loss.

3. A variety of professionals, such as an audiologist and a home-intervention teacher of students who are deaf, enter the family's life changing the family's boundaries and often offering information and advice that sometimes inadvertently undermines the parents' authority (Luterman, 1987).

As noted above, humans have a basic need for acceptance and connection. Communication is critical for transmitting each of those perceptions and emotions. The importance of quality communication between parents and their child with a hearing loss was highlighted by the responses from the successful students and adults presented previously. Similar findings have been made by a variety of well-respected researchers in the field of deaf education with regard to the correlation between language acquisition and early reading, and social-emotional development (e.g., Calderon, 2000; Moeller, 2000) as well as enhanced parent–child relationships (e.g., Jamieson, 1995; Spencer, Bodner-Johnson, & Gutfreund, 1992). In addition, the literature on risk and resilience has reported consistent findings related to the central role of positive communication between families and their children for promoting successful adaptation (e.g., Benard & Marshall, 2001; Clarke-Stewart & Dunn, 2006; Rutter, 2006).

Language provides a means for social interaction as well as a mechanism for thinking (Vygotsky, 1978). Evidence from a variety of sources indicates that the language development of young children is highly dependent on the amount of language input to which they have been exposed to during the first few years of life (e.g., Hart & Risley, 1995, 2003; Huttenlocher, Haight, Bryck, Seltzer, & Lyons, 1991; Wells, 1986). However, when individuals have a hearing loss, the quantity and quality of interactions with significant others as well as with acquaintances and unfamiliar people is often diminished. The reduction in interaction for young children who are deaf often leads to impoverished language skills and beginning school significantly behind their hearing peers (Marschark & Wauters, 2008). And all too frequently, the deficits in language development negatively impact the acquisition of reading skills, academic achievement, and career opportunities (Luckner, 2002).

To offset the potential negative consequences caused by the reduction in interaction that occurs for many children who are deaf, it is essential that family members understand the critical and pervasive role that language has in the development of their child. As explained by Levine (2002):

> Parents should be aware that language is all-consuming in the everyday existence of their children. Obviously, it is the medium for communication with friends, siblings, teachers, pets and parents. It is as well an indispensable ingredient of reading, spelling, mathematics, and writing. Language is a close partner of memory; translating facts and ideas into words (especially their own words) helps kids retain information. Language is raw material from which vital concepts are shaped (such as concepts of "racial harmony" or "ethical behavior"). Language even helps provide some internal control over your child's behavior; it is known that talking through conflicts or temptations, using inner voices, often prevents a child from being rash or lashing out (pp. 120–121).

Second, family members will need to learn how to alter the manner in which they communicate with their children. Often, professionals as well as individuals outside the field of deaf education think that adaptations such as using sign, getting a hearing aid, or a cochlear implant for the child will be sufficient actions to offset the potential impact of a hearing loss. While these actions may improve the quality of the communication between the parent and child, they may not increase the quantity of interactions. For example, with hearing children of hearing parents, significant amounts of incidental interaction occur when the adult carries the child from place to place. While moving, parents talk to the child about where they are going and what they are going to do. This is difficult to do in sign while walking or when the child is unable to look at the parent's face. Simultaneously, often hearing parents and their hearing children have extensive interactions while traveling in the car – parent sitting up front, child in the back seat. Once again, for adults and children with a hearing loss, this leads to compromised communication. For each of these instances, as well as many similar daily events, parents will want to plan to communicate with the child before they move as well after they arrive at their destination. Quite simply, for many children with a hearing loss, it is optimum for adults to think of communication and going places as occurring sequentially, rather than simultaneously.

Third, families will want to recognize that the primary method of promoting the language development of their child is through conversations with their child. Through conversations all aspects of language – pragmatics, semantics, and syntax – come together in an authentic manner. It is also through conversations that children learn about the world, which sets in motion, a cyclical rewarding process. That is, conversing allows children to gather information to share with others while they simultaneously improve their skills in communication and also learning more about the world. Unfortunately, the opposite is also true. Children who have limited communication skills may have difficulty acquiring basic world knowledge, which in turn provides them with less stimuli to converse about and diminished opportunities to increase their world knowledge or to improve their communication skills.

Figure 8.1 provides a visual summary of actions that families can take to plan ways to have conversations with children around shared experiences. It is not essential to have multiple, unique experiences. More important is to have ongoing conversations before, during, and after events. For example, Tabors, Beals, and Weizman (2001) conducted research focusing on three daily events with young children – book reading, toy play, and mealtimes and found that conversations that engaged children in extended discussions provided children opportunities to be exposed to rare words, which was a strong predictor of children's later vocabulary development. Table 8.1 provides a list of developmentally appropriate ways to engage children and youth in conversations.

Additional recommendations for promoting family strengths and for fostering resilience in children and youth reported by Cole, Clark, and Gable (2007) are:

1. Spend quality time with each child at least once a week.
2. Respond to children with patience and respect their feelings and abilities.
3. Encourage family members to share their accomplishments.
4. Visit and, if possible, help at your children's school.
5. Eat a meal together as a family and involve family members in mealtime tasks.
6. Hold family meetings and give each family member an opportunity to share.
7. Develop a family mission statement.
8. Develop and maintain family traditions and rituals.

Promoting Interaction

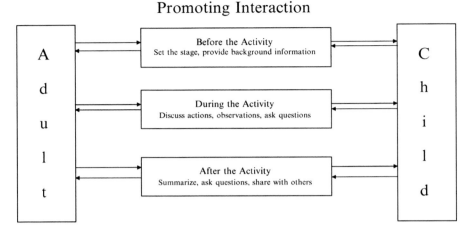

Fig. 8.1 Promoting interaction between adults and children with a hearing loss

Suggestions for Teachers

A variety of writers in the field of resilience (e.g., Duffy, 2007; Henderson, 2007; Henderson & Milstein, 1996; Henry & Milstein, 2004; Richardson, Neiger, Jensen, & Krumpfer, 1990) have summarized the research and key findings and suggested specific models for promoting resilience in children and youth. Five specific elements are found in each model. A brief explanation of each of those key factors is provided below:

- Positive connections – Healthy and supportive relationships give our lives meaning and value. We need to maintain as well as seek out new relationships that support our sense of belonging.
- Clear, consistent boundaries – Creating and enforcing rules help individuals develop a sense of safety as well as security.
- Life-guiding skills – Communication, conflict resolution, problem solving, time management, and self-advocacy are examples of skills that need to be developed, refined, and applied as one progresses through the challenges of life.
- Purpose and high expectations – Clear priorities, goals, and the motivation to achieve them provide the energy needed to grow and develop.
- Meaningful participation – Engagement in family, friends, school, or community events allows us to socialize as well as to help others.

Examples of actions that teachers can undertake on a regular basis that address these five factors are listed in Table 8.2 (adapted from Luckner, 1993; Luetke-Stahlman and Luckner, 1991).

Table 8.1 Suggestions for having conversations with children

Infants and toddlers
  Respond to/talk about baby's prelinguistic communications (e.g., crying, eye contact, wiggles, coos, grunts, pointing, smiles, and laughs)
  Play with the baby – smiles, gentle touches, and games
  Imitate laughter and facial expressions
  Use multiple senses to send messages – exaggerate facial expressions
  Follow the baby's lead (eye gaze, gesture, object, or activity)
  Respect baby's need for "down time"
  Move your hand or body in baby's field of vision
  Move object (e.g., toy) in front of baby, then up toward your face, then communicate
  Tap on object before and after communicating
  Tap on baby to signal "Look at me"
  Teach baby to imitate your actions (e.g., clapping and throwing kisses)
  Repeat words, signs, or short sentences several times
  If using sign, fingerspell
  Talk about routine activities as you do them (e.g., feeding, bathing, and dressing)
  Expand child's utterances/signs
  Read to child, describe, and encourage naming and pointing

Ages 2–4
  Follow child's lead
  Repeat what child says/signs and then expand on what was said
  Wait for replies
  Ask open-ended questions
  Play yes–no game (e.g., Are you a horse?)
  Sing/sign simple songs and nursery rhymes
  Talk about what you or the child is doing
  Read and talk about books
  Begin to use experiences as the springboard for conversations

Ages 4–6
  Follow child's lead
  Continue using experiences as springboard for conversations
  Introduce synonyms, figurative language, and new concepts in context
  Play describing/guessing games (e.g., "I am daddy's favorite dessert")
  Play make-believe games
  Play board, card, and computer games
  Discuss child's favorite television shows
  Do simple chores together
  Engage child in conversations about content subjects
  Read and talk about books

Ages 6–12
  Follow child's lead
  Continue using experiences as springboard for conversations
  Introduce synonyms, figurative language, and new concepts in context
  Involve child in mealtime conversations
  Work on schoolwork together
  Play board, card, and computer games

(continued)

Table 8.1 (continued)

Discuss child's favorite television shows and movies

Use scenarios/role play situations

Engage children in conversations about content subjects

Read and talk about books, magazines, and newspapers

Teach conversation components (i.e., openings, topic initiation, topic maintenance, topic expansion, topic change, and closing)

Teach interactive skills (i.e., attention getting, turn-taking, clarifying, feedback, repair strategies, and signaling transitions)

Ages 12–18

Follow adolescent's lead

Continue using experiences as springboard for conversations

Involve adolescent in mealtime conversations

Teach conversation components and interactive skills for specific situations (good friend, acquaintance, teacher, medical doctor, and work supervisor)

Use scenarios/role play situations

Engage adolescent in conversations about content subjects

Discuss current events

Have conversations about adolescent's postschool aspirations

Table 8.2 Sample actions for teachers to promote student resilience

Positive connections

Send a postcard to new students before school begins. Let them know you look forward to working with them

Try to meet with each student for even a brief time on a daily basis

Actively communicate with students by focusing, clarifying, accepting, and encouraging them

Know and use students' preferred names and name signs

Notice nonverbal indicators that the student is happy, sad, glad, tired, and so on, and communicate these observations

Learn about students' personal interests and activities outside of school

Make positive personal contact with parents

Promote student involvement in clubs, teams, and appropriate organizations

Make an effort to understand the fads, fashions, popular heroes, latest films, and television programs that presently motivate your students. Use them as examples while teaching

Make use of dialogue journals to communicate with each student about personal concerns and interests

Clear, consistent boundaries

Encourage personal responsibility

Avoid ridiculing or shaming students

Accept the fact that students are not adults and that there is a great deal to be learned through experimentation and inappropriate behavior

Help students to understand the consequences of their behavior

Provide incentives for good performance rather than punishment for poor performance

Avoid responding to a situation while you are angry or upset

(continued)

Table 8.2 (continued)

Life-guiding skills

  Organize group discussions for students to communicate about particular issues and feelings that affect them

  Provide methods for students to handle their own grievances

  Provide opportunities for students to self-evaluate their work

  Make use of contracts for behavior and academics

  Encourage students to take risks

  Help students broaden their range of experiences

Purpose and high expectations

  Acknowledge and promote students' special skills and interests

  Help students become aware of the decision-making process

  Teach students how they can influence people in positive ways

  Provide sufficient time for students to complete their assignments

  Provide opportunities for students to make choices, especially when they are of minor concern to you

  Plan activities, seatwork, and homework so that a student's chances of experiencing success are increased

  Preserve student work in a three-ring binder rather than throwing it out or sending it home one piece at a time

  Make use of individual charts and graphs that promote and demonstrate mastery of areas of study

  Provide sufficient opportunities for guided practice and group review prior to having students do individual work

  Relate present learning to future goals of students

  Encourage students to write goals for themselves for the next day, week, or month and to follow through on them

  Read and discuss stories and books about other individuals with a hearing loss

Meaningful participation

  Invite students to talk about their families and some of the things that make their families special

  Make use of cooperative learning procedures and techniques

  Invite parents and members of the community to come to school to discuss their interests and careers

  Expose students to people whom you hold in high regard, either through personal contact, the media, or literature

  Encourage participation in cultural programs and community events

Suggestions for Students

Benard (1991) reported that resilient children and youth usually have four common attributes:

1. Autonomy – A sense of one's own identity and an ability to act independently and exert some control over one's environment.
2. Sense of purpose and future – Goals, aspirations, persistence, and hopefulness.
3. Social competence – Positive relationships with peers and adults.
4. Problem-solving skills – Resourcefulness in problem resolution.

A building block for establishing a sense of identity and for setting goals is being in tune to one's interests, talents, strengths, and aspirations. Taking an inventory of the specific aspects of life that motivate and reinforce us helps individuals develop a sense of self and shape their future. Examples of prompts students can ask themselves, adapted from Luckner and Rudolph (2009) are:

- The three things I like to do most are _____.
- A television show I enjoy watching is _____.
- My favorite foods are _____.
- My favorite book was _____.
- My favorite type of movie is _____.
- My hobbies are _____.
- The things I like to do with my friends are _____.
- The places I like to go in town are _____.
- My favorite vacation was _____.
- Games I like to play are _____.
- My favorite sport is _____.
- My favorite subject in school is _____.
- When I graduate from high school I want to _____.
- Jobs that interest me are _____.
- If I won a million dollars I would _____.
- Something I dream about doing is _____.

Identifying, acknowledging, and building on interests often leads to participation, socialization, and learning related to that activity or topic, which in turn promotes opportunities for goal setting and the development of strengths.

As can be seen by examining Table 8.3 (Hoffman & Field, 2006), a construct aligned with the resiliency attributes noted above by Benard (1991) is self-determined behavior, which "refers to volitional actions that enable one to act as the primary causal agent in one's life and to maintain or improve one's quality of life" (Wehmeyer, 2006, p. 117). Research indicates that individuals with higher self-determination demonstrate more positive adult outcomes related to employment, wages earned, and overall quality of life than individuals with low self-determination (Wehmeyer & Schwartz, 1997, 1998). Concomitantly, research suggests that students can be taught successfully the instructional strategies related to self-determination such as self-awareness, choice-making, goal-setting, problem solving, self-regulation, and self-advocacy (Algozzine, Browder, Karvonen, Test, & Wood, 2001).

The tenets of self-determination are also included in the mandates of the Individuals with Disabilities Education Act of 2004 (IDEA). As noted by Kochhar-Bryant, Bassett, and Webb (2009), these include taking into account and addressing (1) student interests and preferences, (2) transition assessments, (3) postsecondary goal statements, (4) choice of courses of study that reflect their interests and future goals, and (5) student involvement in Individualized Education Plan (IEP) meetings.

In accordance with IDEA and to promote students' ability to become increasingly more self-determined, they can be taught to lead or help facilitate IEP meetings.

Table 8.3 Five-step model of self-determination

Step 1 – Know yourself
  Dream
  Know your strengths, weaknesses, needs, and preferences
  Know the options
  Decide what is important to you

Step 2 – Value yourself
  Accept and value yourself
  Admire strengths that come from uniqueness
  Recognize and respect rights and responsibilities
  Take care of yourself

Step 3 – Plan
  Set goals
  Plan actions to meet goals
  Anticipate results
  Be creative
  Visually rehearse

Step 4 – Act
  Take risks
  Communicate
  Access resources and support
  Negotiate
  Deal with conflict and criticism
  Be persistent

Step 5 – Experience outcomes and learn
  Compare outcome to expected outcome
  Compare performance to expected performance
  Realize success
  Make adjustments

They can begin this at a very early age. For example, in elementary school, students may have the role of introducing their parents to the team and describing what they have been learning in school. In middle school, students may explain their hearing loss, share their interests and strengths, describe the accommodations that are being used currently, and discuss why they are beneficial or why they need to be changed. In high school, students may lead the entire meeting using the steps presented below. They will want to make sure to include information about their preferences and plans for the future so that transition goals and services are documented. A general sequence suggested by Martin, Marshall, Maxon, and Jerman (1996) for student led IEPs is:

1. Begin meeting by stating the purpose.
2. Introduce everyone.
3. Review past goals and performance.
4. Ask for others' feedback.

5. State your school and transition goals.
6. Ask questions if you do not understand.
7. Deal with difference in opinion.
8. State what support you will need.
9. Summarize your goals.
10. Close the meeting by thanking everyone.
11. Work on IEP goals all year.

In addition to developing the appropriate attitudes, knowledge, and skills to be self-determined, students who are deaf also will need to learn to advocate on their own behalf. Self-advocacy refers to an individual's ability to identify the supports needed to succeed and to communicate that information effectively to others, including teachers and employers (Friend & Bursuck, 2009). The development of self-advocacy skills allows students to become actively involved in identifying and meeting their educational, social-emotional, and career goals. Fortunately, students have many opportunities to learn and practice self-advocacy skills in school, while participating in extracurricular activities, and during involvement in community events. Examples of self-advocacy skills that are beneficial for students who are deaf to develop, practice, and use include:

1. Recognizing when they need help.
2. Knowing when and how to request help.
3. Knowing appropriate accommodations and modifications.
4. Asking for appropriate help from peers and adults.
5. Actively participating in setting, establishing, and discussing IEP goals.
6. Understanding legal rights and responsibilities while in school, college, or work.
7. Setting goals and identifying needs and wants.
8. Expressing needs and wants effectively.

Summary and Conclusion

The development of resilience is the process of healthy human development, which is a dynamic process wherein personality and environmental influences interact in a reciprocal, transactional process (Benard, 2007). The construct of resilience should not be viewed as a fixed attribute of some individuals but rather as alterable processes that can be developed and fostered (Waxman, Gray, & Padrón, 2004). As noted by Henry and Milstein (2004):

> Resilient people may have had as many hardships in their lives as those who do not exhibit resiliency, but they cope with them differently. Resilient people bounce back from adversities stronger and quicker, learn from experience, develop new skills, and gain more self-confidence in the process. They are aware of what they need to do to get through difficult situations and bring internal and environmental resiliency building blocks into their lives (p. 249).

A hearing loss of any type – mild, moderate, severe, profound, unilateral, or bilateral – has the potential to change interaction patterns between the individual with the hearing loss and family members, peers, acquaintances, and people in the community. Similarly, a reduction in the quantity and quality of communication with others can negatively affect the development of an intact language system. In turn, impoverished language skills and weak concept knowledge may have adverse effects on the development of literacy and academic skills as well as career achievement.

In order to prevent this downward spiral, persistent attention needs to be directed toward caregiver and attachment relationships, the acquisition of communication skills, mastery motivation, self-regulation, the development of problem-solving skills, and peer relationships.

Simultaneously, a need exists for families, professionals, and students to move beyond focusing on problems and shortcomings and to recognize and build on strengths that help individuals with a hearing loss overcome challenges and to take actions that allow them to achieve personal and professional success.

References

Algozzine, B., Browder, D., Karvonen, M., Test, D. W., & Wood, W. M. (2001). Effects of intervention to promote self-determination for individuals with disabilities. *Review of Educational Research, 71*, 219–277.

Benard, B. (1991). *Fostering resiliency in kids: Protective factors in the family, school, and community*. Portland, OR: Western Center for Drug-Free Schools and Communities.

Benard, B. (2007). The foundations of the resiliency paradigm. In N. Henderson, B. Benard, & N. Sharp-Light (Eds.), *Resiliency in action: Practical ideas for overcoming risks and building strengths in youth, families, and communities* (pp. 3–7). Ojai, CA: Resiliency In Action, Inc.

Benard, B., & Marshall, K. (2001). *Competence and resilience research: Lessons for prevention*. Retrieved December 12, 2008, from http://www.umn.edu/nrrc

Blocher, D. H., Heppner, M., & Johnston, J. (2001). *Career planning for the 21st century* (2nd ed.). Denver, CO: Love Publishing Company.

Calderon, R. (2000). Parent involvement in deaf children's education programs as a predictor of child's language, early reading, and social-emotional development. *Journal of Deaf Studies and Deaf Education, 5*, 140–155.

Clarke-Stewart, A., & Dunn, J. (Eds.). (2006). *Families count: Effects on child and adolescent development*. New York: Cambridge University Press.

Cole, K. A., Clark, J. A., & Gable, S. (2007). Promoting family strengths. In N. Henderson, B. Benard, & N. Sharp-Light (Eds.), *Resiliency in action: Practical ideas for overcoming risks and building strengths in youth, families, and communities* (pp. 199–201). Ojai, CA: Resiliency In Action, Inc.

Covey, S. (1989). *The 7 habits of highly effective people*. New York: Simon & Schuster.

Duffy, T. (2007). Building resilience through student assistance programming. In N. Henderson, B. Benard, & N. Sharp-Light (Eds.), *Resiliency in action: Practical ideas for overcoming risks and building strengths in youth, families, and communities* (pp. 137–141). Ojai, CA: Resiliency In Action, Inc.

Easterbrooks, S. R. (2005, January). *Review of literacy in literacy development and instruction in students who are deaf and hard of hearing*. Retrieved February 11, 2005, from http://www.deafed.net/DeafedForums/ShowPost.aspx?PostID=1964

Friend, M., & Bursuck, W. D. (2009). *Including students with special needs: A practical guide for classroom teachers.* Upper Saddle River, NJ: Pearson.

Garfield, C. (1986). *Peak performers.* New York: Avon Books.

Gerber, P. J., Ginsberg, R., & Reiff, H. B. (1992). Identifying alterable patterns in employment success for highly successful adults with learning disabilities. *Journal of Learning Disabilities, 25*(8), 475–487.

Gottman, J. (1994). *Why marriages succeed or fail.* New York: Fireside.

Haddock, S., Zimmerman, T. S., Ziemba, S. J., & Current, L. R. (2001). Ten adaptive strategies for family and work balance: Advice from successful families. *Journal of Marital and Family Therapy, 27*(4), 445–458.

Hart, B., & Risley, T. R. (1995). *Meaningful differences in the everyday experiences of young American children.* Baltimore, MD: Paul H. Brookes Publishing Co.

Hart, B., & Risley, T. R. (2003). The early catastrophe: The 30 million word gap by age 3. *American Educator, 27*(1), 4–9.

Henderson, N. (2007). Hard-wired to bounce back. In N. Henderson, B. Benard, & N. Sharp-Light (Eds.), *Resiliency in action: Practical ideas for overcoming risks and building strengths in youth, families, and communities* (pp. 9–13). Ojai, CA: Resiliency In Action, Inc.

Henderson, N., & Milstein, M. (1996). *Resiliency in schools: Making it happen for students and educators.* Thousand Oaks, CA: Corwin Press.

Henry, D. A., & Milstein, M. M. (2004). Promoting resiliency in youth, educators, and communities. In H. C. Waxman, J. P. Gray, & Y. N. Padrón (Eds.), *Educational resiliency: Student, teacher, and school perspectives* (pp. 247–262). Greenwich, CT: Information Age Publishing.

Hoffman, A., & Field, S. (2006). *Steps to self-determination* (2nd ed.). Austin, TX: PRO-ED.

Holden-Pitt, L., & Diaz, J. A. (1998). Thirty years of the annual survey of deaf and hard-of-hearing children and youth: A glance over the decades. *American Annals of the Deaf, 143*(2), 72–76.

Huttenlocher, J., Haight, W., Bryck, A., Seltzer, M., & Lyons, T. (1991). Early vocabulary growth: Relation to language input and gender. *Developmental Psychology, 27*, 236–244.

Jamieson, J. (1995). Interactions between mothers and children who are deaf. *Journal of Early Intervention, 19*, 108–117.

Kochhar-Bryant, C., Bassett, D. S., & Webb, K. W. (2009). *Transition to postsecondary education for students with disabilities.* Thousand Oaks, CA: Corwin Press.

Levine, M. (2002). *A mind at a time.* New York: Simon & Schuster.

Lin, P. L. (1994). Characteristics of a healthy family. In P. L. Lin, K. W. Mei, & H. C. Peng (Eds.), *Marriage and the family in Chinese societies: Selected readings* (pp. 9–22). Indianapolis, IN: University of Indianapolis Press.

Luckner, J. L. (1993). Developing independent and responsible behaviors in students who are deaf or hard of hearing. *Teaching Exceptional Children, 26*(2), 13–17.

Luckner, J. L. (2002). *Facilitating the transition of students who are deaf or hard of hearing.* Austin, TX: PRO-Ed.

Luckner, J. L. (2006). Evidence-based practices and students who are deaf. *Communication Disorders Quarterly, 28*(1), 49–52.

Luckner, J. L., & Muir, S. (2001). Successful students who are deaf in general education settings. *American Annals of the Deaf, 146*(5), 450–461.

Luckner, J. L., & Rudolph, S. (2009). *Teach well, live well: Strategies for success.* Thousand Oaks, CA: Corwin Press.

Luckner, J. L., & Stewart, J. (2003). Self-assessments and other perceptions of successful adults who are deaf: An initial investigation. *American Annals of the Deaf, 148*(3), 243–250.

Luckner, J. L., & Velaski, A. (2004). Healthy families of children who are deaf. *American Annals of the Deaf, 149*(4), 324–335.

Luetke-Stahlman, B., & Luckner, J. (1991). *Effectively educating students with hearing impairments.* New York: Longman.

Luterman, D. (1987). *Deafness in the family.* Boston: Little, Brown and Company.

Luthar, S. S., Cicchetti, D., & Becker, B. (2000). The construct of resilience: A critical evaluation and guidelines for future work. *Child Development, 71*(3), 543–562.

Marschark, M., & Wauters, L. (2008). Language comprehension and learning by deaf students. In M. Marschark & P. C. Hauser (Eds.), *Deaf cognition: Foundations and outcomes* (pp. 309–350). New York: Oxford University Press.

Martin, J. E., Marshall, L. H., Maxon, L. M., & Jerman, P. L. (1996). *The self-directed IEP.* Longmont, CO: Sopris West.

Masten, A. S., & Obradovic, J. (2006). Competence and resilience in development. *Annals New York Academy of Sciences, 1094,* 13–27.

Masten, A., & Shaffer, A. (2006). How families matter in child development: Reflections from research on risk and resilience. In A. Clarke-Stewart & J. Dunn (Eds.), *Families count: Effects on child and adolescent development* (pp. 5–25). New York: Cambridge University Press.

Meadow-Orlans, K. P., Mertens, D. M., & Sass-Lehrer, M. (2003). *Parents and their deaf children: The early years.* Washington, DC: Gallaudet University Press.

Mitchell, R. E., & Karchmer, M. A. (2004). Chasing the mythical ten percent: Parental hearing status of deaf and hard of hearing students in the United States. *Sign Language Studies, 4,* 138–163.

Moeller, M. P. (2000). Early intervention and language development in children who are deaf and hard of hearing. *Pediatrics, 106*(3), E43.

National Association of the Deaf. (2000, October 6). *NAD position statement on cochlear implants.* Silver Spring, MD: Author.

National Institute on Deafness and Other Communication Disorders. (2007, May). *Cochlear implants.* Retrieved May 2, 2009, from http://www.nidcd.nih.gov/health/hearing/coch.asp

Ormrod, J. E. (2008). *Human learning* (5th ed.). Upper Saddle River, NJ: Pearson Education, Inc.

Powers, L. E., Singer, G. H. S., & Todis, B. (1996). Reflections of competence: Perspectives of successful adults. In L. E. Powers, G. H. S. Singer, & J. Sowers (Eds.), *On the road to autonomy: Promoting self competence in children and youth with disabilities* (pp. 69–92). Baltimore, MD: Paul H. Brookes Publishing Co.

Richardson, G. E., Neiger, B. L., Jensen, S., & Krumpfer, K. L. (1990). The resiliency model. *Health Education, 21*(6), 33–39.

Rutter, M. (2006). The promotion of resilience in the face of adversity. In A. Clarke-Stewart & J. Dunn (Eds.), *Families count: Effects on child and adolescent development* (pp. 26–52). New York: Cambridge University Press.

Ryan, R. M., & Deci, E. L. (2000). Self-determination theory and the facilitation of intrinsic motivation, social development, and well-being. *American Psychologist, 55*(1), 68–78.

Schirmer, B. R., & McGough, S. M. (2005). Teaching reading to children who are deaf: Do the conclusions of the National Reading Panel apply? *Review of Educational Research, 75*(1), 83–117.

Seligman, M., & Darling, R. B. (1997). *Ordinary families, special children: A systems approach to childhood disability* (2nd ed.). New York: The Guilford Press.

Singer, G. H. S., & Irvin, L. K. (1989). Family caregiving, stress, and support. In G. H. S. Singer & L. K. Irvin (Eds.), *Support for caregiving families: Enabling positive adaptations to disability* (pp. 3–25). Baltimore, MD: Paul H. Brookes Publishing Co.

Spencer, P. E. (2001, January). *A good start: Suggestions for visual conversations with deaf and hard of hearing babies and toddlers.* Retrieved June 4, 2003, from http://clerccenter2.gallaudet.edu/KidsWorldDeafNet/e-docs/visual-conversations/

Spencer, P., Bodner-Johnson, B., & Gutfreund, M. (1992). Interacting with infants with a hearing loss: What can we learn from mothers who are deaf? *Journal of Early Intervention, 16,* 64–78.

Tabors, P. O., Beals, D. E., & Weizman, Z. (2001). "You know what oxygen is?" Learning new words at home. In D. K. Dickinson & P. O. Tabors (Eds.), *Beginning literacy with language: Young children learning at home and school* (pp. 93–110). Baltimore, MD: Paul H. Brookes Publishing Co.

Turnbull, A., & Turnbull, R. (2001). *Families, professionals, and exceptionality: Collaborating for power* (4th ed.). Upper Saddle River, NJ: Merrill Prentice-Hall.

Vygotsky, L. (1978). *Mind in society: The development of higher psychological processes.* Cambridge, MA: Harvard University Press.

Wallerstein, J. S., & Blaleslee, S. (1995). *The good marriage: How and why love lasts.* New York: Houghton Mifflin.

Waxman, H. C., Gray, J. P., & Padrón, Y. N. (2004). Introduction and overview. In H. C. Waxman, J. P. Gray, & Y. N. Padrón (Eds.), *Educational resiliency: Student, teacher, and school perspectives* (pp. 3–10). Greenwich, CT: Information Age Publishing.

Wehmeyer, M. L. (2006). Self-determination and individuals with severe disabilities: Reexamining meanings and misinterpretations. *Research and Practice in Severe Disabilities, 30*, 113–120.

Wehmeyer, M. L., & Schwartz, M. (1997). Self-determination and positive adult outcomes: A follow-up study of youth with mental retardation and learning disabilities. *Exceptional Children, 63*(2), 245–255.

Wehmeyer, M. L., & Schwartz, M. (1998). The relationship between self-determination and quality of life for adults with mental retardation. *Education and Training in Mental Retardation and Developmental Disabilities, 33*(1), 3–12.

Wells, G. (1986). *The meaning makers: Children learning language and using language to learn.* Portsmouth, NH: Heinemann.

Yoshinaga-Itano, C., Sedey, A. L., Coulter, D. K., & Mehl, A. L. (1998). Language of early- and later-identified children with hearing loss. *Pediatrics, 102*(5), 1161–1171.

Young, A., Green, L., & Rogers, K. (2008). Resilience and deaf children: A literature review. *Deafness and Education International, 10*(1), 40–55.

Part IV
Adolescence

Chapter 9
Whose Literacy Is It, Anyway? Strengths-Based Guidelines for Transforming the Developmental Environments of Deaf Children and Adolescents

Martha A. Sheridan

Abstract In this chapter, the literature on resilience is discussed in relation to the results of phenomenological research on a cohort of deaf children and adolescents sharing their perspectives on their lifeworlds (Sheridan, Inner lives of deaf children: Interviews and analysis, Gallaudet University Press, Washington, DC, 2001; Sheridan, Deaf adolescents: Inner lives and lifeworld development, Gallaudet University Press, Washington, DC, 2008). Internal and external protective factors and dispositional attributes of resilience are discussed. Guidelines emerging from the research which were designed to optimize the developmental environments of deaf children and adolescents through multisystemic collaborations with the youth (Sheridan, 2008) are shown to be consistent with a resilience building framework. Through a transcendent, empowering process in collaboration with deaf youth, professionals and parents are challenged to recognize and utilize the existing strengths and talents that deaf children and adolescents possess while simultaneously cultivating their own *deaf – literacies* and *deaf – literate* formative environments.

This chapter examines frameworks from the general literature, which include personal and environmental characteristics that contribute to resilience and what my qualitative research with deaf children and adolescents (Sheridan 2001, 2008) has shown to be applicable for them. I discuss the responsibilities that adults and the professional community have for strengthening and contributing to the development of protective factors in the social worlds of deaf children and adolescents in a way which incorporates, in an empowering and collaborative manner, the existing strengths and talents of deaf children and teenagers. The strengths-based guidelines offered in this chapter aim to help families, professionals, communities, and organizations cultivate constructive long-term effects on the development of deaf children and adolescents and their environments. This chapter views the deaf child and adolescent from a person-in-environment perspective, which explores situations in life presented in the social environments of children and adolescents who happen to be deaf.

M.A. Sheridan (✉)
Department of Social Work, Gallaudet University, Washington, DC, USA
e-mail: martha.sheridan@gallaudet.edu

D.H. Zand and K.J. Pierce (eds.), *Resilience in Deaf Children: Adaptation Through Emerging Adulthood*, DOI 10.1007/978-1-4419-7796-0_9,
© Springer Science+Business Media, LLC 2011

At the core of discussions on risk and resilience are definitions of these two terms. The discussion in this chapter is framed in the belief that *everyone* experiences situations in life that present risk and opportunities to problem-solve, to demonstrate resilience. For *everyone*, challenges, change, disruption, and uncomfortable experiences in life can be opportunities for growth (Earvolino-Ramirez, 2007). As many people like to say, these experiences can make us stronger. In this discussion, resilience is defined as competence and successful adaptation to life stress and/or events perceived as potentially harmful (Greene, 2007; Lazarus, 1999; Masten & Coatsworth, 1998; Pearlin, Aneshensel, Mullen, & Whitlatch 1996; Werner & Smith, 1992).

Discussion of *resilience* necessitates accompanying discussions of risk because resilience implies successfully overcoming a potentially challenging situation. Many resilience studies focus on the adaptations of children born into severe, high-risk conditions of disadvantage (Benard, 1991). These discussions of antecedents and adaptations present a challenge to writing this chapter. As Young, Green, and Rogers (2008) remind us, there has been an abundance of debate over conflicting social constructions and meanings of "being deaf in the world." Conventional medical and pathological views of deaf people portray "deafness" as a condition of disadvantage, deficit, or risk. This viewpoint has been oppressive and created social forces that have marginalized deaf people throughout history. From the medical perspective, deaf children and adolescents are seen as the problem (Brueggmann, 1999) and are left to bear the burden of adaptation (Sheridan, 2008).[1] In contrast to the medical view are social and cultural paradigms, which view the deaf community and the culture of deaf people from a strengths perspective. Central to the debate over social constructions of deaf people is the question of who defines and makes decisions regarding their individual and community well-being. In relation to the topic of resilience, the debate becomes who decides what risk and resilience means in terms of being deaf. Sheridan (2008) states that many hearing people in the social worlds of deaf people are not *literate* in the sociocultural, communication, or linguistic meanings of being deaf in the world, and it is this *audist* (Humphries, 1996) social condition that contributes to the marginalization of deaf people.

Literacy can be defined as a competency one brings to the social world that allows for the achievement of goals in life. By defining *literacy* in this way we can examine the competencies that individuals bring to interactions in various situations in life. In my discussion, risk is defined as a universal experience, since everyone experiences risk in various situations of life. Furthermore, resilience is defined herein as a positive adaptation to challenges, change, or uncomfortable experiences in life. I highlight the strengths, resources, and internal capacities of a cohort of deaf children and teenagers who have shared, through a process of qualitative research, information about their life experiences of being deaf. These children and teens described a breadth of experiences including both positive and negative events, comfortable and uncomfortable experiences, and perceived environmental stressors they have faced in their developmental and social environments. They also discussed how they have dealt with these stressors (Sheridan 2001, 2008).

---

[1] Information in this chapter on research has been adapted from Sheridan (2001, 2008). Both books are available from Gallaudet University Press.

The strengths and competencies exemplified by this cohort of research participants are strongly explanative of their literacies and their resilience. Resulting texts discussing this research (i.e., Sheridan, 2001, 2008) proposed recommendations for maximizing the internal strengths, resources, and capacities demonstrated by these young participants. They also discuss the responsibility that others in the developmental environment have for developing their own *deaf literacies* to achieve successful interaction with deaf children and teens, to strengthen the external environments, and to reduce and remove audist social conditions. This approach is consistent with Bronfenbrenner's (1979) ecological perspective on development, which aims to achieve a "goodness of fit" between the person and the environment. A transcendent (Frankl, 1969), participatory, and empowering method of practice is central to these recommendations. This approach is consistent with the self-determination values of deaf culture and the deaf community.

Resilience research has indicated that developmental environments are important to life outcomes (Cole, Cole, & Lightfoot, 2004; Doll & Lyon, 1998; Masten, 2001; Masten & Coatsworth, 1998). Such research has led to the strengthening of the characteristics of caretaking environments to enhance growth and life outcomes (Doll & Lyon). Deaf children and adolescents, like their hearing peers, face the possibility of alienating experiences in their developmental environments. The differences lie in the unique context of interactional situations involving communication, culture, and perceptions.

The Research

Data about the lives and experiences of deaf children and adolescents have frequently been collected by studying the perspectives of parents and professionals, who are usually hearing (Lane, 1992). Typically, researchers have lacked the skills necessary for studies involving deaf people (Lane, Hoffmeister, & Bahan, 1996; Levine 1960, 1981; Moores, 2001) or have assumed that deaf youth are not reliable sources of information. Recent momentous collections of the reflections of deaf adults on their childhood experiences offer a mature perspective on developmental experiences (Luckner & Stewart, 2003; Oliva, 2004). However, they cannot be generalized to the experiences of deaf children and adolescents in the context of today's social world. Therefore, the perspectives of deaf children and adolescents in a current context are critical to understanding their developmental "lifeworlds" at any given point in time. It is important to note that my research was not about resilience, nor was it about risk, but rather the purpose of my research was to explore and describe what deaf children and adolescents experience and how they interpret their "lifeworlds" (Sheridan, 2001, 2008). This chapter reviews that research and discusses its connectedness to the concept of resilience. The stories and themes presented in this chapter are from the narratives shared by the participants during our interviews. "I set out to understand their perceptions of their 'lifeworlds,' which I define as the synthesis of their experiences, their relationships, their truths; the intersecting physical and psychological systems of self, family, community and beyond; the ways they view their current reality, and the possibilities they see for their futures" (Sheridan, 2008, p. *x*). I sought to understand how they perceive themselves, their experiences, and their interactions with others in the context of their day-to-day social environments.

This research began as a single qualitative study of seven deaf children between the ages of seven and ten. At the completion of this initial study, I returned to interview this same cohort of participants during their adolescent years when they were 13–17 years of age. The longitudinal nature of the study allowed for exploration of the similarities and differences in the participants' perspectives of their lifeworlds across time. The study is now described as having a phase I (childhood) and phase II (adolescence) process.

The phenomenological and naturalistic (i.e., Lincoln & Guba, 1985) methods used in this study allow a researcher to enter the natural environments of the research participants and to learn about the perspectives that they have of their lifeworlds through interviews and observations. Participants shared stories, or narratives, in semistructured interviews, in their own words, of their thoughts, feelings, realities, and experiences. Themes emerged within and across the participants' narratives. Interview methods appropriate for use with children such as projective art and storytelling, direct and indirect questioning, and observation were employed in the phase I study. In the phase II study, the adolescent participants responded to projective storytelling as well as direct and indirect interview questions

My invitation to write a chapter for this pioneering book on resilience in deaf children and adolescents began with the editor's interest in the challenges expressed by my young deaf research participants. While my participants did convey stories about alienating experiences in various situations in life, perhaps the most important contribution that these participants made to our literature was the fact that they shifted our attention to their many positive, joyful experiences and loving relationships, their multiple strengths, their hopes and dreams and the optimistic expectations they have for themselves and their futures, their adaptability and the effective ways in which they tackle whatever challenges that life does present. So much of the focus in research on deaf people has been on expectations that they will encounter overwhelmingly negative experiences in life. Themes in our literature are frequently problem focused because deaf children and adolescents are stigmatized and marginalized. My research participants taught us that their lives are balanced. They also taught us that when they do encounter uncomfortable challenges and alienating experiences they can be expected to use their repertoire of competencies to cope with these events. Rarely do we find studies on deaf children and adolescents that focus on their strengths and competencies and the positive pathways they take in response to stressful or challenging situations that arise.

Resilience Frameworks

The literature on resilience includes a discussion of internal and external protective factors (Benard, 1991; Benson, 1997; Paine & Paine, 2002), dispositional attributes (Werner & Johnson, 1999), assets (Paine & Paine, 2002), and characteristics of resilient individuals (Brooks & Goldstein, 2001). The following traits are characteristic of resilient individuals: social competence, which is defined as prosocial behaviors including "responsiveness, cultural flexibility, empathy, caring, communication skills, and a sense of humor" (Benard, p. 2); problem solving (planning, help-seeking, critical and creative thinking); autonomy (sense of identity, self-efficacy, self-control, self-awareness, and the ability to distance oneself from negative messages and conditions (Berlin & Davis, 1989); and a sense of purpose and belief in a bright future (goal direction, educational aspirations, optimism, faith, and spiritual connectedness) (Benard 1991). Brooks and Goldstein's (2001) characteristics of a resilient mind include feeling special and appreciated; having realistic goals and self-expectations, belief in one's ability to problem-solve and make decisions, recognizing and enjoying one's competence and strengths, social competence, and reliance on effective strategies for coping. The resilient characteristics demonstrated by the cohort of young deaf people discussed herein (Sheridan, 2001, 2008) fit well with the above traits and conceptions of resilient individuals. This section presents some examples.

In both phases of my study, the participants displayed attitudinal assets of self-reliance, optimism, confidence, competence, and a positive future orientation. They had a strong sense of self-directed autonomy, taking responsibility for themselves in situations where barriers existed (Sheridan, 2001, p. 221). In the childhood study, there were instances where the children would motivate themselves in their school work, remove themselves from uncomfortable situations, and identify or create more comfortable circumstances. When sharing stories of communication barriers in their peer relations, they indicated that they would direct hearing children to more action-oriented play activities, which were less dependent on communication; they initiated writing and taught hearing peers to sign, or asked family members to help with communication. They were creative, autonomous, problem solvers who sought help when they needed it. They were caring, empathetic, responsive, and flexible in their social relations. They were self-aware and able to articulate their sense of identity, their self-perception, and their perceptions of others in their lives. They enjoyed a variety of recreational activities including sports, video games, watching closed-captioned television programs, traveling with their families, attending theatre events, as well as solitary play activities with pets and toys. The participants reported comfort and enjoyment in relationships with *self-same* peers (i.e., "deaf like me") and use of technologies (Sheridan, 2008, p. 178). Their perceptions of their futures were mostly optimistic and included positive goals and a variety of educational and career options.

A common theme in resilience research has been the indication that a child's external developmental environment contributes greatly to resilience (e.g. Greene, 2007; Masten, 2001; Masten & Coatsworth, 1998). Protective factors (Benard, 1991) are described as environmental characteristics that may offset potentially negative outcomes of risk and help one to transcend adverse experiences. Three environmental protective factors include: (1) caring relationships which provide for safety and basic trust, (2) high expectation messages focusing on strengths, and (3) opportunities for meaningful participation and contribution (Benard, 1991).

The importance of socialization patterns within the child's family which encourage trust, autonomy, initiative, and connections to others has also been emphasized (Werner & Johnson, 1999). Furthermore, significant and positive attachment relationships with an adult are seen as having an important effect on the potential for resilience (e.g., Luthar, Cicchetti, & Becker, 2000). Constantly changing social contexts and the importance of assessing, understanding, and examining the impact of these historical and evolving circumstances on resilience are critical for professional practice (Greene, 2007).

Resilience in a Cohort of Deaf Children and Adolescents: Challenges, Strengths, and Pathways

Internal Protective Factors: Beneficial Participant Traits and Abilities

Growing up in a predominantly hearing world, which stigmatizes and marginalizes deaf children and adolescents, means that they are likely to receive messages from their environments that could possibly counter their hopes and dreams for the future and shatter a moment's contentment, or even their self-esteem. These messages can be received like a sudden jolt in the context of a particular situation, or they can be disguised in long-standing low expectations for children in their home, school, or community environments. The stories below illustrate some of the stressful, harmful, or alienating social experiences reported by the research participants and their constructive *pathways* or positive responses (Sheridan, 2001, 2008). They illustrate the positive and resilient personal characteristics, assets, or attributes that these participants possess.

Some common themes emerging from this research regarding the pathways these children and adolescents used when faced with challenging or *alienating* experiences include a clear sense of *autonomy* in problem solving, an abundance of comfortable and accessible *relationships*, and *recreational activities*, and choosing to use their skills and resources in *sign language*. *Attachment* and belongingness were evident in relationships with others who the children and adolescents felt comfortable with communicatively, and for the adolescents the *depth and ease* they experienced in relationships with others they identified with was of great importance. Parents, siblings, and peers with whom they could communicate (either deaf or hearing) are referred to as *domesticated others*. The participants were *autonomous* and assertive in their choices to remove themselves from uncomfortable or alienating situations and participate in comfortable relationships. In addition, the participants were *resourceful* and aware of external sources of support should they need them. It was clear that internally they were comforted in the anticipation of doing so. The following examples illustrate many of the themes discussed above.

A 7-year-old deaf boy reported that the majority of his many friends are deaf. He describes his play activities and his happiness with his deaf friends with whom he will "play and play and play" at his residential school identified in his drawing as a school for deaf kids. Prompted to tell us how he would feel should a situation arise where he is with a group of hearing children who do not share his language, he explained that he might feel nervous, awkward, and uncomfortable in a play situation with them, "Well, he might be kind of nervous and... yeah, a little unsure. Because they're hearing and they might not know... he might not know how to use his voice... maybe not comfortable... kind of shy, kind of embarrassed, and kind of hesitant. A little bit afraid if no one signs." (Sheridan, 2001, p. 213). Yet this seems to be of little concern to him because both in his imagination about himself at play and in actual play situations, he is happy, secure, and absorbed in enjoyable interactions with his "many friends" at his residential school for deaf children. In addition, he tells us that if this situation should occur, his hearing sister who signs would help "interpret" and he would be "fine." He exhibits a "taken for granted" attitude about these situations, autonomy, and enjoyment of solitary play situations, which are appropriate to his developmental age. "He has lots and lots of friends... they play 'It' you know where you tag somebody... and then they go on the swing set together." (Sheridan, p. 50) When asked, "Oh they're deaf. All of them.... Sometimes there are hearing friends, but very few of them," and in situations where he is playing with other deaf people he would feel, "Happy" (Sheridan, p. 51).

Another young participant shared stories about the teasing he experienced at the hands of hearing peers at his school, "... people tease... I ask them to stop it. But they still tease and call names and get friends in fights and stuff like that. And we tell the teacher, but the teacher says just 'ignore it.'" (Sheridan, 2008, pp. 94–95). His attempts to elicit help from his teachers and counselors at school have not been successful. He reports that he and his deaf classmates all experience this. At home, however, he had a close relationship with his mother to whom he turned to and whom he perceived as loving and supportive. He makes many references to the support he receives from his mother and sister while continuing to be creative, thoughtful, resourceful, and self-directed in his problem-solving techniques.

While these participants told convincing stories of the love, attachment, and belongingness they experienced at home with their parents, their appreciation of their parents' sign communication skills, and the knowledge that their hearing parents could be relied on to assist with communication when needed, they admitted that the larger the family gathering became with nonsigning relatives, the more isolated and alienated they became. One 14-year old participant whose nuclear family is deaf had this to say about her extended family, which includes hearing cousins: "I have some cousins who are hearing. They're not enthusiastic about sign language. They get together in a group, and ignore the deaf people. It makes me mad because it's hard for me." (Sheridan, 2008, pp. 47–48). This participant autonomously responds to this situation by choosing to ignore it and opts to play with her deaf brothers and sisters. She tells stories of fun and humorous adventures with her deaf family and provides in-depth descriptions and details about each of her family members and family events. This depth of information about her family surpasses the level of knowledge that the deaf children of hearing parents in this current research presented (Sheridan, 2001). As an adolescent, this same girl cherishes her time with her deaf friends where she talks with them "for hours and hours on end... we never stop, we go on and on..."

(Sheridan, 2008, p. 47). Now and then, as this participant responded to my prompts about situations that are not accessible, she responded that it is really "no big deal." She was firmly grounded in a family, as well as an educational and community network of people with whom she was comfortable and could communicate.

However, another adolescent told of his communication experiences with his hearing stepsiblings, "They speak and I ask them what they said, and then they have to sign the same thing. They get sick of it. They say, 'Hold up.' Or they look away and they just ignore me.... There's just so many people around I don't know where to look. I'm lost. It's overwhelming!" (Sheridan, 2008, p. 67). He goes on to talk about how much he enjoys the smaller gatherings when it is just two or three immediate family members who are adept at signing, "There's more signing there. It's a lot better…" He admits to teaching sign language to his sister's boyfriend to help this situation. He goes on to talk about how he now stays in the dorm on weekends, which is more fun for him and has activities that he loves, whereas he gets bored and overwhelmed with communication at home now that his family situation has changed. This adjustment to a blended family situation is significant for him at this point in his life. At the same time, he sees a comfortable and joyful place for himself in his community of peers at school where he participates in sports activities. He speaks openly about his feelings and values the close relationship and quality time he shares with his father.

Another adolescent tells many stories of warm supportive and loving relationships with her parents. She recognizes their love for her and their ability to communicate with her. She shares happy stories of their travels together. She also notes their responsiveness to her naturally curious personality and her eagerness to grow and to succeed in life. She admits that large holiday family gatherings "are not fun when the family is talking. I'll just twiddle my thumbs, focus on my food. I don't know what to do, how to join in the fun with my family. Sometimes I feel really disheartened. Sometimes I'll ask, 'What's wrong?' or 'What's funny?' I scream, 'What's wrong,' and my mother will explain to me and I understand, but it doesn't feel good inside. I wish they could sign. Sometimes… I have to ask (my mother) if she'd mind interpreting, my dad too…. Sometimes I feel frustrated. It's a boost to my self esteem if my relatives are watching TV and I ask them to explain and they set up the closed captioning. It's a relief to know what is going on." (Sheridan, 2008, p. 78) This girl is assertive in these social situations and eager to participate. Her autonomy and assertive attitude and behaviors are some of her strengths in these situations. She is also able to empathize as she talks about how it is difficult for her mother in these situations when she is entertaining a large number of guests to also be her interpreter. Her empathy, assertiveness, and autonomy are also apparent when she discusses her response to a man in her neighborhood who is mentally ill and offered her an alcoholic drink. She responds "No, thank you!" I want to try to help people stop drinking, to get a good life. I try to avoid trouble. Someone will say, "Come here," I'll say, "No. thanks." (Sheridan, p. 76) This teenager is developing independent thinking skills. She talks with her parents and teachers about situations she faces, yet she is able to recognize that she does not always agree with them. She evaluates her risks and weighs possible responses to various situations.

This same participant spoke of the teasing she experienced on the playground when she was younger, "Sometimes the hearing boys would talk and they would yell, and I would gesture, 'What? I can't hear you.' They would be shocked.... The hearing kids would tease me by making fun of my signing.... I'd just look at them." (Sheridan, 2008, p. 78). Her empathy, maturity, assertiveness, autonomy, and competence are evident in this response, "Sometimes hearing people are shy. If they're learning signs they can be embarrassed. But I don't get mad, I don't bite, I understand their feelings. I'll teach them signs, I'll help them with fingerspelling and teach them. Sometimes I'll bring in an interpreter.... Sometimes hearing people are embarrassed, and that's okay. Deaf people are embarrassed sometimes too, but it's fine. That's normal. After a while, they get used to it." (Sheridan, p. 78)

Another teenager describes the ongoing harassment he has received from hearing peers while mainstreamed in hearing elementary and high school programs "... they'll gang up on me, they'll play tricks on me, and I don't like it.... They'll call me names." (Sheridan, 2008, p. 95). He continues, "... in elementary school, it was like, the kids teasing about anything. You'd have to get hands off" quick before they'd go, "Oh he's bothering me" ... And I'd say, "What did I do?" (Sheridan, p. 98). This same participant also received messages of low expectation from one of his teachers: "Like I had a teacher who really thought I couldn't do anything... she really didn't think I would succeed." (Sheridan, p. 109). He also reported "My older brother, he didn't really believe I could do things, but I did. He thought I couldn't play soccer as well as him, but I did." (Sheridan, p. 101). Since elementary school this participant has been open with his mother, sister, friends, teachers, and in these interviews with the researcher about these experiences. He reported that his teachers in elementary school were supportive but were unsuccessful in resolving the difficulties. In high school, however, he took a teacher's advice and succeeded in becoming a peer mediator. This constructive and innovative response put him in a position of authority as a part of the solution (Sheridan). He focused hard on maintaining a high grade point average, getting involved in other leadership activities such as a study abroad group, and the student council, as well as continuing to excel in school athletics despite the teasing, and getting support from friends. This participant adopted assertive, positive strategies in defiance to the teasing he received. He utilized his many competencies and maintained a positive sense of self-respect and confidence in his prospects for the future. In addition to his own competencies, he had this to say about the warm and supportive relationships he has with his mother and his sister, "My mom, she's always been there for me for all my life. And my sister tries to help me. She's almost like my psychologist." (Sheridan, p. 100). "...For many years my mom's been helping, and I really love her. She was there for me" (Sheridan, p. 101).

In terms of *resourcefulness*, sometimes when teenagers begin to emerge further into the community and try out things independently of their parents they may be surprised at what they find. One participant described a situation where he was brushed aside when he attempted to place an order in a fast food restaurant. Although he did not communicate in this interview how he dealt with this situation, he did state that he knew this was wrong and, "I have rights."

Another teenager spoke of how she was working hard to prepare for her future and was aware of many resources available to facilitate her independent functioning in health, employment, and education settings (e.g., interpreters, closed-captioning). She also noted technologies and resources that would be available when she becomes a parent (e.g., baby cry alerts).

In this research, it became apparent that these participants, like any group of adolescents, are not immune to bullying. "I remember when I was around five, at school, there was a boy who was an awful bully. One time he hurt me..." (Sheridan, 2008, p. 75). Bullying may take place in their schools, whether mainstreamed with hearing students who see them as different, or as with hearing students, within their own peer group. Recognizing that bullying and alienation can, and sometimes does, also take place within a deaf youth's own peer group is a fact that the deaf community cannot ignore. The following quote is from an adolescent boy who transferred out of his residential school because of bullying: "I don't go there anymore. I quit. The boys were awful! Yes. It was stupid. They were bullies. I was very upset.... I felt sick to my stomach and felt pressured. I just wanted to go home." (Sheridan, p. 140).

In-group conflict may also exist between factions of students who attend educational programs practicing different language forms. One of the participants attending a school practicing only oral communication admitted that her school has a rivalry with another school in the area where students use American Sign Language, "That school is only for signs, and sometimes we fight" (Sheridan, 2008, p. 184). Another participant, a child of deaf parents, discussed the comfort, identification, and ease she experiences within her deaf family and the deaf community, but stated that sometimes she is ridiculed by her deaf peers for attending a hearing school, "Sometimes they'll insult me, "What do you go to a hearing school for?" (Sheridan, p. 184). Situations such as this, and many others that these participants presented in this research, call for parent, professional (teachers, school, and mental-health personnel), organizational (i.e., schools), and community (i.e., deaf kids clubs, camps, deaf organizations, and community service agencies) response. Such response should be focused on instilling values, building value-based environments of respect, and encouraging community supports for resilience building.

Young people respond to these situations to the best of their abilities, and the participants in this study had many abilities at their disposal. They also respond based on how they have been taught to respond. However, many of the in-group conflicts expressed by the teenagers in the second phase of this study did not include examples of attempted resolution by members of their environment. One child was forced to change schools in response to bullying. The rivalries based on communication and language preferences (oral vs. signed) at deaf education programs expressed by another student did not include information on how the schools attempted to deal with the incident. This may be due in part to the fact that the researcher did not probe for these examples, but it could also be due to the fact that these are situations that necessitate a macro systems level response from their schools and communities which were not forthcoming or visible. Alternatively, these situations may be new to the students who may not have anticipated them or have little experience in responding to such situations. A multisystemic prevention and intervention response including the school, parents, professionals, organizations, and the deaf community would be invaluable. However, one participant showed a remarkable ability to respond to a situation at school where he felt rejected by a group of peers that he wished to interact with. He told a detailed, empowering story of not only the situation and his initial response of disappointment and depression but also how he went home and autonomously developed a strategy to resolve it. He returned to school the next day and began building a circle of friends one by one, thereby surrounding himself with a group of new friends. His story indicated that there was opportunity to discuss the situation with his mother after school, but he did not feel the need to do so.

It is important to note that the negative experiences illustrated above should only be seen as one element of the participants' "lifeworlds." These stressful situations were presented in the author's original publications (Sheridan, 2001, 2008) as one of many themes (i.e., *alienation and disparate others*), which also involved a plethora of strengths, capacities, positive experiences, and future-oriented goals in life (i.e., *attachment and domesticated others; infinity*, positive images of their futures; *strengths, and pathways* such as autonomy, relationships, recreational activities, well thought-out goal-directed problem solving strategies, assertiveness, and resourcefulness). In childhood, the participants took these stressful situations in stride, possessed a "taken for granted" attitude about being deaf in the world, and a ready repertoire of competencies for dealing with these challenges when they arose. The examples above demonstrated the strengths and competencies that the participants possess which helped them cope with these stressful experiences.

Resilience Enhancing Characteristics of the Cohort's Environments

The dispositions exemplified above are internal protective factors or characteristics that the participants possess. This section focuses on external environmental protective factors that may enhance resilience in an individual.

In many instances, the study participants shared stories of *caring relationships* at home, which involved genuine listening and communicated a sense of safety and trust, compassion, respect, understanding, and authentic interest in the youth, which are traits described by Benard (1991). This parallels the theme of *attachment and domesticated others* emerging from the research on this cohort of deaf participants (Sheridan, 2001, 2008). It was apparent that the stronger the communication competencies and linguistic matching between the participants and their family members, the closer their relationships seemed to be. Several of the participants told stories of supportive, loving, and nurturing parents. There was evidence of safety and trust in their relationships with their parents.

As one adolescent boy stated, "My mom, she's always been there for me for all my life." (Sheridan, 2008, p. 100). Another teenager stated, "Like my parents love me, and I'm deaf. They'll say, "Yes we love you. You're sweet!" "I'm thankful. They'll take me to fun places... they spoil me with clothes." (Sheridan, p. 90). This participant spoke of the many things her parents have taught her with regard to her safety and how they have helped her in various situations she has confronted.

High expectation messages are another environmental factor that Benard (1991) considers important to resilience. These are messages of guidance, structure, and challenge, which communicate belief in the teen and the teen's strengths rather than their deficits. Other than from their parents, there was little evidence in the participants' narratives that such high expectations were communicated by adults in their developmental environments. Yet, for many of the participants it appeared that, in the face of the obvious low expectation messages they received from their external environments, they were internally confident in and optimistic about their own capabilities in problem solving, for success in life, and in their relations with others. These participants were goal-oriented and largely purpose-driven. It is important to note that the participants appeared driven to demonstrate their capabilities to those who doubted them. They expected much from themselves in their present and future lives (*infinity*). Through their constructive *autonomous* and resourceful problem solving skills, there were instances where the youth assertively "showed" others, in a good natured manner (Joseph, 1994), what they could do, took it upon themselves to "teach" others how they can interact, devised problem solving strategies for inclusion in peer groups, and worked hard to "learn" information on subjects that are not incidental to them like they are for hearing people so that they would succeed. At the same time, each of these individuals had *self-same* peers with whom they identified and shared deep and lasting friendships with. It appeared that high expectations for deaf individuals were intrinsic in these self-same peer relationships with other deaf youth. These relationships served as a source of self-understanding, which transmitted among them.

Infinity, or positive perceptions of their futures, was another theme arising from the research. The career goals the participants set for themselves included college for many of them: veterinary science, business, professional sports, computers, electrical engineering, English, literature, and social work. They were confident that they would live independent lives, have a social network, intimate partners, and experience a wide range of careers. They took pride in their many talents and capabilities, sports, artistic skills, American Sign Language storytelling, and their interests in such things as travel, history, electronics, etc. Although their perceptions of their futures were largely positive, there were a few instances where participants as adolescents expressed some uncertainty about their future, or the future of other deaf adolescents. This may have represented low expectation messages they received involving discrimination against deaf people in certain career paths (i.e., armed forces, police), the intelligence, or socioeconomic capacity of deaf adults (e.g., one teenager indicated that deaf people are perceived as intellectually inferior to hearing people and that deaf adults typically are not wealthy) (Sheridan, 2008).

The qualitative research methods used in this study enabled the participants to give voice to their perceptions and to participate meaningfully in the creation of a product (the research results and dissemination products) that communicates their understanding of their lifeworlds. It allowed them to contribute to their community through their strengths and talents. This relates to Benard's (1991) third characteristic of resilience enhancing environments – *opportunities for meaningful participation and contribution*. More opportunities for this third protective factor are possible and are discussed further in a later section of this chapter.

From Research to Practice: Cultivating Optimal Developmental Environments

The strengths and talents of the young participants in this study are outstanding, and hence there is a shift in attention to a positive paradigm of deaf children and adolescents rather than to the deficits that many might expect of them; yet it was clear from their narratives that they face unnecessary negative challenges in their environments. Life is relatively unpredictable in terms of the situations we will face and their contexts. There are a number of contextual factors involved in how an individual responds to challenging situations in life including our strengths, options, resources, capacities, and beliefs. Not all children and adolescents possess the resilient characteristics or the number of positive relationships and social supports that were available in the environments of the participants in this study. Children and adolescents are a vulnerable population, and they need adults as allies to create optimal developmental environments. It is important to examine what can be done to strengthen these developmental environments, transforming them into environments that are growth enhancing and less restrictive. In this process, we can capitalize upon and maximize the strengths and talents of the children and teens, allowing them to participate in and contribute to this process in a creative, meaningful, and empowering way, stimulating their own growth and a connectedness to others and their communities. This chapter offers guidelines to facilitate this transformation through connectedness, creative collaborations, and meaningful contributions.

Ideas presented in the guidelines below are based on a strengths perspective facilitating and valuing the deaf adolescent's voice; promoting/facilitating their development, belief in self and capacities and confidence (mastery); development of character, responsibility and leadership competence, tapping into their own capacities; expanding environmental/community/relational and self resources and collaborations; and affirming their self-assessments (Saleebey, 2005) and a sense of ownership.

Families, communities, organizations, social institutions, policy makers, legislators, researchers, professionals, peers, and others in the lives of children and adolescents have a responsibility to serve as critical sources of support and allies to buffer the potential negative effects of societal attitudes and behaviors. As long as there are those who choose to marginalize and label deaf children and adolescents as deficient and inferior, and ascribe low expectations, there will be situations in life where deaf people and our allies must make choices about how to respond. We have a social responsibility to educate, raise awareness about, and change institutional values and practices that perpetuate this marginalization. Being *deaf literate* (Sheridan, 2008), which includes possessing the knowledge, competencies, and values related to being deaf in the world, diminishes audism and is a social responsibility shared by everyone in the deaf child and adolescent's social environment. Framed in existential principles (Frankl, 1969), the approach in this chapter facilitates the deaf person's development of the capacity to exercise freedom and choice, to discover meaning in situations, to transform and transcend stressors, to use their creativity to create solutions, to exercise their belief in things beyond themselves, and to experience connectedness through the use of their existing skills.

The narratives above have illustrated both, the inconsistencies and risk across multiple systems in the environments of deaf children and adolescents and their strengths in adapting to these situations of risk. While it was clear that the participants in the study adapted in a variety of ways to these environmental situations, many of the environments do not reciprocate in this adaptation. Optimal environments for the healthy social/emotional development of a deaf child or adolescent do not leave the burden of responsibility on the child. Rather it involves "multiple systems" that are literate in the language, culture, adaptations, behaviors, needs, strengths, and resources that deaf people bring to their interactions (p. 213). Optimal developmental environments focus on changing the milieu by becoming *deaf literate*, "The absence of deaf literacy is part of the reason audism exists; at the same time, this absence is the reason that multisystemic literacy is part of the solution" (Sheridan, 2008, p. 213).

In my 2008 text I describe three types of *systemic literacies: compatible, partially compatible, and noncompatible systemic literacies* (p. 213) The stories highlighted above show us that the children and adolescents in this study routinely transition across multiple systems (home, school, community, peer, neighborhood, and organizational environments). In doing so, they encountered inconsistent deaf systemic literacies in their developmental environments. Compatible literacy systems are systems that are aware of the factors described above and result in "successful transactions, mutual adaptation, and mutual development." (p. 214). These systems match the needs and goals of the child or adolescent. A deaf child sharing a common language with deaf parents who are able to facilitate positive social, emotional, and linguistic development in the home environment is an example of a system with compatible literacies. "Partially compatible systemic literacies provide for limited interactions and limited adaptation and development" (Sheridan, 2008, p. 214). Limited interactions with peers, family, or others through partially sufficient communication access are an example of a partially compatible systemic literacy. On the other hand, "non-compatible systems fail to match the literacies of the deaf person and may contribute to failed interactions and divergent development where the two systems, such as child and parent, do not mutually adapt to each other" (Sheridan, p. 214). Growth enhancing, *corresponding developmental processes* (Sheridan) should occur in a deaf child's family with hearing parents when the hearing family members respond immediately to the unique developmental needs of their child and develop the literacy skills they both need for communication, cognitive, language, psychological, and social development.

Guidelines for Transforming the Deaf Child's Developmental Environment

This research yielded an abundance of data pertaining to the strengths and competencies of these participants and the adaptations they made in an often uncompromising external environment. Yet, the burden of this adaptation frequently rested upon the children and adolescents. Sheridan (2008) provides recommendations that facilitate optimal developmental environments based upon the expressed values, desires, and strengths of the study participants. This section addresses some of these recommendations for strengthening these external environments so that they are more nurturing and empowering, and illustrate their congruence with those of other researchers. These recommendations are similar to the developmental assets model (Paine & Paine, 2002) for cultivating and enhancing the developmental attributes that children and adolescents possess in that they use existing strengths and dispositional assets as building blocks. A participatory and empowering approach is central to these guidelines, giving deaf children and adolescents empowering opportunities for meaningful contributions. We can help environments escape disempowering low expectations, stereotypes, and stigma and promote transcendence over environmental restrictions by recognizing, promoting, and utilizing the child's internal strengths and resources, or personal resilience characteristics. Protective factors of caring relationships, high expectations, and opportunities for meaningful participation and contributions (Benard, 1991) are shown to be fundamentally congruent with these guidelines. The guidelines are designed to give our youth opportunities for responsibility, decision making, voicing their ideas and beliefs, to contribute their talents and strengths, and develop positive peer relations and a healthy identity. They expose our children and adolescents to successful role models, discourage learned helplessness, and stimulate awareness of their strengths and competencies and areas for continued growth. While building upon existing strengths, this approach also encourages adult, professional and community involvement and responsibility in improving the developmental environments and relations. Furthermore, in keeping with an ecological perspective, it enhances a "goodness of fit" (Bronfenbrenner, 1979) and positive connections and attachment between the youth and the environment.

Reinforcing strengths. As indicated above, deaf children and adolescents have many strengths and talents, yet their strengths and talents have not been the focus of attention from the professionals in their lives. The participants in this research exemplified their personal strengths and optimism in their current and future lives. We should shift our attention to these assets, reinforce them, and use them as building blocks for further development. By recognizing these existing strengths, and believing and expecting that the individual possesses many assets, parents and professionals can adopt a collaborative approach with deaf youth which actively challenges and fosters their continued growth. The remaining guidelines are built upon this reinforcement of strengths and assets.

Collaboration with our students and communities. An empowering and strengths-based approach to working with deaf children and teenagers is important. The contributions of this cohort of informants to their community through their participation in this research process demonstrate that we should expect and value their meaningful participation in environmental change processes and in the development of multisystemic literacies in their many environments. Education and community programs, families, and professional training programs should work with the youth to allow them to use their assets in a manner that facilitates their participation in a meaningful way in their communities and make contributions to their lifeworlds and the lives of others. This process also allows us to continue to challenge and nurture their strengths and assets and leadership skills for their futures. It encourages and reinforces high self-expectations and demonstrates our belief in their capabilities. It is also compatible with a belief in the incremental theory of intelligence (Blackwell, Trzesniewski, & Dweck, 2007), which states that intelligence is a process, not a fixed achievement level.

Bully prevention programs in schools and community organizations. All children and adolescents need safe developmental environments. The study participants shared stories of compassion, love, trust, and safety in their relationships with their parents, who took the time to listen to their concerns and provide them with support. Simultaneously, they stated there were many situations in their lives where they experienced discomfort, rejection, and alienation (e.g., in situations where their rights were violated, or where they were bullied). Schools, homes, and communities need to have clear rules for communication, respect, and responsibility and consequences for all involved in interactions with deaf children and adolescents. Respect and responsibility programs in schools and community organizations should aim to reduce stereotypes and emphasize a deeply ingrained system of institutional values respecting the increasing diversity of deaf youth, their families and communities. These values should be inherent in organizational mission statements and all levels of organizational operations. Prevention programs for bullying, such as the Olweus Bullying Prevention Program (Olweus, 2001), which is currently being adapted for use in educational programs for deaf youth (Weiner & Miller, 2006), should be adopted in schools and other social environments.

Community-based clubs and activities for deaf youth. It is well established in the literature that peer relations have important implications for social and academic success (e.g., Malecki & Elliott, 2002; Oliva, 2004). As children, the study participants alternated between "taken for granted" deaf and hearing play relationships, but as adolescents they projected a strong preference for *self-same* social relations and identification with other peers who are like them in their communication and share their cultural preferences (Sheridan, 2008). As they matured, they reported experiencing *depth*, *ease*, and *comfort* in communication and social relations. These were safe relationships for the participants where they experienced self-expression, understanding, listening, and support. Opportunities for these self-same relationships are infrequent in many geographic areas. Such opportunities are healthy and must be increased. While these opportunities are important for all deaf teens, it is especially true for the many youth who are mainstreamed in educational programs where they do not have self-same peers to interact with.

The study participants responded positively to after school and weekend clubs and activities for deaf children and teens, and during the summer months at camps. These safe "deaf space" or "place" opportunities can be expanded upon through face-to-face or technology-based mentoring and buddy systems using e-mail, social networking, and videophone pals, vlogs, and blogs. They give the deaf youth a safe "space" or "place." Promoting safe and nurturing environments with plentiful opportunities for socialization promotes healthy development of language, cognitive, social, and emotional skills, as well as opportunities for attachment relations. They can involve organized social and recreational activities as well as discussion groups and education around common issues of concern for all teenagers such as dating, drug and alcohol prevention, peer pressure, career and postsecondary choices, self-defense and protection, assertiveness, legal rights, conflict resolution, etc. Mentoring programs with deaf adults in various careers and with deaf college and high school students should be integrated into these programs.

National and international conferences on multisystemic deaf literacies. Such conferences can focus on building agendas and action plans for improving environmental capacity and responsiveness to deaf children and adolescents. Working in collaboration with deaf youth and communities would be an important theme for this conference.

Creative arts and media. Creative arts and media programs have tremendous potential for outreach to deaf children and adolescents who are isolated without a peer group, role models, or significant others in their lifeworlds to provide caring relationships, high expectation messages, and opportunities for meaningful participation and contributions, and for developing life skills. Involving deaf children and teens in such activities allows us to utilize and enhance their strengths and talents, build their communities, and link them to others like themselves. Elementary and secondary educational programs for deaf youth, community organizations such as state associations, community and social service programs for deaf people, and clubs can consider sponsoring theatrical productions about a variety of topics such as the career achievements of famous deaf adults, deaf culture and history, the day-to-day lives of deaf individuals (career, parenting, health-care issues, diversity among deaf people, legal rights, finances, continuing education, socialization, and recreation opportunities). Productions can serve as creative avenues of expression for deaf youth around a variety of issues of interest to them, their goals, their hopes, and their own day-to-day experiences or for psychoeducation and prevention issues. They can provide the students with opportunities to suggest positive changes in their social environments, to enhance positive perceptions of deaf people, and to reinforce their potential.

Education about legal rights, assertiveness, and conflict resolution. In their discussions of alienating experiences faced by this cohort, only one participant mentioned an awareness of legal rights as a resource for problem solving. Educational curriculums and community programs should include opportunities for legal rights education, assertiveness, and conflict resolution strategies that deaf children and teens can utilize.

Programs should also reinforce and reward the positive problem solving skills that deaf youth demonstrate.

Enhance attachment relations with parents and reinforcement of parents' belief that children know they are loved. The participants in this study conveyed a strong sense of attachment in their relationships with their parents and confidence in their parents' love and positive regard for them. Where this is the case, parents should receive reinforcement for their positive attachment enhancing behaviors and caring relations with their children. Early intervention programs can do much to reinforce and encourage this in parent–child relations where it might otherwise be absent. But support for parents in relation to their deaf children should be available throughout the formative years, not just in infancy, because as children develop, their developmental environments must adapt accordingly. Parent support, networking, and education programs can be school- or community-based and offered alongside the extracurricular and community-based activities available to deaf youth.

Mentoring. Mentors have been shown to make important contributions to resilience in adolescents (Hauser & Allen, 2006). Mentoring opportunities for deaf children and teens and their families around a variety of life themes and skills (careers, assertiveness, problem solving, communication and language, parent–child interaction, reading enhancement, deaf culture and awareness, etc.) should be made available to deaf youth and their families. Models such as the Take Your Child to Work Day, and the Laurent Clerc National Deaf Education Center's Shared Reading Project, and Deaf Mentor projects offered by various educational programs for deaf youth are examples of these.

Extended family sign classes and activities. The participants in this study all expressed a sense of alienation and boredom in interactions with their extended families where they were isolated from communication. Their stories revealed that extended family members, stepsiblings, and significant others outside of their immediate families often did not have the language or communication skills, or other deaf literacies, necessary for successful interaction with the deaf family member. Schools and community organizations that offer family learning vacations, which promote sign language proficiency, are critical. These programs should expand their focus beyond the immediate family to include extended family members (grandparents, aunts, uncles, and cousins) and blended family members (stepparents and stepsiblings, stepgrandparents, etc.) in sign language and family education programs. Doing so will enhance the child's comfort, inclusion, and attachment in the family system as a whole and lead to more compatible, growth-enhancing, esteem-building, family environments. Mentoring programs described above should include extended family as well.

Community support workers. Social service and community agencies and educational programs for deaf children and adolescents can do much to support the programs mentioned above by establishing community support positions for social workers to assist with the case management needs of families, daily living skills support, and parent education programs. They would focus on building family support and deaf literacies in the deaf member family system and other community environments interacting with the deaf youth.

Sign language and deaf awareness programs in schools where deaf children are mainstreamed. This research revealed that deaf youth mainstreamed in hearing schools experienced discomfort in relations with their hearing peers and staff who were not "deaf literate." The establishment of ASL and Deaf culture programs for high school credit to make educational settings more deaf literate would be helpful. Deaf students could participate in the planning and delivery of these instructional programs for credit.

Outreach: connecting through technology and transportation-based solutions. School and community partnerships for technology and transportation can be developed as solutions to the isolation that deaf children and teens experience on weekends and summers away from accessible educational environments with peers. Equipment grants for technologies and transportation for rural communities and socioeconomically disadvantaged families can provide a much needed connection to peers, mentors, professionals, information, education, and social interaction. Transportation grants can make it possible for isolated students and their families to attend deaf youth clubs, activities, workshops, camps, and family education programs. Creative technology and transportation innovations can also assist with outreach to immigrant families. Strengthening linkages between community organizations and schools for collaborative programming can also provide opportunities for leadership development in deaf students.

Scholarship/sponsorship opportunities. The participants in this study placed high value on opportunities for learning and social interaction in formal and informal peer group settings (identified above) with others like themselves. Scholarships and sponsorships for financing these opportunities need to be created.

Emergency preparedness. The participants in this study were well aware of the traumatic events of September 11, 2001. Crisis and trauma response programs need to be available and accessible to deaf people, our schools and communities. Deaf education programs of all types should have response plans that are inclusive of deaf students and their families.

Self and program evaluation. In addition the above recommendations from my earlier works, it would also be valuable for deaf children and teens to be involved in the evaluation of the programs and processes identified above, to evaluate their participation and contributions and areas for continued self and program improvement.

Further research on resilience and deaf youth. Finally, since there is such a dearth of research on the topic of resilience and deaf youth, it is critical for us to examine this phenomenon and to evaluate the implementation and outcomes of our programmatic efforts. This will allow us to develop evidence-based practices that reflect the best interests of the children and adolescents that we work with.

Conclusion

In this chapter on resilience in deaf children and adolescents, I have defined risk as a universal, not something that is unique to deaf youth. Risk is seen as challenge, stress, and disruption in life situations, which present opportunities for growth, for resolution, and to demonstrate competencies. Resilience is defined as strengths, competence, and successful adaptations to these life stresses. In a discussion of research into the lifeworlds of deaf children and adolescents and their unique developmental experiences, the participants demonstrated a plethora of strengths and competencies. These strengths and competencies were especially useful when they were faced with challenging situations.

While examining the literature on personal and environmental factors contributing to resilience, this chapter highlighted guidelines for maximizing the existing strengths of deaf children and teenagers and enhanced the literacy of their developmental environments at multiple systems levels. A collective, participatory approach to systems change intent on empowerment, and nurturing the developmental lifeworlds of deaf children and adolescents was presented. The dearth of research on resilience and deaf youth demands that evidence-based approaches to professional practice should be followed and that research into the factors contributing to the strengths and resilience of deaf people needs to be conducted.

References

Berlin, R., & Davis, R. (1989). Children from alcoholic families: vulnerability and resilience. In T. Dugan & R. Coles (Eds.), *The child in our times* (pp. 81–105). New York, NY: Brunner-Routledge.

Benard, B. (1991). *Fostering resiliency in kids: Protective factors in the family, school, and community.* Portland, OR: Western Center for Drug-Free Schools and Communities.

Benson, P. L. (1997). *All kids are our kids.* Minneapolis, MN: Search Institute.

Blackwell, L., Trzesniewski, K. H., & Dweck, C. S. (2007). Implicit theories of intelligence predict achievement across an adolescent transition: A longitudinal study and intervention. *Child Development, 78,* 246–263.

Bronfenbrenner, U. (1979). *The ecology of human development: Experiments by nature and design.* Cambridge, MA: Harvard University Press.

Brooks, R., & Goldstein, S. (2001). *Raising resilient children: Fostering strength, hope and optimism in our children.* New York, NY: Contemporary Books.

Brueggmann, B. (1999). *Lend me your ear: Rhetorical constructions of deafness.* Washington, DC: Gallaudet University Press.

Cole, N., Cole, S., & Lightfoot, C. (2004). *The development of children* (5th ed.). New York, NY: Worth Publishers.

Doll, B., & Lyon, M. A. (1998). Risk and resilience: Implications for the delivery of educational and mental health services in schools. *School Psychology Review, 27*(3), 348–363.

Earvolino-Ramirez, M. (2007). Resilience: A concept analysis. Nursing Forum. *Nursing Forum, 42*(2), 73–83.

Frankl, V. E. (1969). *The will to meaning: Foundations and applications of logotherapy.* New York, NY: New American Library.

Greene, R. R. (2007). *Social work practice: A risk and resilience perspective.* Belmont, CA: Thomson.

Hauser, S. T., & Allen, J. P. (2006). Overcoming adversity in adolescence: Narratives of resilience. *Psychoanalytic Inquiry, 26*(4), 549.

Humphries, T. K. (1996). Of deaf-mutes, the strange, and the modern Deaf self. In N. S. Glickman & M. A. Harvey (Eds.), *Culturally affirmative psychotherapy with Deaf persons* (pp. 99–114). Mahwah, NJ: Lawrence Erlbaum Associates.

Joseph, J. M. (1994). *Parenting today's youth for tomorrow's world*. New York, NY: Plenum Press.

Lane, H. (1992). *The mask of benevolence: Disabling the Deaf community*. New York, NY: Alfred Knopf.

Lane, H., Hoffmeister, R., & Bahan, B. (1996). *Journey into the deaf world*. San Diego, CA: Dawn Sign Press.

Lazarus, R. S. (1999). *Stress and emotion: A new synthesis*. New York, NY: Springer.

Levine, E. S. (1960). *The psychology of deafness*. New York, NY: Columbia University Press.

Levine, E. S. (1981). *The ecology of deafness: Guides to fashioning environments and psychological assessments*. New York, NY: Columbia University Press.

Lincoln, Y. S., & Guba, E. G. (1985). *Naturalistic inquiry*. Newbury Park, CA: Sage.

Luckner, J. L., & Stewart, J. (2003). Self-assessments and other perceptions of successful adults who are deaf: An initial investigation. *American Annals of the Deaf, 148*(3), 243–250.

Luthar, S., Cicchetti, D., & Becker, D. (2000). The concept of resilience: Implications for interventions and social policies. *Development and Psychopathology, 12*, 857–885.

Malecki, C. K., & Elliott, S. N. (2002). Children's social behaviors as predictors of academic achievement. *School Psychology Quarterly, 17*, 1–23.

Masten, A. S. (2001). Ordinary magic: Resilience processes in development. *American Psychologist, 56*, 227–238.

Masten, A., & Coatsworth, J. (1998). The development of competence in favorable and unfavorable environments: Lessons from research on successful children. *American Psychologist, 53*, 205–220.

Moores, D. F. (2001). *Educating the deaf: Psychology, principles and practices* (5th ed.). Boston, MA: Houghton Mifflin.

Oliva, G. (2004). *Alone in the mainstream: A deaf woman remembers public school*. Washington, DC: Gallaudet University Press.

Olweus, D. (2001). *Olweus' core program against bullying and antisocial behavior: A teacher handbook*. Bergen: Research Center for Health Promotion (Hemil Center).

Paine, S., & Paine, C. K. (2002). Promoting safety and success in school by developing student's strengths. In M. R. Shinn, H. W. Walker, & G. Stoner (Eds.), *Interventions for academic and behavior problems II: Preventive and remedial approaches* (pp. 89–112). Bethesda, MD: National Association of School Psychologists.

Pearlin, L. I., Aneshensel, C. S., Mullen, J. T., & Whitlatch, C. J. (1996). Caregiving and its social support. In R. H. Binstock, L. K. George, et al. (Eds.), *Handbook of aging and the social sciences* (4th ed., pp. 283–302). San Diego, CA: Academic Press.

Saleebey, D. (2005). *The strengths perspective in social work practice* (4th ed.). Boston, MA: Allyn & Bacon.

Sheridan, M. (2001). *Inner lives of deaf children: Interviews and analysis*. Washington, DC: Gallaudet University Press.

Sheridan, M. (2008). *Deaf adolescents: Inner lives and lifeworld development*. Washington, DC.: Gallaudet University Press.

Weiner, M. T., & Miller, M. (2006). Deaf children and bullying: Directions for future research. *American Annals of the Deaf, 151*, 61–70.

Werner, E. E., & Johnson, J. L. (1999). Can we apply resilience? In M. D. Glantz & J. L. Johnson (Eds.), *Resilience in development: Positive life adaptations* (pp. 259–168). New York, NY: Kluwer/Academic/Plenum Publishers.

Werner, E. E., & Smith, R. S. (1992). *Overcoming the odds: High risk children from birth to adulthood*. Ithaca, NY: Cornell University Press.

Young, A., Green, L., & Rogers, K. (2008). Resilience and deaf children: A literature review. *Deafness and Education International, 10*, 40–54.

Chapter 10
Building Resilience in Adolescence: The Influences of Individual, Family, School, and Community Perspectives and Practices

Linda Risser Lytle, Gina A. Oliva, Joan M. Ostrove, and Cindi Cassady

Abstract In this chapter we look at the interactive processes of risk and protective factors for deaf adolescents. We start by examining the typical experience of growth and development, looking at skills and experiences common to all deaf children and youth. Although we include the experience of youth in crisis (deaf youth in foster care and in group homes), we discuss not their dysfunctional homes and related challenges, but rather their functioning in terms of how communication, family relationships, and educational experiences affect their lives and shape their sense of self. A focus on the ability to deal effectively with the stresses of normal life, as Masten (American Psychologist 56:22–35, 2001) emphasizes, is an important first step to understanding resilience in deaf people. Our focus is not on the remarkable or exceptional deaf individual, but rather on how deaf adolescents deal with the everyday processes of life and avoid being beaten down by them.

Children and adolescents have little power to affect change in their lives, although as they become older, this power hopefully increases. Because of systemic discrimination, deaf children have even less power to change their circumstances regardless of their individual ability and family support. Audism,[1] a word first used by Humphries in 1975, (Bauman, 2004) is a word that aptly describes the common frustrations, barriers, and oppressions deaf people face. Because audism is an institutionalized response (as well as an individualized one), to address change we must start at the social and institutional levels.

Thornton (2010), in looking at deaf people from a sociopolitical model of disability that embraces a multicultural perspective for understanding others, views change as a social and institutional responsibility. Thornton challenges professionals

---

[1] Humphries' definition of audism includes an assumption of innate superiority of hearing over deaf ways of being, including ability to hear, speak, use language, and be intelligent, successful, and happy. These beliefs and behaviors form discriminatory and oppressive experiences on both individual and systemic levels.

L.R. Lytle (✉)
Department of Counseling, Gallaudet University, Washington, DC, USA
e-mail: linda.lytle@gallaudet.edu

D.H. Zand and K.J. Pierce (eds.), *Resilience in Deaf Children: Adaptation Through Emerging Adulthood*, DOI 10.1007/978-1-4419-7796-0_10,
© Springer Science+Business Media, LLC 2011

to work toward changing oppressive and disabling environments rather than focusing exclusively on the individual deaf client. She argues that focusing on the disabling implications of being deaf simply reinforces the medical view of deaf people, which is disempowering and harmful. The message we want to send to both individuals and systems is that being deaf is part of the fabric of diversity in our society, one to be valued as opposed to one that is viewed as problematic. Thus, it is important to focus not only on promoting individual skills for navigating adversity but also on addressing and changing social and systemic barriers deaf children and adolescents face.

Thornton (2010) proposes that professionals work from a framework of four values: being deaf is an aspect of diversity that is an integral part of society; access is a matter of social justice; creating and advocating for usable, sustainable, and inclusive environments is a shared responsibility; and when inclusiveness is not present, the designer(s) of the system or process becomes the client, rather than the person with a disability. Clearly these values take the burden of change off the individual and put them on the system and social structure, where the problem originates and is owned in the first place.

The framework we use in this chapter borrows heavily from Thornton (2010) and addresses resilience on various levels – the individual level, the family level, the school level, and the community or social level. We address several questions: How can we create greater resilience in deaf adolescents? What can professionals do to provide more opportunities for these adolescents to learn coping skills that will help them in their current lives and in the future? And perhaps the most important, what are deaf adolescents doing for themselves that develops and/or reflects their resilience and creates more strength and success? How can professionals support them in their efforts? What system and social structure changes are needed to create greater opportunities to support resilience? These latter questions give us a positive framework in which to study and work with deaf adolescents, by focusing on wellness, strengths, and opportunities.

In this chapter, we review resilience theory and then explore this concept in adolescents through interviews with three groups – adults who retrospect on their mainstreamed years in Oliva's (2004) study, graduate students in a Master's degree program in counseling, and adolescents in group-home and foster-care settings. We begin with the skills, attitudes, and beliefs these adolescents and young adults have which help them in developing resilience. With this as a framework, we challenge ourselves to think about opportunities that can be designed for them to further enrich their experiences and support their growth. We believe these opportunities must be available to teens across systems of home, school, and community. These opportunities will enable skill development and resilience that will serve them well as they go through life, becoming a part of the fabric of their identity.

Resilience Theory

The concept of resilience, first made popular through Garmezy's (e.g., Garmezy, 1971) studies of children who seemed invulnerable to adverse outcomes despite having grown up in conditions associated with the development of psychopathology, is generally defined through a number of interrelated concepts (see Compas, 2004; Luthar, Cicchetti, & Becker, 2000; Rew, 2005, for reviews). Most of the work on resilience that has generated these concepts and associated theoretical models is based on studies of children who grew up in families characterized by abuse and neglect, extreme poverty, parental substance abuse, or other extremely difficult circumstances. Young, Green, and Rogers (2008) note the challenges of adopting the idea of "resilience" for the study of deaf children. We review some of these challenges below and make our case that many resilience-related concepts are applicable and relevant to the study of deaf adolescents even as we (along with Young et al.) argue that being deaf does not, in and of itself, constitute any particular risk.

Although empirical definitions of resilience vary rather widely (see Luthar et al., 2000 for a review and critique), most definitions used by prominent researchers in the field share some coherent themes. For example, Luthar et al. (2000) define resilience as "the maintenance of positive adaptation by individuals despite experiences of significant adversity" (p. 543), noting also that it is a "dynamic process" (Luthar & Cicchetti, 2000, p. 858). Masten (2001) provides a similar definition, whereby resilience is "a class of phenomena characterized by good outcomes in spite of threats to adaptation or development" (p. 228). These definitions and others also note that resilience is not to be considered "simply" a personality trait or an inherent characteristic of an individual.

The emphasis on process in Luthar and Cicchetti's (2000) work suggests that positive adaptation may be a function of individual or environmental factors or of the interaction of the two (Compas, 2004). These factors are often referred to as "protective factors," or characteristics of the individual, the family, or the broader environment that predict positive outcomes (as opposed to those that predict negative outcomes), often referred to as vulnerability factors. In her review of research on resilience in adolescence, Rew (2005, p. 204) notes the following individual-level protective factors (some of which are, arguably, a function more of the environment than the individual, even if they are usually expressed at the individual level): temperament, sense of humor, positive self-image, beliefs, internal locus of control, skills, early communication, competence in academics, a sense of belonging, engagement in extracurricular activities, and caregiving. Family-level factors that promote resilience include having parents who are caring and available, who have high expectations for academic performance, and who are not separated from their children for long periods of time (Rew, 2005). Finally, community- or environmental-level factors include the presence of other caring adults and positive role models, supportive peers, access to resources, and clear and consistent boundaries (Rew, 2005, p. 209).

Resilience is often discussed in relation to the concept of risk. Risk generally refers to the probability of a negative outcome given a particular circumstance or membership in a particular population (see Compas, 2004). Individual-, family-, and environmental-level factors may constitute risks, and much of the work on both risk and resilience emphasizes the importance of recognizing these multiple and interrelated level factors. An important distinction also exists in the resilience literature between the related concepts of coping and competence. Compas (2004) suggests that "coping refers to *processes* of adaptation, competence refers to the *characteristics and resources* that are needed for successful adaptation, and resilience is reflected in *outcomes* for which competence and coping have been effectively put into action in response to stress and adversity" (p. 274, italics in original).

The very idea that some individuals "make it" against the odds, to survive, or even thrive, in the face of adversity, prompts us to examine carefully the conditions and contexts in which we study resilience. Here we draw extensively from Young et al.'s (2008) critique of resilience in the context of deaf children. Young et al. (2008) note three critical questions in thinking about deaf children and resilience. First, is being deaf itself a risk factor for poor psychological outcomes? As Young et al. (2008) note, although there is evidence that being deaf (especially being profoundly deaf) during childhood is linked with suboptimal outcomes in the areas of educational achievement, employment opportunities, and mental health, that does not mean that being deaf is, in and of itself, a risk factor for those outcomes (p. 43). Instead, depending on other social, familial, and educational contexts, the potentially disadvantaging effects of being deaf have more or less impact.

Second, is being deaf seen as "merely" an audiological condition, or is it considered foundational for a social and cultural identity? If the former is accepted, then efforts to help children develop resilience will be focused on giving them tools to "overcome" their hearing loss. However, if being deaf is considered as foundational for a social and cultural identity, opportunities for developing resilience would be deeply related to opportunities for developing a positive Deaf[2] identity. Indeed, it could be that a connection to a distinct social group composed of individuals like one's self is a protective factor against risks that may be associated with being "deaf" in the audiological sense. Adolescence is a critical time for the development of a sense of identity (e.g., Erikson, 1968); fostering a healthy identity in deaf adolescents may hinge even more critically on the development of resilience in the context of the broader Deaf community.

A final question raised by Young et al. (2008) to consider is whether or not being deaf is an undesirable quality that must be "overcome?" Conceptually, resilience tends to be considered a trait, quality, or set of skills that allow the individual to "overcome" or succeed "despite" something. However, disability and Deaf studies scholars have meticulously challenged the notion of "overcoming" a disability or "succeeding despite being deaf," which "renders any kind of achievement exceptional, thus reinforcing the normative low expectations that society may otherwise have" of deaf individuals (Young et al., 2008, p. 44). Masten's (2001) perspective on resilience is also instructive and related. She documents what she calls the "ordinary magic" of the processes that underlie resilience, offering a critical counterpoint to the idea that there is something "remarkable" or "special" about children who exhibit positive outcomes despite "threats to adaptation or development" (p. 227, 228).

In short, Young et al.'s (2008) critique requires us to understand resilience, especially as applied to deaf children but arguably in all cases, in the broadest social

---

[2]In discussions of culture and identity, the capital D clearly defines a community of people who have common cultural norms and language and we use this throughout our chapter. See Padden and Humphries (1988) for more discussion of this concept.

context possible. Young et al. (2008) make the same argument Thornton (in press) has made. Specifically, it is important to recognize that there are social and institutional perspectives, beliefs, and policies (including systematically discriminatory and audist ones) that impact the lives of deaf children and adolescents. Thus, it is a mistake to individualize deaf children's experiences when studying, and particularly when promoting, resilience. As Young et al. (2008) put it

> seeking to enable resilience is not just a matter of individual capacity-building or family support. It is also a matter of challenging a range of social and structural barriers which also create risk and adversity. For deaf children and young people, the successful navigation of being deaf in a world that faces them with countless daily hassles and which may commonly deny, disable or exclude them, is a key definition of resilience. For such successful navigation to occur, a range of protective resources and repertoires of skills developed through challenging experiences of risk and responsibility have to be promoted.
>
> Young et al. (2008), p. 51–52

What, then, are the conditions under which such protective resources and repertoires of skills are developed? What influences deaf adolescents' propensity to develop the capacity to weather and even challenge the social and structural barriers that exist, and to resist negative societal ideas about their abilities and competence? The remainder of this chapter addresses these questions.

Deaf Adolescents' Experiences with Risk and Adversity

If adversity teaches us important skills, deaf adolescents certainly have a myriad number of opportunities in which to develop such skills. Primarily because of audism, for many deaf adolescents there are daily hurdles to deal with, including communication barriers, literacy challenges, and a shaky, uncertain, or negative sense of self. We believe that the successful development of coping skills and competence in these three areas is foundational for deaf youth in developing resilience. The development of strong skills in communication and literacy, combined with a strong sense of identity, is what allows deaf children to succeed in life. We strongly believe these skills can be (and should be) learned by most deaf children, rather than it being, as Young et al. (2008) note, an "exceptional achievement" by a few. We also believe it is a rare deaf person who does not experience serious challenges and obstacles in at least one of these areas because communication, literacy, and identity/self-concept are intertwined processes and skills; difficulties in one area necessarily impact other areas as well.

The Impact of Inadequate Communication on Development

Similar to hearing adolescents, the boundaries enclosing the world of deaf adolescents consist primarily of home and school. Within this world, deaf adolescents often experience major barriers to communication, particularly dialectical communication. Braden (1994) found that fewer than 4% of deaf children were exposed to a consistent visual language model at either home or school. This lack of language models and communication access defines the greatest risk for deaf and hard of hearing children and adolescents. Adolescents who are not able to easily access rich conversation at home, at school, or in either place are at greatest risk for isolation, depression, and related concerns (Meadow-Orlans, Mertens, & Sass-Lehrer, 2003; Steinberg, 2000).

The barriers deaf students face because of lack of satisfactory communication access in schools are common and well documented (Mayer & Lowenbraun, 1990; Ramsey, 1997), and include issues related to interpreters (Oliva, 2004; Ramsey, 1997). Frequent changes in school placement add another variation to the nature and amount of adversity faced by a deaf adolescent. The annual survey of deaf and hard of hearing children (Gallaudet Research Institute, 2008) notes that sometimes children attend more than one program; however, it does not indicate how many children change placements. However, a further breakdown of statistics from this survey tells us that 4,923 students transferred between programs during the 2007–2008 school year and that the majority of these, 89%, transferred from one mainstream program to another (Kay Lam, personal communication, September 11, 2009). Our experience is that families constantly try to improve on the educational opportunities offered to their deaf children and that many deaf youth experience more than one school placement; most experience several and must adapt each time.

The Impact of Literacy Delays on Development

In addition to the threats to development posed by insufficient communication access and language models at school and home, literacy challenges and educational gaps/delays constitute a second significant threat to the development of resilience in deaf children and adolescents. Of course, communication issues are actually at the heart of these educational shortcomings and illiteracy. Rew (2005) included academic competence in a list of individual-level protective factors. We cannot underestimate the critical impact academic competence has on the successful development of deaf youth and on the future adults they are becoming. In spite of the importance we place on literacy, the scope of this chapter does not allow us to address it fully. We only acknowledge its importance, particularly in the stories youth share with us, and make suggestions for what schools can do that would help foster resilience in areas related to literacy.

The Importance of Identity Development

The development of a clear and positive sense of identity (the major task of adolescent psychosocial development) is another factor that is often mentioned as contributing to resilient adolescents (Masten & Coatsworth, 1998; Werner & Smith, 1992). Lytle (1987), in a study of deaf college women, found that deaf women with the clearest sense of identity had high self-esteem, were self-reliant, and possessed excellent interpersonal skills. They also were able to integrate their feelings about being deaf into their identity. This last finding emphasizes the importance of the development of social and racial identities, which Phinny and Rosenthall (1992) found to be so critical in the lives of ethnic minority youth. Glickman (1986) and Maxwell-McCaw (2001) found that the establishment of a deaf identity was important to the development of a healthy self-concept.

Erikson's (1968) influential theory about adolescent development includes an interesting and useful concept he calls psychosocial mutuality. This concept stresses that an individual's identity is not formed in isolation; indeed how an individual's community (as well as the larger society) views him or her becomes an important factor in the identity process. Adolescents do not have to accept their community's view of themselves, but they cannot ignore it and do have to somehow reconcile this view with their own self-view. For the over 90% of deaf adolescents in hearing families (Braden, 1994) and the 40% educated exclusively in mainstream programs (Gallaudet Research Institute, 2008), this reconciliation of perceptions is crucially important. Adolescents have an uphill struggle to develop strong self-esteem and identity if their communities of home and school have unreciprocated views of their abilities and their very selves. Being seen as "the deaf kid" is not affirming to one's identity. On the other hand, if families and schools work hard to foster respectful relationships with all children, including making sure deaf children and youth have access to peers and adults like themselves, much can be done to support a healthy self-identity and resiliency. Once again, the point is that communities must do their share and not expect individuals to do this work alone.

We must bear in mind that these threats – communication, literacy, and identity – are in addition to the same family and societal issues that all adolescents may face, including abusive homes, alcoholism, psychiatric illnesses, homelessness, and violence. However, we believe it is important to look at the particular stresses and challenges of being deaf and hard of hearing before looking further at dysfunctional environments that can influence any adolescent.

Interviews with Deaf Youth and Young Adults

To take a closer look at resilience among deaf adolescents, the authors examine three separate and disparate groups. First, we summarize relevant information from "The Solitary Mainstream Project" (Oliva, 2004) and explore factors related to social isolation. Second, we review data from a survey and interviews with deaf graduate students at Gallaudet University, in which they were asked to look back on their adolescent years. Third, we summarize interviews with deaf adolescents who are currently living in a group home or in foster care due to serious emotional and behavioral issues. Only one of these groups (youth in group homes and foster care) is clearly viewed as "at risk." Obviously, we are choosing to define resilience not by exceptional achievement, but as a process by which individuals develop skills and abilities, which are internalized to the extent that positive adaptation occurs. In reading the stories from these three groups, we ask the reader to pay special attention to how themes of communication, literacy, and identity play out.

Deaf and Hard of Hearing Adults Retrospect on Adolescence

Deaf participants in the Solitary Mainstream Project (Oliva, 2004) reported many unpleasant experiences in mainstream high schools. They frequently mentioned that their saving grace was exceptional skill in some extracurricular activity, such as a sport, that helped them gain a modicum of peer acceptance. Yet even for the star athlete, being deaf prevents the rich experience of being a fully accepted member of a varsity team.

Let us imagine a high school soccer team that has just won a regional meet. One of their top players is a young deaf woman named Sarah. Her teammates, all hearing, consider her a top scorer. After each home game during the weekends, all the girls gather at a nearby mall food court to hang out. After one particular game where Sarah scores four goals, her teammates rave about this for a while. Then the topic turns to boys, hair, clothes, parents, etc. Soon the team is joined by other friends and several conversations are happening at once. As the minutes tick by, Sarah becomes less and less able to follow any of these conversations. She begins to feel uncomfortable and wonders what excuse she can use to go home. Even though she rarely says anything during these long gab sessions, some teammates protest or make a big deal out of her attempts to leave, making her feel even more uncomfortable. Finally, after a few hours, some of the teens announce they are going to a movie, and she uses that as her cue to escape to the quiet and solitude of her room at home.

While this is a composite story, all of the authors have heard similar stories in their work with deaf adolescents. Teenagers in the mainstream feel increasingly isolated and left out during the high school years, regardless of how athletically or academically successful they are.

Kleiber (1999), a psychologist specializing in leisure studies, focuses on the impact of leisure experiences on human development. He elaborates on the concept of a "fourth environment" as places where people go to hang out and chat – away from home, school, and work. The conversations that take place within these environments are critical to our sense of social support. Adults congregate in coffee shops, or bars, or elsewhere, on some regular basis "just to talk." Adolescents crave these environments. In fact, the propensity to gather together begins during the preteen years – youth can be seen in malls and on street corners and other uniquely designated venues. The fourth environment is defined as "beyond home, school, or work," and is a place to discuss things and make sense of what is happening in our lives. For adolescents in particular, an important element of these environments is the absence of adults. The school bus and the locker room certainly fall within this category. As Kleiber (1999) notes,

The social tasks of adolescence and early adulthood may benefit more from unstructured leisure contexts, since there is more influence over communication and interaction patterns in those situations than when adults are in control. Adolescents in search of companionship and/or romance seek out such fourth-environment contexts as shopping malls, house parties, coffee shops, and swimming pools. And even when activities are organized and structured for children by adults, informal child-centered interaction is likely to persist as part of the experience (p. 76).

How does the deaf high school or college student, who is unable to consistently understand spoken conversation in such settings, accomplish these "social tasks?" What will substitute for this lack of access to the chatter and information sharing through which bonds are formed? Which factors would ensure that this student will develop optimal or even adequate resilience? It is little wonder that those who find their way into the Deaf world, where a visual mode of communication offers a solution to this fourth environment dilemma, usually opt to make this a part of their lives.

We understand of course that the hearing world is as it is and the possibility of full access to communication and language for deaf children and adults will always be, to some degree, limited. In a perfect world, hearing people would all sign, but we do not live in a perfect world and do not anticipate its arrival any time soon. However, that does not mean that our institutions cannot move away from policies and practices that minimize communication and language access.

Conversation in fourth environments is foundational for relationships with others, with the world, and with ourselves. Hearing individuals take their access to fourth environment venues for granted. While isolated individuals or parents of deaf children *may* be concerned about this seriously impoverished access to conversation, virtually never do we find effective policy or programmatic attention to the conversational impoverishment that deaf youngsters experience in fourth environments.

Deaf adults, however, have long recognized this phenomenon of impoverished access to the fourth environment as one that permeated their growing-up years and may continue to permeated their adult lives. Culturally Deaf adults have even developed a sign (e.g., a word) for this phenomenon. The sign looks like this: Imagine two Pac-Man[3] icons; made with your two hands facing each other, snip, clip, chomping away but not going anywhere. They just face each other and chomp. Now, take those Pac-Man-facing-each-other chomping hands and move them around in a stirring-the-cauldron kind of movement. There, you have it – "people blabbing and blabbing all around and as usual I don't have a clue what they are talking about." That is American Sign Language for "hearing-people-bantering around-me-while-I-am-oblivious-to-what-they-are-saying."

Here is a comment by a young adult looking back on her mainstream years that incorporates this awareness:

It was great to be involved (I raced on the swim team and played lacrosse and volleyball), but with this involvement came a lot of stress. I always… missed out on team gossip in between drills (particularly in the pool when I couldn't wear my hearing aids). [I] always

---

[3]Pac-Man is a character in video games that chumps away on any obstacles in its path. In fact, Wikipedia states that the Pac-Man design "came from simplifying and rounding out the Japanese character for mouth, *kuchi* (口) as well as the basic concept of eating."

dreaded the team bus rides to meets because I could never follow all the chatter with all the noise on the bus (I would sit very quiet and feel invisible!). All that soft stuff was an important part of being or feeling part of the team.

Oliva (2004, p. 92)

The Pac-Man-hands phenomenon demonstrates that for deaf individuals, the experience of being unable to access fourth-environment conversations in the "hearing world" is universal. The fact that Deaf people have a sign for this concept powerfully illustrates the awareness of what they are missing. We should further examine the impact this has on the development of resilience.

Informal Survey of Deaf Students in a Master's Level Counseling Program

Today many deaf children experience educational placement in a variety of settings (Gallaudet Research Institute, 2008), and increasingly more are being mainstreamed in their local public schools (Moores, 2006; Stinson & Antia, 1999). Many students who arrive at Gallaudet University have experienced both mainstream and residential settings, as well as settings that fall somewhere in between. Lytle is a counselor educator in the Gallaudet University Graduate School and Professional Programs and often asks her students about their K-12 educational experiences to spark their thinking about the importance of educational experiences in working with deaf clients. Her students typically have strong feelings about their experiences, and they report having attended quite a variety of educational settings. It is rare that students report attendance at only one kind of educational setting. While these deaf students are obviously exceptional in that they are high achievers working on advanced degrees, their reports of their K-12 educational experiences are those that are commonly shared by most if not all deaf students.

In a recent informal survey of K-12 educational experiences of her deaf students (there are also hearing students in this class, but their information is not included), Lytle (2009) found the following: one student reported attending public school; one attended a school for the deaf; one attended public school, transferred to a mainstream program for hard of hearing students and then transferred to a mainstream deaf program; one attended two different mainstream programs and was a solitary[4] in a third school; two attended mainstream programs and spent time as a solitary student in different schools; and five attended mainstream programs, were solitaries, and also attended schools for the deaf.

Students transferred both into and out of schools for the deaf, mainstream programs, and schools where they were a solitary deaf student. It is important to note that several of the students in this informal survey were from Deaf families, and still

---

[4] The word solitary is from Oliva (2004) and used to describe deaf and hard of hearing students who are mainstreamed as the only such child (or one of very few such children) in their school.

their educational experiences were diverse. Families were constantly looking for better educational programs for their deaf child. Often by the time their child was ready for secondary school, parents were willing to allow their child to make their own choice about schooling, which led to transfers into or out of residential schools. Finding programs that allowed for both adequate academic success and adequate social opportunities was a challenge for most.

From the discussions that took place in class, it became clear that schools that truly provided individualized educational experiences as part of a systemized organizational effort were viewed as positive learning environments; in contrast, those that worked with individual deaf students without the systematic support constituted a primarily negative learning environment. For example, students agreed that the communication access they obtained in schools for the deaf allowed their leadership potential to blossom, which likewise strengthened their self-esteem and identity. However, they also spoke highly of large mainstreamed programs that gave them a sense of belongingness to a community of deaf students as well as the richness of a strong academic program. Everyone easily agreed that a program that supported bilingualism – a strong American Sign Language environment along with written English – was the best. The few students who attended schools for the deaf and also had opportunities to be mainstreamed in nearby public schools for part of their school day (bicultural experiences) were viewed by themselves and others as most fortunate. It should be noted that this learning environment is one that requires the most organizational support.

The solitary experience was viewed by far as the most negative, particularly where individual teachers, rather than a well thought-out school-wide plan, drove decision making. One student remembered losing an entire year of education due to an incorrect class placement and the low expectations her teachers had of her. She and her parents had to fight to move her out of special education classes and into the college prep track. Low expectations from teachers and boredom in class because of missed communication were common themes and constitute risk factors inherent in educational settings where organizational support is weak or lacking.

Most of these students remembered negative experiences with their interpreters. The interpreters were over involved in their lives, not sufficiently skilled, or frequently absent. As we noted previously, the individuals in Oliva's (2004) study also spoke strongly about issues with interpreters in the educational setting. The commonly held idea (that is typically held by educators not familiar with deaf education) that interpreters can equalize educational experiences for deaf students is greatly flawed.

Educational environments that provided opportunities to learn with and befriend hearing students were seen as advantageous but fraught with risks. Even with system support present, the advantage was seen as stronger for the hearing students than for those who are deaf. In other words, it was viewed as a positive thing for hearing students and teachers to be exposed to deaf people, but the loneliness and pain of being the solitary deaf student was not mitigated. As one Gallaudet student said, "It was still too hard, even if they [hearing students] did try so hard."

Many of the students in this survey, as well as Counseling Program students from previous years, reminisced about bullying experiences, a prominent risk factor in both residential and mainstream settings. Students who transferred to a school for the deaf without having fluency in sign language were placed in a particularly vulnerable position. Informal (and often underground) hazing of new students is reportedly a common practice and looking back, students reported it as either making (showing they could take it and achieving acceptance) or breaking (transferring out) them. Alternately, in mainstreamed or solitary settings, students typically reported feeling bitterly alone and not able to manage the complicated communication and socialization processes required to avoid victimization.

Despite these negative experiences, students typically remembered protecting themselves from the pain of harassment by convincing themselves that they had done nothing to earn this treatment, that it was temporary, and that it would soon cease. These self-messages seem to be examples of adaptive distancing, a concept Beardsley first made popular in the psychiatric literature (see Beardsley, 1997; Beardsley & Podoresfky, 1988) and later used in resilience research (Benard, 2004; Chess, 1989; Rubin, 1996). Adaptive distancing involves detaching oneself emotionally from dysfunctional and negative messages by consciously choosing to believe that these actions and words against oneself are not earned; thus the messages do not "stick" and self-esteem is protected. From the stories we have heard from young deaf adults, adaptive distancing seems to be a commonly used protective device, one they used in home, school, and community, effectively protecting against harsh, negative messages.

Deaf Foster and Group-Home Youth

Deaf adolescents involved in residential treatment and the foster-care system are not only faced with the obvious adverse interpersonal and family problems, which initially brought them to the attention of the child welfare system, but also subject to adverse audist conditions inherent in the very social and legal systems which purport to protect them from harm. Typically, culturally affirmative or signing foster homes for deaf adolescents are scarce and there are just as few appropriate placements with relatives. The majority of deaf teens are either placed in hearing foster families or they remain in a shelter for extended periods of time. Deaf foster youth report that placement in a nonsigning foster home virtually "guarantees failure" in that home and that they will be returned to the temporary shelter to await yet another foster home placement. This cycle can result in either numerous foster placements within a relatively short period of time or a stay in the temporary shelter that is up to 12 times longer than that of hearing adolescents (L. Miller, social worker with the Deaf Unit, Child Protective Services, San Diego County, personal communication, April 7, 2009).

In interviews with deaf teens who had experienced placement in foster families, those who had lived in nonsigning foster families described the experience as "living in a constant state of frustration," "being uncertain what the rules are," "afraid of being in trouble because of miscommunication," "feeling isolated and lonely," and ultimately, "feeling that no matter how bad conditions were at home, it was better than being in a strange hearing family where no one signs." Deaf youth placed in foster care often believe that they are the cause of the problems in their family, express regret over telling anyone about the abuse or dangerous conditions that existed in their family, and may recant their stories of abuse. Oftentimes, these youth have little, if any, idea why they are being removed, nor do they understand how the legal system works within the context of the reunification process.

Being placed with nonsigning foster families may be perceived by deaf youth as being worse than enduring the abuse at home. The same emotional trauma related to the lack of communication with their hearing parents is once again reenacted with their nonsigning foster parents. Adolescents understandably fail to see how the system is "helping or protecting" them. The foster youth report that nonsigning foster parents become exasperated by the communication challenges and that the deaf child does not feel emotionally supported. Placing deaf adolescents in nonsigning foster families is analogous to retraumatizing them as a result of the foster parents' inability to communicate with the deaf child in his/her own language, and to be emotionally available to them due to their inability to understand the deaf youth.

Deaf Foster and Group-Home Youth: Becoming Resilient

There is a substantial amount of research that has examined resilience, protective factors, and successful adaptation to risk in the hearing adolescent population. (Bell, 2001; Katz, 1997; Rew, 2005) Very little has been written about resilience and the deaf adolescent, and information about deaf youth in foster care or residential treatment specifically addressing their capacity for resilience and adaptability to adversity is virtually nonexistent.

A snapshot picture of the typical deaf youth seen by Cassady in residential treatment in San Diego County will provide the reader with an understanding of the kind of adversity these youth have faced before arriving at the group home. These youth, are between the ages 12 and 18, have typically been raised in a hearing family with minimal or no sign language, have been exposed to chronic and severe sexual, physical, and emotional abuse, have witnessed or were victims of domestic violence, have been exposed to or abusing substances and alcohol, have been separated from their parents and siblings for between 2 and 8 years, and have endured multiple placements in foster homes or other group homes. These youth are also academically delayed by several grade levels because of frequent moves to new foster homes in addition to the usual language, communication, and educational issues that create educational delays. The deaf adolescent in this situation has characteristically been diagnosed, by school and clinical psychologists untrained in evaluating deaf students, as being Mentally Retarded, Conduct-Disordered, or Oppositional Defiant. It is important to note that deaf children who have been previously diagnosed before being placed in the deaf group home are likely to have been misdiagnosed by nonsigning, hearing mental-health professionals unfamiliar with the cultural and linguistic challenges related to psychological assessment of deaf youth.

How is it even possible to conceive of these adolescents as being more similar to their deaf peers who were not in the child protection system than disparate, given the fact they are at high risk and have faced extreme adversity? Cassady (2009) conducted structured interviews using Henderson's resilience interview format (Henderson, 2007, p. 153) to gather information from six deaf group-home adolescents between the ages 14 and 18 to examine this high-risk population's self-perceptions of resilience and adaptation to adversity. The youth were asked a series of nine questions about the struggles they faced in the past or present, how they dealt with those struggles and what beliefs they had about themselves. Other questions inquired about their thoughts and feelings related to people who have helped them, what those individuals had done that made a positive difference in their life, and what would they want to tell other deaf teens if they were going through their situation. Finally, they were asked to explain what advice they would give to adults who were trying to build resilience in other deaf kids.

The concepts of adaptive distancing and "reframing narrative story telling" are useful for describing the psychological tools that may help the deaf adolescent carve out a healthier emotional pathway through the maze of institutionally and socially imposed adversity. As we see through the youths' responses, the adolescents whom Cassady (2009) interviewed were able to build resilience within themselves because a community came together to create a structure of support and removed the barriers of communication, so they could view themselves as successful. It was apparent from the youths' responses to the interview questions that there were three identifiable levels of protective factors that helped build resilience.

Individual Level

At the individual level, several factors served to provide the group-home teen with psychological tools necessary to gain emotional distance from trauma and allow for the possibility of redefining him or herself as resilient rather than as a victim of circumstances. This included factors such as the formation of the youth's self-concept and cultural identity, the ability to reject other's negative perceptions ("adaptive distancing"), the ability to tolerate ambiguity, and the ability to change perceptions about the traumatic events in one's life ("reframing the narrative story").

These youth had similar stories of adversity, and none had parents who could sign. Three of the six teens acquired language after they arrived at the group home and were severely language deprived and cognitively delayed. All of the youth described having weak or nonexistent emotional bonds with their parents due to the lack of communication with their parents in their younger years. Five of the six youth strongly believed that the bad things that had happened to them in the past were not their fault. They did not view themselves as a "bad person," nor did they believe that they had done anything to deserve the traumatic events they had endured. It was common for them to state, "I knew I was not the person they (parents or others) tried to blame me for being. I am a good kid inside but sometimes I acted bad."

Family Level

At the family level, factors typically identified as helping to build resilience in deaf youth included being seen as a valued member of their family or the group home, feeling respected by their parents or group-home staff, having group-home staff or a therapist available to share their day with them when they got home from school, and having someone who could help them with their homework.

Five of the six deaf youth redefined their sense of what "family" meant to them. While understanding the traditional sense of the word, these five youth redefined whom they viewed as being their "family." The youth identified one or two special people in their lives (e.g., school counselors, social workers, therapists) who had known them since they were young and/or who had become connected with them immediately after they were removed from their home. The concepts of transitional objects and transitional stories are very important to deaf foster and group-home youth. Their stories and memories of special times with people of value to them become integrated into the narrative stories they retell many times to make sense of the past and what has happened to them.

As Bell (2001) notes in his discussion about building protective factors in youth, improving the youth's sense of self-esteem by facilitating a sense of connectedness to valued people, places, or things, using role models that the youth can use to make sense of the world, learning to respect the qualities and characteristics about themselves that are unique, and developing a feeling of competence are all key components in building and maintaining resilience in youth. The group-home youth developed a sense of cultural identity through their connections with culturally and ethnically diverse Deaf staff and therapists. They also worked with Deaf mental-health and social work interns from Gallaudet University. The Deaf interns modeled for the youth the importance of education and were living proof that Deaf people can be successful in the academic world and beyond.

Community Level: It Takes a Village

The third level of protective factors in building resilience in youth is found at the institutional or agency level. At this level, in one community, collaboration between professionals, community agencies, child welfare services, and the juvenile court system helped to make creative and innovative systemic changes that ultimately affected the deaf youth in positive and culturally affirmative ways. It is not within the scope of this chapter to address the political and community-wide changes necessary for the conception of the successful group home, but it is important to note that many individuals and agencies worked diligently for a number of years educating supervisors, top-level administrators, attorneys, judges, and public officials about the need for culturally affirmative mental services for deaf youth and families. A Deaf Unit was created at Child Welfare Services in San Diego, modeled after the Deaf Unit in Los Angeles, California. Deaf and signing social workers were assigned cases with deaf children, adolescents, and parents. Deaf parenting classes in ASL were offered to parents involved with Child Protective Services to help them with the reunification process. Many of the deaf youth had a signing attorney. These changes provided the structural bubble within which a supportive, culturally affirmative environment could be created to begin nurturing the growth of resilience in deaf youth.

The response from the Deaf community toward the youth in the group home was overwhelmingly positive. As the youth became more self-confident and more secure, they interacted with both the Deaf and hearing communities in ways that demonstrated passion, motivation, and resiliency on their part. They were proud of their abilities and unique talents. Their activities in the Deaf community and beyond included participation in school extracurricular activities, attending local Deaf culture and community events, and engagement in a summer work program at a Deaf community agency designed to teach them work ethics and job skills.

What These Youth Have Taught Us

On the surface, we could not have selected three more diverse groups. Individuals in one group were struggling to survive their youth, and individuals in another group were developing professional skills, while those from the Solitary Mainstream Project were perhaps doing some of both. However, we found that in important ways the youth in these three separate groups – foster care teens, graduate students, and adults looking back on their solitary years – are not all that different. The themes of struggles in communication, education, and self-identity that permeate their adolescence pull them together rather than apart.

Every one who was interviewed could tell a personal story of painful conversational encounters, although they sometimes turned these painful stories into humorous ones. They all experienced limited opportunities within the school setting and often were dissatisfied with the knowledge and skills they obtained while students. Many of them struggled to find acceptance and belongingness within their families and their communities. We are absolutely convinced that if we were to put all these individuals in one room together, many fascinating conversations would take place, everyone would have a great time, and each one would come away enriched by the experience. In spite of their differences, their commonality as deaf individuals binds them together, as does their capacity for resilience. The remainder of this chapter focuses on ideas for professionals and parents to use for facilitating change and strengthening resilience in youth.

Recommendations for Facilitating Change

Building and strengthening resilience in deaf adolescents will require change in many areas and at all levels. Community and organizational changes are needed the most because of their power to produce significant and lasting effects. In this section, we make recommendations for changes beginning at the highest and broadest levels. These community-level changes may be the most difficult to accomplish as they require a vision, joint cooperation, and major efforts by many disparate administrative organizational structures. However, these are the changes that will make the most difference to individual lives. Once a systems-level change is made, all other changes will be significantly easier. Individuals, families, teachers, and community members will all feel safe knowing that their systems support them and that any problem solving needed will be a shared responsibility. Although we believe that systemic change is most critical, we also make recommendations to strengthen family and individual-level processes.

Community-Level Changes that Work

Affiliation with the Deaf Community

Each and every experience an adolescent has is incorporated into his/her evolving identity. Research on identity tells very clearly that how one feels about oneself as a deaf person is a crucial part of the identity process that can only be developed through meeting others like ourselves (Glickman, 1986; Lytle, 1987; Maxwell-McCaw, 2001). A positive affiliation with the Deaf community is a strong protective factor in the development of self-esteem (Jambor & Elliott, 2005). Learning about the Deaf community and finding one's way toward belonging to this community is one of the strongest, surest ways toward this positive Deaf identity. Jambor and Elliott (2005) found that active involvement in the Deaf community was a strong protective factor for most of the deaf college students in their study for maintaining positive self-esteem while interacting in the sometimes frustrating hearing world. There was a strong positive carryover in self-esteem in individuals who were engaged with the Deaf community as they navigated between both Deaf and hearing communities.

The message is clear. Communities must reach out and find as many ways as possible to provide opportunities for all deaf and hard of hearing youth to begin and maintain affiliation with the Deaf community. As deaf children are increasingly being educated in mainstream programs and fitted with cochlear implants, this need for affiliation with the Deaf community becomes even more important. The shared experience many deaf people feel when they arrive at Gallaudet University and feel for perhaps the first time in their lives, that they are "home," should not be the exclusive provenance of the handful of youth who come to Gallaudet or other large Deaf educational communities, such as the National Technical Institute for the Deaf or California State University, Northridge. This rich experience of "home" should be owned by all. We need to create more opportunities for these experiences of being understood, of being important, and of belonging to a community of others like ourselves.

An interesting and troublesome finding by Jambor and Elliott (2005) was that the protective factors of minority group membership and Deaf community membership did not extend to all members. Students of color in their study did not measure as high in self-esteem as did the white students. This finding does not surprise us. People of color (as well as deaf youth with secondary disabilities) need to find validation and support from both the Deaf community and their ethnic/racial communities, and this is extremely hard to acquire. Fortunately, there are organizations whose main goal is to bring deaf people of common backgrounds together, although we believe that most youth and their parents are not aware of these organizations. Organizations such as Latino Deaf Association, Asian Deaf Association, Deaf People of Color, and the National Black Deaf Advocates all need to submit their mission and goals to educators, counselors, and parents so that they can be strong supports for deaf youth of all races and ethnicities. Educators need to do their part in seeking out more information about organizations specifically dedicated to deaf people of color.

Membership in a affirming community supports the important fourth environment needs of youth. The deeper socialization needs that cannot be met by families, schools, and local communities need to somehow be filled and it behooves the community (the Deaf community and the professional communities that serve them) to take concrete actions to fill in these gaps and provide rich social environments. Some members of these communities have in fact recognized these unmet needs and have taken steps to create programs that can serve as fourth environments for deaf and hard of hearing youth.

Weekend and Summer Programs

The American Camping Association (ACA) is one organization that seems to agree there is a need for "immersion"[5] programs for deaf children. There are approximately 70 summer camps for deaf children listed on the Web site of the Gallaudet University Clerc Center, http://www.clerccenter.gallaudet.edu/Clerc_Center/Information_and_Resources/Info_to_Go/Resources/Summer_Camps_for_Deaf_and_Hard_of_Hearing_Children.html. Oliva's ongoing study of these programs has revealed that more than half of them have been founded since 1995. Interviews with directors and counselors of these programs demonstrate that these individuals (many of whom are

[5]ACA members use the term "immersion camps" to refer to programs geared to a specific population such as youth with diabetes, cancer, etc. This term stands as opposed to the concept of "inclusion," which to ACA members refers to mainstreaming a "special needs" camper into a "regular" summer camp.

deaf, or are very closely involved in educational programs for deaf children and youth) *are* very cognizant of resilience needs, of the need for experiences that will build identity, and for opportunities to provide fourth environment experiences.

Many of the individuals who run these programs summer after summer do so as a voluntary activity. They share a common goal of providing a week or 2 weeks of enriching activities in an "all deaf" environment with the accompanying "full access to conversation," and they share a common challenge in always needing to seek funds and volunteers to stay afloat. Because these program directors are rarely full-time employees, there is little time for a higher level of involvement – that of networking with other programs to find common solutions and to instill continuous improvement beyond a myopic view of their own program's functioning.

What is needed is a higher level of involvement from individuals who are concerned about what mainstreamed deaf children are *not* getting as they live 24/7 in the hearing world. Program directors need to be concerned about the social capital of the children they serve and pay special attention to the kind of fourth environments that are uniquely suited to the needs of these children. Some specific examples of needed change are: (a) more volunteerism and philanthropic contributions from both the Deaf community and the Deaf human services community, (b) more research focused on the short- and long-term benefits of these summer and weekend programs, and (c) local, regional, and state-level efforts to have summer and weekend programs be part of students' IEPs and transition plans.

Systemic and Organizational-Level Changes

Legal and Social Agency Challenges

The systemic changes required to promote positive change for deaf children and youth in the foster care system must happen in both the legal and social services domains. Greater awareness of and sensitivity to the special linguistic and cultural needs of deaf children and adolescents in foster care and residential treatment is needed by social workers and the legal system. Deaf or signing social workers and mental-health professionals are needed, as are juvenile dependency attorneys and judges who are sensitive to the unique needs of deaf youth to avoid needless multiple placements.

School Systems Working Together

We would like to see school systems work together to provide creative, flexible, truly individualized programs and services for deaf children and adolescents.

It is time for school systems to acknowledge that there is often not one "right" school for every child and that the best programming for a deaf child is very likely a combination of various programs. Deaf and hard of hearing children today want both the support and solidarity that comes from the Deaf community while simultaneously developing their interests and talents within the broader world. We would like to see school systems working collaboratively across systems so that children can be full participants in educational and extracurricular opportunities offered by both programs for deaf students and by regular public schools. This really is the best of both worlds. Residential schools are rich with opportunities to develop one's identity, self-esteem, and leadership by connection with deaf peers and adults, while public and private schools offer chances to develop other skills through more diverse academic programming and relationships with hearing children and adults. Such programming would offer opportunities to develop bicultural skills, which contribute positively to self-esteem (Jambor & Elliott, 2005). Deaf children deserve both worlds. Importantly, increasing opportunities to participate in both kinds of educational programs would also decrease the dilemma faced by parents (and adolescents) to choose either this program (and its particular communication/language approach) OR that program (and its communication/language approach). Collaboration in offering programs, rather than an either/or choice, would solve a multitude of problems and offers a vital richness in educational environments.

Wilkens and Hehir (2008), exploring social capital development in deaf children, also endorse such a creative educational programming approach and stress the importance of collaborative educational programming on the successful development of both academic skills and "strong social and relational ties to deaf peers and adults around them" (p. 279). They offer many suggestions for making such programming work, including creative out of school programming, coteaching (for example, between a teacher at a school for the deaf and the public school), and job shadowing. Developing strong academic skills and social ties to peers and adults are both crucial to building and strengthening resilience.

Participation in the community at school and/or out of school is also a protective factor. Residential schools offer the most opportunities in this area. Many students transfer to residential programs for their high school years so that they can fully participate in extracurricular activities and sports. High school students are often able to demand such educational changes for themselves and sometimes their parents listen. In mainstream programs, full participation would mean that extracurricular activities must be available to deaf teens in a way where they feel fully involved and fully welcomed rather than where they are on the periphery and merely tolerated. Community and religious institutions are other avenues through which such involvement can be attained. Involvement and leadership opportunities are often easier for deaf and hard of hearing young people in smaller organizations or activities such as youth groups in the church.

What Can Individual Schools Do?

A positive school climate where attitudes, assumptions, and policies reflect a belief that each student is equally valued reflects a strong systemic effort toward change. In such a school, everyone works to solve problems and care for each other, with the result that all feel involved, respected, and connected. Building a strong mainstream program would result in such actions as a conscious attempt to hire deaf teachers, ASL being taught both in the curriculum and in extracurricular clubs and classes, and signing being a normal thing for a majority of students and staff, starting with the school principal. In fact, that would be the ideal to which all community members would aspire. In such a school, classroom media would naturally be captioned, and interpreters would be respected and valued support personnel. Creative, well-planned programs would be funded and evaluated year after year so that they develop and grow. Mantua Elementary school in Fairfax, Virginia is a model example of such a school (Rodia, 2001). At Mantua, the philosophy of inclusion – not only of deaf children but also of children of all cultures – is put into practice in creative, committed ways. Although Rodia's article was written in 2001, Lytle visited this program as recently as November 2008 and found many of the innovative aspects still being implemented.

Within supportive school structures it is easier to make small changes to help individual students who are struggling with self-esteem or isolation. Without such a structure, small changes fall heavily on the shoulders of individual teachers and counselors, but they are still worthwhile tasks. Teachers could pay attention to classroom dynamics and plan for more collaborative, interactive activities where deaf students are more easily able to show their skills and where communication access or language differences are minimized. Isolated students can be given responsibilities outside of class to help them grow in self-esteem and/or in the eyes of their classmates. For example, they could be a messenger, help in the health room, attendance room, or other school office. These are all recognized responsibilities within the school and are respected by peers and adults alike. Sometimes, using extreme care, responsible, mature students can be asked to befriend isolated deaf students so that they have someone to hang out with and avoid the pain of eating alone each day.

Mentoring programs such as Big Brothers and Big Sisters, which offer sustained and intense relationships, have been shown to be successful in discouraging drug and alcohol use and promoting academic success for many adolescents (Benard, 2007). These programs should be equally effective for deaf adolescents. With the technology available today through videophones and internet, it is exciting to think of mentoring opportunities that can be developed and offered for students in geographically dispersed programs as the mentor and the mentee no longer need to be physically in the same location. Given the increasing number of students who are being mainstreamed (Moores, 2006) and thus often isolated, being able to connect with other deaf peers and adults from a distance is potentially life changing; that is true for both mentee and mentor.

As professionals, we need to constantly look for ways to create opportunities for increased involvement of all students, to be proactive, and to not simply accept the status quo. Sometimes this means changing the system and sometimes it means asking the help of others to make small positive changes in the daily life of a student.

Sometimes small changes are all that are needed to make significant improvements for a lonely, shy, isolated, or stigmatized deaf student.

Family Level Changes

What can parents, guardians, and parent advocacy groups do? First, and most important, especially if the parents are hearing, they must be sure their deaf or hard of hearing child has deaf and hard of hearing peers. Parents should do this from toddlerhood on, while also searching for other parents of deaf children and for Deaf adults to share with and learn from. Without friendships with others like oneself, it will be very difficult, if not impossible, for their child to develop a positive identity.

Second, parent groups can provide educational programs for parents that emphasize the need for special programs that will provide opportunities for the development of resilience. All parents of deaf and hard of hearing children should be aware of the powerful impact summer programs and camps can have on the development of self-esteem, social skills, and resilience, and they should plan for their child to attend as many summer and weekend programs as possible during his/her K-12 years. Parents should become familiar with the programs available, advocate for their inclusion into their child's IEPs and ITPs, and plan family vacation time accordingly.

As stated earlier, youth who have experienced trauma and disastrous family relationships often redefine who their family is. Caring relationships in the family are a strong protective factor. If supportive family relationships are strongly lacking, individuals outside of the family can also make a difference. The more caring individuals in one's circle, the more protection is in place. Clinical experience with deaf and hard of hearing youth makes it clear, however, that it only takes one sincere solid connection with a caring adult to make a difference. While communication issues make this more of a challenge for deaf and hard of hearing adolescents, the one-on-one nature of such caring individual relationships makes this reasonably attainable.

Support at the Individual Level

As we well know, individuals have skills (both based on their temperament and developed through life experiences) that enable them to cope with hardship, to succeed, and to become resilient youth and adults. The skills discussed in the following section are skills we see some youth using, and often using very well. Other youth could use adult support in developing and strengthening these individual coping techniques. We acknowledge that this section addresses not recommendations for change, but rather gives recognition to deaf individuals for skills they have developed for themselves.

Adaptive Distancing

The group-home adolescents used adaptive distancing in much the same way as the deaf youth who were faced with being alone in a mainstream school and the graduate students trying to make sense of their experiences. Through adaptive distancing, individuals were able to protect their self-esteem and identity from painful, negative messages because they clearly knew the messages were not earned or true. However, for the group-home youth, there was a struggle between accepting responsibility for their negative behavior or emotional problems and distancing themselves from accepting responsibility or blame for them. The youth who had been living in the group home longer were less likely to engage in denial and more likely to utilize adaptive distancing appropriately, which suggests this is a skill that can be learned. As discussed earlier, membership in validating communities (the Deaf community and other communities) can strengthen self-esteem and identity, making it possible to use adaptive distancing more successfully.

Communication and Ambiguity

The experience of growing up with minimal language and struggling to make sense of the world and others is an appallingly frustrating task many deaf children and youth needlessly face. Children with severe language deprivation illustrate clearly the consequences of and the adaptations developed to cope with ambiguity in communication. However, nearly all deaf children are faced with similar issues, thus the "Pac-Man" sign, which so clearly illustrates the concept of conversation taking place without the deaf person's participation. The Gallaudet students compared their lives to "foreigners in the hearing world learning to adapt to the hearing world's values and customs as we work our way around to fill in the gap in communication" (Duran, Kuehne, & Odland, 2009, p. 1).

When deaf children and teens are faced with ambiguous or vague social or interpersonal situations, they create their own interpretation of meaning where information is lacking. This is a natural, inherent human response for individuals, deaf or hearing. We attempt to create meaning where we have none to understand and to be understood. Therefore, we suspect the deaf child who has been deprived of accessible language and conversation and who struggles to discern meaning from everyday events and interactions is developing strong inner resources for coping in a hearing world. We suspect living in ambiguity, while painful, possibly has healthy implications, which ultimately serve to increase the ability to be resilient.

Reframing the Narrative Story

Retelling the past in the form of a narrative story empowered all of the individuals we interviewed to gain a sense of psychological and emotional mastery over their behavior and their lives as they began to reframe how they viewed the past and looked forward to their future. The adults who were mainstreamed youth were enthusiastic in sharing how much they benefitted from telling their stories to Oliva (2004), often thanking her for the opportunity and staying in touch long beyond the time associated with the research itself. The graduate students surveyed were required to dialogue in journals and small dialogue groups, exploring their individual and family lives as a part of their training to become counselors. Within 3–6 months of being immersed in a language-rich environment with adult Deaf staff, the language-deprived 14- and 15-year-old deaf foster youth were able to begin to tell their stories, which became richer and more detailed each time they were told as they acquired more and more ASL vocabulary.

American Sign Language is not a written language, and Deaf culture includes a reverence for the art of storytelling as a way to pass on rich heritage: the history, language, traditions, and culture of Deaf people. One young adult at the group home mesmerized his audience of peers and staff alike, as he told stories that were both tragic and hilarious of past memories of foster homes and other group homes. Through his exquisite storytelling in ASL, the audience was magically transported to the Colorado Rockies for a camping trip and a hike to the top of a rocky mountain crag covered with magnificent, fragrant pines, and into (and out of!) a makeshift tent at night after the kids cooked beans for their dinner. Through his vivid renditions in ASL, he served as an excellent cultural and language role model for the other deaf youth in the group home who held him in high esteem and strove to emulate his signing style.

Steinberg (2000), a psychiatrist who works with deaf children and adolescents, writes about witnessing the power of deaf adolescents' shared language and narrative stories to change the meaning of their lives into something more positive and to form resilient identities. Rather than focusing on the difficulties for deaf children and adolescents to acquire sufficient language and dialogue skills, she expands on this hunger to know their stories as well as the healing power of telling their stories. She says, "For the child who is deaf, shared language and narrative can heal the trauma of chronic communication isolation and linguistic deprivation" (p. 105). The authors could not agree with this more, as all have witnessed this healing power of telling one's story and being "heard" and understood. We also believe these narrative stories are foundational in the development of resilience and strong, healthy identities as deaf individuals.

Conclusion

What we have learned from deaf children and youth is that when they are at risk for negative outcomes, it is nearly always due to pervasive communication barriers, educational system shortcomings, and restricted opportunities to develop self-esteem and identity. Being deaf or hard of hearing in and of itself does not lead to risk and is, therefore, not something these young people need to "overcome." What they do need is:

- Family, school, and community environments that have high expectations while at the same time supporting their needs, which often means a visual environment
- Adults and peers who support the development of a strong identity, in large part by seeing past "the deaf kid" label and by acknowledging the deaf youth's individuality
- Genuine conversations with others that offer full and equal exchange of information, ideas, feelings, and dreams
- And connections to a community of others like themselves

Systems and organizations are appallingly hard to change. Professionals, parents, and community members using advocacy skills can support one another in the battle to facilitate changes within systems. Deaf and hearing partnerships – professionals, parents, and the youth themselves – are the most effective change agents. It takes amazing energy and persistence to educate and to facilitate change within legal, social service, and educational systems, and there are not nearly enough culturally knowledgeable professionals doing this work, but the payoff for success is huge for deaf children and youth.

As professionals, we can help deaf youth to develop resilience by asking, "What can I do and what opportunities can I provide to support or jumpstart the process of growth and resilience development?" Accepting such a personal sense of shared responsibility could be a first step toward dismantling barriers and creating success.

References

Bauman, H.-D. (2004). Audism: Exploring the metaphysics of oppression. *Journal of Deaf Studies and Deaf Education, 9*(2), 239–246.

Beardsley, W. (1997). Prevention and the clinical encounter. *American Journal of Orthopsychiatry, 68*, 521–533.

Beardsley, W., & Podoresfky, D. (1988). Resilient adolescents whose parents have serious affective and other psychiatric disorders: The importance of self-understanding and relationships. *American Journal of Psychiatry, 145*, 63–69.

Bell, C. (2001). Cultivating resiliency in youth. *Journal of Adolescent Health, 29*(5), 375–381.

Benard, B. (2004). *Resiliency: What we have learned.* San Francisco: WestEd.

Benard, B. (2007). Mentoring: Study shows the power of relationship to make a difference. In N. Henderson (Ed.), *Resiliency in action: Practical ideas for overcoming risks and building strengths in youth, families, and communities* (pp. 111–116). Ojai, CA: Resiliency in Action, Inc.

Braden, J. (1994). *Deafness, deprivation, and IQ.* New York: Aenum.

Cassady, C. (2009). *Self perception of resiliency: Interviews with deaf teens.* Unpublished raw data.

Chess, S. (1989). Defying the voice of doom. In T. Dugan & R. Coles (Eds.), *The child in our time: Studies in the development of resiliency* (pp. 179–199). New York: Bruner/Mazel.

Compas, B. E. (2004). Processes of risk and resilience during adolescence: Linking contexts and individuals. In R. M. Lerner & L. Steinberg (Eds.), *Handbook of adolescent psychology* (2nd ed., pp. 263–296). Hoboken, NJ: Wiley.

Duran, J., Kuehne, J., & Odland, R. (2009). *Sharing views journal submitted to Gallaudet University Department of Counseling, Counseling Deaf People course.* Unpublished manuscript.

Erikson, E. (1968). *Identity: Youth and crisis.* New York: Norton.

Gallaudet Research Institute (GRI). (2008). *Regional and national summary report of data from the 2007–08 annual survey of deaf and hard of hearing children and youth.* Washington, DC: Gallaudet University.

Garmezy, N. (1971). Vulnerability research and the issue of primary prevention. *American Journal of Orthopsychiatry, 41,* 101–116.

Glickman, N. (1986). Cultural identity, deafness and health. *Journal of Rehabilitation of the Deaf, 20,* 1–10.

Henderson, N. (Ed.). (2007). *Resiliency in action: Practical ideas for overcoming risks and building strengths in youth, families, and communities.* Ojai, CA: Resiliency in Action, Inc.

Jambor, E., & Elliott, M. (2005). Self esteem and coping strategies among deaf students. *Journal of Deaf Studies and Deaf Education, 10*(1), 63–81.

Katz, M. (1997). *On playing a poor hand well.* New York: W.W. Norton.

Kleiber, D. (1999). *Leisure experience and human development: A dialectical interpretation.* New York: Basic Books.

Luthar, S. S., & Cicchetti, D. (2000). The construct of resilience: Implications for interventions and social policy. *Development and Psychopathology, 12,* 857–885.

Luthar, S. S., Cicchetti, D., & Becker, B. (2000). The construct of resilience: A critical evaluation and guidelines for future work. *Child Development, 71,* 543–562.

Lytle, L. R. (1987). *Identity formation and developmental antecedents in deaf college women.* Unpublished doctoral dissertation, The Catholic University of America, Washington, DC.

Lytle, L. R. (2009). *Survey of educational programs attended by students in counseling deaf people course.* Unpublished raw data.

Masten, A. S. (2001). Ordinary magic: Resilience processes in development. *American Psychologist, 56,* 22–35.

Masten, A. S., & Coatsworth, D. (1998). The development of competence in favorable and unfavorable environments: Lessons from research on successful children. *American Psychologist, 55,* 205–220.

Maxwell-McCaw, D. (2001). *Acculturation and psychological well-being in deaf and hard-of-hearing people.* Unpublished doctoral dissertation. George Washington University, Washington, DC.

Mayer, P., & Lowenbraun, S. (1990). Total communication use among elementary teachers of hearing impaired children. *American Annals of the Deaf, 135,* 257–263.

Meadow-Orlans, K., Mertens, D., & Sass-Lehrer, M. (2003). *Parents and their deaf children: The early years.* Washington, DC: Gallaudet University Press.

Moores, D. (2006). Comments on "w(h)ither the deaf community?". *Sign Language Studies, 6*(2), 202–209.

Oliva, G. A. (2004). *Alone in the mainstream: A deaf woman remembers public school.* Washington, DC: Gallaudet University Press.

Padden, C., & Humphries, T. (1988). *Deaf in America: Voices from a culture.* Cambridge, MA: Harvard University Press.

Phinny, J., & Rosenthall, D. (1992). Ethnic identity in adolescence: Process, context, and outcome. In G. Adams, T. Bullotta, & R. Montemaoyor (Eds.), *Adolescent identity formation* (pp. 145–172). Newbury Park, CA: Sage.

Ramsey, C. (1997). *Deaf children in public schools: Placement, context, and consequences.* Washington, DC: Gallaudet University Press.

Rew, L. (2005). *Adolescent health: A multidisciplinary approach to theory, research, and intervention.* Thousand Oaks, CA: Sage.

Rodia, B. (2001). Mantua: A school powered by people. *Teaching Pre K-8, 31*(8), 36–40.

Rubin, L. (1996). *The transcendent child: Tales of triumph over the past.* New York: Basic Books.

Steinberg, A. (2000). Autobiographical narrative on growing up deaf. In P. E. Spencer, C. J. Erting, & M. Marschark (Eds.), *The deaf child in the family and at school: Essays in honor of Kathryn P. Meadow-Orlans* (pp. 93–108). Mahway, NJ: Earlbaum.

Stinson, M., & Antia, S. (1999). Considerations in educating deaf and hard-of-hearing students in inclusive settings. *Journal of Deaf Studies and Deaf Education, 4*(3), 163–175.

Thornton, M. (2010). The ethics of doing business as usual: Rethinking our practices, reframing our roles. In C.Wu, N. Grant, L.R.Lytle, & R. Beach, (Eds), *Proceedings from the 2008 National Counselors of the Deaf Association Conference.* Available from the Gallaudet University Department of Counseling, Washington, DC.

Werner, E., & Smith, R. (1992). *Overcoming the odds: High risk children from birth to adulthood.* New York: Cornell University Press.

Wilkens, C., & Hehir, T. (2008). Deaf education and bridging social capital: A theoretical approach. *American Annals of the Deaf, 153*(3), 275–284.

Young, A., Green, L., & Rogers, K. (2008). Resilience and deaf children: A literature review. *Deafness and Education International, 10,* 40–55.

Chapter 11
Community Cultural Wealth and Deaf Adolescents' Resilience

Jason Listman, Katherine D. Rogers, and Peter C. Hauser

Abstract Adolescence is the period when a child's identity is developing and evolving. During the identity development period, deaf students could also build resilience as deaf individuals living in a society where the majority is hearing. This chapter, which focuses primarily on academic success, discusses the protective factors that ethnic minorities acquire from their cultural communities. These protective factors seem to support minority groups in building resilience. With this concept in mind, could the same factors apply to deaf adolescents' psychosocial and resilience development? Clearly, cultural capital and community cultural wealth plays a huge role in these areas of development and there is some empirical support in relation to this notion. These findings appear to support a theoretical framework which could be helpful in designing deaf adolescents' resilience-building programs. The authors propose that deaf-centric aspirational, family, social, linguistic, resistant, and navigational capitals can be learned from the deaf community, role models, and teachers and parents. The availability of such resources could promote resilience and foster academic success in deaf adolescents.

There is much written on how hearing ethnic minorities develop resilience during the adolescent period. This has led the authors to ponder as to how to foster the development of deaf[1] adolescents' resilience, for both deaf signers and oral individuals. In this chapter, we propose that the cultural wealth of the deaf community

---

[1] "deaf" is used here to refer to both deaf and hard of hearing individuals. Following Young, Green, and Rogers (2008), the term "deaf" is used throughout to indicate all degrees of deafness in audiological terms. It is not used to discriminate by language or technology (hearing aid, cochlear implant) used otherwise indicated. A capital "D" in Deaf is used specifically when referring to culturally Deaf signing individuals.

J. Listman (✉)
Department of American Sign Language and Interpreting Education, National Technical Institution of the Deaf (NTID), Rochester, NY, USA
e-mail: Jason.Listman@rit.edu

D.H. Zand and K.J. Pierce (eds.), *Resilience in Deaf Children: Adaptation Through Emerging Adulthood*, DOI 10.1007/978-1-4419-7796-0_11,
© Springer Science+Business Media, LLC 2011

provides deaf adolescents with a tool kit for navigation in life, to enable them to successfully and positively face barriers and succeed academically. The chapter commences with an operational definition of resilience, followed by a discussion of how the deaf community's cultural wealth may serve as a protective factor, supporting deaf adolescents to develop resilience. The theoretical framework discussed here could guide the development of resilience training programs for deaf adolescents.

There are many definitions of resilience in literature relating to hearing individuals (see McCubbin, 2001, for review), but it is generally agreed that resilience has two critical conditions, namely exposure to adversity and successful positive adaptation during the adolescent's psychological and behavioral development (see Lee, 2006; Luthar & Zigler, 1991). Adversity could include, but is not limited to, poverty, trauma, or discrimination. The experience of adversity ultimately depends on the individual's sensitivity to it (i.e., it being perceived as an adverse event). When an adolescent is affected by adversity, their ability to positively navigate their resources (internal and/or external) enables positive adaption to occur and serves toward the maintenance of mental well-being and self-efficacy. Resilience does not mean one has immunity against adversity, however, but rather having the ability to recover from negative events (e.g., Garmezy, 1991).

One of the definitions of resilience, adopted here, is weighted by the amount of *protective factors* which counter *risk factors* to enable the individual to successfully adapt and transform in the face of adversity as well as experiencing healthy psychosocial development (Luthar, Cicchetti, & Becker, 2000). According to Werner's (1989) model of resilience, the interaction of two types of factors, protective factors and risk factors, seem to determine the individual's outcome from any type of adversity. Protective factors may serve as a buffer against the risk factors, and may help prevent the risk from occurring, or may interrupt the processes through which the risk factors operate (also see Norman, 2000). Poor parental and peer attachment (Fass & Tubman, 2002), preexisting mental health issues (Andrews & Wilding, 2004), and community instability (South, Baumer, & Lutz, 2003) are possible risk factors that could have a negative impact on academic outcomes. Some claim that protective factors such as familial support, good communication skills and autonomy are key to promoting positive adaptation in the face of adversity (e.g., Werner, 1995). Additionally, Lee (2006) states that protective factors, such as involvement in school life and activities, having positive relationships with peers, and having strong family and community ties, are important in enabling an individual to develop resilience and achieve positive academic outcomes. However, the specific factors that may serve as "protective" may vary across communities and cultures.

Young, Green, and Rogers (2008) state that caution is necessary when defining resilience as a response to risk or adversity, because it could lead to the assumption that deafness is an adversity. The first issue discussed by Young et al. is how being deaf is not a risk factor, but rather the external factors surrounding the deaf person (e.g., communication barriers) contribute to risk. Secondly, Young et al. address how resilience could be defined from a socio-political perspective in outcome terms, where someone is a member of a Deaf community and has a Deaf identity despite the range of influences which serve to reinforce the medical perspective of deafness, whereby it is viewed as a problem to be fixed. A further issue is how identifying an academically successful deaf adolescent as resilient might run the risk of reinforcing mainstream society's low expectations in relation to deaf adolescents and academic success (Young et al., 2008). Here, we support the claim that being deaf is not a risk factor in itself, but the lack of a wealth of deaf community resources can be considered as a risk factor for deaf adolescents.

Psychosocial Development and Cultural Knowledge

Adolescence is a transitional period when psychological and societal outlook changes (e.g., Cole, Cole, & Lightfoot, 2005). The construction of the self develops through experience and making sense of the world (Pervin, 2003). Some of the changes experienced, such as moving to high school, will present new questions and challenges for an individual's sense of self. Adolescents' relationships constantly influence their beliefs and opinions about their perceived world (Muus & Porton, 1999). This change in the view of one's self is also true for deaf individuals (see Hauser, O'Hearn, McKee, Steider, & Thew, 2010; Hauser, Wills, & Isquith, 2006).

According to Erikson (1965, 1968), during this age period, adolescents seek an identity as they explore and understand their role in life. Erikson emphasizes the importance of individuals having contact with adults with whom they can identify, believing that interaction with group members within a particular culture can help adolescents to develop their own identities. How a culture is formed and recognized is dependent upon the social construction of the individual's immediate environment. The social, political, and religious practices in Western society have been formed in consistence with the values of individuals with privilege. People with stigmatized status, who are members of, for example, racial, gender, and sexual orientation minority groups, view the world differently to those who are not members of the minority groups and who have a more privileged status (Rosenblum & Travis, 2004). To illustrate this point, an African American adolescent most likely knows the values of their own community but also those of the privileged community, while white adolescents might only know the values of their own community, in order to succeed academically and vocationally. The two groups have different experiences of the world, inside and outside of the educational system.

The educational system and many workforces operate primarily on the socially constructed model and values of the privileged dominant culture. For example, considering the role of gender in the education system, the difference in activities given to different genders can be seen in the physical education curriculum, which may reflect from the social construction of gender (Brown & Evans, 2004). Adolescents from minority groups may know and acquire the social norms and values of the dominant culture; yet, some might resist social norms of the dominant culture and still be successful if they have resilience. For example, civil rights leader Dr. Martin Luther King resisted the social norms of the dominant white culture and encouraged equality for African Americans instead of accepting a minority role within society. His actions set a precedent and example for other minority groups to follow in the future, establishing norms that were contrary to American culture at the time.

Many deaf adolescents struggle to acquire a positive identity or self-concept (Maxwell-McCaw, 2001). Consequently, many deaf adolescents will not have the opportunity to develop the extensive self-theory that is necessary for a healthy identity until they are exposed to deaf role models. Holcomb (1997) states that in order to achieve a well-founded self-theory one requires a common language for effective and meaningful interactions. Deaf adolescents have more positive self-esteem if they identify with others within the deaf community and have a rich sense of language and heritage through being part of a vital cultural group (see Bat-Chava, 1993 for review). This outcome of a healthy deaf identity is not surprising, given that hearing minority individuals who identify with their minority groups have higher self-esteem than those who do not (Crocker & Major, 1989).

However, the role that culture plays in adolescents' identity development and how this is related to resilience development is not fully understood. This might be partially due to the fact that culture is a complex concept with many aspects. Culture is not something static, but rather a process that evolves. To begin to conceptualize the relationship between culture and resilience, it is necessary to first explore different aspects of cultures that adolescents learn.

Cultural Capital

Imagine a college freshman raised by parents who have graduate-level education and work in environments where their colleagues also have graduate-level education. Imagine another college freshman raised by parents who were not college educated and work in minimal wage employments. The discussions the two adolescents had at home while growing up were probably very different. The first freshman's parents might have talked about their college experiences and talked in a way similar to that of the people at the freshman's university. The other freshman's parents might never have talked about college, as this was not in their experience – this student most likely had more to learn on the spot than the other freshman, upon the beginning of the first semester. This is because of the *cultural capital* that the first student's parents provided through their discourse at home; their sharing of experiences aided their child's adaptation to college and resilience. Cultural capital involves educational, social, and intellectual knowledge that parents with privilege often pass to their children (Bourdieu, 1986).

Using Critical Race Theory from the discipline of Legal Studies, Yosso (2005) challenges the traditional interpretation of cultural capital, as it suggests that non-privileged individuals are lacking something rather than subscribing to the view that all groups have capital that is beneficial, but that privileged groups establish barriers for those who do not have the same capital. Instead, Yosso (2005) argues that all communities have what she terms *community cultural wealth*, which consists of aspirational, familial, social, linguistic, resistant and navigational capital. She believes that educational systems do not recognize or take into consideration the community cultural wealth which minority students acquire from their communities.

We and others (see Lee, 2006) believe that the cultural knowledge which ethnic minority adolescents can learn from their own cultural communities can help them build resilience. Trueba (2006) describes the relationship between culture and resilience:

> Resilience is intimately related to self-identity. The most resilient individuals demonstrate an ability to use multiple identities. Resilient individuals from minority groups can code-switch and interact-with ethnic persons and white persons, with less educated community members and with highly trained educational leaders. This ability is based on their multicultural experiences, on their skill in various languages and on their ability to live in different worlds culturally and cognitively. (p. xiv)

This is relevant to the deaf adolescent, who needs to develop an identity as a deaf individual living in a society made up of primarily hearing individuals. They need to understand how people like themselves think, behave, and might value things differently than the predominantly hearing culture. There are some differences between the two communities in terms of humor, social practices, and life experiences (see Hauser et al., 2010, for discussion).

Swidler (1986) claims that culture provides a "tool kit" (p. 273) for hearing individuals, consisting of knowledge and skills learned through interacting with others within one's community, based on stories, rituals, and worldviews that help individuals solve problems. It is proposed here that Yosso's (2005) six forms of capital that comprise community cultural wealth provide deaf adolescents a tool kit to build resilience and succeed academically. Before we can understand how community cultural wealth can help adolescents build resilience, it is necessary to discuss each of the six forms of capital that comprise community cultural wealth.

Aspirational Capital

Yosso (2005) defines aspirational capital as follows:

> ...the ability to maintain hopes and dreams for the future, even in the face of real and perceived barriers. This resilience is evidenced in those who allow themselves and their children to dream of possibilities beyond their present circumstances, often without the objective means to attain those goals. (pp. 77–78)

Aspirations and hopes of parents for their adolescent and the adolescent's own academic aspirations are an important factor in their motivation to learn. This could be viewed as a protective factor. For example, a study undertaken in Mexico found that mothers' academic aspiration predicted whether their hearing children and adolescents were in the correct grade for their age or were behind (or not attending school) (Ferguson, 2006). In an Australian study, educational achievement was predicted by students' educational aspirations (Marjoribanks, 2005).

The development of aspirational capital is not straightforward when hearing parents give birth to a deaf child. In their expectation of the arrival of a baby, parents often envision what their child will grow up to be like. When hearing parents discover their child is deaf, their expectations for their child's future often change (Erting, 1985). Hearing parents may never have met or personally known a deaf adult. Their imagination of what their deaf child's future could look like might be limited. For parents, this limitation may take the form of low, negative, or even false expectations; hence, it should be considered as a potential risk factor. If parents do not meet deaf professionals or learn that there are deaf individuals in all walks of life, it might be a challenge for them to provide aspirational capital to their child during adolescence.

An example of hearing parents' poor aspirations for their deaf adolescent was found in a survey of parents of 184 deaf students in their last year of secondary school in the United Kingdom. Sixty-one percent of the parents reported that they would like their child to go to college, but only 20% felt that it would be likely to happen (Polat, Kalambouka, & Boyle, 2004). Lower aspirations for deaf students are not only held by hearing parents but also by hearing teachers. A study that focused on deaf parents' perceptions of their deaf children's education stated that parents reported concerns about teachers' low expectations of their children's educational abilities (Thumann-Prezioso, 2005). Clearly these findings support the idea that parental aspiration is crucial for resilience development in adolescents. Lack of aspirational capital because of parents' limited perception as to what their deaf children may achieve academically could be considered as a risk to their child's development.

According to Bodner-Johnson (1986), family involvement/interaction, guidance/knowledge, encouragement to achieve, and adaptation to deafness are associated with achievement in reading and math. This suggests that the more parents involve themselves in their deaf adolescent's life, the more likely it is that the child will succeed in school. In addition to Bodner-Johnson's (1986) study, children who performed well on reading were more likely to be from families who had high expectations. This could support the notion that adolescents still need parental support with school issues in order to do well in school. In a related study, based on themes from interview data on nine African American deaf older adolescents who were academically successful, Williamson (2007) found that all of them were resilient and all participants reported that their families were actively involved in their lives while they attended college, providing support and encouragement and communicating with them frequently. These parents had high expectations and thought education was important for their children. Examples of protective factors that Williamson (2007) identified in his study, included understanding and acceptance of deafness, development of leadership skills, positive family, and cultural identity and assertiveness.

Familial Capital

Through the family, including extended family and non-blood "relatives" who are considered family, one learns *the importance of maintaining a healthy connection to our community and its resources*" (Yosso, 2005, p. 79). The family models lessons of caring and coping, informing the individual's emotional, moral, educational, and occupational consciousness. Li (2007) illustrated the impact of familial capital on education through an interview with two Chinese families living in America with nonnative English-speaking parents who were financially worse off than other families that were also interviewed. These two families made greater use of public libraries to access English books for their hearing children than the other families. These parents also made an effort to keep the closed captions available on TV so that their children could see the words being spoken and they also set aside time every day to talk with their children about their school experiences. Additionally, they made efforts to build a social network with the English-speaking community (see social capital below). In contrast, where other families were better off financially, parents could not spend time with the children or encourage them to interact with the community because of their commitment to their careers. Their children's exposure to English print was limited. Although all the families in the study were similar in their educational aspirations for their children, how they fostered their children's second language learning (English) at home was different. It seems that how a family uses their familial capital and in what ways it is invested in their children's learning plays a central role in constructing a positive learning environment.

Over 95% of deaf adolescents are born to hearing parents (Mitchell & Karchmer, 2004), most of who have had no experience in raising a deaf child before. They may also have no idea how to communicate with deaf individuals or how to include them in the daily family discourse. Hauser et al. (2010) discusses how many deaf individuals experience a "*dinner table syndrome*" where they are not able to participate in family dialogue during meals. This appears to have a negative impact on their family attachment and psychosocial development. Luckner and Velaski (2004) found that deaf students who feel cared for, accepted, and supported by their hearing family become healthier, happier, and more competent than others who do not feel that way. In a meta-analysis of 42 studies on deaf individuals' self-esteem (Bat-Chava, 1993), it was found that those with a higher self-esteem had (a) parents who had a positive attitude toward deafness, (b) availability of clear and accessible communication at home, and (c) an identification of the deaf individual with others in the deaf community (also see Bat-Chava, 2000). In general, the family functions as a safety net for adolescents as they go through the trials and errors of young adult life. If parents can communicate with their deaf adolescents and accept them the way they are, then the familial capital these deaf students obtain from their families most likely would serve as a protective factor.

Social Capital

This form of capital represents one's networks of people and community resources. Yosso (2005) explains that *"these peer and other social contacts can provide both instrumental and emotional support to navigate through society's institutions"* (p. 79). Looking at hearing children, Kao and Rutherford (2007) found that parental knowledge of a child's and adolescent's friends names and those of their parents was, as well as parental involvement in school life, a predictive factor for the child's grades and test scores. Similarly, Ferguson (2006) found that the number of connections mothers had with their neighbors strongly predicted their hearing children and adolescents' school status. Humans are social beings and many community and occupational opportunities are obtained through social networks and acquisition of general life information.

One study (Hintermair, 2000) found that parents of deaf children and adolescents who had contact with other parents of deaf students showed lower stress scores than parents who did not. Parents of deaf adolescents can exchange social capital with each other. They can share information with each other including information on resources and things they might have tried with their deaf adolescents. Similarly, another study (Calderon, Greenberg, & Kusche, 1991) illustrated that the more mothers acquired reliable strategies for raising their deaf child (e.g., asking other parents for advice), the better chance their child had of developing emotional sensitivity, reading competence, and problem-solving behavior. In addition to this finding, the children also show less impulsive behavior, higher cognitive flexibility, and better social competence. This finding could also apply to deaf adolescents. If the deaf child already receives good support from the parent, then it may be suggested that when the child becomes an adolescent, they will continue to show less impulsive behavior, higher cognitive flexibility, and better social competence due to having parents who uses good child-rearing strategies.

Parents who have close contacts with deaf adults have been found to exhibit lower stress scores, compared to the parents who do not. It has been suggested that parents can acquire many useful resources and tools from deaf adults (Hintermair, 2000). Deaf adults can share their experiences of growing up, provide useful advice and serve as a role model to deaf adolescents. Overall, parents' social resources were seen to be helpful and necessary in reducing their emotional strain, thus having a positive impact on their deaf adolescent's psychosocial well-being (Hintermair, 2006). Parents' sense of coherence, competence as a parent, degree of social support and their deaf child's communication competence also predicted their parental stress experience (also see Meadow-Orlans & Steinberg, 1993). Nevertheless, parents cannot be fully responsible for providing social capital to their deaf adolescent because they often do not have all the resources or knowledge necessary. Qualitative research has shown, for example, that some deaf students were made aware of deaf colleges by school teachers, not their parents (Foster & MacLeod, 2004). Schools and teachers for the deaf need to assume a greater responsibility for providing social capital to deaf adolescents than they would if they were working with hearing adolescents (see Wilkens & Hehir, 2008, for review).

Linguistic Capital

Yosso (2005) defines linguistic capital as the *"intellectual and social skills attained through communication experiences"* (p. 78). The linguistic capital that is most highly valued by the majority in the USA (parents, teachers, and educational administrators) is English-based literacy. While many individuals in the world are bi- or multilingual, many Americans seem to see native fluency in a non-English language almost as a "disability" because this might mean it would take more time for these individuals to develop adequate English fluency. Some of the nondominant groups develop excellent bi- or multilingual skills, oral literacy skills, and/or metalinguistic skills (i.e., from interpreting for others) that are not valued or even recognized by the educational system, as these skills do not significantly benefit the dominant culture's ways of living. In cognitive research, bilinguals, when compared to monolinguals, show a number of superior executive control abilities such as impulse control and cognitive flexibility (e.g., Bailystok, Craik, & Ryan, 2006).

Medical and speech and language professionals often tell parents not to teach their deaf child a signed language because it would exert a negative impact on the child's spoken language development and consequently their independence – a claim that is not based on empirical research (Marschark, 2007). A recent study in the UK showed that deaf young children who learn British Sign Language and English had a greater vocabulary than those who are taught only one language (Woll, 2009). Almost all deaf education systems in the USA place a higher value on the acquisition of English over the acquisition of American Sign Language (ASL). The majority of schools for the deaf do not offer formal sign language classes as a part of the curriculum, or make any other moves to enhance greater fluency among deaf students. Bienvenu (2008) refers to the cultural value of one language over another as *linguisticism*. This neglect of signed language competency contrasts with hearing students who undergo rigorous training and evaluation of their spoken language skills.

As mentioned earlier, many deaf adolescents born to hearing families have experienced the dinner table syndrome, where they have spent years at the dinner table watching close hearing family members and friends converse with each other but have been unable to decipher what is being said (Hauser et al., 2010). Some deaf adolescents also experience this isolation at school if they attend a mainstream program where there are few, if any, other deaf individuals. Such isolation is especially common during school recess times and lunchtimes. Whereas a hearing adolescent would be able to follow spoken English conversation, gossip and banter quite easily, a deaf adolescent would not (e.g., Keating & Mirus, 2003; McKee, 2008). Where there is no or limited access to their preferred form of communication, deaf adolescents are deprived of incidental learning opportunities. An enormous amount of incidental learning is lost to the deaf adolescent, while hearing children and adults have full access to this information. Deaf adolescents who do not have full access to everyday communication are unlikely to see how adults express their thoughts and feelings, how they negotiate disagreements or how they cope with stressors (Hauser et al., 2010).

This lack of access and the resulting reduction of incidental learning opportunities may have a negative impact on deaf individuals' *physical health* (e.g., Mann, Zhou, McKee, & McDermott, 2007), *mental health* (e.g., Hindley, Hill, McGuigan, & Kitson, 1994), and *academic achievement* (e.g., Traxler, 2000). For example, the rates of presentation for injury in emergency room visits by deaf children and adolescents were more than twice that of hearing children, even after adjusting for age, race, sex, and the number of hospital or emergency department encounters for treatment of non-injury-related conditions (Mann et al., 2007). Parents typically verbally preinstruct or immediately warn children of dangers as they grow up, and children and adolescents learn about risks and dangers by being directly instructed or by passively listening to conversations of others. The absence of incidental learning about possible dangers may be one cause for the above findings, indicating that deaf children and adolescents might not be aware of risks and dangers (Hauser et al., 2010).

Language and communication are necessary for humans to develop healthy relationships. Relationships (attachments) are generally accepted and viewed as an essential component of healthy emotional development in adolescents and maintenance in adults. Attachment style involves the willingness of the individual to explore his or her environment. Likewise, curiosity can be thought of as the interest of an adolescent in seeking out new information from his or her environment. Adolescents with secure attachment styles are likely to express more interest in their environment, as the individual feels secure in exploring and knowing there is a "safe base" to which he/she can return. Those with insecure attachment styles are likely to be less interested in seeking out new information, as the inherent risk-taking involved in satisfying curiosity would be increased due to the lack of a feeling of safety. Thus, the cognitive resources are not available to encourage curiosity about the environment and to seek out new information. Secure attachment styles are related to an increase in health-enhancing behaviors and, conversely, insecure attachment styles are linked with participation in fewer health-enhancing behaviors. Attachment style has also been shown to predict anxiety and depression (Feeney & Ryan, 1994).

Steider (2001) found that secure attachments positively predicted greater curiosity and health-enhancing behaviors in a sample of deaf older adolescents and young adults (college students). Deaf individuals have reported being securely attached with other deaf adults, yet insecurely attached with hearing adults (McKinnon, 1999). Deaf children and adolescents and hearing parents are more likely to have insecure relationships or attachments due to communication difficulties (Lederberg, 1993). The communication difficulties seem to cause problems and there appears to be a higher rate of abuse among deaf children and adolescents (see Dobosh, 2002, for review).

Living and growing up in a life where one experiences the dinner table syndrome at home and school also influences deaf individuals' mental health. Foster (1989) pointed out that many deaf adolescents experience the frustration and pain of isolation at home, school, and in the neighborhood. A study conducted in the United Kingdom found the prevalence of anxiety disorders to be as high as 50.3% among deaf children and adolescents, with greater prevalence among children in main-streamed educational settings than those at schools for the deaf (Hindley et al., 1994). Deaf adolescents' need for strong linguistic capital cannot be stressed enough, not only for reasons of physical and mental health but also for their future academic and vocational success.

Resistant Capital

This form of capital *"refers to those knowledges and skills fostered through oppositional behavior that challenges inequality"* (Yosso, 2005, p. 80). The perception that there is a difference based on the body (e.g., the perceived imper-fection of bodies) is a concept common to racism, sexism, and audism (Humphries, 2008). African American mothers teach their daughters to assert themselves as intelligent, beautiful, strong, and worthy of respect (Robinson & Ward, 1991; also see Pinderhughes, 1995) as a way to help them resist racism, specifically the concept that they are less valued members of society. Similarly, Latina mothers teach their daughters to value themselves and be self-reliant (Villenas & Moreno, 2001, cited in Yosso, 2005). African American mothers have been shown to provide their deaf children with capital related to resisting prejudice (Borum, 2007). Although the mothers in this study did not mention helping their deaf children and adolescents in resisting audism per se, they men-tioned that they tried to help them resist any form of injustice based on their race, gender, or perceived disability.

This perception of disability leads to the assumption that deaf bodies are unwanted, inferior, and subject to repair. To the extent that deaf people do not hear and do not speak, they are seen as less intelligent, less capable, and less human (Bauman, 2004). Embedded within cultural practices and coded into social and cultural institutions, audism often appears in the form of treatments, therapies, and interventions connected to a psychology of deficit (Lane, 1992). Economic effects (workplace discrimination, class struggle, under-education, and under-utilization) are a legacy of audism in the United Kingdom as well as the USA (Turner, 2007). Yet perhaps the most salient impact of audism today is the bring-ing of identities into question among deaf people. The struggle of deaf people to maintain a sense of identity in the face of others' definitions of them has created among deaf people an uncertainty about their own linguistic, cultural, and social identities. Thus, a final defining characteristic of audism is the turning of people against themselves as they internalize this dominant and dominating ideology of others (Humphries, 2008).

Interaction with other in-group members is important, as resistant capital appears to be a protective factor that deaf adolescents learn from other deaf individuals. It appears to be a challenge for some hearing parents and teachers to provide deaf adolescents with resistant capital, as hearing individuals do not experience nor often witness audism. Thew (2007) found that deaf students who attended a residential school for the deaf (with commuters) had higher resilience, as measured by self-reports on their experience of events, their recovery and their long-term consequences, than those who attended mainstream programs, with or without support services. It is possible that deaf adults who attended schools for the deaf developed more resistant capital through shared stories and by observing how other deaf individuals reacted when they experienced audism.

Navigational Capital

This form of capital *"refers to skills of maneuvering through social institutions"* (Yosso, 2005, p. 80). Knowing how to navigate a system such as the education system (e.g., college) or a business corporation is one tool which supports an individual to achieve their goal without allowing the system to hinder their success. People from minority groups use various social and psychological navigational capitals to maneuver through structures of inequality permeated by racism (e.g., Pierce, 1995; Solórzano & Villalpando, 1998, cited in Yosso, 2005). In the context of education, an example of navigational capital can be found in a study illustrating a program that used role models from the same ethnic group to motivate hearing adolescent girls from racial minority backgrounds to stay in school and read more (Hudley, 1992). Having a role model who shared the same language and culture seemed to serve to motivate young people to attain their goals. The program invited successful Latina and African American women professionals to come to school during lunch and discuss their experiences in overcoming barriers to achieve academic competence and career success. Their presentations were informal and they selected written materials that helped them put their own life struggles into perspective. The adolescent girls who attended the program developed better attitudes toward education, school behavior, peers, and parents after meeting the role models. Also, after meeting the role models, these students enjoyed reading significantly more often and had a greater interest in peer tutoring.

There are a few services in both America and the United Kingdom, which make it possible for a deaf child and their family to meet deaf adults (Watkins, Pittman, & Walden, 1998; Young, Griggs, & Sutherland, 2000). These services are mainly limited to children and only infrequently include adolescents. As adolescents transition into adulthood and begin to question their own future contact with deaf adults the time is ripe for them to be given an opportunity to benefit from such role model experiences. As deaf adolescents begin to move away from parental influence and to develop a sense of independence, the introductions of deaf role models would serve to promote a positive sense of self.

One of the benefits of meeting deaf adults has been that parents and their deaf children have access to sign language and the deaf community (Takala,

Kuusela, & Takala, 2000), often resulting in an improvement in the communication competence of the deaf child (Watkins et al., 1998). However, little is known about the outlook upon life from the deaf child's perspective before meeting deaf adults and afterwards. We do not know how much of a difference this may make to a deaf child in terms of taking on a positive attitude toward life as a deaf person and knowing how to resist possible oppression.

Resilience-Building Programs

Lee (2006) provided a theoretical model that was aimed at rethinking how people of ethnic minority groups develop the resilience that eventually helps them succeed in college. Lee's model looked at how identity construction processes proceeded in stages of development, from preschool to college, taking into consideration what these students had learnt of Yosso's (2005) six forms of capital comprising community cultural wealth. Lee's model for resilience training could be applied to deaf adolescents, despite being based on the needs of ethnic minority students. While the experiences of ethnic minorities and deaf adolescents are different, there are some similarities in the experiences of oppression and discrimination. Ethnic minorities are often in schools and colleges that are predominantly white, in parallel to how many deaf adolescents and young adults are predominantly in hearing schools and colleges. Deaf adolescents and young adults who attend deaf schools and colleges also would benefit from resilience training because their internships and future careers may still take place in a predominantly hearing environment. Additionally, deaf individuals who are from ethnic minorities would gain additional benefits from resilience training.

Lee (2006) followed Heiss' (1981) definition of personal identity, which involves comparing one's own definition of self with how others see one. The "others" in this instance are the groups of people with whom one interacts – family, people from the neighborhood, people of the same ethnic group and those at school. Lee believes that if ethnic minorities learn the six forms of capital that comprise community cultural wealth as their identity develops, they will consequently develop healthy academic resilience. Lee's model was applied to four resilience training programs designed for adolescents and young adults from ethnic minorities. A discussion on each of the programs is beyond the scope of the chapter; however, we will discuss one of the programs that used Lee's model (Colyar, 2006), the Neighborhood Academic Initiative: Connecting Culture and College Preparation (NAI), to illustrate how the six forms of capital can be used for resilience training.

The NAI program (Colyar, 2006) involved middle school and high school students from Black and Hispanic backgrounds. The goal of the program was to help these adolescents develop community cultural wealth that would help them develop the resilience necessary for succeeding in college. The NAI program

Table 11.1 Examples of how the six forms of capital that comprise community cultural wealth are used in the NAI program

Aspiration capital	Terming the students "scholars" to help to inspire them
Family capital	Working with parents to encourage their children to study at home and to attend a parents' monthly meeting
Social capital	Building a relationship with the high school and university to provide resources
Linguistic capital	Providing sessions in English and Spanish for parents
Resistant capital	Having teachers in the program remind students that there are different ways to overcome discrimination
Navigational capital	Providing a counselor to discuss social and emotional issues linked with adolescence

(Colyar, 2006) addressed the six forms of capital to foster these students' academic success (see Table 11.1).

As yet, there is no empirical support for the long-term success of NAI or other such programs identified by Lee (2006) as resilience-building programs. Nor is there any available empirical support relating to the long-term impact of the acquisition of cultural capital and resources by minorities. As is also true of this chapter, Lee and Yosso's theories are based on different pieces of qualitative and quantitative research that support aspects of their theories, although the theories themselves have not yet been fully tested. Nevertheless, we believe that the work of Yosso (2005) and Lee (2006) provides a theoretical framework for the development of resilience training programs for deaf adolescents designed for preparing them for college. This does not need to be limited to college but may apply to any kind of academic and career opportunities.

There are very few resilience programs designed for the deaf population. Williamson's (2007) Resilience Program for black deaf students is a notable exception. Williamson claimed that families of deaf young people could serve as one of the protective factors in helping African American deaf students to achieve academic success, alongside schools and community. This particular resilience program was created with the aim of promoting success for African American deaf students, based on ideas from the themes that emerged from her study interviews with nine deaf students. The essential features of the program are to enhance understanding and respect for cultures such as African American culture and Deaf culture, promote academic achievement and healthy development of social and emotional awareness and skills. However, there is no follow up on how the program may benefit black deaf students or make a difference in developing resilience in black deaf children.

We believe that a resilience training program designed for deaf adolescents should take advantage of the community cultural wealth that students might have acquired thus far. The program should also aim to further facilitate the learning of more capitals. Ethnic minorities often learn community cultural wealth from their families, friends, and neighbors – in a similar way to many white adolescents.

We do not know how much community cultural wealth or cultural capital deaf students learn from their hearing parents, friends, and neighbors. Even if they learn some, hearing individuals often cannot serve as role models for the resistant or navigational capitals. These require the deaf adolescent to learn from deaf role models by observing and by listening to their stories.

One possible avenue to promote community cultural wealth is by proving access to social capital in schools. Wilkens and Hehir (2008) recommend schools promote social networking to improve the ties between primary, secondary, and postsecondary schools where there are deaf students. Schools for the deaf and deaf mainstream programs need to adopt some of the responsibility by providing deaf adolescents with opportunities to learn deaf community cultural wealth. All parents need to be involved in facilitating their child's resilience but many hearing parents may be unsure how to go about this and would need guidance from schools. Encouraging participation in deaf summer camps for deaf adolescents is another tool that could help them develop community cultural wealth and resilience.

Conclusion

The authors would like to emphasize that little is yet known about what the aspects of cultural (hearing) capital are for deaf adolescents and how much parents and schools should provide to maximize deaf adolescents' acquisition of cultural capital. Most schools (mainstream or schools for the deaf) have traditionally focused on teaching cultural capital informally. Within the family setting, we believe it is possible that deaf adolescents may acquire less cultural capital than, for example, hearing siblings if families do not make communication accessible to these deaf adolescents. We do know that social economic status, including parental educational level and income, is one of the greatest predictors of academic success in hearing students (see Li, 2007 for discussion), but we do not know whether this is also true for deaf students.

There is a need for further research on the protective factors deaf adolescents need to build resilience. We believe that the six forms of capital that Yosso (2005) asserts comprise community cultural wealth could serve as protective factors and the door could be opened for deaf adolescents to succeed academically and career-wise, as well as maintain healthy relationships. Researchers and educators need to further investigate the possible factors that could enrich all aspects of community cultural wealth, including the possibility of additional capitals that are not included in Yosso's (2005) model. In the context of deaf adolescents and their family, additional capital factors are to be anticipated, as one of the differences between deaf individuals and those of other minority groups is that they may not share the same identity, language, and culture as their parents. On a final note, we believe that being deaf, in and of itself, is not a risk factor, but that parents and teachers who are ill-prepared to guide deaf adolescents how to live in this world as deaf beings are risk factors to those adolescents' resilience development.

Acknowledgments This work was partially supported by the National Science Foundation under grant number SBE-0541953 to the Gallaudet University Science of Learning Center on Visual Language and Visual Learning. Special thanks to Betsy MacDonald, Alys Young, and Team HaDo for feedback on earlier drafts of this chapter.

References

Andrews, B., & Wilding, J. M. (2004). The relation of depression and anxiety to life-stress and achievement in students. *British Journal of Psychology, 95*, 509–521.

Bailystok, E., Craik, F. I., & Ryan, J. (2006). Executive control in a modified antisaccade task: Effects of aging and bilingualism. *Journal of Experimental Psychology: Learning, Memory, and Cognition, 32*(6), 1341–1354.

Bat-Chava, Y. (1993). Antecedents of self-esteem in deaf people: A meta-analytic review. *Rehabilitation Psychology, 38*, 221–234.

Bat-Chava, Y. (2000). Diversity of deaf identities. *American Annals of the Deaf, 145*, 420–428.

Bauman, D. (2004). Audism: Exploring the metaphysics of oppression. *Journal of Deaf Studies and Education, 9*, 239–246.

Bienvenu, M. J. (2008, October). *Deaf culture and deafhood.* Keynote address, Campus Week of Dialogue, Rochester Institute of Technology, Rochester, NY.

Bodner-Johnson, B. (1986). The family environment and achievement of deaf students: A discriminant analysis. *Exceptional Children, 52*, 443–449.

Borum, V. (2007). African American mothers with deaf children: A womanist conceptual framework. *Families in Society, 88*(4), 595–604.

Bourdieu, P. (1986). The forms of capital. In J. G. Richardson (Ed.), *Handbook of theory and research for the sociology of education* (pp. 241–258). New York: Greenwood.

Brown, D., & Evans, J. (2004). Reproducing gender? Intergenerational links and the male PE teacher as a cultural conduit in teaching physical education. *Journal of Teaching in Physical Education, 23*, 43–70.

Calderon, R., Greenberg, M. T., & Kusche, C. A. (1991). The influence of family coping on the cognitive and social skills of deaf children. In D. S. Martin (Ed.), *Advance in cognition, education, and deafness* (pp. 195–200). Washington, DC: Gallaudet University Press.

Cole, M., Cole, S., & Lightfoot, C. (2005). *The development of children.* New York: Worth.

Colyar, J. E. (2006). Neighborhood academic initiative: Connecting culture and college preparation. In M. B. Lee (Ed.), *Ethnicity matters: Rethinking how Black, Hispanic, & Indian students prepare for and succeed in college* (pp. 39–54). New York: Peter Lang.

Crocker, J., & Major, B. (1989). Social stigma and self-esteem: The self-protective properties of stigma. *Psychological Review, 96*, 608–630.

Dobosh, P. K. (2002). *The use of the Trauma Symptom Inventory with deaf individuals who have experienced sexual abuse and assault.* Unpublished Doctoral Dissertation, Gallaudet University, Washington, DC.

Erikson, E. H. (1965). *Childhood and society* (2nd ed.). New York: W. W. Norton & Company.

Erikson, E. H. (1968). *Identity: youth and crisis.* New York: W. W. Norton & Company.

Erting, C. J. (1985). Cultural conflict in a school for deaf children. *Anthropology & Education Quarterly, 16*(3), 225–243.

Fass, M. E., & Tubman, J. G. (2002). The influence of parental and peer attachment on college students' academic achievement. *Psychology in the Schools, 39*(5), 561–573.

Feeney, J., & Ryan, S. (1994). Attachment style and affect regulations: Relationships with health behavior and family experiences of illness in a student sample. *Health Psychology, 13*, 334–345.

Ferguson, K. M. (2006). Social capital predictors of children's school status in Mexico. *International Journal of Social Welfare, 15*(4), 321–331.

Foster, S. (1989). Social alienation and peer identification: A study of the social construction of deafness. *Human Organization, 48*, 226–235.

Foster, S., & MacLeod, J. (2004). The role of mentoring relationships in the career development of successful deaf persons. *Journal of Deaf Studies and Deaf Education, 9*(4), 442–458.

Garmezy, N. (1991). Resilience and vulnerability to adverse developmental outcomes associated to poverty. *American Behavioral Scientist, 34*, 416–430.

Hauser, P. C., O'Hearn, A., McKee, M., Steider, A., & Thew, D. (2010). Deaf epistemology: Deafhood and deafness. *American Annals of the Deaf, 154*, 486–492.

Hauser, P. C., Wills, K., & Isquith, P. K. (2006). Hard of hearing, deafness, and being deaf. In J. D. Farmer & S. Warschausky (Eds.), *Neurodevelopmental disabilities: Clinical research and practice* (pp. 119–131). New York: Guilford.

Heiss, J. (1981). *The social psychology of interaction*. Englewood Cliffs, NJ: Prentice-Hall.

Hindley, P., Hill, P. D., McGuigan, S., & Kitson, N. (1994). Psychiatric disorder in deaf and hearing impaired children and young people: A prevalence study. *Journal of Psychiatry and Psychology, 35*, 917–934.

Hintermair, M. (2000). Hearing impairment, social networks, and coping: The need for families with hearing-impaired children to relate to other parents and to hearing-impaired adults. *American Annals of the Deaf, 145*(1), 41–53.

Hintermair, M. (2006). Parental resources, parental stress, and socio-emotional development of deaf and hard of hearing children. *Journal of Deaf Studies and Deaf Education, 11*(4), 493–513.

Holcomb, T. K. (1997). Development of deaf bicultural identity. *American Annals of the Deaf, 142*(2), 89–93.

Hudley, C. A. (1992). Using role models to improve the reading attitudes of ethnic minority high school girls. *Journal of Reading, 36*(3), 182–188.

Humphries, T. (2008). *Audism*. Unpublished manuscript, University of California, San Diego.

Kao, G., & Rutherford, L. T. (2007). Does social capital still matter? Immigrant minority disadvantage in social capital and its effects on academic achievement. *Sociological Perspectives, 50*, 27–52.

Keating, E., & Mirus, G. (2003). Examining interactions across language modalities: Deaf children and hearing peers at school. *Anthropology & Education Quarterly, 43*, 115–135.

Lane, H. (1992). *The mask of benevolence: Disability and the deaf community*. San Diego, CA: DawnSignPress.

Lederberg, A. (1993). The impact of deafness on mother-child and peer relationships. In M. Marschark & M. D. Clark (Eds.), *Psychological perspectives on deafness* (pp. 93–119). Hillsdale, NJ: Earlbaum.

Lee, M. B. (2006). *Ethnicity matters: Rethinking how Black, Hispanic, & Indian students prepare for & succeed in college*. New York: Peter Lang.

Li, G. (2007). Home environment and second language acquisition: The importance of family capital. *British Journal of Sociology of Education, 28*(3), 285–299.

Luckner, J. L., & Velaski, A. (2004). Healthy families of children who are deaf. *American Annals of the Deaf, 149*, 324–335.

Luthar, S. S., Cicchetti, D., & Becker, B. (2000). The construct of resilience: A critical evaluation and guidelines for future work. *Child Development, 71*, 543–562.

Luthar, S. S., & Zigler, E. (1991). Vulnerability and competence: A review of research on resilience in childhood. *American Journal of Orthopsychiatry, 61*, 6–22.

Mann, J. R., Zhou, L., McKee, M., & McDermott, S. (2007). Children with hearing loss and increased risk of injury. *Annals of Family Medicine, 5*, 528–533.

Marjoribanks, K. (2005). Family background, adolescents' educational aspirations, and Australian young adults' education attainment. *International Education Journal, 6*(1), 104–112.

Marschark, M. (2007). *Raising and educating a deaf child: A comprehensive guide to the choices, controversies, and decisions faced by parents and educators*. New York: Oxford University Press.

Maxwell-McCaw, D. (2001). *Acculturation and psychological well-being in deaf and hard of hearing people*. Unpublished doctoral dissertation, The George Washington University, Washington, DC.

McCubbin, L. (2001, August). *Challenges to the definition of resilience*. Paper presented at the Annual Meeting of the American Psychological Association, San Francisco, CA.

McKee, R. L. (2008). The construction of deaf children as marginal bilinguals in the mainstream. *International Journal of Bilingual Education and Bilingualism, 11*, 519–540.

McKinnon, C. (1999). Relationship representations of deaf adults. *Dissertation Abstracts International: Section B: the Sciences & Engineering, 59*(9-B), 5132.

Meadow-Orlans, K. P., & Steinberg, A. G. (1993). Effects of infant hearing loss and maternal support on mother-infant interactions at 18 months. *Journal of Applied Developmental Psychology, 14*, 407–426.

Mitchell, R., & Karchmer, M. (2004). Chasing the mythical ten percent: Parental hearing status of deaf and hard of hearing students in the United States. *Sign Languages Studies, 4*(2), 138–163.

Muus, R., & Porton, H. D. (1999). *Adolescent behavior* (5th ed.). Boston: McGraw Hill.

Norman, E. (2000). Introduction: The strengths perspectives and resiliency enhancement: A nature partnership. In E. Norman (Ed.), *Resiliency enhancement: Putting the strengths perspectives into social work practice* (pp. 1–16). New York: Columbia University Press.

Pervin, L. A. (2003). *The science of personality* (2nd ed.). New York: Oxford University Press.

Pierce, C. (1995). Stress analogs of racism and sexism: Terrorism, torture, and disaster. In C. Willie, P. Rieker, B. Kramer, & B. Brown (Eds.), *Mental Health, racism and sexism* (pp. 277–293). Pittsburgh, PA: University of Pittsburg Press.

Pinderhughes, E. (1995). Empowering diverse populations: Family practice in the 21st century. *Families in Society, 76*, 131–140.

Polat, F., Kalambouka, A., & Boyle, B. (2004). After secondary school, what? The transition of deaf young people from school to independent living. *Deafness and Education International, 6*(1), 1–19.

Robinson, T., & Ward, J. V. (1991). A belief in self far greater than anyone's disbelief: Cultivating resistance among African American female adolescents. *Women and Therapy, 11*, 87–103.

Rosenblum, K. E., & Travis, T. C. (2004). Experiencing difference. In J. F. Healey & E. O'Brien (Eds.), *Race, ethnicity, and gender: Selected readings* (pp. 31–43). Thousand Oaks, CA: Pine Forge.

Solórzano, D. & Villalpando, O. (1998). Critical race theory, marginality, and the experience of minority students in higher education. In C. Torres & T. Mitchell (Eds.), *Emerging issues in the sociology of education: Comparative perspectives* (pp. 211–224). New York: SUNY Press.

South, S. J., Baumer, E. P., & Lutz, A. (2003). Interpreting community effects on youth education attainment. *Youth & Society, 35*(1), 3–36.

Steider, A. M. (2001). *Attachment, curiosity, and health behaviors: A study of inter-relationships among deaf and hearing populations.* Unpublished Doctoral Dissertation, Gallaudet University, Washington, DC.

Swidler, A. (1986). Culture in action: Symbols and strategies. *American Sociological Review, 51*, 273–286.

Takala, M., Kuusela, J., & Takala, E. (2000). "A good future for deaf children": A five-year sign language intervention project. *American Annals of the Deaf, 145*(4), 366–374.

Thew, D. (2007, August). *School to work transition for deaf and hard of hearing: Acculturation stress and resilience.* Poster presented at the Convention of the American Psychological Association, San Francisco, CA.

Thumann-Prezioso, C. (2005). Deaf parents' perspective on deaf education. *Sign Language Studies, 5*(4), 415–440.

Traxler, C. B. (2000). Measuring up to performance standards in reading and mathematics: Achievement of selected deaf and hard of hearing students in national norming of the 9th Edition Stanford Achievement Test. *Journal of Deaf Studies and Deaf Education, 5*, 337–348.

Trueba, E. T. (2006). Forward. In M. B. Lee (Ed.), *Ethnicity matters: Rethinking how Black, Hispanic & Indian students prepare for and succeed in college* (pp. xiii–xv). New York: Peter Lang.

Turner, G. (2007). 'I'll tell you later': On institutional audism. *Deaf Worlds: International Journal of Deaf Studies, 22,* 50–70.

Villenas, S., & Moreno, M. (2001). To valerse por si misma between race, capitalism, and patriarchy: Latina mother-daughter pedagogies in North Carolina. *International Journal of Qualitative Studies in Education, 14,* 671–688.

Watkins, S., Pittman, P., & Walden, B. (1998). The deaf mentor experimental project for young children who are deaf and their families. *American Annals of the Deaf, 143,* 29–34.

Werner, E. E. (1989). High-risk children in young adulthood: A longitudinal study from birth to 32 years. *American Journal of Orthopsychiatry, 59,* 72–81.

Werner, E. E. (1995). Resilience in development. *Current Directions in Psychological Science, 4,* 81–85.

Wilkens, C. P., & Hehir, T. P. (2008). Deaf education and bridging social capital: A theoretical approach. *American Annals of the Deaf, 153*(3), 275–284.

Williamson, C. E. (2007). *Black deaf students: A model for educational success.* Washington, DC: Gallaudet University Press.

Woll, B. (2009). *Positive support: A UK study of deaf children and their families.* Paper presented at the 8th Early Hearing Detection and Intervention Conference, Dallas, TX.

Yosso, T. J. (2005). Whose culture has capital? A critical race theory discussion of community cultural wealth. *Race Ethnicity and Education, 8,* 69–91.

Young, A., Green, L., & Rogers, K. (2008). Resilience and deaf children: A literature review. *Deafness and Education International, 10*(1), 40–55.

Young, A. M., Griggs, M., & Sutherland, H. (2000). *Deaf child and family intervention services using deaf adult role models: A national survey of development, practice and progress.* London: RNID.

Chapter 12
Promoting Resilience in Deaf Adolescents

Pamela Luft

Abstract This chapter examines the unique conditions and circumstances that both promote and prevent deaf adolescents from successfully preparing to assume roles and responsibilities of adulthood. As adolescents, their life path has begun to assume a certain trajectory with developmental successes and challenges resulting from circumstances, events, and decisions that occurred much earlier. Therefore, this chapter examines some of the antecedent factors and conditions that can intensify over time and ultimately become important influences on adolescence and early adulthood.

This chapter focuses on deaf adolescents born with a hearing loss or who acquired it before age two; these individuals are identified as having congenital (at birth) or prelingual hearing losses. The majority of deaf children with prelingual hearing losses are born to hearing parents who often struggle to communicate clearly with their deaf infants (Zaidman-Zait, J Deaf Stud Deaf Educ 12:221–241, 2007; Zaidman-Zait & Young, J Deaf Stud Deaf Educ 13:55–59, 2008). Hearing loss prevents the spoken language that surrounds the infant from mapping onto the language centers of the brain (Easterbrooks & Baker, Language learning in children who are deaf and hard of hearing: Multiple pathways, 2002). The evidence for this is significant delays in language development that begin in the deaf child's infancy and often extend throughout their school years (Friedmann & Szterman, J Deaf Stud Deaf Educ 11(1):56–75, 2005; Mayne, Volta Rev 100:1–28, 1998; Moeller, Pediatrics 106:1–9, 2000; Newcomer & Hammill, Test of language development-primary 3, 1977). And despite having normally distributed range of intellectual abilities, the majority of deaf students graduate high school with reading and academic content knowledge 5 or more years below their normally hearing peers (Moores, Educating the deaf: Psychology, principles, and practices, 2001; Traxler, J Deaf Stud Deaf Educ 5:337–348, 2000). One of the important markers of potential risk for deaf children is failure to meet age-appropriate milestones, beginning with language.

P. Luft (✉)
Department of Special Education, Deaf Education Program,
Kent State University, Kent, OH, USA

D.H. Zand and K.J. Pierce (eds.), *Resilience in Deaf Children: Adaptation Through Emerging Adulthood*, DOI 10.1007/978-1-4419-7796-0_12,
© Springer Science+Business Media, LLC 2011

Introduction: How Hearing Loss Results in Risk

Given their poor language and academic achievement outcomes, children with prelingual hearing losses are a group who would benefit from activating mechanisms of resilience. Several definitions offer insights into how this could be done. Young, Green, and Rogers (2008) identify resilience as "the factors, processes, and mechanisms which, in the face of significant risk/trauma/adversity/stress/disadvantage, nonetheless work to enable an individual, family or community to thrive and be successful" (p. 42). Regardless of other child and family characteristics or factors, deaf children qualify as being at risk using this definition and therefore, potentially resilient. The second part of the definition focuses on the set of "factors, processes, and mechanisms" that promote success across an individual, family, or community, suggesting multiple options for identifying or creating pathways to success. In another definition, Harney (2007, p. 75) identifies individual responses to conditions and factors as "a multiplicity of psychological characteristics that are inextricably shaped throughout the lifespan by the ecological interplay of relational, social, and cultural contexts." This expands the factors, processes, and mechanisms in the definition by Young et al. (2008) to include the individual and the multiple and mutual interrelationships between all of the elements. Combining these definitions offers maximal comprehensiveness in examining how to enable and activate resiliency in deaf children and their families.

In the past several decades, social science research has increasingly recognized the importance of multiple factors in yielding both positive and negative outcomes in individuals. Several researchers have utilized multifactor theories to examine characteristics and processes of resiliency. One example is Masten and Shaffer's (2006) descriptions of ecological and systems theories for conceptualizing risk and resilience processes. Child development is viewed as embedded within the family system, which is embedded in other systems including the community and culture. An important and widely used ecological theory that focuses on child development was created by Bronfenbrenner (1976, 1988, 1989, 1999, 2001). His theory has been utilized across several social science disciplines, including resilience, to examine ways in which people and conditions interact to enhance development and positive lifelong effects (Goodnow, 2006).

Bronfenbrenner (1988, 1992) has pointed out that previous research models using solitary-effect models that linked select variables with specific outcomes were inaccurate or misleading. In contrast, his ecological theory examined socioeconomic status (SES) to find not only a solitary effect but also links with other related variables. Specifically, individuals with higher income levels had greater access to resources and subsequently different childrearing strategies, which also were influenced by their generally higher educational levels. Brendtro (2006) is another researcher who has used Bronfenbrenner's (1976, 2005) theory to examine the influence of family, school, and peer group that surround each child. Factors that enhance resilience included a healthy ecology and family system, in which the child bonded to caregivers and received positive discipline. The school should have supportive teachers and provide opportunities for academic success, with a peer group that offered acceptance and prosocial values. In contrast, a high-risk ecology would consist of a family with which the child feels insecure bonds and experiences with family members, inconsistent discipline in a school environment in which she or he has conflict with teachers; experiences academic failure; and whose peer group fosters conflict and antisocial values (Brendtro, 2006).

The application of this model to child development yields a more complete analysis of the interrelationships that influence individuals across characteristics of home, neighborhood, and school environments, and the activities and beliefs of those within these environments. This aligns well with resilience literature and the extensive individual variation in people's responses to similar experiences (Rutter, 2006). Applied to deaf adolescents, we should expect each to have different reactions to their hearing loss, which are further mediated and influenced by the reactions of family members, peers, school environments, and personnel, neighborhoods, and communities. The result is a highly unique confluence of risk and resiliency factors – and this example is focused only on this one aspect of their lives. The model is complex, yet without a comprehensive examination of factors, the field risks a single-factor approach or intervention that is unlikely to persist across multiple levels and factors that have created an adolescent's current life situation.

Although this chapter addresses adolescents and young adults, both ecological theory and resiliency literature posit that major recovery can take place at any point, if the later environment is of sufficiently high quality and represents a radical change (Rutter, 2006). Therefore, even if an adolescent's current developmental and academic outcomes are very low, activating resources and mechanisms can help to ameliorate and redirect negatively focused life trajectories.

As with Harney's (2007) definition of resilience, the interactive nature of this ecological theory also views the developing person as an active agent who contributes to his or her own development. Each individual has the potential to alter or create a particular response in an external environment and to affect the course of his or her own growth (Bronfenbrenner, 1992). Therefore, each deaf adolescent has personal characteristics and life experiences that can be further activated and enhanced. Concurrently, activating the interactive relationships and links between key individuals and environments means that the deaf adolescent will not need to face critical or defining life moments alone.

From this theoretical framework, the chapter now begins an examination of the research on outcomes typical of deaf adolescents. Although the ecological theory suggests multiple ways and means for supporting resiliency, it is also critical to have a comprehensive understanding of the extent and nature of the risks that deaf adolescents face. Knowing these risks will lead to a more realistic assessment of each deaf adolescent's personal, familial, and environmental elements that can serve to mediate or ameliorate potentially negative outcomes.

The next section describes the developmental and academic risks that result from barriers to developing fluent language and communication. Following that will be research on transition outcomes across independent living, postsecondary performance, and employment which are the critical markers of adult success.

From that, the chapter reviews the developmental challenges that adolescents face and the unique issues that often confront deaf adolescents while they are simultaneously attempting to acquire transition-age competencies. The final sections utilizes Bronfenbrenner's ecological model to examine risks and protective factors for deaf children and their families with an examination of resilience research. The chapter concludes with a model of the factors to promote resilience and its application to identified risks.

Impacts of Delayed Linguistic Acquisition

As noted earlier, the linguistic delays and deficits that begin in early childhood for deaf children often become lifelong. The linguistic center of the brain decelerates in its ability to naturally acquire language as the individual enters middle childhood (Mayberry, 1993). Therefore, if deaf children do not arrive at school with abilities to understand and utilize adult-level grammatical structures that characterize their normally hearing peers (Bernstein & Levey, 2002; Kuder, 2008), it is unlikely they will ever catch up. Newcomer and Hammill (1977) found that delays persisted through 20 years of age, the highest age tested, with linguistic skills that reached a plateau at preadolescent levels. Even children with mild-to-moderate hearing losses do not typically achieve language fluency levels significantly better than children with severe-to-profound hearing losses (Friedmann & Szterman, 2005; Mayne, 1998; Moeller, 2000). Language development is a critical milestone that should spur us to aggressively activate multiple resilience processes.

The issue of a deaf child developing a spoken or signed language seems to be irrelevant. Deaf children of deaf parents have shown higher levels of reading and academic performance than children of hearing parents, documented initially with studies done by Meadow (1968) and Vernon and Koh (1970). These higher outcomes were a surprise to the professional community because the deaf parents used American Sign Language (ASL), rather than English to communicate. The early and fluent acquisition of ASL appeared to allow bilingual transfer to the learning of English. Bilingual research on deaf children since then has emphasized the importance of first language acquisition (cf. Bailes, 1999; Marschark, 2000). Other studies have shown an association between native ability in ASL and reading achievement (Prinz & Strong, 1998; Singleton, Supalla, Litchfield, & Schley, 1998).

The consequence of never acquiring adult-level linguistic fluency is a barrier in communicating age-appropriate thoughts and ideas to parents, siblings, peers, and the world (Bosso, 2008; Moore, 2008; Steinberg, 2000). Despite legislation that assures deaf students the right to access the general education curriculum (IDEIA, 2004), such access is of minimal benefit if students lack the necessary linguistic skills to learn the identified academic content. This is borne out by research showing that deaf students remain far behind their peers in academic performance (Karchmer & Mitchell, 2003; Traxler, 2000; Wagner, Newman,

Cameto, & Levine, 2006). Their linguistic deficits compromise their abilities to learn at commensurate levels within the general education curriculum and according to their cognitive abilities. The decisions that parents make about communication and the success of these approaches in their child's acquisition of a fluent language by the time they enter school will enhance their child's resilience if successful, or result in a language deficit that may become a lifelong language impoverishment that will negatively impact all relationships, interpersonal interactions, and learning abilities, and will be a major risk factor to the development of resilience.

Although new hearing aid and cochlear implant technology would appear to ameliorate many of the barriers of hearing loss, research has not shown the dramatic improvements hoped for. Children with cochlear implants function more like hard-of-hearing children than they do like hearing children (Marschark, Rhoten, & Fabich, 2007). They remain disadvantaged in developing phonology (speech) and in accessing incidental language and cognitive information through spoken language in their environments. Although their reading typically is better than their peers who use more standard hearing aids, it still lags substantially behind their normal-hearing peers (Marschark et al., 2007). A longitudinal study by Meyer, Svirsky, Kirk, and Miyamoto (1998) examined more than 70 children up to 8.5 years after receiving cochlear implants and found that their auditory perception test scores increased only from 50 (chance) to 65% (slightly above chance). Geers and Moog (1994) showed that implanted children had expressive and receptive language skills that were above the 60th percentile relative to normally hearing children after 36 months of implant use and intensive auditory-oral instruction. However, Moeller and Schick (2006) found that implanted children did not differ significantly from children who used conventional hearing aids with respect to language (productive syntax) or false belief (cognitive development) skills. Both groups showed highly varied and delayed syntactic production skills when compared to normal-hearing children. More recently, Barker et al. (2009) studied 116 severely and profoundly deaf children 1.5–5 years in a postimplant analysis and found that these children had significantly more language, attention, and behavioral difficulties when compared to normal-hearing peers.

The linguistic delay of deaf students is a risk factor that can increase with age, as their hearing peers continue to develop and build more sophisticated language, cognitive, and academic skills. Deaf students may enter adolescence with compromised language fluency and skills, at a time when their brain reorganizes to allow complex logical and analytical thinking and leaves language learning behind. Piaget described the major cognitive task of adolescence as developing skills in formal operations (Quigley & Paul, 1984). Yet because this involves manipulation of abstract concepts, relationships, principles that are embedded within language skills, individuals without fluent and sophisticated language skills will lack the tools with which to complete this development. Erikson described the psychosocial task of adolescence as resolving identity vs. role confusion and isolation vs. intimacy in early adulthood (Scheetz, 2004). These tasks are similarly dependent upon acquiring language fluency. Much of our self-identity is influenced by others' perceptions and valuing of our abilities, ideas that we learn through skillful and clear communication.

Significant language delay leads to other developmental delays for deaf adolescents and a developmental gap with their hearing peers that increases each year. Therefore, at school and as they move into the community to prepare for adulthood, they need accommodations not only for their hearing loss but also for their linguistic delays and insufficient cognitive and academic skills that are the sequelae of inadequate language skills. Without clear communication, deaf adolescents will have limited understanding of the world of work and of adulthood. Unlike their hearing peers, they will likely need specific interventions to expose them to and prepare them for moving out of high school and into postsecondary training, employment, and independent living environments (Luft & Huff, in press)

Impacts of Language Fluency on Academic Performance

The importance of developing equivalent academic skills has been intensified by the No Child Left Behind (NCLB, 2001) requirements for grade-level and graduation tests. Without passing these, deaf students may not qualify for an academic diploma, thereby limiting their potential employment and post-high-school options, including vocational or postsecondary training. Although the intent of NCLB was to ensure high expectations, quality teaching, and high student achievement, the law does not address the foundational language and communication issues that impact deaf students before they enter school and thereby creates an additional barrier to positive post-high-school outcomes.

The Stanford Achievement Test – version nine standardization scores (Traxler, 2000) provide some compelling data on the consequences of early language delay on deaf adolescents. The national median reading comprehension score for deaf 18 year olds is at the fourth grade level, and only those students scoring in the 80th percentile achieve at sixth grade levels. Median language levels are approximately at grade 4.5 for 18 year olds, and slightly under eighth grade for those at the 80th percentile. Median spelling scores are approximately sixth grade for 18 years olds and grade 9.5 at the 80th percentile. Karchmer and Mitchell (2003) compiled these results to find that from the second to eighth grade, only those deaf students at the ninth decile achieved near or slightly below the median score of hearing students; thus, only the highest-achieving deaf students perform at the average level of their hearing peers. The result is that the majority of deaf young adults struggle to read about or competently discuss the academic content they will need to pass graduation tests and to succeed in vocational or postsecondary training or degree programs. In addition, they are likely going to have to make great efforts to understand contracts for renting, purchasing, or getting credit, registering to vote, and participating as an informed citizen.

Mathematics achievement also is suppressed due to the impact of language in communicating increasingly abstract and complex representations and processes within secondary-level content. The median mathematics achievement score for problem solving for 18-year-old deaf students is slightly below fifth grade and at the ninth grade for those at the 80th percentile (Traxler, 2000). Median mathematics procedures scores are slightly higher, near sixth grade for 18 year olds, and approximately ninth grade at the 80th percentile. The majority of deaf students do not perform much above elementary levels of mathematics.

The National Longitudinal Transition Study-2 (NLTS2) also performed academic achievement testing which provides comparisons across 12 disability groups (Wagner et al., 2006). Deaf student means were 75.6 for reading passage comprehension which was seventh across the 12 disability groups. They were also seventh for social studies with a score of 80.5. They improved to a rank of third for mathematics calculation (91.5) which often utilizes less language and reading, but their means were fifth across disability groups for applied mathematics problems (83.9). Their mean score for science was ninth across the 12 disability groups (75.4) suggesting this is an area of academic weakness (Wagner et al., 2006). Overall, these scores show that deaf students did not perform among the higher achieving students with disabilities. In comparison, scores for students with visual impairments were comparatively much higher with two rankings as first and second across the 12 disability groups.

Rates of graduation with diplomas are increasingly important for post-high-school employment and training options; however, data results are quite varied. The federal data identifying reasons for leaving school show that only 43.67% of deaf students receive a diploma (OSEP/Westat, 2007). An additional 12.34% receive a certificate; however, this typically does not qualify them for postsecondary or vocational training nor for certain full-time employment positions. Another 8.4% of deaf students drop out of school, also greatly reducing their positive post-high-school options. In comparison, NLTS2 used parent interviews and reported that 97.3% received a regular diploma, which was one of the highest rates across 11 disability groups studied (Wagner et al., 2005). Newman, Wagner, Cameto, and Knokey (2009) used latter data to calculate that 88.6% of the deaf group had completed high school with a diploma or certificate, which was better than the 80% average rate across all disabilities. It is not clear why these rates are so varied; however, as more states implement graduation tests to comply with NCLB, rates of graduation with a diploma can be expected to decline.

Transition Outcomes of Deaf Adolescents and Young Adults

Population Demographics of Transition-Age Students

An important factor in maximizing these adolescent's efforts to become successful adults is the size of this group. The Gallaudet Research Institute (GRI, 2008) data show that 10–13 year olds comprise 26.9% of the K-12 population, with 14–17 year olds as 27.7% and those 18 and older as 10.8%. Thus, high school students (14 and older) comprise 38.5% of the population with the middle school group (10–13 year olds) comprising more than 25%. As a whole, this secondary age group is nearly 2/3 (65.4%) of the deaf school-age population. It is this group that is now engaged in, or will soon begin, transition planning and preparation for adulthood. This very large group is likely to strain the school services where they are enrolled to accommodate their language, communication, and academic and cognitive challenges that influence the content and strategies they will need for successful preparation and entry into the adult world.

Particularly for those who attend public (rather than specialized or residential) schools, these deaf students rarely receive the specialized or relevant career and adult-life knowledge and skills preparation that they need (Punch, Hyde, & Creed, 2004). Of related concern is research on special education teachers that has found instructional preparation for transition and postschool living, often receiving minimal focus in K-12 school programs (Carlson, Chen, Schroll, & Schein, 2003). Although these teachers used best practices for reading, inclusion, and behavior management, they rarely did so for transition. Many teachers also did not believe they had time to conduct transition planning activities (Carlson et al., 2003). An additional factor may be in results of a study that found most entry-level special educators had little training in transition (Wandry et al., 2008). These studies suggest that public school transition services may not be adequate to address deaf student needs.

The size of the secondary deaf group compounds the instructional time and training of teachers in planning for and implementing instruction for their students' transition needs. Deaf students who attend residential schools are more likely to have specialized services including staff who focus on career and transition training (cf. Stinson & Kluwin, 2003). However, the vast majority (86.41%) of deaf students attend public school programs, and only 12.36% are educated in separate facilities (OSEP/Westat, 2007).

As described earlier, the struggles that deaf students have with reading and communicating often means that they will also have difficulty with many of the tasks and expectations of adulthood. Finding an apartment requires that they know appropriate sources of information and how to use them, can calculate or budget for what they can realistically afford, and can understand their rental contract and credit contracts if they wish to purchase a major appliance or a car. Unequal language and communication skills also results in reduced learning and practice opportunities to develop reasoning and problem solving skills (cf. Lundy, 2002; Moeller & Schick, 2006), skills that are so important to successful adult functioning. Those who are ethnically diverse may have additional academic and linguistic challenges.

Transition Preparation for Community and Independent Living

Independent Living and Self-Sufficiency

A number of studies have identified a variety of transition need and challenges for deaf adolescents. The first National Longitudinal Transition Study (Valdes, Williamson, & Wagner, 1990) contacted parents and students with disabilities to gather data on post-high-school outcomes. Parent interviews found that only 39% of parents rated their deaf children as doing "very well" on functional skills (reading signs, telling time, counting change, etc.). These parents expected that only 12.5% "definitely will" graduate from a 4-year college and only 45% said that their deaf child "definitely will" get a paid job. Bullis, Bull, Johnson, and Peters (1995) supported these expectations with data finding that deaf young adults earned substantially less than their normal-hearing peers and were less likely to be involved in productive activity (work, school, and homemaking) after leaving high school.

The NLTS2 data (Newman et al., 2009; U.S. Department of Education, 2002) is a 10-year study collecting data on youths with disabilities who were 13–16 years of age and received special education services at grade 7 or above on December 1, 2000. These latter studies are done in "waves" with repeated data collection every 2 years. The NLTS2 found higher parental ratings of deaf young adults' self-care skills, at 99.3%, which was the highest overall rating across 11 disability groups (Wagner et al., 2005). Parents also rated deaf young adults at 84.1%, or third in comparison with the other disability groups, for functional cognitive skills. Other NLTS2 analyses also reported more positive parental expectations in comparison with 1989 interview data: 68% expected that their deaf child "definitely will" graduate with a regular diploma and 45.3% expected their child "definitely will" attend any postsecondary schooling (Newman, 2005). This dropped to 22.7% for those who "definitely will" complete any type of postsecondary training programming.

Parental ratings for independent living of their deaf adolescents also were generally positive with 74.9% who "definitely will" live alone without supervision and 50.7% who "definitely will" be financially self-supporting (Wagner et al., 2005). However, comparisons between Wave 1 and Wave 2 data of deaf adolescents living with their parents showed a minimal 7.4% decrease from 89.1 to 81.7% for those living with their parents. This rate was tenth when compared across the 11 disability groups in this analysis suggesting that deaf young adults are not moving into independent living situations at the rate of most other students with disabilities.

Another item of concern is that of those deaf young adults who were living independently with a spouse or partner, 74.6% had an annual household income of $5,000 or less which was the second largest group among the 11 disability groups (Wagner et al., 2005). This also suggests that few deaf young adults are financially self-sufficient. Later analyses that targeted students who had left secondary school by 2005 (67% of the total Wave 3 data collection) found that only 18.5% of deaf young adults were living independently and 12.9% living semi-independently (Newman et al., 2009). This was seventh across the 12 disability groups; however, 79.4% of this deaf group was satisfied with these living arrangements. These results indicate a substantial disparity with nearly 75% of parents who expected their deaf young adult children would live alone after high school and the 18.5% who were actually doing so (Wagner et al., 2005).

NLTS analyses also compared the 1987 (Cohort 1) and 2000 (Cohort 2) individuals and found that deaf young adults had statistically significant lower scores for self-care skills (−0.2) and household responsibilities (−1.7) during this time. No other disability group was as low in average household responsibilities (U.S. Department of Education, 2002). Other analyses show that 68.3% of the deaf population was more than two standard deviations below the mean across NLTS2's broad measures of independence (Wagner et al., 2006). With more than two-thirds of the deaf population scoring so low on these measures *this* suggests that parental ratings may not be completely accurate (forms of) predictors for outcomes. These low scores for independence, the low (18.5%) rate of independent living, and relatively low levels of self-care skills and household responsibilities identify that the skills required for independent living need to be targeted for aggressive intervention. A more positive result is that 78.5% of deaf adolescents had obtained a driver's license or learner's permit (third highest rate) and 76.5% of those eligible were registered to vote (fourth highest rate; Newman et al., 2009).

Other more positive results included a 47.5% increase in the number of deaf young adults who had a checking account between Wave 1 and Wave 2 of NLTS2 (10.6–58.1%), the largest increase across the 11 disability groups, and those with a charge account or credit card increased from 5.8 to 26.6% (Wagner et al., 2005). By Wave 3, 64.7% of deaf young adults had a savings account, 62.9% had a checking account, and 36.8% had a credit card (Newman et al., 2009). However, in terms of income, 93.8% earned $25,000 or less per year suggesting that although they had accounts to manage their money, they are likely to have considerable struggles with financial independence and self-sufficiency.

Another important set of adult skills is participation in the community, including having friends and positive activities outside of work or school. Deaf young adults had a 13.8% increase in seeing friends at least weekly (18.1–31.9%) between Wave 1 and Wave 2 although this was not statistically significant (Wagner, 2005). By Wave 3, 81.9% saw their friends at least weekly and 39.4% communicated at least daily using the computer (Newman et al., 2009), both of which are large increases.

Social and Community Participation

In terms of community group, participation (sports teams, hobbies, and religious groups) between Waves 1 and 2 deaf young adults decreased by 7.2% (49–41.8%), although this was the second lowest decrease across disability groups and ultimately, their overall community involvement across multiple activities remained at the second highest across 11 disability groups. The deaf group's volunteer or community service for Wave 2 was a participation rate of 46.9% (not a statistically significant change), the second highest across disability groups (Wagner, 2005). In Wave 3, 26.3% participated in volunteer or community service and 26.4% were in a community group with 58.8% being involved in some type of activity, the third highest rate of participation across disability groups (Newman et al., 2009). This suggests that deaf young adults actively participate in their community and are involved with friends after they have left high school. This suggests that they are successfully identifying others with whom they can communicate and enjoy doing so and/or are identifying ways to accommodate their needs. These are very positive outcomes and reinforce the existence of facilitative factors within every deaf adolescent and his or her environment that can be used to overcome risks and barriers.

Post-High-School Employment and Training

The employment market's movement from industrial to technological markets requires better educated and more skillful workers although there is a growing class of low-paying and low-skilled jobs as well (Punch et al., 2004). As described earlier, deaf young adults often have difficulty in entering and completing postsecondary training, as well as later competing in the job market (Allen, Rawlings, & Schildroth, 1989; Bullis et al., 1995; Schildroth et al., 1991; Valdes et al., 1990). For deaf individuals who are able to complete some type of postsecondary education, they typically have better rates of employment success (El-Khiami, 1993; Moore, 2001; Schroedel & Geyer, 2000). They also tend to have higher levels of financial self-sufficiency (81%) with salaries that increase by education level even though these are still significantly below their hearing peers (Schroedel & Geyer, 2000).

Postsecondary Training

Gaining entrance into vocational or postsecondary training presents challenges as a result of graduation and entrance achievement exams. An ongoing difficulty is that even deaf individuals who qualify for postsecondary admission often are not adequately prepared for the challenges of this new educational environment (Bat-Chava et al., 1999). Their often constrained world knowledge and academic preparation leaves them less prepared than their peers. However, postsecondary enrollment for both deaf individuals has been increasing since the 1970s (Moores, 2001), although enrollment in the 1990s was only 35% for hard of hearing and 28% for deaf individuals (U.S. Department of Education, 1995). Later data from NLTS2 report that 35.9% of deaf young adults were working and attending postsecondary education, and an additional 5.9% were attending postsecondary only (Wagner et al., 2005). The rate of postsecondary attendance with employment was nearly the same (36.2%) for Wave 3 data for those deaf individuals who had left post-high school up to 4 years prior, with 13.1% attending postsecondary training only, and 17.4% combining postsecondary with job training and employment (Newman et al., 2009). Only 13.9% reported no engagement in any of these activities which was the third lowest rate across the 12 disability groups, another comparatively positive outcome for deaf young adults.

NLTS2 Wave 3 data on those who had left high school also showed that 95% were enrolled to attain a diploma, certificate, or license (Newman et al., 2009). However of those who had been, but were not currently enrolled in postsecondary or training programs, only 15.4% of deaf students had graduated or completed their program. This reinforces the findings of Bat-Chava et al. (1999) that deaf youths frequently struggle to remain in degree or certificate programs. However, deaf young adults generally were positively engaged in education, employment, or training with 86.1% having been engaged at some point after leaving high school, which was the median across 12 disability groups (range of 64.6–92.4%).

It is not only participation in higher education, but also lack of vocational training or apprenticeship training that can leave deaf young adults vulnerable to workforce marginalization (Schroedel, Watson, & Ashmore, 2003). Moore (2001, 2002) researched vocational rehabilitation services and outcomes of deaf individuals and found that those who were provided with college/university training, business/vocational training, on-the-job training, or job placement services were significantly more likely to achieve competitive jobs and also significantly higher income levels.

Employment

In general, deaf young adults are more often unemployed or underemployed (working in positions that are not equal to their level of training and experience; Moores, 2001). NLTS2 employment data comparing Wave 1 and Wave 2 outcomes show that deaf young adults increased their rate of employment from 39.2 to 44.2%, an increase of 5% (Wagner et al., 2005). Although this is a very positive trend across a 2-year period, it ranked 9 of 11 disability groups with three groups increasing 19% or higher. However, even among the groups with the largest increases, none were statistically significant and none achieved the work rate (63%) of their peers without disabilities (Wagner et al., 2005). Rates of employment increased to 53.9% by Wave 3 (Newman et al., 2009), a further increase of 9.7% suggesting ongoing positive outcomes. Nearly 2/3 (65.5%) of the deaf young adults also had been employed at some point after high school and 25.4% had held a job for more than 12 months, this being in the median range across 11 disability groups.

NLTS2 data reported that for deaf young adults, their most frequent type of employment was food service (13.4%), clerical/computer support (12.4%), and child care/teacher's aide (9.2%) although the category "other" employed 33% of this group (Newman et al., 2009). Only 1.5% were employed as unskilled laborers and only 4% were employed as skilled laborers. The low rates of skilled labor reinforces Schroedel et al.'s (2003) concern about reduced access to vocational training and apprenticeships. NLTS2 data reported that deaf young adults worked an average of 28.7 h/week which ranked as seventh across 11 disability groups, with the highest being 34.8 h (emotional disturbance). Of the deaf group, 40.8% worked 35 or more hours per week. Overall, they ranked 7.5 for hourly earnings at $7.50/h, with the highest average being $10 (Newman et al., 2009). Less positive was that the deaf group ranked ninth of 11 in receiving any work benefits (31%). In general, their employers were aware of their disability (60.2%) although only 12.3% reported receiving accommodations. A relatively positive result is that the deaf group were among the more positive about liking their jobs "very much" (52.9%)

or "fairly well" (39.9%). Overall, they felt that they were treated well by others at work (90.1%), were paid pretty well (77.9%), and 53.3% had received a raise in their most recent or current job (Newman et al., 2009). Of those who had left their previous or most recent job, 50.2% of the deaf group had quit and only 4.7% had been fired. Of those looking for work, 48.3% had found their job on their own, with 17.1% having help from a family member and 20.1% from a friend or acquaintance (Newman et al., 2009). Across the other 11 disability groups, 8 used family members more than friends or acquaintances. The deaf and learning disability groups were the only two groups who reported using friends and acquaintances more often than family. For the deaf group, this may be at least partially the result of ongoing communication difficulties with family members.

Much of these data suggest positive trends toward increasing employment of deaf young adults over time with 40.8% working 35 or more hours per week, although only 31% received any benefits from employment. This suggests that many of these positions may be entry-level or initial jobs rather than long-term career positions. In addition, most of these young adults found their jobs themselves or with the help of friends. Somewhat surprising is that only 7.7% used an employment agency of some kind. Deaf individuals typically qualify for vocational rehabilitation services, and transition legislation is designed to ensure that these services are invited to be present at Individualized Education Plan (IEP) meetings for high school students. These findings suggest that greater linkages between deaf individuals, families, schools, and vocational rehabilitation may result in career-focused employment positions that require skills and training, lead to higher income, and include work benefits.

Challenges that remain are improving the rates of vocational and postsecondary training that tends to result in financial self-sufficiency and increased competitiveness in the workforce. Although postsecondary attendance rates are high, and few deaf young adults are involved in neither work nor training opportunities (13.9%), the historical difficulties that deaf young adults have in completing degree or certificate programs are again reinforced with a 15.4% completion rate for those not currently attending a postsecondary program. The fact that deaf young adults show positive trends in many areas, despite struggles in meeting adult expectations that involve reading, writing, communication, reasoning and problem solving, and academic content knowledge and skills, suggests that they are indeed resilient. They also "very much" (52.9%) or "fairly well" (39.9%) liked their current jobs and felt that they were treated well by others at work (90.1%), suggesting that they have many of the characteristics they need in order to lead productive, happy, and fulfilling lives.

The lack of a fluent primary language and the barrier it creates for communicating with others has literacy, academic achievement, and long-term impacts on the skills adolescents need for successfully assuming adult roles and responsibilities. These risks are summarized in Fig. 12.1. The arrows on the left of the model shows how language delays and deficits have several impacts on academic achievement and ultimately, poor employment outcomes. The right side shows how language delays and deficits influence communication on the right side of the model, leading

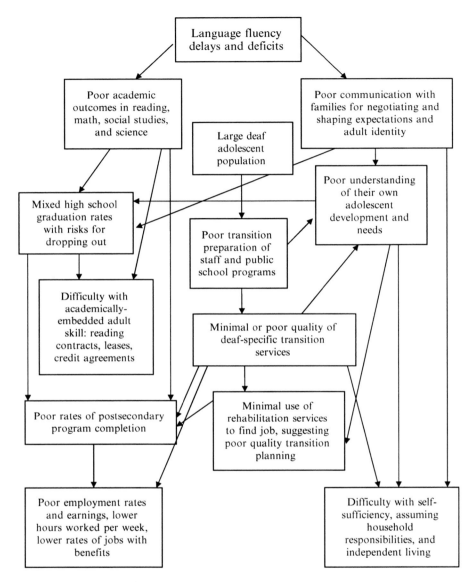

Fig. 12.1 Model of risk factors

to poor self-understanding, poor use of vocational rehabilitation services, and ultimately poor self-sufficiency.

In addition to the risks, we have identified a number of positive outcomes and indicators of resiliency; these are shown in Fig. 12.2. It begins with warm and supportive family relationships with high expectations and firm oversight. One the left are factors that show enjoyment of school and learning, high rates of positive

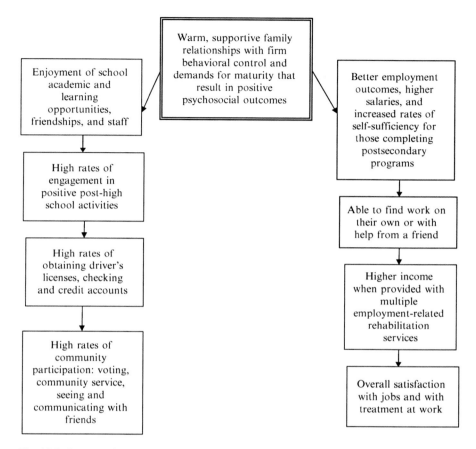

Fig. 12.2 Research-indicated resiliency factors

activities after leaving high school, high rates of obtaining adult-level privileges (driver's license, credit and bank accounts), and high rates of community participation. The right side shows the series of positive employment outcomes that have been identified for deaf young adults.

This next section describes the important changes during adolescent development that deaf students may not fully understand. This is represented in Fig. 12.1 by the second box on the right of the model. These entail some of the key changes that deaf adolescents face; yet, without having adults in their environments with whom they can communicate freely and easily, these adolescents may have very different conceptions of this period in their lives. These substantial challenges occur at a time when they also must begin to confront the adult expectations to which society will hold them. It is a difficult time for all adolescents, but for deaf adolescents the experience is likely to be accompanied with fewer supports and resources than are available to their hearing peers.

Developmental Challenges Facing Deaf Adolescents

During the time that deaf adolescents are confronting the cognitive and academic challenges of secondary school, exploring the nature of their hearing loss as it impacts their current and future capabilities, and beginning to plan for their adult life and how this can be achieved, they are also living through all of the profound physical, intellectual and cognitive, emotional and affective, and moral reasoning changes that will transform them into adults. They may face a critical barrier to understanding the nature and extent of these changes unless they have developed clear and caring communication with parents or other adults who can help guide them. If they have had limited language development and communication with others during childhood, they may struggle to comprehend the depth and breadth of the changes that they now face.

Opportunities for meaningful and multifaceted conversations with family members, peers, and other significant individuals become increasingly important during adolescence. It is also the family interpersonal and relational processes that are the foundations of development and that shape adolescents' patterns of adaptation (Granic, Dishion, & Hollenstein, 2003). Sheridan's (2000) study of seven deaf school children identified students' sense of attachment as occurring primarily in the company of others they see as similar to themselves, and that personal communication methods were important for their sense of belonging and acceptance of others. They showed a sense of attachment, belonging, self-assurance, and fulfillment in relationships with others where communication was accessible, regardless of their hearing status. The importance of clear communication is further emphasized by results of the NLTS2 study that found parents rated their deaf adolescents 41.1% in experiencing no trouble with communication, the lowest rating across 11 disability groups (Wagner et al., 2005). No other group was rated lower than 50% including those with multiple disabilities (54.5%) and mental retardation (55.2%). Family communication patterns that are difficult between teenage children and parents are unlikely to be remedied without targeted interventions and substantial change. This can leave deaf adolescents unsure of the multiple changes they are experiencing and how to successfully negotiate their fluctuating emotions and moods with the increasing level of academic and personal responsibilities expected of secondary-age students.

One set of changes that adolescents often experience are expanded behavioral opportunities and choices that were not available during childhood. This can include such things as how much to study, smoke, or drink and which parties to attend or school clubs to join (Rodgers & Bard, 2003). Some behaviors are unhealthy such as risky sexual behavior, reckless driving, drinking to excess, or drug use. Others are more healthy and socially normative such as joining sports teams or other groups and reading to expand their personal interests. Typical adolescents may use some of these behaviors to overtly or covertly signal their maturity and proximal adulthood (Rodgers & Bard, 2003). However, deaf adolescents with limited world experience or understanding as a result of their reduced access to communication may have a very different perspective on these behaviors and their potential consequences.

Some researchers identify hormonal changes as the source of many of these physiological changes, which then lead to substantial behavioral impacts (Granic et al., 2003; Rodgers & Bard, 2003). Hormonal changes can potentially influence self-esteem, happiness, concentration, aggression and behavior problems, and social relationships (Rodgers & Bard, 2003). For deaf adolescents, these changes can be complicated by communication difficulties with their parents, teachers, and hearing peers which also impacts social relationships, self-esteem, happiness, aggression, and behavior. In typical families, the impacts of the adolescent's combined physical, cognitive, and emotional changes often lead to subtle but wide-ranging modifications in social interactions and environments: the adolescent's world responds in kind and in ways that influence long-term developmental outcomes (Granic et al., 2003). For deaf adolescents, neither families nor the environments may respond in typical ways, or they may experience substantial struggles and misunderstandings in their efforts to be supportive to the unique confluence of developmental and adolescent social forces that are impacting a particular young adult.

Cognitive changes in early adolescence indicate the onset of formal operational thinking and occur as the brain undergoes substantial reorganization. A critical acquisition is the capacity to think abstractly and plan sequential activities that can lead toward accomplishing a future goal (Granic et al., 2003). Adolescents also develop the ability to consider and manipulate abstract concepts, including the development and testing of personal theories about the world around him or her (Granic et al., 2003). Another critical skill is the regulation and resolution of emotional experiences. Adolescents often are preoccupied with understanding themselves in relation to others and may display different personality characteristics in different relationships (Granic et al., 2003). Parental figures also become deidealized when adolescents see that they can be wrong in their opinions or inconsistent in their beliefs and values.

The extent and nature of the many changes across multiple domains associated with adolescence can lead to disagreements in parents' and adolescents' expectations for one another. Often these can involve changes in power relationships and family dynamics as the adolescent seeks to further define himself or herself. In typical families, these relationships continue to shape adolescents' patterns of adaptation and in turn these behavioral adaptations influence family relations (Granic et al., 2003). For deaf adolescents, a limited sense of attachment, belonging, or identification with parents and other family members may alter the nature and extent of these relationships and how they respond to changing adolescent needs.

A review of research on family relationships during adolescence supports the importance of warm, supportive family environments in yielding a variety of positive psychosocial outcomes including high self-esteem, self-confidence, and competence in areas of school achievement (Granic et al., 2003). High scores on parent limit-setting were characteristic of successful European-American families who were not at higher risk (Granic et al., 2003). However, low scores on parent limit-setting were characteristic of successful African American families, suggesting that a firm, strict parenting style meant something different for the two communities. Cooperation with family members (family chores) has been found to be a key process that contributed to adolescents' prosocial development. NLTS2 results showing limited involvement in chores suggest that this is an area that many families could utilize to promote more positive outcomes for their deaf adolescents.

Other family characteristics that promote healthy development across different cultures include parenting that displays high degrees of warmth and responsiveness, with firm behavioral control and demands for maturity, which are important for promoting healthy development (Granic et al., 2003). Responsive parenting during adolescence includes encouragement of independence, negotiation through verbal "give-and-take" and warmth and support. Parental monitoring is critical for minimizing problem behaviors; however, adolescents often have learned parental expectations and parents generally trust that these expectations will be met.

One important conclusion from this research review is the importance of family. Despite adolescent desires for growing control over his or her life, and the ability to make choices and decisions about an increasing array of self-selected opportunities, the role of family in monitoring behaviors and providing guidance remains essential. For deaf students who have limited communication with their families, where it is neither easy nor fluent, creating trustful interdependence may be particularly difficult. Much of one's behavioral and emotional control is guided by cultural and familial expectations; however, if these cannot be easily communicated or reinforced between the family and child, the deaf adolescent may experience an additional development barrier: she or he has limited access to an adult who can mediate and support the extensive changes that come with adolescence and the expectations with moving into adulthood. This can leave the deaf adolescent uncertain about his or her own emotions and how to manage them as well as vulnerable to peers and other adults who may have neither healthy nor beneficial motivations.

Communication and ongoing relationships are also fundamental to learning about the range of adult options for employment, community participation in hobbies and clubs, and independent living including preferred lifestyle. With each new adult role and freedom, also comes a set of responsibilities. Adolescents who have acquired the logical reasoning to understand consequences of their actions or of neglecting the responsibilities that accompany new rights, are more likely to be successful in negotiating adult boundaries. However, if they have unclear or uncertain communication with their primary family members, they are likely to acquire only the most superficial understandings of the adult roles and responsibilities that society will expect of them (Bosso, 2008; Luft & Huff, in press; Moore, 2008; Steinberg, 2000). As a result, they may engage in behaviors that are unhealthy or highly risky, because they are unaware of the consequences or because "trial and error" learning provides the clearest example of what is tolerated in an otherwise confusing "hearing" world.

Adolescents are expanding their worlds beyond their families, and the range of environments with which they are increasingly involved offer additional opportunities and venues through which to positively support their movement through adolescence into adulthood. Communication remains foundational to much of their success, however. They need the reasoning and abstract cognitive abilities, mediated through language, to understand and subsequently manage their developmental changes (Quigley & Paul, 1984; Scheetz, 2004).

Deaf students face not only the typical challenges of adolescents and young adults, but also often bring language, communication, and gaps in academic achievement as well as potentially limited understandings of adult role expectations and their world. Much of their developmental trajectory centers around family relationships, and as adolescents, they are beginning to move beyond this center. They need relationships and social opportunities in order to explore and formulate their identity and life goals. Their own communication preferences will become increasingly important as they assume increasing responsibility for identifying individuals and environments that provide them the clearest and most caring access to what they need to negotiate the enormous set of adolescent life changes.

Promoting Resilience Through Ecological Approaches

Having described many of the negative, and some of the positive, outcomes that face deaf adolescents, we now apply the ecological theory to support resilience in deaf adolescents. The heart of Bronfenbrenner's theory is a hierarchy of four progressively more comprehensive levels of interaction, focusing on the individual and his or her various environments. These four levels are key to understanding and effectively applying the theory, in this case, to deaf children and families, and how resilience can be supported. These four levels consist of the following (Bronfenbrenner, 1988, 1989, 2001, 2005):

Microsystem: The social, physical, and symbolic aspects of the immediate setting that encourage, allow, or suppress, engagement in sustained, progressively more complex interaction with and activity in the immediate environmental structures and processes taking place in an immediate setting containing the developing person, which are typically the home and the classroom.

Mesosystem: The linkages and processes taking place between two or more settings containing the developing person, essentially, a system of microsystems that accounts for the relations between, for example, home and school, school, and neighborhood.

Exosystem: The linkages and processes between two or more settings, at least one which does *not* ordinarily contain the developing person, but that contains factors and events that influence processes in that setting, for example the home relationships with the parents' work and their influence on child, or the school and neighborhood group's relationships and their influence on the child.

Macrosystem: The overarching pattern of micro-, meso-, and exosystem characteristics of a given culture, subculture, or other extended social structure, with particular reference to the developmental belief systems, resources, hazards, lifestyles, opportunity structures, life course options, and patterns of social interchange that are embedded in such overarching systems overarching pattern of ideology or beliefs, and the organization of the social institutions common to a particular culture or subculture which includes the pattern of micro-, meso-, and exosystems that are characteristic of a given society, or the social blueprint for a particular culture or subculture.

An additional factor that applies across these levels is the context of time and historical era within which the individuals live. For today's transition-age deaf students, the current economic climate has greatly contracted, typically reducing the range and availability of potential employment positions and employer ability to accept paid internships and supports available through service agencies (Hoff & Holsapple, 2009). In addition, family circumstances may have changed if one or more parents has been laid off; the family may be experiencing stress regarding its survival. Parents may have fewer resources for supporting adolescent employment or living expenses and less emotional tolerance in negotiating changing power relationships. The school system may have cut personnel and programs that provided specialized work or transition training services to students. Federal and state cuts in funding may mean that vocational rehabilitation counselors may no longer be able to provide the extent and range of independent living, training, and employment services that they had in the past.

Positive changes include a wider acceptance of the use of ASL and the recognition of Deaf individuals as subscribing to a unique culture that has occurred in the past decade. More schools are providing ASL coursework that qualifies as a foreign language leading to its broader use in the general population. Growing national diversity also is leading to greater recognition of different lifestyle and life goal choices that reduces social marginalization of those who are "different" including those who are deaf or hard of hearing. All of these factors contribute to a need to individually identify the particular challenges and strengths of the ecological systems within which each deaf adolescent lives.

Applying the Ecological Systems Framework to Deaf Adolescents and Families

The benefit of using the ecological model to examine resilience of deaf adolescents is that it encourages examination of multiple factors across each of the levels, including the adolescent, and the interrelationships between the factors and individuals for facilitating positive developmental change. The following examines research with deaf individuals across each of the four systems, including research on resilience. The ecological model can help us all, researchers, parents, and professionals to identify important factors and interrelationships between them, that can be utilized to support resilience and optimize deaf adolescent and adult outcomes.

Microsystems

Families

The primary microsystem of the deaf adolescent remains the home and family members. Other important environments are the neighborhood, their school, and their community. One of the critical early tasks of children is to develop attachment to their parents and family members, which then helps structure their adolescent assumption of increased independence. Without clear and caring communication, deaf children and adolescents may experience a different or reduced sense of attachment with their families.

Jackson and Turnbull (2004) reviewed 17 studies on families of deaf children and found that everyday parenting activities were crucial for conveying social norms, values, and accepted behavior. However, these could be challenging when family members did not have full access to shared language and communication. This suggests that adolescents may not have acquired family norms and values to the same extent as their siblings. Bodner-Johnson (1986) examined families and identified four main factors related to school achievement that included family involvement and interaction, guidance and knowledge, a press for achievement, and adaptation to deafness. Children who did well in reading were more likely to come from families who reported integrating their child into family interactions and having high expectations.

Research on students in special education has shown parental influence to be important to adolescents. Whiston and Keller (2004) found parents to be more influential than peers in career development of students with disabilities. Similarly, Lindstrom, Doren, Metheny, Johnson, and Zane (2007) found that relationships with parents, family involvement in school and activities, family support and advocacy, parental expectations, as well as intentional career-related activities were important to career development. Hudson, Schwartz, Sealander, Campbell, and Hensel (1988) found that of 40 successfully employed young adults 19–25 years of age, 90% felt that family support was an important personal resource for their success. Heal, Gonzalez, Rusch, Copher, and DeStefano (1990) found that home support was one of several significant factors discriminating between successful and unsuccessful employment outcomes. Halpern, Doren, and Benz's (1993) 3-year follow-along study showed that informal student supports (e.g., from families) were more important than the program supports. Although these studies were not done with deaf students and families, they emphasize the importance of family involvement with their adolescent children's activities and career decisions.

NLTS2 (2003) provides data tables on key variables, some of which examine parental interactions with their child. Parents of deaf adolescents reported in Wave 2 data collection that 88.8% regularly spoke to their child about his or her school experiences and 9.7% occasionally did so. Parents also reported that 9.5% helped their child with his or her homework five or more times each week, 12.6% helped 3–4 times each week, 37.6% helped 1–2 times each week, 25.7% helped less than once a week, and 14.6% never helped. Discussions between parents and deaf adolescents about post-high-school plans occurred regularly for 78.2%, occasionally for 19.1%, and rarely for 2% (NLTS2, 2003). This suggests that many deaf adolescents have parents who are involved in their lives and with whom they communicate frequently, offering strengths from which to increase a number of transition outcomes including independent living, postsecondary success, and obtaining higher paying employment positions with benefits.

Schools

The school environment is an important microsystem for the developing adolescent. An important change in schooling has resulted from PL 94-142 legislation with approximately 85% of deaf children currently being educated in local districts (OSEP/Westat, 2007). Many parents prefer to have their child attend local schools rather than residential programs, although these special schools have historically been viewed as cultural centers for the deaf (Moores, 2001; Schirmer, 2001). Some have criticized them for having lower academic outcomes; however, Karchmer and Mitchell (2003) found that deaf students who were minimally integrated into regular education classes scored lower than students who attended special schools for the deaf or those students who were fully integrated into classrooms. This suggests that attendance at special and residential schools may not lead to negative academic impacts. Many residential and special schools also have specialized services that include transition preparation, on-site vocational rehabilitation counselors, on-campus and off-campus work experiences and training, and deaf-specific career and academic-preparation programs (Stinson & Kluwin, 2003). Bull and Bullis' (1991) also found that residential schools implemented more desirable transition practices and that their students had more positive postschool activities. For parents and professionals working with deaf adolescents in public school programs, identifying the necessary resources to offer specialized academic and transition services may require strong advocacy. It is potentially through collaborative efforts, the target of mesosystem analyses, that resources can be combined across environments, agencies, and individuals to result in more effective programming and services.

Individual Characteristics

The adolescent's own personality, cognitive, and physical characteristics also are important factors that can enhance or diminish resiliency. The growing number of diverse families in this population (GRI, 2008; OSEP/Westat, 2007) represents a service challenge to many schools and agencies, including early intervention and preschool services. These programs may struggle to successfully address the dual issues raised by deaf and diverse adolescents and often are staffed by individuals who are neither deaf nor minorities. Diverse deaf students typically are at increased risk of low academic achievement, vocational tracking, and reduced financial success (Allen, 1994; Harmon et al., 1998; Schildroth et al., 1991; Moores, 2001; Wheeler-Scruggs, 2002, 2003).

Another group of deaf students that challenge school services are the nearly 50% who have disabilities in addition to hearing loss (GRI, 2008). This is a group that has been poorly served and that shows even lower academic outcomes and post-high-school opportunities for training and employment, as well as fewer independent living options (Bowe, 2003, 2004; Harmon et al., 1998). Yet, cost effectiveness studies show that monies spent on this group yield positive long-term outcomes (Bowe, 2004).

Using the ecological model, deaf adolescents both experience and create impacts on the school environment. Some measure of this interrelationship may be seen in NLTS2 (2003) interviews of students asked to rank their favorite aspects of school on a scale of 1–10. Deaf adolescents gave a score of 52.6% for friendships and free time are their favorite aspects of school, 33% for academics, 24.9% for learning and studying, 19.6% for computers/cooking/sports activities, and 18.1% for school personnel. Friends and free time were generally ranked high across the disability groups, although deaf adolescents rated learning/studying and academics more highly than a majority of the other disability groups and was in the higher group in rating teachers. This suggests a positive interrelationship between schools and deaf students.

Other analyses reported on adolescent self-determination activities (NLTS2, 2003) and characteristics they perceived in themselves. Deaf adolescents reported that they planned weekend activities: every time they had the chance – 32.8%, most of the time – 35.8%, and sometimes – 27.3%. The NLTS2 Direct Assessment tables (2003) reported deaf adolescents doing schoolwork to improve their career chances: every chance – 29.9%, most of the time – 35.9%, and sometimes – 26.3%. They also make long range career plans: every chance – 27.4%, most of the time – 33.3%, and sometimes – 27.5%. They reported that they knew how to make up for their limitations: always – 26.8%, usually – 48.9%, sometimes – 21.6%, and never – 2.7%, and were confident in their abilities: always – 44.7%, usually – 35.1%, and sometimes – 35.1%. The NLTS2 (Newman et al., 2009; U.S. Department of Education, 2002) reports of low rates of independence and self-care skills suggest that some of the adolescents' self-appraisals may be unrealistically high; however, it is also important that they do not demonstrate lack of confidence and low self-esteem as they face the challenges of adulthood. The capabilities and perceptions of the deaf adolescents are important variables in enhancing resiliency and paths to positive adult outcomes. Abilities to plan activities and linking what they do with long-term employment goals are very important skills for successful adulthood.

Peer environments and relationships. As adolescents assume greater control of their lives, they move to expand their environments with increasing influence given to their peers, although the primary environmental influences for this age remain through family and school. The NLTS2 (2003) studies also examined friendships and reported that 74.5% of deaf adolescents can find a friend when they need one, 22.4% can sometimes find a friend, with 3.1% report that they cannot. Only 5.5% are lonely at school, 21.5% are sometimes lonely, and 73.1% are not lonely. This is relatively positive given that 85% attend public schools and may not have other deaf peers with whom they can easily communicate and make friends. The same skills will be important in the workplace and other adult environments, few of which are likely to have many deaf adults.

Resilience Research at the Microsystem Level

Communication remains foundational to acquiring many of the skills and abilities that deaf adolescents will need in adulthood, beginning with family relationships but extending to teachers, peers, extended family, and other influential adults including coaches or club organizers. The factors associated with hearing loss conditions may promote or impede processes of resilience factors in ways that are not found in research with other children. However, several studies have examined factors associated with deaf children and youths. Young et al. (2008) identified that potentially extreme communication deprivation can occur between some deaf children and their parents that often negatively impacts family and social relationships. Steinberg (2000) also described communication between deaf children and hearing parents as commonly disrupted and degraded, with subsequent impacts on developmental environments. When shared communication between child and caregiver is poor and inconsistent, then information, knowledge, and experience about the world is difficult to acquire. She suggested that deaf children in these environments are left with few internal resources to make sense of their world. Charlson, Bird, and Strong (1999) did case studies of several resilient deaf high school students. The common characteristics appear to be above-average or higher intelligence and the ability to bond with another person, even if relationships with parents were disrupted or non-positive.

Research on children similarly supports the importance of early attachment as strategic in the development of resilient functioning (Harney, 2007). Using an ecological systems perspective, Harney (2007) found that fewer family disruptions contributed to resilience, and that attachment and competence were important factors for resilient children. Some of the positive developmental processes were linked to specific caregiver practices, reduced self-blame, and social support including size and complexity of social networks. However, specific processes were successful in specific contexts with self-mastery being a factor within cultural contexts that valued individuality rather than group-oriented values.

Roberts, Kuncel, Shiner, Caspi, and Goldberg (2007) reviewed literature to compare the influence of personality traits with socioeconomic status and cognitive ability on life outcomes. They found that in general, specific personality characteristics were equally predictive of positive outcomes as effects reported for SES and cognitive abilities; all produced small- to medium-effect sizes. Masten, Herbers, Cutuli, and Lafavor (2008) examined several factors across the microsystem and identified effective schools with positive school experiences as providing protective factors to children. For both families and schools, positive factors included warm relationships, a supportive climate, high expectations, and orderly structures with consistent rules. Other protective factors were child-specific and included intelligence, problem-solving skills, achievement motivation, persistence, self-regulation, effective stress management, positive friends, and positive belief systems about oneself and life's purpose. Many of these characteristics are either encouraged or suppressed by environmental factors as well.

The next two levels examine the interactions between these environments, which provide important ways in which each environment can be used to support each other. Given the current economic stresses faced by both of these environments, it is the strength of this model that no one environment has to assume sole responsibility for optimizing adolescent outcomes.

Mesosystem

This level examines the relationships between the settings in supporting the developing child or adolescent. Meadow-Orlans, Mertens, Sass-Lehrer, and Scott-Olson (1997) conducted a national survey of parents with 59% reporting having received information on choices for future school placement for their deaf child. Parents rated teachers as the highest source of support, and 19–20% reported medical doctors as a source of help. However, non-white families reported significantly less support from schools and rated services less favorably. Latina mothers expressed more negative feelings toward deafness than white mothers.

Prior research has described the influence of parents on future career and adult living choices. One of the primary avenues for parental involvement in these decisions is through the IEP and the transition planning page. Newman (2005) studied parental involvement in their deaf adolescents' plans and found that slightly more than one-half of parents were involved in developing IEP goals; however, one-third wanted more involvement in IEP decision making. Schools that encourage greater parental involvement can also use this as a strategy that leads to more successful employment-related outcomes (cf. Schalock et al., 1986).

NLTS2 Wave 2 data tables (2003) examined several factors related to the family–school relationship. Parents who attended their deaf child's IEP reported that IEP goals were developed mostly by schools (40.1%), mostly by the respondent or youth (28.6%), or by a combination (31.3%). Parents reported that they strongly agreed with these goals (31.3%), agreed (60.6%), disagreed (5.9%), or strongly disagreed (2.3%). A mutually supportive relationship would generally yield goals by a combination of participants that were strongly agreed upon by all. Levels of disagreement are low, which is a positive result.

The same data tables reported that 26.2% of parents of deaf students wished to be more involved in the IEP decisions, 73.4% felt they were involved the right amount, and none wished to be less involved (NLTS2, 2003). Parents also reported that post-high-school transition planning was "very useful" (46%), "somewhat useful" (44.2%), "not very useful" (5.4%), and "not at all useful" (4.4%). Parents reported that 51.4% met with their child's teacher to set transition goals in Wave 1, which increased to 70.6% in Wave 2. It is interesting that although over two-thirds of parents met with their teachers about transition goals in Wave 2, those who felt transition planning was "very useful" in Wave 2 was 46%. This suggests that parents' meetings with teachers about transition goals may not have transferred into the IEP/transition planning document that they had anticipated. Parents who are willing to attend additional meetings in order to develop meaningful IEP and transition plans is an opportunity that should be maximized in building positive relationships and ultimately, more successful outcomes.

Also important at IEP meetings is the role taken by the deaf adolescent. Data showed that 30.5% reported the adolescent being present with little involvement, 47.9% reported that she or he provided some input, and 21.6% reported that she or he took a leadership role (NLTS2, 2003). As deaf adolescents leave high school and begin receiving adult services, it is very important that they are able to clearly advocate for themselves and demonstrate abilities to take a leadership role in planning and describing their own abilities and plans. Supporting deaf adolescents in assuming an increasing role would simultaneously encourage a positive parent–school relationship.

Resilience Research at the Mesosystem Level

Research on resilience has found that children's positive relationships with their family members and members of their social network, which included supportive relationships with teachers, promotes resilience (Jaffee, Caspi, Moffit, Polo-Tomás, & Taylor, 2007). This reinforces the importance of positive relationships across key settings. These authors also indicate that children identified as resilient at one point in time may not be considered as such at a later point in time. Therefore, it is important to continue to monitor and support resilience across the developmental span. They also found that exposure to multiple family and neighborhood stressors increased children's risk of being non-resilient, regardless of other factors with special importance given to the interactions among risk and protective factors within the individual's context (Jaffee et al., 2007). Schweiger and O'Brien (2005) found that the quality of parent–child relationships affected the child's school adjustment and peer relationships. Again, this demonstrates the interrelatedness of developmental factors and processes within and across key settings.

Another study used Bronfenbrenner's model with interviews done with adolescent males in a correctional facility. Feinstein, Baartman, Buboltz, Sonnichsen, and Solomon (2008) found that these programs could build internal resiliency such as a positive identity and future expectations. External program factors that contributed to adolescent resiliency were consistency, structure, support, and good relationships with the adults in their lives. This suggests that the same qualities are important for families and schools.

Exosystem

This level examines events and characteristics across settings that indirectly affect the child's primary settings, such as parental support from the school and social networks, the influence of parents of the students' friends, work site stress that affects the parents, or events at siblings' schools or with their teachers. These are relationships that do not involve the child directly such as parental relationships with school personnel.

One example is research that has demonstrated how poor family relationships with schools can have both direct and indirect impacts on the child. A study by Calderon, Bargones, and Sidman (1998) found that 28% of families with a deaf child reported changing residences to be closer to adequate services. These were the result of direct effects (when the child receives services that parents feel are inadequate) as well as indirect effects (when the parents believe the identified services will be inadequate). This also shows how effects may occur across and among levels, in this case across mesosystem (direct effects) and exosystem (indirect effects) levels. Another indirect relationship can be seen in work by Zaidman-Zait (2007) and Zaidman-Zait and Young (2008) who conducted studies with parents of deaf children. Parents described professionals as instrumental in supporting their sense of competence in interacting with their deaf child and in supporting successful coping experiences (Zaidman-Zait, 2007; Zaidman-Zait & Young, 2008). Acquiring these interaction and coping skills would ultimately improve their relationship with their deaf child.

Other indirect effects are shown in a study by Hintermair (2000) that found parents of German deaf children who had strong social networks had several more positive child outcomes. Those who frequently contacted other parents of deaf children showed stronger attachment with, and acceptance of, their child and a close, trusting relationship with their child. They also had less social isolation and demonstrated improved responsivity to their child. Parents who had many contacts with Deaf adults reported less depression and a greater sense of competence. Both also reduced social isolation and increased interactional responsivity to their child. It is interesting that only 9.5% of parents reported frequent contact with Deaf adults, although 27.2% had frequent contact with other parents.

A number of studies have found positive exosystem effects of social networks. Bronfenbrenner (2005) described three studies by Crockenberg (1981, 1985, 1987) that found positive effects of social networks on mother–infant interactions finding the amount and type of supports that could be important factors. Steinberg, Darling, and Fletcher (1995) found that networks of families and degree of social integration of neighborhoods could have important impacts and not always positive. Socially integrated neighborhoods with a high proportion of poor parents had a harmful effect on adolescents' school performance and their behavior.

Few studies of resilience have specifically examined exosystem relationships, although Swick and Williams (2006) described the stress of parents' work as negatively impacting their relationships within the family. They also described a number of issues that cross multiple levels, including the exosystem: parental drug abuse and chemical dependency, and parental violence which often is the result of influences prior to the child's birth, both of which are maintained through multiple levels of influence. Homelessness also is typically the result of external conditions but which substantially impact family and child relationships (Swick & Williams, 2006).

Macrosystem

This level examines how larger cultural and national belief systems impact the developing person. This would include governmental policies and procedures as well as how subcultures, such as deaf culture, are viewed by larger cultural entities. The greater acceptance of ASL as a language and as appropriate for educational programs, the greater positive visibility of deaf people and deaf culture, and the growing use of cochlear implants all impact families at this level. Recent legislation includes the Newborn Screening act as well as recent funding cuts to schools, state agencies, and support services that work with the children or the families of deaf children.

Cultural norms and values and how ethnically diverse families and adolescents negotiate differences between their native and national expectations have impacts throughout the other three levels of the ecological model. Research showing poorer academic results, tracking of diverse students, and lower rates of success for the individual (cf. Allen, 1994; Harmon et al., 1998; Karchmer & Mitchell, 2003; Schildroth et al., 1991; Wheeler-Scruggs, 2002, 2003) reflects multiple interactions across the ecological levels. The task of addressing cultural differences also means that no one single ecological level can be targeted without also accounting for key influences from other levels that may be maintaining majority control. Much of an adolescent's and family's vision of his or her future will have strong cultural foundations beginning with perceptions of hearing loss: identity of the adolescent as a deaf person and/or as a member first of the cultural majority or minority, the support of the family in these identities, and the level of ongoing involvement and attachment to the developing young adult. Culturally inclusive/exclusive and supportive/suppressive definitions of successful adulthood across the family, school, neighborhood, community, and across all of their interactions will either encourage or discourage continued student and family involvement in the school-based planning processes and ultimately their outcomes (Luft, 2008).

Using the ecological model to examine deaf adolescents' resilience has identified the importance of families, schools, neighborhoods, and communities as the building blocks of later success. This suggests that home schools serve as an optimal environment for working within the local settings, with which they would be familiar. However, if these schools have little or no understanding or expertise in working with deaf students and their families, it is unlikely they would be sensitive to the factors and processes that are uniquely important to this group. In contrast, specialized and residential schools are likely to have the expertise but neither frequent access to nor knowledge about the adolescent and family's local community and setting factors. This suggests the importance of building relationships across these settings: direct mesosystem relationships with key personnel and family members, indirect exosystem relationships with administrators and state-level coordinators that will promote supportive organizational structures, and overarching macrosystem values that invest in children and families' critical settings and encourage cross-district and mixed-funding collaboration. It is a positive finding that small effects made early in life can have important lifelong consequences (Roberts et al., 2007). Thus, small changes that impact multiple levels may have long-lasting and far-reaching effects.

These research results are summarized in Fig. 12.3 across the four levels of the ecological system. Each of the factors within each level has a mutual and reciprocal interrelationship with every other variable in the level. The broad arrows at each level indicate that all factors combine to support and impact the next level; thus, the macrosystem factors influence all of the exosystem factors, which influence all of the mesosytem variables and which ultimately impact all of the microsystem variables.

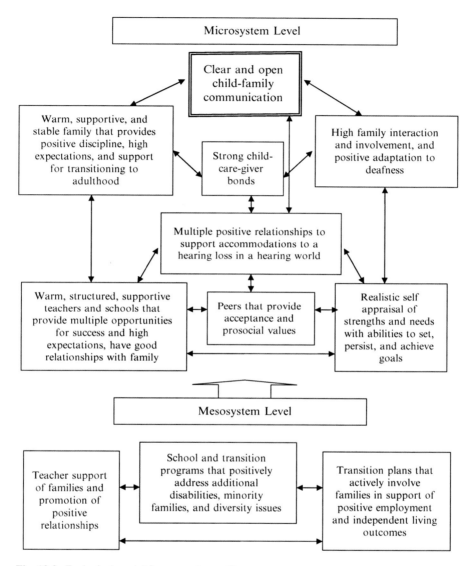

Fig. 12.3 Ecological model for promoting resilience

Implementing the Ecological Resilience Model

This model can be used to identify and conceptualize ways to support and activate an adolescent and his or her family's resilience and to address specific risk factors such as identified in Fig. 12.1. Once risk factors and their potential interrelationships are identified, planning should similarly identify multiple processes and levels

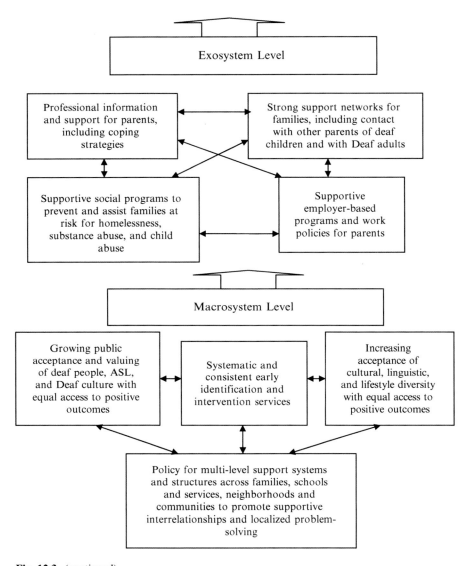

Fig. 12.3 (continued)

in order to thoroughly address and support the creation of strong, positively focused factors and interrelationships (Bronfenbrenner, 1988, 1992).

One way to evaluate potential risks is through comparison with developmental norms. Deaf children with normal cognitive abilities should perform within the normal range for most language and academic skills. This chapter's review of transition and employment outcomes identified assumption of household responsibilities, independent living, financial self-sufficiency, and obtaining work benefits as areas in which deaf young adults did not perform comparably to higher functioning students with disabilities. These also offer comparisons that suggest risk factors.

An example in utilizing the ecological resilience model (Fig. 12.3) is to address risk factors posed by limited communication between family members and the deaf adolescent. Figure 12.1 identifies poor communication as linked to poor academic outcomes in high school and beyond, as well as creating an incomplete means for shaping an adult identity or understanding oneself and the developmental changes of adolescence. Figures 12.2 and 12.3 suggest clear family communication, warm supportive family interactions, positive adaptation to deafness, and strong caregiver bonds as key factors for supporting resilience and for maximizing the deaf adolescent's transition outcomes. A multilevel intervention approach would concurrently address the microsystem relationships, with supportive networks from the mesosystem and exosystem levels. The family should identify opportunities for increased communication and ways to remove current barriers. Activities could include discussing homework, future plans, and also address setting clear and consistent parental expectations with follow-up monitoring. Mesosystem supports would examine strengthening school–family and community–family links and training opportunities to address communication barriers using teachers, extended family, and community activities. Exosystem supports would examine ways to enhance or expand parents' networking opportunities with other parents of deaf children of all ages and to meet or work with Deaf community members or mentors. Such a system of interventions would utilize successes in one area to encourage persistence in other areas that may pose greater challenges.

Another example utilizing the ecological resilience model is to address the challenges posed by the size and diversity of the deaf adolescent population. There often are limited specialized resources for deaf adolescents, particularly for the 85% who attend public school programs. Applying a multilevel approach would identify available school and community programs and individual adolescent and family resources as well. This is likely to yield a much broader range of supports and options, including further networking opportunities with other agencies or community services. Families may have relatives or friends who can provide work experiences, career, or training information. Family involvement in transition planning can result in greater adolescent assumption of household duties and self-care.

Ethnic communities often have their own supports and resources that can be very helpful (Luft, 2008). They may also know of vocational and employment opportunities and encourage responsibilities of contributing to the community. In addition, many residential schools offer outreach and support services across the state that can help provide expertise that local public schools do not have (Stinson & Kluwin, 2003). Transition planning (IDIEA, 2004) requires that all key individuals be present at annual meetings providing a legislated opportunity to plan multilevel interventions. In addition, it allows the adolescent and family to begin forming trusting relationships with key individuals who will be important in adult agencies and settings as they move out of the high school setting and into new microsystems.

Conclusion

This chapter has described a number of risk factors, resiliency factors, and a multilevel model for promoting resilience and result in positive transition outcomes. Although the chapter's figures were based on existing research, one substantial area of need is to research the success of such a comprehensive model. This is a significant challenge, for although we can conceptualize the multidirectional influences with direct and indirect effects, statistical analyses such as structural equation modeling and path analyses do not allow for multiple interactions between variables (Bronfenbrenner, 1988). Therefore, we are still limited to researching pieces of such a model, although professionals now recognize the multiple factors that result in most life outcomes. Much of the research reviewed in this chapter addressed single or multiple factors leading to single outcomes making firm conclusions about multilevel effects unattainable at this point.

One important area of research is identifying multiple intervention paths that result in improved outcomes. For example, Steinberg et al. (1995) found differential effects of authoritative parenting on adolescents' academic achievement that varied by ethnicity. African American and Asian American youths did not benefit from authoritative parenting in the ways that other groups did. The deaf adolescent population is very diverse, and similarly we must never assume just one path to a positive outcome. The ecological resilience model helps to ensure that multiple pathways are always considered and present.

Another very important area of research is on optimizing relationships between families and service providers. Trusting, warm, and supportive relationships between family members and schools have been found to be important antecedents of positive outcomes for children (Masten et al., 2008). Research-supported strategies that professions can utilize when facing challenging situations are needed, including multiple strategies to address diverse families and their life circumstances. Swick and Williams (2006) recommended that early childhood professionals first understand families and the situations they are experiencing, across the multiple levels and complexities that impact their lives. They recommended that professionals engage in the following five practices to:

1. Help families develop caring and loving microsystems.
2. Help families to become more empowered across exosystems (sites indirect influence).
3. Nurture in families ways to help them use mesosystems to better respond to stressors they face.
4. Advocate for stronger family support strategies in the macrosystem contexts.
5. Help families learn from their personal, family, societal, and historical lives in using local resources.

Building strong relationships with families helps schools and agencies build strong relationships within families, which remain of primary importance throughout a deaf child's adolescence. Research suggests that these result in improved transition outcomes for deaf adolescents. Masten and Obradović (2006) describe the interconnected systems of families, schools, and neighborhoods as key factors in promotion resilience in children. Their work has identified several key adaptive systems and individual factors that encourage resilience across the four levels of the ecological model:

Cognitive learning systems: Problem solving, information processing
Mastery motivation system: Self-efficacy processes, reward systems related to successful behavior
Stress response system: Fear or alarm and recovery systems
Self-regulation systems: Emotional regulation, executive functioning, activation and inhibition of attention
Attachment system: Close relationships with caregivers, friends, romantic partners, and spiritual figures
Family system: Parenting, interpersonal dynamics, expectations, cohesion, rituals, and norms
School system: Teaching, values, standards, and expectations
Peer system: Friendships, peer groups, values, and norms
Cultural and societal systems: Religion, traditions, rituals, values, standards, and laws

Once again, these systems suggest comprehensive research analyses that are currently challenging. Resilience integrates well with an ecological model for analysis. It is neither a single trait nor a solitary process, thereby allowing multiple pathways to facilitate positive attributes and processes (cf. Masten & Obradović, 2006). Yet, because an individual's resilience traits are embedded in cultural, developmental, and historical contexts, they may not be easily recognized. In addition, the presence of several risk factors in a deaf adolescent's and family's environments may mask or lead professionals to overlook factors of resilience. The individual combination of these factors that represent the deaf adolescent's ecological system also is very unique. This means that what has been successful with one set of individuals and settings may not apply successfully to the circumstances of others. In addition, each deaf adolescent will engage in distinctive responses to each person and setting characteristic, and each intervention program we may devise, all of which are mutually interrelated and likely to evolve and change over time. The ecological resilience model's multifactor and multilevel approach encourages a comprehensive approach that will enhance an individual's own characteristics of resilience as well as offer multiple options for creating positive adult outcomes. The unique individual and family ecology is well accommodated in this flexible model.

A very opportune aspect of school programming for deaf adolescents is the IDIEA (2004) legislation that requires family and school approval of annual Individualized Education Plans. The transition mandates in this law require postschool agency representation, which provides a venue for cross-setting and cross-agency collaboration that can increase transition resources and supports (Baer, 2008; IDEIA, 2004). Adolescents and families also have opportunities to form relationships with important postschool personnel from potential postsecondary institutions, with vocational rehabilitation counselors, and with current or future employers. From a resiliency-building perspective, these are occasions of enormous potential for optimizing processes that encourage resiliency and future success. No single setting, program, or agency will have the full complement of resources needed to address the heterogeneous and diverse deaf population. Building from each individual's and agency's strengths is the most cost-effective way to ameliorate shortages. Cross-agency relationships then become the foundation for expanding opportunities across the diverse deaf population and its desired adult living options and outcomes.

It has been a very positive development that deafness and hearing loss is no longer an invisible disability, with a much greater acceptance of deaf individuals as contributing members of society. In addition, the Americans with Disabilities Act (1990) has greatly expanded access to postsecondary and job training, and employment positions with many more options for positive adult outcomes than were available only a few decades earlier. However, the need for English literacy to succeed in an increasingly information- and internet-based world continues to present substantial barriers to deaf individuals who must now compete in the global marketplace. However, increased access to real-time and remote captioning, videophone services, and other technologies are reducing prior barriers to employment and community participation and equalizing access in increasingly pervasive ways.

Adolescence is an ecological transition point for all developing individuals but has particular significance for deaf students. At this time in his or her life, many of the earlier developmental processes and outcomes merge to impact both the possible and practical realities of future adulthood. Many of the risk factors, if left unaddressed, may become substantial and lifelong barriers. However, maturational processes will not cease upon high school graduation or leaving. Although academic and employment success will become the consequence of childhood developmental processes, they also serve as an initiator of adult development. Ongoing biological and internal changes will interact with new settings, environmental conditions, and persons within these new settings to continually influence the deaf young adult. From the research and models provided in this chapter, it is hoped that this will result in insights into the factors and processes that promote and optimize factors of resiliency that will serve deaf adolescents through the rest of their life.

References

Allen, T. E. (1994). *Who are the deaf and hard-of-hearing students leaving high school and entering postsecondary education?* Paper submitted to Pelavin Research Institute, A Comprehensive Evaluation of the Postsecondary Educational Opportunities for Students who are Deaf or Hard of Hearing, funded by the U.S. Office of Special Education and Rehabilitative Services. Retrieved from http://www.gallaudet.edu/~cadsweb/whodeaf.html
Allen, T., Rawlings, B., & Schildroth, A. (1989). *Deaf students and the school-to-work transition.* Baltimore, MD: Paul H. Brookes.

Americans with Disabilities Act of 1990, 42 U.S.C.A. § 12101 et seq.

Baer, R. (2008). Transition planning. In R. W. Flexer, R. M. Baer, P. Luft, & T. J. Simmons (Eds.), *Transition planning for secondary students with disabilities* (3rd ed., pp. 317–339). Upper Saddle River, NJ: Pearson.

Bailes, C. N. (1999). Deaf-centric teaching. In L. Bragg (Ed.), *Deaf world: A historical reader and primary sourcebook* (pp. 211–233). New York: New York University Press.

Barker, D. H., Quittner, A. L., Fink, N. E., Eisenberg, L. S., Tobey, E. A., & Niparko, J. K. (2009). Predicting behavior problems in deaf and hearing children: The influences of language, attention, and parent–child communication. *Development and Psychopathology, 21*, 373–392.

Bat-Chava, Y., Rosen, R. B., Sausa, A., Meza, C., Shockett, S., & Deignan, E. (1999). An evaluation of a college preparatory and readiness program for deaf students. *Journal of Rehabilitation, 65*, 51–59.

Bernstein, D. K., & Levey, S. (2002). Language development: A review. In D. K. Bernstein & E. Tiegerman-Farber (Eds.), *Language and communication disorders in children* (5th ed., pp. 27–94). Boston: Allyn & Bacon.

Bodner-Johnson, B. (1986). The family environment and achievement of deaf students: A discriminant analysis. *Exceptional Children, 52*, 443–449.

Bosso, E. (2008). Testing, accountability, and equity for deaf students in Delaware. In R. C. Johnson & R. E. Mitchell (Eds.), *Testing deaf students in an age of accountability* (pp. 167–180). Washington, DC: Gallaudet University Press.

Bowe, F. G. (2003). Transition for deaf and hard-of-hearing students: A blueprint for change. *Journal of Deaf Studies and Deaf Education, 8*, 485–493.

Bowe, F. G. (2004). Economics and adults identified as low-functioning deaf. *Journal of Disability Policy Studies, 15*, 43–49.

Brendtro, L. K. (2006). The vision of Urie Bronfenbrenner: Adults who are crazy about kids. *Reclaiming Children and Youth, 15*, 162–166.

Bronfenbrenner, U. (1976). *The ecology of human development.* Cambridge, MA: Harvard University Press.

Bronfenbrenner, U. (1988). Interacting systems in human development. Research paradigms: Present and future. In N. Bolger, A. Caspi, G. Dowey, & M. Morehouse (Eds.), *Persons in context: Developmental processes* (pp. 25–49). New York: Cambridge University Press.

Bronfenbrenner, U. (1989). *The developing ecology of human development: Paradigm lost or paradigm regained.* Paper presented at the Biennial Meeting of the Society for Research in Child Development, Kansas City, Missouri, April 27–30.

Bronfenbrenner, U. (1992). Ecological systems theory. In R. Vasta (Ed.), *Six theories of child development: Revised formulations and current issues* (pp. 187–249). London: Jessica Kingsley.

Bronfenbrenner, U. (1999). Environments in developmental perspective: Theoretical and operational models. In S. L. Friedman & T. D. Wachs (Eds.), *Measuring environment across the life span: Emerging methods and concepts.* Washington, DC: American Psychological Association.

Bronfenbrenner, U. (2001). The bioecological theory of human development. In N. J. Smelser & P. B. Baltes (Eds.), *International encyclopedia of the social and behavioral sciences* (Vol. 10, pp. 6973–6970). New York: Elsevier.

Bronfenbrenner, U. (2005). *Making human beings human: Bioecological perspectives on human development.* Thousand Oaks, CA: Sage.

Bull, B., & Bullis, M. (1991). A national profile of school-based transition programs for deaf adolescents. *American Annals of the Deaf, 136*, 339–348.

Bullis, M., Bull, B., Johnson, B., & Peters, D. (1995). The school-to-community transition experiences of hearing young adults and young adults who are deaf. *Journal of Special Education, 28*, 405–423.

Calderon, R., Bargones, J., & Sidman, S. (1998). Characteristics of hearing families and their young deaf and hard of hearing children: Early intervention follow-up. *American Annals of the Deaf, 143*, 347–342.

Carlson, E., Chen, L., Schroll, K., & Schein, S. (2003). *SPeNSE (study of personnel needs in special education): Final report of the paperwork substudy*. Washington, DC: U.S. Department of Education. Retrieved September 24, 2008, from http://Ferdig.coe.ufl.edu/spense/Finalpaperworkreport3-24-031.doc

Charlson, E., Bird, R. L., & Strong, M. (1999). Resilience and success among deaf high school students: Three case studies. *American Annals of the Deaf, 144*, 226–235.

Crockenberg, S. B. (1981). Infant irritability, mother responsiveness, and social support influences on the security of infant–mother attachment. *Child Development, 52*, 857–865.

Crockenberg, S. B. (1985). Professional support and care of infants by adolescent mothers in England and the United States. *Journal of Pediatric Psychology, 10*, 413–428.

Crockenberg, S. B. (1987). Support for adolescent mothers during the postnatal period: Theory and research. In C. F. Z. Boukydis (Ed.), *Research on support for parents and infants in the postnatal period* (pp. 3–34). Westport, CT: Ablex.

Easterbrooks, S. R., & Baker, S. (2002). *Language learning in children who are deaf and hard of hearing: Multiple pathways*. Boston: Allyn & Bacon.

El-Khiami, A. (1993). Employment transitions and establishing careers by postsecondary alumni with hearing loss. *Volta Review, 95*, 357–366.

Feinstein, S., Baartman, J., Buboltz, M., Sonnichsen, K., & Solomon, R. (2008). Resiliency in adolescent males in a correctional facility. *Journal of Correctional Education, 59*, 94–105.

Friedmann, N., & Szterman, R. (2005). Syntactic movement in orally trained children with hearing impairment. *Journal of Deaf Studies and Deaf Education, 11*(1), 56–75.

Gallaudet Research Institute. (2008). *Regional and national summary report of data from the 2007–08 annual survey of deaf and hard of hearing children and youth*. Washington, DC: GRI, Gallaudet University. Retrieved August 8, 2009, from http://gri.gallaudet.edu/Demographics/2008_National_Summary.pdf

Geers, A. E., & Moog, J. S. (Eds.) (1994). Effectiveness of cochlear implants and tactile aides for deaf children: The sensory aids study at Central Institute for the Deaf. *Volta Review, 96*, 1–231.

Goodnow, J. J. (2006). Research and policy: Second looks at views of development, families, and communities, and at translations into practice. In A. Clarke-Stewart & J. Dunn (Eds.), *Families count: Effects on child and adolescent development: The Jacobs Foundation series on adolescence* (pp. 337–360). Cambridge: Cambridge University Press.

Granic, I., Dishion, T. J., & Hollenstein, T. (2003). The family ecology of adolescence: A dynamic systems perspective on normative development. In G. R. Adams & M. D. Berzonsky (Eds.), *Blackwell handbook of adolescence* (pp. 60–91). Malden, MA: Blackwell Publishing.

Halpern, A. S., Doren, B., & Benz, M. R. (1993). Job experiences of students with disabilities during their last two years in school. *Career Development for Exceptional Individuals, 16*, 63–73.

Harmon, M., Carr, N., & Johnson, T. (1998). *Services to low functioning deaf and hard of hearing persons*. 1998 PEPNet Conference Proceedings: Empowerment Through Partnerships. April 29–May 2, 1998. Retrieved September 28, 2008, from http://www.pepnet.org/confpast/1998/pdf/harmon.pdf

Harney, P. A. (2007). Resilience processes in context: Contributions and implications of Bronfenbrenner's person–process–context model. *Journal of Aggression, Maltreatment, and Trauma, 14*, 73–87.

Heal, L. W., Gonzalez, P., Rusch, F. R., Copher, J. I., & DeStefano, L. (1990). A comparison of successful and unsuccessful placements of youths with mental handicaps into competitive employment. *Exceptionality, 1*, 181–196.

Hintermair, J. (2000). Hearing impairment, social networks, and coping: The need for families with hearing-impaired children to relate to other parents and to hearing-impaired adults. *American Annals of the Deaf, 145*, 41–53.

Hoff, D., & Holsapple, M. (2009, March). Maintaining a focus on employment in tough economic times. *Community Services Reporter (CSR)*, monthly newsletter of the National Association of

State Directors of Developmental Disability Services (NASDDDS), Retrieved October 7, 2010, from http://www.nasddds.org/pdf/MaintainingFocusOnEmployment.pdf

Hudson, P. J., Schwartz, S. E., Sealander, K. A., Campbell, P., & Hensel, J. W. (1988). Successfully employed adults with handicaps: Characteristics and transition strategies. *Career Development for Exceptional Individuals, 11*, 7–14.

Individuals with Disabilities Education Improvement Act of 2004 (IDIEA), 20 U.S.C. § 1400.

Jackson, C. W., & Turnbull, A. (2004). Impact of deafness on family life: A review of the literature. *Topics in Early Childhood Special Education, 24*, 15–29.

Jaffee, S. R., Caspi, A., Moffit, T. E., Polo-Tomás, M., & Taylor, A. (2007). Individual, family, and neighborhood factors distinguish resilient from non-resilient maltreated children: A cumulative stressors model. *Child Abuse and Neglect, 31*, 231–253.

Karchmer, M. A., & Mitchell, R. E. (2003). Demographic and achievement characteristics of deaf and hard-of-hearing students. In M. Marschark & P. E. Spencer (Eds.), *Oxford handbook of deaf studies, language, and education* (pp. 21–37). New York: Oxford University Press.

Kuder, S. J. (2008). *Teaching students with language and communication disabilities*. Boston: Pearson.

Lindstrom, L., Doren, B., Metheny, J., Johnson, P., & Zane, C. (2007). Transition to employment: Role of the family in career development. *Exceptional Children, 73*, 348–366.

Luft, P. (2008). Multicultural and collaborative competencies for working with families. In R. W. Flexer, R. M. Baer, P. Luft, & T. J. Simmons (Eds.), *Transition planning for secondary students with disabilities* (3rd ed., pp. 54–81). Upper Saddle River, NJ: Pearson.

Luft, P., & Huff, K. (in press). How prepared are transition-age DHH students for adult living? Results of the transition competency battery. *American Annals of the Deaf.*

Lundy, J. D. B. (2002). Age and language skills of deaf children in relation to theory of mind development. *Journal of Deaf Studies and Deaf Education, 7*, 41–56.

Marschark, M. (2000). Education and development of deaf children – Or is it development and education? In P. E. Spencer, C. J. Erting, & M. Marschark (Eds.), *The deaf child in the family and at school: Essays in honor of Kathryn P. Meadow-Orlans* (pp. 275–291). Mahwah, NJ: Lawrence Erlbaum Associates.

Marschark, M., Rhoten, C., & Fabich, M. (2007). Effects of cochlear implants on children's reading and academic achievement. *Journal of Deaf Studies and Deaf Education, 12*, 269–282.

Masten, A. S., Herbers, J. E., Cutuli, J. J., & Lafavor, T. L. (2008). Promoting competence and resilience in the school context. *Professional School Counseling, 12*, 76–84.

Masten, A. S., & Obradović, J. (2006). Competence and resilience in development. *Annals New York Academy of Sciences, 1094*, 13–27.

Masten, A. S., & Shaffer, A. (2006). How families matter in child development: Reflections from research on risk and resilience. In A. Clarke-Stewart & J. Dunn (Eds.), *Families count: Effects on child and adolescent development* (pp. 5–25). Cambridge: Cambridge University Press.

Mayberry, R. I. (1993). First-language acquisition after childhood differs from second-language acquisition: The case of American Sign Language. *Journal of Speech and Hearing Research, 36*, 51–68.

Mayne, A. M. (1998). Expressive vocabulary development of infants and toddlers who are deaf or hard of hearing. *Volta Review, 100*, 1–28.

Meadow, K. (1968). Early manual communication in relation to the deaf child's intellectual, social, and communicative functioning. *American Annals of the Deaf, 113*, 29–41.

Meadow-Orlans, K., Mertens, D., Sass-Lehrer, M., & Scott-Olson, K. (1997). Support services for parents and their children who are deaf or hard of hearing: A national survey. *American Annals of the Deaf, 142*, 278–293.

Meyer, T. A., Svirsky, M. A., Kirk, K. I., & Miyamoto, R. T. (1998). Improvements in speech perception by children with profound hearing loss: Effects of device, communication mode, and chronological age. *Journal of Speech, Language, and Hearing Research, 41*, 846–858.

Moeller, M. P. (2000). Early intervention and language development in children who are deaf and hard of hearing. *Pediatrics, 106*, 1–9.

Moeller, M. P., & Schick, B. (2006). Relations between maternal input and theory of mind understanding in deaf children. *Child Development, 77*, 751–766.

Moore, C. L. (2001). Disparities in job placement outcomes among deaf, late-deafened, and hard-of-hearing consumers. *Rehabilitation Counseling Bulletin, 44*, 144–150.

Moore, C. L. (2002). Relationship of consumer characteristics and service provision to income of successfully rehabilitated individuals who are deaf. *Rehabilitation Counseling Bulletin, 45*, 233–239.

Moore, P. (2008). The potential harm to deaf students of high stakes testing in California. In R. C. Johnson & R. E. Mitchell (Eds.), *Testing deaf students in an age of accountability* (p. 181). Washington, DC: Gallaudet University Press.

Moores, D. F. (2001). *Educating the deaf: Psychology, principles, and practices* (5th ed.). Boston: Houghton Mifflin.

National Longitudinal Transition Study 2. (2003). *NLTS2 data tables*. Retrieved August 5, 2009, from http://www.nlts2.org/data_tables/index.html

Newcomer, P., & Hammill, D. (1977). *Test of language development-primary 3*. Austin, TX: Pro-Ed.

Newman, L. (2005). *Family involvement in the educational development of youth with disabilities*. A special topic report of findings from the National Longitudinal Transition Study-2 (NLTS2). Menlo Park, CA: SRI International. Retrieved July 17, 2009, from http://www.nlts2.org/reports/2005_03/index.html

Newman, L., Wagner, M., Cameto, R., & Knokey, A.-M. (2009). *The post-high school outcomes of youth with disabilities up to 4 years after high school. A report from the National Longitudinal Transition Study-2 (NLTS2)*. Washington, DC: Institute of Educational Sciences, National Center for Special Education Research, U.S. Department of Education. Retrieved August 2, 2009, from http://www.nlts2.org/reports/2009_04/index.html

No Child Left Behind Act of 2001, P.L. 107-110, Title IX, Sec 9101 (23) (A&B).

OSEP/Westat. (2007). *Annual report tables (IDEA)*. Washington, DC: Author. Retrieved March 6, 2009, from (IDEAdata.org) https://www.ideadata.org/arc_toc9.asp#partbLRE

Prinz, P. M., & Strong, M. (1998). ASL proficiency and English literacy within a bilingual deaf education model of instruction. *Topics in Language Disorders, 18*, 47–60.

Punch, R., Hyde, M., & Creed, P. A. (2004). Issues in the school-to-work transition of hard of hearing adolescents. *American Annals of the Deaf, 149*, 28–38.

Quigley, S. P., & Paul, P. V. (1984). *Language and deafness*. San Diego: College-Hill Press.

Roberts, B. W., Kuncel, N. R., Shiner, R., Caspi, A., & Goldberg, L. R. (2007). The power of personality: The comparative validity of personality traits, socioeconomic status, and cognitive ability for predicting important life outcomes. *Perspectives on Psychological Science, 2*, 313–345.

Rodgers, J. L., & Bard, D. E. (2003). Behavior genetics and adolescent development: A review of recent literature. In G. R. Adams & M. D. Berzonsky (Eds.), *Blackwell handbook of adolescence* (pp. 3–23). Malden, MA: Blackwell Publishing.

Rutter, M. (2006). The promotion of resilience in the face of adversity. In A. Clarke-Stewart & J. Dunn (Eds.), *Families count: Effects on child and adolescent development: The Jacobs Foundation series on adolescence* (pp. 26–52). Cambridge: Cambridge University.

Schalock, R. L., Wolzen, B., Ross, I., Elliott, B., Werbel, G., & Peterson, K. (1986). Postsecondary community placement of handicapped students: A five-year follow-up. *Learning Disabilities Quarterly, 9*, 295–303.

Scheetz, N. A. (2004). *Psychosocial aspects of deafness*. Boston, MA: Pearson/Allyn & Bacon.

Schildroth, A., Rawlings, B., & Allen, T. (1991). Deaf students in transition: Education and employment issues for deaf adolescents. *The Volta Review, 93*, 41–53. Retrieved from http://www.gallaudet.edu/~cadsweb/transiti.html.

Schirmer, B. R. (2001). *Psychological, social, and educational dimensions of deafness*. Needham Heights, MA: Allyn & Bacon.

Schroedel, J. G., & Geyer, P. D. (2000). Long-term career attainments of deaf and hard of hearing college graduates: Results from a 15-year follow-up survey. *American Annals of the Deaf, 145*, 303–314.

Schroedel, J. G., Watson, D., & Ashmore, D. H. (2003). A national research agenda for the post-secondary education of deaf and hard of hearing students: A road map for the future. *American Annals of the Deaf, 148*, 67–73.

Schweiger, W. K., & O'Brien, M. (2005). Special needs adoption: An ecological systems approach. *Family Relations, 54*, 512–522.

Sheridan, M. A. (2000). Images of self and others: Stories from the children. In P. E. Spencer, C. J. Erting, & M. Marshark (Eds.), *The deaf child in the family and at school: Essays in honor of Kathryn P. Meadow-Orlans* (pp. 5–19). Mahwah, NJ: Lawrence Erlbaum Associates.

Singleton, J. L., Supalla, S., Litchfield, S., & Schley, S. (1998). From sign to word: Considering modality constraints in ASL/English bilingual education. *Topics in Language Disorders, 18*, 16–29.

Steinberg, A. (2000). Autobiographical narrative on growing up deaf. In P. E. Spencer, C. J. Erting, & M. Marschark (Eds.), *The deaf child in the family and at school: Essays in honor of Kathryn P. Meadow-Orlans* (pp. 93–108). Hillsdale, NJ: Lawrence Erlbaum Associates.

Steinberg, L., Darling, N. E., & Fletcher, A. C. (1995). Authoritative parenting and adolescent adjustment: An ecological journey. In P. Moen, G. H. Elder Jr., & K. L scher (Eds.), *Examining lives in context: Perspectives on the ecology of human development* (pp. 423–466). Washington, DC: American Psychological Association.

Stinson, M. S., & Kluwin, T. N. (2003). Educational consequences of alternative school placements. In M. Marschark & P. E. Spencer (Eds.), *Oxford handbook of deaf studies, language, and education* (pp. 52–64). New York: Oxford University Press.

Swick, K. J., & Williams, R. D. (2006). An analysis of Bronfenbrenner's bio-ecological perspective of early childhood educators: Implications for working with families experiencing stress. *Early Childhood Education Journal, 33*, 371–378.

Traxler, C. B. (2000). The Stanford Achievement Test, 9th edition: National norming and performance standards for deaf and hard-of-hearing students. *Journal of Deaf Studies and Deaf Education, 5*, 337–348.

U.S. Department of Education. (2002). *Twenty-sixth annual report to Congress on the implementation of the Individuals with Disabilities Education Act*. Washington, DC: author. Retrieved July 27, 2009, from http://www.ed.gov/about/reports/annual/osep/2002/index.html

U.S. Department of Education, Office of Special Education Programs. (1995). *Seventeenth annual report to Congress on the implementation of the individuals with disabilities education act*. Washington, DC: Author. Retrieved from http://www.ed.gov/pubs/OSEP95AnlRpt/index.html

Valdes, K. A., Williamson, C. L., & Wagner, M. M. (1990). *The national longitudinal transition study of special education students. Statistical almanac, volume 7: Youth categorized as hearing impaired*. Washington, DC: SRI International, prepared for the Office of Special Education.

Vernon, M., & Koh, S. D. (1970). Effects of early manual communication on achievement of deaf children. *American Annals of the Deaf, 115*, 527–536.

Wagner, M. (2005). *Chapter 7: The leisure activities, social involvement, and citizenship of youth with disabilities after high school. After high school: A first look at the postschool experiences of youth with disabilities: A report from the National Longitudinal Transition Study-2 (NLTS2)*. Washington, DC: Institute of Educational Sciences, National Center for Special Education Research, U.S. Department of Education. Retrieved August 2, 2009, from http://www.nlts2.org/reports/2005_04/index.html

Wagner, M., Newman, L., Cameto, R., Garza, N., & Levine, P. (2005). *After high school: A first look at the postschool experiences of youth with disabilities: A report from the National Longitudinal Transition Study-2 (NLTS2)*. Washington, DC: Institute of Educational Sciences, National Center for Special Education Research, U.S. Department of Education. Retrieved August 2, 2009, from http://www.nlts2.org/reports/2005_04/index.html

Wagner, M., Newman, L., Cameto, R., & Levine, P. (2006). *The achievement and functional performance of youth with disabilities: A report from the National Longitudinal Transition*

Study-2 (NLTS2). Washington, DC: Institute of Educational Sciences, National Center for Special Education Research, U.S. Department of Education. Retrieved August 2, 2009, from http://www.nlts2.org/reports/2006_07/index.html

Wandry, D. L., Webb, K. W., Williams, J. M., Bassett, D. S., Asselin, S. B., & Hutchinson, S. R. (2008). Teacher candidates' perceptions of barriers to effective transition planning. *Career Development for Exceptional Individuals, 31*, 14–25.

Wheeler-Scruggs, K. (2002). Assessing the employment and independence of people who are deaf and low functioning. *American Annals of the Deaf, 147*, 11–17.

Wheeler-Scruggs, K. (2003). Discerning characteristics and risk factors of people who are deaf and low functioning. *Journal of Rehabilitation, 69*, 39–46.

Whiston, S. D., & Keller, B. K. (2004). The influences of the family of origin on career development: A review and analysis. *Counseling Psychologist, 32*, 493–568.

Young, A., Green, L., & Rogers, K. (2008). Resilience and deaf children: A literature review. *Deafness and Education International, 10*, 40–55.

Zaidman-Zait, A. (2007). Parenting a child with a cochlear implant: A critical incident study. *Journal of Deaf Studies and Deaf Education, 12*, 221–241.

Zaidman-Zait, A., & Young, R. A. (2008). Parental involvement in the habilitation process following children's cochlear implantation: An action theory perspective. *Journal of Deaf Studies and Deaf Education, 13*, 55–59.

Part V
Emerging Adulthood

Chapter 13
Self-Efficacy in the Management of Anticipated Work–Family Conflict as a Resilience Factor Among Young Deaf Adults

Rinat Michael, Tova Most, and Rachel Gali Cinamon

Abstract Various studies have shown ties between different types of self-efficacy and resilient behaviors. The belief in one's ability to manage anticipated work–family conflict is a recent studied type of self-efficacy. This self-efficacy has been found to be a central key of young people's career development. However, it has been examined mainly among normal developed participants. The current chapter discusses the concept of anticipated work–family conflict management self-efficacy, presents results from a study conducted on deaf young adults and offers suggestions for intervention directed for the enhancement of this type of self-efficacy among deaf people.

Abbreviations

F→W	Family to work
HH	Hard of hearing
SCCT	Social cognitive career theory
W→F	Work to family
WFC	Work–family conflict
WFF	Work–family facilitation

R. Michael (✉)
Department of Counseling and Special Education, School of Education,
Tel Aviv University, Tel Aviv, Israel
e-mail: freskori@post.tau.ac.il

D.H. Zand and K.J. Pierce (eds.), *Resilience in Deaf Children: Adaptation Through Emerging Adulthood*, DOI 10.1007/978-1-4419-7796-0_13,
© Springer Science+Business Media, LLC 2011

Introduction

Self-efficacy is a belief in one's ability to perform specific tasks. Such a belief helps determine individuals' willingness to initiate specific behaviors, as well as their persistence and emotional reactions when confronting barriers and conflicts (Bandura, 1986). In other words, perceived self-efficacy makes a difference in how people feel, think, and act (Bandura, 1997). Self-efficacy can be defined as an appraisal of how well one can execute the course of action required to deal with a specific prospective situation – how well one can cope with a situation. Self-efficacy judgments influence choice of activity, amount of effort expended, and persistence in the face of obstacles or adverse experiences (Lent, Brown, & Hackett, 2000).

Thus, it is reasonable that self-efficacy also governs risk and resilience behaviors in various life domains. The role that self-beliefs play in the realm of risk-taking behaviors has been the object of many studies (e.g., Dilorio et al., 2001; Hanson, Downing, Coyle, & Pederson, 2004). In addition, research has shown that self-efficacy beliefs are related to adjustment to a variety of stressful life events (e.g., Chwalisz, Altmaier, & Russell, 1992; Cutrona & Troutman, 1986).

Self-efficacy beliefs were studied in various domains such as academic achievements (e.g., Hackett, Betz, Casas, & Rocha-Singh, 1992) and social relations (e.g., Hagedoorn & Molleman, 2006). One domain which has been receiving growing attention is the domain of career development. Variables such as career choices (Tang, Fouad, & Smith, 1999) and aspirations (Nauta, Epperson, & Kahn, 1998) were found to be related to self-efficacy beliefs. A specific area in the field of career self-efficacy which has not received sufficient attention is the belief in one's ability to manage conflict between work and family roles.

Work and family functioning play a central role in the life of Western society. Changes in the nature of families and the workforce, such as growing numbers of dual career couples and working mothers with young children, have increased the likelihood that male and female employees today have both substantial household obligations as well as major work responsibilities (Allen, Herst, Bruck, & Sutton, 2000; Bond, Galinsky, & Swanberg, 1998). Therefore, these factors are important components in assessing the functioning of persons with disabilities.

Although agreement exists regarding the importance of addressing work–family issues as part of students' career programs (Barnett, Garies, James, & Steele, 2003; Cinamon & Rich, 2004), very little research has been conducted in this area in general and among populations with disabilities in particular. In addition, the critical period of emerging adulthood, when young persons are exposed but not yet committed to different jobs and intimate personal relationships, has not been sufficiently researched with regard to work and family roles and their interrelations (Cinamon, 2006; Friedman & Weissbrod, 2005). The current chapter introduces research on work and family issues among people with disabilities, focusing on the deaf population. The challenging task of blending these two demanding roles will be discussed in relation to self-efficacy as a resilience factor. Practical implications for counseling interventions with young deaf adults will close this chapter.

Disabilities and Work–Family Issues

Work and family play a crucial role in our life. These two roles help to define who we are, they influence what we do, how and with whom we interact, and also what we think and how we feel. Indeed, Freud (1930) contended that success in work and love is the hallmark of mental health. Although his blueprint for success highlights these domains simultaneously, the realms of work and love/family have often been researched separately. This separation of the worlds of work and family is not consistent with the experiences of people whose lives do not conform to neat and tidy boundaries (Blustein, 2001).

Most of the research on the functioning of adults with disabilities focuses on the work domain. The accumulative knowledge indicates that adults with disabilities, in general, exhibit dramatically high rates of unemployment and underemployment (Burkauser & Houtenville, 2003), which can adversely affect economic and social status and self-image. According to developmental theories in the field of vocational psychology, these difficulties start earlier (e.g., Super, 1990), and even at the period of emerging adulthood, young adults with disabilities face challenges in establishing a career. They are often slower in launching a career than their nondisabled counterparts (Benshoff, Kroeger, & Scalia, 1990). Some young adults with disabilities may begin to think of themselves as people of lower worth and less deserving of good jobs and may set their career aims too low (Dipeolu, Reardon, Sampson, & Burkhead, 2002; Lustig, Strauser, & Donnell, 2003; Saunders, Leahy, & Frank, 2000). Inasmuch as individuals with disabilities are less likely to hold part time jobs in their teenage years, they face greater hurdles in testing their skills and abilities (Lustig et al., 2003). Consequently, they tend to be slower in crystallizing their career interests in young adulthood (Shahnasarian, 2001) and demonstrate lower aspiration levels which have a negative impact on their vocational choices (Babbitt & Burbach, 1990; Jones, 1997; Saunders et al., 2000).

Similar results were reported in studies regarding career-related variables in deaf people. They too tend to suffer from higher rates of unemployment and underemployment (e.g., McLeod-Gallinger, 1992; Schroedel & Geyer, 2000). In addition, they often earn less money and have fewer promotion opportunities than their hearing colleagues (Luft, 2000). Schroedel's (1992) review of the literature on deaf individuals' occupational expectations concluded that deaf people had relatively low expectations; they more often indicated that blue-collar jobs were more suitable for them than did hearing persons. Weisel and Cinamon (2005) showed that deaf adolescents expressed biased evaluations of deaf women's competence and did not find highly prestigious occupations as suitable for deaf adults.

The literature on career barriers of deaf people focused mainly on environmental barriers such as background noise in the workplace and telephone requirements (e.g., DeCaro, Mudgett-DeCaro, & Dowaliby, 2001), as well as attitudinal variables such as stigma and discrimination (Punch, Hyde, & Power, 2007). For example, the main vocational obstacles for deaf people, as perceived by employers, were communication difficulties, lack of managerial skills and colleagues' support, and specific skill impairments such as poor reading and writing (Arkansas Rehabilitation Services, 2002). These findings, as well as others, led researchers to the conclusion that environmental and attitudinal barriers contribute to the difficulties experienced by many deaf people in gaining employment and career advancement (e.g., Punch, Hyde, & Creed, 2004).

An additional factor which was taken into account was academic functioning. Many researchers noted that the deaf population tends to have poor academic achievements (e.g., Moores, 1996) and that this fact has significant implications for their further educational options and their ability to compete in the workforce (Arkansas Rehabilitation Services, 2002).

As stated, the accumulative knowledge in the field of career development in general and of people with disabilities in particular lacks a broader perspective, having focused mainly on the work domain, disregarding the family domain and, in particular, the relationship between the two. Such way of inquiry contradicts established and accepted theories emphasizing the mutual influences between social systems (e.g., Bronfenbrenner, 1989; Super, 1990). A wider perspective that investigates these two important and demanding domains simultaneously and the mutual relations between them may be more precise and more suitable for understanding human development in "real life" (Blustein, 2001; Cinamon & Rich, 2002).

Work and Family Relations

Work and family play a major role in the lives of many Western adults who divide their time and energy between these two demanding spheres (Greenhaus & Powell, 2003). Active participation in both work and family may benefit the individual but also might accrue high costs and stress, due to ongoing and, frequently, relentless demands on the individual's time and energy (Cinamon & Rich, 2004). Occupational health researchers commonly cite a widespread effect of this stress: the work–family conflict (Frone, 2003).

Work–family conflict (WFC) comprises a form of interrole conflict in which pressures from work and family roles are incompatible (Greenhaus & Beutell, 1985). Research has shown two types of conflict, each with its own unique domain-specific antecedents and unique negative outcomes: work interfering with family (W→F) and family interfering with work (F→W). Research has consistently demonstrated that W→F conflict surpasses F→W conflict among working adults with families (for a review, see Frone, 2003).

WFC has been associated with a number of dysfunctional outcomes in the work and in the family domains such as work and family dissatisfaction or distress (Carlson & Kacmar, 2000; Frone, Barnes, & Farell, 1994; Frone, Yardley, & Markel, 1997). Research also revealed this conflict's negative correlation with employees' mental health, physical health, and health-related behaviors, and positive correlation with psychological distress (Kirchmeyer & Cohen, 1999; Marks, 1998), self-reported poor physical health (Grzywacz & Marks, 2000), and life dissatisfaction (Netemeyer, Boles, & McMurrian, 1996).

Alongside the conflictual relations between work and family, there are facilitatory aspects as well. Work–family facilitation (WFF) is a less established concept than WFC, going by various labels and definitions. Following Wayne, Musisca, and Fleeson (2004), we define WFC as occurring when, by virtue of participation in one role, performance or functioning in the other role is enhanced. As in WFC, bidirectionality also exists for facilitatory relations. Work can facilitate family life (W→F), and family can facilitate work (F→W) (Wayne et al., 2004). The few existing studies in this area indicated positive outcomes of facilitation such as better mental health (e.g., Grzywacz & Marks, 2000; Hammer, Cullen, Neal, Sinclair, & Shafiro, 2005). Furthermore, studies demonstrated significantly higher levels of F→W facilitation than W→F facilitation (Hammer et al., 2005; Wayne et al., 2004).

The investigation of anticipated work–family relations among adolescents and young adults is a relatively new area of research which is based upon the crucial role of expectations in human behavior (Cinamon, 2006). Studies that investigated work and family plans and expectations reported that young adults are aware of the possibility of future conflict between work and family (Barnett et al., 2003), they differentiate between the two types of conflict (they realize that work can interfere with family, and that family can interfere with work) (Cinamon, 2006), and that conflict expectations influence career plans by reducing vocational aspirations in favor of family plans, or by abandoning family plans in favor of demanding vocational aspirations in order to avoid the expected negative consequences of the conflict (Barnett et al., 2003; Lundgren & Barnett, 2000; Weer, Greenhaus, Colakoglu, & Foley, 2006).

A former study conducted by the authors (Cinamon, Most, & Michael, 2008) investigated hearing and deaf young adults' attributions of importance to both work and family roles and anticipated work–family relations among 101 unmarried young adults aged 20–33 years: 35 with hearing impairments (19 hard of hearing and 16 deaf) and 66 with normal hearing. Results indicated that young adults with hearing impairments are aware of the possibility of future conflict between the domains, and that hearing status was a significant variable in predicting anticipated conflictual relations among all participants. The deaf participants demonstrated a significantly higher level of commitment to work, but anticipated the significantly lowest level of conflict between work and family. Mode of communication was a significant predictor of conflictual relations among the hearing impairment group.

Such influence of conflict expectations upon the career development of young adults emphasizes the need to increase our understanding of variables that influence work–family expectations, especially among vulnerable populations with disabilities. One of the variables that carries a potential explanatory power of these expectations is self-efficacy. Given the crucial role that self-efficacy plays in the adjustment to a variety of stressful life events and the various occupational difficulties encountered by deaf people, the study of self-efficacy in managing anticipated WFC among this population and its relation to anticipated work–family conflict and facilitation may be of theoretical and practical value.

Career Self-Efficacy

Self-efficacy theory proposes that the probability of engaging in an activity and executing it successfully is determined in part by the degree to which individuals believe they can effectively perform the behavior (Bandura, 1986). According to Bandura and colleagues (Bandura, Barbaranelli, Caprara, & Pastorelli, 2001), self-efficacy beliefs influence various personal factors such as level of motivation and perseverance in the face of difficulties and setbacks, resilience to adversity, causal attributions for successes and failures, and vulnerability to stress and depression. Schwarzer and Renner (2000) related self-efficacy to proactive coping, counting "coping self-efficacy" as one of the personal resource factors that boost resilience and moderate stress. They defined it as an optimistic self-belief of being able to cope successfully with the particular situation at hand.

Social cognitive career theory (SCCT; Lent, Brown, & Hackett, 1994) applied Bandura's (1986) concept of self-efficacy to career development processes and pinpointed it as an important personal variable for understanding career development. Lent et al. (1994) partitioned SCCT into two complementary levels of theoretical analysis. The first level presents cognitive-person variables (such as self-efficacy) that enable people to exercise personal control within their own career development. The second level of analysis considers the paths through which several additional sets of variables – such as physical attributes (e.g., gender, race, and disability/health condition) and features of the environment – influence career-related interests and choice behavior. This means that, in addition to self-efficacy beliefs, having a disability may affect the individual's career development.

Empirical research on career self-efficacy reported positive correlations between career decision-making self-efficacy and career decision-making tasks and behaviors among youth. For instance, adolescents' high self-efficacy in a specific occupation was found to correlate positively with their willingness to choose that occupation (Tang et al., 1999) and with their high career aspirations for that occupation (Nauta et al., 1998). Similar patterns emerged in research dealing with self-efficacy in family roles. First, parental self-efficacy (referring to persons' beliefs about their ability to succeed in the parental role/tasks) correlated positively with good adaptation to the parental role (Ardelt & Eccles, 2001). Second, marital self-efficacy emerged as a predictor of marital satisfaction (Finchman, Harold, & Gano-Phillips, 2000).

However, similar to studies in career development, most of the research in the area of self-efficacy focused solely on the ability to perform a specific task in one distinct domain – academic, vocational, or family, disregarding the connections between different life roles. Cinamon (2006) emphasized the importance in investigating self-efficacy to manage WFC, due to the crucial role of self-efficacy as a resilience factor. In her study, she defined self-efficacy to manage WFC as the individual's beliefs in his/her ability to manage future WFC, or in other words, the individual's confidence in his/her ability to successfully handle interference from work to the family and interference from family to work. Results of her study indicated that self-efficacy to manage future conflict between work and family roles is negatively correlated with expectations for this type of conflict among young adults (Cinamon, 2006). Young adults that are confident in their ability to successfully handle interference from the work domain to the family expect less W→F conflict, and those who are confident in their ability to success-fully handle future interference from the family to work expect less F→W conflict.

These findings support the social cognitive career model and illustrate how self-efficacy beliefs influence expectations regarding future work–family relations. We also know from previous studies that these expectations influence work and family plans (Barnett et al., 2003; Lundgren & Barnett, 2000; Weer et al., 2006). It seems, therefore, that self-efficacy is an important factor in understanding and enhancing career development of young adults. Nonetheless, the above studies focused on normally developed participants and not on young adults with disabilities. Thus, it is important to investigate the role of self-efficacy among young adults with special needs in order to evaluate its resilience potential impact. Furthermore, addressing such issues may enlarge the body of knowledge regarding young adults' work and family plans as well as the influence of disabilities on career development. The following section will discuss anticipated WFC management self-efficacy among deaf young adults.

WFC Managing Self-Efficacy Beliefs
Among Deaf and Hard of Hearing Young Adults

In this section, we will present a study which is part of a larger research project that examined work–family issues among young adults with and without hearing impairments (for additional results, see Cinamon et al., 2008).

The study goals were (a) to examine the contribution of hearing status to self-efficacy beliefs in managing anticipated WFC, (b) to study the relations between self-efficacy and anticipated WFC and WFF, and (c) to locate background variables in addition to hearing status which may explain different levels of self-efficacy among participants with different hearing status. In order to study the impact of disability, the present study focused on emerging adults with normal hearing and with two different levels of hearing loss and modes of communication. The distinc-tion between deaf and hard of hearing was made according to the participants' mode of communication. Those who used primarily spoken language were consid-ered hard of hearing whereas those who used sign or simultaneous language were considered deaf. This distinction was based on a former study that showed that mode of communication was the main differentiator between the two groups (Cinamon et al., 2008).

Participants were 101 unmarried young adults (50 males, 51 females) aged 20–33 years ($M = 25$; $SD = 2.88$ years) from central Israel: 35 with hearing impairments and 66 with normal hearing. Among participants with hearing impairments, 19 (12 females and 7 males) used spoken language as their main mode of communication and would be referred to as the hard of hearing group (HH), and 16 (7 females and 9 males) simultaneously used spoken and signed language and would be referred to as the deaf group. All participants completed the self-report questionnaire individually and voluntarily.

The first issue investigated was the differentiation between two types of self-efficacy. The question whether the participants differentiated between the ability to manage W→F conflict vs. F→W conflict was in focus. In general, factor analysis indicated two types of distinct factors with the expected items. Furthermore, the correlation between the two factors was .50 ($p < .001$), which means that only 25% of one type of efficacy is explained by the other type of efficacy. Pearson product–moment correlations for each group of participants separately indicated significant differences (see Table 13.1).

Significant positive correlations emerged between the two self-efficacy types among the hearing and the deaf participants but not among the HH participants. 49% and 29.16% of the variance of one self-efficacy type was explained by the other among hearing and deaf participants, respectively. These findings suggest a differential perception of the two types of efficacy by the different groups, with the HH making the most differentiation between the two types of efficacy.

Comparisons between the two types of self-efficacy through paired sample t tests indicated across all participants, as well as within each group separately, higher levels of self-efficacy to manage W→F conflict than self-efficacy to manage F→W conflict (see Table 13.2).

Table 13.1 Correlations between types of self-efficacy

Group	Correlation
Hearing	.70**
Hard of hearing	.09
Deaf	.54*

$*p \leq .05; **p \leq .01$

Table 13.2 Means, standard deviations, and t values of self-efficacy types

Group	Self-efficacy subscale	M	SD	t
All participants	W→F conflict	6.92	1.55	5.14**
	F→W conflict	6.09	1.69	
Hearing	W→F conflict	6.86	1.58	4.22**
	F→W conflict	6.20	1.65	
Hard of hearing	W→F conflict	7.07	1.97	2.41*
	F→W conflict	5.57	2.02	
Deaf	W→F conflict	7.00	0.66	2.69*
	F→W conflict	6.22	1.38	

$W{\rightarrow}F$ work to family, $F{\rightarrow}W$ family to work
$*p \leq .05; **p \leq .01$

Table 13.3 Pearson product–moment correlations between self-efficacy and anticipated work–family conflict and work–family facilitation variables among hearing,
hard of hearing, and deaf participants

		Anticipated WFC		Anticipated WFF	
		W→F	F→W	W→F	F→W
self-efficacy to	Hearing	−.23*	−.14	−.02	.26*
manage W→F	Hard of hearing	−.40*	−.29	.40*	.16
conflict	Deaf	−.05	−.44*	.08	−.23
self-efficacy to	Hearing	−.26*	−.27*	.11	.26*
manage F→W	Hard of hearing	−.29	.15	.43*	.01
conflict	Deaf	.11	−.36	−.25	−.68**

WFC work–family conflict, *WFF* work–family facilitation, *W→F* work to family,
F→W family to work
*$p \leq .05$; **$p \leq .001$

A multivariate analysis of variance (MANOVA) did not find significant group
difference in self-efficacy, $F (4, 184) = 0.52$; $p = .72$; $\eta = .01$. However, when additional variables were considered, significant findings emerged, as will be presented
later on.

As for the relationships between self-efficacy and anticipated WFC and WFF,
different results were found among the three groups of participants (see Table 13.3).
In regards to self-efficacy to manage W→F conflict, significant negative correlations
were found with anticipated W→F conflict among the hearing and HH groups and
with anticipated F→W conflict in the deaf group, and positive correlations were
reported with anticipated W→F facilitation among the hard of hearing and with
anticipated F→W facilitation among hearing participants. As for self-efficacy to
manage F→W conflict, significant negative correlations were found with the two
types of conflict among the hearing group and with anticipated F→W facilitation
among the deaf participants, and significant positive correlations emerged with
anticipated F→W facilitation in the hearing group and with anticipated W→F facilitation among the HH.

The above results indicate that high levels of WFC management self-efficacy
beliefs are related to low levels of anticipated WFC and high levels of anticipated
WFF. However, these correlations were not significant across all groups. This may
imply that although a general pattern was found between self-efficacy to manage
WFC and anticipated WFC and facilitation, the different groups in the study may
be affected differently by additional variables which in turn influence their self-
efficacy levels.

In order to examine the contribution of background variables (gender, employment status, engagement with intimate relations, and participation in education) to
differences in self-efficacy among the three participant groups, multivariate analyses of variance (MANOVAs) were conducted. No significant differences were

found on any of these variables. However, significant interactions were found in relation to gender and self-efficacy to manage F→W conflict [F (4, 184)=3.94; η =.08], employment status and self-efficacy to manage W→F conflict [F (4, 182) = 2.91; η =.06], and engagement in intimate relations and self-efficacy to manage F→W conflict [F (4, 184)=6.83; η =.13]. Figures 13.1–13.3 present these interactions according to gender, employment status, and engagement in intimate relations, respectively.

As presented in Fig. 13.1, whereas hearing and deaf male participants showed lower levels of self-efficacy to manage F→W conflict than female participants, HH males reported higher levels of self-efficacy to manage F→W conflict compared to HH females. HH participants showed different levels of self-efficacy also in regards to employment status (see Fig. 13.2). Whereas, hearing and deaf employed participants reported higher levels of self-efficacy to manage W→F conflict than non-working participants, HH working participants showed lower levels of this type of efficacy compared to nonworking ones. In contrast, the HH group resembled deaf participants in relation to engagement in intimate relations and self-efficacy to manage F→W conflict. Both groups reported higher levels of efficacy among participants with no intimate relationship than among participants who were engaged in an intimate relationship. In the hearing group the results were in the opposite direction.

The study's findings point to the impact that hearing impairments have on self-efficacy beliefs when considering variables of gender, employment status, and

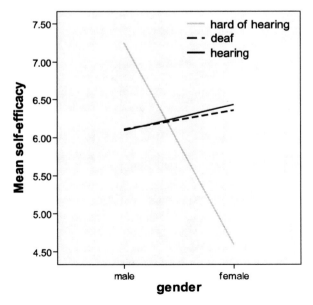

Fig. 13.1 Gender and self-efficacy to manage F→W conflict

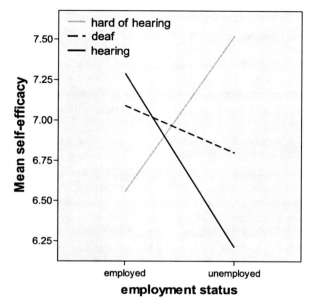

Fig. 13.2   Employment status and self-efficacy to manage W→F conflict

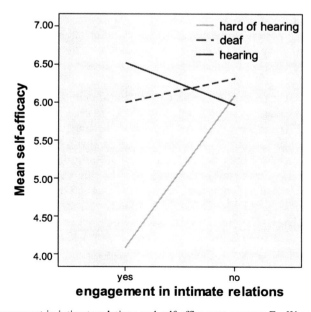

Fig. 13.3   Engagement in intimate relations and self-efficacy to manage F→W conflict

engagement in intimate relations. In addition, some of the results suggest that deaf and normal hearing young adults often tend to think alike and to be influenced in similar ways. First of all, the two groups did not distinguish between self-efficacy to manage W→F conflict and self-efficacy to mange F→W conflict, whereas the HH group did. Secondly, their self-efficacy was affected similarly by gender and employment factors, as opposed to HH persons. However, when concerning intimate relations factors, HH and deaf people show resemblance in self-efficacy.

These results support the notion that HH and deaf are distinct groups (e.g., Weisel & Reichstein, 1990). However, when concerning intimate relations, they tend to resemble one another. This may be partly explained by the types of romantic partners they tend to chose for themselves. For example, Pimentel (1978), one of the few researchers who explored this topic, reported that among married adults with hearing impairments in general, 79.5% had partners with severe to profound hearing loss, meaning that not only do hearing impaired persons tend to marry other hearing impaired individuals, but that the hearing loss of these individuals is significant to their functioning. Nevertheless, Pimentel did not distinguish between HH and deaf persons. In addition, this study was conducted more than 30 years ago and might not be relevant to the twenty-first century.

Suggestions for Intervention

Since many male and female employees today suffer from the stress of WFC, and insufficient solutions are provided by employers, it is important to seek additional strategies to promote mental and physical health and reduce this conflict. Various scholars have called for primary prevention to help young adults prepare for the complex task of balancing work and family lives (Machung, 1989; Weitzman, 1994).

Since self-efficacy serves as a resilience factor, it is important to help people to develop it. However, when dealing with WFC management self-efficacy and persons with different hearing status, the above findings suggest the need for a differential intervention model. A counselor working with hearing imparied youth must first find out how they define themselves – being deaf or HH and to what extent this definition is central in their identity. The importance of hearing impairment in the individual's identity can be explored through the intervention section. Then, counselors should address work and family issues differently, since deaf people's self-efficacy is more similar to hearing ones when it is affected by gender and employment factors. However, when concerning intimate relations variables, HH and deaf people show resemblance in self-efficacy.

The enhancement of WFC management self-efficacy could be based on Bandura's (1977, 1997) four sources of efficacy information: past performance accomplishments, vicarious learning, social persuasion, and emotional arousal. Creating a strong sense of efficacy may be through mastery experiences.

However, if people experience only easy successes, they come to expect quick results and are easily discouraged by failure. A resilient sense of efficacy requires experience in overcoming obstacles through perseverant effort. Thus, in order to promote a strong sense of WFC management self-efficacy, an effective intervention may include emphasizing participants' successful past performances in managing simultaneously two or more life roles (such as dealing with school demands along with having an intimate relationship) together with creating an awareness that some setbacks and difficulties serve a useful purpose that success usually requires sustained effort.

A second way in which counselors may strengthen self-beliefs of efficacy is through the examples of similar others. This may include introducing HH and deaf young adults to a hearing impaired person who manages to combine both a successful career and a rich family life. Such an exposure may raise participant's beliefs that they too posses the capabilities to succeed. In addition, such a model may transmit knowledge and teach effective skills and strategies for managing work and family demands.

Social persuasion is a third way in which counselors can strengthen young people's self-efficacy. They can help raise their beliefs in their capabilities by verbal encouragement. However, positive appraisals may not be enough. Counselors are advised to structure situations in ways that bring success and to measure success in terms of self-improvement rather than by complete triumphs.

The forth source of self-efficacy, according to Bandura, is emotional arousal. People with low sense of efficacy tend to interpret their stress reactions and tension as signs of vulnerability to poor performance. Hence, an additional way of modifying young adults' self-efficacy may be to reduce their stress reactions toward potential work–family conflicts and alter their negative emotional proclivities and misinterpretations of their physical state. This can be done through various relaxation techniques such as deep breathing and visualization.

Summary and Conclusions

The significance of self-efficacy is in its ability to affect the capability to realize desired and undesired futures. A durable sense of self-efficacy requires experience in overcoming obstacles through perseverance and effort (Bandura, 1995). In other words, self-efficacy is closely tied to resiliency. Only a few studies have examined self-efficacy beliefs in managing anticipated WFC among young adults. These studies focused on participants with normal development and did not explore the impact of disability on this type of self-efficacy. The current chapter addressed the issue of work–family management self-efficacy among young adults with hearing impairments and presented a part of a larger study which was conducted regarding work and family issues among this population.

Examination of hearing impaired young adults suggests that hearing status has a central role in their self-efficacy beliefs regarding management of anticipated

WFC. However, hearing status alone cannot explain variances in self-efficacy. Additional variables such as gender, employment status, and intimate relations engagement must be taken into consideration. In addition, the different self-efficacy beliefs are correlated differently with expectations regarding future conflict and facilitation between work and family roles.

It should be noted that the study presented here is limited in scope. First of all, the direct effect of self-efficacy in the area of WFC on resilience was not investigated. We only addressed this topic theoretically. Future studies should empirically examine the relationship between these two variables. Second, our study focused on Israeli young adults. In order to explore cultural effects, it is important to repeat it in other contexts and with other populations.

References

Allen, T. D., Herst, D. E., Bruck, C. S., & Sutton, N. (2000). Consequences associated with work to family conflict: A review and agenda for future research. *Journal of Occupational Health Psychology, 5*, 278–308.

Ardelt, M., & Eccles, J. S. (2001). Effects of mothers' parental efficacy beliefs and promotive parenting strategies on inner-city youth. *Journal of Family Issues, 22*, 944–972.

Arkansas Rehabilitation Services. *Arkansas Rehabilitation Services RT-31 20th Summative Report.* (2002). University of Arkansas, Rehabilitation Research and Training Center for Persons who are Deaf or Hard of Hearing. Retrieved 02/05/07, from http://www.uark.edu/depts./rehabres/center.html.

Babbitt, C. E., & Burbach, H. J. (1990). Note on the perceived occupational future of physically disable college student. *Journal of Employment Counseling, 27*, 99–104.

Bandura, A. (1977). Self-efficacy: Toward a unifying theory of behavioral change. *Psychological Review, 84*, 191–215.

Bandura, A. (1986). *Social foundations of thought and action: A social cognitive theory.* Englewood Cliffs, NJ: Prentice Hall.

Bandura, A. (1995). *Self-efficacy in changing societies.* New York: Cambridge University Press.

Bandura, A. (1997). *Self-efficacy: The exercise of control.* New York: Freeman.

Bandura, A., Barbaranelli, C., Caprara, G. V., & Pastorelli, C. (2001). Self-efficacy beliefs as shapers of children's aspirations and career trajectories. *Child Development, 72*, 187–206.

Barnett, R. C., Garies, K. C., James, J., & Steele, J. (2003). Planning ahead: College seniors' concerns about career-marriage conflict. *Journal of Vocational Behavior, 62*, 305–319.

Benshoff, J. J., Kroeger, S. A., & Scalia, V. A. (1990). Career maturity and academic achievement in college students with disabilities. *Journal of Rehabilitation, 56*, 40–44.

Blustein, D. (2001). Extending the reach of vocational psychology: Toward an inclusive and integrative psychology of working. *Journal of Vocational Behavior, 59*, 171–182.

Bond, J. T., Galinsky, E., & Swanberg, J. E. (1998). *The 1997 national study of the chancing workforce.* New York: Families and Work Institute.

Bronfenbrenner, U. (1989). Ecological system theories. *Annals of Child Development, 6*, 187–249.

Burkauser, R. V., & Houtenville, A. J. (2003). Employment among working-age people with disabilities: What current data can tell us. In R. M. Parker & E. M. Szymanski (Eds.), *Work and disability: Issues and strategies in career development and job placement* (2nd ed., pp. 53–90). Austin, TX: PRO-ED.

Carlson, D. S., & Kacmar, C. M. (2000). Work-family conflict in the organization: Do live role values make a difference? *Journal of Management, 26*, 1031–1054.

Chwalisz, K., Altmaier, E. M., & Russell, D. E. (1992). Causal attributions, self-efficacy cognition, and coping with stress. *Journal of Social and Clinical Psychology, 11*, 377–400.

Cinamon, R. G. (2006). Anticipated work-family conflict: Effects of gender, self-efficacy, and family background. *The Career Development Quarterly, 54*, 202–215.

Cinamon, R. G., Most, T., & Michael, R. (2008). Role salience and anticipated work-family relations among young adults with and without hearing loss. *Journal of Deaf Studies and Deaf Education, 13*, 351–361.

Cinamon, R. G., & Rich, Y. (2002). Attributions of importance to work and family roles: Implications for the work family conflict. *Journal of Counseling Psychology, 49*, 212–220.

Cinamon, R. G., & Rich, Y. (2004). A model counseling intervention program to prepare adolescents for coping with work-family conflict. In E. Frydenberg (Ed.), *Thriving, surviving, or going under: Coping with everyday lives* (pp. 227–254). Greenwich: Information Age Publication.

Cutrona, C. E., & Troutman, B. R. (1986). Social support, infant temperament, and parenting self-efficacy: A meditational model of postpartum depression. *Child Development, 57*, 1507–1518.

DeCaro, J. J., Mudgett-DeCaro, P. A., & Dowaliby, F. J. (2001). Attitudes toward occupations for deaf youth in Sweden. *American Annals of the Deaf, 146*, 51–59.

Dilorio, C., Dudley, W. N., Kelly, M., Soet, J. E., Mbwara, J., & Sharpe Potter, J. (2001). Social cognitive correlates of sexual experience and condom use among 13- through 15-year-old adolescents. *Journal of Adolescent Health, 29*, 208–216.

Dipeolu, A., Reardon, R., Sampson, J., & Burkhead, J. (2002). The relationship between dysfunctional career thoughts and adjustment to disability in college students with learning disabilities. *Journal of Career Assessment, 10*, 413–427.

Finchman, F. D., Harold, G. T., & Gano-Phillips, S. (2000). The longitudinal association between attributions and marital satisfaction: Direction of effects and role of efficacy expectations. *Journal of Family Psychology, 14*, 267–285.

Freud, S. (1930). *Civilization and its discontents*. London: Hogarth.

Friedman, S. R., & Weissbrod, C. S. (2005). Work and family commitment and decision making status among emerging adults. *Sex Roles, 53*, 317–325.

Frone, M. R. (2003). Work-family balance. In J. C. Quick & L. E. Tetrick (Eds.), *Handbook of occupational health psychology* (pp. 143–162). Washington, DC: APA.

Frone, M. R., Barnes, G. M., & Farell, M. P. (1994). Relationship of work-family conflict to a substance use among employed mothers: The role of negative affect. *Journal of Marriage and the Family, 56*, 1019–1030.

Frone, M. R., Yardley, J. K., & Markel, K. S. (1997). Developing and testing an integrative model of the work family interface. *Journal of Vocational Behavior, 50*, 145–167.

Greenhaus, J. H., & Beutell, N. J. (1985). Source of conflict between work and family roles. *Academy Management Review, 10*, 77–88.

Greenhaus, J. H., & Powell, G. N. (2003). When work and family collide: Deciding between competing role demands. *Organizational Behavior and Human Decision Processes, 90*, 291–303.

Grzywacz, J. G., & Marks, N. F. (2000). Reconceptualizing the work family interface: An ecological perspective on the correlates of positive and negative spillover between work and family. *Journal of Occupational Health Psychology, 5*, 111–126.

Hackett, G., Betz, N. E., Casas, J. M., & Rocha-Singh, I. A. (1992). Gender, ethnicity, and social cognitive factors predicting the academic achievement of students in engineering. *Journal of Counseling Psychology, 39*, 527–538.

Hagedoorn, M., & Molleman, E. (2006). Facial disfigurement in patients with face and neck cancer: The role of social self-efficacy. *Health Psychology, 25*, 643–647.

Hammer, L. B., Cullen, J. C., Neal, M. B., Sinclair, R. R., & Shafiro, M. V. (2005). The longitudinal effects of work-family conflict and positive spillover on depressive symptoms among Dual-Earner couples. *Journal of Occupational Health Psychology, 10*, 138–154.

Hanson, C., Downing, R. A., Coyle, K. K., & Pederson, L. L. (2004). Theory-based determinants of youth smoking: A multiple influence approach. *Journal of Applied Social Psychology, 34*, 59–84.

Jones, G. E. (1997). Advancement opportunities for persons with disabilities. *Human Resources Management Review, 7*, 55–77.

Kirchmeyer, C., & Cohen, A. (1999). Different strategies for managing the work/non work interface: A test for unique pathways to outcomes. *Work and Stress, 13*, 59–73.

Lent, R. W., Brown, S. D., & Hackett, G. (1994). Toward a unifying social cognitive theory of career and academic interest, choice, and performance. *Journal of Vocational Behavior, 45*, 79–122.

Lent, R. W., Brown, S. D., & Hackett, G. (2000). Contextual supports and barriers to career choice: A social cognitive analysis. *Journal of Counseling Psychology, 47*, 36–49.

Luft, P. (2000). Communication barriers for deaf employees: Needs assessment and problem-solving strategies. *Work, 14*, 51–59.

Lundgren, L., & Barnett, R. C. (2000). Reduced-hours careers in medicine: A strategy for the professional community and the family. *Community, Work & Family, 3*, 65–79.

Lustig, D. C., Strauser, D. R., & Donnell, C. (2003). Quality employment outcomes: Benefits for individuals with disabilities. *Rehabilitation Counseling Bulletin, 47*, 5–14.

Machung, A. (1989). Talking career, thinking job: Gender differences in career and family expectations of Berkeley seniors. *Feminist Studies, 15*, 35–58.

Marks, N. F. (1998). Does it hurt to care? Caregiving, work-family conflict, and midlife well-being. *Journal of Marriage and the Family, 60*, 951–966.

McLeod-Gallinger, J. E. (1992). The career status of deaf women: A comparative look. *American Annals of the Deaf, 137*, 315–325.

Moores, D. F. (1996). *Education the deaf: Psychology, principles, and practices* (4th ed.). Boston: Houghton Mifflin.

Nauta, M. M., Epperson, D. L., & Kahn, J. H. (1998). A multiple-group analysis of predictors of higher level career aspirations among women in mathematics, science, and engineering majors. *Journal of counseling Psychology, 45*, 483–496.

Netemeyer, R. G., Boles, J. S., & McMurrian, R. (1996). Development and validation of work-family conflict scales. *Journal of Applied Psychology, 81*, 400–410.

Pimentel, A. T. (1978). Some implications of deafness on family life. In L. von der Lieth (Ed.), *Life in families with deaf members, Proceedings of the Fifth World Conference on Deafness* (pp. 159–161). Copenhagen, Denmark: National Federation of the Deaf in Denmark.

Punch, R., Hyde, M., & Creed, P. A. (2004). Issues in the school-to-work transition of hard of hearing adolescents. *American Annals of the Deaf, 149*, 28–38.

Punch, R., Hyde, M., & Power, D. (2007). Career and workplace experiences of Australian university graduates who are deaf or hard of hearing. *Journal of Deaf Studies and Deaf Education, 12*, 504–517.

Saunders, J. L., Leahy, M. J., & Frank, K. A. (2000). Improving the employment self-concept of persons with disabilities: A field-based experiment. *Rehabilitation Counseling Bulletin, 43*, 142–149.

Schroedel, J. (1992). Helping adolescents and young adults who are deaf make career decisions. *The Volta Review, 94*, 37–46.

Schroedel, J. G., & Geyer, P. D. (2000). Long-term career attainments of deaf and hard of hearing college graduates: Results from a 15-year follow-up survey. *American Annals of the Deaf, 145*, 303–314.

Schwarzer, R., & Renner, B. (2000). Social-cognitive predictors of health behavior: Action self-efficacy and coping self-efficacy. *Health Psychology, 19*, 487–495.

Shahnasarian, M. (2001). Career rehabilitation: Integration of vocational rehabilitation and career development in the twenty-first century. *The Career Development Quarterly, 49*, 275–283.

Super, D. E. (1990). A life-span life space approach to career development. In D. Brown & L. Brooks (Eds.), *Career choice and development: Applying contemporary theories to practice* (2nd ed., pp. 197–261). San Francisco: Jossey-Bass.

Tang, M., Fouad, N. A., & Smith, P. L. (1999). Asian American career choices: A path model to examine factors influencing their career choices. *Journal of Vocational Behavior, 54*, 142–157.

Wayne, J. H., Musisca, N., & Fleeson, W. (2004). Considering the role of personality in the work-family experience: Relationships of the big five to work-family conflict and facilitation. *Journal of Vocational Behavior, 64,* 108–130.

Weer, C. H., Greenhaus, J. H., Colakoglu, S. N., & Foley, S. (2006). The role of maternal employment, role-altering strategies, and gender in college students' expectations of work-family conflict. *Sex Roles, 55,* 535–544.

Weisel, A., & Cinamon, R. G. (2005). Hearing, deaf, and hard-of-hearing Israeli adolescents' evaluation of deaf men and deaf women's occupational competence. *Journal of Deaf Studies and Deaf Education, 10,* 376–389.

Weisel, A., & Reichstein, J. (1990). Acceptance of hearing loss and adjustment of deaf and hard of hearing young adults. *Journal of the American Deafness and Rehabilitation Association, 24,* 1–6.

Weitzman, L. M. (1994). Multiple-role realism: A theoretical framework for the process of planning to combine career and family role. *Applied and Preventive Psychology, 3,* 15–25.

Chapter 14
Psychological Well-Being in Emerging Adults Who Are Deaf

Jill Meyer and Susan Kashubeck-West

Abstract This chapter examines signs of independence, transitioning to adulthood, and well-being in emerging adults aged 18–30, who are deaf. Possible protective and resilience factors are explored, with a more complete examination of psychological well-being as a multidimensional resilience factor. To further empirical research with this population, preliminary exploratory analyses were conducted on a small set of data ($N=21$). Age, satisfaction with life, self-esteem, and socioeconomic status were examined in relation to psychological well-being for emerging adults who are deaf compared with the general population.

According to Arnett (2000), emerging adults are young adults spanning the ages of approximately 18–25 who are engaged in self-exploration and other developmental activities. Emerging adults are quite unique and demonstrate a range of diversity in vocational endeavors, education, and living arrangements. As a whole, they tend not to feel that they have attained adulthood (Arnett, 2000; Galambos, Barker, & Krahn, 2006). Typically, such individuals gain autonomy in the areas of finance, employment, and residential arrangements; however, the rate and order in which these occur for emerging adults is highly variable (Cohen, Kasen, Chen, Hartmark, & Gordon, 2003).

In addition to external changes, there are also internal developmental changes that occur during emerging adulthood, such as psychological regulation (i.e., well-being) and role adaptation (i.e., becoming a parent). Emerging adults experience an increase in emotional stability as they learn to retain employment and develop relationships with romantic partners. Overall, the goal during emerging adulthood is general adaptation and the development of autonomy (Cohen et al., 2003; Galambos et al., 2006).

Research on emerging adults suggests that gains in psychological well-being during this life stage are typical. For example, Galambos et al. (2006) examined three markers of psychological well-being (self-esteem, depression, and anger) in

J. Meyer (✉)
Columbia's Missouri Institute of Mental Health, University of Missouri, St. Louis, MO, USA
e-mail: Jill.Meyer@mimh.edu

D.H. Zand and K.J. Pierce (eds.), *Resilience in Deaf Children: Adaptation Through Emerging Adulthood*, DOI 10.1007/978-1-4419-7796-0_14,
© Springer Science+Business Media, LLC 2011

emerging adults aged 18–25 from a school-based community sample. As predicted, their results indicated that anger and symptoms of depression decreased as the emerging adults aged and that self-esteem increased with age. Gottlieb, Still, and Newby-Clark (2007) studied themes of growth and decline among emerging adults newly transferred to university settings. About half of the participants reported that they experienced growth in the domains of relating to others, personal strength, and new opportunities. During this period, experiences with adversity lead to dependency on others, yet overtime adverse events became positive growth experiences. Thus, research findings indicate that psychological well-being improves during this life period. At the same time, relationships deepen, increasing social support, which in turn promotes health and creates a buffer against stress. Likewise, during this time period, emerging adults learn that intimacy can also lead to vulnerability and disappointment in relationships.

Emerging Adulthood and Deafness

Deafness alone does not constitute a risk for unsuccessful transition for deaf emerging adults. Deafness may create vulnerability, but in and of itself deafness does not account for the process or mechanisms that render an emerging adult less likely to adapt, or succeed in transition, or later in life (Young, Green, & Rogers, 2008). Instead, there is typically an interaction of individual and environmental variables affecting adaptation that result in resiliency and competency for emerging adults who are deaf (Masten & Obradovic, 2006).

Much of a deaf person's environmental experiences may be determined by the modeling of disability displayed by significant others (family and friends) and the surrounding community. According to Olkin (2002), there are three models that represent the most common ways in which people frame the concept of disability. The moral model frames disability as a defect caused by moral failings and views the disability as a source of shame and something to hide. The medical model, the most common framework in the USA, frames disability as a failure of a bodily system and advocates for cures. Therefore, medical and technological developments that ameliorate the effects of the disability are sought. Olkin (2002) pointed out that both of these models locate the source of the disability within the individual and both are associated with stigma. The medical model can result in a paternalistic view of the person with a disability as someone who needs charity. Finally, the social model frames disability as rooted in environments that do not include and accommodate people who have disabilities; hence, the problem is an oppressive environment that fails the segment of society that lives with disabilities (Olkin, 2002).

For example, consistent with the social model described above, Young et al. (2008) acknowledged the importance of having a deaf identity, as a linguistic minority. Young et al. (2008) defined possible resilient outcomes as having a deaf identity and belonging to the deaf community. Such an identity may help deaf emerging adults feel a sense of belonging and community with others who share similar experiences. A potential drawback to such an identity may be greater academic difficulties because the individual is not as facile with oral language, which could reduce the likelihood of success and resiliency (Young et al., 2008). Another view of the disabled community that arises often from those holding a medical model of disability is that of the "super-disabled," the belief that a success-ful person with a disability must be an amazingly exceptional person. It is the mindset that a person with a disability must overcome the disability rather than be whole with it and embrace it as a part of one's self. Young et al. (2008) pointed out that accepting this belief sets low expectations of success for individuals who are deaf. While a person who is deaf may not embrace such a belief, others in the indi-vidual's environment may, resulting in the provision of minimal services because the person may be perceived as not being able to gain achievement.

Transition of Deaf Emerging Adults

Emerging adults with special needs, including those who are deaf, have access to transition services to help adjust to and become successful in the adult world. Although the period of transition to adulthood may last longer and be more variable for this group, the goals are usually the same as emerging adults who are not deaf – to gain financial freedom, to live independently, to develop deep romantic relationships, to obtain gainful employment, and to have families. According to Valentine and Skelton (2007), transition is no longer a linear process; it is fragmented and unpre-dictable and typically full of struggle. Although it appears that adolescents are having sex at an earlier age, they are, however, leaving parental homes at a later age and/or are returning after a number of years. Some transition milestones for emerging adults are being met such as transitioning from school to work, yet at the same time, emerg-ing adults may not secure independent living (Valentine & Skelton, 2007).

As mentioned throughout this volume, most deaf children are born into hearing families (Valentine & Skelton, 2007), often making parents' first introduction to their child one of grief and fear. Hearing parents of deaf children often have little knowledge of communication needs, available services, and deaf culture,[1] which can result in children who feel a sense of isolation due to the lack of communication and low expectations from others. According to Valentine and Skelton (2007), poor language and literacy skills of many deaf children can also be connected to the low expectations of instructors in mainstream schools. Interviews with deaf participants resulted in numerous participant reports of being withdrawn from academic classes,

---

[1] Deaf culture refers to the group of individuals who are deaf and share a similar identity (Maxwell, Poeppelmeyer, & Polich, 1999). Deaf culture is a minority, linguistic group, who have endured oppression and paternalism, through which they have created a common bond and identity (Nikolaraizi & Makri, 2004; Young et al., 2008).

specifically English and language courses, and being admitted to more "practical" courses such as art. Many emerging adults who are deaf lack awareness of the wide range of career options open to them (Valentine & Skelton, 2007).

In a paradoxical manner, having too many needs met is also detrimental for emerging adults who are deaf (Valentine & Skelton, 2007). Having proper services may be essential to success, but when too many questions are answered and too many needs are met, one does not learn how to solve problems, or develop a sense of independence leading to issues with autonomy. As emerging adults, deaf individuals who do not have the necessary "life skills," such as self-efficacy and problem-solving knowledge, experience "transition shock" when leaving supportive school environments and upon entering the adult hearing world (Valentine & Skelton, 2007).

According to Valentine and Skelton (2007), much of the transition research with deaf participants, as with much of the research on individuals with other disabilities, has focused on negative issues such as the lack of success, barriers, unemployment, and health problems. Indeed, such research has shown that psychological problems are common in deaf young people. However, deaf people are also characterized by resilience and success; aspects that need more attention from researchers and practitioners alike.

Using Masten's (1994) definition of resilience as environmental effectiveness that is achieved, sustained, or recovered in spite of adversity; Valentine and Skelton (2007) indicated that deaf youth achieve resilience by learning sign language and accessing deaf culture. Learning a signed language and finding the Deaf community are not only signs of independence and transition, they often reflect a sense of "coming out" and identifying oneself as Deaf. As meaningful as this achievement may be to an individual who is deaf, family members often measure or judge independence based on the youth's ability to communicate orally. If oral skills are absent, the deaf child may be seen as lacking competence and therefore considered not to be independent. Unfortunately for many emerging adults who are deaf, measures of success are based on hearing standards, which are both academic and oral. A Deaf identity is important to many individuals who are deaf, but is not always recognized by the hearing community with the same level of importance. Family members may not recognize the need for such membership or may fear a cultural divide. Encouraging a hearing/oral identity may hamper the development of the Deaf identity, hindering independence and autonomy. In addition, success in the hearing world can cause difficulty with acceptance in the Deaf community (Valentine and Skelton, 2007). Hence, well-meaning families and others who operate more from a medical model of disability may inhibit the development of resilience, as defined by Valentine and Skelton. On the other hand, such families may promote the development of resiliency, if the emerging adult is able to overcome the adversity of such beliefs within his or her family. To summarize, Valentine and Skelton (2007) felt that resilience in individuals who are deaf is promoted by three factors: (1) acquisition of a signed language, (2) access to the deaf culture, and (3) transition to a Deaf identity, all of which lead to the pathway of autonomy and independence.

Resilience and Psychological Well-Being

To be judged as resilient, a person has to have experienced significant adversity, yet managed to successfully adapt (Masten, 1994). Adaptation is demonstrated via external markers, such as success in school and with relationships with peers, and internal factors, such as psychological well-being, self-esteem, and physical health (Masten & Obradovic, 2006). Young et al. (2008) identified three categories of internal characteristics necessary for resilience: (1) psychological traits, such as intelligence, self-esteem, and psychological well-being, (2) psychosocial competencies, such as good communications, social competence, and positive relationships, and (3) sociocultural characteristics, such as faith and spirituality.

Ryff, Singer, Love, and Essex (1998) discussed resilience and adult life in terms of psychological well-being. In their review of the literature, the authors documented different definitions of resilience: (1) positive reactions to adverse events and stress, (2) the ability to function and adapt following incapacity, and (3) retained competence under adversity. Much of the research on resilience has been from a developmental perspective focusing on children. However, Ryff et al. (1998) focused on exploring resilience within adults both as an outcome and as a process from an integrated mind–body perspective. From this perspective, Ryff et al. (1998) defined resilience as "the maintenance, recovery, or improvement in mental or physical health following challenge" (p. 74). Resilience is more than just the absence of illness; it is the ability to flourish after hardship and stress, more specifically, moving toward a state of physical, mental, and emotional wellness. Like Masten (1994), Ryff et al. (1998) also incorporate the concept of adaptation to environmental circumstance after a negative experience into the definition of resilience. According to Ryff et al. (1998), one must be integrated in mind and body to successfully flourish after childhood or early adolescent experiences in troubled environments. Ryff et al. (1998) conceptualized protective factors that explain positive reactions to negative events as factors that ameliorate stressful situations so that adaptation is possible, including positive family relationships, social supports, high IQ, autonomy, affectionate, outgoing, possessing positive self-concepts in adolescence, problem-solving ability, good parenting, stable families, and high socioeconomic status (SES).

According to Ryff et al. (1998), protective factors that buffer stress and promote physical and mental health under challenging conditions occur at three levels: (1) sociological (e.g., education, income, occupation, and SES), (2) psychological (e.g., coping and personality characteristics), and (3) social interactional (e.g., social supports and family relationships). These factors along with the mind–body model have yet to be examined regarding resilience in emerging adults who are deaf.

As can be seen in the varying definitions of resilience, psychological well-being appears to be both an outcome of resilience and a factor that promotes resilience. Outcomes from resilience after a negative experience may range from positive physical health and healthy behavior (diet and exercise) to continuing to engage in life's challenges. As a process, resilience is a combination of factors including SES, coping, adaptation, and networks of social supports, including family that allows for continued growth and development and even far-reaching success. Ryff et al. (1998) explained that it is these factors in combination with biological factors such as healthy functioning, immunological status, and cerebral activity that account for how one handles negative situations in a positive or successful manner. Thus, resilience and psychological well-being seem to be interdependent.

Ryff (1989a, 1989b) defined psychological well-being as engaging in and rising to the challenges of life. Psychological well-being accounts for growth and change which takes place during the course of a lifetime. Well-being in addition to other biological and environmental factors contributes to the successful positive adaptation of individuals who have experienced adversity. Incorporating the many theories of well-being, Ryff (1989a) developed a six-dimensional model of psychological well-being, which is currently recognized as the standard of measure (Lent, 2004). Ryff's (1989a, 1989b) model of well-being includes six factors, which are autonomy, positive relations with others, personal growth, self-acceptance, purpose in life, and environmental mastery. Taken as a whole, these factors make up overall psychological well-being.

Psychological Well-Being and Deafness

Examination of Polat (2003) and Valentine and Skelton (2007), revealed that much of the research on emerging adults who are deaf had a pathology-oriented focus and explored issues such as psychological distress, unemployment, and so on. Research is needed that focuses on positive psychological constructs, such as psychological well-being and life satisfaction. A review of the literature related to emerging adulthood for deaf individuals and Ryff's (1989a, 1989b) six dimensions of psychological well-being unfortunately revealed little empirical research. The following six domains comprise Ryff's model of well-being.

Self-acceptance. Ryff (1989a, 1989b) defined self-acceptance as the ability to integrate all personal events, positive and negative, into one's self-concept. Self-acceptance involves self-approval – being accepting of one's traits, habits, characteristics, values, and decision. Few authors have explored self-acceptance in young adults who are deaf. Sevigny-Skyer (1990) wrote about growing up deaf and needing approval from parents to gain self-acceptance and how the lack of parental acceptance of deafness can lead to shame, guilt, and difficulty with future relationships. A second author, Antia (1994) reviewed effective peer interaction strategies for young students who are deaf and noted that effective social skills are important to the development of self-acceptance for children who are deaf.

Positive relations with others. Ryff (1989a, 1989b) defined this domain as having caring, loving relationships with significant others. The ability to have strong, healthy relationships is essential for positive mental health. This domain also encompasses having an active social life. According to Leigh and Stinson (1991), positive relationships with others, in particular family and close friends, are influenced by experiences that are salient to each individual. Individuals who are deaf are at risk for low self-esteem and may feel as though they have less control over the environment than hearing peers, which may affect the development of important relationships. Leigh and Stinson (1991) also examined the social and emotional benefits of residential versus mainstream placements. Students in residential placements reported greater social satisfaction and increased opportunity to create positive relationships. Similar findings were reported by Polat (2003), who indicated that residential school settings were associated with better psychosocial adjustment among deaf students. However, Polat (2003) also noted that research in this area is contradictory and difficult to conduct and results should not be overgeneralized.

Leigh and Stinson (1991) noted three components that are essential to the development of relationships: (1) participation or frequency of interaction, (2) relatedness or one's emotional security, and (3) perceived social competence, the ability to create and succeed in relationships. Depending upon the social group, an individual who is deaf will need different communication skills to succeed in developing relationships. Leigh (1999) reported that through relationships with both deaf and hearing peers, children who are deaf can improve identity, self-esteem, and well-being. Technology can also assist with improving relationships with others, as Polat (2003) reported that the use of hearing aids was associated with better psychosocial adjustment in deaf students. Polat advocated that better language skills and academic achievement associated with hearing aid use resulted in better social acceptance and, therefore, better relationships with others, which outweighs the stigma of wearing hearing aids.

Leigh and Stinson (1991) concluded that, above all, it is most important that parents accept children's hearing loss. Lack of acceptance can significantly affect identity, self-esteem, significant relationships, and ultimately, emotional health, or well-being. Polat (2003) agreed that parental acceptance is important, but also argued that variables yet unaccounted for explain the majority of variance in psychosocial adjustment in deaf young people.

Autonomy. Autonomy, as defined by Ryff (1989a, 1989b), is the self-determination to resist peer pressure and the ability to control one's behavior. Autonomous individuals have self-directed standards of measurement and do not conform blindly to social standards and pressure. Autonomy, a term that means self-directed in the quality of existence, has not always been a characteristic associated with people who are deaf, in that they did not direct their existence and control their quality of life throughout history. According to Humphries (1996), autonomy in the Deaf community came from fighting the grips of oppression and control. People who were deaf created their own autonomy.

Many authors (Arnold, 1984; Leigh, Robins, Welkowitz, & Bond, 1989; Pipp-Siegel & Biringer, 1998; Richardson, Long, & Foster, 2004; Sanders, 1983; Venn & Wadler, 1990) have discussed education, communication, and parenting in combination with the autonomy of individuals who are deaf. These authors all imparted with the same theme – autonomy is necessary in the lives of individuals who are deaf. Exercising autonomy in all areas of life is not a foreign concept for most people, but for a group that has been oppressed and devalued, autonomy is vital.

Environmental mastery. As described by Ryff (1989a, 1989b), environmental mastery is the ability to manage and direct the external environment in an effort to maintain health and well-being. This includes being able to take advantage of external opportunities to grow and meet needs, learning to adapt to and to influence the environment to create success. Kennedy (1994) stated that individuals who are deaf develop an external locus of control overtime due to experiences of oppression and decision making that is controlled by others. Due to this mindset, individuals who are deaf have developed an external locus of control. In addition, according to Donahue-Jennings and MacTurk (1995), and MacTurk, Meadow-Orlans, Koester, and Spencer (1993), a child with sensory loss may find the environment nonresponsive due to difficulty with sending or receiving information. Parents and others who interact with a child with a disability may not respond to requests or cues appropriately, therefore reinforcing the child's inability to impact the environment.

Purpose in life. This dimension is defined as those factors that make life worth living. Ryff (1989a) described this as having a sense of purpose and direction in life, goals, and objectives. As time evolves, so do goals, redefining one's purpose in life and constantly giving new meaning to life. Sheridan (2001) explored this concept indirectly through vignettes in which a sense of purpose in life was evident. Sheridan (2001) noted that for some individuals, purpose in life was found through culture and personal attachments to significant others during the course of a lifetime. Having a sense of community and belongingness is important to individuals who are deaf, as it is for most people. Self-direction is evident when an individual who is deaf chooses to communicate or not communicate with others who are hearing or decides to join the Deaf culture. Self-direction is displayed through decisions that demonstrate the purpose reflected through culture and community.

Personal growth. Ryff (1989b) defined personal growth as continued development and openness to change over a lifetime. To be able to handle constant change in the world, one has to be invested in continuous personal growth. Growth is an effort put forth to evolve as an individual. Greenberg and Kusche (1993) found that self-awareness is created during the development of language. During this developmental period, children begin to symbolize relationships through language, learn self-control, and develop self-awareness, which is ultimately important to personal growth. Kusche, Garfield, and Greenberg (1983) demonstrated that emotional development is not only solely attributed to maturation but also to the development of language and communication skills. Calderon and Greenberg (2000) stated that personal growth should be made part of "educational goals" for children who are deaf, as personal growth is so interconnected with development.

Apparent from the above review, there is continued need for empirical research on many components of well-being in emerging adults who are deaf. One study of interest conducted by Kashubeck-West and Meyer (2008) examined psychological well-being in a sample of women who had experienced postlingual, late-deafness (onset of deafness after the age of 12). Their results indicated that the women reported lower levels of psychological well-being and satisfaction with life compared with samples from the general population. Within-group differences were also found, in that women from lower socioeconomic groups indicated lower levels of psychological well-being, life satisfaction, and self-esteem compared with women from middle and upper class backgrounds. Importantly, Kashubeck-West and Meyer (2008) found that two popular measures of well-being, Ryff's (1989b) psychological well-being measure and the Satisfaction with Life Scale (SWLS; Diener, Emmons, Larsen, & Griffin, 1985; Pavot & Diener, 1993), showed solid internal consistency reliability and convergent validity (and partial discriminant validity) with the sample of women who are late deafened. These findings suggest that these two measures are appropriate for use in samples of individuals who are late-deafened.

Exploring Psychological Well-Being in Deaf Emerging Adults

Given the lack of empirical data on psychological well-being in emerging adults who are deaf, we chose to explore potential relationships among variables related to well-being in a subset of the data collected by Kashubeck-West and Meyer (2008), namely, emerging adults aged 18–30. Although the subset of data is small ($n = 21$), we felt that preliminary exploratory analyses might provide ideas for further research with this population. First, we examined levels of well-being in our sample compared with those reported for emerging adults in the general population. Next, we examined the relations between age and the different dimensions of well-being in our participants, given that findings reported by Arnett (2007), Galambos et al. (2006), and Gottlieb et al. (2007) showed that psychological well-being seems to improve as young adults age. Relatedly, Polat (2003) reported that teachers rated older deaf students higher in psychosocial adjustment than younger deaf students. We also examined whether greater self-esteem would be associated with greater psychological well-being and life satisfaction, given consistent findings in this direction reported by Arkoff et al. (2006), Jambor and Elliott (2005), and Rosenberg, Schooler, Schoenbach, and Rosenberg (1995). Indeed, researchers often include self-esteem as part of their definition of psychological well-being. Kashubeck-West and Meyer (2008) reported that among the women in the sample, lower social class was associated with less psychological well-being, lower self-esteem, and lower life satisfaction. Therefore, we examined whether these findings would exist in our small subsample of male and female emerging adults. Another variable that might relate to resilience well-being, as noted by Valentine and Skelton (2007), is connection with the Deaf community and ability to use sign language. Thus, we examined whether emerging adults who identified as culturally Deaf or who could use sign had greater well-being than those who did not identify in this way.

Participants

The participants for this examination were 16 females and 5 males that had an average age of 25 (SD = 3.66, range of 18–30). Most of the sample was White (81%, $n = 17$) with two biracial/multiracial individuals (9.5%), one African-American participant (4.8%), and one person who selected other (4.8%). All of the participants identified as heterosexual, 29% reported being working or lower middle class, 38% reported being middle class, and 33% reported being upper middle class or upper class. The participants were well-educated, with six indicating some college, nine a college degree, and five attendance in graduate school. Over three-fourths of the sample (76%) reported that they were employed. Nine individuals (43%) indicated that they considered themselves to be culturally Deaf, whereas 12 individuals (57%) indicated that they were not culturally Deaf. Turning to the use of sign language, 57% ($n = 12$) of the sample reported having this ability. More than half of the sample (57%) preferred to use oral communication, a third preferred to sign, one individual preferred text, and one person preferred a combination of these three methods.

Measures

Ryff's (1989b) 84-item measure was used to assess psychological well-being. Participants responded to items using a six-point scale ranging from *strongly disagree* (1) to *strongly agree* (6). Ryff's (1989a) six dimensions of well-being are each measured by 14 items, these are autonomy: "I judge myself by what I think is important, not by the values of what others think is important"; environmental mastery: "In general, I feel I am in charge of the situation in which I live"; positive relations with others: "Maintaining close relationships has been difficult and frustrating for me"; personal growth: "For me, life has been a continuous process of learning, changing, and growth"; self-acceptance: "When I look at the story of my life, I am pleased with how things have turned out"; and purpose in life: "Some people wander aimlessly through life, but I am not one of them." Higher scores on each subscale indicate higher self-ratings on that dimension of psychological well-being. The six subscale scores are summed to form an overall psychological well-being score, ranging from 84 to 504. The emerging adult sample in this study obtained a Cronbach's alpha of 0.98 for the overall measure and alphas ranging from 0.84 to 0.93 for the individual subscales of well-being. Reading levels for the items range from third grade to fifth grade.

Satisfaction with life. The SWLS (Diener et al., 1985; Pavot & Diener, 1993) was used to assess global satisfaction with one's life. Participants responded to five items on a seven-point scale ranging from 1 (*strongly disagree*) to 7 (*strongly agree*). Responses are summed (range 5–35) and higher scores reflect greater satisfaction with life. The Cronbach's alpha for this study was 0.92. The SWLS has a third-grade reading level.

Self-esteem. The Rosenberg Self-esteem Scale (RSES; Rosenberg, 1965) was used to assess global self-esteem. Its ten items are responded to on a four-point scale ranging from 1 (*strongly disagree*) to 4 (*strongly agree*). Item scores are totaled (range 10–40), with higher scores reflecting higher levels of self-esteem. Test–retest reliability for the RSES has been reported as 0.85 in a sample of late adolescents (Silber & Tippet, 1965). A Cronbach's alpha of 0.72 was obtained with the sample in this study. The RSES has a third-grade reading level.

Procedure

Kashubeck-West and Meyer (2008) sent potential participants a Web-based announcement of the study with a hypertext link through the Association for Late Deafened Adults (ALDA) listserv, the MODeaf listserv, and other Deaf-related listserv groups from Yahoo. Individuals who were late-deafened (had lost their hearing at approximately age 12 or later but before the age of 66) were recruited. When potential participants accessed the survey Web site, they were presented with an informed consent page. After reading this page, participants could click on a link to the online survey. Although the study announcement requested individuals who had lost their hearing after the age of 12, a number of individuals who had lost their hearing prior to this age completed the survey anyway. For the sample described here, males and females between the ages of 18–30 who had lost their hearing at any age were included.

Results

With such a small sample size the risk of a Type II error was magnified; therefore, we used a p value of 0.10 to denote significance. Although this p value increases the risk of a Type I error slightly, we felt that the ramifications of a Type II error could be more costly in terms of missed opportunities for understanding well-being in deaf emerging adults. First, we compared the levels of well-being reported by the deaf emerging adults with data from the general population. Means and standard deviations were calculated for the psychological well-being variables and compared with those reported by Arkoff et al. (2006) from their sample of first-year college students. For two of the six subscales of psychological well-being, autonomy and purpose in life, the t tests (df=55) were significant, $t=2.01$, $p<0.05$ and $t=1.73$, $p=0.09$, respectively. Examination of the means revealed that the emerging adults in this sample scored higher on autonomy and purpose in life than did the first-year college students in the Arkoff et al. sample. The t tests for the other four dimensions of psychological well-being were not significant, indicating no differences between the deaf emerging adults in this sample and the sample of Arkoff et al. Next, we compared the life satisfaction scores of the participants with those reported by Robitschek and Kashubeck (1999) with their sample of college students. The t test was not significant, t (df=313)=0.16, $p=0.88$. Thus, there were no differences in life satisfaction between the deaf emerging adults in this sample and a sample of college students from the general population.

To examine the relations between age and psychological well-being, correlations between overall psychological well-being and each of six dimensions with age were examined, as was the correlation between age and life satisfaction. None of these correlations was significant; r values ranged from -0.06 to 0.26. Next, correlations were calculated between self-esteem and psychological well-being (both overall well-being and each of the six dimensions) and life satisfaction. Self-esteem was positively correlated with each psychological well-being dimension, overall psychological well-being, and life satisfaction. The correlation values ranged from 0.58 to 0.79. Finally, correlations were run between ability to sign and psychological well-being and between identification as culturally deaf and psychological well-being. None of these correlations were significant; r *values* ranged from 0.05 to 0.33.

An examination of socioeconomic differences across three groups (working/lower middle class, middle class, and upper middle/upper class) in overall psychological well-being, self-esteem, and life satisfaction indicated that the overall MANOVA was significant, $F (6, 26) = 2.10$, $p < 0.09$, partial $\eta^2 = 0.33$. Follow-up univariate ANOVAs showed that significant differences across socioeconomic groups were found across each dependent variable: overall psychological well-being, $F (1, 14) = 7.86$, $p < 0.005$, partial $\eta^2 = 0.53$; self-esteem, $F (1, 14) = 3.93$, $p < 0.05$, partial $\eta^2 = 0.36$; and life satisfaction, $F (1, 14) = 11.46$, $p < 0.001$, partial $\eta^2 = 0.62$. Post hoc tests ($p < 0.05$) indicated that deaf emerging adults who reported working/lower class backgrounds reported less overall psychological well-being and life satisfaction than participants with middle class or upper middle/upper class backgrounds. In addition, individuals with working/lower class backgrounds reported less self-esteem than participants with upper middle/upper class backgrounds.

Finally, a set of one-way ANOVAs was conducted using identification as culturally Deaf (yes/no) as the grouping variable and the six dimensions of psychological well-being, self-esteem, and life satisfaction as dependent variables. None of these ANOVAs were significant: autonomy, $F (1, 15) = 0.05$, $p = 0.82$; environmental mastery, $F (1, 15) = 0.03$, $p = 0.86$; personal growth, $F (1, 15) = 1.36$, $p = 0.26$; positive relations with others, $F (1, 15) = 0.09$, $p = 0.77$; purpose in life, $F (1, 15) = 0.05$, $p = 0.82$; self-acceptance, $F (1, 15) = 0.84$, $p = 0.37$; self-esteem, $F (1, 15) = 0.92$, $p = 0.35$; and life satisfaction, $F (1, 15) = 0.00$, $p = 0.97$. Thus, there were no differences among the deaf emerging adults in well-being based upon identification as culturally Deaf.

Discussion of Findings

The first set of analyses compared the well-being of our small sample of emerging adults who were deaf with the well-being reported for samples from the general population. We were not able to find a study using Ryff's (1989b) measure with emerging adults who were not college students. However, all but one of the emerging adults in this sample had attended college so we deemed the samples to be comparable with respect to education. The results indicated that the participants in our sample scored equivalent to the general population college student sample on four of the six psychological well-being scales and scored higher on the other two scales, autonomy and purpose in life. In addition, the life satisfaction scores of the deaf emerging adults were not different from the life satisfaction reported in the general college student sample. Thus, the emerging adults who were deaf were similar to (and better-off in terms of autonomy and purpose in life) their hearing peers in psychological well-being and life satisfaction. It is important to note that our sample was older than the (2006) sample of Arkoff et al., and thus it is quite possible that the higher autonomy and purpose in life scores are reflective of that age difference. It is also possible that the sample of emerging adults discussed here were not typical of the broader population of deaf emerging adults, as their level of education was quite high and not reflective of the general population. These participants may have had higher levels of resilience and psychological well-being that enabled them to overcome obstacles to attending college and obtaining employment. Thus, they may be a select sample of deaf emerging adults who have more internal resources to draw upon than the general population of deaf emerging adults. In any case, it is important to be aware that these deaf emerging adults are reporting levels of well-being that are at least comparable to those reported by college students in the general population.

Although we had expected that age might serve to predict psychological well-being and life satisfaction in this sample of deaf emerging adults, the correlations were not significant. Given the small sample size, it is clear that the correlations would have to be fairly large for there to be enough power to detect significance. It is quite possible that with a larger sample some of the correlations would have been significant. However, it is also possible that greater age is not associated with more well-being in deaf emerging adults who may face increased challenges compared with their hearing peers related to creating autonomy, establishing positive relations with others, building self-confidence, and so on.

Consistent with findings on emerging adults from the general population (Arkoff et al., 2006), psychological well-being in the deaf emerging adults in this sample was related strongly to self-esteem. If one's goal is to help emerging adults who are deaf develop positive self-esteem, increasing various components of psychological well-being such as autonomy and positive relations with others may result in improving self-esteem.

A robust finding from this small data set was that deaf emerging adults who come from working/lower socioeconomic backgrounds have greater challenges with regard to psychological well-being, self-esteem, and life satisfaction than deaf emerging adults who come from more privileged backgrounds. This finding is consistent with that found in larger society, as Horton and Shweder (2004) noted that socioeconomic status and well-being are positively related. About 76% of the participants in this sample were employed; individuals with disabilities are typically unemployed and underemployed in higher rates than their nondisabled peers, although most people with disabilities want to be employed (Bureau of Labor Statistics, 2009; Sue & Sue, 2008). Thus, it is possible that the participants experienced financial struggles related to underemployment or lack of employment. It is important to remember that the data reported here come from a single point in time; thus, there is no way to determine whether the disabilities of participants were a factor in their socioeconomic status or whether their socioeconomic status was established prior to their hearing loss.

Valentine and Skelton (2007) felt that resilience in individuals who are deaf is promoted by three factors: (1) acquisition of a signed language, (2) access to the deaf culture, and (3) transition to a deaf identity, all of which lead to the pathway of autonomy and independence. However, the results of this study failed to demonstrate a correlation between the use of a signed language and psychological well-being or between identifying as belonging to deaf culture and psychological well-being. In contrast, these results support concepts presented by Young et al. (2008) that resilience may be fostered by characteristics such as self-esteem and psychological well-being and psychosocial competencies, such as good communications and social competence.

As noted by Kashubeck-West and Meyer (2008), the data are limited by their self-report nature, the fact that participants were recruited via D/deaf Web sites and that the study was not available in American Sign Language. Additional limitations are that the sample was primarily White and heterosexual. Specific limitations related to this chapter center primarily around the small sample size of 21 emerging adults. More analyses on potential within-group differences in well-being related to employment status and preferred communication mode were not conducted due to a lack of power. Similarly, a lack of power may have resulted in one or more Type II errors.

Conclusion

A theme of this chapter is the lack of research on emerging adults who are deaf that focuses on positive aspects of life, rather than mental health problems or educational difficulties. Using Ryff's (1989a) definition of psychological well-being as a guide, the scant literature related to the six dimensions of psychological well-being in deaf emerging adults was reviewed. A small data set was used to explore dimensions of well-being in deaf emerging adults. These results, which need to be viewed cautiously, given the small sample size suggest that deaf emerging adults may be very similar to their hearing peers with regard to overall life satisfaction, self-esteem, and psychological well-being. Such findings, if replicated in larger samples, could lead to new perspectives on the resilience of deaf emerging adults.

References

Antia, S. (1994). Strategies to develop peer interaction in young hearing-impaired children. *The Volta Review, 96*(4), 277–290.
Arkoff, A., Meredith, G. M., Bailey, E., Cheang, M., Dubanoski, R. A., Griffin, P. B., et al. (2006). Life review during the college freshman year. *College Student Journal, 40*(2), 263–269.

Arnett, J. J. (2000). Emerging adulthood: A theory of development from the late teens through the twenties. *American Psychologist, 55*(5), 469–480.

Arnett, J. J. (2007). Suffering, selfish, slackers? Myths and reality about emerging adults. *Journal of Youth and Adolescence, 36*, 23–29.

Arnold, P. (1984). The education of the deaf child: For integration or autonomy? *American Annals of the Deaf, 129*(1), 29–37.

Bureau of Labor Statistics. (2009). *Labor force statistics from the Current Population Survey: Employment status and disability status, March, 2009.* Retrieved April 13, 2009 from http://www.bls.gov/cps/cpsdisability_032009.htm

Calderon, R., & Greenberg, M. T. (2000). Challenges to parents and professionals in promoting socioemotional development in deaf children. In P. E. Spencer, C. J. Erting, et al. (Eds.), *The deaf child in the family and at school; Essays in honor of K. P. Meadow-Orlans* (pp. 167–185). Mahwah, NJ: Lawrence Erlbaum Associates.

Cohen, P., Kasen, S., Chen, H., Hartmark, C., & Gordon, K. (2003). Variations in patterns of developmental transitions in the emerging adulthood period. *Developmental Psychology, 39*, 657–669.

Diener, E., Emmons, R. A., Larsen, R. J., & Griffin, S. (1985). The Satisfaction with Life Scale. *Journal of Personality Assessment, 49*(1), 71–75.

Donahue-Jennings, K., & MacTurk, R. H. (1995). The motivational characteristics of infants and children with physical and sensory impairments. *Advances in Applied Developmental Psychology, 12*, 201–219.

Galambos, N. L., Barker, E. T., & Krahn, H. J. (2006). Depression, self-esteem, and anger in emerging adulthood: *Seven-year trajectories. Developmental Psychology, 42*(2), 350–365.

Gottlieb, B. H., Still, E., & Newby-Clark, I. R. (2007). Types and precipitants of growth and decline in emerging adulthood. *Journal of Adolescent Research, 22*(2), 132–155.

Greenberg, M. T., & Kusche, C. A. (1993). *Promoting social and emotional development in deaf children: The PATHS project.* Seattle, WA: University of Washington Press.

Horton, R., & Shweder, R. A. (2004). Ethnic conservatism, psychological well-being, and the downside of mainstreaming: Generational differences. In O. G. Brim, C. D. Ryff, & R. C. Kessler (Eds.), *How healthy are we?: A national study of well-being at midlife* (pp. 373–397). Chicago, IL: University of Chicago Press.

Humphries, T. (1996). Of deaf-mutes, the strange, and the modern deaf self. In N. S. Glickman & M. A. Harvey (Eds.), *Culturally affirmative psychotherapy with deaf persons.* Mahwah, NJ: Lawrence Erlbaum Associates.

Jambor, E., & Elliott, M. (2005). Self-esteem and coping strategies among deaf students. *Journal of Deaf Studies and Deaf Education, 10*, 63–81.

Kashubeck-West, S., & Meyer, J. (2008). The well-being of women who are late deafened. *Journal of Counseling Psychology, 55*, 463–472.

Kennedy, M. (1994). Art-in-therapy: The role of art-communication and picture-art in working with abused deaf clients. In M. Corker (Ed.), *Counseling: The deaf challenge* (p. 202). Bristol, PA: Jessica Kingsley Publishers.

Kusche, C. A., Garfield, T. S., & Greenberg, M. T. (1983). The understanding of emotional and social attributions in deaf adolescents. *Journal of Clinical Child Psychology, 12*(2), 153–160.

Leigh, I. W. (1999). Inclusive education and personal development. *Journal of Deaf Studies and Deaf Education, 4*, 236–245.

Leigh, I. W., Robins, C. J., Welkowitz, J., & Bond, R. N. (1989). Toward greater understanding of depression in deaf individuals. *American Annals of the Deaf, 134*(4), 249–254.

Leigh, I. W., & Stinson, M. S. (1991). Social environments, self-perceptions, and identity of hearing-impaired adolescents. *The Volta Review, 93*(5), 7–22.

Lent, R. W. (2004). Toward a unifying theoretical and practical perspective on well-being and psychosocial adjustment. *Journal of Counseling Psychology, 51*(4), 482–509.

MacTurk, R. H., Meadow-Orlans, K. P., Koester, L. S., & Spencer, P. E. (1993). Social support, motivation, language and interaction: A longitudinal study of mothers and deaf infants. *American Annals of the Deaf, 138*(1), 19–25.

Masten, A. S., & Obradovic, J. (2006). Competence and resilience in development. *Annals of the New York Academy of Sciences, 1094*, 13–27.

Masten, A. (1994). Resilience in individual development: Successful adaptation despite risk and adversity. In M. C. Wang & E. W. Gordon (Eds.), *Educational resilience in inner city America: Challenges and prospects.* Hillsdale, NJ: Erlbaum.

Maxwell, M., Poeppelmeyer, D., & Polich, L. (1999). Deaf members and nonmembers: The creation of culture through communication practices. In D. Kovarsky, J. Felson Duchan, et al. (Eds.), *Constructing (in)competence: Disabling evaluations in clinical and social interaction* (pp. 125–148). Mahwah, NJ: Lawrence Erlbaum Associates.

Nikolaraizi, M., & Makri, M. (2004). Deaf and hearing individuals' beliefs about the capabilities of deaf people. *American Annals of the Deaf, 149*(5), 404–414.

Olkin, R. (2002). Could you hold the door for me? *Cultural Diversity and Ethnic Minority Psychology, 8*(2), 130–137.

Pavot, W., & Diener, E. (1993). Review of the Satisfaction with Life Scale. *Psychological Assessment, 5*, 164–172.

Pipp-Siegel, S., & Biringer, Z. (1998). Assessing the quality of relationships between parents and children: The emotional availability scales. *The Volta Review, 100*(5), 237–249.

Polat, F. (2003). Factors affecting psychosocial adjustment of deaf students. *Journal of Deaf Studies and Deaf Education, 8*(3), 325–339.

Richardson, J. T., Long, G. L., & Foster, S. B. (2004). Academic engagement in students with a hearing loss in distance education. *Journal of Deaf Studies and Deaf Education, 19*(1), 68–85.

Robitschek, C., & Kashubeck, S. (1999). A structural model of parental alcoholism, family functioning, and psychological health: The mediating effects of hardiness and personal growth orientation. *Journal of Counseling Psychology, 46*, 159–172.

Rosenberg, M. (1965). *Society and the adolescent self-image.* Princeton, NJ: Princeton University Press.

Rosenberg, M., Schooler, C., Schoenbach, C., & Rosenberg, F. (1995). Global self-esteem and specific self-esteem: Different concepts, different outcomes. *American Sociological Review, 60*, 141–156.

Ryff, C. D. (1989a). Beyond Ponce de Leon and life satisfaction: New directions in quest of successful ageing. *International Journal of Behavioral Development, 12*(1), 35–55.

Ryff, C. D. (1989b). Happiness is everything, or is it? Explorations on the meaning of psychological well-being. *Journal of Personality and Social Psychology, 57*(6), 1069–1081.

Ryff, C. D., Singer, B., Love, G. D., & Essex, M. J. (1998). Resilience in adulthood and later life. In J. Lomranz (Ed.), *Handbook of aging and mental health: An integrative approach* (pp. 69–96). New York, NY: Plenum Press.

Sanders, F. M. (1983). Communication and the development of autonomy: Reflections on "Children of a Lesser God". *International Journal of Family Psychiatry, 4*(4), 277–293.

Sevigny-Skyer, S. C. (1990). Personally speaking: A difference to be accepted. *Journal of Counseling and Development, 68*, 336–337.

Sheridan, M. (2001). *Inner lives of deaf children: Interviews and analysis.* Washington, DC: Gallaudet University Press.

Silber, E., & Tippet, J. S. (1965). Self-esteem: Clinical assessment and measurement validation. *Psychological Reports, 16*, 1017–1071.

Sue, D. W., & Sue, D. (2008). *Counseling the culturally diverse: Theory and practice* (5th ed.). New York: Wiley.

Valentine, G., & Skelton, T. (2007). Re-defining 'norms': D/deaf young people's transitions to independence. *The Sociological Review, 55*(1), 104–123.

Venn, J. J., & Wadler, F. (1990). Maximizing the independence of deaf-blind teenagers. *Journal of Visual Impairment and Blindness, 84*(3), 103–108.

Young, A., Green, L., & Rogers, K. (2008). Resilience and deaf children: A review of the literature. *Deafness and Education International, 10*(1), 40–55.

Chapter 15
Resiliency and the Emerging Deaf Adult

Jennifer Lukomski

Abstract This chapter is organized into four sections. First, the theoretical perspective is briefly outlined. Second, protective factors and vulnerability factors and mechanisms are summarized. Third, an overview of the research on the resilience characteristics of deaf and hard of hearing individuals is provided. Lastly, the analysis of the archival data is framed within a resilience model and embedded with questions related to the implications of the findings.

In this chapter, the resilience of deaf emerging adults is examined by reanalyzing archival data. The data was originally collected to compare hearing and deaf college-age students' responses on a social emotional adjustment scale (Lukomski, 2007). The deaf college students' self-ratings of their life difficulties such as home stress, school stress, as well as their self-ratings of their coping skills (i.e., social supports and personal competence), were reorganized within a resilience framework. Examining this archival data from a resilience model poses more questions than answers, yet it is instructive in considerations for future study.

Theoretical Perspective

An appropriate theoretical framework to examine resilience among deaf emerging adults is an integrative developmental model used for studying minority youth (Garcia-Coll et al., 1996). This model incorporates and expands on mainstream developmental frameworks by incorporating culturally different/diverse models – cultural specific and bicultural competencies that are needed to promote minority children's prosocial development. The eight major constructs within this social stratification model that are posited to affect the development of minority

J. Lukomski (✉)
School Psychology Program, Rochester Institute of Technology, Rochester, NY, USA
e-mail: jalgsp@rit.edu

D.H. Zand and K.J. Pierce (eds.), *Resilience in Deaf Children: Adaptation Through Emerging Adulthood*, DOI 10.1007/978-1-4419-7796-0_15,
© Springer Science+Business Media, LLC 2011

children are (1) social position variables (e.g., race and gender), (2) racism and discrimination, (3) segregation (social and psychological), (4) promoting/inhibiting environments, (5) adaptive culture, (6) child characteristics, (7) family values, and (8) children's developmental competencies. Many of these constructs are valuable to consider when conceptualizing the deaf young adult's developmental process and resilience.

Whether or not the young adult identifies with the deaf culture and community, a deaf emerging adult daily confronts the hearing world's phonocentrism (Corker, 1998). Phonocentrism can be loosely defined as the pervasive and systematic assumption of the inherent superiority of a certain auditory and speech status and consequent discrimination against others without the same status. In addition to the hearing world's over reliance on and value of speech and audition, stereotypes and prejudices continue to be present about individuals who have a hearing loss (Kersting, 1997). Kersting (1997) found that deaf college students reported encountering stereotyping on a daily basis, defined as the tendency of hearing students to assume that all deaf people were alike, that prevented the hearing students from getting to know the deaf students. In the hearing world, the attribution of pejorative characteristics based on a person's behaviors and speech intelligibility continue to exist. A hearing person who has limited to no awareness of deafness may assume that when encountering an individual who has a muffled, slurred, or monotoned speech pattern that this signifies lower intelligence. The hearing person may not be aware that without hearing sounds it is difficult to imitate sounds. With regards to behaviors, deaf individuals' behaviors such as vigorous waving of a hand to get a person's attention, scanning the environment periodically to see who is talking, using one's peripheral vision to alert to the environment, maintaining intense and continual eye contact, touching another person to gain his or her attention, and using animated sign language can be viewed as odd or perhaps intrusive from a hearing persons' perspective (Lukomski, 2008). Unfortunately, many deaf individuals are daily reminded of their inability to hear and are blocked from communication access in many social environments. An occurrence as insignificant as not overhearing a conversation in a bathroom, not hearing an announcement on an intercom, or not being alerted to a loud scuffle outside one's line of vision can create awkward social situations. Most hearing individuals are not aware that in such a situation a deaf person may not have heard the "obvious" and wonder why the deaf person is not responding in an appropriate manner to the situation.

Social and psychological segregation can become a common experience in both promoting and inhibiting environments. In more inhibiting environments, such as a mainstream school setting, deaf youth are frequently excluded from extracurricular activities and feel socially and psychologically isolated (Stinson, Whitmire, & Kluwin, 1996). Furthermore, seating arrangements that separate deaf and hearing students within classrooms segregates deaf peers from their hearing peers (Kersting, 1997). In contrast, when deaf youth attend promoting segregated school settings (e.g., residential schools), they are provided full access to communication and social interactions that facilitate social competencies in deaf youth. All in all, environments that are not sensitive to a deaf individual's communication needs and do not provide full social and communication access are more restrictive, inhibiting and possibly stress inducing. The more and better able the deaf individual is able to communicate with the hearing world, and the more the environment facilitates this communication access, the less isolated the deaf child may feel even when the youth and the youth's family choose a segregated environment.

For most deaf young adults who do not have secondary disabilities, communication and language (literacy, reading levels) are the primary areas that are generally affected by their hearing loss and can cause the most isolation. The loss of access to information, as well as socialization opportunities with a large majority of individuals, can be demoralizing. In college settings, many deaf students rely on the interpreters for access to the lectures. Even the best interpreters are not able to express all aspects of conversation, discussion, or lecture that have direct relevance to the classroom instruction (Schick, Williams, & Kupermintz, 2005). When a deaf person has to rely on an interpreter to actively participate in a class discussion, the lag time between what the instructor and class members have voiced and the interpretation can exclude the student from participating in the class. Relying on an interpreter who is unfamiliar with one's sign language style or relying on an interpreter who has weak receptive skills may cause additional embarrassment, especially when the interpreter does not accurately voice what the deaf person has signed, leaving the deaf person wondering why his/her classmates are either looking at her strangely or responding to her participation/question in an odd way.

In contrast to deaf children who are born to hearing parents, deaf children who are born to deaf parents are frequently provided with early language experiences and socialization opportunities (Meadow-Orlans, 1997; Yoshinaga-Itano, 2003) As the child develops, the deaf child may continue to have access to rich cultural and community interactions; however, as the child matures into a young adult, daily interactions which require access to the hearing environment (i.e., most higher education settings and work settings) can be challenging. Interpreters are not readily available and when available may not be a good match to the communication needs of the deaf person. In many cases, ensuring that an interpreter is available requires time and energy, and additional stress.

Communication and a deaf person's facility with communication may be an important variable that is a critical indicator of resilience for deaf individuals. Communication is both an environmental and an individual variable. Limited access to communication and information can place an individual directly at risk for unique and often distorted perceptions and interactions with the world. These conditions are beyond the individual's control and place the individual at great risk for other stressors (e.g., academic difficulties and failure, feelings of being different), peer rejection or peer standoffishness (Calderon & Greenberg, 2003). The severity of the hearing loss may have an influence on the stress but not necessarily in any one direction. For example, individuals who are hard of hearing who don't identify with the deaf culture may not fit in either the deaf or hearing world causing more vulnerability and isolation. The belief in one's ability to communicate and thereby connect with others is a feature in managing stress and daily activities and may be even more vital for deaf and hard of hearing individuals.

Resilience: Risk and Protective Factors

There are multiple pathways to resilience which vary from individual to individual (Bonanno, 2008; Leipold & Greve, 2009; Rutter, 1985) Although there are discrepancies in the definition and conceptualization of resilience, one broad definition of resilience is the maintenance of positive adjustment under challenging life conditions (Bonanno, 2008; Luthar, Cicchetti, & Becker, 2000). The various definitions of resilience share common personal qualities that are believed to characterize resilience. These skills associated with resilience are modifiable and ordinary in nature (Masten, 2001). Some of the more common characteristics include psychological and dispositional attributes, family support and cohesion, external support systems, personal competence, social competence, and personal structure. The personal and social competence attributes refer to the belief in one's accomplishments and ability in social situations whereas the personal structure attribute refers to the individual's ability to plan and organize daily activities – one's executive functioning (Rutter, 1985; White, Driver, & Warren, 2008). Masten (2001) outlined the primary factors that are associated with resilience as those involving connections to competent caretakers in the family and community, cognitive and self-regulation skills, positive views of self, and self-efficacy. When assessing resilience factors, the person's perception as well as quality of his/her resources and adequacy of his/her personal relationships, is more important that the quantity (Rutter, 1985). Since one individual's strategy for building resilience is not necessarily the same as another's strategy, resiliency is an individualized process that is shaped by what works best for an individual (Newman, 2005).

Frequently, when conceptualizing resilience, both risk and protective factors or processes are examined. Protective factors and risk factors are internal and external conditions that affect an individual's capacity to cope. Risk factors and protective factors are frequently inversions of each other, that is a protective factor such as having a social support can become a risk factor when the person has no social support. In this case, protective and risk factors are linked on a continuous dimension directly related to each other. There is not always a direct link between protective and risk factors (Masten, 2001). Furthermore, high protective factors are not necessarily the same as low risk factors.

The individual constellation of risk factors and protective factors in both quality and quantity is multiple. Typically, a risk factor sets up an individual for a possible negative outcome when the individual confronts additional adversity. A risk factor, itself, however, may be an adverse situation. For example, a person's experience of a past trauma is a risk factor, whereas experiencing a trauma is an adverse situation. Protective factors, in contrast, are the external and internal conditions that increase the individual's well-being, and serve as buffers that allow the individual to effectively deal with an adverse situation. Resilience, in turn, is determined by an individual's ability to utilize one's protective processes to resist or maintain positive adjustment when faced with negative experiences (Rutter, 1985).

Protective factors, although expected to provide the individual with the resources to overcome obstacles are not synonymous with resilience. For example, for the deaf toddler with deaf parents, a genetic hearing loss and early language input are developmental protective factors; however, these protective factors may not mean the child is resilient. As protective factors, these early life experiences can boost the deaf child's coping and adaptation when faced with challenging and stressful situations in later years. Early life experiences do influence later childhood and adolescence circumstances (Rutter, 1985; Spekman, Goldberg, & Herman, 1993). When faced with more challenges and possibly less supportive school and community environments, the deaf child who has the better coping and adaptive skills is predicted to be more resilient. The resilience of the child is demonstrated when encountering the challenging circumstance. Risks, in comparison, are a normal part of life. Some risk factors or challenges can actually promote protection, that is the individual's response to a risk factor in a small quantity or uniquely individual quantity can create resilience protection. For example, resilience has found to be an ordinary occurrence, especially common among children growing up in disadvantaged conditions (Masten, 2001) where children face many challenges. Children who experience frequent residential relocations, high family conflict, and stressful life transitions are at a higher risk for school failure, delinquency, and drug use (Hawkins, Smith, & Catalano, 2004). In the same respect, many children in these environments demonstrate resilience and are able to overcome the many obstacles due to protective factors (Hawkins et al., 2004).

Various risk and protective factor domains include personal and social resources, social conditions, developmental challenges, community, family environment, school environments, and peer-individual factors (Hawkins et al., 2004; Greve & Staudinger, 2006). Risk factors include low SES, gender, limited cognitive ability, and single-parent households. Risk factors pertaining to the school atmosphere include academic failure and low commitment to education. In contrast, protective factors include enjoying school, spending time on homework, and perceiving the coursework as relevant (Hawkins et al., 2004). Peer-individual risk factors affect a child's development as well. Seeking out opportunities for dangerous, risky behavior, including membership in gangs, is another factor that increases the chance for problem behavior. Peer-individual protective factors include religiosity, social skills, and moral standards (Hawkins et al., 2004).

One way of further analyzing risk factors, protective factors, and resilience is by examining those factors that predict Post Traumatic Stress Disorder (PTSD), which is when normal people experience an abnormal adverse situation and are unable to rebound from the experience. Trauma research has found that many individuals with no treatment or with brief immediate crisis intervention treatment do not experience PTSD after a traumatic event (Brewin, Andrews, & Valentine, 2000). These people demonstrate resilience. In comparison, the factors that do predict PTSD are a lack of social support, low intelligence, lack of education, female gender, minority ethinicity, prior psychiatric history and dissociative reactions (Bonanno et al., 2007; Brewin et al., 2000). The inverse or protective factors that buffer the individual from experiencing PTSD have been found to be having social support, high intelligence, male gender, education, no psychiatric history. Furthermore, internal cognitive protective factors such as being committed to finding a meaning and purpose in one's life experiences, the belief that one influence is one's surroundings and the outcome of events, and the belief that one can learn and grow from both positive and negative life experiences are protective factors that help an individual maintain positive adjustment when experiencing an adverse situation (Brewin et al., 2000). These hardy individuals who have this mindset minimize the experience of distress by viewing a potentially traumatic situation as less threatening and they are more capable of activating coping and support systems when they do experience stress (Bonanno, 2008). Two other protective factors that buffer individuals in adverse situations from experiencing PTSD that are considered more maladaptive in normal daily life are self-enhancement related – a quality of high self-esteem and high narcissism, that usually evokes negative impressions in others, and, repressive coping which is avoiding unpleasant thoughts, emotions, and memories (Bonanno, 2008). What is intriguing about these findings is that what is considered maladaptive functioning in everyday life leads to resilience when individuals are faced with adverse situations. For example, repressive copers may experience long-term health costs, but they also may be able to adapt to extreme adversity (Bonanno, 2008).

By encountering a nonsupportive environment and being able to successfully navigate through this environment without a negative outcome provides individuals with an experience that bolsters and revamps their coping skills. In contrast, an overload or too many risk factors can cause the individual to experience a poorer outcome (Rutter, 1985). When in larger doses the events and one's perception of the events may elevate the likelihood of poor adaptation and an unsuccessful outcome (Spekman et al., 1993). A number of the everyday life stressors such as major transitions (i.e., entering school, graduating from school, managing school) can introduce doses of risk which promote resilience. The promotion of resilience, a fluid entity, does not lie in an avoidance of stress but rather in the encounter of is stress. Appropriately responding and mastery of the stressful situation allows self-confidence and social competence to increase.

Although there are certain external and trait characteristics that are commonly considered protective influences, personal state differences are important to assess. Good coping strategies are strong protective factors/processes. Some of these protective coping skills as mentioned above are optimism or having daily positive emotions, perspective taking, perceiving psychological control, problem solving skills, and good self-esteem (Aspinwall & Taylor, 1992; Ong, Bergeman, Bisconti, & Wallace, 2006). Positive emotions promote flexible thinking and problem solving and assist an individual in building enduring social resources. Ong et al. (2006) found that positive emotions are more common among high resilient individuals. Positive emotions quiet or undo the effects of negative emotions. Individuals who can laugh and develop a positive outlook on a negative event, experience better adjustment.

The existence of coping, not necessarily the specific method of coping, is what is important. The finding that deaf college-aged students reported significantly better coping skills than that of the hearing college-age students may be more an indication of having to rely more heavily on coping skills to navigate through the academic and social environments than having superior coping skills (Lukomski, 2007). Again, one's perception of coping resources does not necessarily translate into coping outcomes, and at the same time the amount of coping required of a deaf individual to daily self-advocacy and navigate through a hearing world is possibly not comprehensible to the typical hearing individual.

Factors Specific to Deaf Resilience

Having a hearing loss can be a challenging life condition and presents a deaf individual with daily obstacles, especially when interacting and interfacing with the hearing environment. Is a hearing loss, however, a risk factor? From a medical model, having a hearing loss, or any type of disability, is considered a risk factor or vulnerability factor. In comparison, from a Deaf cultural perspective there is less clarity regarding whether a hearing loss per se is a risk factor. There is a need for both contextual and developmental delimitations when conceptualizing the implications of the hearing loss. A hearing loss for deaf infants and toddlers who are born to deaf parents may not be considered a risk factor for the deaf children in their early years, whereas a hearing loss which is caused by maternal rubella for a child born to hearing parents may be categorized as a risk factor. Young, Green, and Rogers (2008) propose that deafness may be a risk indicator but not necessarily a risk mechanism. Deafness is more of a risk marker than a definitive cause of risk due to the ambiguity in the definition of resilience, the inability to claim that deafness is an adverse experience, and that for a deaf individual the interaction of the familial, social, and institutional contexts can create an adverse or promoting situation.

Identifying the specific characteristics that are related to resilience in deaf individuals has been primarily explored through case studies (i.e., Charlson, Bird, & Strong, 1999; Rogers, Muir, & Evenson, 2003). The question is do deaf individuals have different characteristics related to resilience? Charlson et al. (1999) interviewed 23 deaf students and their parents who were nominated by teachers and administrators as exceptionally resilient and then focused their examination on three students who were representative of the group. The predominant resiliency qualities that were common to most of the deaf individuals were independence, assertiveness, a good nature, and good problem solving abilities.

In comparison, Rogers et al. (2003) interviewed three deaf college graduates regarding their interpersonal relationships, behavior, and environment. They found that there were 15 major assets that marked the resilient deaf adult. Similar to Charlson et al. (1999), they found that interpersonal assets that may be associated with resiliency were a good sense of humor, caring, responsible and committed to worthy goals, a strong sense of social bonds, emotional self-perception, awareness of strengths, and the comfort with solitude. The environmental factors that were important were quality time with caring mentors in college, positive learning partnerships with peers in college, and supportive family environment. The behavioral assets that were associated with resiliency were self-advocacy, self-reliance, goal-directed behaviors and persistent problem solving, religious affiliations, and authentic presentation of self. One of the key protective factors across the various settings was that of social support; when a person believes in and reports having a strong sense of social bonds, the more resilient the individual is when faced with challenges and an unsupportive environment. In comparison to the protective factors for hearing individuals, two protective factors that were more notable for deaf individuals were the authentic presentation of self and a comfort with solitude (Rogers et al., 2003).

Pertaining to the authentic presentation of oneself, Hurt and Gonzalez (1988) found that a deaf individual's communication apprehension can interfere with self-disclosure and authentically presenting oneself. Deaf participants responding to a hearing target reported significantly lower self-disclosure. The continuous anticipation of negative interpersonal outcomes can lead to communication apprehension and the concomitant reduction of appropriate self-disclosures. When there is a reduction in appropriate self-disclosure the establishment of effective interpersonal relationships and positive experiences is inhibited (Hurt & Gonzalez, 1988). Deaf student's anticipation or ratings of not being understood or not perceiving themselves as having intelligible speech reinforces them to avoid oral communication encounters further and this dynamic then supports their belief. Hurt and Gonzalez (1988) found that the state of stress experienced by the deaf sample due to their self-perceived inability to adequately transmit and receive oral messages was significant. These negative interpersonal experiences with the hearing world caused the deaf group to avoid meaningful interpersonal encounters with the hearing world, thus limiting their social contacts.

Reexamination of the Data

The data used for this investigation consisted of social emotional surveys and a communication survey completed by 140 deaf emerging adult college students' (mean age of 18). Fifty-one (51%) were males and 49% were females. The Reading Grade Equivalent level of the students ranged from fifth to 12th grade with the mean Reading Grade Equivalent level at the eighth grade. Participants reported that the age at which they learned sign language ranged from 0 to 22 with 5 being the mean age (SD = 5.5). The communication variables consisted of the participants' ratings of their own speech skills, self-ratings of their sign skills, and self-ratings of their understanding of others' speech (see Table 15.1). The majority (65%) of the respondents rated their own speech skill level at that where others could understand at least half of what they say. Similarly the majority (71%) of the respondents reported understanding at least half of what others say. As for their self-ratings of their sign skills, 35% reported excellent skills, 47% reported good skills, and 2% reported no skills.

To examine the archival data set from a resiliency framework, a risk factors domain and a protective factors domain were created from the items on the Life Difficulties Scale (see Table 15.2). The risk items were selected based on a review of the literature (see above). The items selected included risk factors such as home and school stressors, not having meaning in life, loneliness, mental health indicators (i.e., suicidal ideation and terrible temper) and experience of past traumas that

Table 15.1 Communication variables

	Percent	(n)
Rating of speech skills (n=90)		
None of my words	7	(6)
Only a few of my words	22	(20)
About half of my words	23	(21)
Almost everything I say	39	(35)
Everything I say	9	(8)
Rating of speech understanding (n=184)		
None of what people say	8	(15)
Only a few words	21	(38)
About half of what people say	30	(55)
Almost everything people say	36	(66)
Everything people say	5	(10)
Communication preference (n=170)		
Sign alone	34	(59)
Sign and speech together	65	(111)
Rating of simultaneous communication understanding (n=185)		
None of what people say	1	(1)
Only a few words	3	(6)
About half of what people say	10	(18)
Almost everything people say	35	(66)
Everything people say	51	(94)
Rating of sign skills (n=185)		
No skills	2	(4)
Basic	4	(7)
Fair	12	(22)
Good	47	(87)
Excellent	35	(65)

Table 15.2 Risk and protective factor domains/items

Risk factors

I have had a lot of stress lately at home
I have had a lot of stress lately at school
I often have moments when my life seems lonely and empty
I feel that there isn't much in life that's worth doing
I have very strong fears of particular places or things
I have had a terrible experience that still bothers me
I have sometimes thought about how to kill myself
I am known to have a terrible temper
I get upset at the way teachers and others push me around

Protective factors

I feel okay about my ability to do whatever I set out to do
I have a group of friends with whom I feel comfortable
It's easy for me to get along with other students at school
Most problems in life can be solved by thought and persistent effort
In hard times I always have family or friends to help out
No matter how hard life gets, I have solid values to guide me
When things go wrong, I can usually see a bright side

still bothered the individual. Although a few of the inverses of these factors could be considered protective factors, these items were not used in the protective factors to keep the two factors independent.

Instead, the protective factors were also selected based on a review of the literature and focused primarily on coping factors. Friborg, Hjemdal, Rosenvince, and Martinussen's (2003) Resilience Scale for Adults (RSA) and Connor and Davidson's (2003) Connor Davidson Resilience Scale (CED_RISC) were used as templates for selecting the protective items from the Life Difficulties Scale coping scale. The seven items that make up the protective factors scale include items that addressed personal competence (i.e., I feel okay about my ability to do whatever I set out to do), realistic sense of control and having choices (i.e., No matter how hard life gets, I have solid values to guide me), social support (i.e., I have a group of friends), social competence (i.e., It is easy for me to get along with others at school), and optimism (i.e., When things go wrong, I can see a brighter side).

Examining Internal Consistency

To check the internal consistency of the reorganization of the Life Difficulties Scale items, the reliability of the items for the risk factors and protective factors was calculated for both a hearing sample and the deaf group. Chronbach's alpha for the nine items on the risk factor scale for the deaf group was 0.68, whereas Chronbach's alpha for the hearing sample on the nine items was 0.58 which was lower than the deaf group, yet still in the moderate range indicating that the items were moderately correlated. For the seven items that made up the protective factor domain, the internal consistency coefficient for the deaf group (0.69) was similar to that of the hearing sample (0.67). Within the protective factor for the two subdomains (i.e., personal competence and social support), the internal consistency of the items was also examined. The four personal competence items for the deaf group had a Chronbach's alpha of 0.64, whereas for the hearing group the internal consistency coefficient was 0.53. Noteworthy is that for the hearing sample on the three social support items that made up the social support variable the reliability was 0.50, whereas for the deaf group the low internal consistency (0.33) indicated that these three items were not interrelated.

The three items that make up that social support subscale scale are (1) it's easy for me to get along with other students at school, (2) in hard times I always have family or friends to help out, and (3) I have a group of friends with whom I feel comfortable. These items had a stronger correlation with the overall protective factor than they had with each other. The stronger correlation of these items with the overall protective scale items suggests that these three social support items are measuring the construct labeled as the protective factor, however, are not necessarily measuring a cohesive social domain. For example, for a hearing individual getting along easily with other students at school may actually mean that the hearing individual is socially and psychologically connecting with other students at school. In contrast, for a deaf individual getting along with other students at school may actually mean that the deaf student is peacefully coexisting, not necessarily interacting with the other students at school. Similarly, the endorsement that one has family or friends to help out doesn't necessarily translate into an engaged interaction with the family or friends, whereas having a group of friends with whom I feel comfortable may be more indicative of a socially engaged group. That a deaf person can identify a group of close friends, is able to get along with other students, and in hard times has family or friends to help out are all important protective factors but not necessarily measuring a similar type of support as for hearing individuals.

This finding may suggest that it is important to consider how social relationships and social contexts function differently for deaf individuals. Young et al. (2008) propose that the deaf individuals' experience provides for special conditions which transform the significance and operation of some of the identified resilience features that are seemingly consistent with the nondeaf literature.

It is also important to note here that the comparison with a hearing sample on the internal consistency of these factors may not be appropriate because the premise is that the developmental trajectory for the deaf group is different. On the other hand, the fact that the specific scales were internally consistent or not internally consistent for the two groups may be instructive and indicate that the deaf group has different perceptions and experiences with social networks, yet the overall protective factors and risk factors may be similar across the two groups.

In the future, when measuring deaf emerging adult resilience, perhaps the social support construct needs to be more critically examined. The inclusion of an item related to positive role models may be relevant to social support, especially for deaf individuals. Role models are important in other minority populations for creating a belief in self and possibility of success.

Examining the Communication Variables

For the protective and risk factors the items within the factor were summed and then averaged. For the protective factor the sum was divided by seven (the number of items in the scale) and for the risk factors the sum was divided by nine. After creating the two factors (i.e., protective and risk), a quartile split was used to group the deaf individuals who fell at the lower quartile on the protective factors and the deaf individuals who fell at the top quartile on the protective factor, as well as to group the deaf respondents who fell at the lower quartile on the risk factors and the deaf respondents who fell at the top quartile on the risk factors. By examining the low and high groups and eliminating the middle responders, the comparison could focus on those who fell the highest on coping and the lowest on the coping to better discriminate the two groups. The low and high groups were than examined on a variety of communication strategy variables.

Due to the quasi interval nature of the data and the different group sizes for the two within factors (i.e., protective [high and low] and risk [high and low]) one-way

ANOVAs were used to examine the two protective factor groups and the two risk factor groups on the six dependent variables, four of which were self-reported evaluations and one (i.e., Reading Level) which was an objective measure. The four self-rating variables were self-rating of speech skills, self-rating of speech understanding, self-rating of sign skills, and age when learned sign.

Communication is more than language facility and speech articulation. To communicate one needs to have the willingness (extroverted) and needs to have the ability to understand pragmatics and nonverbal cues. A person's self-rating of his or her communication skills may possibly be a better assessment of the person's engagement in the communication processes than the person's actual level of speech understanding of others and rating of their own speech abilities.

None of the students' self-reported ratings on the four communication variables and Reading Grade Level performance were significantly different between the high risk factor and low risk factor groups (see Table 15.3).

In contrast, the students' self-reported ratings on three of the communication variables and Reading Grade Level were significantly different between the high and low protective factor groups (see Table 15.4). The mean of the reading grade level was significantly higher for the high protective factor than for the low protective factor. For two of the communication variables (i.e., understanding others speech, others understanding my speech) more individuals in the high protective factors group endorsed that they understood "almost everything" to "everything" and that others understood "almost everything" to "everything" that they said. In contrast, in the low protective group significantly more participants rated their sign skills as "excellent" in comparison to the high protective factor group. Age of learning sign was not significantly different between the two groups.

Table 15.3 Mean differences for communication strategy variables for the two risk groups

	Low risk ($n=33$)	High risk ($n=73$)
Rate of speech skills	3.55	3.25
Rating of speech understanding	3.52	3.14
Rating of sign skills	3.76	4.07
Age of learning sign	6.55	5.27
NTID reading grade equivalent	9.25	8.78

Table 15.4 Mean differences for communication strategy variables for the two protective groups

	Low protective ($n=68$)	High protective ($n=72$)
Rating of speech skills	2.91	3.33*
Rating of speech understanding	2.75	3.14*
Rating of sign skills	4.22*	3.92
Age of learning sign	4.58	5.01
NTID reading grade equivalent	8.33	9.10*

$*p<0.05$

A multiple regression analysis was completed to determine which of these four significant variables best predicted membership in either the high or low protective factor group. The rationale for the use of the regression analysis was to investigate which of the significant communication variables best predicted whether an individual fell in the high or low protective group. A function of the analysis is to search for the predictor variables that help to explain significant variation between the high and low protective group.

The only variable that was a significant predictor ($p=0.004$) was the participant's reading grade level. The participant's reading level explained 5% of the total variance of group membership. This finding is consistent with the hearing literature regarding reading level being a protective factor. Perhaps reading level has a more powerful protective influence for a deaf person as it is one way of accessing information that is not dependent on the environment.

Within the protective factor groups there were no gender differences on the communication strategies variables. In contrast, for the risk group there was a gender difference for one of the self-ratings. Females rated their speech skills as higher than the males rated their speech skills ($F(1,92)=2.82$, $p<0.04$). Considering that there were no differences between the low and high risk groups on the selected communication variables it may be that risk factors are not as informative for examining resilience in deaf college students as are protective factors. That is, examining the stressors or characteristics that place an individual at risk do not differentiate as well between groups of deaf emerging adults in a college setting.

Several caveats must be taken into consideration when interpreting these data. This sample of deaf individuals may be considered skewed in many ways regarding resilience. In some respects, it can be inferred that many of the deaf students who have attained admission to college are a sample of resilient deaf youth. Young et al. (2008) propose that the deaf individuals' experience provides for special conditions which transform the significance and operation of some of the identified resilience features that are seemingly consistent with the nondeaf literature. That is, unlike most of their hearing peers who attend college, most of the deaf students had to successfully navigate through academic and environmental barriers. This may be one reason why for the emerging deaf adult college-aged students it may be more informative to examine protective factors and coping skills. From a developmental perspective, most deaf students who attend college are a selective group who are asking what is working and doing more of what is working to make themselves successful and more productive.

Nonetheless, since protective influences operate over time and in a multifaceted way this type of cross-sectional analysis that treats the variables as if they interact at one point in time does not properly describe the protective influences (Rutter, 1985). For example, resilient youth place themselves in healthier contexts, generating opportunities for connecting and creating more promoting experiences (Masten, 2001). Similar to babies with easy going temperaments, where caretaker and baby are in a dynamic relationship that creates better developmental outcomes for the baby, resilience does not lie solely in the individual. The timing of interactions between the individual and the environment, and the various situations the individual encounters are multiple. More apparently and salient to discussing resilience within this population is the need for longitudinal research that can highlight the resilience processes. Within the college setting, following the students who persevere, remain in college and graduate would be most informative.

The finding that more of the individuals in the low protective factor group rated their sign skills as "excellent" in comparison to the high protective group ratings of their sign language as "good" is puzzling. Perhaps, deaf individuals who rate their signing as "excellent" only use sign to communicate, which can be restrictive when in an academic setting with both hearing and deaf students. The academic environment tends to favor individuals who are comfortable using both sign and voice. Individuals in the low protective group may be limited by the environmental communication barriers and their self-belief in competence and social support are not viewed as high. Because resilience is domain specific, examining academic resilience in deaf college-age students having excellent sign skills may not be a strong protective factor. In addition, the high protective group had a communication preference for sign and voice, possibly indicating that the high protective group was more bicultural and/or had more flexible communication strategies. Students who self-report feeling comfortable and having a preference for sign and voice may feel comfortable with both sign and voice, whereas students who have a preference for sign only may not feel as comfortable with the two different modalities.

Limitations and Conclusions

Of course, these findings and study have many limitations. Some of which have been alluded to in the above discussion. For example, this analysis does not examine resilience mechanisms. That is, an individual's resilience is a process that emerges and subsides over time. As an individual undertakes the process of negotiating challenging/stressful and risky situations the question becomes what are the protective mechanisms that are utilized for a specific individual to be successful in negotiating the challenge? The question then becomes how much challenge is beneficial and how much challenge sends the individual into a negative outcome (Masten, 2001)? Resilience then is not only about positive adjustment but also about adaptive flexibility (Leipold & Greve, 2009).

The transactional aspect of resilience, where the environment and social community respond and interact with the individual, must also be considered. For deaf youth, it may be of interest for future research to examine the caregivers and peer support group resilience (White et al., 2008). The mechanisms involved in the individual's life trajectory (Rutter, 1985) are more salient in this dynamic concept of resilience than the individual characteristics. The static variables limit capturing the fluidity of the process. In addition, due to the multidimensional nature of resilience, there is an unevenness in functioning across domains and fluctuations in resilience across time (Luthar et al., 2000). An individual may have resilience in one setting and not another. For example, in this study the resilience in question is limited to the educational domain (i.e., college attendees).

Another limitation of this study is the use of archival data that has been reconfigured to fit a model that the data was not intended. This creates many problems. The variables examined were limited to what variables were available to be analyzed. Another limitation may be that even though the protective factors and vulnerability factors were selected based on the literature, which included the few deaf case studies that do exist, the factors were limited to a primarily hearing framework. For example, based on the limited research it would have been interesting to have an item labeled comfort with solitude in the protective scale which may be a unique resilience feature for deaf individuals. Examining the relationships between communication, comfort with solitude and authentic presentation of self would also be of interest. A final limitation was that the data was primarily self-report.

Despite these limitations, the findings offer further discussion points. For example, how does the social world of deaf individuals operate differently from that of hearing individuals and function as a protective factor? Would the inclusion of role models whose hearing status is the same as the respondents be considered a social support more so than the ability to get along with other students? Would greater exposure to teachers of the same hearing status be an important protective feature? It could be useful for future research to determine the degree to which students actually prefer and actively seek out role models of their own and different hearing statuses.

In conclusion, this chapter proposes more questions than supportive findings. Resilience operates at multiple levels that are intertwined with no one single indicator. The deaf emerging adult, nonetheless, is a segment of the deaf population that shows potential for future study to focus on with regard to resilience.

References

Aspinwall, L. G., & Taylor, S. E. (1992). Modeling cognitive adaptation: A longitudinal investigation of the impact of individual differences and coping on college adjustment and performance. *Journal of Personality and Social Psychology, 63*(6), 989–1003.

Bonanno, G. A., Galea, S., Bucciarelli, A., & Vlahov, D. (2007). What predicts psychological resilience after desester? The role of demographics resources, and life stress. *Journal of Consulting and Clinical Psychology*, 75(5), 671–682.

Bonanno, G. A. (2008). Loss, trauma, and human resilience. Have we underestimated the human capacity to thrive after extremely aversive events? *Psychological Trauma: Theory, Research, Practice, and Policy*, S(1), 101–113.

Brewin, C., Andrews, B., & Valentine, J. (2000). Meta-analysis of risk factors for posttraumatic stress disorder in trauma-exposed adults. *Journal of Consulting and Clinical Psychology, 68*(5), 748–766.

Calderon, R., & Greenberg, M. (2003). Social and emotional development of deaf children: Family, school, and program effects. In M. Marschark & P. Spencer (Eds.), *Oxford handbook of deaf studies, language, and education* (pp. 177–189). New York: Oxford University Press.

Charlson, E. S., Bird, R. L., & Strong, M. (1999). Resilience and success among deaf high school students: Three case studies. *American Annual of the Deaf, 144*(3), 226–235.

Connor, K., & Davidson, J. (2003). Development of a new resilience scale: The Connor-Davidson resilience scale (CD-RISC). *Depression and Anxiety, 13*, 76–82.

Corker, M. (1998). *Deaf and disabled, or deafness disabled?* Bristol, PA: Open University Press.

Friborg, O., Hjemdal, O., Rosenvince, J. H., & Martinussen, M. (2003). A new rating scale for adult resilience: What are the central protective resources behind healthy adjustment? *International Journal of Methods in Psychiatric Research, 12*(2), 65–76.

Garcia-Coll, C., Lamberty, G., Jenkins, R., Pipes McAdoo, H., Crnic, K., Hanna Wasil, B., et al. (1996). An integrative model for the study of developmental competencies in minority children. *Child Development, 67*, 1891–1914.

Greve, W., & Staudinger, U. M. (2006). Resilience in later adulthood and old age: Resources and potentials for successful aging. In D. Cichetti & D. Cohen (Eds.), *Developmental psychopathology* (2nd ed., Vol. 2, pp. 796–840). New York: Wiley.

Hawkins, J. D., Smith, B. H., & Catalano, R. F. (2004). Social development and social and emotional learning. In J. E. Zins, R. P. Weissberg, M. C. Wang, & H. J. Walberg (Eds.), *Building academic success on social and emotional learning. What does the research say?* (pp. 135–150). New York: Teachers College Press.

Hurt, T. H., & Gonzalez, T. (1988). Communication apprehension and distorted self-disclosure: The hidden disabilities of hearing impaired students. *Communication Education, 37*(2), 106–117.

Kersting, S. (1997). Balancing between deaf and hearing worlds: Reflections of mainstreamed college students on relationships and social interaction. *Journal of Deaf Studies and Deaf Education, 2*(4), 252–263.

Leipold, B., & Greve, W. (2009). Resilience: A conceptual bridge between coping and development. *European Psychologist, 14*(1), 40–50.

Lukomski, J. L. (2007). Deaf college students' perceptions of their social-emotional adjustment. *Journal of Deaf Studies and Deaf Education, 12*(4), 486–494.

Lukomski, J. L. (2008). Best practices in planning effective instruction for students who are deaf and hard of hearing. In A. Thomas & J. Grimes (Eds.), *Best practices in school psychology* (Vol. V, pp. 1819–1822). Maryland: NASP.

Luthar, S. S., Cicchetti, D., & Becker, B. (2000). The construct of resilience: A critical evaluation and guidelines for future work. *Child Development, 71*(3), 543–562.

Masten, A. (2001). Ordinary magic: Resilience processes in development. *American Psychologist, 56*, 227–238.

Meadow-Orlans, K. P. (1997). Effects of mother and infant hearing status on interactions at twelve and eighteen months. *Journal of Deaf Studies and Deaf Education, 2*, 26–36.

Newman, R. (2005). APA's resilience initiative. *Professional Psychology: Research and Practice, 36*(3), 227–229.

Ong, A., Bergeman, C., Bisconti, T., & Wallace, K. (2006). Psychological resilience, positive emotions, and successful adaptation to stress in later life. *Journal of Personality and Social Psychology, 91*(4), 730–749.

Rogers, S., Muir, K., & Evenson, C. R. (2003). Signs of resilience: Assets that support deaf adults' success in bridging the deaf and hearing worlds. *American Annals of the Deaf, 148*(3), 222–232.

Rutter, M. (1985). Resilience in the face of adversity: Protective factors and resistance to psychiatric disorder. *British Journal of Psychiatry, 147*, 598–611.

Schick, B., Williams, K., & Kupermintz, H. (2005). Look who's being left behind: Educational interpreters and access to education for deaf and hard-of-hearing students. *Journal of Deaf Studies and Deaf Education, 11*(1), 3–20.

Spekman, N. J., Goldberg, R. J., & Herman, K. L. (1993). An exploration of risk and resilience in the lives of individuals with learning disabilities. *Learning Disabilities Research & Practice, 8*(1), 11–18.

Stinson, M. S., Whitmire, K., & Kluwin, T. N. (1996). Self-perceptions of social relationships in hearing-impaired adolescents. *Journal of Educational Psychology, 88*, 132–143.

White, B., Driver, S., & Warren, A. (2008). Considering resilience in the rehabilitation of people with traumatic disabilities. *Rehabilitation Psychology, 53*(1), 9–17.

Yoshinaga-Itano, C. (2003). From screening to early identification and intervention: Discovering predictors to successful outcomes for children with significant hearing loss. *Journal of Deaf Studies and Deaf Education, 8*(1), 11.

Young, A., Green, L., & Rogers, K. (2008). Resilience and deaf children: A literature review. *Deafness and Education International, 10*(1), 40–55.

Epilogue

Debra H. Zand and Katherine J. Pierce

We first envisioned preparing a book on what it means to be resilient and deaf 8 years ago when our daughter turned two and was diagnosed with a "profound hearing impairment." As parents, we needed to know that our daughter would be okay. We live in a centrist society and wanted to know that our daughter would be successful among her peers. In these early years, we mostly read about outcomes and negative trajectories. We learned that among youth, social and academic competence levels of the deaf and hard of hearing fell behind that of their hearing peers (Bain, Scott, & Steinberg, 2004; Holt, Traxler, & Allen, 1992). We read that it is was not uncommon for deaf and hard of hearing adults to experience social isolation in the workplace and to perceive fewer opportunities to advance professionally than their hearing coworkers (Backenroth, 1997). We did not want this for our daughter.

We then began to hear about the "exceptions": deaf doctors, deaf lawyers, deaf psychologists; deaf individuals who had overcome the odds and had become successful. During this period, the diagnosis of a "hearing impairment" signified an adversity which we believed our daughter needed to overcome. We adopted the mainstream definition of resilience as positive adaptation within the context of adversity. Concretely, for our daughter, this meant achieving developmental competencies in the context of being deaf. For us, as her parents, this meant finding ways to facilitate the processes of making this happen. We "knew" that being deaf and resilient was not the norm, it was the exception.

We were so wrong on so many accounts. Raising our daughter, while birthing the present book, has been a painful, joyous, confusing, complicated, enlightening, and incredibly rewarding process. As our daughter and chapter authors have taught us, resilience within the context of being deaf is a complex construct and is not easily transferred from the hearing to the deaf world.

The chapter authors' definitions of adversity, within the context of being deaf, were as diverse as the deaf population itself. While some authors adopted a traditional definition of adversity, identifying hearing loss as the key hardship, others began to challenge the concept itself. For the latter, adversity became a dynamic process that was contextually dependent and focused primarily on communication. Throughout the book, underpinning all definitions was a tension regarding the onus

D.H. Zand and K.J. Pierce (eds.), *Resilience in Deaf Children: Adaptation Through Emerging Adulthood*, DOI 10.1007/978-1-4419-7796-0,
© Springer Science+Business Media, LLC 2011

of the adversity. Conventional viewpoints typically assumed that the burden was on the individual. Specifically, the individual's hearing loss placed him/her at risk. Following this logic, modifying risk primarily focused on professionals (and parents) working with deaf individuals to facilitate their mastery of developmental competencies within mainstream environments (e.g., learning to speak, read, write, etc.). Straying from the time-honored view of resilience as "ordinary magic," (Masten, 2001) with the majority of children "at risk" doing just fine, this "hearing-loss risk" view placed only a select few as overcoming the odds (Werner, 2000), with the majority of deaf persons never achieving positive developmental trajectories. Challenging this belief, other authors placed the burden of the risk outside of the deaf individual. For these authors, deaf unfriendly environments, which impeded communication, were to blame. Modifiers of risk included the environment changing to become language accessible to all and to value diversity. In the absence of such change, resistance to the environment and the development of self-worth and a deaf identity became protective processes. Interestingly, in the "environment-risk" view, the concept of equating socially constructed outcomes with positive adaptation became nebulous and potentially harmful. Instead, the question of "at risk for what?" became fodder for discussion. A new concept of positive adaptation was introduced and defined as the process by which deaf individuals navigate their environments.

The study of resilience among deaf populations is in its infancy, and the current edited volume represents an early attempt to disentangle the elements of this construct. Ultimately, the book raises more questions than it answers, including whether resilience is a relevant area of inquiry. For parents, it may offer hope. For professionals, it may offer new possibilities for interventions and for investigation. For others, it may represent a new packaging of old views that deafness equates with adversity. What remains to be asked, however, is what it means to the youth. Although the present authors generally adopted the mainstream definition of resilience as positive adaptation in the face of adversity, less agreement occurred on how adversity and positive adaptation were defined. Clearly, more theoretical work surrounding definitional issues needs to be conducted. It will be important for scholars to define explicitly the components of resilience and to develop culturally relevant measures of the construct. Akin to the mainstream resilience literature, the study of resilience among deaf populations will undoubtedly move in waves (Masten & Wright, 2010). Clarifying definitional issues will pave the way to studying complex, integrative processes and to testing interventions. This process may indeed be transformative.

References

Backenroth, G. A. (1997). Social interaction in deaf/hearing bicultural work groups. *International Journal of Rehabilitation Research, 20,* 85–90.
Bain, L., Scott, S., & Steinberg, A. G. (2004). Socialization experiences and coping strategies of adults raised using spoken language. *Journal of Deaf Studies and Deaf Education, 9,* 120–128.

Holt, J., Traxler, C., & Allen, T. (1992). *Interpreting the scores: A user's guide to the 8th edition Stanford Achievement Test for educators of deaf and hard-of-hearing students.* Washington, DC: Gallaudet Research Institute, Gallaudet University.

Masten, A. S. (2001). Ordinary magic. Resilience processes in development. *The American Psychologist, 56,* 227–238.

Masten, A. S., & Wright, N. O. (2010). Resilience over the lifespan: Developmental perspectives on resistance, recovery, and transformation. In J. W. Reich, A. J. Zautra, & J. S. Hall (Eds.), *Handbook of adult resilience* (pp. 213–237). New York: Guildford.

Werner, E. (2000). Protective factors and individual resilience. In J. Shonkoff & S. Meisels (Eds.), *Handbook of early childhood intervention* (pp. 115–134). Cambridge: Cambridge University Press.

Index

LaVergne, TN USA
27 February 2011
218070LV00005B/9/P